THE PAPERS OF DANIEL WEBSTER

CHARLES M. WILTSE, EDITOR-IN-CHIEF

SERIES ONE: CORRESPONDENCE

THE UNIVERSITY PRESS

OF NEW ENGLAND

Sponsoring Institutions

BRANDEIS UNIVERSITY

CLARK UNIVERSITY

DARTMOUTH COLLEGE

UNIVERSITY OF NEW HAMPSHIRE

UNIVERSITY OF RHODE ISLAND

UNIVERSITY OF VERMONT

The Papers of
Daniel Webster

Correspondence, Volume 1

1798–1824

CHARLES M. WILTSE, EDITOR

HAROLD D. MOSER, ASSOCIATE EDITOR

PUBLISHED FOR

DARTMOUTH COLLEGE BY THE

UNIVERSITY PRESS OF NEW ENGLAND

HANOVER, NEW HAMPSHIRE 1974

This edition of the Papers of Daniel Webster is published by Dartmouth College with assistance from the National Historical Publications Commission and the National Endowment for the Humanities.

Acknowledgments

The collection, editing, and publication of the Papers of Daniel Webster, in microfilm and selectively in letterpress, was first conceived by Francis Brown, Dartmouth '25, then editor of the *New York Times Book Review*, and Edward Connery Lathem, '51, then assistant librarian of the College. Although the project quickly outgrew their original conception of it, they have continued to give it unfailing and indispensable support.

Webster papers are scattered throughout the United States, with more than a handful in other countries. The task of locating and collecting them brought the editors into contact with virtually every library, records depository, and historical society in the country, with manuscript dealers, and with private collectors. The number of institutions and individuals who have contributed in one way or another to the final product is far too great to permit special mention of them all, but their contribution is hereby gratefully acknowledged. Individual credits for published or listed items are given with each document or entry.

Those to whom our debt is greatest, by virtue of the magnitude of their contributions, include, in alphabetical order, Brandeis University, the British Public Record Office, the Buffalo and Erie County Historical Society, the Canadian Public Archives, Dartmouth College, Harvard University, the Library of Congress, the Massachusetts Historical Society, the National Archives and Records Service, the New Hampshire Historical Society, the New York Public Library, the University of Virginia, and Yale University.

For invaluable aid in the collecting phase of the project as well as for production of the microfilm edition of the papers from which materials for this and subsequent volumes have been selected, grateful thanks are due University Microfilms of Ann Arbor, and especially to its retired board chairman, Eugene B. Power, and its president, Robert F. Asleson.

The faculty and staff of Dartmouth College have been uniformly helpful, but a few individuals must be singled out for special thanks: President John G. Kemeny and President Emeritus John Sloan Dickey; Leonard M. Rieser, Vice President and Dean of the Faculty; Louis Morton, Chairman of the History Department; Edward Connery Lathem, Librarian of the College, and Richard W. Morin, Librarian Emeritus; Kenneth C. Cramer, College Archivist; Herbert W. Hill, Professor of History Emeritus and Past President of the New Hampshire Historical Society; William B. Durant, Jr., Executive Officer for the Faculty of Arts and Sciences, who has cheerfully assumed the role of financial adviser to the project; and Foster Blough, Director of Sponsored Programs in the Comptroller's Office.

Cosponsors of the project with Dartmouth College have been the National Endowment for the Humanities and the National Historical Publications Commission. At the Endowment thanks go particularly to William E. Emerson, Director of its Division of Research and Publication; at NHPC, we are especially indebted to the Chairman, James B. Rhoads, Archivist of the United States, to Oliver W. Holmes, former Executive Director, to E. Berkeley Tompkins, his successor, and to Fred Shelley who has capably served as Deputy to both.

Others who have contributed directly or indirectly to the preparation of this volume include E. Charles Beer, George E. Carter, Richard W. Etulain, Alexander Evarts, and Carol S. Moffatt, all of whom were staff members for the microfilm edition; Mary V. Anstruther, who has worked with both microfilm and the present letterpress volume as combined secretary and editorial assistant; Peter Klarén, who served for a time as an assistant editor; Margaret Abbott of New London, N.H., who has done the bulk of the transcribing; and David G. Allen, National Historical Publications Commission Fellow for 1972–73. Mr. Allen's predecessor as NHPC Fellow, Harold Dean Moser, has made an outstanding contribution as associate editor of this volume.

Alfred Konefsky, editor of the Legal volumes in this series, and Kenneth E. Shewmaker, editor of Webster's Diplomatic Papers, have been available at all times for consultation.

Hanover, New Hampshire
February 1, 1974

C. M. W.

Contents

For the page number on which each document of the Papers begins, see the Calendar.

A section of illustrations follows page 230.

Introduction

Daniel Webster was one of a handful of public men who dominated the first half of nineteenth-century America. It was an age of persistent, often acrimonious, and sometimes violent controversy, centering upon measures but inevitably engulfing those who advocated or opposed. Webster was no exception; yet more than most he influenced his times and left an enduring heritage for succeeding generations. His ideas, expressed in legal and political argument; his contributions as advocate, as legislator, and as diplomatist; the impact of his opulent personality upon his contemporaries—all helped to mold and direct the course of the fledgling United States. The image that emerges from his papers is that of a many-faceted man, a little larger than life, strong-minded and strong-willed, gregarious, acquisitive, ambitious, basically honest, with a sure sense of reality and an unshakeable faith in the destiny of his country.

The outcome of the American Revolution had been resolved at Yorktown just three months before Daniel Webster was born at Salisbury, New Hampshire, on January 18, 1782. He was six when his father, a Revolutionary veteran and devoted admirer of Washington, served as delegate to the State convention that ratified the Constitution, a document soon fixed in young Webster's memory. He was a student at Dartmouth when the repressive Alien and Sedition laws threatened to tear the country apart, and was reading law in the office of a prominent Federalist politician when the Louisiana Purchase led other New England Federalists to scheme for a Northern Confederacy. Webster had just entered practice in Portsmouth, then New Hampshire's principal city, when Aaron Burr was acquitted of treason charges, growing out of a similar attempt to form a new Confederacy in the West. He was already active in local politics when Jefferson's embargo again brought the national government into ominous conflict with New England. His first election to Congress, in 1812, was as an outspoken opponent of commercial restrictions, and of the second war with England.

For the next forty years, until his death in 1852, Webster was active on the public stage. During these same four decades the face of America was irrevocably changed as the industrial revolution took root. The factory, powered by steam or falling water and subsidized by a tariff, largely replaced hand manufacture in the home. Eli Whitney's system of interchangeable parts became the basis of all mass production. The river barge and the stage coach gave way to the steamboat and the railroad. The telegraph and the rotary press combined to speed communication and to change the quality of life. The tide of settlement surged westward from the Appalachians to the Pacific coast. The Constitution, so admirably drawn by the revolutionary generation, was interpreted to provide guidelines for a different, rapidly changing world. The forms of administration were established much as they remain today, and the respective spheres of nation and states were delimited. The United States assumed her place as an equal in the family of nations, bearing her share and more of the world's commerce.

It was also during this period that sectionalism, born of geographical, climatic, and economic differences and deepened by the moral issue of human slavery, reached crisis proportions; and that an offsetting nationalism, strong enough to withstand even the shock of civil war, came into being.

In each of these movements of change, but most especially in the rise of American nationalism, Daniel Webster played a conspicuous and often a leading part. His correspondence is at once an illuminating commentary on men and events and a revealing picture of the everyday life of his times. His legal papers come near to being in themselves a history of American commercial and constitutional law, which they both illuminate and criticize. His diplomatic papers throw light upon crucial issues in foreign relations and outline new departures in policy. The northeastern boundary was only the best known of his contributions; he was also responsible for our first treaty with China and for the opening of Japan. He did as much as any single individual to define the legal framework of an expanding economy that shared in equal measure an agricultural, an industrial, and a commercial interest—an economy in which a subsidy to one interest might well work hardship upon another. He made himself an international authority on central banking, and on currency reform. He dealt incisively with all of the controversies of his day, most generally taking a position that came to be a milestone in the mainstream of national development. In a word, one cannot fully understand the first half of the nineteenth century without taking account of Daniel Webster. His papers constitute an indispensable source for the political, economic, legal, intellectual, and social history of his times.

It is a source that has hitherto been available only in fragmentary form to those who had not the time nor the money to search collections in literally hundreds of manuscript depositories. The purportedly definitive National Edition of the *Writings and Speeches of Daniel Webster* in 1903 was in fact little more than a reprinting of the 1851 edition of the *Works*, edited by Edward Everett with Webster's overt assistance, together with the two volumes of *Private Correspondence* published in 1856 by Fletcher Webster, and miscellaneous additions drawn largely from official files. Up to 1971, when a microfilm edition of Webster's correspondence, prepared by the present editor, was issued, no more than perhaps 20 percent of Webster's letters had ever been published. The percentage in print of letters to him was still smaller, and of his legal and diplomatic papers a hardly noticeable fraction.[1]

Documents included in the present volume cover the period from Webster's New Hampshire childhood to his emergence as a man of nation-wide fame and unlimited potential. Early papers comment on his schooling at Exeter and Dartmouth, his training in the law with staunch Federalist preceptors in Salisbury and Boston, and the launching of both legal and political careers. In both areas he soon outgrew the possibilities for advancement offered by his native state. His move to Boston in 1816 brought a more exacting but more lucrative legal practice and an opportunity to serve as political representative of widely varied interests. With the Dartmouth College case, the first of the Bank cases, *McCulloch* v. *Maryland,* and the steamboat case, *Gibbons* v. *Ogden*—all argued during this period—Webster achieved the very first rank among constitutional lawyers. Each of these cases dealt broadly with the division of power between nation and states. In each Webster spoke for national primacy, and each case was decided by the Marshall court in favor of his client.

In December 1819, with his Massachusetts Memorial opposing the Missouri Compromise, Webster took his first public stand against slavery. The following year he served as a respected and influential member of a convention to revise the Constitution of Massachusetts, where he gave utterance to the often-quoted phrase "power *naturally* and *necessarily* follows property." When he was returned to the House of Representatives from Boston, six years after the second of his two New Hampshire terms expired, it was as the acknowledged spokesman for New England Federalism, moribund as a party but alive and proselytizing as a body of political and economic doctrine. The volume ends as the year 1824 comes to a close, leaving Webster at the threshold of his brilliant career as a national statesman.

1. The provenance and publication history of the Webster papers will be found in the *Guide* to the microfilm edition, published by University Microfilms, Ann Arbor, Mich.

PLAN OF WORK

From its inception the Papers of Daniel Webster was planned as an integrated project, using both microfilm and letterpress publication. The persistent pressure of time and the steadily rising cost of book publication were important factors in the choice of the dual media, but the overriding consideration was the desire to bring all of Webster together, without abridgment or gloss, for those who were equipped to use it that way, while providing the less dedicated scholar and the general reader with the essential Webster in convenient annotated form. The microfilm edition, in four different groupings, is as complete as the surviving records permit. Webster's correspondence, including letters received as well as letters sent, together with miscellaneous notes, memoranda, briefs, drafts, formal writings, reports, petitions, and business papers have been issued with printed guide and index as *The Papers of Daniel Webster* by University Microfilms, Ann Arbor, Michigan. *The Legal Papers of Daniel Webster,* also issued with guide and alphabetical list of cases by University Microfilms, consists of records drawn primarily from the county courts of New Hampshire and Massachusetts and from the state and lower federal courts in New England. Records of the Department of State and of the Supreme Court are available on film from the National Archives and Records Service of the General Services Administration, but the user must select for himself the reels that may contain Webster material.

The value of this film, including as it does virtually all known Webster papers, cannot be overstated; but its very magnitude makes it unmanageable. It is relatively expensive, requires special equipment to use, is hard on the eyes, and effectively buries the grains of wheat by mixing them unevenly with an enormous amount of chaff. The user of the film, moreover, must decipher for himself often difficult or faded handwriting. He must search out the identity of persons and the nature of events alluded to, and finally he must rely upon his own judgment as to the significance of the given document. In the letterpress edition all this has been done for him, even to the selection of documents in terms of their significance, by editors totally immersed in the time and place and almost as familiar with the central characters as was Webster himself.

The letterpress edition in effect complements and renders more useful these various microfilm collections, whose very existence has made it possible to select more rigorously the documents important enough to be offered to the larger audience reached by the printed book. Each volume of correspondence, moreover, includes a calendar of letters written in the same time period but not selected for publication. For each of these the microfilm frame number is cited, as is volume and page citation for any document now available only in a printed version. Footnote references are also made to the film wherever appropriate. For the general reader and for the student of the period rather than of the man, the editors believe the selection of items printed will be ample. The biographer, and the scholar pursuing an in-depth study of some segment of the times, will need the film, to which he will find the printed volumes an indispensable annotated guide.

The letterpress edition is being published in four different series, overlapping in time but not in content, in order to make maximum use of subject matter specialists as technical editors. The edition has been planned in a total of fourteen volumes, of which seven are correspondence, three are legal papers, two are diplomatic papers, and two are speeches and formal writings. The present volume, including the period through 1824, is the first of the correspondence series.

EDITORIAL METHOD

Letters and other documents included in this volume are arranged in chronological sequence, irrespective of whether Webster was the writer or the recipient. The only exception is for letters that were sent as enclosures in later correspondence. These have been placed immediately after the document which they accompanied. Date and point of origin have been placed at the upper right of each letter. If all or part of this information has been supplied by the editors, it appears in square brackets, with a question mark if conjecture. The complimentary close, which in the original manuscripts often takes up three or four lines, has been run continuously with the last line of the text.

All letters are reproduced in full except in rare instances where the only surviving text is incomplete or is from a printed source which did not reproduce it in its entirety. Needless to say, texts from printed sources are used only when the original manuscript has not been found, but the letter is of sufficient importance to warrant its inclusion.

The letters themselves have been reproduced in type as nearly as possible the way they were written. Misspellings have been retained without the annoyingly obtrusive "(*sic*)"; and abbreviations and contractions have been allowed to stand unless the editor feels they will not be readily understood by a present-day reader. In such cases the abbreviation has been expanded, with square brackets enclosing the letters supplied. Punctuation, too, has been left as Webster and his correspondents used it, save only that dashes clearly intended as periods are so written. Superscript letters in abbreviations or contractions have been brought down, but a period is supplied only if the last letter of the abbreviation is not the last letter of the word abbreviated. In all other cases, periods, apostrophes, dashes, and other forms of punctuation have been left as Webster and his contemporaries used them. The ampersand, far more frequently used than the spelled out "and," has been retained, but diacritical marks over contractions have been omitted even where the contraction itself is retained.

Canceled words or passages that are obvious slips, immediately corrected, have been left out altogether; those which show some change of thought or attitude or have stylistic or psychological implications have been included between angled brackets. Interlineations by the author have been incorporated into the text, but marginal passages, again if by the author, have been treated as postscripts and placed below the signature.

In order to keep explanatory footnotes to a minimum, general notes have been interspersed from time to time with the letters that constitute the text of the volume. These serve to indicate what Webster was doing at a particular time or to explain a sequence of events that may help to clarify subsequent correspondence. Footnotes are used to identify persons, places, events, situations, problems, or other matters that help to understand the context of a particular reference.

Individuals are identified only once, generally the first time they are mentioned. For the convenience of the reader who may have missed this first reference, the appropriate index entry is printed in bold face type. Well-known individuals—those in the *Dictionary of American Biography* or the *Biographical Directory of the American Congress*—have not been identified at all unless the context seems to require it. The extent of footnoting has been reduced by adding given names and initials in square brackets where text references are to surnames only.

Immediately following each document is an unnumbered note indicating the provenance of the document and if appropriate, giving some information about the writer or recipient. Symbols used in these provenance notes are the standard descriptive symbols and the location symbols developed by the Union Catalog Division of the Library of Congress. Those appearing in the present volume have been listed under Abbreviations and Symbols below.

Webster Chronology, 1782–1824

1782	*January 18*	Daniel Webster born in Salisbury, New Hampshire, second son of Captain Ebenezer Webster and his second wife, Abigail Eastman.
1784	*January*	Family moved to Salisbury Lower Village, three miles east of Daniel's birthplace.
1796	*May 27*	Entered Phillips Exeter Academy, at Exeter, New Hampshire.
	December	Withdrew from Phillips Exeter at close of fall term, probably for financial reasons.
1797	*February*	Began college preparatory study with Rev. Dr. Samuel Wood, Boscawen, New Hampshire.
	August	Entered Dartmouth College.
1799/1800		Family moved to "The Elms," Salisbury (later Franklin), New Hampshire.
1800	*July 4*	Delivered Independence Day address at Hanover, New Hampshire.
1801	*August 26*	Graduated from Dartmouth.
	August	Began to study law in the office of Thomas W. Thompson, Salisbury, New Hampshire.
1802	*January*	Began teaching school at Fryeburg Academy, Fryeburg, Maine.
	September	Returned to Salisbury and resumed legal studies with Thompson.
1804	*July 20*	Entered law office of Christopher Gore in Boston as a student.
1805	*February*	Published anonymously *An Appeal to the Old Whigs of New Hampshire;* his first substantial political essay.
	March	Admitted to practice before the Court of Common Pleas in Boston.
	April	Opened his own law office in Boscawen, New Hampshire.
	December 13	Abigail Webster Haddock, one of his two older sisters, died.
1806	*April 22*	Captain Ebenezer Webster, Daniel's father, died at the age of 67.

	July 4	Delivered Independence Day address at Concord, New Hampshire.
	August 26	Delivered address on "The State of our Literature" before the Phi Beta Kappa Society of Dartmouth.
1807	*May*	Admitted as Counselor in the Superior Court of New Hampshire.
	June 22	U.S. Frigate *Chesapeake* fired upon by British warship off Hampton Roads.
	September	Moved to Portsmouth, New Hampshire, and established law practice there.
	December 22	Embargo Act became law.
1808	*May 29*	Married Grace Fletcher of Hopkinton, New Hampshire.
	March to November	Campaigned for Federalist candidates.
	October	Published pamphlet, "Considerations on the Embargo Laws."
1809	*March 1*	Non-Intercourse Act in effect.
1810	*April 29*	Webster's first child, Grace Fletcher Webster, born.
1811	*March 19*	Sarah Jane Webster, Daniel's youngest sister, died.
	June 26	Appointed, with Jeremiah Mason and John Goddard, to committee to revise the criminal code of New Hampshire.
1812	*June 18*	Congress declared war on Great Britain.
	July 4	Webster used Independence Day address before the Washington Benevolent Society of Portsmouth as an instrument for taking issue with the war policy of the Madison Administration.
	August 5	Rockingham Memorial opposing war, prepared by Webster on behalf of New Hampshire Federalists, approved at party rally.
	November	Webster elected to Congress on Federalist ticket.
	December 2	Madison chosen President by Electoral College.
1813	*May 24*	Took his seat in House of Representatives. Clay and Calhoun were beginning their second term.
	May 28–29	Battle of Sackett's Harbor.
	June 1	Destruction of the *Chesapeake*.
	June 10	Introduced resolutions designed to reopen

		debate on origins of the war, and in support of them made his first speech in Congress.
	June 21	Resolutions passed. Webster delivered them to the President.
	July 23	Second child, Daniel Fletcher Webster, born.
	December 22	Webster's Portsmouth home destroyed by fire while he was on the way to Washington for the second session of the 13th Congress.
1814	*January 14*	Delivered major speech in opposition to enlistment bill.
	February	Admitted to practice before the Supreme Court of the United States.
	March 12	Presented first argument before the Supreme Court.
	July 4	Mehitable Webster, remaining older sister, died.
	August 24	British captured Washington, burning the Capitol and the White House.
	August 29	Re-elected to Congress.
	September	Portsmouth Committee of Defense, chaired by Webster, organized to defend the city against expected attacks by British forces.
	December 15	Convening of Hartford Convention.
	December 24	Treaty ending war with Britain signed at Ghent, Belgium.
1815	*January 8*	Battle of New Orleans won by Andrew Jackson.
1816	*April 10*	Second Bank of the United States chartered.
	April 25	Abigail Eastman Webster, Daniel's mother, died.
	April	Challenged by John Randolph over misunderstanding in the House of Representatives; disagreement settled without a duel.
	April 30	Passage of Webster's resolutions on the currency.
	August 14	Moved from Portsmouth to Boston.
	December 4	Electoral College elected James Monroe President.
1817	*January 1*	Second Bank of the United States opened.
	January 23	Daughter, Grace Fletcher Webster, died.
	March 4	Second term in House of Representatives ended. His move to Boston had precluded his seeking re-election from New Hampshire.

	September 19	Appeared with Jeremiah Smith and Jeremiah Mason for the plaintiff in *Dartmouth College* v. *Woodward* before the New Hampshire Superior Court of Appeals, Exeter, New Hampshire.
1818	January 16	Third child, Julia, born.
	March 10	Delivered main argument in the Dartmouth College Case before the Supreme Court of the United States.
	May–September	President Monroe's northeastern tour, symbolizing "era of good feelings."
	July 4–25	Published defense of General Israel Putnam in the Boston *Columbian Centinel*.
1819	February 2	Chief Justice Marshall, speaking for a majority of the Court, sustained Dartmouth College in terms reminiscent of Webster's argument: A corporate charter is a contract, as defined by the Constitution.
	February 22	Argued the case for the Bank of the United States—the real plaintiff—in *McCulloch* v. *Maryland*: A state may not tax an instrumentality of the Federal Government because the power to tax involves the power to destroy.
	February 22	Adams-Onís Treaty, by which Spain ceded Florida to the United States, signed in Washington.
	August	Publication of report of arguments in Dartmouth College case.
	December	Presentation to Congress of Massachusetts Memorial on Missouri question, drafted by Webster.
1820	March 3	Missouri Compromise passed. Though not in Congress, Webster opposed it.
	July 20	Fourth child, Edward, born.
	November	Named a presidential elector for Massachusetts.
	November 15/ January 9	Delegate to Massachusetts constitutional convention.
	December 22	Delivered oration commemorating bicentennial of the landing of the Pilgrims, Plymouth, Massachusetts.
1821	December 31	Fifth child, Charles, born.

1822	*January*	Made his first appearance before the Spanish Claims Commission.
	February 22	Spain ratified Florida Treaty.
	May 30	Took seat in Massachusetts General Court, representing a Boston district.
	September	Spanish Claims Commission began hearing cases.
	November 4	Elected to House of Representatives from Boston on the Federalist ticket.
1823	*February*	Named adviser to the Boston branch of the Bank of the United States.
	December 2	Monroe Doctrine announced in President's annual message to Congress.
1824	*January 19*	Spoke in behalf of Greek independence.
	February 4	Argued in the Supreme Court for the plaintiff in *Gibbons* v. *Ogden*, the case that clarified and extended Federal jurisdiction over internal commerce. Decision rendered March 2.
	March 30–31	Clay coins phrase "American System" in speech before House of Representatives.
	April 2	Delivered antitariff speech in House.
	September	Visited Marshfield, Massachusetts, for first time.
	November	Re-elected to House of Representatives from Boston.
	November	Jackson led Adams, Crawford, and Clay in Presidential election, but lacked majority of electoral vote.
	December 9/21	Visited Madison and Jefferson.
	December 19	Son, Charles Webster, died.

Abbreviations and Symbols

MBBS	Bostonian Society
MBNU	Northeastern University
MBevHi	Beverly Historical Society, Beverly, Mass.
MH	Harvard University
MHi	Massachusetts Historical Society, Boston
MWA	American Antiquarian Society, Worcester, Mass.
MWalB	Brandeis University
MWelC	Wellesley College
MdHi	Maryland Historical Society, Baltimore
MeBP	Pejepscot Historical Society, Brunswick, Me.
MeHi	Maine Historical Society, Portland
Mi–U	University of Michigan
MiU–C	William L. Clements Library, U. of Michigan
NHi	New-York Historical Society, New York City
NIC	Cornell University
NN	New York Public Library
NNC	Columbia University
NNPM	Pierpont Morgan Library
NNS	New York Society Library
Nc–Ar	North Carolina State Department of Archives and History, Raleigh
NcU	University of North Carolina, Chapel Hill
Nh	New Hampshire State Library, Concord
Nh–Ar	New Hampshire Division of Records Management and Archives, Concord
NhD	Dartmouth College
NhExP	Phillips Exeter Academy, Exeter, N.H.
NhHi	New Hampshire Historical Society, Concord
NjMD	Drew University, Madison, N.J.
NjP	Princeton University
NjR	Rutgers, The State University, New Brunswick
OCHP	Cincinnati Historical Society
OClWHi	Western Reserve Historical Society, Cleveland
PHi	Historical Society of Pennsylvania
PPAmP	American Philosophical Society
PPIn	Independence Hall National Park
PPL	Library Company of Philadelphia
RHi	Rhode Island Historical Society
RPB	Brown University Library
ScHi	South Carolina Historical Society, Charleston
ScU	University of South Carolina

ViU	University of Virginia
WaU	University of Washington

SHORT TITLES

ADC	George T. Chapman, *Sketches of the Alumni of Dartmouth College*, Cambridge, Mass., 1867.
Curtis	George Ticknor Curtis, *Life of Daniel Webster*, 2 vols. New York, 1870.
mDW	Microfilm Edition of the Papers of Daniel Webster, Ann Arbor, 1971. References followed by frame numbers.
mDWs	Microfilm edition of the Papers of Daniel Webster, supplementary reel, Ann Arbor, 1974.
MHi Proc.	Proceedings of the Massachusetts Historical Society.
PC	Fletcher Webster, ed., *The Private Correspondence of Daniel Webster*, 2 vols. Boston, 1856.
Van Tyne	Claude H. Van Tyne, ed., *The Letters of Daniel Webster*, New York, 1902.
W & S	James W. McIntyre, ed., *The Writings and Speeches of Daniel Webster*, National Edition, 18 vols. New York, 1903.

THE PAPERS OF DANIEL WEBSTER

CHARLES M. WILTSE, EDITOR-IN-CHIEF

SERIES ONE: CORRESPONDENCE

The Papers, 1798–1824

The fragment of autobiography reproduced in the following pages was written in 1829, after Webster had recovered from the first shock of his brother Ezekiel's death in April but before his courtship of Caroline Le Roy, the second Mrs. Webster began, probably in November. It was prepared, according to Fletcher Webster, for Mrs. Eliza Buckminster Lee, who retained the manuscript in her possession until after Webster's death. Eliza Buckminster was an intimate and indispensable family friend from her girlhood. She may, indeed, have been related to Grace Fletcher, the first Mrs. Webster, whose half brother, James W. Paige, refers to her on at least one occasion as "cousin Eliza." (See below, Paige to DW, December 19, 1824.)

The Autobiography begins in leisurely fashion but hurries toward the end and terminates abruptly with a few scattered references to events of 1816–1817. It is chiefly valuable for the picture it gives of the Webster family and of Daniel's early life, education, and political beginnings, but it is notable for the fact that he took time to write it in a crowded and emotionally charged year, to serve no purpose but to gratify a friend. Webster was born January 18, 1782, on a farm near Salisbury, New Hampshire, the fourth child of Ebenezer Webster (1739–1806) and his second wife, Abigail Eastman Webster (1739–1816). The farm, once the northernmost cleared land in New England, supported a large family, adequately if not in luxury. No attempt has been made to annotate the Autobiography. Discrepancies, if they are significant, are noted in connection with the contemporary evidence of the correspondence reproduced later in this volume.

[AUTOBIOGRAPHY]

My earliest ancestor, of whom I possess, at present any knowledge, was Thomas Webster. He was settled in Hampton, N. Hamp, as early as 1636; probably having come thither from, or thro' Mass, tho he may have come by way of Piscataqua. From him to myself the descent may be found regularly recorded in the Church Records & Town Records of Hampton, Kingston, (now East Kingston) & Salisbury.

The family is, no doubt, originally from Scotland, altho' I have not been able to learn how far back any Scotch accent was found lingering on our tongue. Probably enough, the emigrants may have come last from

England. The characteristics of the personal appearance of the Websters
are pretty strongly marked, & very generally found with all who bear the
name in New England. They have light complexions, sandy hair, a good
deal of it, and bushy eyebrows; & are rather slender, than broad, or cor-
pulent. Dr Noah Webster, the author of the Dictionary, is a *vera effigies*
of the race. Revd. Mr Webster, now of Hampton, the large family in the
County of Grafton, & the various remnants of the old stock still to be
found in Kingston, & its neighborhood, bear the same general appearance.

My uncles were formed & marked, in the same manner. No two persons
looked more unlike than my father, & either of his brothers. His mother
was a Bachelder, a descendant of the Revd. Stephen Bachelder, a man of
some notoriety, in his time, in the County of Rockingham. This woman
had black hair, & black eyes, & was, besides, as my father, who was her
eldest son, has told me, a person of uncommon strength of character. I
learn the same thing, from the elderly inhabitants of Kingston. My father
resembled, in complexion & appearance, his mother; his brothers resembled their father. Of my own Brothers, only one had the *Bachelder*
complexion; the others, (three) ran off into the general characteristics
belonging to the name.

My first distinct & clear recollection of my fathers appearance was
when he was at the age of fifty. I think it was rather striking. He was tall,
six feet, or six feet within half an inch, erect, with a broad & full chest,
hair still of unchanged black, features rather large & prominent, a Roman nose, & eyes of brilliant black. He had a decisive air, & bearing,
partly the effect, I suppose, of early soldiership. My late brother, at the
moment of his decease, was nearly of the same age, & most strongly resembled him; except that his hair had turned white, his eyes were larger,
& not quite so black, & his mouth & teeth hardly as perfect. In subsequent
periods, my father suffered much ill health, from rheumatism, & other
complaints, which a good deal changed his appearance.

He was born at King[s]ton, now East King[s]ton, in 1739; the eldest
son of Eben[eze]r Webster, & Susannah Bachelder. His father was a
farmer, as we somewhat improperly call persons of his condition. That is
to say, he was a small freeholder, tilling his own acres with his own
hands, & those of his boys, till they grew up to manhood, when they were
to look out, in the Country round them, for acres of their own to till. From
about the age of 12 or 15, he lived several years in the family of a Col
[Ebenezer] Stevens, the most considerable person then in the vicinity; &
then, as Major Dalgetty would say, he *took service* in the troops, raised in
the Provinces, to carry on the French War. His first engagement, I believe, was in Robert Roger's company of Rangers. He was with the Army
of Genl Amherst, when that commander made his way by Albany, Os-

wego, Ticonderoga &c, into Canada. When Canada was conquered, his occupation was gone; but that event opened new scenes of enterprise, more pacific, but promising more permanent good, to those who had strong hands, & determined purpose.

Previous to the year 1763, the settlements in N.H. had made little or no progress inward, into the Country, for sixty or seventy years; owing to the hostility of the French, in Canada, & of the neighboring Indians, who were under French influence. This powerful cause of repression being effectually removed by the cession of Canada to England, by the Peace of Paris, in 1763, companies were formed in various parts of New England to settle the wilderness, between the already settled parts of New England & New York, & Canada. Col Stevens, already mentioned, & other persons about King[s]ton, formed one of these companies, & obtained from Benning Wentworth, Govr. of the Province of New Hamp, [a grant] of the township of Salisbury, at first called Stevens' town. It is situated exactly at the head of Merrimac River, & very near the center of the State. My father joined this enterprise, & about 1764 (the exact date is not before me) pushed into the wilderness. He had the discretion to take a wife along with him; intending, whatever else he might want, at least not to lack good company. The party *travelled out the road*, or path, for it was no better, somewhere about Concord, or Boscawen; & then were obliged to *make* their way, (not *finding* one) to their destined places of habitation. My father *lapped on* a little beyond the other comers, & when he had built his log cabin, & lighted his fire, his smoke ascended nearer to the north star, than that of any other of his Majesty's New England subjects. His nearest civilized neighbor on the north, was at Montreal.

His story of this early settlement was interesting, at least to me. The settlers doubtless suffered much. The mountainous nature of the Country, the very long winters, with prodigious depth of snow, & the want of all roads to communicate with the Country below, often induced great hardships. The settlement increased, & when the Revolutionary War broke out, ten or eleven years after, the town contained near two hundred men capable of bearing arms. My father was their Captain, & he led them forth, with the other N. Hampshire troops, almost every campaign. He commanded a Company at Bennington, at White Plains, at West Point, at the time of Arnold's defection &c. I have some little articles, the *spolia proelii* of Bennington, which I keep, *honore parentis*. The last time I ever saw Genl Stark, he did me the compliment to say, that my complexion was like that of my father, & that his was of that cast, so convenient for a soldier, that burnt gun powder did not change it.

I was born, January 18th. 1782. My Father, by two marriages, had 5 sons, & 5 daughters. I am the youngest son, & only surviving child. I have nephews & nieces, both of the whole & the half blood; that is to say, sons & daughters of my brothers & sisters, of both of my father's wives.

"The year following my birth, my father removed from his first residence, which was on the hills, to the [Merrimac] River side, in the same town; a distance of three miles. Here, in the meadow land, by the River, with rough high hills hanging over, was the scene of my earliest recollections; or, as was said in another case, "here I found myself." I can recollect *when it was* 1790; but cannot say that I can remember farther back. I have a very vivid impression, indeed, of something, which took place some years earlier; especially, of an extraordinary rise in the River. I remember how the deluge of rain beat, for two days, on the house; how all looked anxiously to see the River overflow its banks, how the waters spread over the meadows, how the boat, coming from afar, on the other side of the river, was rowed up till it almost touched the door stone, how Mr G's 'great barn', fifty feet by twenty, full of hay & grain, sheep, turkies & chickens, sailed down the current majestically before our eyes, & how we were all busy in preparing to fly to the mountains, so soon as our house should manifest a disposition to follow Mr. G's barn.

I remember, or seem to remember, all these things. I did indeed see as much of them as a child of five years could see, (for I think it was in 1787), but still I am of opinion that my impression is from narrative, & not from remembrance of the vision. Plain, intelligible & striking things, of this kind, I have learned, make an impression on young minds, in recital, which it is difficult afterwards to distinguish from actual personal recollection.

I do not remember when, or by whom I was taught to read; because I cannot, & never could, recollect a time when I could not read the Bible. I suppose I was taught by my mother, or perhaps by my elder sisters. My father seemed to have no higher object in the world, than to educate his children, to the full extent of his very limited ability. No means were within his reach, generally speaking, but the small town schools. These were kept, by teachers sufficiently indifferent, in the several neighborhoods of the township, each a small part of the year. To these I was sent, with the other children. When the school was in our neighborhood, it was easy to attend; when it removed to a more distant District I followed it, still living at home. While yet quite young, & in the winter, I was sent daily two & a half or three miles to the school. When it removed still farther, my father sometimes boarded me out, in a neighboring family, so that I could still be in the school. A good deal of this was an extra care, more than had been bestowed on my elder brothers, & originated in a conviction of the slenderness & frailty of my constitution, which was thought not likely ever to allow me to pursue robust occupation.

In these schools, nothing was taught but reading & writing; &, as to these, the first I generally could perform better than the teacher, & the last a good master could hardly instruct me in, writing was so laborious, irksome & repulsive an occupation to me always. My masters used to tell me, that they feared, after all, my fingers were destined for the plough tail.

I must do myself the justice to say, that in these boyish days there were two things I did dearly love, v[i]z reading, & playing; passions, which did not cease to struggle, when boyhood was over, (have they yet, altogether), & in regard to which neither the *cita mors*, nor the *laeta victoria* could be said of either.

At a very early day, owing I believe, mainly to the exertions of Mr [Thomas W.] Thompson, the Lawyer, the Clergyman [Thomas Worcester], & my father, a very small circulating library had been bought. These institutions, I believe, abt. that time recd an impulse, among other causes, from the efforts of Dr. [Jeremy] Belknap, our N. Hamp. historian. I obtained some of these books, & read them. I remember the Spectator among them; & I remember, too, that I turned over the leaves of Addisons criticism on Chevy Chase, for the sake of reading, connectedly, the song, the verses of which he quotes, from time [to time], as subjects of remark. It was,—as Dr Johnson said in another case,—the poet was read & the critic was neglected. I could not understand why it was necessary that the author of the Spectator should take so great pains to prove that Chevy Chase was a good story. That was the last thing I doubted.

I was fond of poetry. By far the greater part of Dr. Watts' Psalms & Hymns I could repeat, memoriter, at 10 or 12 yrs of age. I am sure no other sacred poetry will ever appear to me so affecting, & devout. I remember that my father brought home from some of the lower towns Popes essay on Man, published in a sort of Pamphlet. I took it, & very soon could repeat it, from beginning to end. We had so few books, that to read them once or twice was nothing. We thought they were all to be got by heart. I have thought of this frequently since, when that sagacious admonition of one of the Ancients (was it Pliny?) has been quoted. Regere *multum*, non *multa*.

I remember ·one occurrence, that shews the value then attached to Books. The close of the year had brought along the next year's Almanac. This was an acquisition. A page was devoted to each month, & on the top of each page were four lines of poetry;—some moral, some sentimental, some ludicrous. The Almanack came in the morning, & before night my brother & myself were masters of its contents—at least of its poetry, & its anecdotes. We went to bed upon it; but awaking long before the morning light, we had a difference of recollection about one word, in the third line of *April's* poetry. We could not settle it by argument, & there was no umpire. But the *fact* could be ascertained by inspection of the Book. I arose, groped my way to the kitchen, lighted a candle, proceeded to a distant room, in search of the Almanac, found it, & brought it away. The disputed passage was examined, I believe I was found to be in the wrong, & blew out my candle, & went to bed. But the consequences of my error had well nigh been serious. It was about two oclock, in the morning, & just as I was again going to sleep, I thought [I saw] signs of light, in the room I had visited. I sprang out of bed, ran to the door, opened the room, & it was all on fire. I had let fall a spark, or touched the light, to some thing that had communicated fire to a parcel of cotton clothes, they had communicated it to the furniture, & to the sides of the room, & the flames had already begun to shew themselves thro' the ceiling, in the chamber above. A pretty earnest cry soon brought the household together. By great good luck, we escaped. Two or three minutes more, & we should all have been in danger of burning together. As it was, I think the house was saved by my father's presence of mind. While others went for water, he seized every thing movable, which was on fire, & wrapped it up in woolen blankets. My maternal grandmother, then of the age of eighty, was sleeping in the room.

I recollect no great changes happening to me till I was 14 yrs old. A great deal of the time I was sick, & when well was exceedingly slender, & apparently of feeble system. I read what I could get to read; went to School when I could; & when not at school, was a farmers youngest boy, not good for much, for want of health & strength, but expected to do something. Up to this period, I had no hope of any education beyond what the village school house was to afford. But now my father took an important step with me. On the 25th day of May, 1796, he mounted his horse, placed me on another, carried me to Exeter, & placed me in Phillips Academy, then & now under the care of that most excellent man, DR. BENJAMIN ABBOTT. I had never been from home before, & the change overpowered me. I hardly remained master of my own senses, among ninety boys, who had seen so much more, & appeared to know so much more than I did. I was put to English Grammar, & writing & arithmetic. The first I think I may say, I fairly mastered, between May & October; in the others I made some progress. In the Autumn, there was a short vacation; I went home, staid a few days, & returned at the commencement of the quarter; & then began the Latin Grammar. My first exercises in Latin were recited to JOSEPH STEVENS BUCKMINSTER.[1] He had, I think, already

1. Joseph Stevens Buckminster, destined for a brief but brilliant career as a Unitarian minister, was at this time only 12 years old. He had already completed his own academic work at Exeter, but was felt by his

joined College, but had returned to Exeter, perhaps in the College vacation, & was acting as usher, in the absence of Dr. Abbott, then absent thro' indisposition. It so happened, that within the few months during which I was at the Exeter Academy, Mr [Peter Oxenbridge] Thacher, now Judge of the Municipal Court of Boston,[2] & Mr [Nicholas] Emery, the distinguished Counsellor at Portland, were my instructors. I am proud to call them both masters.

I believe I made tolerable progress, in most branches which I attended to, while in this school; but there was one thing I could not do. I could not make a declamation. I could not speak, before the School. The kind & excellent Buckminster sought, especially, to persuade me to perform the exercise of declamation, like other boys, but I could not do it. Many a piece did I commit to memory, & recite & rehearse, in my own room, over & over again; yet, when the day came, when the School collected to hear declamations, when my name was called, & I saw all eyes turned to my seat, I could not raise myself from it. Sometimes the instructors frowned, sometimes they smiled. Mr Buckminster always pressed, & entreated, most winningly that I would venture—but I could never command sufficient resolution. When the occasion was over, I went home & wept bitter tears of mortification.

At the winter vacation, Decr 1796, or Jany, 1797, my father came for me, & took me home. Some long enduring friendships I formed, in the few months I was at Exeter. J. W. Brackett, late of N York, deceased, Wm Garland, late of Portsmo[uth], deceased, Govr. [Lewis] Cass, of Michigan, Mr Saltonstall, & James H. Bingham, now of Claremont, N. Hampshire, are of the number.

In Febry. 1797, my father carried me to the Revd. Saml Wood[']s, in Boscawen, & placed me under the tuition of that most benevolent & excellent man. It was but half a dozen miles from our own house. On the way to Mr Wood[']s, my father first intimated to me his intention of sending me to College. The very idea thrilled my whole frame. He said, he then lived but for his children; & if I would do all I could, for myself, he would do what he could for me. I remember that I was quite over come— & my head grew dizzy. The thing appeared to me so high, & the expense & sacrifice it was to cost my father so great, I could only press his hands, &

---

father, the Reverend Joseph Buckminster of Portsmouth, to be too young to enter college. Webster calls attention to the name by double underlining (here rendered by small capitals) because Buckminster was the older brother of Eliza Buckminster Lee for whom the autobiography was written.

2. Webster does not mention his own agency in securing the judgeship for Thacher. See DW to Gov. John Brooks, December 25, 1821, below.

shed tears. Excellent, excellent Parent! I cannot think of him, even now, without turning child again.

Mr Wood put me upon Virgil & Tully; & I conceived a pleasure in the study of them, especially the latter, which rendered application no longer a task. With what vehemence, did I denounce Cataline! with what earnestness struggle for Milo! In the Spring, I began the Greek Grammar, & at midsummer, Mr Wood said to me—"I expected to keep you till next year—but I am tired of you, & I shall put you into College next month." And so he did; but it was a mere breaking in. I was, indeed, miserably prepared, both in Latin & Greek; but Mr. Wood accomplished his promise, & I entered Dart. Col. as a freshman, Aug. 1797. At Boscawen I had found an[other] circulating Library, & had read many of its volumes. I remember, especially, that I found Don Quixote, in the common translation, & in an edition, as I think, of three or four duodecimo volumes. I began to read it; & it is literally true that I never closed my eyes till I had finished it; nor did I lay it down for 5 minutes; so great was the power of that extraordinary book on my imagination.

Of my College life, I can say little. Tho' death has made great havoc, in our class, some yet live, who were intimate with me;—especially Mr Bingham, before mentioned. Revd. Mr [David] Jewett, of Gloucester, (Sandy Bay), Revd. Mr [Caleb Jewett] Tenney, of Weathersfield, Revr. Thos Abbott Merrill, of Middlebury, Judge [Henry Weld] Fuller of Augusta, Mr [William] Farrar, of Lancaster, Judge [Sanford] Kingsbury, of Gardiner, & several others of the Class are still living. I was graduated, in course, Aug 1801. Owing to some difficulties, (haec *non* meminisse juvat) I took no part in the Commencement exercises. I spoke an oration to the Society of the United Fraternity, which I suspect was a sufficiently boyish performance.

My College life was not an idle one. Besides the regular attendance on prescribed duties & studies, I read something, of English history, & English Literature. Perhaps my reading was too miscellaneous. I even paid my board, for a year, by superintending a little weekly newspaper, & making selections for it, from books of literature, & from the cotempor[ar]y publications. I suppose I sometimes wrote a foolish paragraph myself. While in College, I delivered two or three occasional addresses, which were published. I trust they are forgotten. They were in very bad taste. I had not then learned, that all true power, in writing, is in the idea, not in the style; an error, into which the *Ars Rhetorica*, as it is usually taught, may easily lead stronger heads than mine.

I must now go back, a little, to make mention of some incidents connected with my Brother, Ezekiel Webster. He was almost two years older than myself, having been born March 11. 1780. He was a healthy, strong built, robust boy. His intellectual character, as it afterwards developed itself, was not early understood, at least in its full extent. He was thought to have good sense, but not to have, & perhaps had not, great quickness of apprehension. The older brothers were married & settled. My father's plan was, that this brother should remain with him. This was the domestic state of things, when I went to College, in Aug 1797. But I soon began to grow uneasy about my brother's situation. His prospects were not promising, & he himself saw & felt this; & had aspirations, beyond his condition. Nothing was proposed, however, by way of change of plan, till two years after. In the Spring of 1799, at the May vacation, I being then Sophomore, I visited my family, & then held serious consultation with my brother. I remember well, that when we went to bed, we began to talk matters over, & that we rose, after sunrise, without having shut our eyes. But we had settled our plan. He had thought of going into some new part of the Country—that was discussed, & disagreed to. All the *pros* and *cons* of the question of remaining at home were weighed & considered.— & when our Counsel broke up (or rather *got* up) it's result was, that I should propose to my father, that he, late as it was, should be sent to School, also, & to College. This, we knew, would be a trying thing to my father & mother, & two unmarried sisters. My father was growing old, his health not good, & his circumstances far from easy. The farm was to be carried on, & the family taken care of; & there was nobody to do all this, but he would [who] was regarded as the main stay, that is to say, Ezekiel. However I ventured upon the negotiation, & it was carried, as other things are often, by the earnest & sanguine manner of youth. I told him, that I was unhappy myself, at my brother's prospects. For myself, I saw my way to knowledge, respectability, & self protection; but as to him, all looked the other way. That I would keep school, & get along as well as I could—be more than four years in getting thro' College, if necessary, provided he also could be sent to study. He said at once, that he lived but for his children; that he had but little, & on that little he put no value, except so far as it might be useful to them. That to carry us both thro' College, would take all he was worth—that for himself he was willing to run the risk, but that this was a serious matter to our mother, & two unmarried sisters. That we must settle the matter with them, & if their consent was obtained, he would trust to Providence, & get along as well as he could.—The result was, that in about ten days, I had gone back to College, having first seen my brother take [leave] of the meadows, & place himself in school, under a teacher in Latin. Soon afterwards, he went to Mr Wood[']s, there pursued the requisite studies, & my father carried him, with me, to College, in March 1801, when he joined the then Freshman class.

Being graduated, in Aug 1801, I immediately entered Mr Thompson's Office, in Salisbury, next door to my fathers house to study the law. There I remained till Jan, following, v[i]z Jan: 1802. The necessity of the case required, that I should then go somewhere and earn a little money. I was written to, luckily, to go to Fryeburg, Maine, to keep school. I accepted the offer—traversed the Country on horseback— & commenced my labors. I was to be paid at the rate of 350 Dlls per annum. This was no small thing; for I compared it, not with what might be before me, but was actually behind me. It was better, certainly, than following the plough. But let me say something in favor of my own industry; not to make a merit of it, for necessity sometimes makes the most idle industrious. It so happened, that I boarded, at Fryeburg, with the Gentleman, (James Osgood Esq) who was Register of Deeds of the then newly created County of Oxford. He was not *Clerical*, in & of himself; & his registrations were to be done by Deputy. The fee for recording, at full length, a common deed, in a large fair hand, & with the care requisite to avoid errors, was *two shillings & three pence*. Mr Osgood proposed to me, that I should do this writing, & that of the two shillings & three pence for each deed, I should have one shilling & six pence, & he should have the remaining nine pence. I greedily seized on so tempting an offer, & set to work. Of a long winter's evening I could copy two deeds— & that was half a dollar. Four evenings in a week earned two dollars — & two dollars a week paid my board. This appeared to me to be a very thriving condition; for my 350 Dlls salary as a Schoolmaster was thus going on, without abatement or deduction for *vivres*. I hope yet to have an opportunity to see once more the first volume of the Records of Deeds for the County of Oxford. It is now near thirty years, since I copied into it the last "witness my hand & seal."—& I have not seen, even its outside, since. But the *ache* is not yet out of my fingers; for nothing has ever been so laborious to me as writing, when under a necessity of writing a good hand.

In May, of this year, (1802) having a weeks vacation, I took my quarter's salary, mounted a horse, went straight over all the hills to Hanover, & had the pleasure of putting these, the first earnings of my life, into my brother's hands, for his College expenses. Having enjoyed this sincere & high pleasure, I hied me back again, to my School, & my copying of deeds. I staid at Fryeburg only till September. My brother then came to see me, we made a journey together, to the lower parts of Maine, returned to Salisbury, I resumed my place in Mr Thompson's office, & he went back to College.

At Fryeburg, I found another Circulating Library & made some use of it. I remember to have read, while at Fryeburg, Adams' defence of the American Constitutions, Mosheims Ecclesiastical History, Goldsmith's history of England, & some other small things. I borrowed Blackstones Commentaries, also, & read I think two or three vols of them. Here also I found Mr Ames' celebrated speech, on the British Treaty, & committed it to memory.

From September 1802, to Feb. or March 1804, I remained in Mr Thompson's Office, & studied the law. He was an admirable man, & a good lawyer himself; but I was put to study, in the old way, that is, the hardest books first, & lost much time. I read Coke['s] Littleton through, without understanding a quarter part of it. Happening to take up Espinasse's Law of Nisi Prius, I found I could understand it, & arguing that the object of reading was to understand what was written, I laid down the venerable Coke *et alios similes reverendos*, & kept company for a time with Mr Espinasse, & other [of] the most plain, easy & intelligible writers. A boy of twenty, with no previous knowledge on such subjects, cannot understand Coke. It is folly to set him upon such an author. There are propositions in Coke, so abstract, & distinctions so nice, & doctrines embracing so many conditions, & qualifications, that it requires an effort, not only of a mature mind, but of a mind both strong & mature to understand him. Why disgust & discourage a boy, by telling him that he must break into his profession, thro such a wall as this? I really often despaired. I thought I never could make myself a Lawyer; & was about going back to the business of school keeping. A friend has recently returned to me a letter, written by me to him, at that time, shewing my feelings of despondence & despair. Mr Espinasse, however, helped me out of this, in the way I have mentioned; & I have always felt greatly obliged to him. I do not know whether I read much, during this year & a half, besides law Books, with two exceptions. I read Hume, tho' not for the first time, but my principal occupation with books, when not law books, was with the Latin Classics. I brought from College a very scanty inheritance of Latin. I now tried to add to it. I made myself familiar with most of Tully's orations, committed to memory large passages of some of them, read Sallust, & Caesar, & Horace. Some of Horace's odes I translated, into poor English rhymes. They were printed. I never have seen them since.

My Brother was a far better Latin scholar than myself, & in one of his vacations we read Juvenal together. But I never mastered his style, so as to read him with ease & pleasure.

At this period of my life, I passed a great deal of time alone. My amusements were fishing, & shooting, & riding; & all these were without a companion. I loved this occasional solitude then, & have loved it ever since, & love it still. I like to contemplate nature, & to hold communion, unbroken by the presence of human beings, with "this universal frame, thus wondrous fair." I like solitude, also, as favorable to thoughts less lofty.

I like to let the thoughts go free, & indulge in their excursions. And when *thinking* is to be done, one must of course be alone. No man knows *himself*, who does not thus, sometimes, keep his own company. At a subsequent period of life, I have found that my lonely journies, when following the Court on its Circuits, have afforded many an edifying day.*

Before proceeding to state some events which happened in 1804, I ought to say, that it would not have been possible for us to have got along, had it not been for the small income derived from my father's official situation. As soon as the war of the Revolution was over, & the pursuits of peace returned, he was elected into such Public Offices, as it might be supposed he was qualified to fill. His qualities were integrity, firmness, decision, & extraordinary good sense. His defect, was the want of early education. He never saw the inside of a School House, in the character of a learner; & yet the first records or some among the first, of the Town of Salisbury, are in his hand writing. What he knew, he had taught himself. His character was generous & manly, & his manners such as gave him influence with those around him. Early & deeply religious, he had still a good deal of natural gaiety, he delighted to have some one about him that possessed a humourous vein. A character of this sort, one Robert Wise,— with whose adventures, as I learned them from himself, I could fill a small book,— was a near neighbor, & a sort of humble companion for a great many years. He was a Yorkshire man—had been a sailor—was with Bing [Admiral John Byng] in the Mediterranean—had been a soldier deserted from the Garrison of Gibraltar—travelled thro' Spain, & France— & Holland—taken up afterward & severely punished—sent back to the Army—was in the battle of Minden—had a thousand stories of the yellow haired Prince Ferdinand—was sent to Ireland, & thence to Boston, with the troops brought out by Gen Gage—fought at Bunker Hill —deserted to our ranks—served with the New Hampshire troops in all the succeeding campaigns, & at the peace built a little cottage in the corner of our field, on the River's bank, & there lived to an advanced old age. He was my *Isaac Walton*. He had a wife, but no child. He loved me, because I would read the Newspapers to him, containing the accounts of battles in the European wars. He had twice deserted from the English King, & once, at least, committed treason, as well as desertion, but he had still a British heart. When I have read to him the details of the victories

---

* The argument in the D. Col. case was mainly arranged, during a journey, on professional business, from Boston to Barnstable & back. John Adams' Speech was composed (not in Philadelphia, in 1776) but in Mass, in 1826, in a New England Chaise. The Address for Bunker Hill was, in great part, composed in *Marshpee Brook; testibus, Johanne de Trutta, et D. F. W. puero.* [DW's note].

of Howe, & Jervis, &c, I remember he was excited almost to convulsions, & would relieve his excitement by a gush of exulting tears. He finally picked up a fatherless child, took him home, sent him to school, & took care of him, only, as he said, that he might have some one to read the Newspaper to him. He could never read himself. Alas, poor Robert! I have never so attained the narrative art, as to hold the attention of others, as thou, with thy Yorkshire tongue, hast held mine. Thou hast carried me many a mile on thy back, paddled me over, & over, & up & down the stream, & given whole days, in aid of my boyish sports, & hast asked no meed, but that, at night, I would sit down, at thy cottage door, & read to thee some passage of thy Country's glory! Thou wast indeed, a true Briton.

My father was of such consideration among his neighbors, that he was usually in such public employment, as they had to bestow. He was a member of the Legislature, & a Senator; & about the year 1791, I think, appointed a Judge of the Court of Common Pleas for the County. This place afforded three or four hundred Dollars a year, a sum of the greatest importance to the family. He lived just long enough to witness my first appearance, & hear my first speech in Court.

In the winter of 1804, it had become necessary for either my brother or myself to undertake something, that should bring us a little money; for we were getting to be "heinously unprovided". To find some situation for the one or the other of us, I set off, in Febry, & found my way to Boston. My journey was fortunate. Dr. [Cyrus] Perkins had been in the instruction of a school, in Short Street; he was about leaving it, & proposed that my brother should take it. I hastened home, & he had just then finished a short engagement in school keeping, at Sandbornton, or was about finishing it, it being near the end of the winter vacation, & he readily seized the opportunity of employment in Boston. This broke in upon his College life, but he thought he could keep up with his class. A letter, stating the necessity of the case, was sent to the authority of College, & he went immediately to Boston. His success was good, nay great; so great, that he thought he could earn enough, to defray, in addition to debts & other charges, the expense of my living in Boston, for what remained of my term of study. Accordingly, I went to Boston, in July, to pass a few months in some Office.

I had not a single letter, & knew nobody, in the place to which I was going, except Dr. Perkins, then a very young man, & like myself struggling to get on. But I was sanguine, & light hearted. He easily persuades himself that he shall gain, who has nothing to lose, & is not afraid of attempting to climb, when, if he fail in his first step, he is in no danger of a fall. Arrived in Boston, I looked out for an Office, wherein to study. But since I knew none of the legal Gentlemen, & had no letters, this was an affair of some difficulty. Some attempts to be recd into a Lawyer's office failed, properly enough, for these reasons; altho' the reminiscence has since sometimes caused me to smile.

Mr [Christopher] Gore had just then returned from England, & resumed the practice of the Law. He had rooms in Scollay's buildings, &, as yet, had no clerk. A young man, as little known to Mr Gore as myself, undertook to introduce me to him! In logic, this would have been bad— "*ignotum, per ignotum*". Nevertheless, it succeeded here. We ventured into Mr Gore's rooms & my name was pronounced. I was shockingly embarrassed, but Mr Gore's habitual courtesy of manners gave me courage to speak. I had the grace to begin, with an unaffected apology—told him my position was very awkward—my appearance there very much like an intrusion— & that if I expected any thing but a civil dismission, it was only founded in his known kindness & generosity of character. I was from the Country, I said, had studied law two years—came to Boston to study a year more—had some respectable acquaintances in N. Hampshire, not unknown to him—but had no introduction— That I had heard he had no clerk—thought it possible he would receive one—that I came to Boston to work, & not to play—was more desirous, on all accounts, to be his pupil, & all I ventured to ask, at present, was, that he would keep a place for me in his office, till I could write to N.H. for proper letters, shewing me worthy of it. I delivered this speech, *trippingly* on the tongue—tho' I suspect it was better composed, than spoken.

Mr Gore heard me with much encouraging good nature. He evidently saw my embarrassment,—spoke kind words, & asked me to sit down. My friend had already disappeared! Mr G. said, that what I had suggested was very reasonable— & required little apology. He did not mean to fill his office with Clerks, but was willing to receive one or two, & would consider what I had said. He inquired, & I told him what Gentlemen of his acquaintance, knew me, & my father, in N. Hampshire. Among others, I remember, I mentioned Mr Peabody, who was Mr. Gore's classmate. He talked to me, pleasantly, for a quarter of an hour; & when I rose to depart, he said, "My young friend, you look as if you might be trusted—you say you come to study, & not to waste time—I will take you, at your word. You may as well hang up your hat, at once, go into the other room, take your Book, & set down to reading it— & write, at your convenience, to N. Hamp. for your letters."

I was conscious of having made a great stride onward, when I had obtained admission into Mr Gores Office. It was a situation which opened to me the means of studying books, & men, & things. It was on the 20th. of

July, 1804, that I first made myself known to Mr Gore; & altho' I remained in his Office only till March following, & that with considerable intervening absences, I made, as I think, some respectable progress. In August the Supreme [Court] sat. I attended it constantly, & reported every one of its decisions. I did the same, in the Circuit Court of the United States. I kept a little journal, at that time, which still survives. It contains little besides a list of books read. In addition to Books on the common & municipal Law, I find I read Vattell, then for the third time in my life, as is stated on the Journal, Ward's Law of Nations, Lord Bacon's elements, Puffendorf's Latin History of England, Giffords Juvenal, Boswell's Tour to the Hebrides, Moore's Travels, & many other miscellaneous things. But my main study was the common Law; & especially the part of it which relates to special pleading. Whatever was in Viner, Bacon, & other books then usually studied, on that part of the science, I paid my respects to. Among other things, I went thro' Saunders Reports, the old folio Edition, & abstracted & put into English out of Latin & Norman French the pleadings, in all his reports. It was an edifying work. From that day to this the forms & language of special Pleas have been quite familiar to me. I believe I have my little abstract yet.

I remember one day, as I was alone in the office, a man came in, & asked for Mr Gore. Mr Gore was out, & he sat down to wait for him. He was dressed in plain grey clothes. I went on with my book, till he asked me what I was reading, & coming along up to the table, I held out my book, & he took it, & looked at it. "Roccus," said he, "de navibus et naulo" —"well, I read that book too when I was a boy"— & proceeded to talk not only about "ships & freights," but insurance, prize, & other matters of maritime law, in a manner "to put me up to all I knew"; & a good deal more. The grey coated stranger turned out to be Mr [Rufus] King.

On my aforesaid Journal, "Some characters at the Boston Bar, 1804". They are drawings, not worth preserving; but I quote what I find is written, at least a part of it, on one.

"T[heophilus] P[arsons] is now about 55 years old, of pretty large stature, & rather inclining to corpulency. His hair is brown, & his complexion not light. His face is not marked by any striking feature, if we except his eye. His forehead is low, & his eye-brows prominent. He wears a blue coat, & breeches, worsted hose, and a brown wig, with a cocked hat. He has a penetrating eye, of an indescribable color. His manner is steady, forcible, & perfectly perspicuous. He does not address the Jury, as a mechanical body, to be put in motion by mechanical means. He appeals to them as men, & as having minds capable of receiving the ideas in his own. Of course, he never harangues; he knows by the Juror's countenance, when he is convinced, & therefore never disgusts him by arguing that of which he is already sensible, or which he knows it is impossible to impress. He is not content with shining on occasions; he will shine every where. As no cause is too great, none is too small for him. He knows the great benefit of understanding small circumstances. It is not enough for him that he has learned the leading points in a cause; he will know every thing. His argument is therefore always consistent with itself, & its course so luminous that you are ready to wonder why any one should hesitate to follow him. Facts which are uncertain, he with so much art connects with others well proved, that you cannot get rid of the former, without disregarding also the latter. A mind thus strong, direct, prompt, & vigorous, is cultivated by habits of most intense application. He has no fondness for public life, & is satisfied with standing where he is, at the head of his Profession."

These paragraphs, which I have transcribed without altering a word, were written when I was 22 years old, & T.P. 55, after studying him a month in Court, but never having spoken to him, nor come nearer to him than the Students seat, in the outer row of the Bar, in the Old Court House. They do not fully describe P's character, but they do not altogether mistake it. About seven years afterwards, I was introduced to him, for the first time; & passed two or three evenings with him, much to my delight.

There is a page or two, on this Journal, for S[amuel] D[exter] as next following T.P. I transcribe only one paragraph, intended to exhibit the different modes of argumentation, adopted by these distinguished persons.

"P. begins with common maxims, & his course to the particular subject, & the particular conclusion, brightens, & shines more & more clearly, to its end. D. begins, with the particular position which he intends to support. Darkness surrounds him. No one knows the path, by which he arrived at his conclusion. Around him, however, is a circle of light, when he opens his mouth. Like a conflagration seen at a distance, the Evening mist may intervene between it & the eye of the observer, though the blaze ascend to the sky, & cannot but be seen."

I will here transcribe one other thing from this little journal, the record of an occurrence which had entirely escaped my recollection. I copy the paragraph *Verbum post verbum*.

"Mar. 5. This day, in one of the rooms of the State House, in presence of Isaac P. Davis, & Samuel A. Bradley, & Timo. Dix Jun, I examined the letters to Callender from Jefferson. Mr Dix told me he had often

seen the signature of Mr J. & on being asked whether he doubted that
Mr. J. really signed the letters in question, he said he did not. I preserve
this precious confession against time of need."

In March 1805, I was admitted to practice, in the Suffolk Court of Common Pleas. The practice then was, for the patron to go into Court, introduce the pupil to the Judges, make a short speech commending his diligence &c, & move for his admission to the Bar. I had the honor to be so introduced by Mr Gore. I remember every word of his speech. It contained a prediction, which I firmly resolved, *quantum in me fuerit,* should not go entirely unfulfilled.

In the January preceding my admission, I was the subject of a great honor. The Clerk of the Court of Common Pleas for the Co. of Hillsborough resigned his place. My father was one of the Judges of the Court, & I was appointed to the vacant Clerkship. This was equal to a Presidential election. The office had an income of fifteen hundred dollars a year. It seemed to me very great, & indeed it was so, rebus consideratis. The obtaining of this object had been a darling object with my father. Its possession would make the family easy— & he hastened to send me tidings that the prize was won. I certainly considered it a great prize, myself, & was ready to abandon my profession for it; not that I did not love my profession, & not that I did not hate the clerkship, & all clerkship[s]; —but simply from a desire to reach that high point of terrestrial bliss, at which I might feel that there was a *competency,* for our family, myself included. I had felt the *res angustae &c* till my very bones ached. But Mr Gore peremptorily shut me out from this opening paradise. When I went to him, with my letter in my hand, to communicate the good news, he said it was civil, in their Honours of the Bench, & that I must write them a respectful letter; that they intended it as a mark of confidence in me, & of respect, probably, for my father, & that I was bound to make civil acknowledgements. This was a shower bath, of ice water. I was thinking of nothing but of rushing to the immediate enjoyment of the proffered Office; but he was talking of civil acknowledgment, & decorous declension. Finding my spirits, (& face too, I suppose) falling, he found out the cause, & went on to speak, in a serious tone, against the policy & propriety of taking such an Office. To be sure, his reasons were good, but I was slow to be convinced. He said, I was nearly thro' my professional preparation, that I should soon be at the Bar, & he saw not why I might not hope to make my way, as well as others; that this office was, in the first place, precarious; it depended on the will of others, & other times & other men might soon arise, & my office be given to somebody else; &, in the second place, if permanent, it was a stationary place; that a Clerk once, I was probably nothing better than a clerk, ever; and, in short, that he had taken me for one who was not to sit with his pen behind his ear; —"go on,["] said he, "& finish your studies; you are poor enough, but there are great[er] evils than poverty; live on no man's favor; what bread you do eat, let it be the bread of independence; pursue your profession, make yourself useful to your friends, & a little formidable to your enemies, & you have nothing to fear."

I need hardly say that I acquiesced in this good advice; tho certainly it cost me a pang. Here was present comfort, competency, & I may even say riches, as I then viewed things, all ready to be enjoyed, & I was called on to reject them, for the uncertain & distant prospect of professional success. But I did resist the temptation; I did hold on to the hopes which the law set before me. One very difficult task, however, remained to be performed; & that was, to reconcile my father to my decision. I knew it would strike him, like a thunder bolt. He had long had this Office, in view, for me; it's income would make him, & make us all, easy & comfortable; his health was bad, & growing worse. His sons were all gone from him. This office would bring me home, & it would bring also comfort & competency "to all the house". It was now mid winter; I looked round for a Country *sleigh*, (Stage Coaches then no more ran into the centre of N. Hampshire, than they ran to Baffin's Bay) & finding one that had come down to the 'Market, I took passage thereon, & in two or three days was set down at my fathers door. I was afraid my own resolution would give way, & that, after all, I should sit down to the Clerk's table. But I fortified myself, as well as I could; & put on, I remember, an air of confidence, success, & gaiety. It was evening. My father was sitting before his fire, & recd me with manifest joy. He looked feebler than I had ever seen him, but his countenance lighted up on seeing his *Clerk* stand before him, in good health, & better spirits. He immediately proceeded to the great appointment, — said how spontaneously it had been made, how kindly the Chief Justice proposed it, with what unanimity all assented, &c &c &c. I felt as if I could die, or fly. I could hardly breathe. Nevertheless, *I carried it through,* as we say, according to my plan.— Spoke gayly about it—was much obliged to their Honors—meant to write them a respectful letter— if I could consent to record any body's judgments should be proud to record their honors, &c &c &c. I proceeded in this strain, till he exhibited signs of amazement, it having occurred to him, at length, that I might be serious, in an intention to decline the Office:—a thing, which had never entered into his imagination. "Do you intend to decline this Office,"? said he at length. "Most certainly,["] said I. ["]I cannot think of doing otherwise. I should be very sorry if I could not do better at present, than to be Clerk, for fifteen hundred Dollars a year, not to speak of future prospects!

I mean to use my tongue, in the Courts, not my pen; to be an actor, not a register of other men's actions. I hope yet, Sir, to astonish your Honor, in your own Court, by my professional attainments.["] |

For a moment, I thought he was angry. He rocked his chair, slightly— a flash went over an eye, softened by age, but still black as jet—but it was gone, & I thought I saw that parental partiality was, after all, a little gratified, at this apparent devotion to an honorable profession, & this seeming confidence of success in it. "Well, my son, your mother has always said that you would come to something, or nothing, she was not sure which. I think you are now about settling that doubt for her." This he said, & never word spoke more to me, on the subject. I staid at home a week— promised to come to him again, as soon as I was admitted, & returned to Boston. Being admitted to the Bar, as already stated in March, I went to Amherst, where the Court was then sitting, & where he was; & from Amherst to his own house. My design was to settle in the practice at Portsmouth; but I determined not to leave my father, during his life. Accordingly I took a room, in the little adjoining village of Boscawen, & there commenced the practice of the Law. My father lived but another year. He died in April 1806, & lies in the burial ground, in his own field, just at the turn of the road beneath the shadow of a tall pine. Beside him repose my mother, my three own sisters, & Joseph, my youngest half brother. Alas!—while the living all change, the tabernacle of the dead remain unaltered. To me, my little native village is now hardly known, but by its sepulchres. The villagers are gone. An unknown generation walk under our elms. Unknown faces meet & pass me, on my own paternal acres. I recognize nothing, but the tombs! I have no acquaintance remaining, but the dead!

In May 1807, I was admitted as Attorney & Counsellor of the Superior Court, and in September of that year relinquished my office in Boscawen to my Brother, who had then obtained admission to the Bar, & removed to Portsmouth, according to my original destination.

The two years & a half which I spent in Boscawen were devoted to business & study. I had enough of the first to live on, & to afford opportunity for practice & discipline. I read law, & history; not without some mixture of other things. These were the days of the Boston Anthology, & I had the honor of being a contributor to that publication. There are sundry reviews, written by me, not worth looking up, or remembering.

September 1807, I went to Portsmouth, there to practice my Profession. June 24, 1808, I was married* [( )See note)[3]

I lived in Portsmouth nine years, wanting one month. They were very

3. Webster did not insert an explanatory note here.

happy years. Circumstances favored me, at my first beginning there. Owing to several occurrences, there happened to be an unfilled place among leading Counsel, at that Bar. I did not fill it; but I succeeded to it. It so happened, & so has happened, that with the exception of instances, in which I have been associated with the Atty Gen of U. S. for the time being, I have hardly ten times in my life acted as Junior Counsel. Once or twice with Mr [Jeremiah] Mason, once or twice with Mr [William] Prescott, once with Mr [Joseph] Hopkinson, are all the cases which occur to me. Indeed for the nine years I lived in Portsmouth Mr Mason and myself, in the Counties w[h]ere we both practiced, were on opposite sides, pretty much as matter of course. He has been of infinite advantage to me, not only by his unvarying friendship, but by the many good lessons he has taught, & the example he set me in the commencement of my career. If there be in the Country a stronger intellect, if there be a mind of more native resources, if there be a vision that sees quicker, or sees deeper, into whatever is intricate, or whatever is profound, I must confess I have not known it. I have not written this paragraph, without considering what it implies; I look to that individual, who, if it belong to any body, is entitled to be an exception. But I deliberately let the judgment stand. That that individual has much more habit of regular composition, that he has been disciplined & exercised in a vastly superior school, that he possesses, a faculty of illustration, more various, & more easy, I think may be admitted. That the original reach of his mind is greater, that its grasp is stronger, that its logic is closer, I do not allow.

My professional practice, while living in Portsmouth, was very much a Circuit practice. I followed the Superior Court, in most of the Counties of the State. It was never lucrative. There was a limit, & that a narrow one, beyond which gains could not be made from it. I do not think it was even worth fairly two thousand Dollars a year. Business, too, fell off much, by the war; & soon after that event I determined on a change of residence.

I never held office, popular or other, in the Govt. of N. Hamp. My time was almost exclusively given to my profession, till 1812, when the war commenced. I had occasionally taken part in political questions, always felt an interest in elections, & contributed my part, I believe, to the political ephemeras of the day. Indeed I always felt an interest in political concerns. My lucubrations for the Press go back, I believe, to my sixteenth year. They are, or ought to be, all forgotten; at least most of them; & all of this early period.

When I visited my father, from Boston, in Jany. (or Feb.) 1804 [1805], a severe political contest was going on, between Govr. [John] Gilman & Govr. [John] Langdon. The friends of the former, [(]& they were my friends) wanted a *pamphlet,* & I was pressed to write one. I did the deed, I believe, at a single sitting of a winter's day & night. Not long ago, I found a copy of this sage production. Among things of a similar kind, it is not entirely despicable. It is called an "Appeal to the Old Whigs." Like other young men, I made 4th of July orations; at Fryeburg, 1802; at Salisbury, 1805; at Concord, 1806, (which was published); at Portsmo. 1812—published, also. Aug. 1812 I wrote the Rockingham Memorial. It was an Anti War paper, of some note in its time. I confess I am pleased to find, on looking at it now, (for I do not think I have read it in all the 20 yrs that have rolled by since I wrote it) among all its faults, whether of principle or in execution, that it is of a tone & strain less vulgar than such things are prone to be.

Before this period, I think in 1808, I had written the little pamphlet, lately rescued from oblivion, called "considerations on the Embargo Laws".

In Nov. 1812 I was elected member of Congress, & took my seat at the extra session, May 1813.

In Aug. 1814 I was reelected. Of the little that I did, & the little that I said, while a member of Congress from N Hamp, the account is to be found in the history of the public proceedings of those times. I recollect some interesting occurrences, connected with important subjects, which I cannot narrate without refreshing my recollection of dates by reference to the Journals. My efforts in regard to the Banks, at different times projected, and in regard to the currency of the Country, I think were of some small degree of utility to the public. Other subjects were temporary, & whatever was done or said about them has passed away, & lost its interest. To these endeavors to maintain a sound currency, I owe the acquaintance & friendship of the late Mr [George] Cabot; who was kind enough to think they entitled me to his regard.

In the session of 1815 & 1816 I also made the acquaintance of Mr Francis C. Lowell. He passed some weeks at Washington. I was much with him, & found him full of exact practical knowledge, on many subjects. At the same session I made an acquaintance with our friend Mr [Theodore] Dwight, or renewed & cultivated a slight one of longer standing. His friendship & advice very much influenced my subsequent resolution of coming to Boston, when I left Portsmouth. I balanced, at the time between Boston & Albany; but finally settled to do, what I soon did. I could carry my practice in New Hampshire no further; I could make no more of it; & its results were not competent to the support of my family. Having resolved on a change, I accomplished it at once. In June 1816, I came over, with my wife, to see about a House. On the 16. of August I left Portsmouth forever, & the same day arrived, with my wife & children at

Boston. My children were then Grace, & Daniel Fletcher. We staid two or three weeks, at Mrs Delanos, & then went to house-keeping, in a house of Mr J. Mason, on Mo[u]nt Vernon [Street]. I think I never went into a N Hamp. Court again, except when I went down the following September, in the Dart. Col. cause.

When I moved to Boston, I had still one session to serve in Congress. Mr Mason was a Senator, at that time. We went to Washington, in Nov. with our families, & took lodgings together. But my wife & myself were called back, by the illness of our daughter. We left Washington the 1st. day of January, & found her living. She died, the 23rd of January. I returned to Washington, soon after, mainly on account of business in Court. On the rising of Congress & the Court, I came back to Boston, & entered with diligence, on the labors of my profession.

I have hurried over my residence in Portsmouth. There are incidents, of no public concernment, yet interesting to me & mine, not mentioned. In Decr. 1813, I being gone to Washington, my house was burnt, in what is called the great fire. My wife & children had just time to escape. I had recently bought the House, for 6000 Dlls; its loss, with the loss of what was burnt with it, was no small matter. It was in no part insured.

AD. MHi. Published in PC, 1: 3–27; W & S, 17: 3–27.

As a student in the local schools around Salisbury, at Phillips Exeter Academy, and at Dartmouth College, Webster quickly and easily formed friendships, many of which continued throughout his life. Among those close friends were Joseph Warren Brackett (1775–1826; Dartmouth 1800), Samuel Ayer Bradley (1774–1844; Dartmouth 1799), James Hervey Bingham (1781–1859; Dartmouth 1801), George Herbert (1778–1820; Dartmouth 1801), and Habijah [Henry] Weld Fuller (1784–1841; Dartmouth 1801), all of whom like Webster later studied law.

At Dartmouth, Webster and his friends revealed an early interest in politics and political journalism. In 1799, they formed an organization to study political developments. When Moses Davis (1777–1808), a native of Concord, proposed the establishment of the Dartmouth Gazette in Hanover the same year, Webster quickly offered his assistance, and over the next several years published numerous essays and poems in it, usually signed "Icarus." He also published at least one poem, "The Hermit," in Davis' Literary Tablet (June 26, 1805); on occasions when Davis was absent from Hanover, Webster superintended his paper. In his Autobiography, p. 10 above, Webster recalls that he paid his board for a year by this means.

TO JOSEPH WARREN BRACKETT

[22 Dec. 1798]

Well, you need not complain, you have no postage to pay, just look, and see who signed this, and commit it to the flames. But stop, it may be that you will read it, if so, I tell you plainly, Joseph, I want to see you, but what of that, you dont care for me. You are now, perhaps, in a lively circle of Misses, where humour and hilarity prevail; while I, on the contrary, am dozing over a musty volume of Rollin. But, Brackett, you have an advantage still greater; in another respect, wherever you may be, however far removed from your friends, yet you are always sure of the company of Celestial Muses, who, alone, are sufficient to transport you to the fields of Elysium, and fire your soul with heavenly raptures. But, Joseph, I raped one of these Gypsies yesterday, and shall make it known next Tuesday, but, your ear wont be hurt with grating jargon. I expect to carry on here through vacation, but dont you write to me, because it will be too much trouble to you, but if you have patience to read this letter, I shall think myself infinitely obliged to you. But why do I pay such respect to you, I'm a sophomore, am as good as you, and wish you good night.

D. Webster.

ALS. NhD.

[July 1799]
CONSTITUTION OF THE FEDERAL CLUB.

This Society, formed for improvement in political information, and the acquirement of useful knowledge; is established on professed friendship and unanimity.

It supposes each member[1] enjoying equally, its privileges, which are to be granted to such, only, as deserve the name of Philanthropists, Gentlemen and Scholars.

So many News-Papers, or other periodical Publications, shall be taken by the Society; as it may think convenient; and such shall be read every meeting, by some member, as the President may appoint.

Each member of the Society shall be entitled to the presidency, for one meeting, in alphabetical order. The President shall receive the papers from the Post Office, lay them before the Society, and keep order in the meetings. He shall, likewise, produce on the meeting succeeding that, of his Presidentship, a short account of the contents of the late papers; and this shall be given to the Treasurer, for preservation, in the Society Journal.[2]

The Treasurer shall be annually chosen, by ballot, on the first meeting of the Society in July, out of the Sophomore, or Junior Class. He shall in the name of the Society transact all its business with Printers, Postmasters &c. He shall exhibit, to the Society, all amounts which are brought against it, and make an equal distribution of expenses among the members, and settle their respective accounts once a Quarter; reckoning the first, as commencing on the Second Friday of July A.D. 1799.

He shall likewise do the duty of a Secretary, he shall keep all papers belonging to the Society, record all votes, preserve and read this Constitution to all candidates for admission.

These are the motives, for which we have associated, and the general principles of our society government.

For the support of which, we pledge our honour and fidelity.

> Joseph Warren Brackett
> Benjamin Clark.
> Nathaniel Coffin
> John H. Crane
> Alexander Conkey
> Tristram Gilman
> George Herbert,
> Warren Peirce
> Danl. Webster.

Copy. NhHi. Fletcher Webster probably made this copy from the original loaned him by Mrs. George Herbert or the Reverend C. D. Herbert. See Mrs. [George] Herbert to the Reverend C. D. Herbert, March 6, 1856, in *PC*, 1: 74–77.

1. All of the members of the Federal Club were Dartmouth classmates of DW. For details on their careers, see *ADC* and appropriate annotations to letters below.

2. Journal not found.

TO MOSES DAVIS

Aug. 27, 1799.

Mr Davis,

Having seen your Proposals for printing a Newspaper, under the respectable title of the "Dartmouth Gazette," I have presumed to come forward, and cast in my mite, to increase, if not to enrich your weekly repast. Should you think the productions of my puerile pen worthy a place in your new "vehicle of Knowledge," you may depend on a number weekly. As I am unable to treat any subject with that knowledge and accuracy it deserves, you will permit me as a compensation for want of abilities, to range the whole field of nature, in order to collect those productions, which fortune may throw in my way. With the most sincere wishes for your success, I subscribe myself ever Yours,   Icarus.[1]

Copy. NhHi. Published in *Dartmouth Gazette*, August 27, 1799, along with an essay on "Hope"; and in *W & S*, 16: 3.

1. For Webster's other contributions under the "Icarus" name, see mDWs and the *Dartmouth Gazette,* August 27, October 21, 28, November 25, December 2, 9, 1799; February 17, 24, April 21, 28, December 6, 13, 1800; February 21, 1801; July 10, August 7, 1802.

TO JAMES HERVEY BINGHAM

Salisbury, February 5, 1800.

The political events of Europe, my friend Hervey, are so novel and unexpected, revolution succeeds revolution in such rapid succession, that it is sufficient to overpower the understanding and confound the calculations of the most sage politician. These events are attended with such important circumstances, involve so many and so various interests, that schemes either of aggrandizement or of defence are agitated and devised in every cabinet of Europe. Nor is it to be expected, at this eventful crisis, that the decisions of our Executive are to be uninfluenced by considerations of transatlantic occurrences. Were we, like China, divested of every commercial engagement, we might, like that empire, remain unmoved, while convulsed Europe tottered to its base. To suppose that the liberty of United America, depends on the balance of power on the Eastern continent, is an idea exploded by every whig of '76, and which ought to be deemed absurd and preposterous. But our connections with foreign nations are such, that to preserve unaffected our commercial interests, while revolutions are making such monstrous strides in Europe, is beyond the reach of human sagacity. Adams, however, has hitherto conducted us in tolerable safety through the dangers which have beset us, and on him, under the guidance of an overruling Providence, we must rely, as the only rock of our political salvation. I, who am a mere novice in the science of politics, have done calculating. I have heretofore applied logical, metaphysical, mathematical, and philosophical theorems, but have found them all insufficient to solve one political problem.

Who thought, six months ago, that Bonaparte, who was then represented as lying with his slaughtered army on the plains of Egypt, to taint the air, and gorge the monsters of the Nile, would at this time have returned to France, have destroyed the Directory and Legislative Councils, have established a triumvirate, and have placed himself at its head—which is saying, have virtually made himself sovereign of France? Who could have predicted that the Duke of York, who so late was marching victoriously through Holland, should ere this time have entered into a convention, by which he was to give up all his booty and prisoners, and evacuate the country? Or, whoever supposed that Paul, emperor of Russia, who so lately was raising one hundred and eighty thousand men, to reinforce his armies, should now order Suwarrow, with his veteran Cossacks, to quit the field and return home? The occurrences hitherto would have warranted the most extravagant expectations; but these events must have been, I think, unprepared for. What unknown cause has wrought these changes? I cannot determine. I am weary of conjecture. But, when baffled in attempting to scan the horizon of European politics, could I turn my eyes home and be presented with such a prospect as was afforded five years ago, I should lift my heart to Heaven in a transport of devotion, and exclaim, "Let France or England be arbiter of Europe, but be mine the privileges of an American citizen." But, Hervey, our prospect darkens; clouds hang around us. Not that I fear the menaces of France; not that I should fear all the powers of Europe leagued together for our destruction. No, Bingham, intestine feuds alone I fear. The French faction, though quelled, is not eradicated. The southern States in commotion; a Democrat the head of the Executive in Virginia; a whole county in arms against the government of [Thomas] McKean, in Pennsylvania; Washington, the great political cement dead, and Adams almost worn down with years, and the weight of cares. These considerations, operating on a mind naturally timorous, excite unpleasant emotions. In my melancholy moments, I presage the most dire calamities. I already see, in my imagination, the time when the banner of civil war shall be unfurled; when Discord's hydra form shall set up her hideous yell, and from her hundred mouths shall howl destruction through our empire; and when American blood shall be made to flow in rivers, by American swords! But propitious Heaven prevent such dreadful calamities! Internally secure, we have nothing to fear. Let Europe pour her embattled millions around us, let her thronged cohorts cover our shores, from St. Lawrence to St. Marie's, yet, United Columbia shall stand unmoved; the manes of her deceased Washington, shall guard the liberties of his country, and direct the sword of freedom in the day of battle. Heaven grant that the bonds of our federal union may be strengthened; that Gallic emissaries and Gallic principles may be spurned from our land; that traitors may be abashed, and that the stars and stripes of United Columbia may wave triumphant! So much for politics.

I have received your letter,[1] as you must know by my delaying to visit you. I shall visit you next Saturday, other things being equal. You wonder I did not write, and are about to conclude that my friendship for you had decreased; but, James, form no rash conclusions. I did write soon after your departure;[2] I wrote very soon; I wrote then. I prepared a letter too long, and too nonsensical to be read with patience, and determined to send it by Mr. [James] Wilson,[3] but did not see him. I then despatched the *animal* by another conveyance, but after a few days travelling it returned. However, after a little refreshment, the *gentleman* moved again, and I conclude by this time is arrived at Sanbornton; where I presume you will deal with his honor according to the fitness of things, that is to say, read till you are tired, then burn him. By last mail I had a letter from [Habijah Weld] Fuller—all well. N. and B. were to go last week. S.F— —er, and Mary, *la bonne*,[4] have gone. Thus you see the circle is broken; well, Hervey, let us then apply ourselves more closely to study. I have to impart to you from Mr. Fuller, the love of all the— — —. My school increases fast enough.[5] Instead of twenty, I have fifty, and shall have more; five English grammarians, I mean students in English, and two Latin scholars. I had a letter not long since from J[ohn] Nelson,[6] and hope to see him on Saturday at Sanbornton. Much speculation is made here on the scribblers for the Dartmouth Gazette. Old Icarus is handled without ceremony. I shall tell you hereafter some pretty things about it. Our family would reciprocate their respects.

I am, Sir, with much respect, yours in the indissoluble bonds of fraternal love.   D. Webster.

Text from *PC*, 1: 77–80. Original not found.

1. Not found.

2. Not found.

3. Wilson (1766–1839; Harvard 1789), New Hampshire lawyer, legislator (1803–1808, 1812–1814), and congressman (1809–1811).

4. Probably Mary Woodward, daughter of Bezaleel Woodward, Dartmouth professor of mathematics and natural philosophy. Others not identified.

5. No other reference to DW's teaching school in February 1800 has been found. Webster had earlier taught a district school in Salisbury in the winter of 1797, shortly after he left Exeter and before he entered Dartmouth College.

6. Letter not found. Nelson (1778–1838; Dartmouth 1803), lawyer in Haverhill, New Hampshire.

[ARGUMENT FOR ACQUISITION OF THE FLORIDAS]

Dec. 25. 1800

Question. Would it be advantageous to the United States to extend their territories?

It might be supposed that a Republic, whose territorial jurisdiction encircles a more extensive portion of the earth's surface, than falls to the share of almost any sovereignty in Europe, would never exert her energies for her Dominion. It is true, on general maxims, that our country is sufficiently large for a Republican government, but if, by an inconsiderable extension of our limits, we can avail ourselves of great, natural advantages, otherwise unattainable, does not sound policy dictate the measure. We reduce the question to a single point; would not the acquisition of the Floridas be advantageous to the United States? Here let it be remembered, that that part of the territory of our government, which lies North of

Florida, and West of the Allegany mountains, including the NorthWestern territory, Tennessee, Kentucky, and a part of Georgia, is, by far, the most fertile part of the Union. No where does the soil produce in such exuberance, no where is the climate so mild and agreeable. The agricultural productions of this quarter, must then, in a few years, become immense, far exceeding those of all the Atlantic States. The next inquiry is, how shall this super abundance be disposed of? how shall the lumber, wheat and cotton of this country be conveyed to a West India or European market? The only practicable method of transportation is down the Mississippi, and the other rivers, that run into the Mexic gulf; and we have here to reflect, that these rivers all run thro' a country, owned by the king of Spain; a monarch, capricious as a child, and versatile as the wind, and who has it in his power, whenever interest, ambition, or the whims of his fancy dictate, to do us incalculable injuries, by prohibiting our Western brethren from prosecuting commerce thro' his dominions. Suppose the Spanish sovereign should, this day, give orders to the fortress of New Orleans, to suffer no American vessel to pass up or down the river. This would be an affliction, not to be born by those citizens, who live along the banks of the Mississippi, but what steps should our government take in the affair? Must they sit still, and fold their hands, while such an intolerable embargo presses our commerce? This would be an ill expedient; we might as well give Spain our whole Western territory, as suffer her to control the commerce of it. The only way we could turn ourselves, in this case, would be to declare war against Spain, and vindicate our claims to free navigation by force of arms. Here then we are under necessity of extending our territories, by possessing ourselves of all the country adjacent those rivers, necessary for our commerce; or of giving up the idea of ever seeing Western America a flourishing country. Therefore, since we are liable, every day, to be reduced to the necessity of seizing on Florida in a hostile manner, or of surrendering the rights of commerce, it is respectfully submitted, whether it would not be proper for our government, to enter into some convention with the king of Spain, by which the Floridas should be ceded to the United States.   D. Webster.

ADS. MHi. Published in *Proc MHi* (1869–1870), pp. 329–330.

TO GEORGE HERBERT (Extract)

Dartmouth College, January 7, 1801.

I find, brother George, that if I would allure an answer to my letters, I must exalt my subject from those trifles which effeminate our sex, to those affairs which mark the man of information and business. I shall

likewise, perhaps, find it necessary to round my periods with more attention, and endeavor to grace my sentences with the flourishes of rhetoric.
For the sake of continuing a correspondence, I would willingly attempt
any thing within the compass of my capacity, but the frog must not strive
to swell to the size of the ox.

Two things I can't say I like; Jefferson's election to the Presidency, and
Hamilton's letter.[1] Of the two, I prefer the former. There is some consistency in the Jacobins raising Thomas to the Executive Chair; it is in
conformity to their avowed principles. But Hamilton's letter is void of
congruity.

Let us just notice one absurdity, which you have undoubtedly observed.
Hamilton proposes to prove that there are certain essential defects in the
character of Adams, I forget the particular expressions, which unfit him
for the office of Chief Magistrate; he labors hard to substantiate this
point, and thinks he has done it. What is his conclusion? He does not wish
to withhold a vote from Mr. Adams. Now mark the consistency. He thinks
there are a hundred men in the United States better calculated for the
Presidency than Mr. Adams, for there certainly are that number who do
not possess these essential defects; yet he wishes, or professes to wish,
every vote given to Mr. Adams. Is this consentaneous to all that independence which he sets out with? Is it agreeable to that rigid republican-
ism which glowed in the breasts of Aristides and Cato?

We are every day expecting the electioneering for governor to commence in this State with warmth. I never yet drove my quill in such a
case, perhaps never shall. I may laugh a little! [John] Langdon,[2] it is expected, will be the anti-Federal candidate. [John Taylor] Gilman,[3] the
Federal; if he declines, [Oliver] Peabody, of Exeter.

Hem! Hem! I am clearing my throat. George P. [Woodward],[4] the son
of Professor [Bezaleel] W[oodward], observed the other day, (as it was
spoken in confidence, I will allow you to make more of it than of general
report): "I am told," said he, "that Herbert is somewhat unwell, and I
believe there is a weed growing round our house, which would cure him.
Mary [Woodward] is also somewhat sick, and I am told there is an herb
now growing in the western part of Massachusetts, which would help
her." These observations were made in Mary's hearing, who replied:
"Since you have discovered a weed which you suppose would be beneficial
to Mr. Herbert, you are in duty bound to communicate your discovery to
him." I pledge myself, Herbert, for the truth of this; but shall tell you no
more of the good or bad things said of you here, till I know more distinctly
your intention. If you are seriously and honorably inclined, I can tell you
enough to give you perfect confidence of success; if you only wish to
amuse yourself, and sport with the girl, I beg you not to make me your

instrument. This however I know you cannot intend. I know the nobleness of your soul and the purity of your heart. Command my service in any way, not inconsistent with the character of a Christian and a gentleman, and I will serve you to the *ne plus ultra* of my talents.

Since you have not answered my other letter,[5] I fear I have offended; I hope not; for surely you will not accuse me of vanity, if I tell you that you have not a friend in existence who means better than

Danl. Webster.

Text from *PC*, 1: 72–74. Original not found.

1. *Letter from Alexander Hamilton, concerning the Public Conduct and Character of John Adams, Esq. President of the United States.* New York, 1800.

2. John Langdon was not an active candidate in the campaign; Timothy Walker was the leading anti-Federalist candidate.

3. John Taylor Gilman won the election.

4. Woodward (1776–1836; Dartmouth 1793), Haverhill lawyer.

5. Not found.

Question.

IS DECEPTION EVER JUSTIFIABLE?

Senior Composition, Dartmouth College, May 4, 1801

That the end sanctifies the means, is a doctrine, too pernicious, in its consequences, to be generally admitted. But there are cases, in which the good to be obtained is far greater than the evil resulting from the use of means, otherwise wrong. So deception, though commonly not justifiable, sometimes produces so much good, that we are warranted in the use of it.

No one supposes, for example, that it is wrong to deceive a mad man, in order to disarm him; or to deceive a highway-man, for the sake of saving life; or to use stratagem in a just war. The reason I apprehend to be this; the highway-man, when he sets out on his business of plunder, expects that every man, whom he assaults, will deceive him if possible: the author of an unjust war, too, looks out for stratagem from the enemy. In these cases, deception has the nature of a covenant between the parties, and is, therefore, every way justifiable.   Daniel Webster.

ADS. NhD.

After his graduation from Dartmouth in August 1801, Webster began to read law in Salisbury with Thomas W. Thompson, a neighbor and friend of the Webster family. Thompson (1766–1821; Harvard 1786), state legislator, congressman, United States senator, and trustee of Dartmouth College, was a leader in the revitalization of the Federalist Party in New Hampshire.

TO JAMES HERVEY BINGHAM

Salisbury, October 26, 1801.

O BINGHAM, and Bingham forever! There is a kind of magic in your pen; I know not how it is, but if you write in a language perfectly unknown, you afford me more pleasure than a well-penned and intelligible letter from a common friend. Of all folks in the world I should last think of flattering you; but, in honesty, I knew not how closely our feelings were interwoven; had no idea how hard it would be to live apart, when the hope of living together again no longer existed. However it may be thought rebellion against nature, I must confess, if I were this day to embark for Europe, my regret at leaving any other person would not be greater than at leaving you. You may judge therefore, whether your letters are not acceptable.

I rejoice most heartily to learn that you are settled so agreeably. Charlestown must be a pleasant place. Though your cousin Solon [Stevens][1] be absent, yet you will, no doubt, find friends. I agree with you, that Mr. [David] Hale[2] is one of the best "*fraters*." So far as I know him, I highly respect him.

Report speaks extremely well of Mr. [Benjamin] West;[3] representing him as the oracle of the law, in Cheshire County. The only objection I ever heard against him, is his unwillingness to enter into public employment, at a period when the perverse nature of the times renders his talents and character necessary. You must, I think, make proficiency with him; if I judge from your progress hitherto, you will take your leave of me soon. You have actually read almost as much law as I, though you have been at it not half so long. I was reading Shakespeare, when I received your letter, but soon laid him by, and took up Blackstone.

Mr. Thompson has gone to Boston, Mr. [Daniel] Abbott[4] to Salem, and I am in consequence alone, and shall be probably for some weeks. I have made some few writs, and am now about to bring an action of trespass for breaking a violin. The owner of the violin was at a husking, where "His jarring concord, and his discord dulcet" were making the girls skip over the husks as nimbly as Virgil's Camilla over the tops of the corn, till an old surly creature caught his fiddle and broke it against the wall. For the sake of having plump witnesses, the plaintiff will summon all the girls to attend the trial at Concord.

If the Funeral Oration be thought decent, I am contented; equal to the subject it is not. The death of [Ephraim] Simonds[5] was a theme on which the first writers ought to be proud to point their pens. "*Hei mihi! Qualis erat!*" I know not how many times I have been asked, whether you were not to read law in this quarter. A lady observed, she should be very well pleased to have Mr. B. in the office. Surely she would not be more pleased than I. My old friend [John Adams] Harper[6] is expected here soon, to finish his reading. A rich acquisition to the gallantry of our office. The scarcity of company here renders it impossible to spend time pleasantly abroad; for entertainment, I betake myself to Mr. T.'s *belles-lettres* library, which affords a pretty variety of reading. How Mr. Harper will relish our amusements is not to be told; I wish he may be pleased.

Friend Lemy [Bliss] is at Mr. [Samuel] Wood's,[7] reading the best of all professions. He certainly has gained cent. per cent. the last year. [Daniel] Campbell[8] went to Concord after Commencement, and rode round with Miss Abbott; he's gone! Cupid has bored his heart through like a sieve. Doctor [G.] Gridley[9] is really doing well; he thinks you neglect him in not writing to him.

"Powerful," indeed, is our representation to Congress. [Elizur] Goodrich, [Gideon] Granger, [Pierpont] Edwards,[10] step ye aside! I have not heard a word from F[rederick] Hunt; nor from [George] Herbert. Am alarmed at intelligence from [Benjamin] Clarke; he is said to be declining visibly! [Joseph W.] Brackett,[11] I believe, is in good health . . .

Afternoon.—The most unpleasant information I have yet to communicate. The "state of things" renders it highly doubtful whether I stay in this office two weeks! I certainly shall not under present circumstances. My father sets out on a journey next week, the issue of which will determine me. It mortifies me, beyond expression, to relinquish my study at this period; but I cannot, cannot help it! Necessity is unrelenting and imperious. If I should leave this place, I look to the Province of Maine for residence; or perhaps Salem. Am I to run [John Flavel] Carey's race? O! O! Dear Hervey, how changeable is fortune! Seven weeks ago I was fixed, and you wavering; now you are settled, and I probably on the point of removing. I never was half so much dispirited as now. Though I make myself easy as I can, yet I am really very unpleasantly circumstanced. Well, I owe submission to the awards of Providence. I will submit. I must see you before I go, if I should go, for probably I shall not meet you again very soon.

I look with great anxiety to the termination of next week. May it be successful!! Good-bye, James, may mercy take care of you. Accept all the tenderness I have.   D. Webster.

Mr. Thompson is made Trustee of Dartmouth College.

Doctor [Samuel] Gerrish[12] is anxious to see you. Of nobody he talks so much when I see him. I tell him you will no doubt visit Sanbornton in the winter, and we calculate on having a good interview. But I am resolved to see you before winter, else, perhaps, I shall see you not at all. [Andrew] Lovejoy[13] is happy as a churchman with his new little wife. All the rest of Sanbornton is just as you left it. Doctor G. lives in his own house; has taken in a family.

I thank you for your receipt for greasing boots. Have this afternoon to ride to the South road, and in truth my boots admit not only water, but peas and gravel-stones. I wish I had better ones. As for my new "friend tobacco," he is like most of that name; has made me twice sick and is now dismissed.

Heigho! A man wants a remedy against his neighbor, whose lips were found damage feasant on his, the plaintiff's, wife's cheek! What is to be done? But you have not read the law about kissing. I will write for advice and direction to Barrister Fuller.

N.B. Let no one know that I think of quitting these realms.

Write often, my best friend, for these conveniences of correspondence may not last long. As you once told me, "write soon, write very soon, write now!"

Text from PC, 1: 95–98. Original not found.

1. Stevens (1778–1809; Dartmouth 1798), lawyer.

2. Hale (1783–1822), Newport, N.H., lawyer, who read law with Bingham.

3. West (1746–1817; Harvard 1768), lawyer, of Charlestown, with whom Bingham read law.

4. Abbott (1777–1853; Harvard 1797), fellow student with DW in Thompson's law office.

5. Ephraim Simonds, classmate of DW at Dartmouth, had died on June 18, 1801. On August 26, at the commencement exercises, DW pronounced the eulogy (see mDW 78).

6. Harper (1779–1816), a law student of Thomas W. Thompson and later New Hampshire representative (1809–1810) and congressman (1811–1813).

7. Wood (1752–1836; Dartmouth 1779), pastor of the Congregational Church at Boscawen, had prepared many students for college, including DW and his brother Ezekiel. Lemuel Bliss (Dartmouth 1801) was then studying divinity under Wood.

8. Campbell (1781–1849; Dartmouth 1801), lawyer and later clergyman.

9. Concord physician.

10. Relying heavily upon the advice of Connecticut representatives Pierpont Edwards and Gideon Granger, President Jefferson had removed the Adams appointee, Elizur Goodrich, from the post of customs collector of New Haven on May 23, 1801, in order to strengthen the weak Republican Party in the state. Webster was exalting the strength of New Hampshire's Federalist representation in Congress in comparison with the party leaders, both Federalist and Republican, in Connecticut.

11. All Dartmouth classmates of DW.

12. A Sanbornton physician.

13. Storekeeper in Sanbornton.

A shortage of money constantly pressed on the Webster clan. In the spring of 1801, Daniel's older brother, Ezekiel, had matriculated at Dartmouth, making the shortage particularly acute. To assist Ezekiel and his parents with their mounting expenses, Daniel Webster left Thompson's law office to accept a teaching post at the Fryeburg Academy in January 1802. He was back in Thompson's office in September, but not before he had made lasting friendships in Fryeburg.

TO JUDAH DANA

Salisbury Dec. 26th. 1801

Dear Sir

Your letter[1] containing an invitation to accept the charge of Fryeburg Academy came to hand more than twenty days after date. I cannot but consider it as a mark of attention to be called to the head of a respectable Institution, and you will be pleased, Sir, to present to the Honbl. Gentlemen of the Trust my sincere and grateful acknowledgements.

It is finally my determination to accept the proposal you communicate, and to be at Fryeburg soon as is convenient. The long passage of your letter and the badness of the roads will not, perhaps, permit me to reach Fryeburg the very *first* of January, though I hope to be there as soon as the fifth or sixth, as I expect to accompany Mr. R[obert] Bradley[2] in his return.

I beg leave to consider myself engaged but for two quarters; my prospects and engagements will not allow a longer absolute engagement.

You kindly insinuate that we are not absolute *strangers*. The observation is pleasing, and will constitute a part of my happiness.

Accept my thanks for the manner in which you convey the invitation of the Trustees, and believe that with the warm attachment of a younger brother, I am respectfully yours   Daniel Webster

ALS. NhD. Dana (1772–1845; Dartmouth 1795), lawyer and politician in Fryeburg.
  1. Not found.

2. Prosperous farmer, storekeeper in Fryeburg, and brother of Samuel A. Bradley.

TO JAMES HERVEY BINGHAM

Fryeburg February 25th 1802

My good Hervey,

The date of this will inform you where I am. Yes, James, I am at Fryeburg. I came here six weeks ago, and took charge of the Academy. My engagements are for two quarters, and the probability is I shall then leave them. It is quite an object with me to put myself in to some *urbanic* place the time I am out of study. Nothing here is unpleasant; there is a pretty little society. The people treat me with kindness, and I have the fortune to find myself in a very good family. I see little female company, but that is an item with which I can conveniently enough dispense. Your old acquaintance Mrs [Judah] Dana,[1] lives next door. I am frequently there—they live in a neat, handsome, social stile. Nabby [Ripley][2] is somewhat expected here soon; Mr & Mrs Dana are now gone to Han[over] and will wish her to return with them. O! Bingham!—(but a schoolmaster must not sigh). Having said so much about myself, I will next talk of you. You are not noted, that I know of for paying your devoirs to that uncertain gossip called fame, yet the creature, through some un-accountable fancy, seems disposed to treat you with caresses. Mr [Abel] Hutchins[3] from Concord was here lately, and told me the proprietors of their public school had determined to write you a pressing invitation to accept the instruction of it. I gave him no encouragement, for I thought you in better business, but told him you was the man if they could obtain you. If you should go, you will find every attention. [Samuel] H[aines][4] is attempting to instruct there in Music, and has rendered himself abso-lutely ridiculous. His Jacobinism has encreased his infamy, for having written a frothy, silly, senseless, ungramatical, mis-spelt letter to some of his Democratical friends, it, perchance, got into the columns of the Courier, and was fine sport for our brother students who live in that quarter. [Jesse L.] Billings is keeping school at Sanbornton, he boards with [Andrew] Lovejoy. I was there on my way hither, and pressed Phoebe [Lovejoy]'s[5] hand, and enquired if she thought Mr Billings a clever man; she said he was not clever like Mr Bingham. I told her there were differ-ent ways of being clever; she smiled significantly, and was silent.

I have heard nothing from Hanover since 'Zeke [Webster] left it. He had just arrived at Salisbury when I set out for Fryeburg. Fan[ny H—n][6] wrote me that she was going to Connecticut. I wish her every blessing, but cannot tell what may arise hereafter. I don't know but my happiness must be sacrificed to hers. She said you had a letter for me, and intimated strongly that she wished me to see it. You may, if you please put it into the mail, & direct to me in Fryeburg.

Solon [Stevens], I fear is shot out of business. The Judiciary Bill[7] is knocked on the head. [Jeremiah] Smith[8] will probably return to the Bar. "This is a land of Liberty and the Constitution"—huzza!

Do write me the very next mail, and add one more to that long chain of obligations which bind to your bosom your everlasting friend

D. Webster

To my best friend on earth.

ALS. NhD. Published in *PC*, 1: 102–104.

1. The former Elizabeth Ripley, youngest daughter of Professor Syl-vanus Ripley of Dartmouth College and the granddaughter of Eleazar Wheelock, the first president of the college.

2. Elizabeth Dana's sister, Abigail.

3. One of the proprietors of the "bell Schoolhouse" in Concord, N.H.

4. Haines (1780–1825; Dartmouth 1803), lawyer in Sanbornton.

5. Billings (Dartmouth 1803); and Phoebe Lovejoy, Andrew's sister.

6. One of DW's female friends from Hanover; for correspondence from Fanny, see below, "Fanny" to Webster, May 29, 1823. Bingham identified her in the endorsement of the letter as "F. H—n."

7. Federalists generally anticipated that the Republicans would repeal the Federalist Judiciary Act of 1801; the Republican bill had passed the Senate on February 3. On February 22, 1802,

the Hartford *Connecticut Courant* (copying from the *Gazette of the United States*) reported: "The passage of the bill to destroy our judiciary may be obstructed, but *it will pass*. Mr. Jefferson has set his heart upon this measure; 'tis his favorite measure and his party will (whatever scruples some of them may feel about the unconstitutionality of it) make this desired offering to his revengeful spirit." As predicted, the Republican bill did pass the House and Jefferson signed it into law on March 31, 1802 (*Annals of Congress*, 7th Cong., 1st sess., pp. 510–797; Charles Warren, *The Supreme Court in United States History* [Boston, 1928], 1: 204–209).

8. It was feared that Smith might lose his judgeship by the repeal of the Federalist Judiciary Act.

TO JAMES HERVEY BINGHAM

Fryeburg, May 18, 1802.

Dearly Beloved,

Suffer me to bespeak your attention for about six hours, to the volume I am about to write to you. Having just rambled to the adjacent intervals, which on account of the late rains are all overflowed, and exhibiting almost a "shoreless ocean," I set myself down by the parlor fire to improve a moderate degree of health and spirits, in addressing almost the earliest friend I have on earth. I have a good many things to talk about, and am not disposed to curtail the conversation. Since I wrote you before, I have been within forty miles of you; but stay, I am too far forward. About three weeks ago we had our semi-annual exhibition. The performances of the school were such, I believe, as gave satisfaction to the Trustees. In truth, I was not much ashamed of their appearance. The Trustees were pleased to pass a vote of thanks, as also to present their preceptor a small extraordinary gratuity.[1] Following exhibition was a vacation of 2½ weeks. Forgive me for writing in figures. I shall be glad if I can find paper for all I have to say to you, without stating my ideas by Algebra. This vacation I had devoted to the reading of Sallust, but on the day of Exhibition I had a letter informing me that 'Zeke' was very sick at college. I had heard also that a young man at Salisbury,[2] who was just about marrying my oldest sister, was on the verge of death, and had expressed very particular and urgent reasons for seeing me once more. Under these circumstances I immediately set out for New Hampshire. I went directly to Hanover, where I found my brother on the recovery, though much out of sorts. There also I saw Fanny and kissed her, nobody else. She was in decent health when I first saw her, but was taken with the cramp the night I arrived. I said but little to her. I also saw Sophia;[3] the palpitation at her heart will not, I fear, suffer her to be a great while company for us mortals. She has frequently, you know, been charged with having palpitations of that organ, but I think she has one attached to her now that may produce greater evils than any preceding one. I had not opportunity to chat with her save in company. Mary Woodward I shook by the hand, and was treated by her with more respect than that family have ever before shown me. [Caleb Jewett] Tenney was there; he had a hard time with the measles, though some thought the measles had the hardest time. I met with [Thomas Abbott] Merrill; we have agreed to correspond. He mentioned with much satisfaction some letters he had received from you. I said "Yes, Sir" to [Nathaniel] Shattuck,[4] winked at [Habijah Weld] Fuller, and shook hands with Freeborn [Adams], and drank an Indian health with [Elisha] Hammond, [Amos J.] Cooke,[5] &c. Nabby was at Woodstock. I saw her not, yet I think I looked that way to see about the weather. Being so near, I wished beyond expression to ride to that place where my Hervey lives; but the vacation was so short I could at most have tarried but one night, which would have been tantalizing to my feelings. I therefore adjourned it till September, when I expect to leave this place, and when, if it please Providence to preserve me, I shall spend a week with you, certainly, certainly.

When I reached Salisbury, I found that the young man whom I mentioned in the first page of this document, had been dead several days. To the last he appeared oppressed with something he would reveal to no one living but myself, and that opportunity never occurred. What this was, I cannot conjecture; it might be something important, and it might be a whim of a sick man's fancy. If he had done me any injury for which he wished forgiveness, God knows I heartily forgive him. Peace to him!

I saw our classmate, [Josiah] Noyes,[6] in Concord; a brother pedagogue. The Hon. Sirs. Merrill, Noyes, and Webster I would have called, from their profession, Messrs. "Syncope," "Verbum Personale," and "Nominativo Gaudent;" these would be pompous and sonorous names, significant of the high honors we bear, being clothed, like Mr. Jefferson, "in the mantle of our country's confidence." By the way, if the mantle of public confidence be such a robe as I consider his Excellency wearing, it would be my preference to wander about like the prophets of old, in sheep-skins and goat-skins; but we shall talk more of politics in the next volume. I will go right on with my story,

"And jog on steady by the road,"
"Nor wander into episode."

I spent a few days at Salisbury, and thence took my departure again for this place. Had a pleasant journey, save the inconvenience which arose from bad roads and bad taverns. I came to one innkeeper's by name Knight. From his appearance I thought he could be no Knight of the 'Garter,' or of the Bath, but because I was much annoyed by a creature that stood in the corner, I put him down for a Knight of the Blue Dyepot.

I arrived here last night; but must fill this page by relating a little anecdote that happened yesterday. I accidentally fell in with one of my scholars,[7] on his return to the academy. He was mounted on the ugliest horse I ever saw or heard of, except "Sancho Panza's" pacer. As I had two horses with me, I proposed to him to ride one of them, and tie his bag fast to his Bucephalus; he did accordingly, and turned her forward, where her odd appearance, indescribable gait, and frequent stumblings, afforded us constant amusement. At length we approached Saco River, a very wide, deep, and rapid stream, when this satire on the animal creation, as if to revenge herself on us for our sarcasms, plunged into the river, then very high by the freshet, and was wafted down the current like a bag of oats! I could scarcely sit on my horse for laughter. I am apt to laugh at the vexations of my friends. The fellow, who was of my own age, and my room-mate, half checked the current, by oaths as big as lobsters, and the old Rosinante, who was all the while much at her ease, floated up among the willows far below on the opposite shore.

END OF THE FIRST VOLUME

P.S. I am now going in to see Mrs. Dana; when I return, I will go about the remainder of the work.

VOLUME II.

I will in this volume, my dear Hervey, give you some account of my circumstances, feelings, and prospects. The salary afforded me is three hundred and fifty dollars exclusive; board is one dollar and seventy-five cents; this is my academic engagement. Fortune, like other females, does not always frown. My landlord is Register;[8] and as he is extensively in business I do the writings of his office; this is a little decent perquisite. If I will tarry, the Board will increase my salary, and do every thing for me in their power. A compensation annually of five or six hundred dollars, a house to live in, a piece of land to cultivate, and, *inter nos solos,* a clerkship of the Common Pleas, are now probably within the reach and possession of your friend, D. W.

What shall I do? Shall I say "Yes, Gentlemen," and sit down here to spend my days in a kind of comfortable privacy, or shall I relinquish these prospects, and enter into a profession where my feelings will be constantly harrowed by objects either of dishonesty or misfortune; where my living must be squeezed from penury, (for rich folks seldom go to law,) and my moral principle continually be at hazard? I agree with you that the law is well calculated to draw forth the powers of the mind, but what are its effects on the heart; are they equally propitious? Does it inspire benevolence and awake tenderness; or does it, by a frequent repetition of wretched objects, blunt sensibility and stifle the still, small voice of mercy?

The talent with which Heaven has intrusted me is small, very small, yet I feel responsible for the use of it, and am not willing to pervert it to purposes reproachful or unjust, nor to hide it, like the slothful servant, in a napkin.

Now, I will enumerate the inducements that draw me towards the law. First and principally, it is my father's wish. He does not dictate, it is true, but how much short of dictation is the mere wish of a parent, whose labors of life are wasted on favors to his children? Even the delicacy with which this wish is expressed, gives it more effect than it would have in the form of a command. Secondly, my friends generally wish it. They are urgent and pressing. My father even offers me—I will some time tell you what—and Mr. Thompson offers my tuition gratis, and to relinquish his stand to me.

On the whole, I imagine I shall make one more trial in the ensuing autumn. If I prosecute the profession, I pray God to fortify me against its temptations. To the winds I dismiss those light hopes of eminence which ambition inspired and vanity fostered. To be "honest, to be capable, to be faithful" to my client and my conscience, I earnestly hope will be my first endeavor. I believe you, my worthy boy, when you tell me what are your intentions. I have long known and long loved the honesty of your heart. But let us not rely too much on ourselves; let us look to some less fallible guide, to direct us among the temptations that surround us.

Good-night; to-morrow I will finish this. How pleasant would be this eve, if I could chat it away with J. H. B.

Wednesday Morning. In politics, my friend, we coincide in sentiment. With you I believe that the present administration cannot long be popular. Our Constitution has left, it is true, a wide field for the exertions of democratic intrigue, while it has strongly fortified against executive encroachments; this is the general nature and construction of governments perfectly free. They are much better secured against tyranny than against licentiousness. Yet it has been said with as much truth as eloquence, that "the thunderbolt of despotism is not more fatal to public liberty, than the earthquake of popular commotion." It would be a phenomenon in history, it would be like a comet which appears but once in a hundred centuries, if there should be found a government advancing to despotism by regular and progressive encroachment. The path to despotism leads through the mire and dirt of uncontrolled democracy. When this government falls, it will owe its destruction to some administration that sets out in its career with much adulation to the sovereign people, much profession of economy and reform, and it will then proceed to prostrate the fairest institutions of government by the pretext of saving expense, but really for the sake of destroying constitutional checks.

The late Congress have done wonders; they, however, have greater wonders to perform, if they can convince the people of America universally that they have done right. The business of destruction has progressed charmingly, and its effects have been felt. Bayard, Morris, and Tracy have produced a change in the public sentiment which will continue.[9] The nation, I hope in Heaven, will awake to some view of her situation. Boston and New York have determined to return to their first love; the commercial interest will follow them, and we shall have an "opening to better times." This Commonwealth, you see, continues strong in the service and in the faith. Federal characters have bestirred themselves; if I may be allowed a play upon words, they have turned out strong, to keep in [Caleb] Strong.[10]

Every advice I have from you gives me pleasure; pleasure it is indeed to hear that you are rapidly progressing in knowledge and reputation, almost the only things worth living for. I learnt at Hanover that your situation was very pleasant at Charlestown; that your virtues had secured you friends and admirers, and that your industry was proverbial. I find you are leaving the friends of your youth in the background; but remember, Jemmy, we will not suffer you to run away with all the reputation without a contest.

I shall occasionally address you a volume through the summer, and am happy in the opportunity which this affords me of expressing my eternal attachment, to my dearest J. H. B.   Dan'l Webster, *Ped[agogus]*

Text from *PC*, 1: 107–112. Original not found.

1. The Trustees of Fryeburg Academy had requested DW to "accept five dollars as a small acknowledgement of their sense of his service this day performed."

2. Not identified.

3. Not identified.

4. Tenney (1780–1847; Dartmouth 1801; Yale, D.D. 1829), was then a divinity student; Merrill (1780–1855; Dartmouth 1801), was a schoolteacher, tutor at Dartmouth (1803–1804), and later clergyman; Shattuck (1774–1864; Dartmouth 1801), later entered law.

5. Adams (1774–1812, Dartmouth), South Carolina physician; Hammond (1774–1829; Dartmouth 1802), later became a teacher in South Carolina and Georgia; and Cook (1778–1836; Dartmouth 1802), followed DW to the Fryeburg Academy post.

6. Noyes (1776–1853; Dartmouth 1801), teacher and later physician in New York.

7. Not identified.

8. James Osgood, Register of Deeds, for whom DW copied deeds in the evenings and at night.

9. The Republican-dominated Congress, in addition to repealing the Federalist Judiciary Act of 1801 in March, repealed the internal taxes on April 6, and on April 26 passed a law providing for the redemption of the public debt. The repeal of the Judiciary Act had provoked the greatest Federalist opposition; the chief opponents of repeal had been Delaware Representative James A. Bayard, New York Senator Gouverneur Morris, and Connecticut Senator Uriah Tracy.

10. Federalist governor of Massachusetts.

TO EZEKIEL WEBSTER

Salisbury Novr. 4th 1802

Now Zeke, you will not read half a sentence—no not one syllable before you have thoroughly searched this sheet after *scrip*— But my word for it—you will find no scrip here. We held a sunedrion[1] this morning on the subject of cash—could not hit upon any way to get you any—just before we went away to hang ourselves thro' disappointment, it came into our heads that "next week" might do. The truth is, Sir[2] had an Exe[cuti]on vs Hubbard[3] of N. Chester for about $100—the money was collecting & just ready to drop into the hands of the Creditor, when Hubbard suddenly died. This you see stays the Exeon till the long process of administering is completed. I have now by me two Cents in lawful Federal currency—next week I will send them if they be all—they will buy a pipe— with a pipe you can smoke—smoking inspires wisdom—wisdom is allied to fortitude—from fortitude it is but one step to Stoicism, & Stoicism never pants for this world's goods. So perhaps my two Cents by this process may put you quite at ease about cash.

Write me this minute if you can. Tell me all your necesities—no—not all—a part only—and any thing else you can think of *to amuse me.* You may tell [John] Nelson that I forwarded his letters to Gilmanton next day after my return, and attended to his other business.

Hon Mr Marston[4] has a young son, which in token of past acquaintance his wife thinks of naming for you. We are all here just in the old way— always behind and lacking—boys digging potatoes with frozen fingers, and girls washing without wood. I shall not stir from the Office again till winter that I know of—nor then unless I go for you.

Pray attend to the little request about paragraphs &c. I shall depend on you. Soon you will know if—or not.

Good bye—be a good child "mind your books and strive to learn."

D. WEBSTER

ALS. NhD. Published in *PC*, 1: 122–123.

1. Transliterated Greek word for Sanhedrin.

2. DW and Ezekiel commonly referred to their father, Ebenezer, as "Sir."

3. Not identified.

4. Not identified.

TO JACOB MCGAW

Salisbury Dec. 18th. 1802

EXORDIUM

I will relate to thee an event, Dear Jacob, that will require all thy credulity. Unless thy belief will stretch like a soaked sheepskin you will not give me credit. But I can prove my positions by all the laws of Evidence.

FACTS

Moses Eastman Esq[1]—can you guess what is to follow? O Yes! you guess pretty well—Moses Esq is appointed Post Master in this place in vice Mr [Thomas W.] Thompson[2] removed!

ARGUMENTUM AD HOMINEM

From the *Man*, I conclude this business is entirely of party, and altogether a wide shot from convenience. Such a torrent of absurd consequences follows this removal of the Office that even the meek Moses himself smells difficulty. The Haverhill Mail you perceive, when it arrives here from Coos, must make an episode of four pretty miles to find the Office & may then if he please return & pursue his rout[e]. This will be fine! But the Contractor says, & swears to it, that he will never carry the mail up there —that it is entirely out of his agreement to quit the usual road to chase round after Post Masters. This will be finer still—to have the mail pass thro' town without going to the Office.

PERORATION, OR CONCLUSION OF THE WHOLE MATTER

Now, with leave to waive this plea and make a stronger one next Court, I will venture, speaking after the manner of men, to call him the aforesaid Moses & all his associates in this dirty trick of a party, a pack of Jackasses— & I pray your honor's judgment on the premises.

Well, now good Pilgrim, do you feel edyfied by your ramblings? This seems to distinguish you from other pilgrims—they worship *dead* saints, & you *living ones*—I suppose. I am sorry that E And[over] was not in your way &c.

Once more I have had the MEASLES— & pretty seriously. Nearly a fortnight ago I was shopped, & this is the first time I have used my pen since I became better. In conscience I hope this time will suffice—lips very sore—do mention this grievance to the ladies whom we love and ask of them a remedy. Head ache can they cure that? O they can do any thin[g]—even to the easiment[?] of the heart. Good bye—eyes 'aching— head throbbing—heart beating—lips parching—fingers freezing & measles jumping. Once more Farewell.   D. WEBSTER

I write Saml [Osgood] Esquire as soon as I am well—pray ask Mr. [illegible][3] if he means to write me.

I remember to owe Doctor [Joseph] Benton[4] something for *operating* upon me when sick. You may please to discharge his Bill,—put all your items together, add fee enough to make the sum round numbers, & send me the Amt. I will forward it by mail.

Accompanying is a letter from Mr. T[hompson] to E. Andover. You will oblige by endeavoring to forward it by some private conveyance.   D W

ALS. NhD. McGaw (1778–1867; Dartmouth 1797) was a lawyer in Fryeburg, Maine.

1. Eastman (1770–1848), a lawyer in Salisbury, had been appointed postmaster in 1801.

2. Thompson had served as postmaster in Salisbury since 1798.

3. The difficulty arises from the progressive deterioration of DW's

handwriting as he nears the end of this letter. Words run together, spelling goes by the board, and calligraphy becomes a jest. The reader does not need DW's confession that he has the measles to realize the writer is indeed ill.

4. Benton had settled in Fryeburg in 1795.

TO SAMUEL AYER BRADLEY

Salisbury June 30th. 1803—

My good Friend,

By this time you are safe in Boston[1] as I suppose, & if not too closely intent on business may be willing to hear from a friend. I recollect you invited me to write you, to give a statement of my *case*, & promised me *advice & counsel.* Well, then, here you have it in full. The first & greatest circumstance in my case is poverty—the next a little spice of ambition for professional respectability, & the last, a strong wish to "live while I live". You know under what conditions I live here—no perquisites & no tuition. To live in some Commercial Town is at present my ardent wish. But on cool contemplation, I cannot see a possibility of effecting my purpose. I *might,* perhaps, effect it by troubling my friends, but to that condition I cannot consent. 'Tis a sad return for past favors, to put one's self in the way of meeting others. I have thought a good deal of the idea of a school in Boston, but our Lawyers talk that to keep school six hours in the day would bar one from having a moment's time allowed, if he should pursue the business a thousand years. So Adieu to school keeping! Well, what next? Why, next, I will—will—will—I don't know what I will, finally— & there is a very wise conclusion for you! I have written to our Friend [Joseph Warren] Brackett in the State of N York. Him I expect to see at Commencement at our old mother Dartmouth, & if he encourages me, I shall migrate Southward; otherwise I shall wait for the completion of the destinies respecting me. It is weakness to repine at what is our fortune. I utter no pathetic exclamations against poverty, because that is not the best way to be rid of it. If I am presented with an opportunity to amend my circumstances, I shall do my duty & earnestly embrace it; if no prospect of better times opens, 'tis proper to moderate my wishes to the state of my affairs. The amount of my worldly wishes is to render my self & friends tolerably happy. If I fail of this object, I shall be disappointed, but I trust not chagrined.

Travelling to Vermont, I met St. John[2] at Hanover on the 24th Inst.

The white aprons were quite numerous, & all heads a little mellow. The Ladies, blessed creatures, were all *nice & pretty*. I thought as how 'twould be well enough to tie one's self up fast to some one of the Virgins, but, & but, & but—and so I concluded it would *not* be well enough.

From Concord I have heard nothing since I saw you there.

Pray hold me in remembrance the first leisure hour, & oblige your friend   Daniel Webster.

N.B.— I presume to direct to S.A.B.

ALS. NhD.

1. Bradley had recently gone to Boston to read law in John Heard's office.

2. Probably John Lord (1773–1839; Dartmouth 1799), then a divinity student in Connecticut.

TO SAMUEL AYER BRADLEY

Salisbury 24th Septr. 1803

The Candidate, who is disappointed of his Election, the Lover discarded by his mistress, & the maiden Lady, whose gallants have disappeared together with her dimples & her teeth—all these folks think Johnson a surly old stoic, when he says, that no misfortune is deserving of pity, except Poverty. But I believe he was about right. In comparison with this, other evils scarcely are worth the name, & "for my single self," I verily declare that I would rather lose an Election [(even] that of Grace) together with my Mistress, & my teeth to boot, than to crawl along thro this world of ours without a competent number of rascal Dollars. You see I am in a mode to lecture on Poverty, & depend, I could give some excellent precepts, not how to remedy, but how to endure it. But Adieu to all this! I am rich! rich as any Hebrew! I have a Nag of the full value of $20—an old coat worth 3 stivers, & a pair of boots which are worth, *in Pigwacket*[1] *currency*, a "Sous Marker"—besides, I have three whole segars, & a half one — & in addition to all these articles of immense wealth, I have a parcel of friends, whom I would not exchange for the whole Louisiana purchase! So, Gentlemen & Ladies, take me all in all, I am a downright rich fellow. Yours by Mr. [John] Heard did not find me at Commencement. Counting up all things, I concluded that the whole routine of Com[mencement] would hardly be worth ten dollars. I had no *special reason* for wishing to attend, for you laughed me out of all my Love, when I saw you last— Your letter[2] was brought down by my Brother, & was "graciously received." You observe, that you have neglected to write for particular reasons, & that soon you would address me at Salisbury. Did you think, when you wrote that sentence that you should put my heart in a flutter? Did you suppose, that thro' so small an opening, mighty hopes would rush into my mind? Indeed, Bradley, fancy is the best friend a fellow who is [in no] very eligible circumstances has. I often flatter myself in contemplating the time when I may be residing in Boston—yet in my sober moments, I see that it is much more a matter of hope, than of probability —that it cannot be accomplished without troubling my friends, which would be quite too great a price to pay for the advantage.

I have thought, latterly, of turning my views to Vermont. It is possible I might go into some Man's family there, & be fitted for practice in that State without immediate expense.[3] Of all these things, however, I say nothing. When I see a way to put them in practice, I shall reveal them.

Life passes rather dully with us this season. I have no companion, but books, & long ago I forswore them. At present I see no way so good to get out of difficulties, as to court me a rich wife. In this undertaking personal beauty & accomplishments promise me much, & the abundance of females increases the probability. Depend, however, I shall not take this step without advice of Council. Before I take her by the foretop in the "name of seizin," you shall view her, shape & limb, from top to toe, & if after due examination, you shall pronounce her not *sea-worthy,* I will never attempt to navigate her.

Yours in fidelity   D Webster

ALS. NhD.

1. The Pequawkets were an Indian tribe of the Abnaki nation who had earlier lived and cultivated the land in the vicinity of Fryeburg, Me.

2. Not found.

3. DW probably thought of entering the office of Charles Marsh (1765–1849; Dartmouth 1786), lawyer in Woodstock, Vt., congressman (1815–1817), and a trustee of Dartmouth College (1809–1849).

TO JAMES HERVEY BINGHAM

Octobr. 6th 1803

Hervey,

One Joseph W. Brackett probably handed you an *urbanic* letter from me written at Hanover, in which I promised to send you soon an epistle "three feet long," in answer to several questions you ask respecting my wanderings to & fro.[1] Here then you shall have the three feet.

And first; my Father has an important suit at Law pending before the Supreme Court of Vt.[2] This has frequently called me into that realm, in the course of the past Summer. Mr. [Charles] Marsh of Woodstock is of counsel to us, wherefore I have made him several visits, in arranging the necessary preliminaries to trial. This circumstance, I fancy originates the suggestion that I contemplated reading in his Office. In reality, I have no such idea in my head at present. Heretofore I have been inclined to think of Vt as a place of practice, & as preparatory therefor have thought it possible that I might read a year in that State, but I never carried my views so far as to fix on an Office, & at this time have no views at all of that kind.

Secondly; You have heard that I contemplated finishing my studies in Massachusetts. There is more foundation for this, than the other. It is true I have laid many plans to enable myself to be some time in Boston, before I go into practice, but I did not know as I had mentioned the circumstance abroad, because it is all uncertain. I believe that some acquaintance in the Capital of New England would be very useful to us, who expect to plant ourselves down as Country Lawyers. But I cannot control my fortune—I must follow wherever circumstances lead. My going to Boston is therefore much more a matter of hope, than of probability. Unless something like a miracle puts the means in my hands, I shall not budge from here very soon. Depend on it, however, James, that I shall sometime avail myself of more advantages than this smoky village affords. But when, or where, you & I know equally well. If my circumstances were like Yours, I would by all means pass a six months in Boston. The acquaintances you would be likely to form there, might help you to much business in the course of life. You can pass that time there just as well as not, & I therefore advise to it, as far as I ought to advise to anything. But "some men are born with a silver spoon in their mouths, & others with a wooden ladle"! (Would not you thank me to mend my pen?)

If you can tell what it is to read Coke in black letter on a day too warm for a fire, & too cold to be without one it will save me any description of myself. When tired of old Coke, I look at Smollets continuation of Hume's history. The whole of my reading, however, does not amount to much. I can hardly be called a *Student* at Law. The Law question that now puzzles us in this quarter, is, Whether Buonapartte, when he shall have gone to John Bull's palace & taken hold of the ring of the door in the name of seizin of the whole Island, will be such a king against whom it will be treason in a Englishman to fight? But they may settle this among them —you & I will not give our opinion without a *fee*.

I shall be alone here for three weeks. Why will you not just take your horse & gallop down here? do come, pray do. 'Twill take but just a day from your Father's. I will tell you when you must come—on the 15th Inst. I shall be at Warner, which is not more than 25 m[ile]s from Lempster— come then & find me there—will you not be there? Say, "aye[?]," do. I shall look for you.

I am, as have been time whereof the memory of man runneth not to the contrary, Your Friend   D. Webster.

ALS. NhD. Published in *PC*, 1: 144–145.

1. See DW to James Hervey Bingham, September 28, 1803, mDW 240.

2. No record of the case has been found. Vol. 104 of the Vermont Supreme Court records, 1799–1805, is missing in the Rutland County Clerk's office, and such a case is not listed in the court docket.

TO JAMES HERVEY BINGHAM

Salisbury, March 16, 1804.

GOOD OLD COMPANION,

I have a thousand things which are secrets, and as many which are no secrets, to say to you in this letter. I hardly know where to begin, for there is such a struggle in my brain as to what shall be said first, that likely enough I may run over two pages before I say any thing.

Yours of 22d February,[1] was received March 12. "Hope deferred maketh the heart sick." I pray you never to delay writing so long again for any event; for even one so important as the commencement of your labors as a lawyer, hardly atones for so long waiting.

By this time you have decided where you intend to advertise writ making; let me know about it directly.

Several gentlemen of the profession have mentioned to me two or three towns, in Cheshire county, where an industrious young man might probably make a moderate living. Washington, Westmoreland, and Chesterfield have been named. As to the first, if you settle at Lempster, as I suppose you will, it will be too near to you; so let that go. The other two I wish you to write me about as particularly as you can. I know I am in great season, as I have a year longer to read, but there are some other reasons, which induce me to wish to know generally what part of the country I shall inhabit. It is more than probable that I shall be leaving this place in April or May. If I could think it likely that I should hereafter find a resting-place at some town in Cheshire, I should be fond of reading in that quarter a while. Now, you know, if I could have my wish, I should be as fond of being in Mr. [Benjamin] West's office as anywhere. Silence! Don't whisper a word; don't ever think aloud; but ponder these matters a little at the bottom of your heart, and write me. Inquire if any charitable clever fellow at Charlestown would keep me, and get his pay when he could. Utter not a word for the soul of you; but let me hear from you forthwith.

So, by the help of a little good testimony, you came off victorious in your first attempt. Well, that is a good omen; go on as you have begun, always, unless when your client's cause is an unjust one.

I was lately in Concord, where I heard of our friend Mary. I shall not put down here all the civil things that were said of her, because, you know, I should make a bad figure in reciting compliments. My brother Zeke has made his bow, by letter, to President [John] Wheelock, and gone to Boston. He has there taken a school, which I engaged for him in January,[2] for you must know that I have been at Boston since I last wrote you, and has the prospect of making something a little decent. [Thomas Abbot] Merrill was this way at the close of the last term. He is quite a beau for a tutor.

[Jabez Bradford] Whitaker[3] has opened his office in Providence. [Habijah Weld] Fuller wrote me about two months ago,[4] he will probably settle in Augusta.

As the last dull paragraph to a very dull letter I will tell you, that I have been out of health for some weeks, that writing is very uneasy to me, and that this is, I believe, the only letter of friendship, which I have undertaken to write these two months.

Sick or well, however, I am not the less your friend,   D.W.

Write me forthwith.

Text from *PC*, 1: 159–160. Original not found.

   1. Letter not found.

   2. Ezekiel taught at the school conducted by DW's college friend Dr.

Cyrus Perkins (1778–1849; Dartmouth 1800).

   3. Whitaker (Dartmouth 1801), lawyer.

   4. Letter not found.

TO JAMES HERVEY BINGHAM

P.S. The top of a letter is a new place for a postscript; excuse it, for its design is to beg you to give my love to your and my friends P. and E.[1]

Salisbury, April 3, 1804.

Good Hervey,

I am really much obliged by your ready attention to my requests; as also by your saying, that as Mr. [Benjamin] West leaves the matter with you, I "may venture to jog on." Captain Enos[2] is precisely the man for me; if ever I eat bread at "No. 4,"[3] it will be at his table. The distance from the office is not too great in dry weather, and in wet times one has nothing to do in Charlestown, but just to step "the other side of the street."

I am now going, James, to give you a full survey of the "whole ground," as it respects my prospects, hopes, and wishes. The great object of a lawyer is business; but this is not, or ought not to be, his sole object. Pleasant society, an agreeable acquaintance, and a degree of respectability, not merely as a lawyer, but as a man, are other objects of importance. You and I commenced the study, you know, with a resolution which we did not say much about, of being honest and conscientious practitioners. Some part of this resolution is, I hope, still hanging about me, and for this reason I choose to settle in a place where the practice of the bar is fair and honorable. The Cheshire bar, as far as I have learned, is entitled to a preference in these respects over that of any county in the State. You know my partiality for Connecticut River folks generally. Their information and habits are far better, in my opinion, than those of the people in the eastern part of the State. These reasons compel me to say with you, "it is a goodly land," and to make it my wish to settle therein.

E contrà. Many of my friends are desirous that I should make an attempt to live in Portsmouth. Mr. [Thomas W.] Thompson, my good master, knows every thing about the comparative advantages of different places, everywhere in New Hampshire, except Cheshire county. He has frequently suggested to me, that Portsmouth would be a good place for a young man, and the other evening when I hinted my inclination for Cheshire, he said he had a high esteem for the people that way, but added that he still wished me to consider Portsmouth. He says there are many gentlemen of character there, who would patronize a young lawyer, and thinks that even Mr. Attorney-General[4] would be fond of the thing.

Mr. T. will have business, on which I shall be at Portsmouth as soon as the roads are passable, and out of respect to his opinion, I shall make no certain arrangements for my future reading till that time. At present, I do not feel that Portsmouth is the place for me.

In the way of study, my present pursuit is some little knowledge of pleading. I am reading what Bacon has collected on that subject, and yesterday, you will hardly believe me, I travelled through a case in Saunders of eight Latin pages. Saunders inserts all the pleas, and abridges the arguments of counsel; he is therefore, I take it, very useful to those who, like myself, are a good deal ignorant of the forms of pleading. I mean to lay my hands heavily upon him, and in one month I hope to be able to give some account of him. The winter has passsed away more pleasantly than any I ever before passed at Salisbury, as far, I mean, as my health, which has not been the best, would suffer it to be pleasant. Mr. T.'s sisters have been in this realm, and being very excellent folks, added much to what was before very small society in Salisbury. Miss [Emily] Poor is in town, yet. It would please her vastly if you would just call and play a game at backgammon with her again. She says I unreasonably monopolized your company last fall, at the expense of the folks in the house. I told you how all that matter was and would be; I don't see how I can live any longer without having a friend near me, I mean a male friend, just such a friend as one J. H. B. Yes, James, I must come; we will yoke together again; your little bed is just wide enough; we will practise at the same bar, and be as friendly a pair of single fellows as ever cracked a nut. We perhaps shall never be rich; no matter, we can supply our own personal necessities. By the time we are thirty, we will put on the dress of old bachelors, a mourning suit, and having sown all our wild oats, with a round hat and a hickory staff we will march on to the end of life, whistling as merry as robins, and I hope as innocent. Good-bye to this nonsense, and, by way of contrast, good-bye to you.   D.W.

Text from PC, 1: 162–164. Original not found.

1. Not identified.
2. Not identified.

3. Charlestown had been granted to 63 persons under the name of Number Four on December 31, 1735.
4. Jeremiah Mason.

By 1804, Daniel Webster had definitely decided to complete his legal studies at some place other than Salisbury. At first he leaned toward New York City or Albany, but Ezekiel, then teaching in Boston, urged him to consider the Massachusetts metropolis and offered him a temporary position in Perkins' school. Simultaneously, Ebenezer, Daniel's father, obtained for the restless Daniel a clerk's appointment to the Hillsborough Court, in the hope of keeping him near home. The appointment came from Timothy Farrar (1749–1849; Harvard 1767), a prosperous farmer, trustee of Dartmouth College, and judicial officer from Ipswich, N.H., whose son, Timothy, Jr. (1788–1874; Dartmouth 1807), later read law with Webster in Portsmouth and became his law partner in 1813. Daniel, however, diplomatically declined the elder Farrar's offer and proceeded with his plans to join Ezekiel in Boston.

In July 1804, Daniel entered the office of Christopher Gore (1758–1827; Harvard 1776), a leading Federalist politician—Massachusetts senator and representative, governor, United States senator, and commissioner to England under the Jay Treaty—and an equally prominent lawyer. Webster apparently had been assisted by one of his Dartmouth friends, Samuel A. Bradley, in gaining a place in Gore's office, but he tells a somewhat different version in the Autobiography, p. 16 above. He remained with Gore until his admission to the Suffolk Bar in March 1805. The following month he returned to New Hampshire, opening a law office in Boscawen.

FROM EZEKIEL WEBSTER

Boston April 4th 1804

Dear Daniel,

I most readily concur in the opinion that, the present scene of your life as well as of my own is marked with "dark traces and heavy shades." The map of human life is chequered with misfortunes and disappointments. A continual sunshine of prosperity does not accompany man in his transit from the cradle to the grave. Penumbral shadows of doubt, perplexity and anxious care mark the path-way of the most fortunate through the course of life and often the moment of greatest obscuration is the very period when he is about to enter upon a new profession. Yet at solemn and distant intervals a ray breaks through this gloom and opens to the imagination a vista of better times. Let this *ray* cheer and console us. It is a sweet delusion. I am glad that you feel no "depression of spirit." I can not see any reason for an indulgence of melancholy; though there appears abundant cause. Fortune is a mistress not to be melted into pity by the plaintive lamentations of her stricken votary. Persevering enterprise alone withstands her frowns.

Agreeably to your injunction I have thought and meditated upon your letter[1] for three days and for no inconsiderable portion of three nights and I now give you the result as freely as I earnestly wish your welfare. I am directly opposed to your going to New York, and for several reasons. Firstly the expensiveness of a journey to, and residence in that place is with me a material objection. Secondly the embarrassments to which you will be liabble without friends to assist or patronage to support. Thirdly I fear the climate would be destructive to your constitution. I have now told you what I would not have you do and I also tell you what I would that you should do. I would have you *decamp* immediately from Salisbury with all your baggage and march directly to this place. This is the opinion, I have maturely formed, for which might be urged a thousand reasons. They are too numerous to be mentioned nor is it perhaps necessary; for I say to you imperatively *"Come."* It is the most easy thing in the world for a young fellow of any enterprise or ability to support himself here very handsomely without descending to any business incompatible with the situation of the gentleman. Here too is the focus of information. A person ever so obdurate cannot but learn something. Ever so impenetrable a few *ideas* will enter his head. I will state to you a single circumstance which I think will remove all doubt paying your way. I have now Eight scholars in Latin & Greek whom I shall be obliged to dismiss unless I can have an assistant, and I dare not at present hire one. The tuition of these Eight scholars will pay for your board. They recite twice a day and will take you about ¾ an hour to hear them each time. Here then you can support yourself for the labour of an 1½ hour each day. If you will spend that time in my school each day I will board you at as genteel a boarding house as you can wish or the place affords. Consult Sir, the family and your friends and start for Boston the next day after the receipt of this letter. Another such an opportunity may never occur. COME and if you don't find every thing to your liking I will carry you back to Salisbury with a chaise and six and pay you for your time. I must say again consult Sir, if he approves take the Patriarchal blessing and come. I am as usual &c. Most affectionately to the family.   Ezek Webster

N.B. Be careful to bring those books. If you do not come write *immediately*.   E.W.

ALS. NhD. Published in *PC*, 1: 164–   1. Not found.
166.

TO EZEKIEL WEBSTER

Salisbury May 5th. 1804

Dear Ezekiel,

Salisbury, you perceive, as yet heads my letters, & how much longer it may I can hardly tell. I know it is much better for me to be absent, & I am zealously laboring to put myself into a new situation. If I recollect I informed you my intention was to depart as soon as it is possible for me to get a little cash, to enable me to rig out—for when I leave this vale, emphatically *a vale of tears,* I am determined to be under no obligation[s] to any body in the neighborhood, except those of gratitude & friendship. I never heard what particular substance Archimedes wished his desired fulcrum to be, resting on which he was going to move the world; but if his design had been to move every thing in it, he would have wished it *cash.* Cash, of all things of a perishable nature, is worth the most—it [deserves?] the most toil. It ever did, does & ever will constitute the real, unavoidable aristocracy that exists & must exist in Society. I had an expectation of putting into execution a plan that would have made me able to see you immediately. It was well laid, & I begged of "Sir" to attend to it last week at Court—*but he forgot it.*

I shall continue to scrape round me, & let you hear how I speed. John Smith[1] has left College—he has never sent me any word about your matters, & believe I have not heard from Hanover since I saw you. I have been thinking that if it can be well dispensed with, you would chuse not to attend Commencement. You have never written me any word about your *finances* at present, but if you could get 40 or 50 in the course of this month, I believe you had better transmit it to me, & send me on to Hanover with it, to intercede with His Excellency[2] about giving a degree without your presence, & to secure the trifles you have there, & to pay the aforesaid 40 or 50 to your Creditors. "Sir" has sent oooo to Mr [Richard] Lang,[3] & dou't he will. I don't honestly see how he can. Let me [hear] from you what you think in respect to this idea. *I should abominate to look over your shoulder in Boston & see you break a seal and read "Dear Sir, The little trifle you owe me—"*

You see I suppose the accounts of our Governor Election as readily as I do. If all the votes be returned, [John Taylor] Gil[man] will creep in on the force of about 150 majority.

Pray write forthwith. Give my love to our friends.   D Webster

ALS. DLC. Published in PC, 1: 168–169.

1. Probably John W. Smith (Dartmouth 1804).

2. John Wheelock, President of Dartmouth College.

3. Richard Lang, merchant in Hanover.

TO EZEKIEL WEBSTER

Salisbury June 10th. 1804.[1]

Dear Ezekiel,

Yesterday evening I returned from Election, in about as good spirits as you would naturally suppose, after being witness to the triumph of Democracy. J. T. Gilman is elected Governor by a majority of 132 votes if I recollect aright. Senate is 7 Demos & 5 feds. Nich. Gilman is President. John Langdon is Speaker of the House by a majority of 12. Nat. Gilman was yesterday elected Treasurer, by 3 votes majority, but on examination it was found that there were several more votes rec'd, than there were voters in the house! What an everlasting disgrace to N. Hampshire, that there are such scoundrels in her Government. This is about as clever as a Boscawen Town Meeting. Today at 10 oclock they were to proceed to a new choice for Treasurer. I have not heard the result.[2] [Samuel A.] Bradley & [James H.] Bingham bring me the only word I have heard from you, since Mr [Samuel] Greenleaf's[3] return from Boston. The former tells me he understands you intend putting your name in some Office forthwith after Commencement. That is right. Make a good choice of an Office—he mentioned old Judge [James] Sullivan's.[4] I should think that might do very well.

Feeling some anxiety about your sheep-skin I wrote to [Thomas A.] Merrill,[5] & begged him to put his finger on the President's pulse, & tell me how it beat. He writes in return,[6] that if you attend commencement, there is no doubt you will have your degree. He said he tho't it would be well for you to prepare an English Oration, for Commencement. I promised to mention the thing to you. If you should have one of the very first stamp, I should like it.

I talk of going for Mr [Thomas W.] T[hompson] to E. Andover to accompany Miss Poor, to her friends. As soon as this is over, I intend going to Boston. For cash, I have made out. Perhaps in 3 weeks you may see me in *Short Street*.[7] Our Cousin Nat[haniel Webster][8] is getting better. Aunt Esther [Jones Adams][9] is about rushing into wedlock—next week, she sets out in life. Zeke, I don't believe but what Providence will do well for us yet. We shall live, & live comfortably. I have this week come within an ace of being appointed Clerk of C[ourt of] C[ommon] P[leas] for Hills[borough] Co:—well, you will say, you are no better off, than if you had not come within an ace. Perhaps I am. Say nothing, but think a good deal, & do not "distrust the Gods."

I shall write you before I go [to] E. Andover, if I go at all[;] if I do not go, I intended seeing you directly.

Keep the contents of this page a close secret, write me immediately & believe me Yours Affectionately   D. Webster

ALS. NhD. Published in *PC*, 1: 173–174.

1. The return address on the cover of the letter (in DW's hand) is Concord, N.H., June 11.

2. The balloting for state Treasurer took place on June 8 and 9, not the 9th and 10th as DW's letter indicates. Nathaniel Gilman was declared elected on June 9.

3. Merchant in Salisbury and later in Boston.

4. Ezekiel Webster subsequently read law with Sullivan in Boston.

5. See DW to Thomas Abbot Merrill, May 1, 28, 1804, mDW 276, 288.

6. Letter not found.

7. Location of Cyrus Perkins' school in Boston, where Ezekiel taught.

8. Son of Ebenezer's brother, William.

9. Her relationship to DW is not known.

TO EZEKIEL WEBSTER

Salisbury June 18th. 1804.

Dear Ezekiel,

Day after tomorrow, if the wind blow from the right point, I start for East Andover. On this tour I expect to be absent about twelve days, & soon after my return here I expect to see Boston. The season is now so far advanced, I intend to make my calculation so as to be merely seasonable in Town to learn the gestion of your school, & be able to manage in it, till you go after your degree. Now I want you to be particular. Some time ago, you mentioned to me a few Latin & Greek Scholars[1]—since then, you keep glued lips on the subject of your school. I desire to know whether you can employ me—how many hours per day—in what doing — & for what reward. All these questions you must certainly answer & have your answers here by the time I return. Tell me into whose Office I better go—whether letters of introduction & from whom would be useful. In short tell me every thing— & as an inducement I will now tell you all I know about our N. Hampshire politics. The propositions in Amendment of the Constitution passed by a majority of 7.[2] It is probable Nich[olas] Gilman or Jonathan Steele will be elected Senator to Congress in the place of Judge [Simeon] Olcott,[3] whose time expires next March. Ben. West will be the Fed. Can[didate]. I know not if this Election is to be made this session. It is said the Representatives to Congress will be chosen by Districts. I know not who are candidates on either Side. The Electors, they say, are to be chosen by the people on a Gen. Ticket.[4] The Democratic candidates are thought to be, [John] Goddard, [John] Langdon, Allen Tarlton,[5] Obed[iah] Hall — &c. The Feds meet this night at Concord to agree on their list. The probability is, it will contain the names of Jere[miah] Smith, Tim[othy] Farrar, Ben[jamin] West (perhaps) T[homas] W. T[hompson] Arthur Livermore, W[illia]m Hale, Oliver Peabody—this is my conjecture—perhaps I am incorrect. The Court have had the grace to add 500 Dols to Chief Justice Smith's salary—this it is thought will keep him on the bench. Apropos: they have passed a set of resolves complimentary to the present administration![6]

In the neighborhood, we have nothing new. Every body is well, except uncle Will[iam Webster],[7] & he has just told me to say to you he is better.

Aunt Jones is married to old uncle Adams. Hymen came down one Eve, & did himself the honor to unite the glowing lips of *youth & beauty.* Mr [Moses] Davis was this way at Election time—he brot nothing from Hanover worthy to be told.

Adieu—pray do not fail to write me so that I may find your letter here when I return. Give my Love to Mrs & Doctor [Cyrus] Perkins.

Daniel Webster

ALS. NhD. Published in *PC,* 1: 176–177.

1. See letter from Ezekiel, April 4, 1804, above.

2. Twelfth Amendment, declared ratified on September 25, 1804.

3. Olcott (1735–1815; Yale 1761), Charlestown lawyer, had been elected to the Senate in 1801 to complete Samuel Livermore's term.

4. The New Hampshire bill to divide the state into districts for the purpose of choosing representatives to Congress passed both houses of the legislature but was not signed by the governor (*Senate Journal,* June 1804, p. 17; *House Journal,* June 1804, pp. 53–55). The bill prescribing the election of presidential electors on a general ticket by the people was approved on June 21, 1804 (7 *Laws of*

New Hampshire 285–286).

5. Probably William Tarleton, state representative from Piermont, 1803–1805, instead of Allen Tarleton. See the Keene *New Hampshire Sentinel,* November 10, 1804, for a list of Republican presidential electors.

6. The resolutions expressed "the fullest confidence in the justice, benevolence and wisdom of the President of the United States," and "their unalterable determination to co-operate with the general government in all necessary and proper measures to preserve the Union, to establish justice, to ensure domestic tranquility . . ." (*Senate Journal,* June 1804, p. 17; *House Journal,* June 1804, pp. 41–43).

7. Webster (1749–1824), younger brother of Ebenezer, DW's father.

TO TIMOTHY FARRAR

Salisbury July 12. 1804

Timothy Farrar Esquire,

Instances of favors conferred sometimes occur, in which it is not a little difficult to determine, whether a respectful silence, or an open acknowledgment is most likely to be well received by him who has obliged us. But though it may be uncertain whether we ought to *speak,* it is yet sometimes difficult to be *silent,* when <u>kind</u> things are done in a <u>kind</u> <u>manner.</u>

My Honoured Father informed me, that on an expected vacancy in the Clerkship of the Court of Common Pleas in this County, you were pleased to mention my name to the Court, as a candidate for that Office. I should be happy, if on this occasion, I could express my Gratitude in terms not likely to offend against the delicacy of your feelings. I confess I was gratified, as well as surprised, by this unexpected mark of distinction; particularly so, as I have not the honor of much acquaintance with you, and am destitute of many of those aids, which make young men known in the world, beyond the sphere of their personal friends.

Office and emolument have, as I hope, their just, and no more than their just estimation in my mind: but aside from the consideration of these, and though I should never, in this case possess them, the nomination will add something to my happiness, as I shall be the better pleased with myself, for having been thought worthy an Office of trust and confidence by Judge Farrar.

I am, Sir, with high respect Your humble servant   Daniel Webster

ALS. NhD.

TO JAMES HERVEY BINGHAM

Boston, September 14, 1804.

Dear Hervey,

I should be glad if I could think of a great many wise and useful things to say to you now, just as you are preparing to clothe yourself in the character of a lawyer. Having however a subject nearer home, for all the admonitions with which my mind furnishes me, I shall leave you unadvised.

I wish you were here. Boston would please you as a place of professional study. I could, however, only wish you here under particular circumstances. You say the want of cash prevents you, and if it were not for that you would pass a six months here. I do not know whether I should advise it. You are now ready to open an office, open; you are ready to make writs, make them; you are ready to go about making money, get it. This is my advice. If I had gone my time, I would not stop to study law anywhere; not because I think it a good calculation to hurry into life; but I am argued into the notion by that all-powerful argument, the necessity of being in business. Write me in less than two minutes after you receive this, and let me know where you are going to fix yourself. Having settled, for I suppose you intend to stay in Cheshire county, I wish you to give your opinion of the then best vacancy in Cheshire, together with the opinion of others whom you hear mention the subject. I mean to stay here, if I can, till my time is out, and in the interim I wish to inform myself, so as to be at no great loss for a stand. If I am not earning my bread and cheese, in exactly nine days after my admission, I shall certainly be a bankrupt. [Habijah Weld] Fuller was lately here. He said much about Bingham, and appointed once or twice to write to you, but something prevented. He had with him a Miss, who is said to be his intended. She appears a very sensible, agreeable girl. Mary Smith is in town. I have made her my humblest bow. Last evening I was at [Cyrus

W.] Perkin's; some one knocked; the door was opened; when, with precisely the old swing, entered that "urbanic and extended figure," Augustus Alden.[1] He is very well; resides at Augusta, a student at law. Adieu, good fellow, adieu,   D. Webster.

Give me information about my newspapers, that I may reimburse your expenditures on the subject. Zeke sends love.

Text from *PC*, 1: 186–187. Original not found.

   1. Alden (1780–1850; Dartmouth 1802), divinity student and later a lawyer in Augusta, Me.

Alarmed by the increasing strength of Jeffersonianism, many New England Federalists attributed their political decline to the three-fifths clause of the Constitution, which gave disproportionate weight to the Southern States. In the 1804 session of the Massachusetts legislature, William Ely of Springfield hoped to restore New England's power in the nation through his proposition for a constitutional amendment repealing the three-fifths clause. To Ely's proposal, Webster, the Boston law student, offered his editorial support.

Webster's earliest political writings had identified him with the Federalist cause, but probably to Thomas W. Thompson and William Plumer he owed his increased activity on behalf of Federalism in 1804. On July 4, Thompson and Plumer had met with four other New Hampshire Federalist leaders in Concord to organize a more effective party in the state. They resolved, among other things, to "write occasional pieces for newspapers." Soon after they organized, the Concord central committee probably enlisted Webster's services, and doubtless those of other eager young men, in the 1804 Federalist campaign. An outgrowth of his participation in the campaign was an anonymous pamphlet titled "An Appeal to the Old Whigs of New Hampshire" published by Webster in February 1805. William Plumer has often been mistakenly credited with the authorship of this political tract.

[October 2, 1804]

FOR THE REPERTORY.

COMMUNICATION.

"The Constitution, as it now stands, gives to the slave, at least partially, the character of man."   *Mr. Morton's Speech.*

Accute must be that eye that can see reason in the above observation. If indeed it were so, that the bondage of the whip galled slave was in any degree lightened by the Consitution *as it now stands*, Federalists would be the last to wish it altered. If it subtract any thing from the horrours of Southern slavery—if it spare a tear to the wretched, for the sake of humanity let it remain as it is. But Mr. [Perez] Morton will not persuade the people of Massachusetts that Mr. Ely's motion is calculated to increase the miseries of the slave.— According to a law of Congress, 33,000 inhabitants are constituted to a Representative in Congress. Now suppose that in a Virginian District, there are but 10,000 whites, but they have so many blacks, that three fifths of them, added to the 10,000 whites, make up the requisite number of 33,000. These 10,000 whites, choose the Representative— Who can shew, now, what difference it makes to the slave whether the Representative be chosen by 10,000 or 33,000 whites? Does the slave acquire any more of "the character of man" from the power of his master? So the Laws of this Commonwealth require that every Elector shall possess property of a given value.— Now suppose the property of a farmer in this county to consist in *oxen*— Suppose farther, that for some reason, it should be thought necessary, that the Elector's should consist in real estate, or something else besides *cattle*— "No," exclaims Mr Morton, "in the name of humanity forebear! The law, as it now stands, gives to the *ox*, at least partiality [partially], the character of man— Will you obliterate that character?— Will you degrade the *ox* still lower than he now is?" This sort of reasoning applies to one case, just as well as to the other. The slave, like the ox, is so much property—a mere marketable article— He gives his owner a certain influence in Elections. Append this influence to all property, and we are content. We ask nothing but that the New England *cattle* should be represented as well as those of Virginia.

Another observation of Mr. Morton and of Mr. [Thomas] Allen [of Pittsfield] has been frequently noticed. Federalists complain, that New England has not her proportionate influence in the Union— Very true, say Messrs. Morton and Allen; but how will you remedy this? Not by wicked oppugnation against Virginia—no, no—that's no way to regain influence. But you must "unite with the party which is now a majority." You must give all your votes for the very measures of which you complain— If Virginia smite one cheek, you must not only offer the other, but to save her trouble, you must smite it yourself. You will then have your part of the influence. If the master chastise his servants, he is not to resist— That would be both unbecoming and unavailing. But while the master is administering stripes, the best policy of the servant, is to take another cat o'nine tails, and like a good catholick, assist his master in lashing his own shoulders— He will thereby regain a due share in the *administration*. W.

Text from the Boston *Repertory,* October 2, 1804. Original not found.

Nearing the end of his legal studies, Webster learned that a general requirement for admission to the bar was three years of preparation. Usually, the member who directed the candidate's reading registered the date of the commencement of study with the secretary of the bar association, but in Webster's case, having read law with several lawyers, no such reports had been made. The oversight forced Webster to solicit statements from his former instructors. Apparently with the intention of being admitted to both the Suffolk, Massachusetts, and the Hillsborough, New Hampshire, bars, Webster requested confirmations of his studying law from Thomas W. Thompson and Judah Dana of Fryeburg. At the same time, pressure was again building for either Daniel or Ezekiel to return to a spot near home. Economic hardships and Ebenezer's recurring illness had placed the family in severe straits. It was primarily in response to this family pressure that Daniel opened his law office in Boscawen following his admission to the Boston bar.

FROM THOMAS W. THOMPSON

Salisbury Oct. 17th 1804

Dear Sir,

I returned from Haverhill & Hanover last Sunday after an absence of nearly three weeks. Upon my return I recd yours of the 27th ult.

Unfortunately the rule of the Bar is as you suspect & the business entirely escaped my mind at Sept. Court. I was at the Court but about an hour. I did not attend Oct. Court at all. I feel criminally negligent, & to quiet my own mind & make you some amends I have written this day a circular letter to each gentleman of the Bar[1] in the county propounding you for admission & preparing their minds to dispense with the letter of the rule considering it was established when the terms were three months only apart. An association of ministers meet this day at Mr [Thomas] Worcesters[2] & your Father has undertaken to disperse the letters by the mail & by those ministers. I flatter myself this propounding will answer your purpose. If not, I feel confident the Court will admit you without the recommendation of the Bar. No exertion shall be wanting on my part to procure you the recommendation of the Bar.

The death of President [Joseph] Willard[3] affected me very sensibly. I not only esteemed & respected him very highly but I loved him. My two years residence at Cambridge as a Tutor gave me an opportunity of knowing him perfectly. To strangers his address was rather of the repellent sort, to his friends he was amiable in the highest degree. My opinion is that the Corporation cannot select a more suitable person to fill the vacancy occasioned by his death than Judge [John] Davis. If Judge Davis had more dignity of person, his appearance would I think be more presidential. This is a trifling exception. I cant help feeling a strong attachment to my Alma Mater & this attachment together with my general regard for the interests of literature & religion creates a strong anxiety to have that chair filled by the very best man that can be had. The influence of a President of that University may be of incalculable importance. Why is not a Professor of Divinity chosen? I wish you to unravel this mystery. I suspect the Corporation have different views upon the subject. Some wish for a calvanist others for an arminian. I conjecture that the difficulty of supplying that vacancy results more from something of that kind than from a lack of candidates of respectability who would accept the appointment. I wish you to inform me.

I am much pleased with the communications signed Mass.[4] & W. & I can assure you they have excited a very interesting enquiry for the authors. The former I recognized. The latter I had not seen till after the receipt of your letter. Go on. Catch every leisure moment. If pecuniary compensation should not follow, you will have a satisfaction of a higher nature.

It gave me no small pleasure to learn that you had found a seat in Mr [Christopher] Gores office & I made an effort, the effect of which I have never learned, to interest Mr. G's feelings in your favor. Mr Saml Torrey[5] is his brother in law & my effort was directed thro' him.

I wish you could persuade [John] Park[6] or some other good soul to preserve a volume of the best eulogies on Hamilton. I am confident a subscription for that purpose would run well. The best I have seen are Notts, Masons, Otis & Ames. Cheethams ought not to be omitted.

If you propose to pass the winter in Boston I should like to know it in order to give you some commissions of a troublesome kind. I shall wish you to write to me often & you must pardon me if I insist upon paying the postage upon my own & your letters. At some distant period I shall not object to your paying your proportion.

I hope you keep up your acquaintance with my friend Capt. Wm Parsons.[7] Say how is this?

We have had as yet very few particulars of the destruction done by the late storm in your quarter. At that time I was at Hanover with my family & was obliged to remain there three days before I dared set out for home & then I was two days & a half travelling home. One person counted 100 trees which were blown across the turnpike between Clough's in Enfield & Thompsons in Andover. The snow in the woods was from one to two feet deep. When I came thro' on Saturday it was upon an average one foot deep, & so solid as to bear me for miles without leaving scarcely any impression of my foot. We were eight hours in the carriage riding eighteen miles. At the plain the snow was about six inches deep after the storm &

very solid. The orchards & woods thro' the country have sustained immense damage.

I have for a long time endeavored to purchase without success Roscoe's life of Lorenzo de Medicis. Will you purchase it for me & send it up by some of our traders. My wife has heard much of a novel called the Minstrel & wishes you to purchase it for us. Please to let me know the prices & I will transmit you the money by the return of the mail.

Should you have occasion to borrow money, please to let me know it & if I have it on hand I will accommodate you with it as long as you please at 6 pct. annually.

Your friends here are in usual health excepting Mrs. Hadduck[8] who is quite unwell, yet.

My regards to Ezekiel.

I am Dear Sir affectionately Yours   Thos. W. Thompson

N.B. I wish you to procure me a copy of the Act incorporating the Exchange Bank or such parts of it as will be necessary to shew the principles of that institution. If it is published with the public acts perhaps you can procure a printed copy & forward to me. Furnish me if you please with any information you may possess that will be useful in understanding the manner in which it is conducted.

Inclosed is a $10. bill for which you will please to give me credit towards the disbursements I have requested.

ALS. NhD. Published in *PC*, 1: 188–190.

1. Neither Webster's letter of September 27 nor Thompson's circular has been found.

2. Worcester (1768–1831), minister at the church the Websters attended in Salisbury. In 1801 he received the honorary Master of Arts degree from Dartmouth College.

3. President of Harvard College, who died on September 25, 1804.

4. The Boston *Columbian Centinel* of September 29, 1804, contains a Federalist poem written by "Massachusetts," again probably written by DW.

5. Boston merchant.

6. Publisher of the Boston *Repertory*.

7. Boston merchant.

8. Abigail, nee Webster, one of DW's older sisters, who died December 13, 1804. "Haddock" was frequently spelled with a *u*, even by DW.

TO EZEKIEL WEBSTER

Albany Novr. 15th 1804

Dear Zeke,

Like other invalids we have made it an important point to visit the springs.[1] Yesterday we were at N. Lebanon. The health of both of us is much benefited by a visit to the medicinal waters of that place. We drank, I believe, nearly a tea spoonful a-piece & after washing it down with a draught of wine, we really thought we felt better. This place, to wit N. Lebanon, & Saratoga will be the Bath & Spa of America. They are now the resort of the well, as well as the sick—of the gay, the rich and the fashionable. Where you look to see every nook and corner crowded by cripples & consumptive skeletons, you find taverns, assembly rooms & billiard tables.

Albany is no despicable place. To be sure it is irregular, and *without form*. It's houses are generally old & poor-looking—its streets are rather dirty—but there are many exceptions. A part of the town is very high—overlooking the river in a very pleasant manner— & affording many fine seats. Some handsome buildings ornament the town. The Dutch reformed Church & the new State Bank would not disgrace State Street. There are all sorts of people. Both Greek & Jew—Englishman & Dutchman, Negro & Indian. Almost every body however speaks English occasionally tho' I have heard them talk among themselves in a lingo which I never learned, even at the Indian charity school. The river is here half a mile wide— that is I should [think] it so, & if I think wrong you must look at Dr. [Jedidiah] Morse[2] and correct me.

Tommorrow, weather being fair, we set out on our return. We shall probably go by way of Hudson, Hartford &c.

Before I get back to Boston, the time will expire in which I was to pay Mr Howard,[3] Codman's Wharf, for the sugar, &c. He was promised his cash by the 20th. Inst. If you will borrow it somewhere and pay him, perhaps I can replace it when I arrive. I am peculiarly desirous of being punctual in this case, because Mr [Elijah] C[hamberlain][4] was surety to Mr Howard that I should be so. Pray get it paid some how before the sun goeth down the 20th. It is about 18 Dols.

Call in at Mr. Chamberlains & give him & his folks my love. I shall be glad to get back again, tell 'em.

Adieu—honest fellow.   D. Webster

And there went abroad over all the land an evil spirit, and it deluded many. Oh, Good old mother Massachusetts![5]

ALS. NhD. Published in Curtis, 1 : 68–69.

1. In November 1804 Daniel accompanied Taylor Baldwin, an elderly acquaintance from Boston, on a pleasure trip to Albany and Saratoga Springs, New York.

2. *The American Gazetteer . . .* (Boston, 1797).

3. Partner in the firm of Howard & Eaton, importers of West Indian goods.

4. Boston merchant.

5. DW presumably is referring to Jefferson's landslide reelection, with even "Good old mother Massachusetts" in the Republican column (Boston *Repertory*, November 9, 13, 16, 1804).

TO THOMAS ABBOTT MERRILL

Boston Novr. 30th 1804

My Dear Friend,

Having been absent from Town some weeks, yours of October 25th[1] did not reach my hand till day before yesterday. All that I know about "evanescent subtenses" or "conterminous arches" might be collected on the pupil of a knat's eye, without making him wink. This however I know, that my Friendship for Merrill is a sentiment in no degree *evanescent,* an *arch,* both ends of which rest in the foundation of my heart. I was sadly grieved that you did not write me sooner. My heart suggested a thousand excuses—"Merrill is busy—new employments fill up all his time—he is making his acquaintances—and has much visiting to do". But I never suspected that you was ignorant of the place of my residence. W[illiam Henry] Woodward Esquire[2] made me your compliments just before I left Salisbury, & in your behalf asked me where a letter would find me. I told him Boston. As Dr [Cyrus] Perkins and my Brother [Ezekiel] were at [Dartmouth] Commencement, I took it for granted you knew that I was in this marvellous Town<*of Boston*>. So much for explanation. I am now here, (believe me) —you are at Middlebury—and let us take care to remind each other of these facts often. Now hear me talk a little about myself—I am in the Office of Christopher Gore Esquire, who has lately returned from London, where he has resided for eight years, as an American Commissioner, to settle commercial claims between the two nations. He is a Lawyer of eminence, & a deep & various scholar. Since I left John Wheelock I have found no man so indefatigable in research. He has great amenity of manners, is easy, accessible & communicative, & take him all in all I could not wish a better Preceptor. My acquaintance here does not extend very far. It were much easier for me to form connexions than to support them. There are many young men of my own age, with whom it would be easy to associate. But a young man who has a fortune to *spend,* is not a proper companion for another who has a fortune to *make.* There are, however, some families into which I have free ingress. Here I resort sometimes to play Back Gammon with the girls, in order to keep off the glooms—"With speech so sweet, so sweet a mien— They excommunicate the spleen". There are many fellows in this Town from abroad, who like myself, fall under the general class of adventurers—some for knowledge, some for fame, & some for cash. A similarity of pursuit attaches these to each other— &, if I must say the truth, I think they are rather envied than despised by the natives of the peninsula. You would be astonished at the portion of the active business of the place, of every kind, that is done by men who moved here from the Country. Yet, as far as my circumstances will admit, 'tis my endeavor to become acquainted with the aboriginal Bostonians. It is not the locality of the town—it is not a sight of Beacon Hill or the Long Wharf that renders Boston useful as a place of residence for a stranger—but the conversation, the acquaintance, the connexion, the intimacy which one has with Boston folks. An English Lord, when he travels to view the continent, carries with him English companions, English servants, & English Books. He will stop no where but at an English inn, & converse with nobody but his Countrymen. How superlatively ridiculous this is! What use is there in going to France, if he must carry England with him? Now this is quite too much the case with young gentlemen who come here from the Country to read professions. They associate together—they almost invariably fall into the same boarding houses, & of the manners of Boston folks they catch none hardly of the spirit—of their habits, they learn few beside the *bad ones.*

Dear Merrill, I reciprocate your wishes for a meeting most cordially. Why was not you at Cambridge Commencement? I explored every countenance I met, with the strictest scrutiny, to see if I could not make M's face out of it—but M's face was gone to Middlebury. Of the heart and the heart's concerns, I can say nothing, for want [of] room to say enough. Merrill, if in your walks you should happen to meet with Wisdom & Folly, in whose hands should you look for the sceptre of this world? For my part, I deny, mente et lingua, pugnis et calcibus, unguibus et rostro, the old Grecian definition of human nature—"animal, bipes, implumis, *rationalis.*" So says Plato of man. I contradict him— & to put the thing beyond doubt, I will write my verdict in poetry, of the *most sublime* kind—favete Musae—audi Merrill—

> What nonsense lurked within the pate, Oh!
> Of definition-making Plato,
> Who sang, in philosophic metre,
> "Man is a *rational* & biped creature."
> Many do think & so do I
> Old codger, that you—told—a lie.
> And yet, perhaps, you surly lout
> There is a hole where you'll creep out.
> *Males* you call rational—but no man
> E'er heard you say the same of woman!

Yet I believe we are pretty much alike. I should rejoice to chat with you & inquire, & inform about all matters & things. Pray write me all you know about Hanover & write me as soon as you receive this—a letter in four or five months, is four or five times too seldom. Adieu! D. Webster

ALS. NhD. Published in *PC*, 1: 194–
196.
  1. Not found.
  2. Woodward (1774–1818; Dart-

mouth 1792), son of Bezaleel Wood-
ward, Hanover attorney, and later
Treasurer of Dartmouth College and
Secretary of the Board of Trustees.

FROM EBENEZER WEBSTER

[Salisbury, December 21, 1804][1]

Dear Sons

Governor [John Taylor] Gilman has called on me for money. He has a
Large payment to make out soon wishes my assistance if you can hire me
forty or fifty pound at Boston and send it on by the next mail I will return it as soon as I can perhaps I can not before March court. I can settle
with Mr. Whitehouse[2] without troubling you but I can not make out for
the Governor as I should be Glad two unless I can hire some money
Nath[a]n[iel] Webster would Like to take your horse and sleigh and meet
you at Dunstable or go on to Boston if you think it best and will write to
us when you wish to Leave Boston. We received a verry acceptable present from you which makes us verry comfortable this cold weather. As to
the place of your settlement you must determine for your self. Esqr [An-
drew] Bowers[3] Mr [Samuel] Greenleaf and others are verry anxious to
have you at the center road. Write by the next mail whe[th]ir you can
obtain the money or not.   Ebn. Webster

ALS. NhD. Published in *PC*, 1: 197–
198; Van Tyne, p. 18.
  1. Ebenezer's note, addressed to DW
and Ezekiel, is a postscript to Sally
[Sarah] Webster to DW, December 21,

1804 (mDW 428).
  2. Not identified.
  3. Bowers (1759–1833), Salisbury
merchant and legislator.

FROM JUDAH DANA

Rochester Jany. 18th. [A]D1805

Dear Sir—

Your favour of Decr. 29th ult.[1] arri[v]ed in my absence; and the necessity of my attending Court in this town immediately after its arrival; prevented me from answering the same until this time—and now in the
bustle of business at Court.

I can not assertain the precise time of your residence at Fryeburg, as
Preceptor of the Academy—but think you came in Novr. or Decr.
[A]D1801 and returned the Sepr. following, making a term of about eight
months. On your arrival, you informed me that, as you had commenced;
you intended to pursue the Study of the Law: and wished for the use of
my Library—during said term, and you had access to the same—and I
expect that you devoted the principal part of your leisure hours, while
you were at Fryeburg to the Study of the Law.[2] If a certificate of the the

above statement will be of any benefit to you I can truly and cheerfully make it. I am, Dear Sir—in much confusion—& with much esteem Your Sincere Friend &c.   Judah Dana

ALS. NhD. Published in Van Tyne, pp. 23–24.

1. See mDWs, for letter in which DW requested an affidavit from Dana certifying that he considered himself *"destined for the profession of the law, & had access to the [Dana's] Library of a practitioner"* while teaching in Fryeburg.

2. Although DW was a frequent visitor at the Dana residence, his extant correspondence from those months fails to mention his reading law. Instead, on several occasions he mentions spending his spare time in copying deeds in James Osgood's office.

TO EZEKIEL WEBSTER

Boscawen[1] Ap. 30. 1805

Dear Zeke,

As yet I find it not in my power to procure any money for the purpose of paying for my books. I therefore am under necessity of requesting you to make my peace with Mr [Samuel] Parker[2]—give him something, if ought you have to give, to indemnify him for his trouble & expense, & ask him to put the books again on his shelves. In the course of the summer perhaps I might find a chance to procure the cash; but probably he would be unwilling to keep the books any longer, in uncertainty. The books which I own, he will give to you, & you may, at some convenient time, send them to me. Considering your circumstances, I do not imagine it to be in your power to borrow the cash for a couple of months in B[oston]. If you should providentially light of a chance, & it should be necessary to procure a surety, be pleased to carry this letter to my friend Mr [Peter Oxenbridge] Thatcher,[3] & I think he will be friendly in the case; as I have in many instance[s] found him so before.

My residence here is tolerably pleasant. I live with Mr [Joel] French.[4] Some little business is done here, & I get a part. In time, perhaps I shall gratify my moderate rational wishes. Mr [Caleb] Putney[5] has failed. Mr [Timothy] Dix [Jr.][6] is convalescent from his sickness of the purse, & expects to be in business again soon. Mr [Andrew] Lovejoy[7] will shortly occupy the store in which Mr Putney traded.

At Salisbury the folks are in usual health. Sir is much better than in the winter. N[athaniel] Webster keeps school in his own District. His health is tolerable. Pray write me often—without Books, & with little business, I have much leisure to peruse & answer letters.

Make my love to my friends. Yours   D. Webster

Since sealing this my Books have arrived all safe. I owe Mr Parker Many Thanks for his friendly conduct respecting them. I do not find a list, or Bill & prices of the Books, among them. I wish you would ask him for it, & enclose it to me. I shall take true care that the contract with him be punctually fulfill'd.

ALS. NhD. Published in *PC*, 1: 204–205.

1. For a discussion of the events which prompted Daniel's return to New Hampshire, see DW to Fuller, March 10, 1805, in *PC*, 1: 199; DW to Merrill, March 10, 1805, mDW 441; and DW to Bingham, May 4, 1805, below.

2. Boston bookbinder.

3. Thacher (1776–1843; Harvard 1796), Boston lawyer, who had been one of Webster's instructors at Phillips Exeter Academy and remained a lifelong friend. See Autobiography, p. 9, above.

4. French (1779–1826), Boscawen merchant and town officer.

5. Boscawen merchant. As agent for the Boston mercantile firm, Gore, Miller, & Parker, DW had been instructed to institute legal proceedings against Putney for the collection of unpaid bills. Much of DW's law practice in Boscawen involved debt collection for Boston and Charlestown merchants (mDW 445, 447, 460, 463, 477, 529, 556).

6. Dix (d. 1813), the father of John Adams Dix, was a merchant in Boscawen and a state legislator.

7. See Lovejoy to DW, April 15, 1805, mDW 455.

TO JAMES HERVEY BINGHAM

Boscawen N.H. May 4. 1805

Dear Bingham,

You must know that I have opened a shop in this village for the manufacture of Justice writs. Other mechanics do pretty well here, & I e'en determined to try my luck among others. March 25. I left Boston—with a good deal of regret, I assure you. I was then bound for Portsmouth, but I found my father extremely ill, & little fit to be left by all his sons, & therefore, partly thro' duty, partly thro' necessity & partly thro' choice, I concluded to make my stand here. Some little business is doing in the neighborhood, & of that little I hope to get a little part. This is all that I can at present say of my prospects. For one thing I ought to be thankful. If poverty brings me so near the wind that I canot stay here, *in duty to my stomach,* I have only to take my hickory & walk. The disagreeable incumbrances of houses, lands & property need not delay me a moment. Nor shall I be hindered by Love, nor fastened to Boscawen by the power of Beauty. Our friend [Andrew] Lovejoy will open a store in this place next week, in which he will put Warren [Lovejoy], his Brother, & Thomas,[1] son of Major Taylor. I shall be glad to have them here. One disaster has happened to me. With the assistance of my friends, I collected 85 Dols & sent to Boston, for the payment of a Bookseller[2] with whom I had contracted for a few volumes. But the cash was stolen from the pocket of the bearer, after he got into Boston—& I lose all. Books, therefore, I must go without for the present.

When I have more leisure I will write you more at length. The object of this is only to tell you that I am here, & pray you to write to me. How much did you pay Mr [Frederick Augustus] Sumner[3] for my New York paper?

Adieu—my old—good—friend   D Webster

ALS. NhD. Published in *PC*, 1: 206–207.

1. Warren Lovejoy (1784–1819), was later a merchant in Boston, and Thomas (1779–1850), of Sanbornton, often drove teams to Boston to pick up Lovejoy's merchandise.

2. DW sent the $85 by John Fifield of Salisbury to Samuel Parker of Boston (mDW 457, 496). On April 29, DW had written Samuel Ayer Bradley (mDW 477) that he had not lost the money.

3. Sumner (b. 1770; Dartmouth 1789, Harvard 1793), lawyer and postmaster in Charlestown.

TO EZEKIEL WEBSTER

Boscawen May 12 1805

Dear 'Zeke,

I have nothing more to say on the subject of books, only, that if you have purse enough to purchase "American Precedents of Declarations," & the set of Espinasse's Nisi Prius which Mr. [Samuel] Parker bound for me, & the stationary which he prepared for me, I will thank you to put them, together with my old Books, into some box or trunk, & forward them.

My business increases—*inter nos*, I think I shall make something this summer. I have drawn 14 court writs, & have half a score of Jus: demands to be sued. Mr. [Timothy] Dix has given me about 40 demands, of various descriptions to collect. All this *inter nos*. I have determined on 500 Dols as the sum which I ought to earn the first year. If I fall much short of that I shall not tarry here—this also, *inter nos*.

I wish you to write largely upon your views & opinions respecting the Clerkship. It is time to form a resolve on that subject. Write also, copiously, on your present situation, the degree of attention you receive from Judge [James] Sullivan, & every thing else pertaining to you. Dilate also, upon Town news & politics &c. With this direction for the formation of your future epistles, I will close this Sunday Morn' lucubration.

Your's   *D. Webster*

P.S. Please inform me whether John Lowell Esquire has returned from Europe.

Mr [Joel] French, Mr [Andrew] Lovejoy, Mr [Joseph] Noyes,[1] Mr [Andrew] Bowers will all have teams down about this time, & by them you can send my box or trunk above mentioned cheaper than by the stage.

ALS. DLC. Published in *W & S*, 16: 6–7.

1. Salisbury merchant.

FROM PETER OXENBRIDGE THACHER

Boston May 17. 1805.

My dear Sir,

Your brother informed me to day of your place of residence. Give me leave to add my good wishes to those of your other friends, who are interested in your success. You may reasonably calculate on a favourable course of affairs, for I believe, that the qualities of your mind will ensure your establishment. I hope that you will give me some account of your situation and prospects, and be assured of my readiness to render you any services in this quarter.

My friends who are engaged in the support of the 'Anthology' have instructed me to thank the author of the criticism on Dr Caustic's "Terrible Tractoration."[1] It is highly pleasing to them & has been favourably received by the public. We have thought, that the author of that piece was well qualified to do justice to the Dr's last publication.[2] I beg your acceptance of the volume, & hope that you will authorize me to say to the gentlemen, that they may shortly expect to receive a review of the work. If you are compelled to confine yourself in a situation remote from the pursuits of cities, still I hope, that you will allow your mind sometimes to pay us a visit. I remind you of all your promises in favour of the Anthology and I hope that you will find nothing in Coke or Rastell, which will impair the obligation.

I wish you would tell your brother, that it will give me pleasure at any time to have him pass an hour in my office. Sometimes I shall use his friendship, he may always use mine. Your sincere friend   Peter Thacher

ALS. NhHi.

1. DW's review of the first canto of Christopher Caustic [Thomas Green Fessenden], *Terrible Tractorian!! A poetical petition against Galvanizing trumpery and the Perkinistick institution* . . . appeared in *The Monthly Anthology*, 2: 167–170. The essay was signed "D.W."

2. Thacher was probably forwarding DW either *Original Poems,* first published in London in 1804, or *Democracy unveiled,* published in Boston in 1805. DW, however, reviewed neither of these works for the *Anthology.*

TO EZEKIEL WEBSTER

[Boscawen, May 25, 1805][1]

Dear Zeke,

You seem to have treated my request to write weekly rather scurvily. Two jaunts to Salisbury P. O. have produced nothing, except a letter from my worthy friend Mr [Peter O.] Thacher, including a note for collection, & containing the information that he had intrusted to you a letter of friendship for me, & a Doctor Caustic. Your condemnation shall be double, if, not satisfied with your own silence, you purloin, & delay the

letters of my friends. I expect, however, that some private hand is bringing me a packet by this time. My hopes of business are yet alive—but
there is no telling how soon fortune may put an extinguisher on them.
Money is scarce as love. In all June I hope to be in Boston, & by fair
means or foul *will bring out some books.* I am to have my Office in Mr
[Timothy] Dix's house—a room is finishing, into which I shall remove in
ten or twelve days. He gives me some countenance notwithstanding I
made a pretty impertinent push upon him, when I first came, on Mr
[John] Gore's[2] debt. A confounded breeze was stirred by shutting up Lt
[Caleb] Putney—but it has subsided.

The *Boston host*[3] looks formidable in a Newspaper, & I hope will prove
themselves so to all rascals & jacobins in the Legislature.

Write me, if you have a finger in the world. Yours cordially   D.W.

ALS. NhHi. Published in *W & S*, 16:
7–8.
　1. The return address on the cover
is Concord, N.H., May 27; Sally Webster's letter to Ezekiel, enclosed with
the above DW letter bears the date of
May 25, 1805.
　2. John Gore & Co. (Gore, Miller, &
Parker).
　3. On April 1, 1805, Suffolk County

voters elected all Federalists to the
state senate; and on May 8, Boston
elected a full slate of Federalists to
the state house. It was most probably
this overall set of recently elected
Federalist lawmakers to which DW referred as the "Boston host" (*Columbian Centinel*, April 3, May 10, 1805;
Boston *Repertory*, May 3, 10, 1805).

TO EZEKIEL WEBSTER

Boscawen, August 9, 1805.
Dear Zeke,
　Mr. [Robert] Fletcher[1] having failed and shut up, it seems probable that
something will now be done about the clerkship. Mr. [Joel] F[rench] is in
your favor, and we shall endeavor to make matters work at September
court.

The legislature have diminished the fees somewhat;[2] but it is now
worth one thousand dollars per annum. Write me by Mr. French, without
fail, whether you wish it.   D. Webster

Text from *PC*, 1: 215. Original not
found.
　1. Fletcher (1762–1809), clerk of
the Hillsborough Court of Common
Pleas in 1805 and an active business-

man in the county.
　2. Approved on June 19, 1805, the
act established the clerk's fee at thirty
cents for every action.

*In addition to politics, Webster showed an early interest in banks and
banking. These institutions were tightly woven into the economy of the*

early nineteenth century. Their notes were currency and their stocks provided both solid investment and a medium for speculation. In one way or another the banks generated extensive legal business. Through Benjamin Porter (1771–1818), Haverhill lawyer and businessman, Webster became associated with the Coös Bank in 1805, two years after its incorporation. His association with the Concord Bank dated from its chartering in 1806.

FROM BENJAMIN PORTER

Newbury Sept. 27, 1805

Dear Sir,

Enclosed is a list of C[oös] B[ank] shares[1] in yr. neighbourhood including some at Haverhill Mass. As there are I am told many *buyers*—I can only recommend to you *dispatch* in any negociations you make with the owners. Be so kind as to acquaint me *early* of any shares you get. Am Sir, with much esteem Yours   Ben Porter

ALS. NhD.   1. Not found.

TO EZEKIEL WEBSTER

Boscawen Octr. 13. 1805.

Dear Ezekiel,

I am exceedingly sorry that you do not find it convenient to make us a visit. Some family arrangements are *absolutely necessary* to be made, & how they can be made without you, I know not.[1] I cannot see the immense peril of leaving your school for two weeks; nor the immeasurable difficulty of getting some one to take care of it for that time; nor how you leave it in the winter more conveniently than now. However, if you are serious in these objections, you have probably your reasons, & if you are not serious, you do very wrong to make light of a subject, on which I was serious & earnest. I will attend to Mr [Samuel] Parker, if possible, but if you leave me to do every thing at home, you must do every thing abroad. I have paid $500 for Father, this Summer, & must immediately make out more. You will judge whether I have any thing to do, & whether I have any other reasons for wishing to see you, than a whim. You may state to me, how much Mr. Parker must have, & I will forward it by next mail, after the receipt of your letter. Pray write me the very moment you receive this.

I have no time to enlarge—all well. Yours affectionately   D. Webster

ALS. DLC. Published in *W & S*, 16: 8.
  1. In addition to pressing family matters, DW himself was under considerable economic pressure. See
Charles H. Atherton to DW, October 5, 1805, mDW 608; and Ezekiel Webster to DW, October 17, 1805, mDW 616.

FROM BENJAMIN PORTER

Newbury Nov. 11, 1805

Dear Sir,

Your letter of the 8th. inst. enclosing the <blank> Certificates, of 10 shares in 'Coos bank' is recd.[1] To obtain you the loan you wished, I adopted the last proposal in yr. letter which was to fill up yr. own blank endorsements on these Certificates & so return yr. own note. The balance due you in case you consider the transaction as a *sale* to me (which it is my wish you should) shall be paid you in any manner & at any time you please.

With respect to future purchases of shares which you think it in yr. power to effect, I wish you to act discretionarily but with some *dispatch*. I hope you will be able to buy for 20 or 25 pr. Ct. advance but I would give even 30 or 33 pr. Ct. Acquaint me as early as possible of any purchases that I may be prepared for them.

For yr. trouble in all this business you have my word that you shall be rewarded here & *better authority* for a *future* recompense.

With much Esteem Am yr. obliged friend   Ben Porter

ALS. NhD.   1. Not found.

Toward the end of 1805 when Thomas W. Thompson, Webster's former law teacher, took his seat in the Ninth Congress, Europe was at war with Napoleon. Congress was debating the policies of President Jefferson and Secretary of State Madison as they related to the warring European powers. Thompson provided Webster with detailed accounts of Federalist opposition to Jefferson's policies, while Webster kept Thompson informed as to political developments in New Hampshire. When Webster himself went to Congress in 1813, he drew on the intimate knowledge he had thus acquired of prewar events to oppose "Mr. Madison's War."

FROM THOMAS W. THOMPSON

City of Washington Jany 10th 1806

Dear Sir

This is the fifth day in succession that the House has been debating with closed doors, upon a most interesting subject.[1] Our lips & pens are under injunctions of secrecy, when that injunction is removed we may have materials for letters to our friends. At present I believe I may say without breach of propriety that a very considerable division exists in each of the three departments House Senate & Cabinet upon a question of great importance. National honor has had a most able industrious persevering advocate in one of our political opponents[2] with whom the federalists have cooperated with infinite pleasure. I fear his eloquence &

exertions will be unavailing & the friends to dignified conduct will have to regret the morbid sensibility of the Legislature.

A show of preparation for war is making on paper. A bill to prohibit the exportation of arms & ammunition—has passed the House.[3] Resolutions have been reported for the appropriation of $1 000 000. to the fortifications of our harbours & building 50 gunboats & six line of battle ships.[4] A bill authorising the President to call out the Militia is before us.[5] A bill reestablishing with some amendments the rules of war[6]— & some other things indicate an intention on our part to be ready for "the unprofitable contest of trying which can do the other the most harm"—but I fear that the preparations will be on paper only & not one single solitary measure of energy will be adopted. I hope I wrong the powers that be & that they will before the end of the Session convince me of my error.

I conclude that negotiation & remonstrance will be the weapons of defense our Gov will use agt Great Britain France & Spain, our relations with whom exhibit a dismal aspect. The clouds continue to gather & thicken in the political atmosphere. We expect soon to hear the thunder roll— & it is not impossible that ere long our political chief may wish to surrender the car of State as on a former occasion to some other hand more skilled &.practiced in guiding it thro' the tempest of war. This very day he has made a communication to the Senate consisting of letters from the Gov of France to our Gov. requiring us in terms of insolence (I am told[,] I have not seen them) to interdict our commerce with St Domingo.[7] The new pamphlet "War in disguise" supposed & believed to be the language & doctrine of the British Ministry[8] threatens the annihilation of a vast proportion of our foreign commerce, Spain—poor humbled Spain cocks her nose at us & bids us take our own course. The Genevan[9] I believe is alarmed for the revenues & fears his darling object the payment of the public debt will not be accomplished so soon as he calculated if ever. I rather think he wishes some of the internal taxes were in existence.

I have made intimations herein to you that my friends to whom I have read them say they would not or have not dared to make to their friends. Hence I must request you to make a prudent use of them.

I thank you for yours of the 29th ult.[10] It gave me particulars that were very interesting. I hope you will continue to write me whenever leisure permits. I am my dear Sir Yours Sincerely   Tho W Thompson

The British Minister has recd official intelligence that Prussia has joined the coalition. News arrived this day from Norfolk Virg. that Bonaparte entered Vienna the 16th of Nov.

ALS. NhD.

1. Under discussion was Jefferson's special message on relations between the United States and Spain.

2. John Randolph of Roanoke.

3. The bill passed the House on December 12, 1805, but it failed in the Senate.

4. "A resolution appropriating a sum for building gunboats," reported on December 23, 1805.

5. "A bill authorizing a detachment of the militia."

6. "A bill establishing rules and articles for the government of the armies of the United States."

7. General Louis Turreau to Secretary of State, October 14, 1805; Turreau to Madison, January 3, 1806;

Charles M. Talleyrand to General John Armstrong; Talleyrand to Armstrong, August 16, 1805—all in American State Papers: *Foreign Relations*, 2: 725–727.

8. By James Stephen, who later denied that the work had been written at the request of the ministry of William Pitt (Bradford Perkins, *Prologue to War: England and the United States, 1805–1812* [Berkeley, 1961], pp. 77–79).

9. Albert Gallatin.

10. Not found.

FROM THOMAS W. THOMPSON

City of Washington Jany. 29. 1806

Dear Sir,

At length the spirit of the American nation has shewn itself in the democratic majority of this House by the introduction of a resolve to prohibit commercial intercourse with G. Britain and her colonies.[1] It appears to be the result of a caucus, & of course sanctioned with the approbation of their wisest leaders. It stands committed to a com[mittee] of the whole house on the State of the union. My conjecture is that they offer it principally to shew their patriotic indignation, apprehending no great inconvenience from it in consequence of the general peace in Europe which has or will soon take place. In this I imagine they will find themselves in an error. Extraordinary indeed must be the combination of events which will induce G. B. to yield to Bonaparte the supremacy of Europe, & quietly sit down under the immense accession of power wch. the peace with Austria will necessarily give him. No I believe they will continue to sweep the seas of French Spanish & Dutch vessels.

D[e] Yrujo has entered the lists with the Executive in some degree a la mode de' Genet[2] by a newspaper publication wch you will soon see. The Minis[terial][3] paper will not even notice it. Yours   Tho. W. Thompson

ALS. NhD.

1. Earlier in the day Pennsylvania Representative Andrew Gregg had introduced resolutions for a ban on imports from Great Britain and her colonies.

2. In mid-January, the Marquis de Casa Yrujo, Spanish minister to the United States, had allowed a protest to the administration's request for his recall to be published in Federalist newspapers. A few years earlier, Edmond Charles Genet, first minister of the French Republic to the United States, had similarly gone over the heads of the government to the press for support.

3. Meaning "administration."

FROM THOMAS W. THOMPSON

City of Washington
Feby. 14th 1806

Dear Sir

I am inclined to believe that a variety of incidents are the subjects of conversation here the remembrance of which is not tho't worth preserving but mention of which would engage the attention of our friends. Hence I conclude we might write oftener than we do & afford as much if not more amusement than we now do. We now think that unless we have *pith of moment*—events of great national consequence to mention that it is not worth while to write. If my indolence does not prevent I have determined to adopt this idea & carry it into practice.

From a variety of circumstances I am led to believe that Jefferson is becoming unpopular amongst the leaders of his own party & in the middle states they venture to instruct their subalterns to confuse & belittle him. We hear his High Mightiness spoken very disrespectfully of by democrats of the minor classes & we perceive no incense offered to him by the higher orders. Conjecture states that in New York the Clintonians & Burrites have made a treaty offensive & defensive & that their object is to provide a candidate to·run against Madison or Munroe for the Presidential chair. In Virginia & several of the other S. states symptoms of division of opinion on the subject of Pres. candidate appear. These circumstances very naturally lead those who are opposed to Madison, Jeffersons apparent candidate, to lessen Jeffersons influence. If the object was worth a mighty exertion I have no doubt such is the strength of the federal party in the States & such the unusual division amongst the democrats, that at the next Pres. election we might obtain the least exceptionable candidate if not a federalist.

The Secy of the Navy Robert Smith has been appointed a Judge in Maryland & is very much inclined to accept the appointment & it is said will accept it if Mr Jefferson does not once more overpersuade him to continue in the navy department. It is clear that Jefferson finds great difficulty in procuring respectable men of his party to accept that office or any other. His number of respectable characters is small & the gentlemen of that number have generally very little inclination for office.

This week [Louis Marie] Turreau[1] the French Minister inserted an advertisement in the National Intelligencer which you may have observed the only object of which was to prevent his wife from being trusted. They live in a quarrel. He even beats her. She has once fled his house. He is a savage. And she was the daughter of a butcher & as vulgar a termagant as need be. He occasionally calls in half a dozen of the handsomest cyprians he can procure & makes them dance before him in proprius personis

—in a state of nature,—absolutely without any kind of covering on any part. This is the same man who commanded at Vendee & caused so many inhuman butcheries there. All these things circulate here for facts but I wish not to have the reports traced back to me. His looks confirm all these stories. One thing is fact Madisons wife will not answer him when he speaks to her. A gentleman demo the other evening seeing Turreau exclaimed "I wish to G— Napoleon would send us at least a better looking man for his Minister." But I conclude that Randolph was right when he said At Paris we have no character—it is gone!—yes Sir gone!— We are down on the same list in Tallyrand's bureau with Spain Holland & Italy &c. Like them we shall be required to replenish Napoleons exchequer so long as French rapacity exists on the one hand & American cullibility on the other.—We have fine weather here. The season can hardly be called Winter. In Jany we had one morning nearly snow enough to cover the ground which disappeared the same day. This is all we have had. We have no frost in the ground & have not had for nearly a month. Yours truly   Tho W Thompson

ALS. NhD.

1. Turreau (1756–1816), had arrived in the United States on November 16, 1804.

FROM WILLIAM HENRY WILKINS

Portsmo. 22 Feby [1806]

Danl.

You have not paid a visit to this town, as you said when you was here before. The business before the court, has been important; & managed with all the ability that could be expected. We have had three Lawyers of note: [Jeremiah] Mason, [Edward St. Loe] Livermore, and [Joseph] Story (of Salem) all persons with whom you are acquainted; the two latter came from Mass., to rival Mason; & believe me Danl. when I say I think they did in a great measure. Here the young class cant shine, there wants to be a person that is not affraid to assume his right; as much as to say, there never was a time when a person possessing a large share of Bar talants could Do better than at this time & in this place I am not alone it is the general cry therefore excuse me if I urge a pointt which you seem to treat with indifference. You understand me.

It is now some time since I have heard from you officially. There is one thing that seems to stick in Gizzar, or, rather I dont see thro it i.e. L[ucy Hartwell]'s[1] pa[r]ticular attachment; from what you both have told me, there never could be any lasting fondness, on either side; but when I was at Boscawen, I saw something, which I thot, the reverse of former assertions. Danl. if you can consistant with your generosity inform me whether I am correct or not in thinking you will not have a lasting partiality pray do. You must pardon me for asking such a favor and answer it if you will. You must make my respects first to Mrs. [Abigail Wilkins] Dix then to Lucy[2] and so on till you have gone thro the family. When you have [done] that then accept of the esteem of your affectionate

William Henry Wilkins

ALS. NhD. Wilkins (1780–1854), born in Amherst, N.H., settled in Portsmouth, where he imported European and Indian goods for the retail market. Economic troubles, however, soon forced him to close his business, and he moved to Burlington, Vt., where he resided for the remainder of his life.

1. See Wilkins to DW, August 6, 1806, mDW 767.

2. Wife, and youngest daughter of Timothy Dix, Jr.

TO THOMAS W. THOMPSON

Boscawen Mar. 5. 1806

Dear Sir,

Yours of the 10th[1] & 14th Feby. I received as I returned from Hav[erhill] Court the 1st Inst.

You are entirely correct in the opinion you express of the topics of epistolary conversation— Matters of *pith and moment* get to us in the newspapers, but the thousand small incidents, private anecdotes, &c which happen at the theatre of national business come not in that channel. These seeming trifles are far from being uninteresting to us. The chit chat of a Congressional party is a very important business, when transported from the Potomac to the Merrimac. I think I cannot envy you and your friends the happiness of your seats. With the best men, I think the present circumstances of the Country would be embarrassing, & with infatuated, self sufficient, insufficient Democrats I think them still more embarrassing. There is a degree of responsibility attached to every member of Congress, even tho' he may, in the main, oppose the measures which are adopted. A considerable portion of the community are incapable of separating the ministerial phalanx from the opposition phalanx— & it seems to me nothing can be worse on earth, than to be accountable for measures adopted in opposition to our opinions.

I hope the division in the democratic party will create the possibility of chusing the less evil, & that a union with the better part will, once in a long while, give feds the pleasure of voting with a majority. Yet, I consider a minority the place where a great politician is made. In the history of parliamentary warriors we find no distinguished combatants who did not learn their art of political fencing by exercising against a superior enemy.

At this season you will <expect> suppose us engaged in electioneering. But really nothing, or very little of that business is doing. The

Federalists have hardly made a nomination. An indifferent paragraph at Keene and Amherst has the names of O[liver] Peabody and T[imothy] Farrar as candidates for the chair. No Senator is mentioned for our District. In this Town we mean to choose B[enjamin] Little Esq.[2] Rep. if we can—the chance is I think about even. In Salisbury there is no general understanding among Federalists—a circumstance which I regret exceedingly. The Democrats give up [John Collins] Gale, having no hopes of electing him, & there will never be a better opportunity, I fear never so good, to restore the federalism of the Town. The Democrats are something broken, but I suspect they will eventually unite in Moses Eastman Esq, & from the unaccountable & highly censurable apathy of the feds you must not be surprised to hear that he is chosen. In Concord Mr [Stephen] Ambrose will be the Federal candidate, & S[amuel] Green the democratic. The [Timothy] Walkers, it is said will have a third candidate— probably Mr [Jonathan] Wilkins.[3]

If Mr Eastman should be chosen in Salisbury, & should accept, he must resign his Post Office. Would it not be well to seize that opportunity & compel, Mr [Gideon] Granger, vi & armis, to place the Office at the river again?

At Haverhill I had the pleasure of making my most respectful bow to Mrs Thompson, shaking hands with Lucia, hearing William tell a story & propose a riddle, & patting the plump cheek of Francis[4]—all in fine health and spirits. Haverhill Court was a still one. Judge [Samuel] Emerson, it was said, had made up his mind, to retire before next Term, & from Senator [Moses Paul] Payson I learnt that [Moses] Dow, [William] Tarlton, & [Jesse] Carleton[5] would be candidates to succeed him. A Smart, a Noyes, & one other whose name I do not recollect, were apprehended at Hebron some ten days ago for passing counterfeit twenty dollar Bills of U. S. Bank. They are lodged in Haverhill Jail. C. Putney was caught in this Town about five weeks ago, & imprisoned at Amherst. About twenty days since, he, & Stark & Aikin &c escaped from jail & fled. They were afterwards apprehended in Barre, Vermont, & recommitted. Many names are mentioned as being implicated in the escape, some of whom it is to be hoped, are guiltless of the charge. To you I may venture to say, that Mr Everitt[6] is *suspected,* at least. Pray do not communicate the report.

My Father has been more poorly for a week or two—is attended with considerable fever, & is quite dangerous.

You shall hear from me after Election.

Yours, with great esteem & affection,   D. Webster

ALS. CSmH.
1. Not found.
2. Peabody (1753–1831; Harvard

1773) was a lawyer and politician; and Little (1760–1846), a legislator from Boscawen.

3. Gale (1750–1812) was a Salisbury farmer, store- and tavern-keeper; Ambrose (1770–1845), a trader, town officer, and state legislator; Green (1770–1851), a lawyer, state legislator, and later judge of the Superior Court; and Wilkins (1755–1830; Dartmouth 1779), a farmer and trader.

4. Elizabeth Porter Thompson, wife of Thomas W., and their three children.

5. Samuel Emerson of Plymouth, a Revolutionary veteran, was at this time Judge of the Court of Common Pleas for Grafton County; Payson (1770–1828; Dartmouth 1793) was a Grafton County lawyer and legislator; Dow was appointed Judge of the Court of Common Pleas for Grafton County in 1808 and also served as a New Hampshire legislator; Tarlton (1753–1819), a hotel-keeper and Grafton County sheriff, 1809–1813; and Carleton, a Revolutionary veteran who had moved to Bath from Boxford, Mass.

6. Not identified.

FROM THOMAS W. THOMPSON

City of Washington Mar 10. 1806

Dear Sir

This is the fifth day in succession that we have had [Andrew] Greggs resolution[1] under discussion. The Federalists have not & probably will not utter a syllable upon the subject. The southern demo's have very generally either in conversation or on the floor expressed their disapprobation of it & the demo's from the middle & eastern states have made but a feeble defence—very feeble defence. [James] Elliot has been the only eastern man that has fairly met the subject & he in a speech of two hours length effected but little.[2] But the ground taken against it to me appears hostile [to] the interest of the Eastern States—its true but not a[dmis]sible basis is—we will not sacrifice our interest to support yours. They declare that the trade in question is generally fraudulent & that portion of it wch is honest is so inconsiderable as renders it inexpedient to involve the nation in a war for its defence—a war they consider (& I rather think they are right) the necessary consequence. They also declare that the number of impressed seamen is too small to require measures of this nature. The resolution will probably be run down—but from present appearances [Joseph H.] Nicholsons motion[3] will prevail.

[John] Randolph has made a violent attack upon the President & treated Madisons host with ineffable contempt. I hope soon to have it in my power to forward you his Speech. If it appears on paper as he delivered it, the impression it will make on the public mind must be great. Jefferson here is evidently loosing popularity with his party. It has been conjectured that Randolphs object is to prepare the way for Munroe to the Presidential chair.[4]

The federalists here are of much more consequence than I expected. Such is the division amongst the democrats, that they acknowledge it to be in our power to effect or prevent many of the principal measures proposed. Yours truly   Tho W. Thompson

ALS. NhD.

1. See note 1, Thomas W. Thompson to DW, January 29, 1806, above. Not until April 18, 1806, did the substance of Andrew Gregg's resolutions become law.

2. Elliot, Federalist representative from Vermont, delivered his speech on Gregg's resolutions on March 8, 1806.

3. On February 10, 1806, Nicholson, Maryland congressman, had introduced a milder set of nonimportation resolutions than Gregg's.

4. See Thomas W. Thompson to DW, January 10, 1806, above.

TO THOMAS W. THOMPSON

Boscawen March 15. 1806

Dear Sir,

I sit down to fulfil the promise which I made in my last, of writing you after our elections.[1] In Salisbury, to begin at the Town for which you probably feel the most interest, the event was better than I apprehended. The Demo's put up Benj. Pettingail for Rep—& after several trials they were vanquished, & Mr [Andrew] Bowers elected by a majority of 7. or 8. The old Clerk & Selectman. In Boscawen, I think I told you we intended to choose B[enjamin] Little Esquire. The Demos felt strong, but the issue was against them— C[aleb] Knight had 112—Major [Henry] Gerrish 2—Little 127— & was chosen   Some pains was taken to unite the Federalists, which was no easy business. Moderator, Clerk, & Selectmen are Federal. N[athaniel] Green was up for several Offices, but obtained none. We had a fair majority in every thing.

In Concord, S[amuel] Green esq. is chosen by a majority of 8. In Pembroke, Asa Robinson. New Chester, E[benezer] Kimball—*almost* run down *by John Wadleigh*—Bridgwater, T[homas] Crawford—Alexandria & Danbury, Peter Ladd—federal—Plymouth W[illiam] Webster. Wentworth & Rumney—[Abraham] Burnham—Warren Bartlett—Orford, [Joseph] Pratt—Haverhill, Major N[athaniel] Merrill—Andover, *Doctor [Jacob Bailey] Moore*—Warner, the great James Flanders—to match the Gentleman from Bridgwater—*par nobile fratum*—Loudon—J[onathan] Clough—Democratic—Canterbury, Obadiah Clough—Northfield, the same as last year— & so at Hopkinton, and Dunstable—Merrimac J. Thornton. Sandbornton & New Hampton, the same as last year.[2]

For Gov. the Federal votes are much divided between [John Taylor] Gilman, [Oliver] Peabody, [Jeremiah] Smith & [Timothy] Farrar. Few Federal votes are given.

I have fears that [Daniel] Bla[i]sdel will be run down as Counciller by [William] Tarleton, & [Moses P.] Payson as Senator by [Peter] Carleton. [Benjamin] Peirce is no doubt reelected, & so is [John] Bradley—

I am waiting impatiently to know what Congress will do with John Bull. I think he [may] be found surly— Another recess, without [doing] something for the protection of commerce, [will] I think, put a period to the popularity of the administration. If the cities are awakened, they will awaken the country. The nation may cease to sleep, and the paltry politicians who govern it, may be shaken from their seats. Yours, as ever,

D. Webster

ALS. MHi. Published in *Proc MHi* (Dec. 1927), 79–80.

1. See letter of March 5, 1806, above.

2. Jonathan Ayer (Northfield), Benjamin B. Darling (Hopkinton), Frederick French (Dunstable), James Thornton (Merrimac), Samuel Prescott (Sanbornton), Daniel Smith (New Hampton). All were candidates for the New Hampshire House of Representatives.

FROM BENJAMIN PORTER

Newbury May 19, 1806

Dear Sir,

Our Bank[1] of late have been very sparing of discounts & in the five instances where any have been made the sums have been very small—that I almost dispair of rendering you any assistance [(] in which I should personally be much gratified) in obtaining the loan for your friend.[2] Shall attend at the bank today & effect what I can. I did not ask the bearer of yr. letter[3] if a part of the sum would be any accommodation.

Hastily am with esteem Yours &c   Ben Porter

I send $15 collected of Simonds. Did you receive the Goodenough money?

ALS. NhD.

1. Coös Bank.

2. Not identified.

3. Not found.

During the summer of 1806, Webster delivered two occasional addresses: one, on July 4 at Concord and published by George Clough; the other, the Phi Beta Kappa oration, "The State of our Literature" (mDW 776), at Dartmouth College on August 26. He also extended and amplified his interest in banking. In the June session of the New Hampshire legislature, he and several of his friends had obtained the incorporation of the Concord Bank. In their efforts to get the bank in operation, differences developed among the incorporators on its management and operation, resulting in a split into the "upper end" and "lower end" interests. Webster and Thompson identified with the "lower bank," headed by Joseph Towne, Stephen Ambrose, Ebenezer Dustin, Joshua Darling, and John Collins Gale.

TO THOMAS W. THOMPSON

Boscawen Aug. 23. 1806

T. W. Thompson Esquire,

I have reconsidered my thoughts, & have, on the whole, concluded to go to [Dartmouth] Commencement.

Pray are you not mistaken, in saying, the [Concord] Bank meeting is *next* Monday. Seems to me, it is the first Monday in *Septr*.

Lt. Atkinson has notified Mr Green to attend the taking of your deposition Monday morning next, at Mr Bowers[1]—7 'clock.

Yours &c   D. Webster

ALS. DLC.   1. None identified.

FROM CYRUS PERKINS

Boston Sepr. 3d. 1806.

My dear friend,

We are well home. As I passed Concord I called on Mr. [Asa] McFarland;[1] and speaking of your Φ. B. K. Oration, he told me he was informed you refused a copy for the press. I hope, however, his information is not correct. I shall be sorry to be deprived the pleasure of perusing it myself; and it is [not] a thing I think good to die with the breath which gave it utterance and be blown away by the wind—you *must* not persist in a refusal—I shall write the Secy. to put me a doz or two—Why! have you not let me know that you oratorized at Concord 4th July? you will confer a great obligation by sending one of yr orations, immed[iatel]y per mail. I am, dear Sir, with much esteem your cordial friend   Cy. Perkins

Remember me affectionately to brother Ezekiel—whom I hope to see with you, when you come to town.

ALS. NhD.   College, 1809–1822, and Concord
    1. McFarland (1769–1827; Dart-   clergyman.
mouth 1793), trustee of Dartmouth

TO SAMUEL A. BRADLEY

Boscawen Nov. 21, 1806.

Dear Bradley,

The enclosed Ex[e]c[utio]n[1] I wish you to put on your files for immediate collection. [Benjamin] Simson[2] left Canterbury some few weeks ago, & I suspect will never be more able to pay than now. The money is not needed excessively; but, like Falstaff's taylor, we insist upon security. If Simson will furnish that, he may have a few weeks to pick up his shreds.

I have just finished a long letter to Saml. Fessenden,[3] touching his touching thot, which all authors who have ever written touching the subject, say he ought not to have touched. (My [- - - -]! I have touched off that sentence with many inimitable touches—)

I wrote in answer to a letter rec'd from him,[4] in which I tho't he manifested more low spirits than became him. I hope you do your best to keep him up. You have done him much service heretofore—I doubt not the fountain of your heart is still unexhausted.

Some three weeks after I saw you, I met with *Counsellor* [Samuel] *Haines*,[5] whom you *smoked* so nicely at College. "Pray[,"] says he to me, ["]what can be the reason, that the marriage was not consummated— Mr. B. told me, in confidence however, that there was no doubt of the thing!" Poor H's impatience all vanished! Ah, you wicked rogue! I was to give the counsellor the belief of his consequence and then let him down again to poor stupid Sam Haines. [Samuel] Fessenden has a fine son.[6] I have not seen him, but he is said to be the image & superscription, & to carry proof of his parentage in his countenance. When about a week old, he was put out at nurse.

I wish you to inform your Bro' Robert that the Concord Bank is not yet in operation. Somehow, the Legislature when they made the charter, were so vigorous as to beget twins, for truly there are now, two sets of men, who call themselves the Concord Bank Corporation. Each set has its directors. T[imothy] Walker, J[ohn] Bradley, C[aleb] Stark, B[aruch] Chace, & J[oseph] Clough—are one board of Directors. J[oseph] Towne, S[tephen] Ambrose, Eben[ezer] Dustin, B. B. [Joshua] Darling, & J[ohn] C[ollins] Gale, the other. Walker & Towne are the two Presidents. A very fine vault is building for Judge Walker's bank, and it is said they will issue their bills shortly. It is said the other set will go into operation in a few months, & leave it to the Superior Court to decide which is the real Bank. A novel spectacle, this. For my own part, having no money to place at usury, I have never intermeddled with the dispute,[7] farther than I were obliged by happening once to represent a grantee's right at a meeting. I am, on the whole, inclined to the opinion that the Towne Bank will prevail. It is very deeply entrenched in the minds of the Community; this will give their Bills a circulation, & I believe it will be difficult to sustain a prosecution against them and in the restraining act, so called. I am told that Walker shall find no sale in Boston, or anywhere on the sea board, & I know that shares in the other bank are eagerly bought up, both in Towne & Country.

I have tho't it proper to suggest these remarks to your Bro', as knowing that he has contemplated some connexion with the Bank. I have heard, but I know not with how much truth, that your Father & Jos. Clough intend resigning their offices as directors.

I am anxious to hear how our lottery business succeeds. Pray give me a line on that and other subjects.

Give my love to your Bro's family, & believe me to be Your's for ever

D. Webster

Typed copy. NhD. Original not found.
1. Not found.
2. Not otherwise identified.
3. Letter not found.
4. March 20, 1806, mDW 714.
5. Haines (1780–1825; Dartmouth

1803), lawyer in Sanbornton.
6. William Pitt Fessenden, for whom DW stood godfather.
7. By 1808, DW was a stockholder in the "lower bank" (mDW 39499).

TO THOMAS W. THOMPSON

Boscawen Dec. 2. 1806

Dear Sir,

On Saturday the 29 Novr. the Concord Bank made its first appearance.[1] Some nine or ten hundred three dollar bills had been procured from [Joseph] Callender,[2] Boston, a part of which were in circulation, and a board up, over [John Collins] Gale's north room Saturday Morning. I believe no mortal of the other party dreamed of such an event. It was, *magna componere parvis*, like Buonapartte's battle of Austerlitz, a "clap of thunder". It took, however, mightily with the people, & on the whole I think was a very wise step. Yesterday was Stockholders meeting. A great many people were present, & all in great glee. Some considerable specie was paid in, on shares, & the sale of the remaining shares was instantaneous. They can now be sold above par. Director [Benjamin] Gale[3] was not present! I declare I am not much in love with your friend this same Col. [Samuel] G[reely].[4] I fear he is a bad bargain. He has done nothing, since you left us, towards promoting the views of the institution, &, what is much worse, he speaks of it, at Salisbury, in a faint, discouraging tone; the consequence of all which is, that not a mortal attended the meeting yesterday from Salisbury except J[oseph] Noyes.

Your subscription paper has not been returned. I conclude you left it with Col. G. If it be not returned, the shares will probably be disposed of by others of the Committee. Shall I write a line today to Col. G. to forward it, if he has it, to Concord, or at any rate, to inform me, what number of shares stand against your name, that the assessments may be paid? I rec'd your Power of Atty. from Boston.[5]

After the meeting was over last Eve', a message came to the Directors from Judge [Timothy] Walker,[6] with a proposition, that the two sets of Directors should meet, & confer on the means of a reconciliation! What does this look like? But Messrs [Stephen] Ambrose & al were disposed to play the Roman. They informed the messenger, (Mr. [William]

Whittle)⁷ that they knew no other set of directors, than themselves—that they should not accredit any gentlemen, in capacities which they had wrongfully assumed, & therefore could not agree to any such meeting as was proposed! They condescended however to say, that they desired no unnecessary contest, or difficulty; & should be happy if the persons, disaffected with their proceedings could be reconciled. In short, they sent the Judge back this consolation, that if he wished for shares in the Concord Bank, which were now all taken up, they would use their influence to persuade some of their friends to part with a portion of their own shares, to accomodate him!

So much for the Concord Bank—which, as it is now the only topic of conversation here, hath spread itself over the greater portion of this sheet. I count the days since your departure, & the computation sets you down, this day at the door of your boarding house, in the City of W. Surely I congratulate all your sound bones, & compassionate your broken ones. Such a *jam* in the stages, I should dread more than the circumnavigation of the globe.

The weather is remarkably mild yet. There is no snow, & people are ploughing their grass lands.

I had the pleasure of seeing Mrs Thompson, and family, Thanksgiving Eve'; all well.

I am, Dear Sir, With much esteem, Your's   D. Webster

ALS. CSmH.
  1. The "lower bank."
  2. Engraver.
  3. Gale (1772–1822), one of the incorporators of the bank.
  4. See Stephen Moody to DW,

October 26, 1808, below.
  5. Document not found.
  6. Walker (b. 1767), farmer, town officer, and judge in Salisbury.
  7. One of the incorporators of the bank.

TO THOMAS W. THOMPSON

Boston Dec 26. [18]06

Dr Sir,

Rumour reached us at home some six or eight days since, that the Bills of the C[oncord] Bank were not current in this Town, owing to the refusal of the Ex[change] Off[ice]¹ to receive them as deposites. I was dispatched by the Directors, to inquire into the fact, & enter into some negotiation to secure the friendship of the Office. I have found, that it will be difficult if not impossible, to procure the bills as credits here, without such an arrangement. The Office offer, to become interested with us, by taking 100 of our shares—or by securing a considerable sum, for a given time, without interest. For myself, I thot it more adviseable to give them shares; & that being the opinion of Mr [Joseph] Towne, who is here with me, they will probably be told that 100 shares shall be reserved for them. If this business be satisfactorily adjusted, I have no particle of fear from any thing which can be done by [Timothy] Walker & Co:[2] I am persuaded they will never take another step.

While I write this, Judge [James] Sullivan is closing the cause of the Commonwealth vs Selfridge.[3] Messrs [Christopher] Gore & [Samuel] Dexter were heard yesterday. Mr Gore was remarkably impressive, & eloquent. He is really the most courtly, polished Speaker I ever heard. Dexter closed the defense, & certainly I never before heard any thing that could be called oratory, in comparison with his speech. He was up 3½ hours. Public opinion is every moment becoming more favorable to Selfridge, & the prevaling opinion is, that the Jury will acquit.

In haste, & with esteem Your Obedt Servt   D. Webster

ALS. NhD.

1. Boston Exchange Office, of which Andrew Dexter, Jr., was proprietor. Dexter (1779–1837), a graduate of Brown University and a Boston lawyer had secured the incorporation of the Exchange in 1804, the purpose of which was to purchase country bank notes at a discount and return them for payment at face value, thus restraining inflation and checking note depreciation. The Exchange Office, however, soon adopted the policy of delaying rather than expediting note collection. Extending his influence in New England Dexter obtained control of the Glocester Bank in Glocester, R.I., the Berkshire Bank in Pittsfield, Mass., and the Bangor Bank, Bangor, Me. He sought but failed to gain similar control over the "Towne" Bank in Concord. In August 1808, when his financial empire was at its peak, Dexter owned the legal limit of 100

(out of 1,000) shares in the Concord Bank. With the rise of considerable opposition to his various schemes for controlling money circulation in New England, Dexter's financial power over the country banks declined. He left the state and founded Montgomery, Alabama (Dividend Ledger, 1807–1840, Concord Bank, NhHi; Bray Hammond, *Banks and Politics in America* . . . , Princeton, 1957, pp. 172–176).

2. Timothy Walker, President of "the upper bank."

3. Thomas Oliver Selfridge, Federalist lawyer of Boston, had been accused of killing Charles Austin, a Republican. In this case with political overtones, the jury pronounced Selfridge "Not Guilty." For a discussion of *Commonwealth v. Selfridge,* see Carl Seaburg and Stanley Paterson, *Merchant Prince of Boston: Colonel T. H. Perkins, 1764–1854* (Cambridge, 1971), pp. 172–176.

FROM MOSES LEWIS

Charlestown Feby 1st. 1807

Dear Sir

You will see at one view by the inclosed Papers the bargain I have made with Mr. [Andrew] Dexter [Jr.] which was the best I could do, he states that the blank may as well be filled with 3000 dol, as a less sum which is the sum I have thought best to have, then say we can have two thousand dollars to do as we please & one thousand to keep on hand if we need for Exchanging. Should that be the Case our money will cost us nine Pr Cent Which I think a good Bargain. The bills are in good Cr[e]d[it] in Boston with a number & with others not so good but they all say they think they will get in circulation. I think the bills will be in better Cr[e]d[it] that we had any Idea, of, your filling the blanks & signing & sending them to me by the Tuesdays Stage will enable me to bring the money on with me on wednesday which I will do & will call & make such a division & ar[r]ange the Security in such a way as will be to your satisfaction. It has not been any Material damage in not receiving the money at Mr Blanchards[1] as was talked of by us but shall be in receipt of it—on tuesday night if conveniently in your power to send it, & further if you can send me 2 or 3 hundred dollars more than we talked of I'll replace the same the monday following as you well know where the money is that I am to have at that time. I think you can write to Mr [David] Smiley[2] to enter the actions brought before me on thursday next & have them continued to monday following. I wish you to be Particular in giving the Haverhill Stage man directions to shift in the Papers &c into the Hands of him that comes to Parmers & the Papers &c I'll receive at said Par[mers] from the hand of the Stageman. I shall set for home on Wednesday morning if alive and well at all events am Sir your obt Servt.

Moses Lewis

ALS. NhD. Lewis (b. 1770), a resident of Bridgewater, N.H., frequently represented that town in the New Hampshire legislature, where he promoted industrial development and internal improvements.

1. Not identified.
2. Smiley, lawyer in Bridgewater, Grafton County, in 1808 and 1809.

FROM CYRUS PERKINS

Boston Feby. 3d. 1807—

My dear friend,

You perceive by the date of my letter that I have got to Boston. I went to Andover that eveng. I left you—to Em's Tavern a distance of 41 or 2 miles—where I put up and had a very good nights rest! I had a most agreeable ride—charming place your turnpike is for undisturbed meditation—not even an owl inhabits its neighborhood.

I immediately on my arrival called on Mr. [George] O[diorne][1]—and took your check for $336.08. I counted your money and made it as you did 120$. I wish you to use all conven[ien]t diligence in purchasing *shares* in the bank—less than 20 could hardly be worth the looking after of a man of *my consequence!*—to increase the number you have already bought give what you think proper— as I have a number in hand a few dollars premium to make that num[be]r respectable can be no object with me. You can probably buy some at *par*, some for 5 dols. and if twice 5 should be necessary to raise my no. to 25 or 30 shares or more you *will* buy.[2] I do not believe that these bank shares can be VERY *valuable*—the bank is too near Boston—all will depend on *cunning management*. If we have a goodly no. of shares in the bank we can the more confidently make a "talk" to the interests, of it—and have the preference to those who are not stockholders or less ones—this is some object. I don't want to be an *insignificant* stock holder i.e. from numbers. If it should not be convenient for you to do this thing with the money in your comm[an]d do, my friend, write me immed[ia]t[el]y and I will replenish my funds—in the mean time drop a letter into the care of your *faithful* post master who keeps letters under *consideration* a week before he mails them! From conversation I heard in the bank I have no doubt you will be able to get any no. of sh[are]s you may choose.

If you *can* do it before you come—get my shares or even *a part of them* transferd and take out some cash for me on them & bring it with you. Mr. [Joseph] *Towne* is coming before you; I hope he will bring me some money & I will give him a new note. If he will come before next Saturday, or indeed a week from that time and bring me some 1. 2. & 3 dol. bills— I can dispose of them advantageously for the bank without being myself at much trouble as I am going a journey—where for *years* they will not see Concord. If Mr. Towne should not do this perhaps you can when you come *next week*. Either let me the money on good security as shall be produced at this time or I will get the money Changed and "return" other money.

I am, dear sir, your sincere friend   Cy Perkins

ALS. NhD.
  1. Odiorne, Treasurer of the Boston Exchange Office.

2. By September 1809 Perkins held fifty-eight shares in the "lower" Concord Bank.

FROM CYRUS PERKINS

Boston Feby. 27. 1807.

Dear Sir,

It is now almost five weeks since I was at Concord & you [wa]s comeing to Boston in a fortnight. But I have not only not seen you, I have not even heard from you—in the mean time I have written to you, at least, twice and in one of my letters, pressd. you closely to say something by the next mail.[1] There seems, somehow, a very strang[e] fatality attending the Concord mails at least as far as I have been concerned.

Before I was at Concord I wrote and recd. an answer in about 4 weeks. Your Concord Post Mastr. kept your letter in his office 7 days then our

P. M. kept it about as much longer before he would own he had any such letter. If my letters take the same course it just about makes up the month! Presuming my last letter will finally arrive at its place of destination before the present I will not trouble you with any repetition or re-capitulation of the business it contained.

I wish to know whether any arrangements have been made for an agency and whether any of my propositions will be complied with—if not thro you, & soliciting your good offices in the thing, propose to take from the Bank $10,000 more or less—for which good security shall be given. These bills shall be payable to some name which shall distinguish them from all other bills issued—and as fast as these shall be returnd. to the bank I will [re]deem them with specie or Boston money—so that the Bank shall have [full?] benefit of the discount, & run no hazard of diminishing their specie [as a res]ult. This will be getting 6 pr. cent for the simple impression on [the] signing off the bills— & d' ye hear—I shall make something [on it myse]lf— I wish you would see this done—do. I hope you will, too, [bring the] money or part of it when you come. My shares I wish [discoun]ted—but I don't know yet how many you have obtained. [Unless you] are coming immediately I wish you would write. This m[oney I ver]y much want you to hold onto for me you will confer on [me a ver]y great favour. I should wish you, when you come to be [armed] with this money and to be invested with power to ex[change on sig]ht of such security [for] it as sh[oul]d be satisfactory. I cannot fore-see what objection can be urged against this loan provided the security be good—because it will be mak[ing] *me* pay the specie for the bills when called for instead of its [being] drawn out of the vaults—thereby not en-creasing the risk of a [run?] in the least—as soon as any sum of these bills is returned to your bank let notice thereof be given me immediately and I will deposit and have credited to the P. & Directors of the Concord B—the amt. recd. in the "Boston Bank" a certific[a]te of which shall be forwarded from the bookkeeper to your Cashier. This may thus answer the same purpose as so much specie deposited in the vaults of your own bank because you will be principally called on for payment of bills by people in and about Boston who will prefer a draft on either of the Boston Banks to the trouble of specie from Concord. I wish you to converse par-ticularly on this subject with Col. [William A.] Kent and the other officers of the bank and I am persuaded you will obtain it.

Give me to friend E[zekiel] W[ebster] &c—we are pretty well— I hope I shall see you or hear from you very immediately. I beg of you not to fail. Your attention to these interests of mine will very much oblige your very sincere and devoted friend   Cy. Perk[ins]

ALS. NhD.
   1. Only one of the letters, February 3, printed above, has been found.

TO THOMAS ABBOT MERRILL

Boscawen Mar. 8 1807

My Dear Friend,

Yours of Feb. 13, accompanied by your Election Sermon,[1] were duly [received]. I pray you, receive my most hearty thanks for both. How happy, my good friend, am I, when the tedium of business is relieved by a communication of this sort. And I am more abundantly grateful, if the communication is a little moral, or serious—because I am happy to have my mind called back from the pursuit of ordinary affairs to a contemplation of serious things.

As to your sermon, I cannot say what I think of it, without seeming to flatter you. When I took it up, I took my pen, determined to [mark] such passages as pleased me. I assure you I have blurred & blotted you pretty well. Page 10th contains some paragraphs of excellent ideas—page 14. 15 16 & 17. are favorites with me. The comparison between Rome & Attica, page 21 is entirely new, & I think highly striking & just.

It is indeed alarming, that private character weighs nothing in the scale of qualification for public office—as if a man has *two hearts*—a deceitful, depraved, wicked one towards his neighbor; an honest, [pure & godly] one towards his country! I cannot indulge myself in reflections on the growth of this & a thousand other pernicious sentiments among us, without falling into the horrors.

Indeed I fear that our Country is growing corrupt at a rate, which distances the speed of every other. I do not say that the degree of positive corruption at present [is] so great—but the course towards total depravity is swift. Nevertheless, you say truly "The Lord reigneth"— & while I write that sentence I feel a consolation in my heart, which I would not exchange for the sceptre of Buonapartte. You observe, "however melancholy prospects may be in this Country, they are far more so in Europe". I tho't you was going to say—*they are brighter in Heaven*. As to any human exertions being able to rectify the disorder'd affairs of this world, it is all out of the question. Empires are crushed in a day. All that is ancient, all that is venerable, all that is valued in Europe is overwhelmed by the mighty torrent of French Power. Yet so did *Cyrus*—and so may God do, by means of any instrument, and you & I will endeavor, with his assistance, to rely on his protection.

The times are such I am surprised at nothing. [If] before I rise from my Table, I should [learn] that Buonapartte [was in] London, it would not astonish me. I am persuaded that a great revolution is taking place, not only in Europe but through the world. Society is deeply shaken every where. The minds of men are flying from all steadfast principles, like [an arrow from the bow]. Principles are called prejudices, & duty, scrupulosity. Where all this will end, you and I cannot tell. May we at all times have grace to say, with honest and sincere hearts, "Father in Heaven, th[y will be] done".

I rejoice that you have so comfor[table] a cage. A Bird you cannot but find eas[ily]. [Your] friend W. has neither cage nor bird. How[ever he] lives in hopes.

I have no very *great* objections to sendi[ng you a] copy of my P.B.K. speech.[2] A *small* [one, however,] is, that not being printed, I should [be obliged to write] it off. You *must not* di[sappoint us next] Commencement. A journey [over the mountain] will do you no injury. Pra[y do not fail.]

When I have better health tha[n at present—for] you must know I am now quite [out of health]—I will, I think, write you [a better letter.]

In the mean time remind [me of the] promise.

Adieu—   [D Webster]

ALS (mutilated). NhD. Published in PC, 1: 225–226. Bracketed insertions taken from copy, NhD.

1. Letter not found. DW was probably referring to Merrill's

"Sermon preached before the Vermont legislature on October 9, 1806," which had been published recently at Middlebury, Vt.

2. See mDW 776.

FROM PETER OXENBRIDGE THACHER

Boston April 24. 1807

My dear Sir,

I am much gratified with your account of our [Concord] Bank. The sooner the question of right is decided, the better. I hear nothing in this town injurious to our credit. It will certainly be well, for a time, to issue but a moderate quantity of bills, so that embarrassments may be avoided, and the reputation of the Institution fixed on a solid foundation. I have been thinking on the subject of the agency to the Bank. I consider that all loans are to be effected through him; at least, that you will repose confidence in his information as to the credit of the applicants. This would be a trust which I could not execute with comfort to myself. The property of many merchants in this town depends very much on political events. I observe frequent changes among the young traders. I notice that they are extravagant and are apt to hold out *false tokens*. Such observations as these, added to reflections on the rapid growth of some, the sudden flight of others, the commercial death of some by the natural course of the law, and the moral death of others by suicides, have unqualified me to set at the portals of fortune, and to invite the adventurers into her temple. But perhaps it would have been sufficient for me to say, that my profession requires my whole attention, and therefore I ought not to assume an office which would be attended with care and would require a portion of time, which I could not well afford. I am still ready to do any thing for you, which I can do for the common benefit.

On making enquiry of Andrew Dexter, he told me, that he did not know that any application had been made to his uncle[1] by the other party. I have had no means of ascertaining whether they have applied to Judge [Theophilus] Parsons.[2] I have felt unwilling to ask him the question, and I really do not know how I can obtain information from any other source.

I am much inclined to continue my interest in the bank. But some recent events in my family make it desirable to me to realize, if I can, advantageously, the value of my shares. If you can with convenience sell them on favourable terms, I authorize you so to do. But as I have been indebted to your friendship for the chance, and have subjected you to trouble, I pray you to retain a *quiddam honorarium* for your services.

You may be surprized, that the review[3] which you sent to me some time ago has not appeared. I thought it would be proper to shew it to one of the Fathers and with his advice, something has been added, and something taken away, but not in malice. It so happened that a pressure of materials for the last number, having a prior right, excluded its appearance then but it will appear in the No. which is now in press, with all its several honours. Do not let the cares of the world and the deceitfulness of riches choke the growth of literature in your mind. New Hampshire has yet to produce its portion of eminent men.

I believe that I have now answered your favours. I always wish you health, long life and happiness, and remain Your friend   Peter Thacher

ALS. NhHi.

1. Possibly Samuel Dexter, Jr., for whom Andrew had served as secretary when the former was in Washington.

2. Parsons (1750–1813).

3. Review of *Reports of cases argued, and determined, in the Supreme Court of Judicature of the State of New-York,* by William Johnson, appeared in *The Monthly Anthology,* 4: 206–208. Thacher did the editing of DW's review (Mark Antony De Wolfe Howe, *Journal of the Proceedings of the Society . . . ,* Boston, 1910, p. 104).

Looking toward his settling in Portsmouth, Webster requested the assistance of Nathaniel Adams (1756–1829; Dartmouth 1775), a clerk of the New Hampshire Supreme Court, in finding him suitable lodgings. In late August, Webster moved to New Hampshire's major city.

FROM NATHANIEL ADAMS

Portsmouth June 9th 1807

My dear Sir

Agreeably to your request I have waited upon Mrs. [John?] Wardrobe and have engaged her to receive you as a member of her family—her terms are five dollars P[er] week for which she furnishes <provision> boarding & lodging a setting-room in common with other boarders, a chamber to yourself, furnished in a genteel manner, washing will be an additional expence which you can easily procure in the neighbourhood. I have likewise engaged the chamber over Mr. [William H.] Wilkins's [Dry Goods] Shop at sixty six dollars P[er] year—possession to be delivered the first day of July next. Will you be so obliging as to write me by the next mail & inform me whether I have executed my commission agreeably to your wishes. If I have so done I shall be happy to receive any further orders you may have for me—and by way of encouragement inform you that I have reserved several demands for you to collect at the next court, so that you must be here in season. Yours &c   Nathl. Adams

ALS. NhD.

TO THOMAS WORCESTER

Boscawen Aug 8. 1807

Dear Sir,

The other day we were conversing, respecting confessions of faith. Sometime ago, I wrote down, for my own use, a few propositions, in the shape of articles, intending to exhibit a very short Summary of the doctrines of the Christian Religion, as they impress my mind.

I have taken the liberty to inclose a copy, for your perusal.

I am, Sir, with respect, Your's &c   D. Webster

[Confession of Faith]

I believe in the existence of Almighty God, who created and governs the whole world. I am taught this by the works of nature, and the word of Revelation.

I believe that God exists in three persons: this I learn from Revelation alone. Nor is it any objection to this belief, that I cannot comprehend, how *one* can be *three*, or *three one*. I hold it my duty to believe, not what I can comprehend, or account for, but what my Maker teaches me.

I believe the scriptures of the old and new Testaments to be the will and word of God.

I believe Jesus Christ to be the son of God. The miracles which he wrought establish, in my mind, his personal authority, and render it proper for me to believe whatever he asserts; I believe, therefore, all his declarations, as well when he declares himself to be the son of God, as when he declares any other proposition. And I believe there is no other way of salvation, than through the merits of his attonement.

I believe that things past, present, and to come, are all equally present in the mind of Deity; that with him there is no succession of time, nor of ideas; that therefore the relative terms past, present and future, as used among men, cannot, with strict propriety, be applied to Deity. I believe in the doctrines of foreknowledge, and predestination, as thus expounded. I do not believe in those doctrines, as imposing any fatality or necessity on men's actions, or any way infringing free agency.

I believe in the utter inability of any human being to work out his own Salvation, without the constant aids of the spirit of all grace.

I believe in those great peculiarities of the Christian Religion, a Resurrection from the dead, and a day of Judgment.

I believe in the universal Providence of God; & leave to Epicurus, and his more unreasonable followers in modern times, the inconsistency of believing, that God made a world, which he does not take the trouble of Governing.*

Although I have great respect for some other forms of worship, I believe the Congregational mode, on the whole, to be preferable to any other.

I believe Religion to be a matter, not of demonstration, but of faith. God requires us to give credit to the truths which he reveals, not because we can prove them, but because He declares them. When the mind is reasonably convinced that the bible is the word of God, the only remaining duty is to receive its doctrines, with full confidence of their truth, and practice them, with a pure heart.

I believe that the bible is to be understood, & received, in the plain, and obvious meaning of its passages; since I cannot persuade myself, that a Book intended for the instruction and conversion of the whole world, should cover its true meaning, in such mystery, and doubt, that none but critics and philosophers can discover it.

I believe that the refinements and subtleties of human wisdom, are more likely to obscure, than to enlighten the revealed will of God; & that he is the most accomplished Christian Scholar, who hath been educated at the feet of Jesus, and in the College of Fishermen.

I believe that all true Religion consists in the heart, and the affections; and that therefore all creeds and confessions, are fallible & uncertain evidences of evangelical piety.

Finally, I believe that Christ has imposed on all his disciples, a life of active benevolence; that he, who refrains only from what he thinks to be sinful, has performed but a part, and a small part of his duty; that he is bound to do good & communicate; to love his neighbor; to give food and drink to his enemy; and to endeavor, as far as in him lies, to promote peace, truth, piety and happiness, in a wicked and forlorn world; believing, that in the great day, which is to come, there will be no other stand-

* Dr. Sherlock.[1]

ard of merit, no other criterion of Character, than that which is already established.

By their fruits ye shall know them.

ALS. NhD. Published in *W & S*, 16: 9–10. Thomas Worcester was pastor of the Salisbury Congregational Church at this time. Three of his four brothers were also Congregational ministers. His nephew, Samuel Austin Worcester, went as missionary to the Cherokee Indians in Georgia and became the plaintiff in *Worcester* v. *Georgia*, decided in his favor by the Supreme Court in 1832.

1. Probably Dr. William Sherlock (1641?–1707), a British clergyman.

A significant part of Webster's law practice in New Hampshire involved collecting debts for merchants in Boston and elsewhere. Ebenezer Frothingham, Boston merchant, was only one among many to use Webster's services in this way.

FROM EBENEZER FROTHINGHAM

Boston 1 Sept 1807

Sir

I recd your favr 26th from Portsmouth. Your's from Boscawen has not come to hand.[1] Enclosed you have [Oliver] Davis[2] Note & Other side you have his Bill—the first Bill I sent you at Portsmo. My Agreement with Davis was to pay Intrest after Six Months on Book debts the same as Notes as he some times left town before his ware was packd or the Bill made out—but Expect Intrest will not be allowd. Your Hum Servent

Eben Frothingham

ALS. NhD.
 1. Neither letter found.
 2. Note not found. For additional information on Davis' account with Frothingham, see Frothingham to DW, July 22, 1807, mDW 884.

Webster's two years as attorney in the little town of Boscawen may not have been particularly profitable ones economically, but socially he found the community rewarding. There, at the home of Timothy Dix, he met a schoolmistress, Grace Fletcher (1781–1828), daughter of the Reverend Elijah Fletcher of Hopkinton, whose charm and beauty captivated him. Their courtship continued after Webster moved to Portsmouth, and on May 29, 1808, in Salisbury, the two were married.

TO GRACE FLETCHER [WEBSTER]

[Sept.] 4, 1807

Dear G.

I was fortunate enough be at home Sunday morning, 6 o'clock, after rather a *solitary* ride. The Country from Cambridge to Dunstable is really, as I tho't, much more pleasant, than from Dunstable to Concord. I have not yet seen your friends, but I understand from Mr [Israel Webster] Kelly[1] that they are well. By Mr [Daniel] A[bbott] I send you a small piece of velvet, for the aforesaid 5 pence.

Early in the week after next, I hope to see y[ou] all. Give my love to all the friends & excuse a scrawl written in a Court house. Yours entirely—

D. W.

ALS. NhD. Published in part in *Century Magazine*, 29 (March 1885): 723.

1. Kelly (1778–1857), Grace Fletcher's brother-in-law.

Soon after he moved to Portsmouth, Webster and several of his friends were again running short of money, a situation which required immediate attention. To Ezekiel and to Thompson, he appealed for assistance.

TO EZEKIEL WEBSTER

Portsm. Dec. 16. 1807

Dear Ez,

I have no time, such is the brevity of Mr. [Timothy] Dix's stay here, to sew your shreds & patches together, & send you back a whole garment. Enclosed is a minute[1] respecting my demands, which you will please regard. Mr J[oel] French owes me $100—lent. Ask him, if he can do me the favor to pay 50 of it. Mr. Joseph Atkinson, & Peabody[2] owe me $100—ask them to send me by you 50. At present I have not ten Dollars, sub celo. Pray sue my notes, in some name other than mine.

I wrote you by Mail a week ago[3] but you say nothing of it.

There is no money here, within my reach. I have sued any body I could, & if there is any money I shall have some, one of these days.

Sue every body that ought to be sued.

I doubt whether Mr [Samuel] Haines is admissible to our Bar.[4] Your's in haste.   D. Webster

ALS. NhD.
1. Not found.
2. Not identified.
3. Not found.

4. The Rockingham Bar, in January 1808, postponed a decision on Haines' admission until the August term.

TO THOMAS W. THOMPSON

Portsm. Jany 9. 1808

Thomas W. Thompson Esq.

I have this Eve' received a letter from Doctor [Cyrus] Perkins of Boston,[1] giving a particular account of his misfortune, (of which you have heard,[)] and requesting me to go to Concord, to negotiate some arrangement with the directors [of the Concord Bank]. The Court has not yet risen, and it is therefore out of my power to comply with his wishes. I have thought best to communicate his letter to you, and pray you to read it to the Directors. It is a sad tale, & perhaps not written for such an use, but it relates his story better than I can.

I really feel an ardent wish, that something might be done for his relief. He is really oppressed by the thing, more than he ought to be—& it must necessarily oppress any one in his circumstances much. I have heard from some of his acquaintances in Boston, that he is totally unfit for, & incapable of any business, & walks his rooms, in a constant agony.

In a recent letter to me, he says he is ready to deliver up to the Bank all the property he has, if they will take it, and discharge him. What can be done? Delay would be dreadful to him, & useless to the Bank. If the Directors will not receive the Portland notes, and discharge him, he chuses to deliver up his effects, & pay as far as every thing will go. Will the Directors then discharge him? I know that in any other case, it would seem to be better to defer, & give time to retrieve, in some measure, this misfortune. But from my knowledge of Perkins, & from what I learn from his letters, I am convinced it is preferable for him to deliver up all, even to his shoe buck[l]es, than to delay—for he never can *do any thing* with this calamity hanging over his head. If I can be of any service to Perkins, in your opinion, by going to Concord, I will go up on Monday, after next. But I know not if I can be useful to him. I think the Directors will incline to do what you suggest, & am sure that you can advise more wisely than any of us. Will you be so obliging as to write me, what the Directors me[an] to do.

I am, Dear Sir, With esteem & affection, Your Obedt Sevt
D. Webster

ALS. CSmH.   1. Letter not found.

TO JAMES HERVEY BINGHAM

Portsmouth Feb. 27. 1808

Dear Bingham,

"Friendship, like Love, is destroyed by long absence, though it may be encreased by short intermissions." I this moment read this sentence in one of the numbers of the Idler, & as I read, the idea of my old friend Hervey rushed into my mind. What a horrible thing it is, my dear friend, that I have neither heard from you, nor written to you, for twelve months! How is it, that our lips have been glued so long? I would not have believed such a thing could happen, though ten wise men had foretold it. But so it is. When busied about many things, the mind is easily persuaded to defer untill tomorrow, that, which there is no pressing necessity of doing today.

Since I have seen you, & written you, I have changed my residence from Boscawen to this place. Some brief narration of my life since June

1806 seems necessary, to bring up a view of the present, so that we may go on, in the old way of correspondence—for if ever I neglect writing you for so long a time again, I shall have lost my senses.

My business at Boscawen was tolerable, but not altogether to my mind. A little money might be made there, but no pleasure, of a social sort enjoyed. My Brother Ezekiel was admitted to the Bar in September last, & to him I made an offer of my Office. The truth is, our family affairs at Salisbury rendered it necessary for one of us to reside in that neighborhood, & not being very willing to take charge of the farm, I concluded to indorse over to my Brother both farm & office, if he would take both together. Being thus left to seek a new place of abode, I came to this Town —a measure which I had in some degree contemplated for a length of time. I found myself here the latter part of September— I knew few people here, & Mr [Nathaniel] Adams was the only person who advised to the measure.

Hitherto, I have done as much business as I ought to expect. There are eight or nine of us, who sell writs in Town. Of course my share cannot be large, even if I should take my equal dividend. On the whole however, I am satisfied that I did right to come, & suppose shall meet as much success as I deserve.

I have a pleasant room, in a good situation; have made some additions to my library, which is nevertheless yet very small; have some pleasant acquaintances in Town, & time rolls along pretty agreeably—*jam satis est.* I will expatiate no farther on that endearing subject, self. Now, my dear Bingham, a little account from you, to balance this, would be to me a precious morsel, & I trust I shall not long be without it. Mr [Solon] Stevens, your Cousin, I see often— & the oftener I see, the better I like him. He boards [with] me, when here, & we have become a good deal acquainted. He tells me many things of you, which I am fond of hearing. Among the *good* people of Alstead, I know you must be esteemed, & I fancy *with the bad,* you will not be unpopular.

Pray write me a long epistle, &, in the mean time, give my love to the amiable P–y.[1] I am, dear James, with undiminished affection, Your friend
D Webster

ALS. OClWHi. Published in *PC*, 1: 227–228.

1. Polly Stevens, who became Bingham's wife.

TO EZEKIEL WEBSTER

Portsmo. Mar. 3rd. 1808

D'r E.

I am just now distressed for some Hills[borough] bl[an]ks—I must have 20. If you send a coach with them, let me have that number by next

Wednesday. It would seem a small business to send a boy down upon, but it is of very considerable consequence to me to have them, & if they cannot come otherwise, dispatch J. Gilmore[1]—not telling him, or any body, what the business is.

Money I have none. I shall certainly be hanged before three weeks, if I cannot get some. What can be done—?

Sue every body. I send the copy of the [Daniel] Peterson note—sue Young Doctor, without fail. Mr [John] Ladd, the bearer, is entitled to receive $210 of J. Wilcox,[2]—have you heard any thing about it?

Have you heard from Mr [Bohan Prentiss] Field, of Belfast, about Mrs Martin's[3] matter. If not, press him again. Time is now quite short. We want proof that Martin sold a Lot of land there—inclose Mr F. a little fee to start him, if you can get it. Pray attend to this, *now*—or it may be too late.

I will send the horse, first chance. Dover Court, I have not attended much. I have many things to say to you— & will keep them all till Amherst Court.   D Webster

I shall almost perish, if I have not my 20 Hills: Blanks by Wednesday night.

ALS. NhD. Extract published in *PC*, I: 229.

1. Not identified.

2. Peterson had moved to Boscawen about 1770, becoming the first physician in the town; Ladd (1786–1824), was a cabinet maker in Salisbury; J. Wilcox has not been identified.

3. Field (1774–1843; Dartmouth 1795), was a Maine lawyer; Mrs. Martin has not been identified.

Even though the state capital had moved to Concord, Portsmouth remained the political center of the state for nonlegislative activities. Soon after he settled there, Webster launched an active political career. Although not yet a candidate for office himself, he campaigned vigorously for the Federalist ticket of 1808 and succeeding years. Combining his political interests with his law practice, he became ever more widely known as a dependable and able party man.

TO SAMUEL SMITH

Portsmo. March 6. [1808]

Dear Smith,

We have felt a good deal of alarm here about the Election— & are taking some pains to wake up our folks. I am requested to write to you, & most devoutly to solicit your attention to the subject. The Federalists must be roused, or we shall lose the Election. *You must see to all the Towns around you.*

Send the accompanying letters to New Ipswich *at once*.[1] We should write to [James] Wilson, but suppose he is at Keene. You see what a pickle we should be in, if thro negligence this Election should go wrong. This State, under such a Govt. as we should have, would not be fit for an honest man to live in. I am requested to urge the importance of this Election upon your consideration in the most urgent manner. Ever yrs

D. Webster

ALS. NhD. Smith (c. 1767–1842), one of Peterborough's leading entrepreneurs, investing in retail,

manufacturing, and building enterprises.

1. Letters not found.

TO JOHN H. CRANE

Portsm. May 19. 1808

D'r Sir,

On my return from the Country I received Mr [George] W[oodward]'s letter & yours.[1] I have forwarded about 800 Dols, to be deposited in the Ex[change] Office for the Coos Bank. I will send a bill, if I can purchase one for the residue tomorrow. In haste Yours   D Webster

ALS. NhD. Crane was a Boston lawyer.   1. Neither letter found.

TO SAMUEL AYER BRADLEY

Portsmouth June 28. 1808

Dear Sir,

As your desire is to do good, I suppose you will be willing to assist your friends, in this State, in the ensuing August election. I write you, therefore, to stir you up, on that occasion. In the first place, I promise that I address you by no authority—there is, I believe somebody in the County of Strafford, who will request your services, in a more formal manner— I am merely one of the people. The Federalists have agreed on a Ticket for Reps—Nathl. A. Haven, Wm. Hale, Jas. Wilson, Jno. C. Chamberlain & Daniel Blasdel.[1]

This list is the result of long & mature meditation— & consultation— & if there are men on it, as I hope there [are] none, that you do not like, be assured they are the very best men, who could be persuaded to be candidates. For electors, the choice of whom is in Novr. a list will be seasonably formed.

The Demo's have had some difficulty in their ticket.[2] At a first Caucus, the result was that C[harles] Cutts, [Daniel Meserve] Durell [Jedediah K.] Smith, [Francis] Gardner & Obed Hall should be the men. At this [Clement] Storer's[3] friends were enraged—they said he *must* go—Cutt's friends said *he should go*. At length they broke Obed's neck, & put both Storer & Cutts on the Ticket. So it now stands Storer, Durell, Smith, Gardner &

Cutts. Grafton & Coos are left without any representation—to the great lamentation of all the good Demos that way, more especially of the aforesaid Obed. Your situation will enable you to look after Conway, Eaton, Chatham, &c. A single vote will be of consequence, for it is thought the election will run very even. Pray engage Bro Dana's exertions, & do all you can for us.

I am glad to see Fryeburg returning to ancient principles. Your whole State has done itself much credit, in the eyes of Federalists at least, in your last Elections.[4] I hope we shall partake of your spirit and of your success.

If Mrs [Eliphalet] Ly[man][5] is yet desirous of knowing any thing of the Secty. &c.—please assure her, I shall oblige her by imparting all the knowledge I have.

Give my respects to my friends Your ob ser   D. Webster

ALS. NhD.

1. Nathaniel Appleton Haven (1762–1831; Harvard 1779) was a Portsmouth physician and merchant. Hale (1765–1848), also of Portsmouth, was a merchant and shipowner, and served in the 11th and two succeeding Congresses. John Chamberlain (1772–1834; Harvard 1793) was a Cheshire County lawyer, state politician, and congressman. Daniel Blaisdell (1762–1833) was a schoolteacher, farmer, lawyer, New Hampshire legislator, and congressman from Canaan. In the 1808 campaign, Haven and the full slate of Federalist candidates were elected to the 11th Congress.

2. The *Portsmouth Oracle*, June and July 1808, has lengthy discussions on the caucuses and candidates. See the issues of June 18 and 25, for comments on the Democratic caucus.

3. Cutts (1769–1846; Harvard 1789) was a lawyer, New Hampshire lawmaker, United States senator, and

secretary of the United States Senate, 1813–1825. Durell (1769–1841; Dartmouth 1794) was a Dover lawyer, judge, and state legislator. Smith (1770–1828), Amherst lawyer, was also a New Hampshire legislator, and congressman. Gardner (1771–1835; Harvard 1793), Walpole and Keene lawyer, served in the 10th Congress. Hall (1757–1828) was a Bartlett farmer and innkeeper, state legislator, and New Hampshire representative to the 12th Congress. Storer (1760–1830), a Portsmouth physician and merchant, was also a state legislator and had been elected to the 10th Congress.

4. Despite Christopher Gore's defeat by James Sullivan in the gubernatorial race, the voters of Massachusetts had elected a Federalist plurality to the state legislature. Even in Fryeburg, Federalist support had risen (*Columbian Centinel*, May 14, 28, June 1, 1808).

5. Née Abigail Ripley.

TO MILLS OLCOTT

Portsmouth July 11th 1808

Mills Olcott Esqr.

The arrangement finally made at Concord respecting the Electoral Ticket, is not so well received this way, as I wish it was.[1]

The two Gentlemen from this County[2] are thought not to be the most popular. I have conferred with Mr [William] Kent,[3] & others, on the subject and it is thought best not to publish the Electoral Ticket any more for the present.

It will be time enough after the August election, to newspaper the electors. In the mean time we can consider, whether it is advisable to press the ticket as it is, or to have a change.

As far as I have been able to gather information on the subject of our *prospects,* I am inclined to think that no reasonable expectation which may have been formed of Federalism this way, will be disappointed. I hope that Rockingham & Strafford, together, will give no great, if any majority, for the Demo Ticket. There will probably be a dead weight agt us in Hillsborough—against which Cheshire & Grafton must furnish an offsett—or we fly up. Our sort of folks in this neighborhood are active & in some degree confident.

This will be handed you by Mr [Charles] Tappan, of this town. He is a *bookseller* & wishes an acquaintance with all *book-buyers,* & *book readers.* It is surely a *lucky bit* that *I* should commend him to *you.* Your ob. ser

D. Webster

ALS. NhHi. Mills Olcott (1774–1845; Dartmouth 1790), Hanover lawyer, politician, Treasurer of Dartmouth College, 1816–1822, and trustee, 1821–1845.

1. Although not publicized in their presses in New Hampshire, the Federalist legislators held several caucuses and nominated congressional candidates and presidential electors during the June 1808 session of the legislature at Concord (*Portsmouth Gazette,* July 5, 1808). The list of Federalist electors (Simeon Olcott, Timothy Farrar, John T. Gilman, James Sheafe, Samuel Hale, Robert Wallace, and Jonathan Franklin) had appeared in the Boston *Columbian Centinel,* June 25, 1808. Only hints of the division among Federalists appeared in Federalist newspapers. The Keene *New Hampshire Sentinel* (July 16, 1808), while declaring that the list contained names "of good and true men," dismissed the Boston list as merely a nomination by one person. The *Ports-*mouth Oracle (June 18, 25, July 16, 1808), on the other hand, carried essays and letters denouncing the caucus system of the Republicans and suggesting district nominations of electors. As a result of the divisions in their ranks, the Federalist newspapers did not carry the names of their electors until late September (*Portsmouth Oracle,* September 24, 1808; Keene *New Hampshire Sentinel,* October 8, 1808).

2. James Sheafe and Samuel Hale. Sheafe (1775–1829; Harvard 1794), Portsmouth merchant, had served as assemblyman, senator, and councilman in New Hampshire, in the United States House of Representatives, 1799–1801, and in the United States Senate, 1801–1802. Samuel Hale was also a Portsmouth merchant and shipowner. One other Federalist who appeared on the early list, John T. Gilman of Exeter, former governor of the state, did not appear on the September list of Federalist electors.

3. Kent (1765–1840), Concord

merchant and banker, was one of the six Federalists who met secretly in Concord in 1804 in an effort to rejuvenate the Federalist Party in the state.

TO THOMAS W. THOMPSON

Portsmouth July 25. 1808

Dear Sir,

The Democratic circulars[1] were dispatched from this Town about a week ago. We know not what they contain. They were printed, with the greatest secrecy. Even the Printer was not trusted—a faithful fellow, it is said was posted by the side of the press to see that no straggling copy got away. They are distributed all over the State, & are to be opened on a *particular day*—which day is to be the same throughout the State—they will probably contain assertions that the embargo is off—or shortly coming off. Some such deceitful trick is no doubt intended. You will no doubt, see the propriety of giving caution to the public, not to be gulled in this way. We shall, in this quarter, give the public notice of this contrivance, in the Newspapers & in every other possible way. Your Ob Ser

D. Webster

ALS. NhHi.

1. Signed by Richard Evans, chairman of the Republican caucus at Concord, the Republican circular supported Jefferson's embargo as promoting commerce, which the Federalists denied (Keene *New Hampshire Sentinel*, August 20, 1808; *Portsmouth Oracle*, August 27, 1808).

TO SAMUEL AYER BRADLEY

Portsmouth Octr. 20. 1808

Dear Sir,

I have recd yours of the 15th,[1] & am obliged to you for it. We are well aware, that every effort is making to carry the Madison Ticket, & are preparing to meet these efforts, & prevent their effects wherever we can. Of the occurrences hinted at in your letter, we shall make such use, as may be—Conway, Bartlett, Adams, Eaton, Burton, & Chatham,[2] are very much out of our way. We should be very glad if any thing could be done for them. Conway did better than we expected, on the late election, & we thank our Fryeburg Friends for it. Pray help us again, as much as you can, for we shall need your *help, more than ever*. If any thing can be done, in those Towns, *you must do it*. I fear the next election will run much closer than the last. Our adversaries are now more busy, & more cunning, than they were then.

I hope, & believe, that we shall carry our Ticket, but it will require great industry, & exertion.

I shall take the liberty of sending you a few Oracles,[3] by mail, to be used as you think best.

Sir Richard [Evans][4] is now at Concord, as Editor of the new paper. I do not well comprehend the length & depth of the project, which you mention. Sir Richard is too deep for me—but I suppose it to be a step towards the establishing of a correspondence.

In Cheshire & Grafton our zeal & our strength is in no degree diminished—I have recently come from Haverhill, & have had means of ascertaining this. I am not without fears that Rockingham & Hillsborough will not do as well as they did before—Strafford I think will.

On the whole, I am of opinion that we shall carry the Ticket, by a majority, not quite as large as the last—but this is inter nos.

In the name of all that is patriotic, I conjure you & Brother [Judah] Dana, to do all that can be done, in the Towns in your neighborhood. Yours friend and ob se   D. Webster

ALS. NhD.
1. Not found.
2. Towns on the New Hampshire–Maine border.
3. Portsmouth Federalist newspaper.
4. Evans (1777–1816), a Portsmouth businessman, began publishing the *American Patriot* on October 18, 1808, in Concord. The following spring he sold the paper to Isaac Hill, who changed its name to the *New Hampshire Patriot*.

TO STEPHEN MOODY

Portsmouth Octr. 21. 1808

Dr Sir,

I have just recd yours of the 15,[1] as I arrived in Town from Haverhill. I doubt whether there will be a pamphlet published in this Town—if there be, you shall receive some numbers, as soon as they are out of press. A little book is in the Walpole press[2]—it will be distributed through Cheshire & Grafton. I think you might obtain some numbers at Plymouth. Wherever John Shepherd[3] goes, Col [Samuel] Greely[4] must go after him. I think there will be pamphlets at Plymouth, & perhaps at Concord the first of next week. I wish the Col would take some, & go after Shepherd—or go without them, if he cannot get them.

I think this election very perilous—am glad to hear that Gilmanton is like to do better.

Pray keep a look out on the Towns around you. I consider every thing depending on this election—let us do our utmost, to give it a favorable result. I am, D'r S'r, Yours   D. Webster.

ALS. Mrs. Stephen Hopkins, Waban, Mass. Published in Van Tyne, pp. 24–25. Moody (1767–1824; Harvard 1790), Gilmanton lawyer, moderator, postmaster (1801–1829), county solicitor (1804–1819), and strong Federalist partisan.
1. Not found.

2. Probably *Considerations on the Embargo Laws,* a campaign pamphlet. In his autobiography, DW remarks that "I had written the little pamphlet [in 1808], lately rescued from oblivion, called 'Considerations on the Embargo Laws' (mDW 8261). Isaiah Thomas of Worcester, Mass., and his son Isaiah, Jr., owned and

operated the Walpole, N.H., press.

3. John Shepard (1754–1844), Gilmanton town officer and on occasion delegate to the New Hampshire House of Representatives.

4. Greely (1747–1824), Gilmanton farmer and state legislator, regarded as a "man of property, influence, and respectability."

TO STEPHEN MOODY

Portsm. Oct. 26. 1808

Dear Sir,

Let the good Colonel [Samuel Greely] be dispatched with all good speed —to do all the good he can—if he should expend a little *cash* he will be remunerated. I have had a letter from [Oliver] Crosby[1] on that subject, *which letter I agree to.*

I send you some *news.* I incline to think there is something in it.[2]

D. W.

ALS. Mrs. Stephen Hopkins, Waban, Mass. Published in Van Tyne, p. 24.

1. Crosby (1769–1851; Harvard 1795), a Dover lawyer. Letter not

found.

2. Webster presumably enclosed a clipping, which has not been found.

FROM GEORGE HERBERT

Surry March 13. 1809.

My Dear Daniel,

I & my wife have gotten down here after a water passage of three days to Castine 30. miles distant from this. The time was short, but the sea was worse than I ever knew it. Consequently we were both very sick, but have since recovered. I hope you arrived at Portsmouth well.

My dear fellow I should not have written to you so soon—(I will confess the truth.) had it not been that my own affairs are in so miserable condition owing to the vile policy of our enemies—which has as I have before told you made our *poor people at the best* so poor that I can not have of them what they ought to pay me, without *distressing* them. I might more truly say I can not *have it at all.* Many of our people are pinched even for food & are suffering all the horrors of a famine. One man in Sullivan has had some provisions for sale of late & people have brought their plate Cows, pigs &c. &c. as they had, to barter them for some little food to keep them from starving. Oh my God—where is thy hidden thunder? Oh my country—thou deservest all! Thou hast slighted the warning voice of thy friends—thou has sinned against light. Thou deservest all—nay more. But woe unto them by whom this cometh! It

were better for them—that they had not done this—for the way of trans-
gressors *is hard*— & justice *shall surely overtake them!* If I had come
by Portsmouth I should certainly have availed myself of your kind offer.
As it is, my necessities coming upon me I must send you my note, & if
you can help me you must. If you can not I know not what I shall do—
but I shall live probably. In the last case, you must indorse the note
secured in full & send it back to me. I have no time to write—the post
is here—but I cannot well wait till another mail. If you can let me have
it, send it to John Estess Esqr.[1] Boston by some trusty conveyance—say
an acquaintance. He may be found at Whitney & Dorr's[2]—corner of Milk
& Broad Streets. I wish you well. Mrs H's love to Mrs W. My respects to
her & anc[i]ent friendship to you. Go on & prosper in the good cause—
we must prevail. Your friend   Geo. Herbert
   Write me an answer soon & your Prospects in N. H.

March 13. 1809

   For value received I promise to pay Daniel Webster or order two hundred dollars on demand with interest.   George Herbert
$200—

ALS. NhHi. Extract published in Van   1. Not identified.
Tyne, pp. 25–26.   2. Not identified.

TO MILLS OLCOTT

Portsmouth May 11. 1809

Dear Sir,
   It is thought adviseable for us to take the depo[sition] of Joseph Doe,
to be used in the case of Weeks agt. Cochran & Fox. Doe is now in this
Town. On Friday the 19th Inst at 8 o'clock A.M. before Samuel Elliot
Esqr. at his Office in this Town, Doe will attend to give his depo., provided, you can give notice to Cochran & Fox in season, & send evidence of
that notice here.[1] Your power of doing this may depend on the time of
your receiving this letter. As I do not know the course of the mails, I cannot calculate on the time of the arrival of this letter to your hands. If,
however, you should receive it in such season, as that you can notify
the defendants, & send on to us the evidence, so that the Justice can
certify notice, you will please so to do. If this should arrive too late, &
you should not be able to notify, Weeks must get Doe to go to Plymouth.
Doe thinks he can secure enough to charge both Cochran & Fox. The Gov
& Council meet in this Town tomorrow. I hope I shall be able to learn
their doings, quoad the Senators, before I set out for Plymouth.[2] No great
interest is making, that I can learn, for [Richard] Evans'[3] Judgeship. I
doubt whether any powerful Demos in this town would recommend it.
[John] Goddard is tho't to dislike him— & [John Samuel] Sherburne,[4]
who never *agrees* with G. in any thing, does not probably greatly *disagree*

with him, in this. Citizen [Daniel Meserve] Durell wishes to put on Judge [Paine] Wingate's cocked hat, when the Judge lays it off. But 'tis the common opinion, this way, that no appointment will be made by the present Govr. Citizen Durell, by the way, had occasion recently to exercise his brawny muscle over the head & ears of some ragamuffion, for an offense of a high nature. The offender had the impudence to call him "Squire McDuda"—which said McDuda was the name of the citizen's father—and Duda is still the name of his brothers & cousins. The citizen, however, some years ago, saw fit to convert Daniel McDuda, into Daniel Meserve Durell. He tho't the aforesaid vile appellation of McDuda was a base attempt "to filch from him his good name," & he defended agt. it as valiously as ever thief bestirred himself to defend a stolen horse. T offender protests, that tho' he desires to fight under the nar M. Durell, he shall be Indited for as[saul]t & battery under name of Danl McDuda; as that is the name by which his been indicted for a century.

That he may not leave the bar for the bench, whether und or another, is your wish, & the wish of Yr ob sert. D. Webste

ALS. NhHi.

1. For additional information on the above action, see DW to Mills Olcott, April 10, 1809, mDW 1044.

2. The Governor and Council met to determine the votes for New Hampshire senators. Seven Federalists and five Democrats were elected (*New Hampshire Sentinel*, May 27, 1809).

3. Evans was being consic the post of justice of the Supe Court.

4. Sherburne (1757–1830; Di mouth 1776), lawyer, state legisl and district Judge of the United St in Portsmouth.

5. Wingate, Judge of the Superior Court who retired in 1809.

According to a widely accepted account, Webster first developed his taste for good wine while reading law under Gore. This may well be true, so far as it applies only to good wine, but his fondness for brandy goes back to his Dartmouth days, attested by his account with a Hanover merchant (mDWs). The earliest extant documents relating to his use of wine are those below, detailing the purchase of a hogshead of Madeira through his friend Charles March (c. 1781–1855), formerly of Greenland, New Hampshire, but then a merchant in New York City.

FROM NEWTON, GORDON, MURDOCH & SCOTT

Madeira 25 May 1809

Sir.

By desire of Messrs March & Benson of New York we have shipped for your account on board the schooner Portsmouth Capt Chase a hogshead of the very best pale old London Particular Madeira wine. The bill of lading we have enclosed to these gentlemen the wine being consigned to them & we have drawn on you for the cost (£24Stg) at 30 d[ay]s s[igh]t in their favour. We are Sir Respectfully Yr obt. Serts

Newton Gordon Murdoch & Scott

FROM CHARLES MARCH

New York 17 July 1809.

My Dear Sir

I forward to you a letter from my Madeira Friends, who, as you will observe, have sent us the h[ogs]h[ea]d of Wine which we were to take together. By the first good conveyance I shall send it round to Portsmouth; and after tasting it, I think you will not be disposed to give me up my half to which, as I am already suppled, I shall not object provided you will not refuse a glass when I have the pleasure of seeing you. Madeira never produced better wine than your h[ogs]h[ea]d; and I shall hand you the Bill of Exchange as soon as I ascertain the amount of expenses of freight duty, &c.

If I still am in the recollection of Mrs. Webster, I pray you to remember me to her. And believe me your friend   C. March

ALS. NhHi.

FROM CHARLES MARCH & ALFRED G. BENSON

New York 3 Augt. 1809

Dear Sir—

We have shipped on board the Almira to sail for Portsmouth in a few days, your H[ogs]h[ea]d Wine, and annexed is Capt Blunts rect for the same. We also enclose the Bill of Exchange the Amount of which, with the Charges agreeably to the annexed Statement, you will please remit us here. We are Dr Sir Yr. mo. ob Sts   March & Benson

DW. 1 Half Pipe Wine £ Stg. 24. is $		106.66
Freight	3.50	
Duty	31.32	
Insurance	3.25	
Lighterage	18	
Cartage labor fee	1.25	39.50
		$146.16

New York 3 Augt Received on board the Schn Almira, under my Command—DW—One Hogshead Wine, which I promise to deliver (dangers of the Seas excepted) unto Daniel Webster Esqr. at Portsmouth New Hampshire, on receiving Customary freight.   M. S. Blunt

ALS. NhHi.

Two factors—Jefferson's embargo policy and unsound banking practices —account for much of the economic pressure and hardships in New England between 1806 and 1815. In October 1809, Jeremiah Smith and Daniel Webster were concerned with the acceptance of New Hampshire bank notes in Boston.

TO JEREMIAH SMITH

Portsmouth Oct. 24. 1809

Dear Sir

I have this moment recd. yours of the 21 Inst,[1] & am both surprised & mortified at its contents.

As I believe, I before mentioned to you, the next day after Mr. [George] Woodward gave me *Coos Bills* to purchase Boston money for you, *Coos bills would buy nothing.* I immediately wrote Mr W.[2] that, for that reason, I had been unable to obtain the money for you, & that I had his bills on hand. Since which I have actually returned to the Bank the bills I recd. I supposed [John] Montgomery & [Moses P.] Payson[3] had handed you your money at Commencement, as I never heard any thing from them afterwards. My impression is that under these circumstances, I had better send directly to Haverhill, & if they do not pay the money, give Mr. Stevens' Administrator instant notice. I think Montgomery & Co. (W. is absent) will certainly pay it, together with expenses. My Clerk, Mr [Timothy] Farrar will be the bearer of this to you, & if you think of nothing more expedient, he will either go, or send by some trusty hand, to Haverhill, carrying my letter to Montgomery.

You will believe me when I say that this business gives me the greatest pain & mortification.

I have the honor to be Your ob. ser.   D Webster

Copy. NhHi. Published in *W & S*, 16: 11.
   1. Not found.

2. Letter not found.
3. Incorporators of the Coös Bank; Montgomery was its president.

TO MILLS OLCOTT

Portsmouth Oct 30 1809

Dear Sir,

It would be agreeable to Mr [Jeremiah] Mason to know as soon as may be, whether a trial is to be had at Amherst in the actions agt. the Directors.[1] He does not usually attend that Court, & perhaps would hardly be able to go, on a very sudden call. As soon as you have settled the question of the compromise, please inform us. I shall be in Boston some day this week, but probably not till the latter part of it.

I have been pretty severely dealt with *at home,* for not bringing a better account of Mrs [Sarah] O[lcott] & Miss Murdock.[2] The latter lady is bound by solemn contract to make her appearance in this place in the winter; we shall not let her off from the engagement. I inclose a letter to the Baron.[3] I trouble you with it, because the mail is long, & a little uncertain in its journey to Hanover, & because I wish the Baron to receive it this week, or first of next. I am, Sir, with esteem Yours   D. Webster

ALS. NhD.

1. DW was probably referring to a pending case growing out of the controversy surrounding the two Concord banks.

2. Not identified.

3. Benjamin Joseph Gilbert (1764–1849; Yale 1789), commonly called Baron Gilbert, was a lawyer and state legislator from Hanover. Letter not found.

Daniel and Noah Webster were not related (although Daniel assumes a relationship in his Autobiography) but similar academic and professional interests made them friends. Daniel was keenly interested in Noah's lexicographical studies, and later in Congress worked closely with Noah and others for the passage of a copyright law.

FROM NOAH WEBSTER

New Haven Novr. 4. 1809

Dear Sir,

I take the liberty to inclose to your care, a Prospectus of my Dictionary, for obtaining Subscriptions.[1] It is issued in conformity with the advice of my friends here & in Boston. If any Subscribers should be obtained, the money may be lodged in the hands of Mr George Cabot of Boston, who can easily transmit it to me. I wish you to retain the original paper in your hands— & present it [to] such Gentlemen from the interior country as you may see during the winter. It will be proper that every Subscriber should understand that this application is addressed more to his patriotism than most others of a like kind, & that he advances his money upon the risk of my *life, health & fidelity*. This, I should hope, most men of liberal views would do without much reluctance, when they know that I have hazarded more property than all the Subscribers will do, & given the best portion of my life to the undertaking. I beg you to make my compliments & respects to all my friends in Portsmouth & believe me very respectfully your most Obedt. huml servt   Noah Webster Jnr

ALS. DLC.

1. Noah Webster's prospectus, "To the friends of literature in the United States," was an appeal for support of his efforts to compile and publish his *American Dictionary of the English Language,* which finally appeared in 1828. See *A Bibliography of the Writings of Noah Webster,* Emily Ellsworth Ford Skeel, compiler; Edwin H. Carpenter, Jr., editor (New York: The New York Public Library, 1958), p. 232.

FROM WILLIAM WEBSTER

Plymouth Decr. 4th—1809—

Dear Sir

I Received yours of the 21st of November last,[1] on the 1st of Decr. Instant, in which Letter my Character seems to be Implicated by several Questions therein Proposed by you which Questions I am very willing to answer by making the following statements, viz., I did not receive satisfaction of the Executions vs Haines in Coos Bills wholly, but Part in Coos, part in Cheshire Part in Hillsborough, and Part in Bills of other Banks, and not more than forty or fifty Dollars in Salem, Newburyport, and Concord Bills—and at the time I sent the money above named I did not know that the Coos Bank had refused payment—that I supposed Coos Bills would answer the purpose of the Creditors as well as Bills from any other Bank, the reason why I did not send the Identical Bills I received of said Haynes was a Gentleman in this vicinity who was raising a sum to pay to Coos Bank other than Coos money, whom T. McJames Little,[2] Moor Russell,[3] and S[tephen] Grant,[4] accommodated by exchanging—if the above statement is not satisfactory to the Creditors and yourself I expect to be at Portsmouth the first of Slaying and shall be willing to answer such further Questions as you or they may think proper to propose.

I am Sir your most obedient & very Humble Servant— Wm. Webster

ALS. NhHi.
1. Not found. William Webster was one of many left holding worthless notes by a flurry of bank failures in the New England hinterland following the collapse of Andrew Dexter's banking empire.

2. Not identified.
3. Russell (1757–1839), Revolutionary soldier, town officer, state senator, and one of the incorporators of the Coös Bank.
4. Plymouth lawyer.

FROM SAMUEL R. MILLER & CO.

Boston 23 Decr 1809

Sir

We have not recd the money you proposed to pay, when here, a few days since. We are really in great want of it— & as your expectations may not have been answered, we have thought proper to give you this information.

We are—With Respect Yr. Obedt Sts   S R Miller & Cy

ALS. NhHi. Miller was a merchant and later a banker in Boston.

Webster again proved an effective campaigner as Federalist candidates sought state offices in 1810. He continued to depend on Thompson, then treasurer of New Hampshire, for much of the campaign propaganda.

FROM THOMAS W. THOMPSON

Concord Feb. 17 1810

Dear Sir

We have recd the lines respecting the candidates for No 2[1]— & our list shall be corrected accordingly. We think it advisable that the Oracle[2] should be the first channel of information to the public of the comparative allowances to the Secy under the Fed & Demo administrations— & therefore send you the following minutes to be worked up as shall be tho't expedient.

Allowed for salary & claims of every kind to Secy [Joseph] Pearson[3] & his Dep.

from May 1803 to May 1804	. . . .	557.67
from May 1804 to May 1805	. . . .	416.50
after May 1805	. . . .	392.11

Allowed for salary & claims of every kind to Secy. [Philip] Carigain[4]

from May 1805 to May 1806	. . . .	542.50
from May 1806 to May 1807	. . . .	929.94
from May 1807 to May 1808	. . . .	1342.23
from May 1808 to May 1809	. . . .	wanting
after May 1809	. . . .	400.—

By some blunder I omitted to take the minutes of the amount of Orders issued in favor of Carigain from May 1808 to May 1809 or if I did they are lost. I shall send to [Nathaniel] Parker[5] this evening to take them off & send them to you immediately.

[John] Langdon never accounted for the $1000. contingent fund granted him in June 1808. We understand he allowed [William?] Tarlton[6] $10 for delivering Col David [Webster][7] a letter from Carigain notifying him that he was 70 years old.

You will understand that the allowances to Carigain were exclusive of the fees & perquisities of office.

Pardons

to Jno Stewart	Dec. 21 1808
Jno Haynes	May 16 1809
Leavitt Hill	Feb. 8 1809

all for passing counterfeit money

Ben[jamin] Pierce D[aniel] Gookin[8] & W Tarlton were the Councillors who advised the Governor to notify David Webster that satisfactory evidence had been recd by them that he was 70 years old & consequently disqualified & that they should make a new appointment.

We are all activity here & cannot learn that we have lost any friends in any town unless in the vicinity of Dart. Col. & we are not certain what the effect the digging up will have in a political point of view. Yours

Tho W Thompson

ALS. DLC.

1. A reference to the senatorial nominees of the second district of New Hampshire; the "lines" have not been found.

2. Portsmouth *Oracle*, a Federalist sheet. DW's essay, based on the information furnished by Thompson in this letter, appeared in the *Oracle* on February 24, 1810, under the title "Look to the Money Chest! ! !"

3. Of Exeter, formerly New Hampshire secretary of state.

4. Carrigain (1772–1842; Dart-mouth 1794), lawyer of Concord, who succeeded Pearson.

5. Parker (1760–1812), lawyer of Exeter, who succeeded Carrigain as secretary of state.

6. Councillor from Grafton and Coös counties.

7. Webster (1763–1844), sheriff of Plymouth, Grafton County.

8. Of North Hampton, N.H., Revolutionary War soldier, councillor, Judge of the Court of Common Pleas, and Judge of Probate for Rockingham County.

FROM WILLIAM A. KENT

Feb. 28 [1810]

Dear Sir

I was aware that your professional engagements would prevent your giving us much information while the Court were at Portsmo., & now conclude you are on duty at Dover. Knowing your devotedness to the cause of your country is next to the cause of your clients, I have no disposition to charge you with neglect. I only say when you can give us a line we always receive it with pleasure. Mr T[hompson] and self have laid aside what little modesty we had as you will see by the Patriot.[1] The impudence of these fellows made it a duty. We had a meeting at Stickneys Hall last Thursday evening without disguise, organized as we ought & adjourned to the day previous to the election at 2 *oClock* in the afternoon & we don't care how bright the sun then may shine upon us. I am confident we lose nothing here by taking *tall ground*. I think we shall gain a little in Concord, they say the same of Loudon & Chichester. Andover we have some fears of doing worse as well as Boscawen owing to the Freewill people, who have increased in those Towns. The change however will not be great. They have hopes of New Chester Rep founded upon some changes—from Hanover they write within a few days that things look better & that the importance of *exertion* has taken hold of the minds of many worthy men. [Jeduthun] Wilcox[2] will be aided by [Abiathar G.] Britton[3] in the election at Orford. I have this day recd a line from Walpole and another from Keene. [Roger] Vose[4] says "I can with some confidence state to you generally that I believe any *reasonable* expectation will be realized." [John] Prentiss[5] at Keene says "all is activity *at this time*. Chesterfield will be much better, great hopes are entertained for Walpole: our prospects grow better every day."

No. 2 must I think be safe, can it be possible that the *apostate* will find a majority for *him*? The Demos have not yet agreed for No. 4. There is a division among them as yet. I understand that next Monday they are to meet in this Town to settle it. The eastern part propose J[osiah] Sanborn,[6] this, *Northfield* will it is said object to, much will depend in this district upon the candidate & his local situation. I have some fears of No. 6. Gilmantown is strongly beset by *wolves* and your *dogs* of Lawyers are out of the way. [Thomas C.] *Drew*[7] is to run against *Vose*. There I think we may be easy.

The belief that the Administration wish to connect us with France is daily increasing among us, & the *exhibitions* of various kind relative to our State concerns are calculated to have a good effect. Yours   W A K

I rejoice to learn that Gov [John Taylor] Gilman has consented to receive the votes in Ex[eter] for Rep. This Mr [Oliver] Peabody assures me is fact. The Boscawen people are not yet ready to say *Ezekiel*. You know there is a little *clanishness* there.

ALS. DLC.

1. The Concord *New-Hampshire Patriot*, February 20, 1810, carried a letter by Thompson on the election.

2. Wilcox (1769–1838), Orford lawyer, state legislator, and congressman, 1813–1817.

3. Britton (d.c. 1852), also an Orford lawyer and state representative.

4. Vose (1763–1842), a Walpole lawyer, state senator, and representative in Congress, 1813–1817.

5. Prentiss (1778–1873), printer and editor of the Keene *New Hampshire Sentinel*.

6. Of Epsom, Rockingham County, state representative and justice of the peace.

7. A co-proprietor of the Walpole *Political Observatory*.

TO EZEKIEL WEBSTER

Portsmo. Mar. 2 [1810]

Dear Ezl.

I expected to hear from [you], by Nat[haniel Webster] before now, but suppose want of snow has prevented his coming. I am looking earnestly for a little *rhino*[1] from your quarter.

Mr. [William A.] K[ent] writes[2] that there is reason to fear that Bos[cawen] will not be quite so Fed. as last year. This will never do. Your characters are *committed*. Make Boscawen "toe the mark" once more, as nobly as last year. I will not think you will fail in this Respect. As to the Rep. let that go easy. If the G's & C's[3] are disposed that you should go, go— If not, altogether & heartily, stay. It would be weakening, rather than increasing your personal influence, to go, unless it were nem con. I should like well eno. to gratify the good old Capt. once.

The time is nearly expired, when we promised the Capt.[4] to take up his name. If he wishes it, it shall be done. Please see him immediately on the subject. Enoch G[errish][5] of Cant[erbury] is the man I intend to obtain in his room. It would be expensive for me to go up on purpose— Will you, or can you, effect it for me? Please inform me, by next Post. I must entreat your *especial attention* to this.

We must make an extra effort this time, to bear down all vice & immorality. You may depend on hearing that we do our duty this way. For Reputation's sake, do yours.

Your's &c. D. Webster.

ALS. NhD. Published in part in *PC*, I: 231.

1. "A cant word for gold and silver, or money." Webster, *An American Dictionary of the English Language*.

2. See letter of February 28 above.

3. Possibly a reference to the Gage and Clough families of Boscawen.

4. Not identified.

5. Gerrish (1775–1856), Boscawen merchant.

TO TIMOTHY BIGELOW

Portsmouth March 31. 1810

Dear Sir,

This will be handed you by Mr [Timothy] Farrar, [Jr.] the son of your friend Judge Farrar. He is a student in my office, & is now in Boston, for the purpose of attending the session of the Supreme Court. It was not only his own wish, but also the wish of his worthy Parent, that he might be made known to some of the Professional Gentlemen of Boston, & in an especial manner, to Yourself. He is a young Gentleman of good talents, & excellent habits.

I am, Sir, with great esteem, Your Obt. Sert. Danl. Webster

ALS. NhD. Bigelow (1767–1821), was a Boston lawyer and politician.

FROM BENJAMIN JOSEPH GILBERT

Hanover 2d. April 1810

Dear Sir—

Yours of Mar 14th last[1] giving the votes in 11 Towns, in which the neat federal gain was 301, was duly received—but out of season to promise any thing, the votes from so many of the Towns, & almost all, worser & worser than last year, having been already received as sufficed to convince me [Jeremiah] Smith was a *gone governor*.[2] I have repeatedly said though not in the hearing of many, that the *Divil* is in the people— &

when I have seen the strong efforts of the Democrats, & heard them, as I have often, declare Smith would not, & should not be chosen, I have been ready to adopt the question of Pilate to the Jews, & ask why—what evil hath he done? This day Old Massachusetts casts her hundred thousand votes for Governor—I hope Gore will have three fourths of them.

Are you to come up to Hanover & Thetford & see about your demand against Asa Day? You have not yet sent forward the depositions in Abijah B. Little v James Wheelock. And he has concluded to dispense with your sending them (excepting mine) which he wishes, & I wish you to forward immediately—he intends to take my deposition over again, or to make me go to Hopkinton. There can be no need of my going, certainly & it will be extremely inconvenient for me to go—and I wish you to reply to this & enclose my deposition & say that you think, as the expense would be considerable, you think on the whole, it is not adviseable for me to attend—you see I have to attend meeting of council at Exeter the 16th May. If you will send me a brief of the case I will send you by Mr [James] Wheelock,[3] a particular opinion on it. In great haste, & with high esteem I am your friend   Ben. J. Gilbert

ALS. NhHi.
1. Not found.
2. John Langdon defeated Jeremiah Smith in the New Hampshire gubernatorial election in 1810.
3. Wheelock (1759–1835), brother of Eleazar Wheelock, graduated from Dartmouth in 1776 (ADC, p. 20).

FROM SAMUEL FESSENDEN

New Gloucester June 2d 1810
Dear Sir,

It is now a long time since I have had the pleasure of seeing you, or hearing of your welfare. Except so far as public gratitude has extended your professional fame. And I hope you will not, amidst the profusion of your wealth and honors, think I am troubling you too far, in crouding myself once more upon your notice. More particularly as business is the immediate subject of this letter. Some time last winter a Mr. Plummer, who it seems, is the holder of the note which I gave Green,[1] called on me for the money. I made shift to pay him one hundred dollars, and gave him encouragement that I should be able to pay the residue in June. He stated that the note should be deposited in your hands. Now as Poverty still with unrelenting *haste*, and unwearied diligence pursues me, I find that I shall not be able to meet the residue of the note as I hoped. If it be, as I suspect, deposited in your hands, will you use your endeavour to make him easy for some months to come? I hope you have not so far forgotten me as not to comply with my request. I think a suit against me, at this juncture, would operate as a serious injury. Just entering on the stage of life, it is of great consequence that my credit should stand firm in the public opinion, as confidence is indispensable to the success of a professional man. Be so obliging as to drop a line, per mail, and inform me if the note be in your possession.[2]

I do a little business, and hope to get on by perseverance. But the event is very uncertain. On examination I find myself not possessed of talents which will enable me to rise even to mediocrity, and am now struggling hard to bring down my ambition to a level with my single *talent*. The perfection of philosophy is to pursue without regret the path wisely marked out for us, by *him* who alone is capable.

If I can once attain to that state, when with boldness I can say, not one of my creditors has suffered by me; believe me, I shall resign all pretentions to wealth or fame, with as little regret as the *Cynic* could throw his wallet and staff into the *Styx*. My health is good—and may this find you & Mrs W. enjoying that & every other in the fullest extent which Heaven, can, consistent with the grand plan, allot to share of mortals.

Accept my respect and believe me as ever your obedient & very humble Servt.   S. Fessenden

ALS. NhHi.
1. Neither Plummer nor Green has been identified.

2. DW's response to Fessenden has not been found.

[TO FEDERALIST COMMITTEES IN NEW HAMPSHIRE]
Portsmouth Aug. 1st. 1810.

Gentlemen,

At a meeting of Federal Republicans holden at Portsmouth on the 30th. ult. we were appointed a Committee to request several influential men in the neighbouring towns to aid with zeal & activity the election of the Federal candidates for members to Congress by all honorable means within their power. The ensuing election is every where considered, by men of sagacity & reflection, highly important. The imperial Democrats in the next Congress, unless they are checked by a respectable federal minority, will, beyond doubt, have recourse to another Embargo, or some measure equally pernicious. The Democrats, in many places, notwithstanding the unpopularity of their candidates are active & sanguine. Their efforts can be overpowered only by the continual exertions of correct political men. Our prospect of success at the ensuing election is now flattering, but inattention will be fatal. The result of the election will depend on the labours of the several town Committees. We trust, that you will make such arrangements in your town, as will ensure the attendance at the meeting of every sound political man & that you will use such salutary advice & persuasion, as will induce every doubtful or wavering man to support the Washington ticket.

We are, Gentlemen, your friends & fellow-labourers.   D. Webster
William Garland[1]
Edward J. Long[2]
Edw Cutts Jr.[3]

LS. NhHi.
   1. Garland, Portsmouth merchant.
   2. Long (d. 1824), also of Portsmouth and Secretary of the New

Hampshire Fire and Marine Insurance Company.
   3. Cutts (1782–1844; Harvard 1797), Portsmouth lawyer.

TO EZEKIEL WEBSTER

Portsmo. Aug. 27. 1810.

Dear Ezl.

I send you a small charge for Hillsborough, to which I ask your attention. The Bowers action you may manage after the manner most agreeable to yourself. Get Judgt in the case of Haven v Bell if you can. The action is on a Mortgage, deed & note enclosed.[1]

Aug. 28.

I left off here yesterday to attend Town Meeting, Dr. B.[2] has minutes of the result. If you have all done your duty, the thing is safe. I send you your List of Rock[ingham] actions.[3] You must send for your Ex[ecutio]ns.

In haste Yrs   D. Webster

ALS. NhD.
   1. Not found.

2. Not identified.
3. Not found.

TO EZEKIEL WEBSTER

Portsmouth Novr. 27th. 1810—

Dear Sir,

I am so particularly pushed, that I find it necessary to take some measures to raise some cash. I have proposed to get a note discounted, upon real security, & to accomplish this, now intend to execute a Mortgage on the place at Salisbury. I herewith enclose a deed for your execution, & when we meet the consideration &c shall be adjusted. Please execute it & send it me—send also a copy of the will, if you have one— & also your receipt for the legacy of 200. I should also be glad to procure Mehitable & Sarah (& Eben) [Webster's] discharge, in order to show a complete title. All this, I want here by Saturday night. If you see nobody coming, just send Nat[haniel Webster]—or Gilmore,[1] or somebody on purpose. You may say to Hitty & Sarah, that it is my request that they should execute discharges, & that you are about to do the same. When I am up, I will see them satisfied on the subject. If however, there are difficulties in obtaining these discharges, send your own, & the deed. I should prefer to have all.

Do not fail to let me have a return by Saturday night. I should send on purpose, but Capt Atwood[2] being [here,] I can send by him, & suppose it would be cheaper & easier to send a horse & boy from you to me, than vice versa.

If you can possibly send *any* money—if a little—it will be particularly acceptable. Yours &c.   D. Webster

N.B. Pray send the deed M Lewis to me of the lands appraised. I think it is in your office—otherwise it is at Haverhill—please send for it by 1st mail, & forward it to me. I hope it is [in] your office as I want it.

Perhaps one discharge, signed by all, & releasing to me severally, would be proper.

ALS. NhD.   2. Not identified.
  1. Not identified.

Uncertain though the returns were, speculation in land was one of the major means of economic mobility in the nineteenth century; and throughout his life, Webster found it appealing. Just how he acquired the properties discussed below has not been established. Perhaps they were a part of the Webster family holdings; he may have purchased the property; or the land may have been acquired through mortgage fore-closures or as payment of legal fees.

TO EZEKIEL WEBSTER

Portsmo. March 27. 1811

Dear Sir,

The bearer of this, is Mr Nathl. Banfield,[1] of this Town. He and I are attempting to negotiate an exchange of lands. He owns a pretty valuable farm in this Town; out of which he wishes to enable himself to remove an Incumbrance, & in the next place to procure a tidy little farm in the Country. I have in view to furnish him such a farm as he wishes, & to take his here, removing the incumbrance. My object is, to turn some of our Grafton Co: debts into this farm, which *can be* turned into money. I have made such enquiry and arrangements, as to be certain of doing pretty well with this farm, & have also made provision for removing the Incumbrance, which is a mortgage of about 1500 Dols.

Mr Banfield's farm is worth, say,	3640 Dols
deduct Mortgage—	1500
	2140—say

Twenty one hundred, forty dollars. He now wants a farm, in the Country, worth from 1400, to 1700 dols— & the balance can be accomodated. I have thought of the Saml. Simonds place. I have two hundred dollars, due from Simonds—also a note of 1000 from Col Lewis—in addition to some other. There is also the Kidder debt,[2] of say, 350, which I understand Col L is bound to pay. Now can not some turn be made, so that Mr Banfield can be accomodated? Perhaps some of the lands, of which I am now owner up that way, would suit him. I can do so well with his farm here, that I think it quite an object to bargain with him. He now goes up on purpose to see what you & he can do. You must take two days & go to Bridgwater with him, & between you & Lewis, I am certain he can be suited. I think the Simonds place will suit him. If not, you must make a shift of my debts, or your own, & find one that will. The Watts Emerson farm *would have been* just the thing. If you are engaged when he arrives at Boscawen, he must stay a day—till you can go with him. I rely on your doing something, be[ca]use it will be a great help. He wants a farm of 100, or 150 acres, some part cultivated, with decent little buildings,—hay to keep a small stock, a young orchard &c. Pray lay aside all other concerns & attend to this for 3 days. Any of my debts up that way, may be turned in. What is the Timo. Simonds place? I cannot now recollect very much about it—but know there is an attachment on real estate there. Yrs   D. Webster

N.B. 100 dols, or so should be deducted, if you take real estate for debts —so that it may be put 100—or 150 lower to me, than Mr B. will give me for it.

ALS. NhD.   2. Not identified.
   1. Not identified.

FROM EZEKIEL WEBSTER

April 4th. 1811

I have just this moment returned from Bridgwater. The Farm that suits Mr [Nathaniel] Banfield best is the Capt Tolford Farm in Alexandria of which Lewis will give a warrantee deed. Mr. B. is to take 50 acres north of the road on which stands the house, & 100 acres south of the road on which stands the barn both pieces being in Alexandria. It is agreed how the lines shall run—for which he will give 12 dolls pr acre amtg. to 1800 Dolls. I put it to him at 2.000 Dolls. and as being then very cheap—but mention to him, as you are pretty *notional* you may take 200 Dolls less possibly—rather than not have his farm. It will do to trade with him at $1800—but you know 2,000 will be some better—it will be put to you not over $1700— & I hope some less. Lewis engages to have the *squire* off

any time, he wishes. But if the bargain can be closed irrevocably now &
let him take possession next fall or Winter I should prefer it—for fear
the old man should be some what ugly. However if it should be better to
have him take possession now—just as well.

Mr B. mentions if the bargain is made he can take a lease or deed & let
it be executed when convenient.

The pay to Col. Lewis you know will be easy.

I will write to you again on Saturday. Yours &c   E Webster

ALS. NhD.

*In December 1805, Timothy Dix, Jr., received from the state of New
Hampshire a grant of 29,340 acres of land in Coös County, midway between Vermont and Maine and only some 25 miles south of the present
Canadian border. The grant required Dix to pay to the state $4,500 in
annual instalments of $500, with the first payment due in 1811, and to
secure thirty settlements on the tract. Daniel Webster, Jeremiah Gerrish
(1764–1836), and Stephen Gerrish (1770–1815), all of Boscawen,
served as Dix's sureties for the purchase price.*

*After 1805, Dix found himself under increasing economic pressures
to meet his demands; and by 1811, when the first payment on the land
became due, he was near bankruptcy. Accordingly, payment of the first—
and of subsequent—instalments devolved upon Webster and the Gerrish
brothers, who subsequently became co-owners of the Dixville township.
Following the death of Stephen in 1815, Jeremiah held a two-thirds interest in the township, and Webster, one-third. As late as 1833, Webster
still retained his share.*

TO NATHANIEL GILMAN

Portsmo. May 16. 1811

Sir,

Messrs Jeremiah Gerrish, Stephen Gerrish, & myself are sureties to
Timothy Dix Jr Esqr. on sundry notes in the Treasury, one of which has
been some time due. We have waited thus long, in the hope that Mr Dix
would pay the note. This not being done, we now have taken upon ourselves the payment. I enclose you Two hundred & twenty dollars, towards
the payment, being according to my computation, about my third of the
debt. The other two sureties are, to my knowledge, ready to pay, & probably intend to take the opportunity of your being at Concord. It has been
suggested, however, that it would be convenient that the note should
be paid before the meeting of the Committee on the Treasure[r]'s Accounts. If the Committee should not be together until the first day of

June, this can be done. I am now going into the Country, shall return the latter part of the month, & will undertake that the residue of the note shall be paid on or before the first day of June; which I think will be the Thursday before the meetings of the Legislature.

Please endorse the enclosed as paid by me.

I have the honor to be sir, Your ob ser   D. Webster

ALS. Nh-Ar. Nathaniel Gilman (1759?–1847), state senator and rep- | resentative, was at the time state treasurer.

Webster's legal and political skill won him recognition and respect from both Federalist and Republican leaders in New Hampshire. In 1811 the New Hampshire House of Representatives appointed Webster, Jeremiah Mason, and John Goddard to revise the criminal code. Although the legislature voted them compensation for their services, the revised code was never adopted, possibly because a controversy developed over the revision and the location and disposition of certain documents used by the commissioners. Samuel Sparhawk (d. 1834), Concord banker and then Secretary of State, informed Webster of his appointment.

FROM SAMUEL SPARHAWK

Secretary's Office
Concord June 26th. 1811

Sir

I have the honour to transmit to you herewith an attested copy of a Resolve passed at the late session of the Legislature, appointing yourself, Jeremiah Mason and John Goddard, Esquires a committee for certain purposes therein expressed. Very respectfully Sir yr. obedt. Servt.

Saml. Sparhawk

State of New Hampshire
In the House of Representatives June 20th. 1811

Resolved, that the Hon. Jeremiah Mason, John Goddard and Daniel Webster Esquires be a committee to revise the code of criminal laws, and prepare police laws for the regulation of the State prison, in the recess of the General Court, and report at the next Session of the Legislature.

Sent up for Concurrence
Clement Storer Speaker

In Senate the same day, read & concurred,   William Plumer President
Approved June 21st. 1811   John Langdon Govr.
Attest   Saml. Sparhawk Secry

ALS. NhHi. Published in Van Tyne, p. 26.

FROM PETER OXENBRIDGE THACHER

Boston July 6. 1811

Dear Sir,

After notifying Morrell,[1] I put a writ into the hands of an officer, who used his diligence, but without success, to find his horse & chaise, or other property. From the enquiries which I made, I was well satisfied, that he had no property having been harassed with debts &c for years. I therefore return it to you pursuant to your request.

I have applied at the office of the Secretary of State to procure the pamphlet which contains the regulations of the prison & the laws which you want. I have not yet succeeded to procure one, but will not fail to send to the Superintendant of the Prison & get one for you, as soon as the excessive heat of the weather will permit.

An addition of our Laws in 3 8vo volumes by Manning & Loring has been published under the authority of the Government. It contains the laws as far down as 1807.

Our truly sapient & honest Legislature among a multitude of other things at their last session passed a law in addition to the other laws regulating the State Prison at Ch[arlestown] which will be published, I understand, in a few days. I shall not be inattentive to your wishes & am Dr Sir, with regard Your friend & sert   Peter O. Thacher

ALS. NhHi.   1. Not identified.

Webster always seemed to be short of money; and to meet his own pressing obligations, he frequently had to scrape together funds from wherever and whomever he could. The letter below is typical of many.

TO EZEKIEL WEBSTER

Portsmo. Sep. 14. 1811

Dr E.

C[harles] Cutts has pd. amt. of note & int[erest] & cost of writ to me, viz 63.00—which I have pocketted, & credited you for. My first note to Holden[1] becomes due for 834. in one week from today. It is deposited in the Bank here, & I must pay it. After counting up all my means, I find I shall come short unless I receive something from above. I therefore send Jones[2] to see if you have picked up any. I am depending on the Tarlton money,[3] but if you should have scraped him so close, as that my debts are not paid, I am undone, pro hac vice. I dare not trust to what I may hear at Court. If you have a dollar, you must send it. Give me strength this time to slay the Philistines. Whatever money you send me, or whosever, I will repay at Amherst. This you may be sure of. If you can & will furnish me with some present aid, you need not go to Boston to see about the other two notes, until we meet at Amherst. The [Nathaniel A.] Haven debt I hope is paid—tho that is not to be touched. If the other two Ex[e]c[uti]ons v Tarlton which amt. I think to about 260— or 280— are paid— & you can *add an equal,* or a *larger* sum, I hope to swim.

Inform me what was done with my Ex[e]c[uti]ons—particularly Gore v Lewis, & self v Goodhue—also v Albree.[4] I send you a writ for service on Lay. The first day of October shall sue the Sherriff unless Lay[5] pays up arrearages.

I recd yr notice for Newton,[6] & shall have it served. You will of course send me your orders for Court. Send also Ex[e]c[uti]on vs Varrel[7] by bearer. Did not I give you, at yr house, the Chase[8] note? I hope I did, as I have not been able to find it. If you have got Ex[e]c[uti]on thereon please send it. In Lewis v Varrel there is a special attachment—therefore must have the Ex[e]c[uti]on.

We are all well, send love. Yrs   D. Webster.

ALS. NhD.
1. Not identified.
2. Not identified.
3. DW apparently did not get the "Tarlton money" at this time. He filed three separate suits against William Tarleton at the August 1813 term of the Rockingham County Court of Common Pleas.
4. *Webster* v. *Sam Albree* was de-
cided at the January 1811 term of the Rockingham County Court of Common Pleas; *Gore* v. *Lewis* and *Webster* v. *Goodhue* at the August term.
5. Not identified.
6. Not identified.
7. *Moses Lewis* v. *William Varrell,* decided in the Grafton County Court of Common Pleas, September 1811.
8. Not identified.

TO WILLIAM A. KENT

Portsmo. Oct 24 1811

Wm. A. Kent Esqr.

I have this day recd the enclosed.[1] I have no objection that the Directors of the C[oncord] B[ank] should inform Saml. [B.] Goodhue,[2] or any body, or every body else, how much I am "bound by every principle of honor & Justice" to pay them "money of theirs" in my hands. Nevertheless I think I might be permitted to remonstrate modestly against the statement of *facts* which never existed. Neither the Cashier, nor any Director, nor any other person, ever informed me, by letter or otherwise, that Goodhue, had, or intended to, or had applied to the Bank with a view, to pay his debt to me by cancelling the amount at the Bank. Nor was any suggestion of the kind, ever made to me, directly or indirectly, until after I sent the Ex[e]c[uti]on to be served.[3] Yr humble sert

Danl. Webster

ALS. Nh.

1. Not found.

2. Goodhue (d. 1846; Dartmouth

1792), lawyer of Putney, Lyndon, and Brattleboro, Vt.

3. Not found.

FROM PAUL REVERE & SONS

Boston 29 December 1811

Sir

We hold a note of hand signed by James Leavitt & John Marston[1] jointly & severally Dated 28 Feby 1811 for 205 Dollars 39/100 payable in Sixty days interest after. It was given for a Church Bell for the town of Hampton.

In a P.S. to a letter reced from Mr. Leavitt, Mr Edmd Toppan[2] who is one of the Committee requests that we would apply to you for payment and observes by forwarding the note or a Copy you would transmit the amount in ten days. Very Respectfully Your Humble Servants

Paul Revere & Sons

ALS. NhHi.

1. Both were residents of Hampton, N.H.

2. Toppan (1777–1849; Harvard 1796), Hampton lawyer, postman, and legislator.

FROM JAMES A. GEDDES

Moule Grandtier Gaudaloup
January 17th. 1812

Dear Sir

I mbrace this opportunity by my friend whos name I omit to in form you That I am in Good health & pray God That this will find you and yours injoying the same blessing as it leaves me at Present. Sir I should have made you som[e] remitances, be four this time had it not bin for my being taken sick on my arivail which sickness cost me much Pain & Expences, to raise Cash to pay off my Bill for Board and Doctr. Bill which amounted to 140 Dollars, but thanks be to almity God for his mercey I have got so as to look after my affairs. I have almost brought them to a close in the month of March. I expect to be able to return to the united States with fifty or sixty hhds of muscavadou Sugars, I have be gun to receive them from the Planters. Cash is verry scairce and no sail for sugars aperson who has Cash can purches first quality Brown Sugar at four Dollars pr quentall. You well know Sir that Sugars & Coffee are prohibeted[.] We have Verry little commerce with the united States I don't know how I shall gitt my Property home[.] I am in hopes that we shall have no disturbance with England that Commerce will be banned with that mother Country, that I may once more see you and settle all my affairs.

I intend going to St francois, in few days to see a planter who owes me & my Sister fifty four thousand Livers, if I suck sead in the Settlement of that business, I shall be as well off as my Neighbours at home[.] This is my fifth Letter to you.[1] This gose by way of St Barts to Be forwarded by first opportunity. I hope it will Come safe to hand. I should be happy to hear from you if any off your friends should think fitt to send a vessell to this place with an asorted Cargo they will meat with sucksess in the sails and return. As molasses is verry Cheap it would in able me to send you som remitances which I know would be verry acceptable boath to you and my family. The latter I know must be in want, unless your generosity provides for their Subsistances, I wrote Mrs. Geddes last Sunday Perhaps she may think that I am at St. Barts'.

I remain— Sir your most Obedient & most humble Servt.

James A Geddes.

ALS. NhHi. Geddes was a mariner, resident of Portsmouth, and client of Webster's.

1. None of the other Geddes letters to DW have been found.

On June 18, 1812, with the presidential and congressional campaigns already underway, Congress declared war on Great Britain. Having endured hardships for several years already, under successive embargo and nonintercourse acts, New England's denunciation of the war policies reached an unprecedented level.

In New Hampshire, Webster's was a leading voice of dissent. He was himself for the first time a contender for office, having been named a congressional candidate on the "Peace Ticket" at the Brentwood Convention in early August. Two productions from his pen in 1812 had won him the confidence of the state's Federalist leaders. The first was his Independence Day Address before the Washington Benevolent Society, in which he again took issue with Jeffersonian policies. The second was the "Rockingham Memorial," a public letter addressed to Madison recapitulating New England's grievances. Notified in advance that he would be appointed chairman of a committee to prepare a memorial, Webster completed a draft of it previous to the August 5th gathering at Brentwood, and the other committee members and the convention enthusiastically adopted it. As a result of his efforts, Webster, now regarded as "a gentleman of commanding talents and undoubted patriotism" throughout New England, won the congressional seat in the fall elections, and in May 1813 took his seat in Congress as an opponent of "Mr. Madison's War."

TO TIMOTHY FARRAR, JR.

Portsmo. July 28. [1812]

Dear Sir,

I owe you an apology for not sending you a few of my Orations, as I engaged. The truth is, I have not had any to send. I believe there will be some struck off in a few days, & I will forward a few. I now send you, to the care of Mr. Duren,[1] of Boston, a few of the Addresses of the Minority.[2] They have been printed here for distribution. I hope you will find readers for those sent to you.

We are to have a County Convention next week at Brentwood. It is expected, a great many people will attend. If we can form a *comprehensive* peace party, perhaps the Country may be saved by it. The heavy losses at sea very much discourage and distress the Merchants, & diminish their influence and of course their means of opposition. This, perhaps, is one of the consequences foreseen by Administration. A little feverish, puerile spirit is kept up by the privateering system, otherwise all would be conquer[ed]. If I were now to hazard a conjecture on our future course, *without a change of men*, it would be, that the War will be long & lingering. We shall hardly take Canada in a hurry. Our Southern ports being open to neutrals, the English will go there under Spanish & Portuguese colors & take to themselves the whole benefit of that *Commerce* which we have been accustomed to think the *right* of the Northern States.

I hope to send you word in a few days, about Mattox's Ex[e]c[utio]n. Yours with great respect   D. Webster

ALS. NhHi.

1. Not identified.
2. *An Address of Members of the House of Representatives of the Congress of the United States, to their Constituents, on the subject of the War with Great Britain.* Portsmouth: W. Treadwell, 1812. The *Address* was also published in the newspapers.

On the presidential question in 1812, Federalists throughout the nation were divided, but most were convinced that they could not elect one of themselves. To give direction and unity to their ranks, over sixty Federalists assembled in New York City in September for the purpose of deciding on a candidate, but the resolutions adopted were ambiguous and the hoped-for unity did not emerge. According to the National Intelligencer *of October 15, the convention resolved: "First. That under present circumstances it would be unwise to take up a man notoriously of their own party. Second. That they should support the candidate of the two already in nomination [James Madison and DeWitt Clinton] whose success would best promise the objects of their party. Third. That they would not now make a selection of either as their candidate." The request for information on Federalist politics in New Hampshire, below, was an additional attempt to unite Federalists behind a single candidate. As with Binney, Hopkinson, and Meredith, the disagreements and disunity among Federalists also dismayed Webster.*

FROM HORACE BINNEY, JOSEPH HOPKINSON, AND WILLIAM MEREDITH

Philadelphia, September 26 1812.

Sir

At a meeting of a number of Federal Gentlemen, deputed from eleven of the States, held at the city of New-York on the 15th, 16th, and 17th instant, the Subscribers (with Mr. [Samuel] Sitgreaves, of Easton, and Mr [Thomas] Duncan, of Carlisle,)[1] were appointed a Committee to correspond with such Committees or Persons in each State, on the subject of the Presidential Election, as would be likely to afford us the earliest information, after the Electors are appointed, of the manner in which the Electors respectively may be disposed to vote,—and to transmit the information thus obtained to the same Committees and Persons.

It is in the performance of the duties thus enjoined upon us, that we (the distance of the residence of Messrs. Sitgreaves and Duncan preventing them from co-operating with us) have now the honour to address you, and to request that you will communicate to us the information desired, from the state in which you reside. We beg leave to press upon your attention the expediency of making your communication by the earliest opportunity after your Electors are chosen, because delay would defeat the purpose with which it is requested: and, if in the meanwhile any thing should occur which in your opinion is likely to have an influence upon or may afford a reasonable ground for calculating the result of the choice, we shall be glad to be advised of it.[2]

We have the honor to be
Your most obedient servants,

Your letters may be addressed
  to either of us.

Hor: Binney
Jos. Hopkinson
Wm. Meredith

LS printed. NhHi. William Meredith (1772–1839) was a lawyer, president of the Schuylkill Bank, and a leading figure in Federalist circles.

1. Sitgreaves (1764–1827), a Philadelphia lawyer, Federalist in the 4th and 5th congresses, United States commissioner to Great Britain under the Jay Treaty, local officeholder, and

president of the Easton Bank, 1815–1827; Duncan (1760–1827), a Carlisle, Pa., lawyer, a leading Federalist figure in Carlisle after 1800, and a member of the Federalist State Committee in 1812.

2. No communication of DW's to the Committee has been found.

TO JOSEPH SMITH

Portsmouth Oct. 6. 1812

Dear Sir,

I send you herewith the New-Hampshire Gazette[1] of this morning, containing a very important communication from Doctor [John] Goddard.

You will perceive that that Gentleman does not feel bound by the mandates of a Congressional Caucus, & that if chosen an Elector, his vote would be in favor of such men as are disposed to make Peace, or competent to conduct the War.

I am, Sir, with respect, Your friend & obt. servt.   Danl. Webster

I write to Mr. [Daniel?] Waldron[2]; he will show you the letter.

ALS. MWA. Joseph Smith (b. 1763), was a native of Exeter.

1. Newspaper published in Ports-

mouth.

2. Waldron was a resident of Portsmouth. Letter not found.

TO TIMOTHY FARRAR, JR.

Portsmo. Oct. 9. 1812

Dear Sir,

I avail myself of an opportunity to say something of our political affairs. There is, you perceive, more than an intimation in the public papers, that the Federal votes in N. E. will be given for [DeWitt] Clinton; & yet it does not seem to be said so, in plain terms.[1] I cannot think it becomes us, as a party, to hold oscilating language on so great a subject, & am not wholly able to comprehend the wisdom of the opinion said to be adopted in N. York; that is, to obtain all the votes possible agt. [James] Madison, & dispose of them according to circumstances. I suppose every Federalist in N. E. if he were put to the choice between C. & M. would not hesitate to prefer the former. I suppose also, that there is no one who thinks it possible to elect a Federalist; & yet there seems an unwillingness to say, in so many words, that they will support C. It certainly is not consistent with character to make partial intimations of supporting Clinton, with the design of obtaining Democratic votes, & yet be wholly undetermined how to act. In Mass. they are silent for other reasons. It rests with their Senate, whether they shall have any votes or not. Public discussion is not likely to move that body, & perhaps it is thought the object can be better obtained by keeping quiet. Our Election is now before the Public, & in my opinion we ought to speak out. I do not say, what would have been my opinion upon the original question, of supporting C. or throwing away our votes. But I suppose that is pretty much decided. If so, why not act upon that decision? & act openly?

I have conversed on this point with distinguished characters, in Mass: as well before as since the N. York Convention.[2] If I am not wholly satisfied with the project of supporting Clinton, I now think that nothing else can be done with propriety & consistency.

You will perceive a change in our Electoral Ticket. Dr. [John] Goddard is very decisive on the subject of the War, and of a change of men.[3] We think the ground he takes will have a great effect. From present appearances our success in this Town will be great. It may be defeated, by success in privateering, &c—but if no important events of the War kind occur, we think there will be a majority for the Peace Ticket.

The Meeting at Gilmanton was very large, respectable, & satisfactory. There are parts of Strafford that promise very well.

To recur again to the choice of President, I would observe, that these Federalists who favor C.'s nomination, go on the ground, merely, of his preference to Madison. We have no reason, say they, to hope for a Fed. Administration. The best we can expect, is to infuse some portion of Fed. principles into a Democratic Administration. If C. is chosen by the Northern States, he is sure to encounter the opposition of the South & West. He must rest for support, then, on the Commercial States. He may, it is true, disappoint us. He may act as bad as his predecessors. If so, our hands are clean. He is not our choice. We should have elected [John] Jay, or [Rufus] King, or [John] Marshall if we could. We chose between *your* candidates. If we have taken a *bad* one, we know also that we have *left* a *bad* one. Give us *our own* choice, & he will be a *good* one.

The Federalists will probably take no part in C's Administration. They will leave him to worry his opponents by his own pack, & they will tell him plainly, when they chuse him, that they do it, for no positive qualities of his own, but on account of the negative qualities of his rival.

I do not suppose these ideas new to you. I only state them as being the general run of observations among the Feds, who are favorable to Clinton. I hope you will see that a proper representation of the case goes abroad in your County. The sum of all I wish to say is, that if we support Clinton, we ought to say so, that the Clintonian Demos (& there are many in the lower Counties) may vote with us, if they will.

In a late letter Mr. [Harrison Gray] Otis[4] says, that if the votes of Mass. & this State can be obtained, he verily believes C. will be chosen. Yours with great regard & affection   D. W.

ALS. NhHi.

1. For an article that echoes the comments expressed in this letter, see the Portsmouth *Oracle*, October 3, 1812.

2. The delegates to the convention from Massachusetts, some of whom DW might have spoken with, numbered eight. Those known to have attended were Harrison Gray Otis, Israel Thorndike, William Sullivan, Theodore Sedgwick, and possibly Timothy Bigelow.

3. The announcement of Goddard's political about-face and the Federalist support of him as elector appeared in the Portsmouth *Oracle*, October 10, 1812.

4. Letter not found.

Webster's compaigning in 1812 involved not only a defense of his own views but also the character and views of other Federalists. Most notable of these was Timothy Pickering, who had served as Secretary of State under Washington and Adams, had been summarily dismissed by the latter, and was now seeking a congressional seat from Massachusetts. On October 13, 1812, the New Hampshire Gazette, *a Republican sheet published in Portsmouth, had branded Pickering a "Benedict Arnold." In the letter below, Webster called Timothy's attention to the charge, offering his legal services should the Pickerings decide to sue. They so decided, and a libel suit against William Weeks, publisher of the* Gazette, *was filed, but was dropped in 1813.*

TO JOHN PICKERING

Portsmo. Oct. 15. 1812

Sir,

You will excuse the liberty I take of forwarding the enclosed paragraph cut out of the New Hampshire Gazette of this Week; a paper that has abounded with the most infamous libels against your venerable parent.[1] I wish him merely to be informed, that if a sense of duty should induce him to a prosecution of the Printer, it is believed there is honesty enough in our Courts & Juries to bring him to Justice.

I am, Sir, with much respect, Your Ob ser   D. Webster

ALS. MHi. W & S, 16: 11.
    1. For other comments on the libel issue, see Timothy Pickering to DW, October 29, 1812 (mDW 1405), and December 23, 1812 (mDW 1414);

DW to John Pickering, December 11, 1812 (mDW 1409); and DW to Timothy Pickering, December 11, 1812, below.

TO SAMUEL AYER BRADLEY

Dec. 9. 1812

Dear sir,

Do me the favor to procure a service of this writ.[1] It is possible the def[en]d[an]t may not live in Eaton, but in some neighboring Town. If so the Sherriff may alter the writ, in that particular.

We have just heard that Moscow is burned, by the Russians, to deprive the French Army of Winter-quarters—a city of 300.000 Souls! Such an instance of resolution in a *People* is not on record. Yrs   D. Webster

ALS. NhD.
    1. Writ not found. An endorsement

on the cover reads: "Mr Fessenden gave the writ to B. Osgood, Jr."

TO TIMOTHY PICKERING

Portsmouth Decr. 11. 1812

Sir,

No event of the kind could have caused me more regret, than that my absence when you were here should have prevented me the pleasure of seeing you, and of paying you, in person, the respect which I feel for your character.

Among the consequences which may probably grow out of recent events, I look forward to none with more pleasure, than the opportunity which may be afforded of cultivating the acquaintance of one of the *Masters* of the Washington school of Politics.[1] Wholly inexperienced in public affairs, my first object is, to comprehend the objects, understand the maxims, & imbibe the spirit of the first Administration; persuaded as I am, that the principles which prevailed in the Cabinet & Counsels of that period form the only *anchorage*, in which our political prosperity & safety can find any *hold* in this dangerous and stormy time. If my progress in the science of Washington Policy should be in proportion to my regard for its dead & *living* teachers I shall have no occasion to be ashamed of my proficiency. Intending to visit Boston this winter, I contemplate paying you my respects, at the place of your residence.

By this mail I have written to your son,[2] in relation to the suit agt. the Printer here.

I am, with the utmost respect, Your Ob. Ser   Daniel Webster

ALS. MHi. Published in *W & S*, 16: 12.   tives.
1. Both Pickering and DW had been   2. See DW to John Pickering, Deelected to the House of Representa-   cember 11, 1812 (mDW 1409).

TO SAMUEL AYER BRADLEY

Portsmo. Mar 30 1813

Dear Sir,

Every thing, as to our Election, depends on the Councillor of Strafford.[1] That is, the Government will not be *unique*, if a War hawk is chosen in that County to advise the Governor in the Executive part of Government. We therefore are anxious to obtain exact returns from all the Towns; to which end I wish you to do us the favor to obtain exact returns from *Conway, Eaton*, & if not too inconvenient, *Burton*. If you will on receipt of this, dispatch a hand to Eaton & Conway, & send me the result by the very first opportunity, you will not only confer a favor, but will also be entitled to be remunerated for the expense. We have understood, that in Conway & Eaton, Mr. [Richard] *Odell* had a portion of the Democratic votes. If this be true, to any considerable degree, all will be well.

Your Messenger may as well also take the account of Senator votes, in those Towns; its being not yet ascertained, who is chosen in that District. Our Majorities will be about thus

Gov. [John Taylor] Gilman 6 to 8 hundred
Senators
[Oliver] Peabody   150—
[William] Adams   500

[William A.] Kent	85
[Jonas C.] March	95
[Levi] Jackson	700
[Josiah] Bellows	200
[Daniel] Kimball	800
[Moses Paul] Payson, say 4 or 5 hundred	

We fear [Elijah] Hall is chosen Councillor in this County—[Jedediah K.] Smith doubtless in Hillsbor.—Cheshire & Grafton will be Federal;—tho' it is doubtful whether there is any choice in Grafton.

The House will be respectable—Majority about 30. Of the Bar, are elected [George] Sullivan, [Thomas W.] Thompson, [George B.] Upham, [Henry] Hubbard, [Phineas] Handerson, [James Hervey] Bingham, E[ze-kiel] Webster, [Edmund] Parker, (of Amherst) [Abiel] Wilson, [John] Ham, [Charles] Hodgdon &c also [David] Heald, of Washington & [Nehe-miah] Eastman, of Farmington.

Pray let me have an answer as early as may be. Yrs   D. Webster

ALS. NhD.
1. Nathan Taylor. At the time Webster wrote this letter, the only returns not yet in were from Strafford, and on those returns rested the political complexion of the New Hampshire Council, two war and two peace candidates having already been elected. Taylor, the peace candidate, won the Strafford seat.

FROM GEORGE HERBERT

Ellsworth Apl. 28, 1813.

My Dear Daniel,

Upon the faith of your half-promise when I saw you at Boston, I immediately on my return sent by mail to you a letter[1] containing my note for $200 which I wished you, if you could lend it to me, to deposit with Messrs Peters & Pond[2] Boston[;] since that time I have heard nothing on the subject either from you or otherwise. I fear the note may have fallen into other hands and wish you to inform me what you can about it. We are all here in *misery* the distress of this part of the country is in-conceivable—already starving and *starved*. A woman & 2 children are already dead of the famine as I am informed. Many are sick & famish-ing from want. God preserve us all or we shall all die. Our best livers have already parted with all pretty much that they had for their own subsist-ence and all are in one condition. There is not a cent of money in the country more than provision. It is all drained away & gone. I believe I am the owner of what would in good times be worth $20,000 to me, and I cannot raise a dollar. Can you *now* help me, if you can you will do a deed *of charity*—for all I am worth would not produce $100.

Curse this Government! I would march at 6 days notice for Washington, if I could get any body to go with me—and enough I could if I had but a commission, and I would swear upon the *altar* never to return till Maddison was buried under the ruins of the capitol. All the pleasure I have is anticipating the time when I shall march in armour on the FARTHEST GEORGIA and trample the planters under my feet.—But they must be after all the aggressors in war.—But, again they must be *made* such. And how easy that would be, if we were to exercise one hundredth part of the policy *they* have used to bring about this war. I can almost never pardon Boston & the leaders of the Federal interest there, for their pusylanimous and mean conduct in holding back the country from taking even *one* step—when so many are to be taken; some of which are *preparatory*. Hence it comes we are *ruined—starved*. And this is a light thing forsooth. "O let the country suffer"—with a mighty careless unconcerned air, as they had no duty to perform but to attend festivals of the table the very *crumbs* of which would afford us relief—I wish to God, if I knew myself that Boston was bombarded this moment, I could shrug up my shoulders with much complacency when I saw the *smoke of their torment* ascending up on high. *Thou in thy life time hast had thy good things* &c. let them suffer—let them suffer! [Harrison Gray] Otis[3] has over come all the *good sense* and *humanity* of the town of Boston & Boston has depressed the independent feelings of Mass. & Massachusetts not moving— who else could move till she was ready & how could Mass. move till Boston was ready & How could Boston move till Otis was ready! Heaven preserve us.! *on what a slender thread hang* the destinies of nations! The mere breath of *that man* is a more absolute law with Federalists than the ordonnances of Buonaparte are in Paris. It is time things were otherwise. If they are not soon such is our love of life, wives, children & selves that I will not answer for the consequences. I[f] our neighbours under the *despotic* government of a *King* enjoy such *privileges* without *taxation,* as produces them abundance of all the comforts of life, I doubt whether the time will not soon come when we shall determine [on] the leeks and onions of Egypt rather [than] hunger—we have no manna rained upon us by the Govt. and they intend to force us to live upon air like the chamelions. If so they have a right to expect that we shall change the colour of our coats as soon. And I'll warrant them *we shall*—so help us god! We care for *ourselves.* Shall we care for those whether at *Boston* or *Washington* or any where else who care nothing about us? What is *Country,*— & love of *Country* & liberty? Is *it to stalk about* like *shadows?* and *live on air*—and pay tribute of *more than all we have!*—No—! we will not starve if any nation that has wronged us so little as a *certain nation* we can mention, will provide for us. Boston people are *very* wise. If they do not take care they will over shoot themselves—in starving us into reason. I have known a democrat come about in a moment from the violence of his disease to perfect sanity—at least so far as to swear he was ready to take up his musket and fight, but what he would have better times. These fellows know no distinction between federalism[,] founded as it was really on democracy[,] and monarchy. But *life is sweet and a pleasant thing it is to see* food—sometimes. You may tame the tiger with hunger till he will be as still as any other carcase. And may my children rise up and call me cursed if I starve them to death. I tell you friend the timid counsels of Boston and Boston folks will not do for this meridian. I have only to add God send bombardment upon Boston. I should admire to see how they will stand it & like it. I am not saying this for the *public* ear and am only uttering to *you* the bitterness of my heart.

But the mail is come fare well   G. H.

I wont add my name to this treason.

Write next mail

ALS. NhHi. Published in Van Tyne, pp. 27–28.

1. Letter not found.

2. John Peters and Sabin Pond,

merchants.

3. Boston Federalists, headed by Otis, had honored America's naval heroes at public dinners.

Elected to Congress on the Peace Ticket in November 1812, Webster took his seat on May 24, 1813, at the beginning of the first session of the Thirteenth Congress. The major issues before Congress grew out of the prosecution of the war with England—taxes, loans, the Russian mediation, and other diplomatic questions. Webster's consistent tactic, like that of most other Federalists, was to embarrass the administration, and very early in the session his Federalist colleagues recognized him as an able leader of the antiwar forces. To two people mainly—his brother, Ezekiel, then a state legislator, and Charles March—he reported on the proceedings of Congress.

TO EZEKIEL WEBSTER

Washington May 24 1813

Dear E.

You will be glad to hear of my safe arrival in this place. We got into this city, so called Saturday Eve'. The House are getting together this morning. I have marked myself a seat; or rather found one marked for me, by some friend who arrived here before me. I am in good company. Immediately on my left, [Joseph] Lewis & [Daniel] Sheffey—on my right [Joseph] Pearson,[1] [William] Gaston, & [Timothy] Pitkin. I suppose we shall proceed to chuse a Clerk, in an hour or two. The House seems to be pretty full. Adieu — Yrs   D. Webster

ALS. NhD. Published in Van Tyne, pp. 31–32.

1. All were Federalist congressmen: Lewis (1772–1834), from Virginia, 1803–1817; Sheffey (1770–1830), also from Virginia, 1809–1817; and Pearson (1776–1834), from North Carolina, 1809–1815.

TO CHARLES MARCH

[May 25, 1813]
Tuesday 12 o'clock

The Message is out—Russian Embassy in Front—call for taxes in the rear—*immunity of flag* insisted on &c.[1]

If possible I will enclose a copy before Mail closes.   D W—

ALS. NhHi. Published in Van Tyne, p. 32.

1. See President Madison's May 25, 1813, message to Congress in which he reported a Russian offer to mediate between the United States and Great Britain, stated the case against the impressment of men and materiel on board neutral ships, and called for a new tax to finance the ongoing war (James D. Richardson, *Messages and Papers of the Presidents,* 1: 526–530).

TO EDWARD CUTTS, JR.

Washington May 26. '13

Dear Sir,

I am much obliged to you for yours of the 19th;[1] as I shall be for all similar favors. [Samuel] Ham's[2] death, with the awful suspicions attending it, I had previously heard. It is in truth a most melancholy affair.

I should be willing to adopt the Judicial system, of which you give a general account: not because I think it the best possible, but because it proposes *some advantages,* & because a change is indispensable. Too much cannot be done or said to convince Federalists of the necessity of attending to the subject.

I hope the Legislature will have spirit eno[ugh] to correct the violent proceedings of [William] Plumer & his Council.[3] I think public opinion requires it; at least, that it w[oul]d well bear it. I thank you for your hint, on the defenseless state of the coast. If a fair occasion presents, shall endeavor to make use of it. Mr. [Charles] Cutts[4] is here. It is generally believed, that an attempt will be made to supercede Mr. [Samuel A.] Otis,[5] as Clerk of the Senate, by appointing Mr. C. I understand, pretty directly, that such a project is in being. Messrs [Rufus] King & [Christopher] Gore have not yet arrived. They are on the road. [James A.] Bayard has resigned his seat. The Govr. of Delaware is Democratic, but the Legislature have outwitted him, & have continued to have a session about this time.

They met yesterday. They were called together a good while ago, under pretense of providing defense for the Delaware, but the rumor of Mr Bayard's appointment to Russia getting out, they took the liberty to adjourn, to this time. Messrs [William H.] Wells[6] & [Nicholas] Vandyke are the Candidates.

It is generally believed we shall have the *taxes,* in some shape. The Western People, some of them, say their Constituents are *eager to be taxed.* An excise on certain articles, is I think to be expected. Whether a land tax will be voted is not quite so certain.

I went yesterday to make my bow to the President. I did not like his looks, any better than I like his Administration. I think [Johann Kasper] Lavater[7] could find clearly eno[ugh] in his features Embargo, Non-Intercourse & War.

The House will probably today go into Com[mitt]ee of the whole, on the Message, & refer its parts to Committees. [John] Dawson & [William] Finlay [Findley] are the makers of all motions, which are of course. Finlay makes his from the Journal of the last session, which he holds in his hands & reads. Dawson is as insipid an animal as one would wish to see.

I shall hope to hear from you often, & shall be happy to communicate to you any thing which may be thought to be either important or entertaining. Yrs with great esteem   D Webster

ALS. NhHi. Published in Van Tyne, pp. 32–33.

1. Not found.

2. Ham, a Portsmouth merchant, had died on May 16. According to Edward St. Loe Livermore, Ham "occasioned his death by laudanum" (mDW 1445).

3. Governor William Plumer had sought to improve New Hampshire's judiciary when Judge Jonathan Steele resigned from the Superior Court, but when he nominated Samuel Bell, the council rejected the appointment. Repeated nominations and rejections for the Superior Court post followed, and finally Plumer accepted the Republican councillors' nomination of Clifton Claggett. According to Lynn W. Turner in *William Plumer of New Hampshire, 1759–1850* (Chapel Hill, 1962), p. 217, the Court then consisted of "a judicial despot, . . . a chronic invalid, . . . [and] a mediocrity, while the attorney general who argued the state's cases before the bench was a drunkard," and Plumer found it impossible to remedy the situation. It was this situation apparently, which DW and Cutts wished corrected.

4. Cutts was elected secretary of the United States Senate on October 11, 1814.

5. Otis (1740–1814; Harvard 1759), father of Harrison Gray Otis, Boston merchant, representative in the Continental Congress, and secretary of the United States Senate, 1789–1814.

6. Wells (1769–1829), Delaware lawyer and merchant, United States senator, 1799–1804. On May 28, 1813, he occupied Bayard's vacant senate seat and served until March 3, 1817.

7. Lavater (1741–1801), Swiss theologian and author, "the father of the modern science of characterology."

TO EZEKIEL WEBSTER

Washington May 26. [1813]

Dear E.

The House are now in Committee of the whole, on the President's Message. Mr. [John] Dawson, the mover General, has moved three resolutions, for referring its several parts to select Committees, viz.

> on the Army
> the Navy
> the Revenue

These resolutions carried. Mr. [Felix] Grundy moved a 4th Resolution, referring that part of the Message that relates to foreign affairs to a select committee—agreed to.

Mr. [Henry] Clay, Speaker, offered a further resolution referring to a select Committee that part of the Message, respecting the manner in which the War has been waged by the enemy—agreed to. Clay made a furious speech. On motion of Mr Dawson, the Committee rose. The Chairman reported the five resolutions, & the House adopted them. Nobody said any thing but Clay, Speaker.

Mr. [Thomas P.] Grosvenor[1] moved a reconsideration of the vote of the House, adopting the last resolution for the purpose of amendment—to inquire also into the conduct of our own troops—negatived 62 to—74.

Genl. [Robert] Wright made a flaming speech.

We shall do nothing more today. Yrs   D W

ALS. NhD.

1. Grosvenor (1778–1817; Yale 1800), a New York lawyer and Federalist representative in Congress, 1813–1817.

TO SAMUEL AYER BRADLEY

Washington May 28 '13

Dear Bradley,

Looking at Brother [George] Bradbury's[1] Portland Paper last Evening, I perceived with no little pleasure that you were to represent Fryeburg in the General Court. I presume therefore that this will find you at Boston. It is more than I expected. I thought even Distress, the most powerful of all preachers, would not so soon bring your People to their senses.

We have done nothing here, as yet, but hear the Message, carve it up & deliver its pieces to Committees. Nothing wears much the aspect of Peace. The Message, as you will perceive, shows that the project of a Russian Mediation has as yet not been concurred in, by the English Ministry. They appear to know nothing about it.

There is a general talk of Taxes, among the War members, but it is not improbable that there will be great quarrels, as to the particular taxes which shall be laid.

We have some fine fellows on our side of the House; capable of exhibiting Cabinet measures in their true colors, when the proper opportunity shall arrive. You know how to estimate [Timothy] Pickering, [Egbert] Benson & [Richard] Stockton, and are acquainted with the N. England Representation generally. Among those less known to you, & from whom much seems to be expected, are [Thomas P.] Grosvenor, [Thomas J.] Oakley, [Nathaniel W.] Howell & [Zebulon R.] Shepherd[2] from New York —[Alexander C.] Hanson from Maryland, & [William] Gaston from N. Carolina.

It is midsummer here, while you are just able to find in Massachusetts a flower for an Election nosegay.

Field strawberries are in perfection—lettuce finely headed in the open air; green peas grown on old matter, &c. I am, however, altogether disappointed in the general appearance of this Country. It has not the wealth nor the People which I expected. From Baltimore to this place, the whole distance, almost, you travel thro woods, & in a worse road than you ever saw. There are two or three plantations, looking tolerably well;—all the rest is a desert. It never entered into your imagination, that roads could be so bad, as I have found them, this side of N. York, in many places.

I hope to hear from you often, while in Boston, & shall communicate to you any thing which I may think acceptable to you.

As yet, we have not a single document, nor a communication from the President except the Message.

Yours, with great esteem   D Webster

ALS. NhHi.
1. Bradbury (1770–1823), a Portland lawyer and one of Webster's colleagues in the House of Representatives.
2. Howell (1770–1851), a lawyer, had been state assemblyman and attorney general for western New York before he was elected to the 13th Congress; Zebulon R. Shipherd (1768–1841) had pursued a law career.

TO EZEKIEL WEBSTER

Washington May 29. [1813]

Congress adjourned yesterday, after half an hours session.

Two elections will be contested—Bayley's & Hungerford's—by [Burwell] Basset[t] & [John] Taliaferro.[1] Messrs [Rufus] King & [Christopher] Gore took their seats yesterday. There will be a new Senator from Delaware—[William H.] Wells, or [Nicholas] Vandyke.[2]

There is no present prospect, as I think, of Peace, altho' the Madison men appear to be very confident of such a result from the Russian Embassy. There will be difficulty about the Taxes; in as much as the War party will be divided, in respect to the objects of taxation. The whiskey tax will not be high. The domestic dram drinking interest is astonishingly powerful. I am going to day, with Col. [Timothy] Pickering, Mr. [Richard] Stockton, & a few others to dine with Judge [Bushrod] Washington, at Mt. Vernon. House adjourned yesterday to Monday. Yrs   D.W.

ALS. NhD. Published in *PC*, 1: 244–245.

1. Bassett (1764–1841) unsuccessfully contested the election of Thomas M. Bayly (1775–1834); Taliaferro (1768–1852) unsuccessfully contested the seating of John P. Hungerford (1761–1833) in Congress. All were Virginians.

2. Wells defeated Van Dyke in the bid for James A. Bayard's vacated senate seat.

TO CHARLES MARCH

Monday Morning
31 May [1813]

The French news will have no very great effect with our rulers. They will not believe. Some of the first men of the party here insist that the Emperor's loss last Campaign was inconsiderable;—that it was nothing like an overthrow— & not exceeding the ordinary wear & waste of a large army. While Bona[parte] lives, some of his worshippers will continue to adore him.[1]

The prospect about the Taxes is doubtful. There will be opposition, in the ranks of the Democratic party. The President talked so much about "amicable dispositions," & the effect to be expected from the Embassy to Russia, that some of his party pretend to think Peace so near, that it is unnecessary to lay the Taxes. They are for breaking up this session. Sentiments like these have fallen from [Charles J.] Ingersoll, of Philadelphia; [William E.] Bradl[e]y of Vermont, & others. Others talk of a very small tax on whiskey— & a high tax on some other articles. [John W.] Eppes, I am well informed, says, he can find no two agreeing—& that every one is for taxing every body, except himself and his Constituents. At present, rely upon it, there is great diversity & schism, among the party—how much of this can be remedied, by caucusing & drilling, it is not easy to say. The prevalent impression on our side of the House seems to be to keep quiet, until we see whether the jarring interests on the other side will be reconciled.

I wish to remit 150 Dols, to Capt Charles Coffin,[2] Portsmo. At this moment I have no money here, fit for remission. I would be obliged to you, if convenient to enclose him that sum, & on my account, & I will find something in a few days, which will be proper for remission to you.

I like several of your N. York members very much. Was at M. Vernon, on Saturday, at a dinner party—had a very pleasant time— Judge [Egbert] Benson was present—he & I held fast our integrity to the "Murdoch." We insisted it beat "Hills"[3] & every thing else. The party generally returned Saturday Eve'. The Judge staid over Sunday. Yrs   D. Webster

ALS. NhHi. Published in Van Tyne, p. 35.

1. Defeated in Russia during the last months of 1812 and now facing the combined strength of Russian and Prussian troops, Napoleon's defeat seemed imminent.

2. Portsmouth merchant, engaged in the Russian trade.

3. Wines.

FROM CHARLES MARCH

New York 31 May 1813

Dear Sir

A thousand thanks for your Letters. I am glad to see by the Intelligencer, you are on the Foreign Committee, and wish you had a Majority on your side; that of Truth. Most of your Colleagues are able men. [John C.] Calhoun I don't know personally but have a high respect for his talents. He is young, and if honest may yet be open to conviction. [Langdon] Cheves, I take for granted has displeased Mr Speaker [Henry] Clay by his independent conduct on the subject of the Merchants Bonds last session. If your Committee want a guide in making up their Report, Governour [Caleb] Strongs Speech (an admirable thing) would be an excellent one. It is language indeed fitting a New England Governour, and what was expected of the Venerable Chief Magistrate of Massacts. The proceedings thus far look like anything but a speedy Peace, and a part of the Message, about the immunity of the Flag is in my opinion extremely Warlike. Great Britain will never abandon the right of Search, nor formally that of impressment of her own seamen. Mr Madison knows it. She may waive the right of impressment if our Laws leave to her the use of her own seamen; but the moment she gives up the right of Search, she seals her downfall. The infatuation of our Cabinet is unaccountable. This Country in fifty years will in the common course of Events insist on enjoying, as it will be for her Interest so to do, the very Rights which GB now contends for— What is thought of the late news from Europe: Prussia you see the misfortunes of (whose cheating and cheated Monarch has excited however but little commiseration) has followed the footsteps of Sweden in pressing Russia; and Austria and Denmark were threatening to do likewise. Not a word is said in any of the London papers of the *Mediation,* and they seem to have but little concern in England as to the Duration of the War.

[Stephen] Decaturs Squadron was seen on Saturday 5 PM beating out of the Race which you know is nearly opposite New London; the wind was fair all that night, and it is believed they got to Sea.

Poor [Samuel] Hams Death was melancholy indeed: I saw a Portsmouth man on Saturday whose reports confirmed all the fears I expressed to you. What a Creature is man!

Do you receive the News Papers regularly? Truly Yours   C. March

They talk in Wall Street of the New Importation Act coming off—it must be mere conjecture; as nothing has been done to warrant the conclusion. You must not forget to give me your opinions as to probable Measures. They shall not be abused.

ALS. DLC.

TO CHARLES MARCH

Washington June 3, 1813

Thursday Afternoon—I have just learned that the Senate have *refused* to call for the Russian document by a Maj: of 5. Gen [Samuel] Smith, [Michael] Leib, [John] Lambert[1] &c voted with the Federalists— [William B.] Giles absent.

I cannot say certainly whether the new loan is 5—or 7 millions. Gov [Caleb] Strong's Speech is more determined than any thing I have seen from him. I expect the tone in Mass will be high. Yrs   D. Webster

ALS. NhHi. Published in Van Tyne, p. 36.

1. Lambert (1746–1823), a New Jersey representative and senator.

TO EZEKIEL WEBSTER

Washington June 4 1813

Dear E.

If your Legislature pass any Resolves this Session, on the War, &c, I hope you will not fail to put in a solemn, decided, and spirited Protest against making new States out of new Territory &c. Affirm, in direct terms, that New Hampshire has never agreed to favor political connexions, of such intimate nature, with any people, out of the limits of the U. S. as they existed at the time of the compact.[1] Yrs   D. Webster

ALS. NhD. Published in Van Tyne, p. 37.

1. No such resolves were introduced in the New Hampshire legislature at its June 1813 session.

FROM EZEKIEL WEBSTER

Saturday June 5th 1813

Dear Daniel,

I wrote you last evening[1] giving some account of our doings. We have not done much to day, save the choosing a Senator in Congress. The Senate proceed to choose on their part— & the votes were for John Goddard 8. J[edediah] K. Smith 3. & Caleb Ellis[2]—1: [Josiah] Bellows voting for

Ellis. On motion to concur in the house—the *ex* speaker [Clement Storer] moved the yeas & nays be taken by ballot, (the yeas & nays being called for) [John F.] Parrot made a speech, but I could not ascertain what he wanted. Mr. [Thomas] Page[3] said he had constitutional scruples of voting by yeas & nays. Mr [William] Morrill[4] said it was a novel proceeding & that the Senate had stole a march upon the house. The ex-speaker upon reflection thought that as the proper question was upon the concurrence, his motion to proceed by ballot was not in order, as it was a substitute. The yeas & nays were taken, & were for concurring 108 nays—70. Messrs Morrill & Page voting with the *yeas*. The yeas & nays I believe ferreted them from their dens. I imagine I shall be able to write you monday evening & inform you whether Dr [John] G[oddard] accepts or declines. In case of the latter we shall proceed anew in the choice & shall elect Mr [Jeremiah] Mason. Of this I am confident. It must be so. The Judiciary & the Election Bills are now before committees. Mr. [John Taylor] Gilman has been qualified to day & made his speech.

I am told the Presidents message has a pacific aspect in the apprehension of many federalists in this quarter. I think it very warlike. If he has given the *basis* on which the Russian treaty is to be made, there can be no hopes of a treaty being concluded. If I understand him the British are to surrender the right of search for British goods or British subjects. The war then will be likely to continue as long as even the Kentuckians will desire. I expect no peace till the people make it. It will be, whenever it does come, the peoples' peace. We must make peace by speaking through our representatives. They must give the public mind an impression, a direction & that in its turn will strengthen their hands & encourage their hearts. You are in Congress at a time when men, who love their country, have talents to promote her best interests, would like to be there. It is a time for men to act in. We expect the friends of peace will oppose, taxes, loans, & every measure, calculated to prolong the war. You will be called upon to make the Government *strong*. We should choose to have them made honest. God forbid, that with their present tempers, motives dispositions and principles, they ever should be made stronger. It would be as rational for me to wish that strength might be added to the hurricane, that is laying waste my fields; or to the flames which are consuming my dwellings.

I have recd. three letters from you & hope to receive many more. I should like to see the Intelligencer if it be perfectly convenient. We have heard of the capture of [the Ch]esapeake & we all lament it.[5] It is a great loss.

[M]onday June 7th
We have chosen the old Secretary [Samuel Sparhawk], Treas [Nathan-

iel Gilman] & Asa Dearborn[6] Commissary General. Dr Goddard refuses to come to see you. To morrow morning is assigned for making a choice of Senator.

I will send you his letter next mail. Yours &c &c   E Webster

ALS. NhD. Published in *PC*, 1: 234–235.

1. E. Webster to D. Webster, June 4, 1813, mDW 1501.

2. Ellis (1767–1816; Harvard 1793), a Claremont lawyer who had served in the state House and Senate and in Congress for two years. In 1813, he was appointed a justice of the New Hampshire Supreme Court.

3. Representative from Hawke and Sandown.

4. Legislator from Brentwood.

5. The destruction of the *Chesapeake* off Boston harbor occurred on June 1, 1813.

6. A native of Chester, N.H., born in 1756.

TO CHARLES MARCH

Washington June 6. [1813]

Dear Sir,

The Committee of W[ays] & M[eans] have concluded, I understand, to report all the Tax Bills, as they recd them from the Treasury— & leave their discussion & modification to the House. They will probably be in, Monday or Tuesday. They are so drawn, as to bear most hard on the Atlantic & Eastern States. This was to be expected. The Stamp Tax—for example—is to be imposed, almost exclusively, upon Bank Bills— & notes negotiated at Banks. The Whiskey Tax will be small— & so contrived, as to be easily evaded. It will be laid, not on the gallon but on the *still*, according to its capacity—leaving out all under a certain size. Instead therefore of a few great stills, they will have a thousand little ones. Every effort will be made to force the taxes down—but I continue to think their passage a little doubtful. [Albert] Gallatin made [David] Parish[1] the most solemn assurances of two things— 1. That there w[oul]d be peace —that he himself had been always opposed to the War— & was now going with a full resolution to end it— 2. That the Taxes should be laid. You see in all the Executive Communications, the necessity of Taxes urged.—Nothing of consequence has lately transpired in the Senate.

We were yesterday at the Russian Celebration. It was a pleasant occasion. Many persons of Virginia & Maryland, of the first distinction were present. G[eorge] W[ashington] P[arke] Custis made an Oration, and Hon R[obert] G[oodloe] Harper made an Address to us, at Table, of three quarters of an hour. It was very good. Yrs   D W

ALS. NhHi. Published in Van Tyne, pp. 37–38.

1. Philadelphia banker with "influential connections in all the economic capitals of Europe," who acted as a loan contractor during the War of 1812.

Webster's chief congressional contribution to the efforts of the antiwar coalition was his resolution requesting the President to inform Congress when the United States first knew of the repeal of the Berlin and Milan decrees. Offered on June 10 in the House after the Senate had failed to make public France's duplicity on the decrees, the resolutions became a rallying point for the opponents of the war.

TO CHARLES MARCH

Monday Afternoon [June 7, 1813]

Dear Sir,

We have done nothing today, but hear a case of disputed Election in Tenessee[1]—taxes not in yet—have just heard of the taking of Fort George,[2] & the loss of Chesapeake.

Tomorrow I intend to bring forward a motion, calling for information relative to the famous French Decree, repealing the Berlin & Milan Decrees. Lest some accident should prevent, you will say nothing of this, till you see or hear more of it. If they chuse to oppose it— & to bring on a general battle, we are ready. Some of your N. Y. members are very good fellows— [Thomas P.] Grosvenor, [Zebulon R.] Shepherd, [Thomas J.] Oakley, [Nathaniel W.] Howell &c, as well as the Judge [Egbert Benson], are relied on to give us a lift. [Alexander C.] Hanson is a hero. Yrs   D. W.

I look anxiously for news from N. H. respecting Senator.

N.B. [William B.] Giles has just taken his seat in Senate, & has put a claw on Gallatin. The President will be hard pushed in the Senate.

ALS. NhHi. Published in Van Tyne, p. 38.

1. William Kelly had contested the seating of Thomas K. Harris.

2. The attack on Fort George, on the Canadian side of the Niagara River, below the falls, had first come in October and November 1812, and had recently resumed.

TO CHARLES MARCH

[June 10, 1813]
Thursday Afternoon—

Dr March,

The *resolutions*[1] were offered today—they lie until tomorrow for consideration. What the House will do with them, I cannot say. The question to consider them was carried— 132—to 28. I have done what I tho't my duty—& am easy about the result. A friend will forward them this Evening to the Commercial Advertizer[2]—in which paper you will be likely first to see them. I ask of you the favor to obtain a few of the papers, & send two or three of them to Portsmo. (nobody there takes the paper) & one to each of the following persons—viz. Thos. W. Thompson Esqr,

Concord, N. H., via Boston; Ezl. Webster, Concord N. H.—via Boston—
& Isaac P. Davis³ Esqr, Boston. Send one to Wm. Garland, *Portsmo.*—The
taxes are in today—they make a good many wry faces—they are referred
to a Committee of the Whole, on Monday. They will make the People
stare. Albert Gallatin has not yet got thro. the Senate. After several days
discussion, he is committed to a Committee of 5—viz.—[Rufus] King,
[William B.] Giles, [Joseph] Anderson, [James] Brown & [Jesse] Bledsoe⁴
—*the 3 first are ag[ains]t confirming him.* There cannot be much sleep in
the White-house about this time—let nothing get into the Newspapers,
about the Senate, at present. Yr's in haste— D *Webster*

ALS. NhHi. Published in Van Tyne,
pp. 39–40.
 1. Webster's resolutions on the
Berlin and Milan decrees.
 2. DW's resolutions appeared in the
New York Evening Post, June 14,
1813, and in the *New York Spectator*
(*Commercial Advertiser*), June 16,
1813.

 3. Davis (1771–1855), Boston manufacturer and businessman, close
friend of Webster. In 1841, through
the influence of Webster, then Secretary of State, Davis received an
appointment as Naval Officer of Boston, a post he held until 1845.
 4. Bledsoe (1776–1836), lawyer and
senator from Kentucky.

TO MOODY KENT

Washington June 12 1813

Dear Sir,

 I send you the enclosed report,¹ that you may see how we pass time
here. Today we have been wholly occupied with it, & expect to be a day
or two longer. The only questions are, "will the House *presume* that the
Sherriff *did not* perform his duty, in having the Clerk sworn"; & "can the
name of a man be written, by the initial of his Christian, & the whole of
his surname. For example, if I should put at the end of this letter "D.
Webster," is that "entering my name" upon it, or not. On these knotty
points, we are much divided. Speaker Clay made a vehement speech, in
favor of the report. He said the name must be written at full length—that
both names might be given by initials as well as one &c &c—*Col.* [Tim-
othy] *Pickering* ansd. him. He said, it was required that all Bills &c should
be "signed by the Speaker", & he had observed the constant mode of signing to be "H. Clay." He wished to know, whether this was right or wrong;
& if right, whether a public Law is not a matter requiring as much form,
as a Virginia Poll list. The Speaker spoke no more.

 [Nathaniel] *Macon* was not clear, whether the law wd. presume the
Clerk to be sworn, till the contrary appeared; or whether the other pre-
sumption ought to take place.

 [John C.] *Calhoun* made a long speech to prove the essential policy of
Virginia, in requiring every voters name to be written at *"full length"*. It
was, he said, because there was a land-list, or list of freeholders, & this

served to check the voters by. Therefore the names were required to be written "at full length" on the polls; so that the same names may be found on the land list. This Orator was mistaken only in three unimportant points.

1. The land list is not a check; because every freeholder does not vote in Virginia—

2. The names on the land list are, more than half of them, abbreviated in the same way—

3. The Law of Virginia requires no such thing, as that the name shall be written "at full length"—vid. the report

[Daniel] *Sheffey* demolished all this nonsense, in a very sensible argument, & strewed the dust of the fabric over those who had raised it. How the House will decide is uncertain—The taxes are reported; not acted upon. *I hope they will pass.* All that I have heard from Concord yet, I like very much. My information comes down only to Dr. [John] G[oddard]'s election. Write me, & tell me all the news. Yours &c   D. Webster

ALS. DLC. Published in Van Tyne, pp. 40–41.
1. Report of the Committee on Elec-

tions on John Taliaferro's contesting the election of John P. Hungerford. Report not found with letter.

TO CHARLES MARCH

Washington June 14. [1813]
Monday—

Dear Sir,

All day Saturday, & all today on the disputed Election in Virginia.

Tax Bills yet not acted on. When I am more at leisure, I will say what I think about the prospect of Peace. In the mean time, if any thing looking like a repeal of Non Intercourse should take place, I will give you notice.

You must contrive some way for me to get rich, as soon as there is a peace. Yrs   D W

N.B. The Senate are yet in debate, on [Albert] Gallatin, [Jonathan] Russel[l] &c. Russel[l] was today referred to a Committee, viz. [Rufus] King, [William B.] Giles, [William H.] Wells. Poor Madison! I doubt whether he has a night's sleep these three weeks.

ALS. NhHi. Published in Van Tyne, p. 42.

FROM CHARLES MARCH

New York 14 June 1813

The Resolutions are excellent, and extremely apropos. The House was more civil than I expected; you took them by surprise, and the thing will annoy them not a little. Copies of the Resolutions, which have first appeared in the Morning Papers (Yesterday being Sunday) shall be forwarded as you request. If these Resolutions pass, the last one in particular will be a bitter Pill at the Palace.[1] [John] Goddard declined his appointment, and I am glad of it. You will be as glad as I am to hear that [Jeremiah] Mason is chosen. I shall hope to see him in a day or two. Our state will stand high. Already do our Citizens bow with respect to *The Mover of The Resolutions*. My own opinion is they will not pass; at least in their present shape; [William W.] Bibb wanted time to consult the little occupant of the great White House and will be told to act as may suit the views of the Cabinet. The Essex Frigate is safely blockaded in a Port of the Brazil—St. Salvador I believe.

Yours in haste but most truly   C: March

ALS. DLC.

1. "*Resolved,* That the President be requested, in case the fact be that the first information of the existence of said decree of the 28th April, 1811, ever received by this Government, or any of its ministers or agents, was that communicated in May, 1812, by the Duke of Bassano to Mr. Barlow, and by him to his Government, as mentioned in his letter to the Secretary of State, of May 12, 1812, and the accompanying papers, to inform this House whether the Government of the United States has ever required from that of France any explanation of the reasons of that decree being concealed from this Government and its Ministers for so long a time after its date; and if such explanation has been asked by this Government, and has been omitted to be given by that of France, whether this Government has made any remonstrance, or expressed any dissatisfaction to the Government of France, at such concealment." (*Annals of Congress,* 13th Cong., 1st sess., 1813–1814, p. 151.)

TO CHARLES MARCH

June 19. 1813

I have not time to write you any thing in detail; especially as I intend saying a word, on my Resolutions, Tomorrow Morning.[1]

There is no prospect of Non-Importation coming off. I am watching it very closely, & will give you the first hint. The fact is, the Administration are, for the moment, confounded. They are hard pushed in our house— much harder in the Senate. [Albert] Gallatin not confirmed—a Resolution has actually passed the Senate, that the Offices of Secretary of Treasy. & Foreign Minister are incompatible!! Madison has been several days quite sick—is no better—has not been well eno[ugh] to read the said Resolution of the Senate—the Taxes go heavily— *I fear* they will not go at all. They cannot raise a Caucus, as yet, even, to agree what they will do. They are in a sad pickle. Who cares?—   D. W.

I will steadily watch the Non-Intercourse.

ALS. NhHi. Published in Van Tyne, pp. 42–43.

1. DW's resolutions passed the House on June 21; he did not make a

speech on them. According to the New York *Evening Post,* June 25, 1813, "Webster, Stockton, Pickering, and many others would have been upon the floor, if the debate had been continued." See DW to Ezekiel Webster, June 28, 1813, mDW 1582; and "Notes and Memoranda for a Speech on my Resolutions," printed in *Century Magazine,* 50 (July 1895), 468–471.

TO CHARLES MARCH

June 21. 1813

Dear Sir,

The Resolutions have passed,[1] unaltered, except putting in the usual saving in the last Resolution, which was left out by accident.

The last Resolution passed 93.—to 68. I made no speech. When I came to the House this morning, [John C.] Calhoun told me, the motion for indefinite postponement would be withdrawn—his motion to amend withdrawn— & he, & some of his friends should vote for the Resolutions as they are. I of course could not object— & considering the thing given up on their part, I forbore to speak. They have acted very strangely—a dozen motions, made & withdrawn—some pulling one way—some another. They do not manage like so many Solomons. Adieu— Yrs   D W.

[Alexander C.] Hanson, [Thomas P.] Grosvenor, [Thomas J.] Oakley, [Joseph] Pearson &c have made excellent Speeches.

ALS. NhHi. Published in Van Tyne, p. 43.

1. For the final passage of the reso- lutions, see *Annals of Congress,* 13th Cong., 1st sess., 1813–1814, pp. 301– 311.

FROM CHARLES MARCH

Monday Morning 21 June 1813

My Dear Sir

The British Account of the affair of the Chesapeake is arrived, and you will see it in the Centinel.[1] I thank God that even by their own Account we have lost no honour. The Honour of our gallant little navy remains untarnished. [James] Lawrence (poor fellow) all his Lieutenants, and the sailing Master were all killed or mortally wounded in the Commencement of the Action, and the ship left without anyone to lead or direct: the remaining Crew half of them seasick and strangers to one another. I feel confident that from the result of this brave but ill advised battle our naval character will not be the less respected. Every face is covered with deep gloom by the death of poor Lawrence; but in a national view, I rejoice he fell. Peace to his Manies. Our brave Enemy buried him with every mark of attention & respect. The news from the North is disastrous, but that interests me not much.

I have no letter these three days: The Resolutions I see are brought up, and I anticipate a Continuance of the warm debate which had commenced. [Thomas P.] Grosvenor is a fine fellow. Before they are disposed of, you will give them (the Demos) another heat. Most truly Yours,

C: March

ALS. NhHi.   1. Boston Federalist newspaper.

TO CHARLES MARCH

June 22. 1813.

Dear Sir,

This morning we shall take up the taxes. I have a little draught on New York, which I shall enclose you, either today, or Tomorrow—to repay the sum you sent to Portsmo. I expect this week to have occasion to send 5 or 6 hundred Dollars to Boston. If I do, I shall take the liberty to write to you, & if convenient to you, to get you to send it on, & receive it when I return home.

I know not what course the taxes will take—perhaps at night I can tell you better. Yr   D W

Mr [John] *Rhea*, after my Resolutions passed moved a little Resolution calling for information of the P. Regent's Declaration—passed nem-con.[1] The Speaker has appointed me & *old Rhea* to carry the Resolutions to the Palace!! *I never swear.*

ALS. NhHi. Published in Van Tyne, p. 44.

1. Rhea requested the President to transmit to the House a copy of the

Declaration and Orders in Council (*Annals of Congress*, 13th Cong., 1st sess., 1813–1814, p. 311).

TO CHARLES MARCH

June 24 [1813]— Thursday—

Nothing yesterday & today but "taxes". There is a good deal of objection to the detail—there is great doubt what will be done. Virginia hates a land tax. [Henry] Dearborn has resigned[1]—Madison still sick—[John W.] Eppes sick— &c &c. —I went on Tuesday to the Palace to present the Resolutions. The Presidt was in his bed, sick of a fever. His night cap on his head—his wife attending him &c &c. I think he will find *no relief* from my prescription. —You will see by today's Intelligencer, that the Party are troubled with them. You recollect what R[obert] Smith s[ai]d about his inquiry of [Louis] Serurier. How will Madison answer the part of Resolutions calling for his correspondence with Serurier? In truth, there never was a party acted so awkwardly, as the Demos did thro the whole of that business.

The Senate has done nothing yet. They now have [William] Duane before them, for Adj: Genl. They are not in a hurry to appoint any of Madison's Creatures.

The news is, that the British have recd a vast reinforcement in the Bay, and the lower Country is greatly alarmed. You will see there has been a battle between a frigate & some Gun Boats.

Yrs   D W

ALS. NhHi. Published in Van Tyne, pp. 44–45.

1. Dearborn, commander of the American forces, had not resigned, and President Madison did not request his retirement until July 6, 1813. DW probably based his comment on a rumor circulated by Louis Serurier, French Minister, that Dearborn would likely be replaced by James Wilkinson.

TO CHARLES MARCH

Monday [June 28, 1813]

Dr March,

You are probably tired of receiving letters containing nothing; but I continue to write them. Look at the enclosed; & if you think it worth while, hand it along.

Yr man [Jonathan] Fiske[1] has this day put the Democratic ranks in no small confusion, by moving a Resolution for a tax on whiskey, to be imposed on the *gallon,* not on the *still.* All the West is in arms. It lies over till Tomorrow.

Nothing of any importance has recently occured in the Senate. As to Peace, a part of the Democrats doubtless wish it; a part do not. The West is still fierce for War. Do not credit any report of Mr. [Rufus] Kings opinions[2] without good evidence. I see him sometimes, & think I should know any important sentiment, on these subjects, which he might divulge.

I am fully of opinion, that the Administration now looks forward to its own certain downfal[l], unless it can have a peace. But if it does make Peace, it will have all the West &c in arms agt it. Poor Madison does not know what to do. I can tell you, for yr own ear, that he this day nominated Paul Hamilton, Com[missioner] of Loans for S. C. The Senate will certainly negative it!! This shows his standing with that body. Never was man sinking faster. It is said today, as it is every day that he is better, as to his health. Adieu Yrs   D W

ALS. NhHi. Published in Van Tyne, p. 46.

1. Fiske (1778–1832), New Hampshire native and at the time Democratic representative from New Hampshire.

2. Unlike most Federalists, King had indicated a willingness "to cooperate with the administration if it worked to establish an equitable and permanent tax system." Undoubtedly, DW worried that King's cooperation with the administration on tax proposals might be interpreted by citizens elsewhere as support for the war.

TO JEDIDIAH MORSE

Washington June 28. [1813]

Dear Sir,

I am obliged to you for yours,[1] as I shall be for all similar favors. You have learned, before now, the fate of the Resolutions which I introduced.[2] The debate terminated very strangely. For four days, the other side of the House had opposed their passage, with great vehemence; encountering them with motions to amend, postpone, &c &c. Opposition was then suddenly abandoned;—or rather the debate was abandoned, except by some secondary men on that side;— & some of the chiefs manifested a disposition to vote for the Resolutions just as they were. This was at the moment when I had risen to speak on the subject. It struck me, that I ought not to proceed, after this intimation from the other side. I accordingly resumed my seat, & after a few speeches from the *soldiers* in the opposite ranks, the question was taken, & decided as you have seen. The 5th Resolution, 93 yeas—68 nays. On the 22nd I presented them to the President. *He was in his bed, sick of a fever.* He is still sick. The daily report is, that he is better, but my opinion is, that he is not yet convalescent. His fever I understand is bilious. Probably he is not esteemed to be dangerous by his friends; but I am convinced he is a good deal sick.

The Senate act a very unaccomodating part. [Albert] Gallatin not yet confirmed. They passed a Resolution, that the Offices of Foreign Minister & Secy. of Treasury are incompatible. What Mr. Madison will say to this, is not known.

The taxes are before us. It is generally supposed they will be laid. It is not, however, certain. Public business seems to be in a state of languishment. The President, & the Chairman of the Ways & Means, sick; Mr. Gallatin gone;—the heads of Departments that remain, not supposed to be in the most perfect amity;—the Senate very much inclined to have its own course; the House reluctantly engaging in [more] Taxes; the Commander in Chief resigned. At the same time, the Enemy is in great force down the Bay; has possessed himself of Hampton;— & threatens Norfolk; —Canada not quite conquered;—no money in the treasury, & our expenses going on, at this moment, as is well ascertained, at the rate of 6 millions, & a fraction, per month!

Give my respects to Mr. [Jeremiah] Evarts, & let me have the pleasure of hearing from you often.

Yrs with great regard.   D. Webster

ALS. PHi. Published in *W & S*, 16: 27–28.

1. Not found.

2. On DW's resolutions, see letters to March, June 19, 21, above.

TO EZEKIEL WEBSTER

Washington July 4. '13

Dr E.

You have done a great work, at Concord—may your reward be great. I have recd. the Judiciary bill, &c &c &c—all is right. I have no objection to the candidates you mention for Judicial Offices.[1] I do not hear whether [Arthur] L[ivermore] came into this?[2]

We are yet on the taxes. They will probably pass. It will take so long to adjust the details, & to bring the Bills before the House to be discussed on their general principles, that I very much doubt whether any full discussion of the War will be had this session. For myself, I am determined not to remain here more than ten days. The weather is already very hot—more so than ever I experienced.

The President has sent no answer yet. I must, in decency, stay till he does, if it comes in any season, in order to see if supplementary questions are necessary. He will be followed up on that subject. An inquiry into the failures on the frontiers is talked of— I think there will not be any time this Session.

We have several projects, & a good many good hands to give a lift. We are trying to organize our opposition & bring all our force to act in concert.

There is recently appointed a kind of Committee to superintend our concerns, viz, [Timothy] Pickering, Webster[,] Wm. Reed, [William] Baylies, [Elisha R.] Potter, [Timothy] Pitkin, [Thomas P.] Grosvenor, [Thomas J.] Oakley, [Richard] Stockton [Henry M.] Ridgely, [Alexander C.] Hanson, [Daniel] Sheffey, [William] Gaston[3]—

It will take us this Session to find one another out. Yrs D. W.

ALS. NhD. Published in *PC*, 1: 236–237.

1. Candidates not identified.

2. With the reorganization of the New Hampshire courts, Livermore's position as Chief Justice of the Superior Court was in doubt; he was, however, made an associate justice of the state Supreme Court.

3. All were Federalists: Pickering from Massachusetts; Webster, from New Hampshire; Baylies (1776–1865), from Massachusetts; Potter (1764–1835), from Rhode Island; Pitkin, from Connecticut; Grosvenor, from New York; Oakley, from New York; Stockton, from New Jersey; Ridgeley (1779–1847), from Delaware; Hanson, from Maryland; Sheffey, from Virginia; and Gaston, from North Carolina.

TO CHARLES MARCH

July 10. '13

My dear Friend,

I expected to leave this place Tomorrow, & to be with you by the middle of next week. But understanding that we are to hear from the President[1] either today or Monday, I shall wait a few days longer.

The Senate have decided *against* the Swedish Mission.[2]

Gen [John] Armstrong is going to the frontier to take the command of our discomfited armies! This is not publicly announced, but I have great reason to think it true. Your's as ever,   D. Webster

ALS. NhHi. Published in Van Tyne, pp. 47–48.

1. On DW's resolutions on the Berlin and Milan decrees.

2. President Madison had nominated Jonathan Russell as Minister to Sweden, but the Senate decided such a mission "inexpedient."

FROM RICHARD STOCKTON

Princeton 23d. July 1813

Dear Sir,

Your funny friend Mr [Roger] Vose has for the last week forwarded to me your national Intelligencer—the paper came within a blank cover and I supposed that some of our mess on leaving the city had requested him to forward one of the papers to me. Last evening he wrote me a line by which I first discovered that he expected that I would forward the paper on to you. I shall write to him not to send it longer to me as I am to leave home on Tuesday next—and besides get all I want to hear from the Capital early eno[ugh] in the Phi[ladelphi]a papers. Mr [David] Dagget passed thro' yesterday—he was so eager to meet his wife in N Y: that I could not prevail on him to stay the day with me. He was the last of the mess and had been alone for four or five days. [William] Coxe [Jr.] had left W. before your letter arrived,[1]—so that they lost the amusement it would have afforded. You will see by the late papers that what we made merry about is likely to become serious. The Enemy are coming up to pay their respects at the palace. There seems to be much alarm—for my own part I cannot think that a landing will be ventured on now with the small force they now have. You have doubtless read with becoming disgust Munroes Jesuitical answer to the resolutions.[2] I am sorry so many of our Men have gone off if any discussion is to take place. [Thomas P.] Gro[s]venor [Alexander C.] Hanson and [William] Gaston will I have no doubt expose it as it ought to be exposed. If the people of this Country can believe that the French decrees were expiated within the meaning of our act on 1st. Novr. 1810— That the British orders in Council were not in any manner affected by the repealing act of France of 28 Ap 1811— And that the War is still just necessary and advantageous—they will believe any thing and are fit subjects for the hospital of incurables. The materials for a most vigorous effective opposition next session are accumulating every hour—and when the tax gatherers shall have become our heralds we shall not speak in vain—till then I continue to think that it will [be] spending breath in vain. Believe me Dear Sir with entire respect and Esteem Sincerely yours   Rd. Stockton

ALS. NhD.

1. Not found.

2. The Executive report, prepared by Secretary of State James Monroe, in compliance with DW's resolution requesting information on when the United States first learned of the repeal of the Berlin and Milan decrees, was sent to the House of Representatives on July 12, 1813, shortly after DW left Washington for Portsmouth (*American State Papers: Foreign Relations,* 3: 608–612). For the purport of the document we cannot improve upon Monroe's biographer, who describes it as "a carefully woven fabric of equivocation and evasion, which neither commented on the authenticity of the Decree of St. Cloud nor clearly answered the question whether it had been known in Washington before Barlow had transmitted it." Harry Ammon, *James Monroe* (New York: McGraw-Hill, 1971), p. 321.

From the time he had completed his legal studies, Webster had shown a keen interest in banks and banking, having been involved both professionally and personally in the affairs of the Coös and Concord banks; and despite the many problems those associations had presented, his interest in banking continued unabated. Following his return to Portsmouth from Washington in 1813, Webster became involved in efforts to secure incorporation of the Rockingham Bank, which occurred on November 5, 1813. Beyond this, little has been established regarding Webster's interest in the bank at that time or later. He was not listed in the charter as one of the incorporators.

TO THOMAS W. THOMPSON

[October 1813]

Dear Sir,

Since my return from Washington I have engaged a little in the project for the obtaining a Bank Charter, for this Town. I am inclined to think the Petition will come forward this session, under circumstances as favorable as could be expected to attend such a scheme.

1. The N. H. Bank will not oppose it. I believe there are *many* of its stockholders, (& know there are *some*), who desire the Petition to prevail.

2. The Portsmo. Bank wd. best like us *to fail;* but I fancy will take no steps.

3. The Union Bank, probably pretty indifferent—some of their heaviest stockholders willing the Grant should be made.

4th. It will not be a party question. The whole Representation from this Town will support it.

5. The direction will fall into as *safe* and *responsible* hands as any in Town. When I see you, I can give you names, not on the Petition, which wd. probably be concerned.

6. It wd. gratify the inclinations, & promote the interest, of the most active, *useful & zealous* men in this place; on whom we are chiefly to rely hereafter.

Having myself a pretty deep interest in the Petition, I thought it would be more pleasant to you, that I should state to you, in this way, the circumstances attending the application, than to trouble you with much conversation. If it seems to you safe for the public & the party to pass a Bill on the Petition, we shall be glad of your aid; if not, I for one shall be certain, that you would give us your aid, if you did not think public duty prevented it. If you think it worth while to shew this to [William] Kent & [Moses P.] Payson, I will be obliged to you so to do. I should not like to have it communicated farther.

I intend being in Concord on Thursday or Friday. Next week, I suppose, I must spend at Plymouth. I think we shall have a charming Court, neither the Ch[ief] J[ustice] [Jeremiah Smith] nor [Caleb] Ellis attending. Yrs   D. Webster

ALS. CSmH.

On December 22, 1813, a catastrophe commonly known as the "Great Fire" hit Portsmouth, destroying 272 buildings in the town, 108 of which were residences, before it was brought under control. Webster's was one of the houses destroyed. Uninsured, the destruction of his $6,000 home and valuable library was a great financial loss for him. Not until his arrival in Washington did Webster learn of the fire.

With assurances that his family was safe, he reluctantly turned his attention to Congressional matters. In the second session of the Thirteenth Congress, Webster's role was even more conspicuous than in the first. His leadership there was more noticeable, and his efforts to influence public opinion through the Federalist presses were more effective. Throughout 1814, he contributed numerous essays to newspapers attacking the administration's war program and Republican positions in New England.

In 1814 Webster also made his debut before the Supreme Court, arguing two prize cases at the February term. These were the St. Lawrence, 8 Cranch 434; the Grotius, 8 Cranch 456.

Washington Decr. 29. 1813

Dear E.

I arrived here last Evening, & here learned of the Portsmo. fire, & the consumption of my house. I have only time to say, that the safety of my family compensates the loss of the property. Mr. [Jeremiah] Mason urges me, that Mrs Webster may remain at his House till Spring; I think this will be best—except, perhaps a short visit, if the travelling should be good, into your quarter. I have not time to say more—but thought you wd. be glad to hear, that I am in possession of myself, after the knowledge of such a loss.

I am Yrs   D Webster

ALS. NhD. Published in *PC*, 1: 237.

TO ISAAC P. DAVIS

Jan 6. '14

Dr Sir

Please hand this to Ed: Centinel or of other Paper. Tell him to use it, in whole or in part, & alter it, in any respect, to his mind. My object is merely to alarm N.England at the project of *Conscription*, or *Compulsory draughts;* a measure which is certainly determined on at the White House.[1]

Our Town has met with another conflagration.[2] I heard not a syllable of it, till I reached here. I found a letter from my wife,[3] but so horrible was the general account, which the People about me gave, that it put my firmness to a severe test to open it. When I found nothing lost, but House & property, you may well imagine how much I felt relieved from distress.

You will be glad to learn that my houseless Family have found a good shelter for the Winter. Whether at Mr. Mason's, or with my friends in the Country, I do not yet know. They were offered an asylum at either place.

I had at first almost made up a Resolution to return immediately. Mrs. W. had anticipated such a resolution, & in her first letter advised agt. it. On the whole, considering how critical the times are here, I shall I believe stay thro the Winter.

The great news from Europe comes seasonably; at least to me. It enables one to forget, in some degree, his own misfortunes. We have all been in danger of worse evils than burnings, & exposed to a foe more merciless than all the elements. I trust Providence has delivered us.

Buonapartte's disasters produce a visible effect here. The Administration seems to be appalled. It seems, at present, to be suspending its war measures, & taking time to consider; & perhaps, also, to ascertain whether the voice of the Party is still for War. There are evident symptoms of schism in the Cabinet, & in the Party, in Congress. Some construe the dispatches to be *pacific;* others say they will bear no such construction. That is, those who are still for war, say there is nothing in the dispatches; those who begin to grow sick of it, affect to see new evidences of a pacific disposition on the part of England, in these dispatches, & in the speech of the P[rince] R[egent]. One of the leading Demo. Senators detained me half an hour, to hear his comment on the word "Reciprocity", in the P.R.'s speech. He thinks it a word, full of Peace, & hangs all his hopes on "Reciprocity". [James] Munroe will have it that the Dispatches are pacific; whence it is inferred, that his "thoughts are turned on Peace". In truth, his thoughts are turned principally on the next Election. [John] Armstrong can see nothing in the dispatches, which looks like sentiments of returning justice, in the minds of the British Ministry. He is still for trying the tug of War. Capt. *Hudi[b]ra[s]* doubts. The truth is, I suspect, that the dispatches are, in substance, just like the Speech— England is willing to treat, as she always has been. Madison has not yet determined, whether he had now better break off his French connexions, give up his War, & make peace with the best grace he can, or again rally his friends, & put forth all efforts to do something next Campaign. He is waiting to see which way the Party, generally, incline.

Munroe & Armstrong cannot go on long together. I have no doubt Armstrong will fall. Via.[4] Democratic Press. If any thing prevents, it will be the influence of [Henry] Clay, [Felix] Grundy, & the other lights of the West, who are supposed to be for More War, & for Armstrong.— Excuse a long letter; which, when begun, was meant only for an envelope; Make my respects to Mrs. D., & believe me, with esteem,

Yr's Tr   D. WEBSTER

Typed copy. NhHi. Original not found. Published in part in *PC,* 1: 238–239.

    1. DW's enclosed letter on "Conscription!" appeared in the *Columbian*

Centinel, January 15, 1814.
    2. "Great Fire" in Portsmouth.
    3. Letter not found.
    4. PC reads *Vide.*

TO EZEKIEL WEBSTER

Washington Jan. 30 [1814]

Dear E.

    I enclose you a few creatures called speeches.[1] One of them you will find I have corrected, in some of its printers errors, with my pen—please do the same to the rest before they go out of your hands. I shall send a few to your Townsmen—you will learn who, by looking at the Post Office —for I have not my list by me now, & so cannot say exactly who I shall send to you. Of those that come to your hands, give them, in my name, to those you think proper, Feds, or Demos.

The Speech is not exactly what it ought to be. I had not time. I had no intention of speaking till nine o'clock in the Morning, & delivered the thing about 2— I could make it better—but I dare say you think it would be easier to make a new one than to mend. It was well eno[ugh] recd at the time, & our side of the House said they would have it in this form. So much for Speeches.

What do you do with such a house full of women & children?—especially how do you make out to keep the House quiet, with those two black eyed, brown headed, chattering, romping cousins in it?—& more especially, with that one, which, tho' youngest, is yet biggest; but tho' biggest, I fear not best? As to him who sleeps in his borrowed cradle, & bears the loss of his own with so much moderation of temper, I trust he is born to be a Philosopher. To all these, together with their mothers, you must give my love—for I have not time today to write more than this letter.

To whatever projects for carrying on the War Govt. may adopt they will find obstacles. There will yet be much discussion, in both Houses. Some excellent speeches have been made in the Senate—especially one on the Non-Importation Bill by Mr. [Christopher] Gore. As to the prospect of Peace, my opinion is this. If the Administration can get an Army, they will still contend for Canada. If the high bounty will not obtain men, they will *certainly* try Conscription. If Buonapartte rises, they will rise—if he is kept down, & they can get no Army, they will have peace, if they can get it. Write me often—do you yet talk about the Election? Who are Candidates? &c &c. Yrs as ever   D. W.

Mrs. G. W.

I am sorry the Revd. Ephraim[2] has got our little white house, but we will find another. I hope you will do a great deal of visiting this winter— because it seems to be a leisure time. You must especially go & visit Mrs. [Samuel] Wood & Mr. [Ebenezer] Price[3] & Deacon [Enoch?] Gerrish &c— also all the Squire's[4] neighbors—as well as the Salisbury quality.

ALS. NhD. Published in *PC*, 1: 239–240.

1. Speech opposing "A Bill Making further provision for filling the ranks of the Regular Army, encouraging Enlistments, and authorising the Enlistments for longer periods of men whose terms of service are about to expire," printed in *Annals of Congress*, 13th Cong., 2nd sess., 1813–1814, pp. 940–951. DW's speech of January 14 was subsequently widely

reprinted in pamphlet form by presses in New Hampshire.

2. Not identified.

3. Née Eunice Bliss (1756–1850), daughter of Hezekiah Bliss of Leba-

non, Conn. Price (1771–1863) was a minister of the Congregational church in the Boscawen area.

4. Thomas W. Thompson's.

TO EZEKIEL WEBSTER

Washington Feb. 5 (Friday)
[1814]

Dr E.

I recd. yr's of the 23 yesterday— & G[race]'s of same date.[1] You may depend upon our discussing public subjects here, at least freely & with spirit—of the ability the public must judge. They are determined not to take up my Resolutions this session.[2] Of this I am certain. But on the loan Bill, we hope to get a blow at them. That Bill must go to a Committee of the whole—by the Rules— & the Previous Question cannot be called in Committee of the whole. [William] Gaston & [Thomas P.] Grosvenor are prepared to give great speeches on that subject. I do not think myself of trying again, unless my friends at the North should be of opinion that I can do better.

Mr. [Christopher] Gore's Speech[3]—a very good one—I shall be able to send you, in the course of a few days. On the Maryland Memorial[4] a very animated debate happened in both Houses. Mr. [Rufus] King came out, for the first time. You never heard such a Speaker. In strength, & dignity, & fire—in ease, in natural effect, & gesture as well as in matter —he is unequalled. He did not make a set speech— & did not expect to speak at all—but the Administration hands objected to Printing the Memorial. He made a few remarks on that point—some how, [William B.] Giles got into the debate, on the wrong side. I do not know how it happened—but one thing led to another till Mr. King came out in *plump* terms on the right of remonstrance & of resistance— he said it was a mere question of *prudence,* how far any State w[oul]d bear the present state of things &c &c.

Are you safe in y'r election? Pray be in season in your measures. Who is Councillor for Hills[borough]?—how does the New H[illsborough] Sheriff[5] manage? &c &c. Yrs   D. Webster

I wrote yesterday to G[race].[6] It gives me great pleasure to hear so good a character of a certain young Gentleman in your house. I trust, "he will one day do honor to the name of Pit[t]."

ALS. NhD. Published in *PC*, 1: 240–241.

1. Neither letter found.

2. The documents on DW's resolu-

tions had been submitted to the Committee on Foreign Relations, which had made its report. On January 3, 1814, DW proposed that the executive documents and the Foreign Relations committee report be referred again to that committee in order to get them before the House; his motion, however, was modified and the whole French Decree question was referred to Committee of the Whole (*Annals of Congress,* 13th Cong., 2nd sess.,

1813–1814, pp. 824–825).
3. On the prohibition of certain importations.
4. Memorial of the Maryland House of Delegates "on the awful condition of national affairs in general . . ."
5. Israel W. Kelly.
6. Letter not found.

TO [BENJAMIN J. GILBERT?]

Washington Feb. 8. 1814

Dear Sir,

I enclose you Mr [Christopher] Gores speech on the Non Importation Bill (additional). I think it a very good one. The object of the Bill was (& is) to prohibit all importations, from every quarter, of woolen & cotton goods, & rum. The Bill is now before our house.

We have just this moment learned that the President has nominated G. W. Campbell to be Secy of the Treasury—Richard Rush to be Atty General— & Albert Gallatin to be 5th Commissioner to Gottenberg! ! !

The War passion rages here yet, & the introduction of Campbell to the Cabinet is very unfavorable to Peace. He is the mere creature of [John] Armstrong, & is a great zealot for the War, & the conquest of Canada. I hope our good People will not be led away by the pretenses of love & desire of Peace in the Administration. If the President can get men— & money—& can reconcile the People of the Northern States to it—he will carry on the War, till he has made more attempts on the Canadian Provinces.

The People have nothing to do, but in every way, & especially by the elections, to express their abhorrence of the present war. I should be glad to hear from you, as often as you can find opportunity to write, especially in relation to your prospects of Election.

Yrs &c   D. Webster

ALS. DGU.

TO [?]

Washington Feb. 11 1814

Dear Sir,

I have not been unmindful of you, & more than once intended to write you, on various matters, but, as it happens in other cases, the tares of this world have sprung up & checked the wheat.

As to Massachusetts, her conduct produces an impression on *some*— but others disregard it. Here are Sam Dana,[1] Jeb Carlton,[2] Judge [Joseph] Story &c &c who represent that State as nearly equally divided in political sentiment, & that the present spirit of the Legislature is the effervescence of a heated, tho' small, & perhaps temporary majority. As to N. Hamp— letters from Judge [Clifton] Clagget[3] to [William Merchant] Richardson, & other letters from other parts of the State speak confidently of the election of Govr [William] Plumer![4]   These things, of course, very much diminish the fears of Administration, in regard to the state of things at the Eastward. After all, it is easy to see that there is great anxiety & alarm. By all I learn, it would seem very doubtful, what course public opinion is likely to take in New York. Their Election, of Members of Congress as well as of their own Legislature, takes place in April.

In N. Carolina, [William] Gaston thinks a very great change is working. His friends write him confidently, that if an Election were now to take place, that change would be apparent. But the Southern Federalists, you know, are themselves alarmed at every thing which looks like dissolution. The severance of the Union would give them over to be buffetted. Their wish is that N. England would be moderate, & reserve itself to act hereafter. If the War lasts, they are confident of being able to oust Democracy out of the Genl Government.

My own opinion is, that you ought, in N. E. to go no faster than the People drive you. Take care to carry your elections by strong Majorities; keep alive the public attention; convert the honest; silence the brawlers; let the War & the Embargo drive away from Democracy all men of any honor, principle, or property— &, in the end, if the Government will not relieve you from the evils of its oppression, act as the case shall require. In the mean time, forbear talking *big*—hold a cool but a determined & fixed resolution. They speak a good deal here of the scolding, blustering spirit of Massachusetts.

What do you think, of the ensuing Election in N.H.? Who are Candidates, for Senators, &c? Is the Judiciary Law, on the whole unpopular?[5] On all these points, I should be glad to hear from you.

You know, pretty well, the pleasures of a winter here. Every other day rain—every day, mud. Our business, to sit in our places. Our amusement; —to read the Newspapers. There is, however, controversy enough to keep the spirits alive, & we have some good speaking. It seems to be a talking season. The loan Bill is now under discussion, & I suppose will bring up all the topics of the War. [Timothy] Pitkin & [Daniel] Sheffey spoke at length yesterday, against [John W.] Eppes estimate of the Ways & Means, & on the general subject. Gaston, [Thomas P.] Grosvenor & others, I believe mean to be heard. As to my old matter of the French Decrees, the Adm[inistratio]n folks do not mean to let them be called up. Whether our men will think it best to give Munroe a dart, on the present discussion I do not know.

Great fears are entertained about the Loan—never so great before. The general opinion is, it will not go. The opinion of peace is not so favorable as it was, & all the Banks, from N. York Southward are extremely pressed. The idea of getting up a National Bank, in this District, is agitated. It wd. be a very foolish thing—of no use if it were granted—it probably will not prevail. You have seen the new nominations. [George W.] Campbell is the creature of [John] Armstrong. His accession to the Cabinet is not omenous of Peace. Armstrong has silenced the clamor agt. him—whether they have made a bargain, satisfactory to all parties, about the next Presidency, or merely hushed up their differences, out of present necessity, is not known. Armstrong has had no expectation of Peace, from the Gottenberg Mission—indeed he is said to ridicule the idea. Your friend [clipped] is quite inexcusable for not writing to you, as one of his immediate Constituents. But no wonder. He wont speak— & writing costs more labor than speaking. He is as dull as ever—the same sad, melancholy dog!— It gives half the House the horrors to look at him! I shall remind him of his duty, & ask him to remember his friends.

Make my respects to [clipped] and Mr [clipped] & believe [me] to be, as I am,

Yrs with esteem   D. Webster

ALS. NjP.

1. Samuel Dana (1767–1835), lawyer and congressman from Massachusetts.

2. Not identified.

3. A native of Hillsborough County and judge of the Superior Court of New Hampshire from 1812 to 1813.

4. John Taylor Gilman, the Federalist candidate, was elected governor instead of William Plumer.

5. The act, establishing a Supreme Judicial Court, and Circuit Court of Common Pleas, was approved on June 24, 1813.

TO [NATHANIEL APPLETON HAVEN?]

[Feb. 28, 1814?]

Dear Sir,

If the enclosed, or any part of it, will do any good, at any meeting, &c. you may use it—but do not put into the Paper.

Granger's Affair does in truth make some folks quite raving. G. says he will die a hard death. Yrs   D.W.

ENCLOSURE TO [ISAAC P. DAVIS?]

Washington Feb. 28. 1814

Dear Sir,

I have observed that several of the Eastern Prints are filled with rumors of an Armistice, & a speedy Peace. The circulation of these rumors must be intended only to deceive. There is not the least foundation for them.

No man here, of any party, expects an Armistice, or a speedy Peace. The Government manifests no disposition for an Armistice, & its whole conduct shows that no peace is expected. The greatest exertions are using to press the recruiting service, & fill up the Army to sixty three thousand men. Large sums of bounty money have been sent to all the principal Towns, to the recruiting Officers. Among other places, Ten Thousand dollars, to my knowledge, have been sent to Portsmouth. It is not possible Government could waste so much money, & be preparing to waste so much blood, if they either intended or expected Peace. The truth, is Mr. Madison & the Western People will carry on the War, tho' it should be five years, till they get Canada, Quebec & all, unless the People, by their strong disapprobation, oblige them to make Peace. Members of Congress have expressed the foregoing determination, in so many words. We have just heard that the Camp at French Mills is broken up. It may probably be owing, among other things, to the sickliness of the troops. The public have never known the extent of that evil, the last Campaign. A General Officer, of high character, has told me within three days, that two thousand men found their graves last fall at Sackets Harbor alone!!![1]

Mr. [Gideon] Granger's removal[2] creates a good deal of excitement. Every body asks *why* he is dismissed. The New England Democrats are quite loud in their disapprobation. Among others Genl. [Joseph B.] Varnum & Mr. [Dudley] Chase,[3] of Vermont, have expressed themselves very decidedly. The real truth is, Mr. Granger was opposed to the President in some particulars. He did not altogether approve of the policy of this war. He was therefore dismissed—for as the war is yet to go on, the President seems resolved to have nobody near him who is not zealous for it. There are other New England Republicans, who will soon be removed. I could now point out some, by name, against whom round Robins have been signed by the hottest warhawks & sent to the President. They will follow Granger. I trust the People of New England, throwing aside party distinctions, will ere long unite to save themselves. Yrs &c   D. Webster.

Since I wrote you last,[4] we have nothing new about Conscription. The high bounty will be first tried. If that fails, Col [George Michael] Troup says the other method must be resorted to.

ALS. NhD.

1. It is perhaps indicative of the emotional nature of the opposition to the war that any general officer could have offered such a preposterous figure—or that the usually level-headed Webster could have accepted it. The American deaths in the battle of Sackett's Harbor were in fact no more than fifty. American army battle deaths for the entire war did not reach 2,000. *Army Almanac, 1950,* 411.

2. Gideon Granger, Jefferson's Postmaster General continued in that position by President Madison, had been recently ousted from his post as the result of a patronage dispute over

the appointment of postmaster in Philadelphia. Many administration opponents argued that his dismissal came because of his opposition to the war. On the Granger affair, see Irving Brant, *James Madison: Commander in Chief, 1812–1836* (Indianapolis, 1961), pp. 243–245.

3. Chase (1771–1846; Dartmouth 1791), Randolph lawyer, elected to the United States Senate in 1813. On November 3, 1817, he resigned his Senate seat to become chief justice of the Supreme Court of Vermont.

4. See DW to Isaac P. Davis, January 6, 1814, above.

TO EZEKIEL WEBSTER

Washington Mar 28 1814

Dear E.

I send you today [Daniel] Sheffey's speech. You will at least like its length & substance. We are yet to have one or two more in Pamphlet form, which I will endeavor to obtain & send. In relation to the offer made by England to renew Jay's Treaty, I intend to see, & collect, & carry home what evidence there is on the point.[1] The News brought by the "rambler" has just arrived here—we have not had time to consider it. It is vast & momentous.

Most of the subjects intended to be acted upon this session are thro. One, of great importance, has lately been started—viz. another Bank project. The *loan will fail*, unless they can help it on by a Bank. The Nat. Intelligencer says it is *necessary*— & seems to intimate that consideration ought to supersede *constitutional* scruples. Of course, I cannot desert my post here, while so important a project is in agitation. If this should go by, I may, & think I shall, be at your Hopkinton Court. I have written the Chief Jus[tice] [Jeremiah Smith][2] to to send Judge [Caleb] E[llis] to *Haverhill*. In the Sup. Court I showed myself once, twice, or thrice. In one case I charged a N. Yorker 300 Dls— & in two other cases, 100 Ds each. So much for prize causes &c. There is no man in the Court, that strikes one like Marshall. He is a plain man, looking very much like Col Adams,[3] & about 3 inches taller. I never have seen a man of whose intellect I had a higher opinion.

The Court adjourned about 2 weeks ago. The Yazoo Bill is thro—passed by 8 maj:—It excited a great deal of feeling. All the Feds supported the Bill, & some of the Demo's. The Georgians, & some Virginians & Carolinians opposed it with great heat. [Thomas J.] Oakley made the principal speech, of the Feds, in its support. Our policy was to get the Demo's support of it. [James] Clark, of Kentucky, a pretty clever fellow, made a handsome speech in support of it.

[Jeremiah] Mason is growing to be a great man. He ranks, in the Senate, *I* think, next to [Rufus] King & [Christopher] Gore. He has made some very excellent speeches.

I give you joy of the Election. We had here a great deal of distress about it, & could not have stood a defeat.⁴ You give an enormous vote; nearly 40,000. I do not hear who *rides* for Boscawen, but I suppose some of the Old School. Your vote in B was a glorious one, but nothing gave me more pleasure than the regeneration of Salisbury. I hope that Town may be kept right hereafter. I have sent [William] Gaston's speech to Capt Benj: Pettingail,⁵ who I hear is one of us—if not, it will do him no hurt. I think I shall send a speech, or something to Caleb Knight. These speeches are a little too much like *treatises*. Yr's as ever   D.W.

Give my love to all your numerous family. I have today had a letter, inclosing other letters, enclosing locks &c.⁶

ALS. NhD. Published in *PC*, 1: 243–244.

1. See DW to John Kelly [c. August 12, 1814], below, and essay signed by "Cato" in the *Concord Gazette*, August 16, 1812.

2. Letter not found.

3. Not identified.

4. New Hampshire voters had once again elected John Taylor Gilman, Federalist, governor.

5. Pettingail (1758–1834), Revolutionary War veteran and state legislator from Salisbury.

6. Letters not found.

TO MOSES PAUL PAYSON

[June 20, 1814]
Portsmouth. Monday morn.

Dear Sir,

We heard yesterday that [Elijah] Hall was elected Counsellor in Convention, & we are overwhelmed with mortification. If a Federal Legislature has done this, I shall cease to have faith in men. We know no particulars. I never have seen so much indignation expressed on any occasion as is manifested here. If this choice was effected by the infidelity of a few, they ought to be published immediately, that general odium may have some individuals to rest upon, & not attach to the whole. What little Federalism there is in this town is certainly *extinct*, unless some explanation can be given, of this most strange transaction.¹

After the pains & expense to which our people submitted to reject the Portsmouth votes,—they feel *personally* ill-treated. They think too, that all confidence among ourselves, as a party is destroyed—above all, a Federal Legislature that can so soon forget Josiah Sanborn—what shall I say of it? For Mercy's sake give us some consolation. I can give no answers to the questions put me at every corner of the street. Yrs.

D. Webster

Copy. NhHi. Published in Van Tyne, p. 29.

1. With allegations of a fraudulent election in Portsmouth, the legislature had rejected the votes of the town and proceeded to elect Hall, reportedly a

Democrat, instead of Josiah Sanborn, the Federalist candidate. On the Portsmouth election and the legislative proceedings, see the Portsmouth *Oracle*, June 18, 1814. Federalist response to Hall's election appears in the *Oracle* of June 25.

TO JOHN KELLY

[c. Aug 12, 1814]

Dr. Sir,

The truth relative to the offer of England to renew Jay's treaty is as stated in the enclosed, which I have drawn up in the form of a paragraph for your Paper.[1] The Statement is made on Mr. [Rufus] K[ing]'s authority. You may add, if you think fit, that it was made on "good authority." I think my Brother Ezekiel has a copy of the Treaty negotiated by Munroe; & refused by Jefferson.

Yrs   D. W.

ALS. NhExP. John Kelly (1786–1860; Dartmouth 1804) was a lawyer who at this time edited the *Concord Gazette*.

1. In an attempt to replace the Jay Treaty of 1794, James Monroe and William Pinkney had negotiated and signed a new Anglo-American accord on December 3, 1806. President Jefferson, however, subsequently rejected the treaty since it ignored the controversial issue of impressment. In his "paragraph" in the *Concord Gazette* of August 16, 1814, Webster indicted the Jefferson administration for its failure to approve the treaty and called for new leadership in Washington. The editorial was two-pronged: it was designed to embarrass the Anti-Federalists of New Hampshire and to boost his and other Federalists' chances in the canvass.

Throughout his long career, Webster's position as an anti-administration, peace politician during the War of 1812 plagued him. He faced repeated accusations that he was an active supporter of, if not participant in, the disunion movement of the Hartford Convention; and just as often he denied any association, always appealing to his role as chairman of the Portsmouth Committee of Defense, an announcement of which appears below. Nonetheless, he never overcame the taint of the charges, since some of his political opponents had access to several of the following documents containing his comments on the Hartford Convention.

NOTICE OF PORTSMOUTH COMMITTEE OF DEFENCE

Saturday, Sept. 10, 1814.

ATTENTION!

The Committee of Defence[1] hereby request all the Exempts, within the first regiment, to assemble, in pursuance of the Governor's Orders, on the Parade, in Portsmouth, on Monday Morning next, at 9 o'clock;—as well those who are not yet organized into Companies, as those who are; —every man to bring such arms as he has in his possession, to the end that there may be then a perfect organization of the exempts.

DANIEL WEBSTER,
For the Committee

Printed D. NhHi.

1. On the activities of the Committee, see also Committee for the Defense of Portsmouth (John Goddard,

Jeremiah Mason, and DW) to John Taylor Gilman, September 3, 1814, mDWs.

TO WILLIAM SULLIVAN

Washington Octr. 17 [1814]

Dear Sir,

We are not a little disappointed today, in finding that your proposed Convention is put off till next *August*.[1] What can be the reason of so much delay? You perceive now that there is no hope of Peace. I am perfectly confident you will see in 3 months, that the Govt could not, if it would, protect N England. Indeed its inability so to do is already sufficiently manifest. Why then not prepare to defend yourselves next Campaign?

Our New England People like the Report[2] much. They think it suited to the occasion. And altho' southern Federalists would be glad that N. E. should suffer patiently, until the south is also brought to her senses by suffering, yet I hear no complaint of Mass. The Election in Philadelphia & its neighborhood has cheered us a little—but the probable loss of New Jersey has thrown us again into the glooms.

I do not perceive any favorable change in the views or temper of Administration. They are doubtless in a considerable degree *frightened;* but still they act as if they would go on in the old way. A thick & gross delusion seems to be upon them all, & whoever is doomed to be in Congress is doomed also to hear a repitition of the same folly and nonsense, which have prevailed there so long.

That the States must defend themselves, or be undefended is clear with me—and the sooner they prepare themselves the better.

Yours as ever   D. Webster

P.S. The 20$ you may remit me here in a Boston Bill.

ALS. Watertown Library, Watertown, Conn.

1. There was considerable misunderstanding among politicians in Washington on the decision in Massachusetts for an antiwar convention in

New England. Webster himself had arrived in Washington on October 14, and had apparently only heard rumors of the proceedings of the special session of the Massachusetts legislature which met on October 5. In a second letter to Sullivan on the same day (see below), DW reports that the misunderstanding about the date of the convention had been cleared up. The announcement of the date of the Hartford Convention (December 15) appeared in the *Columbian Centinel,* October 15, 1814.

2. "Otis's Report," adopted by the Massachusetts Senate on October 12 and by the House on October 16. The Report appeared in the *Centinel* of October 12.

TO WILLIAM SULLIVAN

Washington Oct. 17. 1814—

Dear Sir,

The papers recd today have put us right, about the time of your proposed [Hartford] Convention.

We this morning recd the communication of [Alexander J.] Dallas, relative to finances. He differs in some things from [John W.] Eppes. He proposes to increase the land tax 100 pr ct, & most of the present internal duties in the same ratio;— & to lay 25 cts pr gallon on *whiskey,* in addition to the present tax on stills. But his great hobby is a Bank, of 50 millions—6 millions specie—44 millions stocks—Govt. to own 2 fifths—15 directors—President to appoint 5— & to appoint the President—&c &c.

I shall send you the Instructions to our ministers which have been published. You perceive that certain parts are *kept secret.* You will see enough, I think, to be of my opinion, that the British have completely *outgeneralled us.*

Some of our good friends here are fearful that the Federalists in the Bay State are not sufficiently attentive to the ensuing Election for members of Congress. In whatever event, it would seem to be very important to make the Federalists as numerous as possible. Mr. [John] Wilson[1] has just arrived. I perceive he is a little apprehensive that no measures are taking in his District to secure the election of a Federalist in that District. Would it not be very well for your Committee to write immediately to the active men in that District on that subject. It would be excessively disagreeable to have any Jacobins from Massachusetts. We hope also that Mr S[amuel] Dana[2] may be excused from attendance here hereafter. Pardon me for calling your attention, & that of your friends to this subject.

Mr. [John] Randolph has been this way & has gone Northward—I did not see him. I understood he was going to Boston; others say to Philadelphia only. It is now confidently said he will be in the next Congress— & that Eppes will decline the contest.

I shall be very glad to hear from you often. Yrs   D. Webster

ALS. MHi. Published in Van Tyne, pp. 50–51.

1. Wilson (1777–1848), lawyer and congressman from Belfast, Maine

(then a district of Massachusetts).

2. Dana (1767–1835), a Democrat who had been elected to Congress to fill the seat vacated by William M. Richardson's resignation. A lawyer, he had previously served in the Massachusetts House of Representatives and Senate.

In summarizing his October 24 speech in Congress on the question of increasing the direct taxes, the Washington National Intelligencer *of October 25 reported that Webster "explained at considerable length the motives and feelings with what he should vote for this tax, and for the taxes generally. These motives and feelings were of a character wholly adverse to the present administration of the government." Instead of announcing that he would vote for the taxes, Webster had remarked (as given in the printed version of the speech) that "he should not obstruct; he should only hold himself at liberty not to approve, without reason, the course pursued . . . He should not give his vote for the measures proposed, either by way of expressing his approbation of the past, or his expectations of the future." On Thursday, October 27, a clarification of his position and his speech (probably written by Webster himself, as suggested above), appeared in the* Intelligencer. *It was these events which prompted the following letter to Nathan Hale.*

TO NATHAN HALE

[Oct. 25, 1814]

Dear Sir,

I am totally misrepresented in the Intelligencer of this Day. For God's sake let nobody imagine that I am about to vote for the Taxes. Do me the favor to see that no such notice is given of my remarks if published in Boston. I shall publish my objections on *Thursday*.

ALS. MHi.

Still unsure of the position he should take on taxes, Webster had asked Ezekiel for his views on October 20. Ezekiel's reply follows:

FROM EZEKIEL WEBSTER

Oct 29th. 1814

Dear Daniel,

I received yours of the 20th,[1] this morning, and am very glad to hear that you are at your post. The present will be a session of very arduous and difficult duties, and of very great responsibility. On the subject of the taxes my opinion corresponds with yours. Let them have the whiskey tax. In case any money is to be voted the administration the tax on land is perhaps the most equitable. It will bear with a more just and even hand upon the southern and eastern states. The internal taxes perfect the system of "domiciliary vexation." If my hat, my boots my shoes, my horse my chaise, saddle and bridle &c &c are to be taxed, what will be exempted? Most of these taxes, I apprehend will operate very injuriously upon New England. For instance the tax upon spindles in cotton & woolen Factories. I apprehend more than ¾ of these establishments are this side the Potomac. Woolen cloths are almost altogether of N England consumption. Besides I think the faith of the Government is some what pledged not to tax these establishments. It has always professed its desire to encourage them. The restrictive system depriving us of all importations, they are in some degree very necessary to us. The principal part of the cotton clothes worn in this quarter are of our own manufacture. Many factories with the high price of cotton, and under this tax would be obliged to cease their operation.

The proposed tax on leather would likewise be unequal in its operation. It requires not much argument to prove that the same population in N Hampshire have occasion for much more leather, than in Georgia.

Of $100,000 proposed to be raised on playing cards, I imagine Virginia will pay her proportion. It is right they should have this tax. Let Gamblers be made to contribute to the support of this war, which was declared by men of no better principles than themselves.

I am not pleased with the idea of taxing the "process of law". Let justice be administered *freely*. No man ought to be compelled to pay a tax in order to have his right.

There are but a very few of the taxes that I should vote for. I am not sure that I should vote for any, till the administration should change its measures. For what purpose should you put men or money into their hands? You voted last session men and they have been marched to Canada, you voted money & what portion of it has been expended in defending our maratime frontier? With all the men & money asked for how have they defended the Capitol? It is worthy of remark that the defence of the Capitol, under the eye of the administration, and all its officers is more disgracefull than any event of the war. It discovers more imbecillity, & more cowardice. Gen. [William] Hull's surrender was a triumph to it.

I am confident that the people would support almost any attack that should be made on the administration, especially any which should expose their imbecility, and their incompetency to fill their offices. The language towards them ought to be dignified, but at the same time it ought to be plain and intelligible.

They have as many vulnerable points, as their assailants could wish, & I want to see them goaded to the very quick.

It would be better to lash them "naked through the land" for bringing us into these difficulties, than to unite with them to plunge us into still greater. Reformation ought to come from them. It was told them war would ensue from their restrictive system. The progress and events of the war were likewise foretold—but they still persisted in their measures —and they now acknowledge no errors, nor change any of their measures. Ought they to ask for the support of the opposition in this state of things—no. They ought not to ask it, & they *ought not to have it*. Every day demonstrates their incapacity and the folly of their measures, & furnishes the best evidence for not supporting them. Had not any of the predictions of the opposition been fulfilled, they might with some plausibility expect their support.

I hope an occasion will soon happen when some of your people can speak their minds of them. I trust it will be done fearlessly.

I feel very anxious that Judge [Timothy] Farrar should assent to be a Candidate. You proposed to address a letter to him and signed by all our delegation in both branches. I think it ought to be done, immediately.

My Folks are all well. With affection &c Yours   E Webster

ALS. NhD. Published in Van Tyne, pp.   1. See mDW 1711.
52–54.

TO [TIMOTHY FARRAR, JR.?]

Oct 30 1814

Dear Sir,

It is perhaps not one of our smallest difficulties at this time to keep public opinion—or *Federal* opinion right, on political subjects. The first impression made on many by the Despatches,[1] was very incorrect— & pains ought to be taken in every way to get back the minds of the People to a just view of the case. If the terms of England are inadmissible in their present form they are certainly capable of *modification*. At any rate, Federalists ought not to commit themselves on this subject. You have seen what trouble sprang up here by a little haste & inadvertence. It takes time to cure the evil, but I think we shall cure it. Every day diminishes the number of those, who were disposed to join the *war cry*, & *unite* under Madison, tho' protesting all the while against his capacity. Some half dozen Federalists in our house may perhaps vote for the Taxes —but I *now* think they will give their reasons in a style, which shall take away all bad consequences from their votes—at least I hope so. After a good deal of reflection I adopted the course indicated by my remarks[2]— a fuller tone of opposition would have better suited my own feelings, but I did not wish to jostle agt. those, who had felt it their duty to take a different course. In some States—especially Maryland—they are *not able* to defend themselves—they are obliged to look to the Genl. Govt. The popular ground there is—give the Govt. money—take away all excuses— & call on it to defend us. New York, with a Veteran Army on her frontiers, & threatened with a visit from L[or]d [Rowland] Hill[3] to her Capital, feels something of the same sentiment. For these, & many other reasons I thought it necessary to touch lightly— & to leave the way open for Federalists to vote either way, without ceasing to be Federalists. How this will suit you in N. E. I do not know—but I could think of no better course. On the dispatches, my notion is not to commit ourselves at all, by giving any opinion.

I understand Mr. Monroe will send down Exchequer Bills to pay your Militia. I believe he has said he should write immediately to Gov. [John Taylor] Gilman to that effect— & telling him also that he had not one cent of money.

How does the [Hartford] *Convention* suit N. H. Federalists? Should you send Delegates, if the Legislature were together? What is the present tone of feeling among you? How do you like the taxes? How do you like the conscription?

I rely on you & Mr. [John] G[oddard?] to keep the People well informed —I mean those of them who read the Oracle. Let me hear from you. Yrs
D. Webster

ALS. NhD.

1. DW was probably referring to the communications received from the United States envoy and his efforts to negotiate peace with Great Britain. President Madison had transmitted the communications to the House and Senate on October 10.

2. On the question of direct taxes, DW had indicated that he would neither vote for the measures proposed nor "obstruct" their passage (*Annals of Congress*, 13th Cong., 3rd sess., 1813–1814, pp. 464–465).

3. Sir Rowland Hill, whom the British had originally intended to lead the land forces at New Orleans but who instead remained in Europe because of conditions there.

TO EZEKIEL WEBSTER

Oct 30 1814

Dear E—

I shall occasionally enclose you the Telegraph—perhaps pretty regularly—because it is a paper I receive, & because I can as well do it as not. If you find nothing in it worth reading, still the trouble of looking into it long enough to find that out will not be great.

We have as yet done little. The taxes are before us. I have marked out my course respecting them— & shall vote for nothing but the Whiskey Tax. This I am anxious to have laid. It will stop distillation in New England;—a practice which is drawing upon our sources of life, & rendering us far less independent than we otherwise should be upon others for *bread*. A few of our best Federalists feel an inclination to vote *for* the Taxes—owing to circumstances, & the particular state of public opinion in their Districts. A great majority of us shall however probably hold back.

The terms offered by England struck our folks differently at first, from what they do on reflection. For my part, I expected no better; so feeble has the Govt. shewn itself, & so little able to carry on the War successfully.

We have a plan for a Conscription. I think I have sent you its out lines. The Bill is drawn principally on Mr Monroe's *first plan*.[1] Of course, we shall oppose such usurpation all we can.

I should like to hear from you, respecting what is the present tone of public sentiment among you? What do Federalists think we ought to do here? Yrs   D. W.

ALS. NhD. Published in part in *PC*, 1: 245–246.

1. The first of several conscription plans submitted by Secretary of War Monroe, and the plan incorporated into the House bill, is thus summarized in the *Annals of Congress*, 13th Cong., 3rd Sess., 1814–1815, p. 482: "This bill proposes to provide for the division of the whole free male population of the United States, by the assessors, into classes of twenty-five men each; each class to be compelled, under a penalty of —— hundred dollars, to furnish, within —— days after the classification aforesaid, an able-bodied recruit for the service of the United States. The bill is of some length, and contains very full provisions for carrying itself into effect."

TO EZEKIEL WEBSTER

Washington Nov. 21 [1814]

Dear E.

At present we are engaged about a Bank. The project brought in by the new Secretary of the Treasury [Alexander J. Dallas] was calculated only for the benefit of the holders of the stock created since the War. The assessments on the shares were to be paid in, in such stock principally, at par. It being now much depreciated, this was giving its proprietors a great boon. After some days discussion, this plan was abolished, & a new one is now before us. This is, that every share shall be paid for, by the Subscribers, as follows viz one tenth in gold or silver, & nine tenths in Treasury notes—whole Capital to be fifty millions. If this plan succeeds, the capital of the Bank when all paid in, will consist of 45 millions Treasury notes & 5 millions specie. These Treasury notes the Govt. is to issue, in payment of its debts, & it is expected that they will be received, & even bought up, by those who wish to become Stockholders in the Bank. These Treasury notes, after getting into the Bank in this way, are to be turned into Government stock, bearing an interest of 6 pr cent, & payable at the pleasure of Govt. so that the Capital, will then be 45 millions *stock,* & 5 millions specie.

In the present plan all Presidential interference in chusing Directors &c & all obligation to lend the Govt. money is struck out. Federalists have generally voted for the Amendment, in preference to the first plan—but they are pretty indifferent about any Bank.

Mr. [Jeremiah] Mason's Speech[1] is published. It was well received, & is a solid argument.

We cannot learn whether the Conscription will be brought up, on Monroe's plan, in this House. Indeed the party are all in a swamp— & I should not be surprised at any thing's taking place—even the resignation of every one of Mr. Madison's ministers at any day. There is an utter want of confidence in Madison, & his advisers, on all sides. Yrs   D.W.

ALS. NhD. Published in *PC,* I, 247.   For Mason's speech, see *Annals of*
    1. On the bill making further provi-   *Congress,* 13th Cong., 3rd sess., 1814–
sion for filling the ranks of the army.   1815, pp. 77–91.

TO EZEKIEL WEBSTER

Washington Novr. 29. 1814

Dear E.

The man in the patent office is searching to see whether Messrs Gerrishes invention is new. As soon as he finds out, I will let you know.

When Mr. Quimby[1] died he owed me forty dollars, borrowed money. I have no note *that would change the nature of the debt.* If you can secure it, do it.

Sue Theophilus Sanborn,[2] if you think best.

We are here on the Eve' of great events. I expect a blow up soon. My opinion is, that within sixty days Govt. will cease to pay even Secretaries, Clerks, & Members of Congress. This I expect— & when it comes we are wound up.

Every thing is in confusion here. [John W.] Eppes chasing [Alexander J.] Dallas — Dallas chasing every body. The Bank bill finally lost—104— to 49—after a day of the most tumultuous proceedings I ever saw. The conscription has not come up—if it does it will cause a storm such as was never witnessed here.

In short, if Peace does not come this winter, the Govt. will die in its own weakness.

I have recd several letters, especially from Cheshire, relative to Governor & wishing to know what I thought of nominating [Jeremiah] *Mason.* What do you think of it? Would it be popular—decidedly so? My own opinion is he would not *refuse,* if there should be a meeting of Delegates from all the Counties who should agree on him. This *you may take for granted*—but you must not intimate that you have any particular authority for saying so. But who would be Senator? I cannot agree to [George B.] Upham, & if I thought that would be the consequence, I would certainly oppose Mr. M's nomination for Govr—because it may yet happen that the place of Senator may call for a man of firmness & decis[ion.] If we were sure of [Roger] Vose, [John C.?] Cha[mberlain] W. H. Woodward or [Moses P.] Payson, [for] Senator, I should be very m[uch] [in]clined to support Mason for Governor. Write me fully [on] this. In the mean time, [make] no haste to nominate any body. We shall know many things by Jany 15 which we do not know now. Yrs   D. *Webster*

ALS. NhD. Published in Van Tyne,   1. Not identified.
p. 55.   2. Not identified.

TO EZEKIEL WEBSTER

Washington Dec. 22 [1814]
Dear E.

We have done nothing here lately except Taxes. They have all passed this House except the land tax, of 6 millions, (last year 3) which will be read the third time today. [William B.] Giles' Militia Draft Bill, which was altered in this House, so as to reduce the term from *two* years to *one*. The Senate have voted to *disagree* to the amendment. A conference will ensue, & the Senate will in the end probably recede from their disagreeing vote. This Bill, as you will see, cannot be carried into effect, if the State Governments do not lend their aid to it. Of course, it will be a dead letter in New England. Indeed the Bill is as weak and ridiculous, as it is wicked & violent. On a motion to strike out the first Section of this Bill, & on a motion to postpone indefinitely the usual manner of moving to reject a measure, *we made a [few] speeches*—[Richard] Stockton, [Thomas P.] Grosvenor, [Zebulon R.] Sh[i]pherd, [Artemas] Ward [Jr.],¹ [Morris Smith] Miller, &c &c &c. Millers & Stocktons are in the press—I shall send you sundry copies of each. *Mine* I have written out—but upon the most wise reflection, I have laid it up in the drawer. It will not, in my opinion, answer the expectation of those who heard it—and therefore I shall not publish it at present. Perhaps during the Session, we shall have Conscription up in a worse form, tho' I believe the party are a good deal frighted at it.²

We are expecting every day to hear from N. Orleans. It seems certain that the English have sent an Expedition thither. On its result perhaps the question of Peace may depend.

The people must look for protection to the *State Govts*. This Govt. cannot aid them—or will not—or both.

Give my love & duty to our mother, & my love to your family. I intend coming home in Feby.

As to Govr. let the People have their choice—strengthen the State Government as much as possible—especially see if something cannot be done for the Council. Yrs   D. W.

ALS. NhD. Published in *PC*, 1: 248.

1. Ward (1762–1847; Harvard 1783), lawyer and Federalist representative from Massachusetts.

2. On Dec. 9, DW spoke in the House of Representatives on the Conscription Bill. The *Annals of Congress*, 13th Cong., 3rd sess., 1814–1815, p. 800, simply recorded that DW spoke. See mDW 1747 and Van Tyne, pp. 56–58, for his remarks on the Conscription Bill.

The Treaty of Ghent, ending hostilities between the United States and Great Britain, had been signed on December 24, 1814; but Americans, unaware of the treaty until mid-February, were still at war, and many feared that the United States was on the verge of collapse. Financial distress, military reverses, and the sacking of Washington in August had considerably weakened the nation's war efforts. Rumors of British forces collecting at New Orleans and elsewhere discredited the predictions of an early peace, and so did the administration supporters' efforts to pass conscription and tax laws and to create a national bank. Through all the efforts to finance and to wage the war, Webster continued his selective opposition.

TO EZEKIEL WEBSTER

Jan 9. [1815]

Dear E,

As Conscription has gone by, for the present at least, I thought you might like to see the several documents. I send you Monroes letter[1]— [William B.] Giles' bill[2]— & the bill reported by our Military Com[mitt]ee.

The Bank bill has passed our House, in a form very much amended. It will now be harmless, as we think. We had a hard task to prevent its passing in its worst shape.

We hear that the British are near New Orleans. As that place is likely to become the theatre of interesting operations I shall try to send you a map &c.

I have no doubt the British will take it—if so, we get no peace.

I hear you talk of Mr [Benjamin?] West for Govr. If he will accept, & will be acceptable, it will do well. He would make an excellent Govr. I should think Cheshire would give him a great vote.

The taxes have mostly past. They are enormous. The Govt. put off the necessary work so long, that they have been obliged to lay more than I think the People can pay. I have no belief they can be collected.

Mr [Rufus] King is getting a good deal of popularity for having moved the postponement of Giles Bill—it was accidental—unpremeditated— & there was no debate. After we passed the Bill with amendts. it was handed about several days from house to house on account of the disagreeing votes relative to the amendments. Being one day before the Senate, & it being known that public sentiment had *terrified* the vehement Senators, Mr. K. made the motion—some members happened to be out—it was immediately put & carried.

Mr. [Christopher] Gore has recently made a very great speech. I understand it is to be published— & shall send it to you. I know not whether occasion will offer for general discussion in our House soon—but expect it before we go. We shall take up the investigating Report one of these days, & talk over the Bladensburg business.[3]

Give my love to mother & your family. Yrs   D. W.

ALS. NhD. Published in *PC*, 1: 249.

1. Monroe to William B. Giles, October 26, 1814, in *American State Papers: Military Affairs*, 3: 518–519.

2. Bill for "making further provision for filling the ranks of the Army."

3. On October 19, 1814, Webster was named to a congressional committee to investigate the burning of Washington by the British. Dissenting from the majority report of that special committee, Webster declared before Congress that it covered up "in a mass of prolixity and detail what he considered a most disgraceful transaction" (*Annals of Congress*, 13th Cong., 3rd sess., 1814–1815, p. 690; *National Intelligencer*, December 4, 1814).

TO [WILLIAM F. ROWLAND?]

Washington Jan 11 1815

Revd. Sir,

I have recd yours of the 3rd enclosing a Petition from yourself & others,[1] which I shall very cheerfully present. Very many similar petitions have been presented at this session, & are referred to the Postmaster General. There seems to be a strong inclination among many members of Congress to do something on the subject of these Petitions, but whether any measures will be adopted at the present session I am doubtful.

I wish, Sir, it were in my power to give you such a view of our public affairs, as would inspire the hope of peace & prosperity. But it is not. I am fearful the day of peace is still distant. We can hardly see, on the face of the correspondence at Ghent, any thing very important in difference between the parties; &, if we looked no further, we might hope that the negotiation would come to an amicable conclusion. But England, in the mean time, is reinforcing her armies & navies, & incurring great expense in fitting out expeditions against this Country. This looks as if she did not expect peace. We have heard, that the British forces have shown themselves near New Orleans, & we are very fearful the next news will be that that City is in their hands. If so, it cannot but be a great obstacle to peace. We do not exactly know the temper of the Spanish Court at present, relative to our conduct respecting Louisiana & the Floridas; but there is reason to fear it is not very pacific. The closest connexion exists of course between England & Spain. There is reason to apprehend, therefore, that some arrangement has been made between them, ceding Florida to Spain [England];—if so the quarrel about the division line between West Florida & Louisiana will probably be a serious obstacle to peace. *We* say (I mean our Government) that Louisiana extends East to the River Perdido. *Spain* says it stops at the Mississippi. *We* are in actual possession of the disputed territory. Our Government entered upon it, in the fall of 1809—when Spain was in no condition to assert her claim by force. If she has now ceded the territory to England, the latter power will doubtless contend for the boundaries which Spain has always insisted on as the true boundaries.[2]

On the whole, affairs in that quarter are very far from wearing a promising appearance.

Most of the tax bills are passed. The taxes are high; higher, I almost fear, than the People *can* pay, without commerce. The land tax is raised from 3 to 6 millions— & it is to continue till the war debt is paid, or other Revenue of equal amount substituted. Almost every thing is taxed which can be thought of. I lent a helping hand to the tax on domestic distilled spirits. This tax is so high that I am in hopes the practice of distillation will in a great measure cease in New England.

The Conscription Bill, as you will have seen, finally failed in the Senate. I believe some of its friends had become frighted.

For many weeks Congress has been engaged on a National Bank. The plan seems to be to make such a Bank if it is possible, as shall be able to furnish money to Govt. This is found difficult. I take the liberty of sending you, in the paper, some observations of mine on this subject, which may serve to give you a general idea of what is contemplated.

We recd yesterday the proceedings of the Hartford Convention. They are esteemed moderate, temperate & judicious. The Federalists, who belong in the middle & southern states, are very highly gratified.

My own opinion, My Dear Sir, is, that the present state of things cannot last long. When or where or what the change will be, is known only to the all-seeing eye of Heaven; but I think some change must come. If we get peace, our political difficulties will at least subside, & we shall probably have a calm. If peace do not come, I do not pretend to conjecture what will happen. We must leave things to the direction of Providence.

If New England *reforms her morals,* & maintains her religious, literary, & social institutions, she will have the best Securities for her prosperity, which the case admits. These constitute her real strength. With these, if she should be compelled *to take care of herself,* she will have nothing to fear. She is sufficiently powerful to resist all encroachments on her civil liberties; she is so situated as to command more or less commerce; & she has the means of subsistence. <I should exceedingly> All the reflecting men in the nation know how important New England is to the Union; & all the reflecting men in New England feel that the Union also is important to her. I am sure—at least I have a high degree of confidence— that she will never dissolve it. But I do not conceal my apprehension, that if the war last, & our affairs be as much mismanaged as they have been— this Government will almost cease to exist— & dwindle to nothing;— as to the protection & defense which it will be able to yield.

I beg your pardon for troubling you with so long & so hasty a letter.

It will give me pleasure to correspond with you, at all times, while I may be here, & to give you any information relative to public affairs which may be in my power.

May God, in his merciful Providence, preserve us and our Country. I am, Sir, with respect Yrs   D. Webster

ALS. MH. Rowland (1769–1843; Dartmouth 1784), pastor of the Congregational Church at Exeter when Webster was a student at Phillips Exeter Academy. For thirty-eight years, from 1790 until 1828, Rowland served that church.

1. See mDW 40749 for the Exeter petition protesting the transportation and opening of mail on Sunday. The covering letter, of the 3rd, has not been found.

2. In 1810 President Madison proclaimed American authority over the area between the Perdido and Mississippi rivers, and during the War of 1812 there was considerable hope that, if Spain entered the war on the side of the British, the United States would acquire Florida; but Spain remained a nonbelligerent in the war. The settlement of the Florida question did not come until 1819, when the United States and Spain signed the Adams-Onís Treaty.

TO MOODY KENT

Washington Jan 14 [1815]

Dear Sir,

I have just recd yours of the 2nd. & 6th together. I am greatly *surprised* at the resolution taken at the Meeting at Concord.[1]

It seems to be a part of the never ending troubles & embarrassments of our State politics. I hope those concerned will *consider,* & *reconsider* their determination. If my information, which is pretty general, is not altogether incorrect, *schism* would certainly follow that nomination.

I have not time this day to say more—but will [write] you again soon.

In the mean time I have no objection to your saying to any body, you may think proper, my opinion on this. I am sure it is also the opinion of others here much better entitled to give an opinion than myself. Whether we are all of that opinion I cannot say, but will inquire & let you know. I thought it *settled* & *decided* last June that we were to have a new Candidate for Governor—but it seems nothing can be decided, in the politics of our State.

In haste yrs — D. W.

Nothing yet decisive of the fate of N. Orleans—considerable reinforcements were likely to arrive in season.

ALS. NhHi. Published in Van Tyne, pp. 69–70.

1. Neither letter found. The reference is to an internal dispute among New Hampshire Federalists as to their gubernatorial nominee. Some favored the renomination of John Taylor Gilman, who had served as governor from 1794 to 1805 and 1813 to 1815. Webster and his friends favored the nomination of another, and such had been the consensus of a Federalist caucus in June 1814. In a January 1815 caucus in Concord, however, another group of delegates had again nominated Gilman, whom the former caucus had regarded as "utterly incompetent for the office." It was this situation which alarmed Webster and Kent.

[TO NATHANIEL APPLETON HAVEN]

Washington Jan 19 1815

Dear Sir,

I have recd yours of the 14[1]—shall pay the Bill to the Editor of Nat Intell— & am obliged to you for your attendance to the Unity land.

I cannot describe the anxiety we have felt here about the Bank. Never have I witnessed a moment of deeper apparent interest, than when Mr. [Langdon] Cheves gave the casting vote vs [Alexander J.] Dallas' Bill.[2]

The Senate, as you see, in effect disagreed to our amendments—by adding thereto other amendments of their own, restoring the Bill to its original form in most respects.

Yesterday we considered the Senate's Amendments, & disagreed to them by a very small majority; say 5 to 7. This morning, it was discovered, by the strangest & merest accident in the world, that an attempt was this day to be made in our House to *reconsider* the decision of yesterday, & to agree with the Senate; & that a sufficient number was ready to alter their votes; viz [Samuel] Dana, [John W.] Taylor, [Abraham Joseph] Hasbro[u]ck[3] & others. It was also discovered, by the same accident, that the Bill, which ought to have been carried by the Clerk to the Senate early today, was *kept back*, till the morning business of receiving petitions &c was over, & till a motion to reconsider could be made. A subject happened to be then before the House—*some* of our friends agreed to *discuss it*, till others could take the necessary steps to have the Bill returned to the

Senate with our disagreeing votes— We applied to the Speaker about it— he called on the Clerk—the Clerk said he was going to the Senate, with the Bill, when one member of the House (Taylor) called him back— & told him not to go at present. The Speaker directed the Clerk to carry down the Bill—which he did— & thus put it out of the power of our House to reconsider their votes. In fact the Senate had been discussing the subject near an hour, before the contrivers of this little project learned that it had failed. They supposed the Bill was lying quietly in the Clerks drawer.

In the Senate has been today a most animated & interesting discussion. In the issue, [William B.] Giles & [James] Barbour declared themselves in favor of the Bill as we modified it. The Senate, by a majority of 2, receded from their propositions—18 to 16. I suppose you will see the names in Tomorrows paper—[Jeremiah] Mason, [Thomas W.] Thompson, [Christopher] Gore, [William] Hunter, [Rufus] King, [Obadiah] German, [John] Lambert, [Outerbridge] Horsey, [William H.] Wells, [Robert H.] Goldsboro' Giles, Barbour, [John] Gaillard, [James] Brown, [Eligius] Fromentin, Dana, [David] Dagget, & one other whom I do not recollect made the 18.[4]

This being ascertained, [William W.] Bibb, of Georgia, moved the indefinite postponement of the Bill; on the ground that it was worse than no Bank. The Senate adjourned, without deciding this motion.

My opinion is the Bill will pass—in the shape, substantially that it passed our House. But I cannot speak with confidence. A series of wonderful occurrences have happened on this subject.

If a letter, intended for *one* Gentleman, had not this morning, by accident & very innocently, come into possession of *another,* the Bill, in Dallas' form, would inevitably have been a law at this moment,—as far as the assent of both houses makes a law. I will advise you of what may happen hereafter.

With great regard Yrs   DW.

ALS. PPIn.
1. Not found.
2. Cheves succeeded Clay as Speaker of the House, January 19, 1814.
3. Hasbrouck (1773–1845), a Clintonian Democrat from New York, state legislator, and representative in the 13th Congress.
4. Joseph Kerr of Ohio was the other member who made up the eighteen in opposition to the bill.

TO [NATHANIEL APPLETON HAVEN]

Washington Jan 21 [1815]

Dear Sir,

The Bank Bill passed yesterday; the Senate receding from all their disagreements.[1]

The Intelligencer of this morning contains all the news we have from New Orleans.

Another mail is expected today, which will probably give the result. My own opinion is, that New Orleans is lost.[2]

As to the Bank, many think the President will return the Bill. He will certainly be urged so to do by some; but I think he will not.

The Sec. of Treasury has this morning sent to the Com[mitt]ee of W[ay]'s & M[ean]'s a more dreadful account of the finances than every thing heretofore said. It is ordered to be printed, & will make you stare. It proposes a whole list of new taxes—viz: on inheritances & devises; upon legacies; upon last wills; upon legal processes; upon mortgages; a stamp tax on all sorts of instruments; upon wheat flour, 1 Dl. per barrel; upon transfers of stocks; upon all sorts of income &c.

It appears from this letter that all the taxes yet laid will not, in this year, produce enough to pay the interest of what we now owe;—leaving the whole expense of the War & Govt. to be borne by loans.

I cannot conceal my opinion that this disclosure, together with the loss of Orleans, must shake this Govt. to its centre. I shall be surprised at nothing's happening. If I had Treasury notes, & they recd any rise from the passage of the Bank Bill, I should sell them, I think. I never have seen affairs look quite so squally. I will write you again Tomorrow.

Yrs.   D.W.

ALS. DLC.

1. The bill was vetoed by President Madison on January 30. *Annals of Congress*, 13th Cong., 3rd Sess., pp. 189–191.

2. "This day we expect a Mail which is to announce the triumph justly due to the patriotism of Louisianans and their brave fellow-citizens from Tennessee and Kentucky, or to confirm the awful apprehension which we entertain for the ultimate safety of that highly important section of the Union." *National Intelligencer*, January 21, 1815. News of Jackson's victory did not in fact reach Washington until Saturday, February 4, reported in the *Intelligencer* for Tuesday, February 7, 1815.

TO EZEKIEL WEBSTER

Jan 30. [1815]

Dear E.

I send you the Intelligencer containing our latest advices from Orleans.

The President has *negatived* the Bank Bill—so all our labor is lost. I hope this will satisfy our friends that it was not a Bank likely to *favor* Administration. What is to be done next nobody can tell.

One or two more taxes are expected to be passed—one on income, is contemplated—I think the others recommended by the Secretary will not go.

I see Govr. [John Taylor] G[ilman] is to run again. I do not at all like this—but see no way to remedy it now— I think it a very foolish affair. I am glad to see [Mills] Olcot[t]'s nomination. We wanted strength in Council.

My intention is to depart hence in about 8 or 10 days—so as to be home at Court—at which time & place you must come & see me.

I shall not probably find an occasion to say something which I should like to say—but I hope (& think) that Mr. [Jeremiah] Mason will discuss some subjects of interest, in a manner to awaken the attention of the people a little.

We are getting printed a little abstract of reports, Bills, &c, tending to show the design of Govt. on Conscription &c.[1]

I shall send a number of them to you for circulation.

Give my love to our mother & your wife & children. Yrs   D.W.

ALS. NhD. Published in *PC*, 1: 251.
    1. No copy of the "abstract" has been found.

TO [NATHANIEL APPLETON HAVEN]

Washington Feb. 5. [1815]
Dear Sir,

There was a Democratic Caucus on Friday Evening, & a vote passed to attempt again to make a Bank, on the following outline—

    20 millions T. Notes
     5   Do.   Cash
    15 Stocks, without distinction
    10   Do. to be subscribed by Govt.—
making 50 millions Capital.

The proposition is to be brought forward in the Senate. It is thought it will pass; tho' there is no certainty[:] 35 Senators are present—17 are said to be certain *for* the project—16 certain *agt* it—2 doubtful; viz. [Joseph] Kerr, of Ohio, & [Jonathan] Robertson of Vermt. There is to be a fixed loan of 30 millions to Govt. & a suspension of Specie payment.

If it passes the Senate, I think it will go thro our House.

I expect to leave here for home on Wednesday.

Yrs with respect   D Webster.

The papers contain all we know from New Orleans.

ALS. PPIn.

TO [TIMOTHY FARRAR, JR.]

Feb. 11. [1815] Saturday
Washington
Dear Sir,

It is possible I may not reach home the first day or two of the Court. I hope, in that case, you will see as little harm done as possible. The Bank

Bill is in the Senate today, on its third reading. As far as votes yet given indicate, it will pass, 19 to 16. I have, however, half a notion that [Joseph] Kerr, of Ohio, may yet join the opposition in which case, the vote will stand, if all are present—18 for—17 agt. If chance, or ill health, should keep off any one of its friends, the Bill might miscarry, in the Senate. But this is not probable. I expect the Bill in our house on Monday— & have pretty [well] resolved to stop & give my vote on it, on that day. I think it's stay in this House will be short. It will probably pass at on[c]e, by a considerable majority. At any rate it has been so often discussed, & especially it's whole details being settled in Caucus, it will not take much time to decide upon it.

I shall write to [David?] Hale,[1] to your care, to answer, for me, in Bells causes.[2] I shall be at home [in] time to try the issues. There is no material dispute, I suppose about facts—and the question of Law will of course lie over. I recd a letter from Mr. [John] Bell[3] at Albany, requesting my particular attention to the causes.

I shall write you again, perhaps daily—so that the time of my departure & probable arrival may be known.

Yrs   D. Webster

ALS. NhHi.   Bell, February 15, 1815, mDW 1878).
   1. Letter not found.   3. Otherwise unidentified.
   2. *Lord* v. *Bell* (See DW to John

In 1815, a long-standing feud between John Wheelock, President of Dartmouth College, and the Board of Trustees of the College was brought into the open and the lines were drawn for the famous lawsuit of the Trustees of Dartmouth College v. *William H. Woodward. When the case reached the Supreme Court in 1818, Webster appeared with Joseph Hopkinson of Philadelphia for the plaintiff, and William Wirt and John Holmes for the defendant. The Supreme Court rendered its decision in February 1819. A full discussion of the Dartmouth College case will be found in the* Legal Papers of Daniel Webster.

The dispute between the two factions within the college in 1815 erupted when President Wheelock, in his Sketches of the History of Dartmouth College . . . (1815), *charged the Trustees with numerous violations against the institution and its aims. Wheelock quickly followed his list of abuses with a memorial to the legislature, urging them to investigate the College and its affairs. In June 1815 the legislature took up the challenge, appointing an investigating committee, consisting of Daniel A. White (1776–1861; Harvard 1779), a prominent Newburyport lawyer and later Unitarian layman; Nathaniel Appleton Haven of Portsmouth, and the Reverend E. P. Bradford of New Boston. A hearing was scheduled for August, to which Webster was invited by Wheelock. The Dartmouth*

President concluded, on the basis of a conversation at Concord, that Web-
ster was on his side, and enclosed a retaining fee in the letter that follows.
As Josiah Dunham (1769–1844; Dartmouth 1789), former preceptor of
Moor's Charity School, educator, sometime newspaper publisher, and
Wheelock supporter, explains, however, Webster ignored both the invi-
tation and the fee.

FROM JOHN WHEELOCK

                                         Dartmouth College
                                         Augt. 5th. 1815.
Dear Sir,

I take the earliest moment to inform [you] that the Hon. Mr. [Daniel
A.] White has communicated by his letter dated the 21st. Inst. the assign-
ment made by the Committee of the State to meet here on Wednesday
the week preceeding commencement which will be a week from next
Wednesday, on the business for which they were appointed. It is needless
to say how highly we appreciate your distinguished talents & virtues in
whatever concerns the interest of literature & the happiness of society.
You will permit me to express an ardent desire that you would make it
consistent to be here in season to conduct the interesting public cause of
truth & justice, in which a sense of duty has led me to be concerned. It
would be gratifying & useful could you find it convenient to be here by
Saturday next or as long before the meeting as may be. I much regret that
the period is so short & that there was no ground for my giving you information before this instant as I have made dependence on you as counsel, agreeably to our conversation at Concord. The position & relations of
the great object are much as when I had the pleasure of seeing you. I entreat your goodness not to fail. You will please to consider me responsible
to remunerate you honourably to your satisfaction.

With sentiments of very cordial & great respect I am Dear Sir, Your
obliged friend & obedient servant   John Wheelock

P.S. I hope the enclosed $20.00 will reach your hand.

ALS draft. NhD. Published in John M.   *Causes* (St. Louis, 1879), pp. 88–89.
Shirley, *The Dartmouth College*

FROM JOSIAH DUNHAM

[with enclosure: Thomas W. Thompson to Ebenezer Adams]

                                         Hanover Aug. 16. 1815
Dear Sir,

The President is sadly disappointed in not seeing you here, as he informs me you engaged (or had given him encouragement) to come, &
that he had notified you, enclosing a small fee. He has been the more

disappointed, as you did not even answer his Letter, by Mr. [Nathaniel A.] Haven, who says he saw you on business relative to this journey, the moment before he came away.

A friend present informed him, that a letter had appeared, which might throw some light on the subject— & concluded by observing that you *would not come.* I was curious to know what was alluded to and soon after had a Copy of the letter put into my hands—a copy of which I will enclose [to] you.[1] It is a key to and a sample of all their wicked proceedings in order to destroy the President. *They will be defeated.* Nay, this letter alone x x x x[2]— And unless you can extricate yourself from this unpleasant affair, it will be *unpleasant for you.* If great men will manage thus, the Lion's Skin must be stript off.

Judge [Henry] Hubbard[3] has undertaken for the President and he has friends here, who will never forsake him in so righteous a Cause.

Quere— Will you not have to give up your Caucus Nomination of old Judge [Timothy] Farrar [Sr.]? Believe me, you had better undertake to drag old President [Eleazar] Wheelock from his tomb, than Judge Farrar into the Governors Chair. There is no other man, (unless it be [Jeremiah] Mason,) who can run successfully against [William] Plummer, but Govr. [John Taylor] Gilman. I know the feelings of people on this River; and it seems to be generally understood, that a *"Certain Man"* has been deeply intriguing against Gilman and *against Mason,* &c. &c. all with a view to place himself snugly there when he is ready. It won't go—*Ce n'ira pas.* This *certain man* begins to be seen thro'—and he will be "effectually *put down."* Take care, that he does not drag you, along with him, in his fall! —verb. sap. sat.

With very sincere respect & esteem, my dear Sir, I remain, as ever, your friend & very Hum[bl]e Servt.   J. Dunham

P.S. Are not the Trustees & their friends trying to give this College Business a *political* turn, in order to draw in *all Federalists* to help them pull down the President? That the Democrats will try to make use of it to help *their* party I well know. If you Federalists meet them on this ground —*you are gone!* For there are Federalists who know the merits of the Case & who will act conscientiously with the President. But the only course for the Federalists is to act honestly, fearless of consequences, *independently of any party considerations*—not to let it, among Federalists, become a party question. *Otherwise,* it will as certainly revolutionize your State, as that you are now Federal. Mark my words— & mark the result. The President will never consent to be *silently trodden into the earth,* by wicked men, or by wicked means, without exposing their conduct, for fear of injuring Federalism. He has never been a violent politician any way, but has been engaged in literary toils. I think him *orthodox* in politics & religion—but no sectarian. Duty, however, would not require him to sacrifice himself *in silence*, for fear of exposing a few designing men, who call themselves Feds.[4]

N.B. Some here conjecture *from circumstances*, that you have been employed by [Thomas W.] T[hompson] *to feel of Mr.* [*Nathaniel A.*] *Haven*!!! I would much rather suppose that Mr. T. had made use of your name, without any authority, to encourage his friends in their wickedness here.

ALS. NhD.

1. See enclosure, Thomas W. Thompson to Ebenezer Adams, July 13, 1815, below.

2. The sentence is so written in the original, perhaps with the intention of implying more than the document warranted.

3. Hubbard (1784–1857; Dartmouth 1803), lawyer, state legislator, and later congressman from Charlestown.

4. DW's reply (August 25, 1815) to Dunham appears below.

ENCLOSURE: THOMAS W. THOMPSON TO EBENEZER ADAMS

Concord July 13. 1815.

Professor Adams,
Dear Sir,

I have had a *long conversation*, with Mr. D. Webster, *by which it appears*, that a strong desire prevails, that the *Reply*, with the COMMITTEE'S REPORT should *effectually put down a certain man*. Mr. W. Dr. [Asa] MacFarland & I are very desirous, that affidavits should be immediately taken, relative to such facts, as will shew, that person's character, in a just point of view. I can't name all the points to which the testimony should be directed; but you and our friends must hold a consultation and select such points as will be productive of the greatest effect. Full and satisfactory testimony should be taken relative to the matter of usury (a great crime, no doubt, in the good Senator's eye!) and particularly Mr. [Jabez?] Kellogg's[1] deposition—

It will be very useful to obtain testimony (or Documents, if practicable) to shew, that the College had to pay Col. Kinsman[2] $——— in consequence of the Executive neglecting to enforce the laws & orders of the Trustees. Testimony should be had of every *trick, contrivance*, and *management*, of his, to shew his true Character.

On the part of our friends at Hanover, *great, unceasing, & systematic efforts should be made to collect evidence*. (Is it then so hard a thing for the Trustees to justify their conduct?!) It is impossible for the Trustees to obtain it, but through their friends. (They have acted, then, upon the *hearsay* of their friends!!!) *The expense MUST BE CLUB'D AMONGST US!!!!!!*

I intend, IF POSSIBLE, to collect testimony here to shew that with the Democrats he was a democrat,—with every sort of religionist he was one of them;—with Federalists he was a federalist,—and that he descended to base means to make influence.

I have a scrap of the envelope of the communication to the Repertory, which will shew the hand writing. I wish not to communicate my suspicions, till I exhibit it at Commencement. I can say thus much, I think the writer is a president's man. Perhaps this ought not to be mentioned just yet.[3]

I shall depend much upon the exertions of our friends to procure evidence, and shall be much disappointed, if it is not immediately and effectually attended to. Your friend,   Tho. W. Thompson

No notice to the President will be necessary.

(Superscription)
>   Ebenezer Adam[s], Esqr.
>   Professor Mathematics, &c.
>   D. College

This can be proved, by the most undoubted testimony to be authentic— other copy— & that Adams has actually recd. the original in Thompson's own hand. Excuse the comments in the Bracketts. They were intended for another purpose. They were unnecessary for you.

Copy, with notes by Dunham. NhD. Published in Shirley, *Dartmouth College Causes*, pp. 89–90. Ebenezer Adams (1765–1841; Dartmouth 1791) had been preceptor of Leicester Academy and Professor of Mathematics at Phillips Exeter Academy before he returned to Dartmouth in 1809 as Professor of Languages. A year later he became professor of mathematics and natural philosophy.

1. Kellogg (1763–1831), a deacon in the Church of Christ at Dartmouth College.

2. Kinsman had erected the commons building at Dartmouth in the 1790's. Contracted to be built to house 100 students and the dining hall, the commons proved unsuccessful, because many students were excused from living there.

3. Thompson was probably referring to the notice in *The Repertory* (Boston), April 26, 1815, which suggested that a successor to John Wheelock would probably be chosen at the August commencement.

TO [JOSIAH DUNHAM]
>   Portsmo. Aug 25. 1815

Dear Sir,

On my return from Exeter today I found your letter from Hanover. On the subject of the dispute between the President & the Trustees, I am as little informed as any reading individual in Society; & I have not the least inclination to espouse either side, except in proceedings in which my services would be professional. It was intimated to me last Spring, that the President might probably institute process ag[ains]t the trustees for the recovery of money due him from them; that proceedings might also perhaps be commenced in the Courts of Law to determine whether there had been a perversion of the Phillips' fund; & that in case these events should happen, the President would be glad to engage my assistance as Counsel. At Concord, the President suggested, in general terms, that he might wish to obtain my professional assistance, on some future occasion, which I readily promised him.

After Dr. Haven had left this place for Hanover, I recd. the Presidents letter desiring me to be at Hanover at a time which had then already elapsed. I answered it by mail, not quite so soon as I should have done, if I had not expected some private conveyance, & if I had not known that an answer by any conveyance would have been wholly immaterial at that time.

If I had recd it earlier, I could not have attended; because the Court engaged me at Exeter. And I ought to add here, that if I had no other engagements at the time, & had also been seasonably notified, I should have exercised my own discretion about undertaking to act a part before the Committee at Hanover. I regard that certainly as no *professional* call, & should consider myself as in some degree taking side personally and individually for one of the parties, by appearing as an advocate on such an occasion. This I should not chuse to do, until I know more of the merits of the case.

As to the letter you enclose, & the mention made in it of myself, I can only say, that I have no particular recollection of any one conversation in which, more than on any other occasion in which I talked of the subject, I expressed what is there ascribed to me. Undoubtedly, however, the substance of what I should say on that subject at any time would be, that the Trustees should make a Reply, & that whatever they alledge, they should fully prove by affidavits or otherwise. If by "putting down a certain man," is meant a refutation of the charges contained in his publications, I certainly have felt, in common with every body else as I supposed, a very strong desire that the trustees, for many of whom I have the highest respect, should be able to refute, in the fullest manner charges which if proved or admitted would be so disreputable to their characters. My "desire" on the subject is just what I had imagined every one else felt, who wished to see a controversy cleared up, & to learn the truth.

What you are pleased to say about the necessity of my extricating myself from this affair, or of its being otherwise unpleasant to me; as also what you observe of a suspicion entertained by some that Mr. Thompson had employed me to feel Dr. Haven on the subject; give me leave to say, that I should know better how to answer these remarks, if I were not writing to one for whom I have the highest & warmest esteem, & of whose sense of delicacy & propriety very few certainly have had at any time occasion to complain. Be assured, my dear friend, that I feel in no manner of danger;— & towards those who harbour such a suspicion I entertain no sentiment but contempt.

On the merits of this dispute, I perceive you are decided & warm. This is natural to the generosity of your nature, & the sincerity & warmth of your friendship. You speak, in terms of pretty strong derision, of individuals, whom I regard as among the most valuable & honorable men in [the] Community. But on this account, I neither bring accusation nor insinuation against you. No suspicion of the purity of your motives or the uprightness of your conduct has come near my mind.

I am not quite so fully convinced as you are that the President is altogether right, & the Trustees altogether wrong. <Of the general spirit of the President's publications I have never concealed my opinion. I think it> When I have your fulness of conviction perhaps I may have some portion of your zeal. Whenever I have said any thing to either side, it has been to impress the necessity of moderation & candor; as they will do me the justice I trust to acknowledge.

As to political consequences, I am no prophet.

[One or more pages missing] than Govr. Gilman's. <Give me leave to hope, my Dear Sir, that Vermont will next month set us so good an example of Federalism, as to give us leave to trust that our own future prospects are not so gloomy as you imagine. I am, Dear Sir, with entire respect Yrs D. Webster> If the friends of the President *prove* any thing in any degree derogatory to the Judges [Farrar's] character, it will certainly have its weight. But it is not likely that the great body of Federalists in the State will take much on trust of Democratic newspapers. They will look to the result of the inquiry by the Committee.

You may be well assured, that in our nomination of Governor we have regarded nothing but the political interests of the State. I can but flatter myself, that if you were better acquainted with circumstances, you would think less unfavorably of the conduct of your Federal friends. I am quite sure your patriotism & your candor will lead you to a thorough inquiry, before you pronounce your disapprobation. In the mean time give me leave to hope, that Vermont, in which I trust this controversy has not been much felt, will set us so good an example next month, as would make us quite ashamed either of apathy or disunion. I am, Dear Sir, with sincere & great regard Yrs &c   [D. Webster]

ALS draft (incomplete). NhD. Published in *PC*, 1: 251–253.

TO NATHAN HALE

Portsmo. Aug 26. 1815

Dear Hale,

I was sorry to see that somebody inserted a strange Paragraph in [Charles] Turells paper today[1]—pray take no notice of it.

Every body I believe in our little circle reads Yr Paper— & no one has a higher opinion of the manner in which it is conducted than

Your Ob. servt.   D. Webster

ALS. MHi.

1. *Portsmouth Oracle*, of which Turrell was proprietor from September 1813 to July 1821. The paragraph signed by "A Real Federalist," attacked "a certain daily paper" in Boston for so neglecting to report the news of the country that its "political character" could not be easily determined. The only Boston daily newspaper at the time was Hale's *Boston Daily Advertiser*.

The return of peace and the restoration of a modicum of party harmony did not solve the nation's economic problems. The tariff, currency, banking, and bankruptcy remained pressing issues, no longer to finance an unpopular war but to cope with a heavy burden of debt and to prepare the way for national development. With the exception of national bankruptcy legislation, which was not decided until the 1840's, the Fourteenth Congress fashioned laws to deal with the most pressing economic questions.

Webster's role was conspicuous, providing the ablest leadership on his side of the House, but his chief contribution was his currency resolutions, introduced on April 26 and passed on April 30 after considerable debate and various amendments. Known as the Joint Resolutions of 1816, they stipulated that the "revenues of the country ought to be collected and received in the legal currency of the United States, or in Treasury notes, or in the notes of the Bank of the United States, as by law provided and declared," and not in "paper of various sorts, and various degrees of value." It is largely with the postwar economy that the following letter to Ezekiel deals.

TO EZEKIEL WEBSTER

Mar. 7. [1816]

Dear E.

There has been hardly any thing transpiring here this month, out of which one could find materials for a letter.

The great subject is the *currency*. Agt. the express provision of law, [Alexander J.] Dallas receives the depreciated notes of the Banks of the

Middle States for duties &c. They are, say ten per ct below par. He could, it is thought correct the evil, if he would. But he uses this evil as a motive to make a Bank. They say he wants to be Prest. of a great Bank, with 8 or 10 thousand a year &c. The Bank will not be made, after his fashion, & it is quite doubtful whether it will be made at all.

A Bankruptcy Bill is reported—probably it will not be acted upon this Session. A Bill making great alterations in the Judiciary will most likely take the same fate; & indeed I am doubtful whether the important subject of the new Tariff will not be postponed. If these things should all take place, we may adjourn next month. I think we shall.

The spring is coming forward here. The ground is settled & dry—the buds are appearing, & the grass is green. But spring does not rush forward here, as it does in N. H. after it has commenced. It lingers, & gets along by imperceptible degrees.

There are many applications for Mr. [Joseph] Whipple's place.¹ [Timothy] Upham, H[enry Sherburne] Langdon, [John F.] Parrot, E[dward] Cutts, *Jesse Johnson*, & F[rancis] *Gardner*.² I think Upham will succeed; but there is no telling.

All that I know almost about your Election I gather from the papers. They look well; especially Portsmo. & Keene. But before you receive this the matter will be settled—so I will not trouble you on that subject. I imagine you will not be in a condition to like to talk about it—at least I *fear* so.

I have no faith in [William H] Crawford.³ I believe he will *shrink*— & give in— & be paid for his compliance by the seals of State.

Mr. [Rufus] King will stand Candidate for N. York.⁴ There will be a severe contest in that State.

I think the nomination of Genl [John] Brooks a wise measure.⁵

Give my love to mother & your family—   D. W.

& let me hear from you.

ALS. NhD. Published in *PC*, 1: 242–243.

1. Collector of Customs at Portsmouth, a post held by Joseph Whipple from 1801 to 1816.

2. Upham (1783–1855), a native of Deerfield, N.H., was appointed to succeed Whipple. A former military officer, he served as Collector of Customs until 1829. Langdon (1766–1857), educated at Yale, was a prosperous attorney in Portsmouth. Jesse Johnson has not been identified.

3. Recently home from France where he had served as United States minister, Crawford was Secretary of War at the time this letter was written. He was also one of the chief Republican contenders for nomination for president.

4. Daniel Tompkins, the incumbent, defeated Rufus King in the New York gubernatorial election.

5. Federalist nominee and successful candidate in the Massachusetts gubernatorial election.

TO EZEKIEL WEBSTER

Washington, March 26, 1816.

Dear Ezekiel,

I have settled my purpose to remove from New Hampshire in the course of the summer. I have thought of Boston, New York, and Albany. On the whole I shall, probably, go to Boston; although I am not without some inducements to go into the State of New York. Our New England prosperity and importance are passing away. This is fact. The events of the times, the policy of England, the consequences of our war, and the Ghent Treaty, have bereft us of our commerce, the great source of our wealth. If any great scenes are to be acted in this country within the next twenty years, New York is the place in which those scenes are to be viewed. More of this hereafter.

We are now coming to the end of the session. The bank is before the Senate, and in my opinion, will be a law in a week. [Alexander J.] Dallas is to quit the treasury, to be president of it.

The tariff is the only other important article before us. In three weeks I intend to be off. As to circuit, I decline Hillsborough and Cheshire, but perhaps shall be obliged to go to Grafton.

I am very sorry to hear of mother's continued ill health. The weather has now turned warm, and I hope she will experience the benefit of it. Here it has been very cold for three or four weeks; but spring seems now coming in earnest.

Give my love to mother and your family. Ever yours,   D.W.

Text from *PC*, 1: 256. Original not found.

TO EZEKIEL WEBSTER

April 11 1816

Dear E.

I recd yours yesterday,[1] & learned with great sorrow the illness of our mother,[2] & Mary [Webster].[3] I have hardly a hope that the former can now be living. If she should be, on the receipt of this, tell her I pray for her everlasting peace & happiness, & would give her a son's blessing for all her parental goodness. May God bless her, living or dying!

If she does not survive, let her rest beside her husband and our father.

I hope Mary is not dangerously ill. You must write to me, addressed to N. York—where I expect to be on my way home about the 28 or 30th. Inst. Congress will probably rise about 22—or few days later.

We have got thro most of the important public business of the Session.

Give my love to your wife & children & may Heaven preserve you all. Most affectionately Yrs   D. Webster

ALS. NhD. Published in *PC*, 1: 257.

1. Letter not found.

2. Abigail Eastman Webster died on April 25.

3. Mary (November 27, 1809 – July 16, 1816), daughter of Ezekiel Webster.

TO SAMUEL AYER BRADLEY

Washington Ap. 21. [1816]

Dear Bradley

The enclosed[1] will shew you what liberties I have taken with a friend. A. Lucas[2] is from N. Carolina; Mr. [William] Gaston gives an excellent account of him; & his object is to print, not so much a party paper, as a correct journal of congressional proceedings, & the principal public documents.

We shall get away this week. The Bank, you know, is passed; the *Tariff* is nearly finished. These are the principal measures of the Session. As to *party*, we see little of it. There are strange things happening here as well as elsewhere. Whether all our party distinctions are not breaking up, I cannot say. Appearances are very much in favor of such a supposition. Many Federalists voted for the Bank. Indeed Federal votes carried it. On the *Tariff* Federalists as well as Democrats were much divided. The manufacturing interest has become a *strong distinct political party.* This you may rely upon. In short, I believe we are all to be thrown into new forms, & new associations.

If you are in N. H. this spring, pray come by P[ortsmouth] & let me see you.

With great respect Yours   D. Webster

ALS. NhD.

1. Not found.

2. Not identified.

During the tariff debate in Congress, a misunderstanding developed between Webster and John Randolph of Roanoke, when the former objected to the incorporation of a sugar tax in the tariff bill, the inclusion having been urged by Randolph. The disagreement led the Virginian to challenge Webster to a duel, but Webster declined. In the letters below Webster requested and received a copy of his correspondence with Randolph.

TO JOHN RANDOLPH

Tuesday Morning [April 30, 1816]

Mr Webster leaves the city this morning, which is a little earlier than he intended, for the pleasure of the company of Mr. [Charles Fenton?] Mercer & Mr. [Jeremiah] Mason. He would feel it to be a particular favor if

Mr. Randolph would transmit him a *copy*—(Portsmouth N. H.)— & he takes this occasion to make to Mr Randolph an expression of the sincerest sentiments of regard & esteem.

AL. ViU.

FROM JOHN RANDOLPH

> Davis's. 9 Miles from Washington
> on the Baltimore Road,
> Apr. 30. 1816

Sir

Your polite & friendly note was put into my hands this morning, under circumstances that did not permit me to write. I now regret very much that I did not leave George Town with you this morning. I have just dined where you breakfasted this morning with a most pleasant party. That reflection seems to add to the uncomfortable feel of solitariness that now assails me. Below you have the *"copy"* of the paper which you desired me to forward to you. Accept my acknowledgments for the terms in which that request is made & believe me with very high respect & regard

Your obedient Servt.   John Randolph of Roanoke

ALS. NhHi. Published in *PC*, 1: 258.

ENCLOSURE: TO JOHN RANDOLPH

[April, 1816]

Sir

For having declined to comply with your demand yesterday, in the House, for an explanation of words of a general nature used in debate, you now "demand of me that satisfaction which your insulted feelings require & refer me to your friend (Mr———[1] I presume, as he is the bearer of your note) for such arrangements as are usual."

This demand, for explanation, you, in my judgment, as a matter of right, were not entitled to make on me; nor were the temper & style of your own reply to my objections to the Sugar Tax of a character to induce me to accord it as a matter of courtesy.

Neither can I (under the circumstances of this case) recognize in you a right to call me to the field to answer what you may please to consider an insult to your feelings. It is unnecessary for me to state other & obvious considerations growing out of this case. It is enough that I do not feel myself bound, at all times & under any circumstances, to accept, from any man, who shall choose to risk his own life, an invitation of this sort; altho' I shall be always prepared to repel in a suitable manner the aggression of any man who may presume upon such a refusal.

Copy. NhHi. Published in *PC*, I: 258–259.

1. DW's endorsement, "respecting Mr. T[homas] B[olling] Robertson's

challenge," identifies Robertson as Randolph's friend and the "bearer" of the Virginian's note.

At its August 1815 meeting, the Trustees of Dartmouth College had removed John Wheelock and named the Reverend Francis Brown as President. In the political controversy between Brown and Dartmouth College and Wheelock and "Dartmouth University," created by the legislature in June 1816, Webster defended the former.

TO [FRANCIS] BROWN

Portsmouth, June 4, 1816.

My Dear Sir,

I received yours last evening.[1] You do not feel a stronger wish than I do, that nothing may take place at this session detrimental to the college, and I am willing to do any thing in my power to soften the irritated feelings of democracy towards it. I am under engagements to go to Boston to-morrow, and shall be in that town four or five days. From Boston I can go direct to Concord, if it should be thought useful. Mr. [Jeremiah] Mason will go up, I believe, the first of next week. I have some hope that the legislature will do nothing; partly, because I hope they will be satisfied in some measure with the report, and partly from the hopeless state of Dr. [John] W[heelock]'s health. It is a favorite idea with some to create a new college. Would it not be well if this idea could be encouraged, and to let the ill humors work off in that direction? Suppose a proposition should be made for a committee to report at next session, upon the expediency of making a new college at Concord, and what donations, &c., could be obtained for such an object.

"Resolved, that a joint committee of both Houses be appointed to take into consideration the expediency of establishing a Seminary of Learning, in some part of this State, to be called the University of New Hampshire, and to ascertain what endowment for such institution could be obtained from private donation, and also what grants of land or money could be properly and conveniently made to the same by the State; and also to prepare a draft of a charter for such seminary; and to report at the next session of the Legislature."

Perhaps if something of this sort should be brought forward by somebody who has been favorably inclined to Dr. W., but who would wish to prevent violent measures, it might do good.

Mr. [Joseph] Tilton[2] of Exeter, I should think, might do it to advantage. Think of this; Mr. [Charles] Cutts, the bearer of this, is an intelligent friend of mine, and capable of being useful at Concord. I recommend it to you to cultivate his acquaintance, while there. He is intimate with Mr. Tilton, and indeed with most other leading men in the legislature. Any thing that shall postpone the subject, will give time to the present feelings to cool and evaporate.

I am, dear Sir, yours with esteem,   D. Webster

N.B. The resolution might say the charter should be drawn on the following principles: —

1. A board of trustees, to be inserted in the bill by the legislature, to fill up their own vacancies.

2. A board of overseers, viz: governor, senators, counsellors, and speaker of House of Representatives for time being.

3. An unlimited right of conscience, in officers, and students; no test, creed, or confession to be required of either, nor any preference, direct or indirect, of one religion over another. If any thing of this sort be done, it ought to be done early.

Text from *PC*, 1: 259–260. Original not found.

1. Not found.

2. Tilton (1774–1856; Harvard 1797), Exeter lawyer and New Hampshire politician.

When Webster moved to Boston in the summer of 1816, he took one of his former law students, Alexander Bliss (1792–1827; Yale 1812), into his office. From 1816 to 1827 Bliss managed affairs in Boston while Webster was in Washington on legal and congressional business.

TO ALEXANDER BLISS

Portsmouth June 27. 1816

Dear Sir

I see nothing to prevent me from being in Boston in next month, & think the offices which we examined in Court Street should be prepared, as soon as may be, unless you should find better rooms.

I shall send my library up in a week or two, directed to your care. I must trouble you to see cases provided for the books, but it will be in season perhaps to order them when the books come, & when it can be better seen what is wanted. Yours with respect   D. Webster

ALS. DLC.

TO PHINEAS HANDERSON

Portsmo. Sunday Eve' [June 1816]

Dear Handerson

From some observations which I have heard since my return, I am inclined to believe that the feelings of many Republicans in this Town on the subjects of the Court & the College are undergoing a very favorable change. This is one reason, & a strong one why delay should be obtained, if possible. I am well informed that some men of influence, who have been of another way of thinking, have lately expressed sentiments very favorable to the proposition of leaving the college & courts where they are.

On another important subject I am not able to write you this Evening. With great respect Yours   D Webster

ALS. NhD. Handerson (1778–1853) was a Chesterfield lawyer, then a   member of the New Hampshire state senate.

TO [JOSEPH] STORY

Portsmouth, July 30, 1816.

Dear Sir,

In the change which has taken place in the judiciary of this State, I feel a strong desire that a friend of mine should have a proper place in the new establishment. In this wish, I am influenced, I trust, not more by sentiments of personal respect than by a regard to the public interest. I refer to Mr. [Nathaniel] Adams. He has been for many years clerk of the Supreme Court; and during the period in which you honored us with an occasional attendance at our bar, you were sufficiently acquainted with the manner in which he discharged the duties of his office. I think him the best clerk I ever saw. If others do not agree to all this, they will hardly be able to mention many whom they think better. By the new law, the Supreme Court is to have a clerk in each county.[1] Probably some gentlemen intended, by this, to effect a junction of the officers of County Common Pleas Clerk, and County Supreme Court Clerk. But this can only be done by consent of the two courts, for each has by the Constitution the appointment of its clerk.

What would be agreeable to Mr. Adams, and I think useful to the county, is that he should be clerk of both courts for this county. I imagine the justices of the Supreme Court will at once appoint him their clerk for this county. But this office would be very small of itself. It seems necessary to add to it the clerkship of the Common Pleas. I have no doubt Chief Justice [William Merchant] Richardson will use his influence with the Court of Common Pleas for Mr. Adams's appointment. That court consists of Dan. M. Durell, Esq., Chief Justice, and Levi Bartlett, Esq., Associate.[2] There is one vacancy.

I have thought, Sir, that it would be useful on this occasion, for these judges to know, that gentlemen of other States, who have been in our courts, have a favorable opinion of the official conduct of Mr. Adams, and I have ventured to think, that with others you have entertained that opinion, and that the expression of it by you would have its weight. New judges perhaps are not likely to appreciate the force of Lord Bacon's remarks upon the usefulness of a skilful and experienced clerk: and not having seen, some of them, many courts, they may not at once know the difference between good clerks and indifferent ones.

Your professional and judicial life has already been long enough to enable you to estimate these things justly.

Having said so much, may I now beg of you to write on this subject to your friend Chief Justice Richardson? This would give weight to his representation to the justices of the Court of Common Pleas, and if you should also address Chief Justice Durell on the subject, if you know him sufficiently, it would probably be extremely useful. I suppose the appointment will be made soon.

Pardon me for giving you trouble, and accept the assurances of my respect. Your humble servant,   Dan'l Webster.

N.B. The health of the present incumbent renders some change necessary soon in the clerkship of the Court of Common Pleas.

Text from *PC*, 1: 261–263.

1. The act prescribing the appointment of clerks in each county had been approved on June 27, 1816 (8 *Laws of New Hampshire*, 502).

2. Bartlett (1763–1828), a physician of Kingston, Rockingham County, formerly postmaster and executive councillor, appointed Judge of the Circuit Court in 1816.

TO JEREMIAH MASON

Boston Oct 29th. 1816

Dear Sir

Mrs. Webster thinks she cannot be ready for her departure till Monday the 11th & I should think that would be in tolerable season as it w[oul]d give us three full weeks. My plan is to make some bargain for myself & wife to be conveyed to Hartford, independent of your carriage. It is a long & heavy road to Hartford, & I should not think it would be well to add any thing to the burden of your new horses, at their first setting out, & over so hilly a road. I can easily take either a hack, or a gig, & in the last case send our baggage by stage. It will be three days to Hartford, by way of Worcester, & Stafford— & not much less on any road. One day from Hartford to New Haven, & two thence to New York. We shall then have a week to go to & stay in Philadelphia, & another to get to Washington. If we go from here the 7th. or 8th. (Thursday or Friday) as you propose, we shall find ourselves in Connecticut *at a time of the week*, when we could not travel, if we would.

I have written Mr. [John] Coyle, & recd. an answer.[1] He is afraid of turning off his old boarders—at least he says so,— & thinks he cannot take us. You know the true reason. Do you know much or any thing of

Mrs. Hyers?[2] It is the house where [Joseph] Hopkinson & [John] Sargeant lodged last winter. Possibly, when at Philadelphia, we can make an arrangement with them. If you think it useful to write to any body else at Washington at present, I wish you would do it—or if you desire it, I will write to Coyle, (knowing nobody else there) to be looking out a place conditionally,—that is, if we like it.

Our daughter[3] is yet not well. She has a tumor on her neck which we thought the *mumps* but it has remained too long for that. It has for some days appeared to be better, & we believe it is going off. We have made an arrangement to leave our children with Mrs. [Samuel] Webber, at Cambridge.

We saw Mary[4] on Sunday. She was well and I think not *homesick.* Her instructor told me Yesterday, that she began well.

I am, Dr Sir, Yours   D Webster

Copy. NhHi. Published in Van Tyne, pp. 71–72.

1. Coyle, a District of Columbia lawyer, had previously arranged a "mess" for Webster and his friends. Neither of the letters herein mentioned has been found.

2. Proprietress of a Washington boardinghouse.

3. Grace Fletcher Webster (1810–1817).

4. Daughter of Jeremiah Mason.

During his second term in Congress, Webster had two "angels," Nathaniel A. Haven of Portsmouth and Charles March of New York City, businessmen who loaned him money at crucial times. Below, Webster details for Haven the state of his law practice and his prospects for repaying him.

Later, James William Paige (1792–1868), Grace Fletcher Webster's half brother and a prosperous merchant in Boston, became another of his financial supporters.

TO NATHANIEL APPLETON HAVEN

Boston Nov. 9. 1816.

Dear Sir,

I owe you so many obligations, not only of a pecuniary, but of a personal & friendly nature, that I think I ought to render you some account of myself, & am willing to believe that on many accounts you will be willing to hear from me. My principal purpose is to say, that I have found better encouragement here than I expected, & I feel at length, as if I could see thro my embarrassments, notwithstanding the loss of property in the fall of my Country lands, provided my health should continue good. From my Book of receipts, I have copied, as on the other side. This nobody has seen, or will see, but myself. I thought I would shew it to you confidentially, that you might have courage, to hope that I shall be able to pay you, in due season, even tho' the Country lands, should not sell. I would not, of course, wish you to shew it to any person. My receipts have enabled me to pay off some pressing things, & discharge the expenses of establishing myself & household here. If I have ordinarily good fortune at Washington, my earnings, this winter will be respectable, as you will judge by some of the items under. I hope to receive enough there to be able to remit something to you, & also to the N. Hamp. Bank, if necessary.

If I can be of any use to you at W. or can contribute any thing to your information or amusement, I hope you will permit me.

Make our united regards to Mrs. Haven & Charlotte.[1]

I am, Sir, with very sincere esteem Yr's   D. Webster

Came to Boston Aug. 15, 1816

Retainer — of W. N. Boylston, in his dispute with the Town of Boston[2]	30.
of Jno. Gray, in action Wm. Gray v J. Gray & I. Thorndike[3]	50.
Aug — In case of Ariadne, at Washington, by N G & G [torn] note	500.[4]
In the case of the George, at Washington, by draft on Messrs Smedis, New York[5]	500.
of Mr. Beyerman, agent for Cremer & Son, Rotterdam, in action v L. Higgins & Co (a claim of 70,000 Dls)[6]	300.
of James Wilson, in his affairs[7]	20.
of Wms & W., fees in case of Margaretta, U. S. Court[8]	500.
of C. & J. H. Hayward, in case of goods imported into Hampden[9]	125.
of Mr. Colburn for advice, relative to bond to Bank[10]	10.
of Mr Crowningshield, in action Sturgis v. him[11]	20.

I have of course, <many> some charges. The great part of these, are of a nature not likely to recur often. I mean fees &c for cases in U. S. Court at Washington—hope you will burn this—when you have read it. Nobody has before seen it but myself.

ALS. NhD.

1. Mary Tufton (Moffat) and Charlotte Haven, Nathaniel A. Haven's wife and daughter.

2. No information has been found on this entry.

3. No information has been found on this entry.

4. See *The Ariadne*, 2 Wheaton 143

(1817).

5. See *The George*, 2 Wheaton 278 (1817).

6. See *Cremer v. Higginson and Perkins*, 1 Mason 323 (Circuit Court, District of Massachusetts, 1817).

7. No information has been found on this entry.

8. See *The Brig Margaretta v.*

United States 2 Gallison 515 (Circuit Court, District of Massachusetts, 1815), and Appellate Case Files of the Supreme Court, Reel 40, Frames 802–803.

9. The extent of DW's participation in this case has not been determined.

10. Not identified.

11. DW represented Richard Crowninshield for a short period of time in the Circuit Court in Boston. DW, however, was not associated with the case before the Supreme Court in Washington.

TO JAMES WILLIAM PAIGE

New York 18 Novr. [1816]

Dear Sir,

I have drawn on you for fifty Dollars, & when I arrive at Washington, you will hear from me further. Thus far, we have got along very well. We tried the steam boat at N. Haven, but after tossing in the sound all day, (Friday) the weather drove us back; & we had to take land conveyance. We arrived here yesterday Morning. Shall send you a T[reasury] Note. Yrs

D. Webster

N.B. Since writing the above, I have concluded not to draw a formal Bill, but just request you to inclose 50 Dls, in N. Y. Bills, in a letter to me, at this place, care of Messrs [Charles] March & [Alfred G.] Benson, Merchants; & if it does not arrive here until I leave, they will forward.

ALS. DLC.

TO [WILLIAM SULLIVAN]

Washington Jan. 2nd. 1816 [1817]

☞ Do not read this, while you have any thing else to do.

Dear Sir,

I am glad to find you so well employed as in chasing whales, tho. they be dead whales. Having seen you last in your own chamber, I was glad to learn that you have got into court, & are fit to engage in such arduous enterprises as whaling.

Your account[1] reminded me of some very ingenious & laughable remarks of Lord Erskine, in a *crim. con.* case, some twenty years ago. They are in one of the vols of the Annual Register. Mr. Erskine was for the Defendant. His defense was, that the pl[aintif]f had abandoned his wife, & put her to separate maintenance, & having thus voluntarily relinquished the comfort & society of his wife, he could not pretend that the Defdt, by his interposition, had deprived him of these enjoyments. He then went on to say, that the Law of England in respect to wives, was just like the law of the Greenland Fishery in respect to Whales. Whoever struck the whale, had a right to him, *so long as he held on by the line.* However the fish might plunge, or flounce, or curvet; tho' he should go to the bottom, or run away to the temperate or the torrid zone, while the striker held on by his line, the animal, however untamed or untameable, remained his property, & woe betide the wrong doer that should interfere. But the moment he let go his line, the animal in the eye of the law was *ferae naturae*, & became the rightful property of the first taker. So in the case of wives. While the husband holds on by his matrimonial string, however far the wife strays, at whatever great distances she may run out from the path of duty, or however crooked & eccentric her course, the law still regards her in *custodia viri*, & will allow no interference of third persons. But if the husband will chuse to let this little cord drop out of his hand, in an instant all is over. The wife then runs "unclaimed of any man", & like the wounded whale becomes the property of the next striker.

We are doing nothing now but to quarrel with one of our Laws of the last Session, called the *horse* law (not because horses made it—for it was made by asses). It was to pay the Kentucky men for all the horses which died in that Country during the War. So far very well. But there was a section put in to pay for all houses & buildings burned by the enemy on account of having been a *military Deposite*. This played the very Devil. All the Niagara frontier, the City of Washington &c, wherever the enemy destroyed any thing, was proved to have been a *military Deposite*—one tavern (27,000 Dollars) because some officers or soldiers lodged in the house a day or two before the burning—one great rope walk, because a rope had been sent there to mend from the Navy yard— &c &c. Some say the fault is in the Law—some say it is in the Commissioner who executed the Law (Richard Bland Lee). Others say there is no error in either— & others insist there are great errors in both.

I agree with the last, as the most probable proposition[2]

The Bankrupt Bill will be tried next week.[3] It will be hard pressed by [Joseph] Hopkinson but I cannot foresee its fate.

We then have the compensation to repeal which I trust will not take us long. I fear a bare repeal of the law of last Session will take place.[4]

Then the Judiciary projects must be disposed of.

Then comes from the Senate the Conscription Law, as you justly call it.

What inducement has one to resist this or any other abomination? Two years ago with infinite pains & labor, we defeated Mr Monroes conscription. Nobody thanked us for it. Last winter our friends in the Senate got this *Militia Bill* thrown out. Nobody knew or cared any thing about it— For two or three years Massachusetts has been paying from 10. to 25 pr ct more duties on importations than Pennsylvania or Maryland. At the close of the last Session, we tried to do something for her relief. But her Federal

Legislature takes no notice of the abominable injustice done her, or the plain violation of the Constitution & Laws, which has taken place to her great injury. All are silent & quiet. But when her Federal members who come here to be kicked & stoned & abused, in her behalf, think proper to raise their compensation, so that it will defray their expenses, she denounces them, man by man, without an exception. No respect for talents, services, character, or *feelings,* restrains her from joining with the lowest democracy, in its loudest cry.

I will not scold!!—dont fear—at any rate, I am too far off to *strike.*

Indeed I have never felt any emotion but pity and contempt. I pity the *mass,* who meaning right, have not knowledge enough to know what right is. The rest I despise.

Having thus written you a very long & dull letter, & come near to finishing with a fit of the spleen, I will conclude by sending to your household our sincerest gratulations, at the opening of the new year, & our wishes that all its days may be pleasant to you. I must add, also, which you will be sorry to hear, that the illness of our little daughter [Grace Fletcher] at Cambridge has very much alarmed us, & we are in expectation that Mrs W. will be compelled to return. If so, she will be accompanied by her brother [James William Paige], to whom I have written to come here for that purpose, unless I should make such dispositions of my business at the Court as to permit me to return with her, which I do not expect. Yrs truly   D. Webster

ALS. MHi. Published in *PC*, 1: 254–256. The endorsement on this letter is in the same handwriting as those of other known DW to Sullivan letters.

1. The source of DW's news about Sullivan has not been determined.

2. On March 3, 1817, the president signed into law a bill clarifying and amending the provisions of the April 9, 1816, act "to authorize the payment for property lost, or destroyed by the enemy, while in the military service of the United States."

3. On February 24, 1817, Congress postponed indefinitely the bill to establish a uniform system of bankruptcy.

4. On January 23, 1817, the House of Representatives repealed the compensation law of March 19, 1816; on February 6, President Madison signed the bill into law.

Absent from Washington from mid-January to mid-February because of the illness of his daughter, Webster's role in the second session of the Fourteenth Congress was significantly less impressive than it had been during his previous appearances.

On January 23, 1817, about a week after he and Grace reached home, their daughter, named Grace Fletcher for her mother, died from an acute form of tuberculosis.

Boston Jany. 9. 1817.
11 oclock.

Dr. Sr.

I did not know till yesterday that your little girl was in Boston, nor where she was untill this morning.

She is *now* in Mrs. [Samuel] Greenleafs[1] parlor in the arms of a woman who appears to feel great tenderness for her. And Mrs. G. appears to be extremely solicitous and attentive. I will state to you my impressions, from my own observation—and then what I heard from Mrs. G.

She had not any fever to day. I examined her pulse;—she is not very obviously reduced in flesh or strength; she had a proper color in her face, and I should say a healthy color;—her eyes did not look languid; her lips looked dry—but not, to my eye, feverish. She does not speak loud willingly, but whispers. This may be owing to the blister on her breast. She said she had no pain, but on her breast. She did not seem to suffer at all. She coughed once while I was there, and raised phleghm. The woman said she coughed more in the night, than in the day; she thought as often as once in 20 or 30 minutes during the night. Your daughter would not admit that she was very sick, and seemed to resent any intimation that she was so. I am not able to find Dr. [John C.] Warren before the mail closes.

Mrs. G. followed me out—she said she did not express before your daughter any opinion as to her illness, because it was evident that it was displeasing to her as being contrary to the opinion which she entertains of herself.

Mrs. G. told me that she thought she had changed for the worse within ten or fifteen days—that the application of leeches to her back had increased her debility. Although Mrs. G. thought her better to day than she was yesterday, she thought her very sick. She said that Dr. W. thought so —and spoke discouragingly of her. But I must add that Warren has been many years my family physician, and I know that in the case of my wife (once with a fever) and twice on other occasions with children, he has expressed himself very discouragingly, when I entertained a different opinion,—and the cases did not terminate fatally. And yet, I think, from putting all things together it must not be disguised, that your poor little girl is very sick. But to what extent her case is alarming I cannot judge, not having seen a similar case. It seems to me to turn on this, whether she has or has not strength enough to bear the applications which should be made externally. It is certainly very proper that Mrs. W. should come home. I should not think your presence indispensable, unless your own feelings demand it. I shall see Dr. W. to day, & shall see your daughter and him again tomorrow, & shall write a letter to N. Y. by tomorrows mail, & a duplicate to New Haven.

Your friend, Wm. Sullivan.

My wife was confined on Sunday—or I should be able to give you her opinion.

ALS. NhHi.

1. Wife of the former Salisbury (and now Boston) merchant.

TO EZEKIEL WEBSTER

Boston Jan 19 [1817]

Dear E.

Grace's illness has brought us home. We arrived four days ago. She has been declining almost ever since we left her, the middle of November, & was so low on our arrival that we entertained very faint hopes of her recovery. Her case is consumptive, & seems a good deal like dear little Mary's.[1] Since our return her symptoms have been a little more favorable, & might almost encourage a slight hope of ultimate recovery. Dr [John C.] Warren thinks at least that for a week she is no worse. She seems a little less languid, & has coughed less today than any day for a fortnight. My engagements in the court at W. are such that if possible I must return. If Grace should grow no worse I intend going about Thursday or Friday. We found little trouble in opening our house, & collecting our family. Both Hannah & Phila[2] are here. Eliza Buckminster is coming to stay with us a while. We came home very quick. From Philadelphia in four days. Mrs W. stood the journey wonderfully well, & took no cold— I have not been out, so much as to my office.

If your courts do not prevent, I wish you would run down & see the family.

We desire our love to all your family most affectionately, & to Mr [John?] Kelly. Yrs   D. W.

ALS. NhD. Published in PC, 1: 263.

1. Ezekiel's daughter, who died in July 1816 at seven years of age.

2. Hannah was a domestic servant who had been in Webster's family many years, according to Eliza Buckminster Lee. "Phila," probably also a servant, has not been otherwise identified.

TO EZEKIEL WEBSTER

Boston Sunday [Jan. 26, 1817]

Dear Ezl.

Our dear little daughter has followed yours. She died on Thursday Evening, at 11 oclock— & was interred yesterday. Her death, tho' I thought it inevitable soon, was rather sudden when it happened. Her disease, the consumption, had not apparently obtained its last stages. She had suffered very little—the day of her death she was pretty bright, in the forenoon, tho weak. In the afternoon she grew languid, & drowsy. She however desired her friends to read & talk to & with her untill a few minutes before eleven, when her countenance suddenly altered, & in five or six minutes she expired.

Mrs W. tho' in great affliction, is in tolerable health. Our little boy is very well. Tomorrow Morning I set out on my return to Washington.

Eliza Buckminster is with us, & Anne Paige[1] also arrived here last Evening.

We desire our most affectionate regards to Alice,[2] & the children. Ever yrs   D.W.

As to action v Pickering—I have sent every where to find him. I want to give him *notice* before I take jugt.[3] Say these things before the Ct. & get *one* more con[tinuanc]e. I have now inquiries making for him on the *lines.*

ALS. NhD. Published in *PC*, 1 : 263–264.

1. Grace Fletcher Webster's half-sister.

2. Alice Bridge Webster (1784–1821), Ezekiel's wife of eight years.

3. *Brackett Weeks* v. *Samuel Pickering,* in which DW, Ezekiel Webster, and Timothy Farrar acted for the plaintiff. The case was finally decided in the Rockingham Court of Common Pleas on February 3, 1817.

TO EZEKIEL WEBSTER

Boston Sunday Evening
[May 25, 1817]

Dear E.

As soon as you get home from Haverhill, I wish you would come down here. I want to consult you, about divers things. I have a chance of being able to make some disposition of some real estate, say 6 or 8 thousand Dls. I wish you to consider what of our Grafton territories could be taken to make up such an amount. I wd. take all that is in Dr. [Nathaniel A.] H[aven]'s hands.

I want you to bring with you such proof or estimates of value as you may have. There will be no more convenient opportunity for you to come. I shall accordingly look for you this week. If anything should prevent your coming, please write by return of mail.

We are all pretty well & send love. Yrs   D. Webster

ALS. NhD.

The following letter to Jeremiah Mason (who had resigned his Senate seat on June 16) captures the political sentiments of many Federalists shortly before President Monroe made his northeastern tour that summer to demonstrate the unity and good feelings among former political opponents.

Federalists generally believed that Webster had discreetly urged Monroe to make his goodwill northeastern tour. His exact influence on Monroe's decision has not been established, but that Webster was somehow involved seems likely, because during Monroe's stay in Boston George Sullivan proposed Webster, a strong exponent of harmony between the two political parties, as a possible candidate for the post of attorney general in Monroe's cabinet.

TO JEREMIAH MASON

Boston June 28 1817

Dear Sir

I believe your reasons for resigning are tolerably good, & yet I could have wished that you should have remained. It is, I think, very much to be desired that some body should be in each House who would be capable of making out a proper course for Federalists to pursue, in those emergencies which will probably arise, in a year or two.

I fear Mr. [Rufus] King[1] will follow your example, & leave the Senate. Who remains, fit to prescribe any course to us? I thought also that the few Federalists in N. H. who have much intelligence on the subject, were desirous that you should remain, & that you might, under the circumstances, decide a doubtful question by a regard to their satisfaction & gratification.

Nevertheless, it is true that very little political interest exists any where, & that the sacrifices which your situation in Congress required were very great.

Mr. [Harrison Gray] Otis it is said, is balancing, between his two places.[2] He may try to get thro' next winter, without relinquishing either, but in the end, he must probably quit one, & I have little doubt it will be his seat in the Senate. Did you know that [William?] Hunter was gone to England? He has been gone a Month. Has he any object in it?

Mr. [James] Lloyd[3] is in Philadelphia. The meetings of the Directors of U S Bank, when they propose to make new Branches &c., is sometime in July, but I cannot ascertain when. They have a quorum, always, in Philada. & can meet at any time.

I wish you would make Roberts continue his Foul & Laurence cause till Feby. As you will now be at that term, I suppose he can have no great objection. It would be very convenient for us to have this agreement made, as I do not think we can probably be prepared, at any rate, & it wd. put Mr. F. who wishes to attend the trial himself to very great inconvenience.[4]

I found that the College people thought that you made a strong impression, in their cause. It would be a queer thing if Gov. [William] P[lumer]'s Court should refuse to execute his Laws. I am afraid there is no great hope of their disobedience to the powers that made them.

I am coming down the coast pretty soon. I cannot answer for Mrs. W. She has a tour to Monadnock in head, where she may be detained some time.

We see Mary sometimes but not as often as we wish. You have her approbation very decidedly in resolving to quit W[ashington]. We talk of nothing but the Presidents visit, in relation to which we have as much folly as heart could wish. Yr's always   D Webster

Copy. NhHi. Published in Van Tyne, pp. 73–74.

1. King did not resign his senate seat.

2. United States senator from Massachusetts, 1817–1822, and Judge of the Boston Court of Common Pleas, 1814–1818.

3. Lloyd (1769–1831), formerly Massachusetts state senator and United States senator, and at the time director of the Second Bank of the United States.

4. The allusions in this paragraph are to *Laurason & Fowle* v. *Nickerson et al.*, November 1819 term of Massachusetts Supreme Judicial Court.

Nationally, party warfare may have been waning, but in New Hampshire it was much alive. There, in 1817, Dartmouth College was the center of party debate, with Republicans largely siding with John Wheelock and the "University" and Federalists backing Francis Brown and the College.

Webster had long identified himself with the College, but it was probably Jeremiah Smith's invitation, referred to in the letter below, which placed him, Smith, and Mason as advocates for the College before the Superior Court at Exeter in September. That Court, dominated by Republicans and all Plumer appointees, rendered its decision in favor of the "University" in November, and the College forces immediately prepared to take the case before the United States Supreme Court.

TO [JEREMIAH] MASON

Boston, September 4, 1817.

Dear Sir,

We are happy to hear that Mrs. Mason arrived safe, and hope that Jane's[1] illness was not of long continuance. We think it would have been wise in you to have been here at the time of Commencement.[2] It was, I thought, a pleasant occasion. I went to Waltham, and passed a few hours at Mr. [Christopher] Gore's, while Mr. [Rufus] King was there. Mr. King expressed great regret at your leaving him. He thinks you underrate the good which might have been done, but at the same time does not doubt that you will find it more agreeable to be at home.

Mr. Gore was pleased to have given you a mark of the esteem in which the learned hold you. As he is so much confined, it would be a very good thing for you to come and see him, if you should find it convenient, in the course of the autumn.

Judge [Jeremiah] Smith has written to me,[3] that I must take some part in the argument of this college question. I have not thought of the subject, nor made the least preparation; I am sure I can do no good, and must, therefore, beg that you and he will follow up in your own manner, the blows which have already been so well struck. I am willing to be considered as belonging to the cause and to talk about it, and consult about it, but should do no good by undertaking an argument. If it is not too troublesome, please let Mr. [Stephen] Fales[4] give me a naked list of the authorities cited by you, and I will look at them before court. I do this that I may be able to understand you and Judge Smith.

I hope you will do the needful about our lodgings at Exeter. I should not like to be too much crowded at Mr. Gardner's.[5]

Yours, with great regard,   D. Webster

Text from *PC*, 1: 265–266. Original not found.

1. Daughter of Jeremiah.

2. Harvard commencement exercises were held on August 27.

3. Letter not found.

4. Fales (1790–1854), probably then a clerk or partner of Mason's.

5. Not identified.

FROM JOSEPH HOPKINSON

Philad: Nov. 20. 1817

My dear Sir

I have your favour of the 16: inst.[1] and enlist most cheerfully and heartily, under your banner, in the cause you mention—whether on business or pleasure; in social or professional intercourse, I know none with whom I would prefer to associate. From the little knowledge the newspapers gave us of your controversy, I confess I am greatly surprised at the result; unless, indeed, something beside the justice & argument of the cause has found its way into the decision. For such things do happen even in the tribunals of the law from the highest to the lowest; sometimes without a consciousness of their influence; and sometimes more culpably.

When I heard of Mr [James] Lloyd's resignation,[2] which was at a large dinner table, I clapped my hands and proclaimed, ["]Now we shall have Webster there." The company joined in the wish; but, after all, you wont come. Well, I am sure I could not desire you to make a serious sacrifice of your private concerns, either for my gratification, or to serve the publick; and I will be content to hear of your prosperity; and to see you occasionally at the Supreme Court at Washington. Does Mr [Jonathan] Mason consent to be the democratic Candidate?[3] and must we rely on the profession of faith given to him by one of the orators of the democratic caucus? I think Boston federalism is in a fine way—you erect triumphal arches— and glittering thrones, and sing songs of triumph to Mr Monroe, whose path is strewed with flowers by virgins (or those who pass for such) and children who are bona fide so, and all this for harmony & brotherly love; and you conclude the farce, by quarrelling for a place in Congress. To be serious about your reception of the President; I am fully of the opinion that every mark of a dignified & proper respect should have been shewn him, on every account; but really it seems to me that, Yankee like, you pushed the thing to the very borders of the ridiculous. You cannot be moderate in any thing. Like a canadian climate, you either freeze or con- sume whatever you touch. God bless you, Yr hu[mble] S[ervant]

J. Hopkinson

ALS. NhD.

1. Letter not found.
2. Lloyd had resigned his seat in Congress on October 25, 1817.
3. Having been nominated in Suf-

folk County by the Democrats and one faction of the Federalists, Mason was elected to Congress on November 17, 1817.

TO [JEREMIAH] MASON

Boston, November 27, 1817.

Dear Sir,

President [Francis] Brown has written to me respecting the college cause in its further progress.[1] I have engaged to keep hold of it if I go to Washington this winter. He seems desirous of a final decision this winter. To this end it is necessary that the record should be forwarded as soon as possible. If you can have it sent to me, I will send it along. Mr. Brown does not know the necessary steps in order to the getting up and getting along the writ of error, and relies on you and Judge [Jeremiah] Smith. Causes, as you know, are entered at the supreme court, upon the arrival of the record. I should like to know something of the court's opinion; I wish you or Mr. [Timothy] Farrar could get a copy for me. If I go to Washington, and have this cause on my shoulders, I must have your brief, which I should get of course without difficulty, and Judge Smith's.

I must also have somebody to help me at Washington. I can think of nobody better for such a question than [Joseph] Hopkinson.

We have no news here. The court has commenced its session, and the chief justice [Isaac Parker] intends to get through next month. Not a word is said about our congress election, since it is over.

Mr. [Christopher] Gore seemed to be very well, for him, a fortnight ago, and I believe continues so.

Will you inform me whether a copy of Judge [William Merchant] Richardson's opinion[2] can be had, and whether you can devise a mode in which I can get Judge Smith's minutes if I should go to Washington?

With many salutations for Mrs. Mason and the children, I am yours,
D. Webster.

Text from *PC*, 1: 266–267. Original not found.

1. Letter not found.
2. The majority opinion of the New Hampshire Superior Court—that

Dartmouth College was, in fact a public corporation subject to regulation by the state legislature—rendered on November 6, 1817.

TO JEREMIAH MASON

Boston Decr. 8. 1817

Dear Sir,

Judge [Jeremiah] Smith has written for a form of citation &c, in the College cause,[1] which I shall send him, & write to him, for his minutes.[2] My wish is, to see both him & you, before I go to W[ashington]. If I should not be kept in town by the Court, as I do not expect to, I intend seeing you, about Christmas, or New Years.

Every body will expect me at Washington to deliver the Exeter argument.[3] Therefore, the Exeter argument must be drawn out before I go. I will spend a day or two, on this Subject, at Portsmo. or Exeter, if you incline that I should do so. We must have [William Merchant] Richardson's opinion, a little before hand, if we can, that we may consider its weak points, if there be any such.

Gore & Pine[4] has not disappointed me. There is not [one] of them I would trust sixpence with.

I am sorry our College cause goes to W[ashington] on *one* point only. What do you think of an action in some court of U. S. that shall raise all the objections to the Acts in question? Such a suit could easily be brought; that is, Jurisdiction could easily be given to the Court of U. S. by bringing in a Vermont Party. Yrs   D. Webster

ALS. MHi. Published in Van Tyne, pp. 74–75.

1. Letter not found.
2. Webster to Smith, December 8, 1817, *PC*, 1: 267–268.
3. Presented by Smith, Jeremiah

Mason, and DW, the Exeter argument contended that because Dartmouth was a private, charitable institution, its affairs could not be regulated by the state of New Hampshire.

4. Not identified.

FROM ISAAC HILL

Concord, N. H. Dec. 16, 1817.

Sir,

Having been solicited from various quarters to publish an entire view of the College question as lately tried in the superior court of this State, and having the promise of the opinion of the court and the arguments of some of the counsel, it would be peculiarly pleasing to me to be able to add your argument in this case to this publication; which will be in a pamphlet form. You may rest assured that the printer will strive to do justice by faithfully publishing such manuscript as may be presented him by those interested. He will be glad to receive it as soon as the tenth January next.[1]

Your obedient servant,   Isaac Hill

ALS. NhHi.

1. To Hill's request, Webster responded (December 27, 1817) that the Dartmouth case "being still pending, it appears to me to be improper to publish the arguments of Counsel." For the full text of Webster's response, see mDW 2116.

TO [JEREMIAH] SMITH

Boston, January 9, 1818.

Dear Sir,

I was not a little disappointed at your sudden departure from this town. Being under an obligation to go to Cambridge on Thursday, and expecting to meet you at Mr. [William] Prescott's[1] on Friday, it was quite unexpected to hear that you had left us. I wished to have said something on the college case confidentially. I shall now say it to Mr. [Jeremiah] Mason, whom I must see before I go, and he will communicate with you. My hopes of ultimate success are at present somewhat stronger than they ever have been. I must beg the favor of all your notes. I have not assurance enough, although not entirely destitute, to think of arguing this cause on my own strength. To argue it as you did would be more than I shall ever be able to do. I wish to present the cause fully and fairly to the court, and your notes will enable me so to do. If anybody is coming over, pray let me have them soon, and all of them. If you have no opportunity to send them direct, please forward them enclosed, to Mr. Mason. I am writing to him to-day, and will ask him to take care of the packet and to send it to me directly.

I am, dear Sir, with unabated regard, yours,   D. Webster.

Text from PC, 1: 268–269. Original not found.

1. Prescott (1762–1844, Harvard 1783), Boston lawyer, delegate to the Hartford and Constitutional conventions, and Judge of the Boston Court of Common Pleas in 1818.

TO [JEREMIAH] MASON

Boston, January [c. 23?], 1818.

Dear Sir,

I must either accept your proposition to meet you at Newburyport, or persuade you to come here. Our court yet holds on; and since I last wrote you, I have been requested to take charge, at Washington, of a cause of much earlier standing on the docket than any in which I had previously a concern.[1] The consequence is, that I must depart somewhat sooner than I intended, and that I shall be pressed much for time while I stay. If I go to Portsmouth, there are persons who will expect to see me there; and indeed if I only allow the time necessary to go and return, staying a day with you, it will be more than I know how to spare. I must try to get off for Washington this day week. If you cannot come here, I will meet you at Newburyport, say on Sunday morning, if I hear from you to that effect. I hope, however, you will find it convenient to come here. You will have motive enough, in the natural desire of seeing Mary [Mason]. If you will come up on Saturday, my house shall be closed upon us, we being in it, until your departure, on Monday morning, if such is your wish. On any other occasion, or at any other time, I would go a hundred miles to see you. I profess to be a sort of attendant on your course, in your orbit. But at present, if you can vary a little to accommodate the secondary planet, it would be a great favor. In addition to events in the house, I have been engaged for a fortnight, forenoon and afternoon, in indispensable drudgery.

Under the circumstances, I shall wait to hear from you by Saturday morning's mail. I shall contrive to get to Newburyport by Sunday morning, if you so write. But I should esteem it a very particular obligation, which I would not request on slight reasons, if you could any way make it convenient to come here.

Mrs. Webster is getting along very well. The daughter[2] is in good health, and seems to take the world easy.

With unabated regard yours,   D. Webster.

P.S. I saw Judge [Joseph] Story as he went on. He said he had had a correspondence with you about "things;" but company being present, did not say what things. As usual, he told our lawyers here, that Mr. Mason was decidedly the first lawyer in New England.

Text from *PC*, 1: 270–271. Original not found.

1. DW was probably referring to *The United States* v. *William Bevans,*

3 Wheaton 336 (1818). See Thomas L. Winthrop, *et al.*, to DW, January 20, 1818, mDW 2156.

2. Julia, born on January 16, 1818.

TO JEREMIAH MASON

Washington, Feb. 22, 1818.

My dear sir

I have hardly found eno[ugh] to write abt to make a letter, since I have been here. I wrote Judge [Samuel] Bell some time since, & nothing new has occurred in his case since, which you will please inform him.[1] I have hopes it will go over, but it is yet a little uncertain. The docket is not quite so formidable as it was expected. The College case is not yet argued. We expect it on this week. [William] Wirt & [John] Holmes are for Def[endan]t. Wirt is a man of a good deal of ability. He is rather more of a lawyer than I expected. As to Holmes, if he shines no more in court than in Congress, he will not shed much light. He is quite run thro'. I never knew a man so completely disappoint all expectation. Men of all sorts take a pride to gird at him. His political friends are angry at their disappointment—his political enemies rejoice that he is found out. The first scold & call him hard names—the latter laugh. Your friend the Judge [Arthur Livermore] is in pretty much the same predicament, except that he brought up reputation with him, & of course has not fallen quite so far. He does not seem to be of any consideration.

I have been once or twice in the house. Those N. H. members to whom I had ever been known came to see me except the Judge. I have seen nothing of him.

The Bankruptcy Bill I fear will hardly pass, tho' it will come near it.[2]

The Western gentlemen say the Circuit Courts must be established this session.[3] On the whole, I think there is a fair chance for the adoption of the measure.

The Judge volunteered to tell me what correspondence had taken place, & he seems to be fixed in his purpose in that particular. You have a very ardent friend in Col. [John] Williams. I dined with him not long since. He took occasion to speak of you in such a manner, that I had a pretty full conversation with him.

He is a very good fellow— I only wish to say, on this subject, as much as shall let you know that at present all things wear a very favorable appearance.

Mrs. Bagot inquires for Mrs. Mason, and Mrs. DeNeuville asks for *My Brother-in-Law*, Mr. Mason.[4] I informed her that my brother-in-law was very well. The Ministers are hospitable as usual. I have been once at Mrs. [James] Monroe's, it was very full. I have dined with the President. His style of life exceeds his predecessors. Washington is in all things pretty much what it was last year. I hope to get away from here early next month; but I shall stay a week or two if necessary to observe the course of things. Give my love to Mrs. M. ask her to write often to Mrs. W.

Yrs   D. Webster

Typed copy. NhHi. Printed in part in PC, I: 271–272.

1. On the case of *Bullard* v. *Bell* argued before the Supreme Court at the February 1819 term. Because the court was divided, no decision was rendered (5 Wheaton vii). On the case, see Samuel Bell to DW, January 12, 1818, mDW 2144. DW's letter to Bell has not been found.

2. On December 12, 1817, Congressman Joseph Hopkinson introduced a

bill to establish a uniform bankruptcy law. Charging that it would only benefit Northeastern merchant interests, representatives primarily from the South and the West defeated it on February 25, 1818.

3. On February 18, 1818, Congressman Hugh Nelson of Virginia reported a bill from the Committee on the Judiciary "for the more convenient organization of the courts of the United States, and for the appointment of circuit judges." Supreme Court judges would no longer ride circuit, and their number would consequently be reduced over the years from seven to five. As Charles Warren noted, "The demand for this reform had become more and more urgent as the number of States admitted to the Union increased," thus making circuit riding a burdensome chore for the justices. Charles Warren, *The Supreme Court in United States History* (Boston, 1928), 1: 672. Congress failed to pass the Nelson bill as it did other corresponding measures from 1816 to 1826, when finally a weak version lengthening the term of the Supreme Court was enacted into law.

4. The wives of Sir Charles Bagot, British Minister to the United States, and Baron Jean Guillaume Hyde de Neuville, French Minister to the United States, respectively.

TO [WILLIAM SULLIVAN]

Washington Feb. 27. 1818

My dear Sir,

The Divina Pastora has not yet come on, but I have no doubt it will, at this term. I have attended to the case, & am as ready for it as I shall be.[1] The Prosecution agt Palmer & al, adjourned here from Boston, presents many questions much connected with the Pastora.[2] I expected that would be argued first, but it seems at present it will not. I must therefore begin, in the affairs of the Patriots.

The Bankrupt bill is lost—it might have been carried, if all N. E. had been in favor of it. I did not hear the debates—but report speaks well of the efforts of some of the M[a]ss[achusetts] Members—particularly [Elijah Hunt] Mills & [Ezekiel] Whitman. I have hardly been half an hour in either house of Congress since I came here—a proof, I hope you will think—that I have no wish to get back there. Mr & Mrs [Harrison Gray] Otis live within three doors—but I see little of them. Mr [Eli P.] Ashmun[3] I believe has gone home. There are in the City a great number of Bostonians—more than I ever saw before at once. Brother Jno. [F. Parrott?] has arrived— & going to work on Congress pretty much as he does on the N. H. Legislature has got a bill thro. the Com[mitt]ee of the Senate abt. Patents. Col [Thomas Handasyd] Perkins is expected today I believe. Bro. [Rufus Greene] Amory & I are all the brethren of the Boston Bar here— (I forgot Mr [George] Blake).[4] [David B.?] Ogden, & a Mr. [John] Baldwin[5] from N York—[Joseph] Hopkinson—[John] Sergeant & C[harles] J[ared] Ingersoll—Phila[delphi]a—[Robert Goodloe] Harper—[William Henry] Winder—Baltimore—[John] Wickham, [Benjamin Watkins]

Leigh & [Philip Norborne] Nicholas from Virginia—[John M.] Berryan [Berrien]—from Georgia—& the Gentlemen of this District. [William] Gaston was expected—but has not come. Court meets at 11—hears long speeches till 4— & adjourns. I have dined abroad every day since I came *but one*— & the principal reason is, that the only boarding house where I could get a seat at table, is one, in which one would seldom wish to *dine at home*. I have a room and a bed, at a friend's house—Dr [Andrew?] Hunters—& get my coffee in the morning with his family. So on the whole I am better off than most of my neighbors. I am filling up this sheet without saying what I had in view, principally, in writing today—here it is—

There is a prospect that the Bill establishing Circuit Courts may pass at this term—making *one* judge in each Cir[cui]t.

Jno. Holmes— & Levi Lincoln—as well as Mr [George] *Blake* will probably seek to be made judge.

There is some chance, I think, of having a word to say on that subject ourselves. Therefore—I am very desirous—that Govr. [John] Brooks— Ch. Jus [Isaac] Parker—Genl. [George] Sullivan—Mr. [William] Prescot— & other such men, should not commit themselves to any Demo. candidate hastily—on the supposition that there is nothing but a choice of evils. You know Govr. Brooks better than I do—is there not danger of his lending his influence to some person, out of his disposition to oblige, before he knows the whole ground?

What induces me to write this is—that if such an office should be created, certain *Republican* Gentlemen here would make an effort to get the appointment for Mr. [Jeremiah] Mason of N. H.—Judge [Joseph] S[tory] I believe would exert himself to that end. Mr. M. has left a high law character here— & several of the Demo. Senators—from the East & the *West* —would like to shew him their respect by recommending his appointment to such a place. Some of the Demo. Gentlemen from N. H. would also urge his appointment. Now—if Govr. Brooks—& the Suffolk Bar think they can do no better—would it not be well for them to hold themselves free to support Mr. Mason, in case &c.

This of course is pretty confidential. You may mention it, if you see fit to Mr. Prescot—or a few other of your friends—but I wd. not have it spoken of aloud. As soon as the least chance of passing the bill appears— the candidates will spring up. No time shd. be lost to put Govr. B. on his guard, if done at all.

I do not write my wife today—will you let her know of my welfare— & will you make a bow to Mrs Sullivan, & shake hands with her, on my acct. Yours, *Dr. Genl.*   D. Webster

ALS. MHi. Published in *PC*, 1: 272–274.

1. A prize case (4 Wheaton 52–73), in which Webster represented a claimant, a Spanish consul, on appeal from the Massachusetts Circuit Court. Before the Supreme Court, he argued that the privateer violated the laws of neutrality and the Pinckney treaty. The Supreme Court remanded the case to the Circuit Court for further consideration.

2. *United States* v. *Palmer*, 3 Wheaton 610 (1818), a decision which

Chief Justice John Marshall followed in the opinion on the *Divina Pastora*. In the Palmer case, George Blake appeared for the United States; no counsel appeared for the defendants.

3. Ashmun (1770–1819), lawyer and senator from Massachusetts who resigned his seat on May 10, 1818.

4. Amory (d. 1833; Harvard 1778) and Blake (1769–1841) were members of the Suffolk bar.

5. Baldwin (d. 1843), an attorney from Livingston County.

TO [FRANCIS] BROWN

Washington, March 13, 1818.

Dear Sir,

The argument in the cause of the college was finished yesterday. It occupied nearly three days. Mr. [John] Holmes ventured to ask the court whether it was probable a decision would be made at this term.

The chief justice in answer, said, that the court would pay to the subject the consideration due to an act of the legislature of a State, and a decision of a State court, and that it was hardly probable a judgment would be pronounced at this term. You can draw any inference from this which you think warranted. If the court saw no difficulty in coming to the conclusion that the decision in New Hampshire was right, it is not probable that, knowing the state of the college, they would put off the final decision for a twelve months. Mr. [William] Wirt said all that the case admitted. He was replied to in a manner very gratifying and satisfactory to me by Mr. [Joseph] Hopkinson.

Mr. Hopkinson understood every part of the cause, and in his argument did it great justice. No new view was suggested on the other side. I am informed that the bar here are decidedly with us in opinion.

On the whole we have reason to keep up our courage. I am particularly glad that an ejectment is brought. It is just what should be done. You will see the necessity of not giving too much publicity to any thing written by me on this subject. You may say, however, to your friends, and give the students to understand, as far as useful, that the cause looks well here. I think it does look so at present, although I am not perhaps the best judge. The inference, too, to be drawn from the court's postponing the decision, is a very fair one to be used in the extent stated above, by you.

As to the opinions of the bar, you would do well not to state that on my authority, although I believe what I have said to be strictly true. If any thing further occurs relative to the case, I shall write you again.

Yours truly,   D. Webster.

Text from *PC*, 1: 274–275. Original not found.

TO WILLIAM SULLIVAN, ENDORSED TO MRS. GRACE FLETCHER WEBSTER

Washington March 13. [1818]
Friday 2 oclock

Dear Sir,

The Court has announced its intention to rise tomorrow—& will hear no argument except in the cause now before them, which is No. 79.[1]

The Pastora will not be reached. I am exceedingly sorry for this—but could not help it. I insisted to the last—& the Chief Justice was obliged to tell me it was *impossible*—& then I gave it up.

The College case is argued—not decided. There is a difference of opinion on the bench— & some of the Judges have not come to a conclusion in their own minds—so it is to be continued. I shall depart, on the rising of the Court— & make the best of my way home. Yrs   D. Webster

Dr. Madam In a letter which I have seen, it is said—"In the College cause, Webster shone like the sun; and Holmes like a sun fish."—Wm. Sn.

ALS. MHi. Published in *W & S*, 16: 40–41.

1. *McIver's Lessee* v. *Walker, et al.*, 4 Wheaton 444 (1819).

Webster's allusion to "a case," below, referred to other suits, based on diversity of citizenship, which were brought on behalf of the College in late March. The expectation was that they would be heard before Judge Joseph Story during the May term of the Federal Circuit Court, but at that court, the defendants requested and received continuances so that they might better prepare their defenses.

TO [JEREMIAH] MASON

Boston, March 22, 1818.

My Dear Sir,

I arrived last evening from Washington, having left the great city this day week. Of course I have little news to tell you. On the subject of the college cause, you know all I have to say. I send you your brief, and Judge [Jeremiah] Smith's; you may both probably need those hereafter. I believe it is fully expected that a case, raising the question in the amplest form, will be presented at the circuit court. I have given some reason to expect this, and, unless for good causes, should be mortified if it were not so.

Nothing seems likely to be done at Congress this session about the judiciary. I am rather glad of it; for, upon consideration, I am exceedingly doubtful on the constitutional point. Others are the same way of thinking; at least the objection would be plausible.

I conferred with very few on this subject. In general, I found what I thought to be a sincere desire to accomplish an object particularly important to myself and others. One reason why nothing is likely to be done this session is, that members of congress, at least some of them, are willing enough not to be excluded from the list of candidates. I think this weighs with certain Senators of Rome.

Mrs. Webster is not very well. She has had a fair trial of her nursing talent, and is obliged to yield the point.

We are procuring a wet-nurse for the child. When she is obtained, I have little doubt Mrs. Webster will enjoy full health.

I send you three or four seed potatoes. I brought them in my trunk from New Jersey. The species is lately imported from England, and is a great favorite where known.

Be good enough to plant them in your garden, and raise enough to see what they are.

Mrs. Webster desires her love to Mrs. Mason, and beg to add my regards.

Yours, truly,   D. Webster.

Text from PC, 1: 278. Original not found.

In the letter below, Webster acknowledges his deep indebtedness to Jeremiah Mason and Jeremiah Smith for use of their briefs in arguing the Dartmouth College case before the Supreme Court. And whereas he had earlier rejected Isaac Hill's request for copies of the arguments before the Superior Court because the case was yet pending, Webster now had several copies of the arguments printed for private circulation among friends of the College. Shortly, however, a copy of the pamphlet reached Isaac Hill, who reportedly printed and distributed about one hundred and fifty copies of it.

TO [JEREMIAH] MASON
                    Boston, April 23, 1818.
My Dear Sir,
    The plaintiff in the Edson cause requested my attendance at Portsmouth at the Circuit Court.[1] I have agreed to go on his performance of certain conditions precedent; and probably it rests on this, whether I shall attend the court. As to the college cause, I cannot argue it any more, I believe. I have told you very often that you and Judge [Jeremiah] Smith

argued it very greatly. If it was well argued at Washington, it is a proof that I was right, because all that I said at Washington was but those two arguments, clumsily put together by me. I do not mean to hold you answerable for any deficiencies; but in truth have little right to claim the merit, if there be any, in the opening of our case. Since I came home, a young man in my office has assisted me to copy my minutes, and I have been foolish enough to print three or four copies. I committed this folly principally on the motion of some friends here, who were anxious to know something of the grounds of our case, of which they have been most deplorably uninformed. These copies are and will remain, except when loaned for a single day, under my own lock and key. They are hastily written off, with much abbreviation, and contain little else than quotation from the cases. All the nonsense is left out. There is no title or name to it. These precautions were taken to avoid the indecorum of publishing the creature. If I have a safe conveyance, I shall send one to you. You must not let [Timothy] Farrar [Jr.] see it, because he would wish to show it to President [Francis] Brown and all. And perhaps I should do better to burn it, than to send it at all. Judge [Joseph] Story has been recently in town. I have no doubt he will incline to send up the new cause in the most convenient manner, without giving any opinion, and probably without an argument. If the district judge will agree to divide without argument, *pro formâ*, I think Judge Story will incline so to dispose of the cause. A special verdict is the most convenient mode, I think. The verdict in the other cause I think very right, and from the same minutes one can be drawn in the present case.[2] I shall be at Portsmouth whether I hear from Edson or not, unless I should be engaged at Ipswich.

Mr. [William] Prescott is judge, a very good thing for the county of Suffolk, and not so bad a thing for himself as it might at first seem.[3] He will receive about three thousand dollars per annum. He does not wish and has repeatedly declined a seat on the other bench, on account of its great labor, and being willing to leave the bar pretty soon, this seems to be an eligible retirement. We shall endeavor to get along without him at the bar, and bear our loss as well as we can.

We expect Mrs. Mason to see us next month, and she has partly promised to bring her husband.

Yours truly,   D. Webster.

Text from *PC*, 1: 280–281. Original not found.

1. *Caspar R. Edson* v. *Timothy O. Edson*. The case does not appear on the docket of the circuit court.

2. The three Dartmouth College circuit court cases were all subsequently heard at Exeter that September.

3. On April 21 Prescott had been appointed Judge of the Boston Court of Common Pleas.

TO [JEREMIAH] SMITH

Boston, May 12, [1818]

Dear Sir,

I send you by Judge [Oliver] Peabody your argument and [Jeremiah] Mason's, bung[l]ingly put together by me. Right or wrong, I have done the deed. So great, and how great you know, was the want of information on this subject by our best men, that I could endure it no longer. Some few copies are printed, not to be published, but to be read by those who ought to understand the subject a little. I shall take all care I can not to let the things get much abroad. It is, as you see, nameless; and it may go "unclaimed of any man." I have been more than usually silly on this occasion; ascribe it to having been six weeks at Washington. Mr. Wells[1] has received a few new books; not yet opened. If you wish any particular book which he is likely to have, I will look out for it, if you let me know soon. I believe he has the latest reports.

Always very truly yours, D. Webster.

Text from *PC*, 1: 306. Incorrectly dated 1819 by Fletcher Webster.

1. Wells and Lilley, a Boston publishing house.

TO [FRANCIS] BROWN

Boston, July 16, 1818.

Dear Sir,

You are not much accustomed, I believe, to forget your duties; and some apology would seem necessary for reminding you of things, which in all probability you have fully attended to. There are two topics, however, upon each of which I will repeat the expression of a wish. The first is the letter to Mr. [Joseph] Hopkinson; the second, care to prevent any public use being made of our argument. Mr. [Benjamin Joseph] Gilbert informs me that a copy has been given to the students, and I am fearful their zeal in a good cause may lead them possibly to make an indiscreet use of it. I rely on you for safety against such evils. I am quite satisfied our course is right. The argument will cease to do good, if used in any other way than that in which we have used it. Pray caution the students against publishing it, or any part of it. The printer also should be admonished not to say any thing about it.

We have nothing new about the final result. As far as I learn, those who have paid attention to the question are more and more convinced that we have the right side.

Very truly yours, D. Webster.

Text from *PC*, 1: 284–285. Original not found.

Webster's review of Henry Dearborn's Account of the Battle of Bunker Hill *and Daniel Putnam's* Letter to Major General Dearborn, repelling his unprovoked attack . . . on Major General Israel Putnam, *in the July 1818 issue of the* North American Review, *prompted the following response from Daniel Putnam (1759–1831), the son of Israel. Other essays in the Boston* Columbian Centinel *(July 4–25), which Daniel Putnam mentioned, were also subsequently attributed to Webster.*

FROM DANIEL PUTNAM

Brooklyn Con[necticu]t 17th. July, 1818

Sir,

I have read with deep interest, and great satisfaction an article in the North American Review, vindicating the character of General [Israel] Putnam, and his conduct on the 17th. of June 1775. If the attack was violent & unexpected, the defence has been valiant and effectual to the satisfaction of the public mind. For the distinguished part which your love of justice has contributed towards it, I pray you to accept the grateful thanks of the family, and mine own individual acknowledgement of obligation, greater, than it will ever be in my power to repay.

It is due however, to the relation in which I stand to General Putnam, to maintain with modesty, what he always asserted with confidence— that the *command* on Bunker-Hill was his. If this could not be done without taking from the Gallant and deserving [William] Prescott, any part of the glory which always has, and I hope ever will be accorded by his grateful country, for the persevering valour with which he defended the principal object of assault; I should be among the last to make the claim, in favor, even of a Father. But this business has been candidly and I hope satisfactorily stated in the last of a series of Nos. in the Centinal, which do honor to the head and heart of the writer, and give to Putnam and Prescott the commendation appropriately due to each; leaving nothing for the friends of either to wish, or regret.

I have the honor to be, most respectfully Sir, Your most Obt. & much obliged Sevt.   Danl. Putnam

ALS. NhHi. Published in *PC*, 1: 285.

TO JACOB MCGAW

Boston July 27. 1818

My Dear Sir,

The next Term of the C.C.P. in this County is on "the last Tuesday of Septr." I will be obliged to you to alter friend [John?] Hodgdon's writ accordingly, & to give it to a sherriff for service.[1]

I send you with great cheerfulness a "sketch" of our view of the case in the question abt. D. College.

I have never allowed myself to indulge in any great hopes of success; but if even a few such men as Judge [Samuel Sumner] Wilde[2] should think we had made out our case, it would repay the labor. If you should think there is any merit in the manner of this argument, you must recollect that [it] is drawn from materials furnished by Judge [Jeremiah] Smith, & Mr [Jeremiah] Mason as well as from the little contributed by myself. The opinion of the N. H. Court had been a good deal circulated, & I was urged to exhibit in print our view of the case. A few copies only were printed, & those have been used rather cautiously. A respect for the court, as well as general decorum, seems to prohibit the *publishing* of an argument, while the cause is pending. I have no objection to your shewing this to any professional friend, in yr discretion. I only wish to guard against it's becoming too public.

Remember me to Mrs McG & believe me to be Yrs sincerely

Danl Webster

ALS. NhD. Excerpt published in Van Tyne, p. 77.

1. Hodgdon, a native of Ware, N.H.
2. Wilde (1771–1858; Dartmouth

1789), Massachusetts lawyer, delegate to the Hartford and Constitutional conventions, and judge of the Supreme Judicial Court, 1815–1850.

TO EZEKIEL WEBSTER

Boston Aug 27. 1818

Dear Sir,

I have bo't the [John L.] Sullivan[1] lands—for cash—1000 Dlls in 30 d[ay]s—one thousand in sixty, & in[teres]t. I have told Mr Greeley[2] the lands are mine—but not on what t[erms.] I have offered them to him for 2700 Dlls—on his terms of credit.

You are at liberty to take the bargain off my hands—if you see fit. If so, I must know, by Tuesday's mail. Write me before you go to Hopkinton. The 30 d[ay]s— & 60 days—begin to run this day. Will [you] take them. Yrs   D. Webster

I will not sell them under 2700 Dlls—*you* may take my bargain—& sell them for what you please—

ALS. NhD.
1. Boston merchant, who was also

head of the Middlesex Canal.
2. Not identified.

TO [JOSEPH] STORY

September 9, 1818.

Dear Sir,

I send you five copies of our argument. If you send one of them to each of such of the judges as you think proper, you will of course do it in the manner least likely to lead to a feeling that any indecorum has been committed by the plaintiffs. The truth is, the New Hampshire opinion is able, ingenious, and plausible. It has been widely circulated, and something was necessary to exhibit the other side of the question.

I have read the article on "Maritime Law"[1] with the highest delight. There is a great deal that is new to me, and will be most useful to the profession. Your compliment to Chancellor [James] Kent was happily turned, and well deserved. His brother, Moss Kent,[2] of Albany, is a personal acquaintance of mine, and not knowing how many copies of the North American Review might be taken in Albany, I yesterday sent one to him. I think this Number a very good one.

To-day I have been at work for [Henry] Wheaton,[3] although I have not seen the book yet. Whatever I write must pass your revision.

Very truly, your obedient servant,   D. Webster.

Text from *PC*, 1: 287. Original not found.

1. DW's reference was to the review of William Frick's *Laws of the sea with reference to maritime commerce during peace and war—from the German of Frederick J. Jacobsen,* which appeared in the *North American Review,* 7 (September 1818): 323–347.

2. Kent (1766–1838), a lawyer and former state legislator, had been elected to the 13th and 14th Congresses, where DW probably became acquainted with him.

3. Webster was probably preparing a review of the recently published third volume of Wheaton's Supreme Court Reports. See his letter to Wheaton, December 12, 1818, below.

During the Dartmouth College controversy, the College found itself in severe financial difficulty. In the letter below, President Francis Brown discusses with Webster ways of acquiring the necessary funds.

FROM FRANCIS BROWN

Dart. Coll. Sept. 19, 1818.

My dear Sir,

I have received your favour of the 6th.[1] & have seen Mr. [Charles] Marsh.

In regard to the reprinting, I have some little doubt, whether the benefit to be expected would render the measure expedient, considering how soon it may be hoped the *volume* will appear. The very scarcity of the argument, & the half-secret & cautious manner of the distribution, stimulate curiosity, & add somewhat to the *preciousness* of the document. It has already been, or shortly will be, read by all the *commanding* men of New England & New York; & so far as it has gone, it has united them all, without a single exception within my knowledge, in one broad & impenetrable phalanx for our defence & support. N. E. & N. Y. *are gained.* Will not this be sufficient for our *present* purposes? If not, I should recommend the re-printing. And on this point you are the best judge. I prevailingly think, however, that the current from this part of the country is setting so strongly towards the south, that we may safely trust to its force alone to accomplish whatever is necessary. I acknowledge I am sanguine; and, on that account, ought to distrust myself. I, therefore, conclude this topick by saying, if, in your opinion, any thing more *needs* to be done in en-lightening the *most eminent* of the professional men of the country, let a hundred or two copies be struck off without delay. But even in that case, I should recommend the principle of selection in the distribution; for I would not allow the argument to be common, until it is to be sold.

Prof. [Ebenezer] Adams has mentioned your plan for funds, and I hope you will not give it up (unless a better one presents) on account of the free remarks of our excellent friend, Mr. Marsh. He mentioned that he discouraged a loan—the favour must be a *gift*. I agree with him, so far as this mode can be made to succeed; so far as it cannot, the other is un-questionably to be seized with thankfulness. It is true, we shall have to struggle hard, even after we have gained the victory in the legal combat. And therefore it is our duty to provide, in the present exigency, which presents a tangible object to the community, for future emergencies. I do not yet despair of obtaining all, that may be needed, as a gift. We can at least pull on this string for two or three months. Will it not, then, be best to suspend operations for a loan for the present? When January comes, we shall know how we stand, & what more is necessary; and we can then act according to circumstances.

I have received an answer from Mr. [Joseph] Hopkinson.[2] He consents to prepare his part of the argument for publication, and I presume it will be ready in season. The book must be out at the earliest possible day after the opinion of the Court can be procured. Will it be best to print in Bos-ton? What printer shall be employed? Will it be best to have proposals issued beforehand? What terms can be secured? These are inquiries, which have occurred to me, & which I will thank you to consider at some convenient time.

We are under obligations to Dr. [John Thornton] Kirkland for his civili-ties & proffers of aid. I have no question of his sincerity; and I believe he exercises no more caution than other men in eminent stations have thought proper to observe. We will avail ourselves of his kindness at such time & in such manner as may seem best.

I am, my dear Sir, as ever, yours,   Francis Brown

ALS. NhD. Published in Shirley, *Dart-mouth College Causes*, pp. 271–272.

1. Not found.
2. Letter not found.

TO FRANCIS BROWN

Boston Sep. 20. 1818

Dear Sir,

I recd yours from Albany,[1] &, today, that from Reedsboro'.[2] You are probably at home by this time, & will find one from me. I am particularly gratified with the state of things where you have been. I never doubted, for a moment, on which side of such a question C[hancellor James] K[ent]'s mind must ultimately rest. I have studied him (in his works) many years, & think I understand him. He has great talents, great legal learning, & great *firmness* & independence of mind. His opinion will have *weight,* wherever it is known. I hope he will express himself, as occasion may offer.

I returned friday Eve' from Exeter, where I saw Mr [Charles] Marsh. The causes look quite promising. I think there will be little doubt of some or all of them going up. Mr Marsh engaged to attend the Court. I think it important that he should, as things may arise on the trial which strangers may not be able to explain. I hope he will not find many other journies necessary. His exertions are truly commendable.

I heard at Exeter, (& have no doubt of the truth of it) that the University has retained Mr [William] Pinkney. This will occasion another argument at Washington, which I regret, on some accounts. I do not fear that it will increase the danger to our case, which I trust will grow brighter by discussion, but who is to argue it on our side? I do not feel as if I could ever undertake it again, & hardly know what to recommend to you. As Bro. [John] Holmes *retires* probably from the cause the next term, I think it [would] be prudent for me to retire with him. Of all these things we must consult hereafter.

I propose going into N. H. this week—expect to pass next Sabbath at Salisbury. I shall of course see Mr. [Richard] Fletcher.[3]

I hear nothing *discouraging,* as to the probable event of things. C. B. Haddock[4] has been here. His health is a little precarious. He has gone into the Country, & perhaps you may see him. I think he must winter at the South. Yrs truly   D.W.

ALS. NhD. Published in part in Shirley, *Dartmouth College Causes,* pp. 270–271.

1. See Brown to DW, Albany, September 8, 1818, in Shirley, *Dartmouth College Causes,* pp. 264–266, and mDWs.

2. Brown's Reedsboro letter was dated September 15. See mDW 2519.

3. Fletcher (1788–1869; Dartmouth 1806) had read law with DW in Portsmouth and settled in Salisbury. Following his move to Boston in 1819, he served in Congress, on the bench of the Massachusetts Supreme Court, and as a trustee of Dartmouth College.

4. Charles Brickett Haddock (1796–1861; Dartmouth 1816), Webster's

1. Daniel Webster, c. 1804, artist unknown, Dartmouth College Archives.

2. Ebenezer Webster, artist unknown. New Hampshire Historical Society, Concord, New Hampshire.

3. Abigail Eastman Webster, artist unknown. New Hampshire Historical
Society, Concord, New Hampshire.

4. Dartmouth College, by Samuel Hill and engraved by Josiah Dunham. *Massachusetts Magazine*, Volume 5 (February, 1793), facing p. 67.

5. (top left) Joseph W. Brackett, by John Wesley Jarvis. Dartmouth College.

6. (top right) Samuel A. Bradley, artist and engraver unknown. William Willis, *A History of the Law, the Courts, and the Lawyers of Maine* (Portland, Maine, 1863), facing p. 309.

7. (bottom left) Thomas W. Thompson, by Charles Balthazar Julien Fevret de Saint-Mémin, 1807. Corcoran Gallery of Art, Washington, D.C.

8. (bottom right) Christopher Gore, by John Trumbull, 1800. Massachusetts Historical Society, Boston, Massachusetts.

9. Ezekiel Webster, engraver and artist unknown. Charles Carleton Coffin, *The History of Boscawen and Webster [New Hampshire] from 1733 to 1878* (Concord, N.H., 1878), facing p. 453.

10. Grace Fletcher Webster, by Chester Harding, 1827. Dartmouth College.

11. Daniel Webster, by Gilbert Stuart, c. 1825. Dartmouth College.

12. A View of Portsmouth, New Hampshire from the East Shore, by
Joseph F. W. Des Barres, *The Atlantic Neptune*, c. 1780. New Hampshire
Historical Society, Concord, New Hampshire.

13. (top left) Jeremiah Mason probably a copy of the Gilbert Stuart portrait, c. 1815. Harvard Law School, Cambridge, Massachusetts.

14. (top right) Joseph Story, by Gilbert Stuart, 1819. Harvard College, Cambridge, Massachusetts.

15. (bottom left) Nathaniel Appleton Haven, Jr., attributed to Joseph Greenleaf Cole. Portsmouth Atheneum, Portsmouth, New Hampshire.

16. (bottom right) William Sullivan, by G. S. Newton and engraved by W. Warner. Frontispiece of William and John T. S. Sullivan, *The Public Men of the Revolution Including Events from the Peace of 1783 to the Peace of 1815* (Philadelphia, 1847).

17. (top left) Rufus King, by Gilbert Stuart, 1820. Museum of the City of New York.

18. (top right) Timothy Pickering, engraved by T. B. Welch from a drawing by J. B. Longacre after Gilbert Stuart. James Barton Longacre and James Herring, *The National Portrait Gallery of Distinguished Americans* (4 volumes, Philadelphia, New York, 1834–39), I (1834), 90.

19. (bottom left) Joseph Hopkinson, by Gilbert Stuart, 1803. The Historical Society of Pennsylvania, Philadelphia, Pennsylvania.

20. (bottom right) Richard Stockton, Jr., by Edward Ludlow Mooney after Charles B. Lawrence. Princeton University, Princeton, New Jersey.

21. View of Boston and the South Boston Bridge, c. 1820, drawn by Jacques Gerard Milbert. *Itineraire Pittoresque du Fleuve Hudson et Des Parties Laterales D'Amerique du Nord* (Paris, 1828–29), from State Street Bank and Trust Company, Boston, Massachusetts.

22. William H. Woodward, by William H. S. Doyle, 1802. Dartmouth College Archives.

23. Francis Brown, copy by Joseph Ames after Samuel F. B. Morse, 1817–18. Dartmouth College.

24. Thomas Gibbons, artist unknown. William L. Hopkins, Jr.,
Savannah, Georgia.

25. John Inskeep, by Nikol
Schattenstein after Rembrandt
Peale. Insurance Company of
North America, Springfield,
Massachusetts.

nephew. Upon leaving Dartmouth, he studied divinity at Andover for two years, then returned to Dartmouth as a professor. Subsequently, he repre- sented Hanover in the New Hampshire legislature, and from 1850 to 1854 he was chargé d'affaires in Portugal.

TO NATHANIEL APPLETON HAVEN

Boston Sep. 21. 1818.

Dear Sir

It seems too great a sacrifice to sell the Thornton land for 300 Dlls. I would consent to let it go for 400,—on such terms of payment as you should think fit. If Mr Smart[1] does not offer that, I think it would be best to wait till Spring, in hopes of a better offer than his. The two warm summers which have gone over us will, I hope, give some more value to these N. Hamp. lands.

This is a time in which I am not in the receipt of much money. I have <laid> paid 500 Dlls on Mr Rogers[2] draft, for N. H. Bank; & I must be able to do something for you soon. I do not expect, however, to be able to do much under a month or two, unless it should be *indispensable;* in which case I must find ways & means to comply with your requirements. I am going this week to Boscawen, & will try to hasten the payt. of the residue of the Lang[3] note. Yours with great regard   D. Webster

ALS. Douglas R. Gray, Portsmouth, N.H.
    1. Not identified.

2. Not identified.
3. Not identified.

In his frequent appearances before the Supreme Court, Webster met and formed strong personal and professional relationships with the eminent men of the bar from across the nation. Two such friendships were with Thomas Addis Emmet of New York, whose letter appears below, and William Pinkney of Maryland, whose letter follows under the date of December 28.

FROM THOMAS ADDIS EMMET

New York Septr. 29th. 1818

Sir

On my return to this City from the Session of our Court of Errors at Albany, I had the pleasure of receiving yours of the 23rd. Inst.[1] I propose being at Washington next Winter, if I can accomplish it, without interfering with my engagements before the Court of Errors. Indeed until the last adjournment of that Court I had hopes of being able to do so without difficulty. It is now however very clear that I shall not be able to be in

Washington until some where about the middle of February— & probably that may not answer for the business about which you wish me to be employed. I should be extremely happy to be associated with you;[2] & only regret that I am obliged to speak with some kind of indecision, as to the time, & perhaps even the certainty of my being there—for I cannot sacrifice the business, in which I have from the commencement of the suits been engaged, that will come before the Court of Errors next Winter. I however still hope, if I can be indulged with a small delay at Washington, to accomplish both; & shall in that event have great pleasure in receiving your commands.

I am, Sir, with much respect Your Obedient Servant

Thos. Addis Emmet

ALS. NhHi.

1. Not found.

2. DW had probably asked Emmet to appear as counsel with him in *Bullard* v. *Bell*, which was subsequently dismissed by the Court on March 24, 1824. See Emmet to DW, December 19, 1818, below.

Two articles implicating Webster in an unethical stock transaction appeared in the February 10 and March 24, 1818, issues of the New Hampshire Patriot. *They charged him with obtaining $10,000 of Yazoo claim stock for the executor of a Londonderry estate and, "being in want of money," of selling about $4,000 of it for his own use. It was about these charges that Webster had written George Farrar (1778–1858; Dartmouth 1800), a Londonderry physician.*

FROM GEORGE FARRAR

Londonderry Octobr 10th. 1818

Hon. Daniel Webster,

In answer to the letter you wrote me while at Exeter,[1] I give the following—

I had no agency in writing the pieces published in the N. H Patriot to which you allude.

In the second place I state that I had no knowledge of either of those publication[s], before I saw them in the Patriot, except the one to which Mr. [Silas] Betton[2] put his name, and lastly I do not now know who was the author of either of the pieces published in the N. H. Patriot to which you refer. Yours with esteem   George Farrar

ALS. NhHi.

1. Not found.

2. Betton (1768–1822; Dartmouth 1787), Salem lawyer and legislator. In a May 12 letter printed in the *Patriot*, Betton had vigorously denied the charges against Webster. No further reference to the charges has been found.

TO EZEKIEL WEBSTER

Boston Oct. 11. 1818

Dear E.

One thing I forgot—I am about paying something to the Exeter Bank, on my note, & they wish a renewal, by your & my joint & several note for balance. Please [send] me your name, on paper to have a note written over it. I shall not increase but diminish the sum. Let this come by return of mail if you can. Write me about Mrs Quimby.[1] We got home well, & found all well. Yrs   D.W.

ALS. NhD.   1. Not identified.

In the fall of 1818, the Supreme Court had not yet delivered its opinion in the Dartmouth case; and Webster and his colleagues, Hopkinson, Smith, and Mason, were preparing to meet a new legal challenge from the University forces. Webster, however, was reluctant to continue with the cause; and although he declared that his reasons were pecuniary, they may have run deeper: he possibly feared that he could not equal his earlier effort before the Supreme Court. It is also possible that he was simply weary of the subject matter of the case.

Concurrently, Webster, Farrar, and other friends of the College considered the preparation of a full report of the Dartmouth case in the various courts. To Webster fell the collection and preparation of the arguments, while Farrar oversaw the printing. Two major obstacles—obtaining briefs from attorneys and judges and finding a good printer—delayed the appearance of the Report of the Case of the Trustees of Dartmouth College against William H. Woodward (*Portsmouth, 1819*), *until August.*

It is with these two subjects—the Dartmouth case and the "Book"—that much of Webster's correspondence, both incoming and outgoing, deals in late 1818 and 1819.

FROM FRANCIS BROWN

Dart. Coll. Nov. 4, 1818.

My dear Sir,

Your letter to Mr. [Charles] Marsh[1] by Mr. [Job] Lyman[2] is before me.

You will allow me to say, that, in my judgment, & in the judgment of all the friends of the College, we must rely *chiefly* on you, in the contemplated discussions at Washington. Nor do I think this will require a new argument on the old ground. For if you propose to the Court & the adverse Counsel, that the pltffs have nothing to add, & mention this in season, is it at all probable they will require any thing more? <I think not.> But *if they should,* what shall we do? Why, indeed, I know not. For who would be willing to go over the same ground after you, which you would be unwilling to retrace yourself? To me it is clear, that no man in the country would undertake this task. Mr. Marsh mentions, that Judge [Jeremiah] Smith or Mr. [Jeremiah] Mason might, possibly be persuaded to go on. We should repose the most entire confidence in either of them. But what could they say, which has not been said? I despair on this point; and therefore I do not believe they would go. What if you should write a line to Mr. [William] Pinkney, & propose the alternative suggested in your letter to Mr. Marsh? This would at least bring him out, and enable us to proceed with more light. But I beg you to allow us to expect, that you will yourself reply to Mr. Pinkney. The only reason I will mention for this wish, is, that it will be next to impossible for any man, not deeply versed in the history of D. C. and Moor's I[ndian] C[harity] S[chool] to possess the requisite knowledge <in the case> to enable him to unravel & explain all the matters & things, which the will &c. will introduce into the cause. I dislike this addition. It will embarrass the Court; and they will need a very clear historical statement to enable them to understand it. Indeed, a considerable part is unintelligible by any body. The School is *"alter, et idem,"* with the College, as occasion requires. *How* this is Mr. [John] Holmes, by his new arithmetick, must shew; *why* it is so, I will endeavour to explain to you on some future occasion. I have been labouring thro' the "Narratives" &c. &c. of which I intend to attempt something like a digest, & transmit the same to you in due season.

I have obtained a copy of the will. It will go hence to Woodstock on Saturday, & Mr. Marsh will in a few days transmit it to you.

And now, Sir, as to compensation for yourself & Mr. [Joseph] Hopkinson in the new causes, will you tell me what it should be? I intend to make a new effort, if Providence permit, in N. H. & should be glad to know the sum necessary to be raised before you go to Washington. It is my present intention to be in Boston by the middle of January.

I am, dear Sir, as ever yours,   Francis Brown

ALS. NhD. Extract published in Richard W. Morin, "Will to Resist: The Dartmouth College Case," *Dartmouth Alumni Magazine*, 61 (April 1969).

1. Letter not found.
2. Lyman (b. 1781; Dartmouth 1804), Woodstock, Vt., lawyer.

TO [FRANCIS] BROWN

Boston, November 9, 1818.

Dear Sir,

I received yours yesterday.[1] It will not be necessary to decide on the subject of other counsel until I see you. You do not appear to apprehend my reasons exactly, and I can explain them better *ore tenus;* suffice to say, at present, that, although if nothing should be necessary in the way of argument but a reply, Mr. [Joseph] Hopkinson, or myself, might do that, yet if it should be necessary to go over the whole ground again, some new hand must come into the cause. My own impression is to apply, in case of need, to some gentleman there on the spot. Let this rest till January.

As to money and compensation, &c., I hardly know what to say about it. As to myself, considerations of that sort have not added greatly to my interest in the case. I am aware also, that others, whose labors are more useful than mine, are obliged to confer gratuitous services. The going to Washington, however, is no small affair, and is attended with great inconvenience to my practice here. My other inducements to attend the ensuing term are not great, not so much so as last year, while the sacrifice here will be greater.

As to Mr. Hopkinson, he has put the case on such ground, that nothing can be done about his compensation till a final decision. If that should be as we hope, something honorable must be done for him; towards which I expect to contribute in proportion to my means, and in common with other friends. I hope you will be here a little sooner than January 15, as I hope to be able to set off by that time. I rely on you for all necessary knowledge of Moore's Charity School; not caring, however, so much about it as you seem to. The cause has gone too far to be influenced by small circumstances of variance.

I hear nothing unfavorable. Our friends say sometimes that the university people abate nothing of their confidence, which, I confess, a little surprises me, as I think they cannot but observe the general tendency of professional opinion. Mr. [George] Hough[2] says, a hundred and fifty copies of our argument have been printed at the Patriot office and distributed. I hope they will do no hurt.

Yours, very truly,   Dan'l Webster.

P.S. I wish you to understand that if I go to Washington, and am paid for it, anything necessary for new counsel there, I shall pay. It is not my intention that any arrangement of this sort shall increase expense. I am not certain that a new argument will be ordered, and am still more doubtful whether a new opening on our side will be called for. But this is possible, and if so, some gentleman must repeat our view, and add what he or we may have obtained new. This event or course of things is not probable, but possible.

Text from *PC,* 1: 287–288. Original not found.

1. See letter of November 4, above.

2. Hough (1757–1830), the first printer in Concord, having set up a newspaper there in September 1789.

TO [FRANCIS] BROWN

Boston, December 6, 1818.

Dear Sir,

I was very glad to receive yours,[1] as I wished to know something of your health, having heard of your indisposition. I trust you will by no means expose yourself until your recovery is complete. As to money concerns, I am of opinion, which I speak freely, that little is to be accomplished here without you. If the professors, &c. can employ the vacation in recruiting for the immediate wants of the college government, each in that region of the country where he may have most friends, it may be very well. This quarter, I think, had better be left till you shall be able to visit it. As far as relates to any provision for the expenses at Washington, &c., I would have every thing remain as it is, unless you should be able to come down, and would by no means have you come unless your health should be altogether restored. I must try to get along with things as well as I can. However, if you should think fit to try what can be done here without yourself, I think it would be useful, if practicable, to join such a man as Mr. [Moses Paul] Payson or Mr. [Mills] Olcott with such a man as Dr. [Seth] Payson.[2]

I am as yet not well informed on the topics connected with the will, and with the school. I hope your health will enable you to give me some view of this subject. It will save me both labor and time; the latter of which I shall have little to spare between this and the 15th January. I have read the will. The general impression I took from it was not at all unfavorable to our general doctrine. Perhaps a second reading might enable me to see something else. As to the school, if you wish the act of 1807, in the verdict, which is perhaps admissible, I think you had better write to Judge [Jeremiah] Smith on the subject soon. I think I heard that all papers were to be furnished, so as to make up the case by January 1. I do not think it will be easy, perhaps not possible, to get the court to say any thing about the school. They will think that "sufficient," &c. At the same time I should not expect much difficulty about the school, if the question should be decided right with the college.

Let me hear from you every week, respecting your health. If any thing further occurs to me I shall write again. Writing lately to Dr. P. to acknowledge a copy of his "Eulogy,"[3] I took occasion to ask whether Mrs. W[oodward] intended to enter her appearance voluntarily in the suit now at Washington. If not, I am inclined to give her notice so to do.

Yours truly,   D. Webster.

Text from PC, 1: 289–290. Original not found.

1. Not found.

2. Payson (1758–1820; Harvard 1777), Rindge, N.H. minister, state legislator and trustee of Dartmouth

College, 1813 to 1820.
 3. Letter to Seth Payson not found; Webster was probably referring to

Payson's "Eulogy" on William Henry Woodward, who died on August 9.

TO HENRY WHEATON

Boston Decr. 12. 1818

My Dear Sir

I owe you an apology for a few meagre remarks on your Book in the N. A.[1] The truth is, I intended to extend the Article to some length, but being called away on professional business, when I returned I found the printer had set up what I had sent him, & *gone on upon the next Article.*

I can only add, that when another Vol appears, I will endeavor to find some one to do it more justice. I think this vol. particularly valuable, & well executed, in every thing depending upon the Reporter—There will be questions eno[ugh], I think, to make another Vol this winter. There will be sundry cases of capture under Span. Pat. flag; the case abt. taxing U. S. Bank: The D. College Case:—Bullard v Bell: & one or two other cases from this Circuit which will deserve to be reported, & will occupy room. I have no doubt there will be many others.

Your excellent friend the Judge [Joseph Story] is expected in town on Monday to try the pirates, in the *Plattsburgh.* It will raise no questions of Law probably. With very great regard Yrs   D. Webster

ALS. NNPM.
 1. DW's review of *Wheaton's Reports of Cases argued and adjudged in the Supreme Court of the United*

States, February Term, 1818, appeared in the *North American Review,* 8 (December 1818): 63–71.

FROM THOMAS ADDIS EMMET

New York Decr. 19th. 1818

Dear Sir

I have delayed until the present time replying to your two last letters with the enclosures, because I was in daily expectation of being able to speak decidedly as to my being at Washington next Term of the Supreme Court—but it was not until last night that I received the answer on which my determination was to depend. I now take the earliest opportunity of informing you that I shall not attend that Court this Winter— & that Mr. [Samuel] Bell will have to provide himself with another Counsel.[1] I have read his Argument with very great pleasure & instruction, & think he might almost venture to present it without any Counsel to the Court—but as I understand you will be at Washington, I am sure he can suffer nothing by my absence. I shall hold the papers you have forwarded to me to be disposed of in such manner as Mr. Bell or you may direct— & I shall be happy at any future time to be honored with your commands.

I am Dear Sir With much respect & esteem Your Obedt. Servant
Thos. Addis Emmet

ALS. NhHi.
1. See Emmet to DW, September 29, 1818, above.

FROM WILLIAM PINKNEY

Baltimore 28th. Decr 1818.
Sir

I feel very much flattered by the application which you have been so good as to make to me[1] in the Case of Bullard v Bell—and regret sincerely that I have lost the power of profiting by it. I should have taken particular pleasure in becoming your associate in that case—but unluckily the opposite party has engaged my assistance several weeks since without apprizing me in any degree of the nature of the Case.

In the affair of the Bank of the United States (relative to the power of the Legislature of Maryland to tax it) I understand that we are on the same Side. It was my intention to have asked from you an interchange of Ideas in that Cause; but I now suppose it will not be necessary, since it is said that little else than the threadbare topics connected with the constitutionality of the establishment of the Bank will be introduced into the argument, which is expected to take place early in the next Term of the Supreme Court.

Believe me to be with sincere Respect Sir Your most Obedient Humble Servant   Wm. Pinkney

ALS. NhHi.   1. Not found.

FROM TIMOTHY FARRAR, JR.

Portsmouth Jan. 2. 1819.
Dr. Sir,

One of the papers herewith sent to you, is not included in any agreement yet made, viz. the letter from the Trust in Engd. to Eleazer Wheelock. There are three other papers in my hands in regard to which I presume they expect to make some agreement. These are Dr. E. Wheelock's will[1]—Memorial of John Wheelock in the name & behalf of the Trustees to the Legislature in June 1805[2]—and the Grant of the White Mountain land in June 1807.[3] These shall be forwarded to you as soon as copied. If the grant of Landaff[4] goes into the case, would it not be best to be prepared to show its invalidity—the prior grant &c. The grant of land in Hanover Judge [Jeremiah] Smith says is the same land which was reserved in the original grant of the town to Benning Wentworth & by him given to the College. I have not heard from you as I expected since you left this town. Will you be good enough to write to me by Mr Mason upon the subject of our book &c. As it may be useful to you to know the kind of talk which is kept up on the other side—I would just mention that I understand Master Icha[bod Bartlett][5] has lately spoken in a way to induce the belief that there is an open door between him or some of their folks & the judges—that they have expressed themselves very fully upon the subject—and that it is perfectly certain the cause will be decided in their favour &c. It may be he did not intend to be so understood—but my informant supposed from what he said that he wished him to think this was the case. I am, Sir, very respectfully, Yours &c   T. Farrar.

ALS. NhD. Extracts published in Morin, "Dartmouth College Case."

1. Dated April 2, 1779, NhD.

2. Dated June 5, requesting a grant of money for the College, NhD. On June 15, 1805, the legislature responded, by granting the College the sum of $900.

3. The land grant was approved by the legislature June 18, 1807.

4. Landaff, N.H., was site of the original land grant made to the College on December 13, 1769, by Governor John Wentworth.

5. Attorney for William H. Woodward when the case was argued in the New Hampshire Superior Court.

FROM TIMOTHY FARRAR, JR.

Portsmouth Jan. 8. 1819

Dr. Sir,

Herewith you have the copies of the three cases certified from the Circuit Court,[1] the copy of an agreement executed at present only by Mr. [Jeremiah] Mason, a copy of certain parts of Eleazer Wheelock's Will, Copy of a Grant to the Trustees of D. Col June 1807, and a Copy of a Memorial of Jno. Wheelock in the name & behalf of said Trustees June 1805. The copy of the letter of Apl. 25. 1771 from L[or]d Dartmouth & others[2] with Mr [William] Allen's[3] affidavit has been already forwarded. You will notice a provision in Dr. E. Wheelock's Will that in consequence of certain property of his having gone to the benefit of the [Moor's Indian] *Charity School*, it is charged with the payment of an annuity to Ralph Wheelock &c.[4] This annuity I understand has always been considered as due from the College & paid by the Trustees. There is a provision in the act of June 1807[5] by which the Legislature reserve to themselves the right to controul the Trustees in respect to the appropriation of the income of that grant. This grant remains unproductive.

I have received a line from Prest [Francis] Brown respecting our book, and have conversed with Mr. [Jeremiah] Mason on the subject. The Prest. is silent in regard to the plan of it, what the introduction shall contain &c. Mr. Mason is decidedly of the opinion that there should *be none*—that is, that the book should be *wholly* confined to the law or judicial history of the case, without any notion of the ecclesiastical or political or any other part of the preliminary dispute. His reasons are that it is for the interest of the Institution to bury every recollection of this dispute as soon as the cause is ended, and not perpetuate the enmity of the Individuals concerned, or of the party by putting into a permanent form any thing that shall compel them to look upon their own iniquity. This is a matter that you and the President must decide, and let me know how much and what matter the book should contain. Please to acknowledge the rec[eip]t of these papers. Respectfully yours   T. Farrar

ALS. NhHi. Published in Shirley, *Dartmouth College Causes*, pp. 285–286.
   1. The three cognate cases, *Hatch* v. *Lang, Pierce ex dem. Lyman* v. *Gilbert,* and *Marsh* v. *Allen,* which had been brought against the University in the Federal Circuit Court of New Hampshire.
   2. The English trustees to Eleazar

Wheelock, NhD.
   3. President of Dartmouth University.
   4. Wheelock (1742–1817; Yale 1765), the third son of Eleazar Wheelock. Dartmouth College was originally Moor's Indian Charity School.
   5. An Act Granting a Certain Quantity of Land to Dartmouth College.

TO [FRANCIS] BROWN

Boston, January 10, 1819.

Dear Sir,

A letter came to me to-day, addressed to you, bearing the Hanover postmark. As it was not superscribed in a lady's hand, I presumed it might relate to the common cause, and might be intended to communicate information important for me to have. I therefore opened it. It was from Mr. [Roswell] Shurtleff,[1] containing some little account of movements on the other side.[2] I do not think it necessary to send it back to you.

I have nothing new to say. No public or general opinion seems to be formed of the opinion of any particular judge. I hope no judge, if he has formed an opinion, will communicate it, or hint what it is; inasmuch as it would commit him, which would be likely to make him more tenacious, and so be worse for us, if his opinion should be against us, or it might diminish the weight of his opinion upon others, if it should be in our favor. I hope the judges will come together without its being known at all what opinions any particular judge may have formed.

I have received the records from Mr. [Timothy] Farrar, and I believe am prepared with all necessary papers. The book of memoirs[3] I shall not carry. Dr. [Cyrus] Perkins can lend me one, if I should want it.

If any thing new occurs before I leave home, I shall write you. You may expect early and frequent intelligence from Washington.

Very truly, yours,   D. Webster.

Text from *PC*, 1: 299. Original not found.

1. Shurtleff (1773–1861; Dartmouth 1799), minister of the college church, professor of theology, moral philosophy, and political economy, and also College Librarian. Letter not found.

2. Both sides were actively engaged in publicizing their respective positions in the case in hopes of influencing the forthcoming decision.

3. David McClure and Elijah Parish, *Memoirs of the Rev. Eleazar Wheelock*. Newburyport: Edward Little and Co., 1811.

TO TIMOTHY FARRAR, JR.

Washington Feb: 1. 1819.

Dr Sir

The Court met today; present all but [Thomas] Todd. Judge [William] Johnson is here, & I suppose will sit the Term out, notwithstanding he is nominated Collector.[1] Mr. [William] Pinkney will be in town today, & I suppose will move for a new argument in the case vs. Woodward. It is most probable perhaps, that he will succeed, in that object; altho I do not think it by any means certain. Not a word has as yet fallen from any Judge on the cause. They keep their own counsels. All that I have seen however looks rather favorable. I shall send you word, from time to time, of what occurs; altho I hope to be relieved from further anxiety, by a decision for us or agt. us, in five or six days. I wd. not have another such cause for the College plain; & all its appurtenances. Yrs truly

D. Webster

Let Mr. [Jeremiah] Mason know you have heard from me.

ALS. NhHi. Published in Shirley, *Dartmouth College Causes*, p. 243.

1. About this time speculation abounded in Washington as to whether Johnson would resign from the Court and assume the post of Collector of the Port of Charleston. Before writing this day to Farrar, DW

had probably seen the *National Intelligencer* for February 1, which reported the Justice's intention to resign from the Court for a lesser but higher paying post. The rumor proved incorrect. Johnson continued on the Court until his death in 1834.

TO EZEKIEL WEBSTER

Washington Febry. 2. 1819

My Dear E.

All is safe. Judgt was rendered this morning, reversing the Judgt in N. Hampshire. Present, Marshall, Washington, Livingstone, Johnson, Duval & Storey. All concuring but Duval, & he giving no reason to the contrary. The opinion was delivered by the Chief Justice—it was very able & very elaborate. It goes the whole length— & leaves not an inch for the University to stand on. Yrs affectionately   D. Webster in Court

ALS. NhD. Published in *PC*, 1: 300.
See also similar letter to Francis

Brown, same date, mDW 2620, and
PC, 1: 300.

TO TIMOTHY FARRAR, JR.

Washington Feb. 4. 1819

Dear Sir

I suppose *all* the Judges will give opinions to Mr [Henry] Wheaton, to be published, in the College cause. I have not seen or heard any but the Chief Justice's; but I have no doubt they will be very full & able. I think it would be very well to get along the *Book*, but there is one difficulty in it. These opinions are the property of the *Reporter*. His reward for his labors is principally from the sale of his Book; & this case will make a principal part in his next volume. Mr Wheaton is an excellent Lawyer, & in all things disposed to do well, & act liberally. Still, he might think it not his duty to give gratuitously copies of these opinions, as the sale of your Book would a little interfere with his. I have thought of offering him a hundred Dollars, for copies of these opinions, if you think it best to get them. This will compensate him for the loss of a sale of some of his volumes. The Book, if printed at all, must be printed at Boston, & we must get Judge [Joseph] Storey to inspect the proof sheets of the opinions. I suppose we can get the book out by the first of June, or the middle of May; supposing the work to commence pretty soon after my return. Please let me hear from you on this subject.

With my respects to Mrs. F. I am Dr Sir Yrs   D. Webster

If it should be necessary, I could get them copied here, & sent on, so as to get the Book out *in April*. But I suppose *May* is just as well.

ALS. NhHi. Published in Shirley, *Dartmouth College Causes*, pp. 294–295.

TO TIMOTHY FARRAR, JR.

Washington Feb. 7. 1819

My Dear Sir

I have thought I would say a word to you, about preventing the Newspapers from triumphing too much, on the result of this cause. It is our true wisdom to enjoy our victory with moderation. It is great indeed— & needs no flourish of trumpets to usher in the annunciation of it. On all accts a moderate & dignified course becomes us. We have many friends, who feel this victory as their own & who would be grieved & mortified to see it abused. I have written today to Mr. [Francis] Brown— & wish you, if you agree with me, to impress on others a sense of moderation, liberality & magnanimity.[1]

Nothing new has occurred here since I wrote you. Mr. [William] Pinkney *talks* about arguing one of the other causes, but I do not think he will attempt it. I shall endeavor to get the judgt entered as of last term in the case of Mr Woodward. In the other cases, I hope to get a certificate that shall enable Judge Storey to know what to do with them in May.

The court is pressing along with the business. Judge [Samuel] Bell's cause will come on on Wednesday. Tomorrow is the question of the constitutionality of the Bankrupt Laws of the States.[2] I think it likely the Court will sit till March 10th. The Circuit Court bill seems not likely to pass.[3] An attempt will be made for the Bankrupt bill, I fear unsuccessfully.[4] In my opinion this is a *poor* Congress for business.

A horrible duel was fought yesterday near here, between Genl. [Armistead Thomson] Mason, & Mr. [John Mason] McCarty—the quarrel arose at an election two years ago.[5] The parties fought with muskets, loaded with *three* bullets as is said, at a distance of ten feet. Mason fell—his adversary escaped with a small hurt. Taken in all its circumstances it was the bloodiest affair I have heard of.

If Mr [Jeremiah] Mason has returned from Dover court please show him this. Yrs   D. Webster

ALS. NhHi. Published in *New England Register*, 29 (July 1875): 229–230.

1. Among other things, DW was anxious not to aggravate further the already precarious financial condition of the College.

2. *Sturges* v. *Crowninshield*, 4 Wheaton 122.

3. A bill extending the judiciary system, which included reorganization of the circuit courts, was committed by the House Judiciary Committee to the Committee of the Whole on February 2, 1819.

4. The House Judiciary Committee reported a bill to establish a uniform system of bankruptcy throughout the country on November 24, 1819. For all practical purposes this was the same bill that had been reported by the same committee in February and again in December of 1816. The bill had been originally drafted by Joseph Story, at Webster's request. See DW to Story, December 9, 1816, mDW 2007 and W & S, 16: 36–37. Action was indefinitely postponed in 1819 as it had been on previous occasions.

5. Mason (1787–1819), veteran of the War of 1812 and interim senator from Virginia, 1816–1817. The duel, fought with his brother-in-law McCarty on February 6, 1819, at Bladensburg, Md., arose out of a bitter congressional campaign in 1816 in which Mason lost to Charles Fenton Mercer.

During his long absences in Washington on congressional and court matters, Webster and his wife, Grace Fletcher, corresponded regularly about the family and their various affairs. Unfortunately, very few of Webster's letters to Grace survive; and many of those from Grace to Daniel are no longer extant. A fairly typical example of Grace's letters to Daniel follows.

FROM GRACE FLETCHER WEBSTER

Friday evening 19 Feb. 1819
Scene Mrs. Websters Parlor

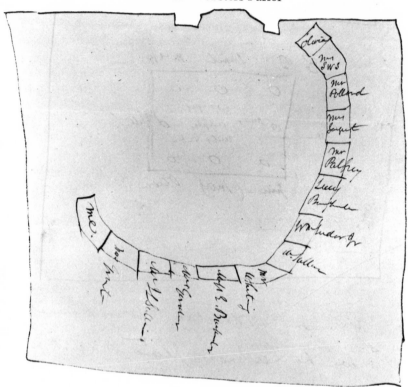

Sunday evening 7. Oclock
[February 21, 1819]

I hope my dear Husband, that this ingenious production of Mr [William] Sullivans will afford you as much amusement as it did us. I shall be very glad to send you something pleasant for I fear I have not given you pleasure by anything that I have written. I have had a small party as you will perceive, or rather a great one for me, and yesterday Eliza [Buckminster,] Daniel[1] and I dined at Mr S[ullivan]s we had a very pleasant visit, and in the evening after Mr S returned he drew this what shall I call it? of our dinner and evening—he was in fine spirits as you will imagine.

Do you know that Mr P[eter] T[hacher] is coming? you will know that he has come when you get this. If I had know[n] I should have sent it by him, I would have written another letter and left this as it was given to me, but I could not bear to let it go without a word from me, as I expected to send it by mail.

Saturday 3 oclock & ½ W.S.
basement Room

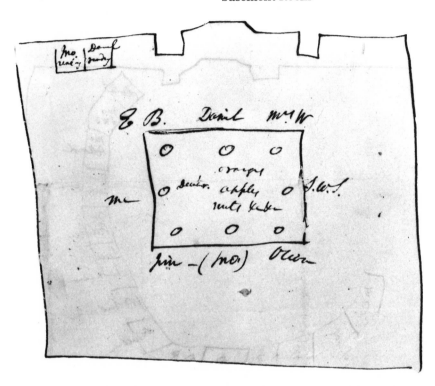

Mr F. Bodowin[2] called and very kindly offered to take anything to you, but I would not trouble him with a letter and I had nothing else to send.

Eliza was to have written a postscript but she has gone to Brookline with Mrs W Sullivan and it is now so late I fear I shall not have it ready in time.

We are all very well and always yours   G W.
                              Goodnight

ALS. NhHi.   Webster.
   1. Daniel Fletcher Webster (1813–   2. Not identified.
1862), son of DW and Grace Fletcher

TO JEREMIAH MASON

Washington Feb. 24. 1819

Dear Sir

Since I wrote you a day or two since[1] we have been talking a little about the College causes. In the action agt. Woodward, judgt is rendered, nunc

Saturday Eveng. Parlor upstairs

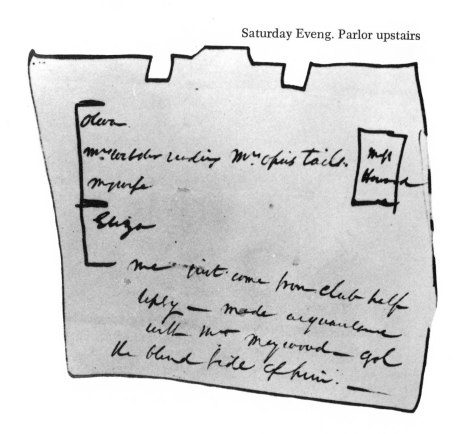

pro tunc, as of last term. The other causes will be remanded, without argument or discussion here. If no alteration shall [be] made in the Verdict, the Circuit Court will know what judgt to render. If the other side should be inclined to attempt to make a different case, he must offer his evidence, & rely on his bill of exceptions, if the evidence should be ruled out, as being immaterial.

In the mean time the opinions in the first cause will be published, & it is not probable that Counsel will see any thing left, whereon to maintain further contest. I thought it upon the whole a great point gained, to make this arrangement, & avoid further discussion here. If they move to set aside this Verdict, it will probably only be granted upon condition of acceding to all the facts, on our part, already in the Verdict. This will secure us agt. the expense & inconvenience of going thro. our proofs again. But I am inclined to think, that when the Election is over,[2] there will be no great inclination to keep up the contest. Our Bank Argument[3] goes on— & threatens to be long. Nothing new respecting Bell's cause.[4] Yours as usual   D. Webster.

ALS. NhD. Published in Van Tyne, p. 78.

1. See DW to Jeremiah Mason, February 23, 1819, mDW 2650.

2. Statewide elections were held in New Hampshire on March 16, 1819.

3. *McCulloch* v. *Maryland*, 4 Wheaton 316. DW argued for the bank representing McCulloch, cashier of the Baltimore branch of the Bank of the United States.

4. *Bell* v. *Bullard*. A divided court rendered no decision. 5 Wheaton, front page.

On February 24, 1819, the United States Senate ratified the Adams-Onís, or Florida, Treaty.

According to its provisions, Washington agreed to renounce all prior claims against the Spanish government in return for Spain's cession of Florida to the United States; it also recognized the Sabine River as the Western boundary of Louisiana.

Article XI of the treaty, providing for the creation of a Claims Commission in Washington to resolve all private claims for damages against the Spanish government on the part of United States nationals, particularly interested Webster. In the letter below, he discusses the opportunity for "pecuniary profit" which the eventual creation of such a commission would provide. Spain did not ratify the treaty until February 22, 1821. Shortly thereafter Congress moved to carry out the provisions of Article XI, and Webster, his clients already secured, prepared to represent claimants before the Commission.

TO [?]

Washington Feb. 24. 1819

Dr Sir

The Spanish Treaty will be ratified, by the Senate either today or tomorrow. I understand it provides for the creation of a board of Commissioners with power to make compensation for Captures &c, not exceeding, in the whole five millions of Dlls. The Insurance Offices in Boston must, of course, have heavy claims of this character. The Commissioners will sit, probably, in this City. I have ventured to think, that those Offices might, usefully to themselves & me, make me their agent, in those claims. A general agency, for all or most of the Offices, would make it worth my attention, & justify me in appropriating as much time to the subject as the nature of it required. If this suggestion should meet your approbation, I hope you will communicate it to the Gentlemen at the Suffolk Office, & also to Mr. [Henry] Cabot.[1] If, however, any, the least, doubt, difficulty, or impropriety occurs, to you or to them, I beg you at once to forbear pursuing the suggestion. I have asked Mr [Jeremiah] Mason to write to Genl. [Samuel A.] Welles' Office[2] on the same subject. I do not remember that I ever before sought any employment with a view to pecuniary profit. No doubt I may make an awkward figure at it, now. Perhaps, too, I misjudge the importance & amount of these claims. But if it be a case in which I might render service, & receive equivalent compensation, it would suit my objects entirely to be employed in it.

I suppose Comm[issione]rs will not be appointed until the Treaty shall be ratified by Spain.

It has been suggested to me, from a pretty high source, that the persons interested in the North might have some influence, in regard to the nomination of one or more of the Comm[issione]rs. It will be in season to think of this hereafter. In the mean time I think no partial recommendation should be forwarded, if it can be avoided.

I suppose our Western boundary is fixed as follows— Beginning at the mouth of the Sabine River, following the western boundary of Louisiana to the Red River; up the Red River to the 100th deg. of W. Longitude;— thence due north to the Arkansaw; up the Arkansaw to the 42nd deg. of N. Latitude, & thence West to the Pacific—giving us about 7 Degs of Latitude on the Pacific— & the mouth of Columbia River. We also get the Floridas, in cons[ideratio]n of the 5 millions paid to our own citizens.

I am, Dr Sir, Very truly Yours   Danl. Webster

ALS. NhD.

1. Cabot (1783–1864), Boston attorney and insurance broker. Upon inheriting a large fortune at the death of his father, Cabot retired from business and professional activities in 1824.

2. President of a Boston insurance firm.

TO [FRANCIS] BROWN

Washington, February 25, 1819.

Dear Sir,

Yours I received last evening.[1] The new causes will be disposed of as I mentioned to you in my last.[2] I am quite satisfied with this arrangement, and do not expect much further trouble in the case. We shall get a judgment, I trust, at May term,[3] even if the friends of the University should be advised that it is worth their while to attempt to renew the contest. I hope they will be better advised, both for their own sake and yours. You need the use of the buildings, and I hope they will admit you to possession without further inconvenience or delay. I am quite confident that there can be no reasonable expectation of changing the decision; and though it may be inconvenient to you, it can do no good to the other side to continue the contest.

I hope to be at home by the 15th March. I should be glad to see you at that time; some things which must be done, may better be done then than afterwards. I shall carry with me the materials for the book; and if it is made, it ought to be put to press without a day's delay. Let me at least find a letter from you at Boston on my arrival, say the 13th. The sooner after that that you are there, the better. Very truly yours,   D. Webster.

Text from *PC*, 1: 303. Original not found.

  1. Letter not found.

  2. See DW to Francis Brown, February 23, 1819, in *PC*, 1: 301–302.

  3. Judge Joseph Story handed down the final judgment, probably on June 10, 1819, at the Circuit Court in Portsmouth.

TO WILLIAM SULLIVAN

Washington Feb. 25. 1819

My Dear Sir

I believe I can now *see thro.* the concerns which I have here, & in all probability shall be able to get away by the 4 or 5 of March, & home by the 12 or 13. I hope this will be in season for the very few law questions in which I am concerned. I will thank you to suggest to the Court, that in those cases in which I am *alone* (I believe they are very few) I should be glad that they might lie to the end of the term, unless other parties, or the Court, should thereby be put to inconvenience; in which case I shall expect no delay. It is possible I may be at home by the 10th.

You have all the news. The two houses are now, *beginning* to be serious. A more *do little* Congress I do not think ever assembled. The sooner it disperses the better.

The Bank cause is not heard thro. yet.[1] Luther Martin & [William] Pinkney are both to speak—after this comes a Militia Court Martial cause from Pennsylvania,[2] & that will nearly wind up the Court. I am grown impatient to be off. Yrs truly   D. Webster

ALS. NN.

  1. *McCulloch* v. *State of Maryland*, 4 Wheaton 316.

  2. DW was probably referring to *Houston* v. *Moore*, 5 Wheaton 1.

FROM JOSEPH HOPKINSON

Washington Mar 11. 1819

My Dear Sir

I am still at this horrible place, and to add to its charms, we have, at this moment a violent snow storm; greater than any we have seen through the winter. Tomorrow (friday) I shall take my departure; and the Court will rise on the next day. Indeed every thing has languished for a week past; and both Judges and Counsel seem to cry "Enough."

I informed you some days since of my obtaining for our College, a Copy of [Adam] Seyberts Statistical Annals.[1] I hoped Judge [Joseph] Story could have taken them on to Boston; but I find it will be inconvenient to him. I will therefore take them to Philad. myself; and look out for an opportunity there to forward them to you.

I have not followed the *hint* or *suggestion*, I mentioned to you; but yesterday the proposal was made to me directly; or rather the question asked whether I would accept.[2] It was stated that there is a multitude of applications, strongly supported. The offer therefore is the greater compliment for a *federalist*. I know that our friend [David] Daggett—and Mr [Eligius] Fromentin[3] are among the Candidates. *Keep this entirely to yourself;* for should I determine to decline, it would not be proper to have the proposal known. I am satisfied that as to pecuniary matters I can do infinitely better with the agency for the claimants; but I confess I am greatly tempted by the consideration of the evidence the appointment would afford of the independence and correctness of my short political career in Congress; since even those to whose faith I do not belong give me this publick mark of confidence. I wish you would write me pretty fully your views of the matter. Still one should not be too unmindful of what the knowing ones call the *main chance.*

I am here entirely alone. [John] Sergeant went yesterday. This solitude of houses is intolerable; and my prospects of a journey, dismal enough. But that cannot be very unpleasant which takes me out of Washington; and brings me every hour nearer to home.

Truly & affectionately Yours   Jos. Hopkinson

ALS. NhD.

1. *Statistical Annals; embracing views of population, commerce, navigation, fisheries, public lands . . . of the United States of America . . .* Philadelphia, 1818.

2. Commissioner on the Spanish claims commission, membership of which was then being considered in anticipation of ratification of the Treaty by Spain. Hopkinson was recommended by General Samuel Smith of Baltimore. See Diary of J. Q. Adams, March 4, 1819, MHi.

3. Fromentin (d. 1822), Louisiana lawyer, judge, and United States senator, 1813–1819.

TO TIMOTHY FARRAR, JR.

Boston March 12th. 1819

My Dear Sir,

I arrived here on the eleventh. Yours went to Washington,[1] &, arriving there the day I left, has followed me here. I expect Mr [Francis] Brown will be here in a day or two, if his health will permit, & some decision must then be made abt. the *Book.* I incline to think it must be made; &, if at all, I am clear, it must be done *at once.* Judge [Joseph] S[tory] must prepare his argument *before* Hopkinton Court. I can now furnish copies of the opinions. As to the obstacle you speak of, as being created by my letter, that shall not stand in the way. If Mr. Brown should be here in a day or two, can you come up & see him? I have no objection to the Book's being printed at Exeter, if it can be done there best. I will only repeat, that if any thing is done, it must be done *immediately*. Please inform me, by return of mail, whether you can come up here, on notice of Mr Brown's arrival. Yrs   D. Webster

ALS. NhHi.   1. Letter not found.

TO TIMOTHY FARRAR, JR.

Boston Mar. 22. 1819.

Dear Sir,

I have no *records:* all I can furnish will be the argument at Washington, decision, opinions, mandate &c. I shall wish to see the *proofs* of the Washington case, which I suppose can be easily accomplished. Please let me know when the Printer will need the matter from me, or any part of it. Mr [Francis] Brown's opinion seems to be in favor of confining the Book very much to the law case, in which I concur. Even then it will be large. Yrs as usual   D. Webster

ALS. NhHi.

TO JOSEPH HOPKINSON

Boston March 22. 1819

My dear friend,

I thank you for your several favors from Washington. As to the *"hint"*, which has more recently been stated to you "distinctly", I am clear for your accepting it.[1] I have thought a good deal of it, & am decidedly of opinion you ought not to refuse. Under the circumstances, it will be very *honorable* to you; & not unprofitable. I hope you will not hesitate.

I found President [Francis] Brown here. Our *Book* must go on, &, on looking over your minutes, I perceived, very soon, how much better you could write them off than I could. I would cheerfully take the labour; but as it is a Book which is to make some noise in the world, I wish your part of it to be done up to your own satisfaction. *You must therefore write out your argument.* I will examine, compare, correct, & edit it; and take any other labor about it; *but you must write it, & give it the impress of your own style & manner.* This is a work which you must do for *reputation.* Our College cause will be known to our children's children. Let us take care that the rogues shall not be ashamed of their grandfathers. We shall want your argument for the press in about three weeks—or a month. Three mornings will give you time to complete it.

I believe we shall have little further trouble with the University, altho. she does not seem to die with grace. The instruction in it is broken up, &

the College scholars are in possession of the buildings.[2] The story is, that a Gentleman, coming that way, brought off *two* of the classes of the University in his *gig*. Most of the Boys have I believe joined the College. The decision has given the greatest satisfaction to a great majority of the people. The Trustees are to meet the 28th. of April, after which time you will immediately hear from them. Yours as ever   D. Webster

ALS. NhD. Published in *W & S*, 16: 46–47.

1. Only one letter, Joseph Hopkinson to DW, March 11, 1819, above, has been found.

2. For a discussion of the closing of the University, see Leon Burr Richardson, *History of Dartmouth College*, 2 vols. (Hanover, N.H., 1932), 1: 366–367.

TO JEREMIAH MASON

Boston Mar. 22. 1819.

Dr Sir,

I agree that the *Book* ought to be confined very much to the law case, except a general preface, giving a short view of the history of the College. Such is Mr [Francis] Browns opinion, & as the Book is to be made in N. H. you must see that it is made right. The Princeton People have requested me to be their agent in looking up their legacy. They expect no difficulty, as Mr [William] Allen has written them that he shall give them all facilities. I have recd. a power of Atty, to *you* & *me,* jointly & severally. All that at present seems to be necessary is to appoint some one to see to the rents & taxes. There is a quaker, by the name of [John] Williams,[1] the best man I at present think of, to manage such a concern. He was a sort of land agent & adviser to Dr. [John] Wheelock, & knows all about the property. Mr Brown thinks him much the best man in the neighborhood. I propose to write to him, sending a list of the lands devised, & requesting him to call on the tenants to pay *him* the rents from the time of notice. The judgt in the College cause is entered *Feb. 1818* declaring the Acts not valid. I suppose that must meet the provision in Dr W's will. Having written as above to Friend William[s][2] I propose to do nothing further at present. If I am not right, thus far, please to put me right.

I cannot go to Portsmo. at present, altho I wish very much to see you. Perhaps May Court may bring me down. I should be glad to know whether [Ichabod] Bartlett & [George] Sullivan intend to do any thing further in their causes or not; but I suppose they do not know themselves.

With affectionate remembrances to Mrs Mason & the children, Yrs as ever   D. Webster

ALS. MHi. Published in *W & S*, 16: 47–48.

1. Williams (1769–1849), a resi-

dent of Hanover, N.H.

2. Letter not found.

TO JEREMIAH MASON

Boston March 23. 1819

Dear Sir,

I enclose you the copies of the Record above, in the two causes in the Circuit Court defended by the University folks.[1] Perhaps these may as well be filed with the Clerk at once. I understand the University Gentlemen still keep up the talk of another trial. I am inclined to think it adviseable to give them immediate notice that we shall endeavor to bring the causes to judgement at May Term. Let them try it, & see what they can make of their *new facts*. I will try to be at the Court, if they threaten to attempt any thing.*

Upon reflection, I have concluded to do nothing for the Princeton People at present, except to write to Mr [Mills] Olcott[2] to give us advice about a proper Agent.

Our Law term finished today, after a duration of three weeks. I think there have been few great causes. Judge [Charles] Jackson will sit at Nisi Prius three or four weeks. Then I must see the Circuit Court thro., in which I have very little to do— &, after that, if we are all alive & well, I am for a summer of rest & play. Yours as always   D. Webster

* I find this to be a very modest paragraph. I only meant to say, if there is a probability of *trouble*, I wd. be present to bear my part of it. ALS. NhHi.

1. The collateral causes referred to are *Hatch* v. *Lang* and *Marsh* v. *Allen*. A third case was *Pierce ex dem. Lyman* v. *Gilbert*.

2. See DW to Mills Olcott, March 25, 1819, mDW 2692.

TO JOSEPH STORY

Boston Thursday Eve' [March 25, 1819]

My Dear Sir,

We have been looking for you two or three days; but on sending to the Marshall's today, he sent me word you were at home *unwell*. So I have been considering whether I ought not to write you, to tell you how glad we should be [to] see you here, if you should find it convenient to come up. I send you a few English Newspapers, which may amuse you. Ch[ief] Baron Richards,[1] it seems, is appointed by Letters Patent Prolocutor of the House of Lords, during the absence of the L[or]d Chancellor from indisposition. Perhaps this shews who is to be L[or]d Eldon's[2] successor.

I have no new law Books; Wells and Lilley[3] expect some by an early arrival.

One of the things I wish to see you most about relates to our College book. Arrangements are made to print it in Exeter. Judge [Jeremiah]

Smith will see to the N. H. case; the proofs of the opinions of the Judges will be sent to you, & of the rest of the Washington case probably to me. At any rate you are to see the proofs of the opinions. Lest this book should not get on fast enough for [Henry] Wheaton, I intend having the opinions copied immediately. But, before they are copied, I wish to go over the Chief's [John Marshall's] & Judge [Bushrod] W[ashington]'s *with you,* & to see that every word & letter be right. On this account I wish to see you for *two hours,* soon. If you cannot come up, I must go to Salem; which is not quite convenient as Judge [Charles] Jackson is holding our N. P. Court at this time. Pray let me hear from you Yrs as ever   D. Webster

P.S. The opinion in the Bank cause is universally praised.[4] Indeed I think it admirable. Great things have been done this Session. I send a N. York paper, in which you will see what Judge [Thomas] Todd has been about, if you have not seen it before.

ALS. MHi. Published in *W & S,* 16: 46.

1. Sir Richard Richards (1752–1823) was appointed lord chief baron of the exchequer in 1812. Upon the illness of Lord Eldon, then Chancellor, in January 1819, Richards assumed the speakership of the House of Lords.

2. John Scott, first Earl of Eldon (1751–1838) became Lord Chancellor of England in 1801.

3. Boston publishing house.

4. *McCulloch* v. *Maryland* was decided unanimously in favor of the plaintiff on March 6.

FROM LANGDON CHEVES

Bank of the United States
April 2d. 1819

Sir

I have been directed by the Directors of the Bank of the United States to present to you their respectful thanks for your very able and successful exertions on the part of the Bank in the case of McCullo[c]h vs. the State of Maryland and to ask your acceptance of an additional fee of Fifteen Hundred Dollars which the Cashier of the Office at Boston has been directed to pay.

I have great personal pleasure in making this communication.

I have the honor to be with great respect Your obt. Servt.

L Cheves Presidt

LS. NhHi.

TO TIMOTHY FARRAR, JR.

Boston April 3. 1819

Dr Sir,

I do not know that there is much preference between the two modes of printing the Charter. I should rather prefer the distinct *paragraphical* manner, unless there be objections which have not occurred to me.

I hope to be able to furnish the Washington case, as fast as you want it. I shall look over my argument, make two notes, (for the Appendix) & can send it down at once. I wd. not care much abt. *subscriptions.* I think the Book will certainly *sell.* It will be a great point to get the vols in the Market, here & at Concord, before the legislatures rise. I am expecting [William] Wirt's argument daily. Yrs   D. Webster

ALS. NhHi.

TO JEREMIAH MASON

Boston April 6. 1819

Dear Sir,

I enclose you Mr. [Francis] Brown's letter,[1] that you may judge of the propriety of giving formal notice to [George] Sullivan & [Ichabod] Bartlett, that we intend to proceed in the actions at May Term.[2] I wish to finish them. The topic has been long eno. under discussion. I am persuaded the Court will see the propriety of a speedy decision of all the remaining questions, if there be any remaining questions. Yrs   D. Webster

ALS. NhD. Published in *W & S*, 16: 52.

   1. Letter not found.

2. The cognate Dartmouth College cases which were before the Circuit Court at Portsmouth.

TO JEREMIAH MASON

Boston April 10. 1819

Dear Sir

My own interest would be promoted by *preventing* the Book. I shall strut well enough, in the Washington Report, & if the "Book" should not be published, the world would not know where I borrowed my plumes. But I am still inclined to have the Book. One reason is, that you & Judge [Jeremiah] Smith may have the credit which belongs to you. Another is, I believe, Judge [Joseph] Story is strongly of Opinion it would be a useful work, that Wheaton's Reports go only into the hands of Professional men, but that this Book might be read by other Classes &c &c. If it should be decided, at May term, that another cause should go to Washington, I should be very unwilling to have the book published—but I have hitherto had a strong belief we should finish the Actions, at May Court. I think so still; but very probably may be disappointed. I should be for pressing the Judge to adjourn for a short time, rather than continue the causes. I think he will feel the propriety of settling the controversy, as far as may be done.

I shall come down, accidents excepted, & very possibly Mrs. W[ebster] may attend the same Court—she has not determined, however, as yet, whether she shall go that Circuit. Solicitor Genl. [Daniel] Davis[1] goes down to try *Bullard* v. *French*. By what I learn he intends to go to issue on a new premise in that case.

In a newspaper Report, I see that Mr. Justice [John] Bayley,[2] of the King's bench, said lately "—Debt will not lie by indorsee of a Bill of Exchange vs. Acceptor, for want of privity.["] Yrs   D W.

Copy. NhHi. Published in Van Tyne, pp. 80–81.

1. Davis (1762–1835), Massachusetts and later Maine lawyer; United States attorney; and legislator.

2. Bayley (1763–1841), was judge of the King's Bench from 1808 to 1830. *DNB*.

TO JEREMIAH MASON [Excerpt]

Boston, April 13, 1819.

My Dear Sir,

. . . I was yesterday at Salem. Judge [Joseph] Story has lost a daughter (the one who has so long been an invalid), and Mrs. Story is quite unwell but convalescent. He says he wishes the circuit had commenced, that he might have employment and occupation. As to the College Cause, you may depend on it that there will be difficulty in getting delay in that case, without reason.[1] I flatter myself the judge will tell the defendants, that the new facts which they talk of, were presented to the minds of the judges at Washington, and that, if all proved, they would not have the least effect on the opinion of any judge; that unless it can be proved that the king did not grant such a charter as the special verdict recites, or that the New Hampshire General Court did not pass such acts as are therein contained, no material alteration of the case can be made. Our course will be to resist the introduction of evidence—on the ground of immateriality—being very liberal as to the sort of evidence which we care for, provided the facts proposed to be proved be admissible. Let Mr. [Ichabod] Bartlett continue to understand that we shall resist all delay. You may take another thing for true,—[William] Pinkney sent back this cause to get rid of it. He talked, however, and blustered, because among other reasons the party was in a fever and he must do something for his fees. As he could not talk *in* court, he therefore talked *out* of court. I believe his course is understood. Let us hope for the best, and by all means oppose protraction. Yours truly,   D. Webster

N.B. To take away pretense of delay, suppose you tell Bartlett that we shall not require strict proof of any known fact if the court should think the fact material.

Text from *Memoir and Correspond-ence of Jeremiah Mason* (Cambridge, Mass., 1873), pp. 222–223. Also pub-lished in *W & S*, 16: 49. Original not found.

1. Frustrated by DW in his attempt to introduce "new facts" into the case at the Supreme Court level, Pinkney nevertheless continued to try to re-open the case by way of the cognate causes now before Judge Story at the Circuit Court at Portsmouth.

TO [FRANCIS] BROWN

Boston, April 14, 1819.

My Dear Sir,

I am happy to hear that Mrs. [Eliza] Woodward[1] is so well advised as to be disposed to surrender the property according to agreement. I should be equally happy to see the President of the University [William Allen] wise enough to deliver the books and apparatus, and retire from the con-test without giving anybody further trouble. His own reputation and character, I should think, would be as much benefited by that course as your convenience. If he thinks otherwise, however, he has a right to judge for himself. I do not know any thing which is necessary to be done by way of preparation. I have written to Mr. [Jeremiah] Mason repeatedly. Mr. [Mills] Olcott must be there; his presence will be essentially necessary on many accounts: I wish him to bring with him your affidavit of the notice given by you to Mr. [William] Allen and Dr. [Cyrus] Perkins, of our in-tention to proceed to final judgment in these causes this term, and the time of giving such notice. Mr. Mason has given notice to the counsel. I flatter myself the cause will not be put off to October term without reason.

The University folks should understand, very distinctly, that we are resolved to bring this controversy to an immediate end, and that they are to have no delay, except such as they can obtain by law. There is a fable of the old man and the boy who stole his apples, which it would be edify-ing for the gentlemen connected with the University to read.

I think of nothing necessary to be done by the trustees particularly.

As to the proposals, I hear little of them. Mr. [George] Lamson[2] of Exeter was here, and finding nothing done, attempted gratuitously to do something; and I helped him as I could. Nothing effectual will be done from Portsmouth on that subject.

Text from *PC*, 1: 303–304. Original not found.

1. Wife of William H. Woodward, treasurer of Dartmouth College and defendant in the Dartmouth College case. Prior to the decision in the case, William Woodward died, on August 9, 1818. Eliza Woodward, acting as executrix of his estate, turned over to the trustees the records, seal, charter, and other papers of the College in May.

2. Lamson (1794–1826), was an Exeter lawyer and publisher of the *Exeter Watchman*, a post he held for two years. In 1823 he moved to New York City and entered the business of bookselling.

FROM JOSEPH HOPKINSON

Bordentown Apl. 19. 1819

My dear friend

It is but time and labour thrown away to attempt to do that which we know to be impossible. This proposition seems to me to be so clear that nobody, but Luther Martin, who delights in amplitude; or P[hilip] Barbour, whose logical head disdains to take any thing for granted, would give a moment to prove it. I shall presume that you admit it; and proceed to say that this is precisely the case in relation to make up either the speech I did make, or one I did not make, in our College cause, from the notes which served well enough to guide me through the argument at the time of the trial. The chain of connection, the whole course of thought, are now so entirely lost, and gone with the things "beyond the flood", that they are as much out of my power as Noah's ark or Jacob's ladder. All I can do is to give good counsel instead of a bad speech; to wit, that it be stated in its proper place in the big book, that the argument of Mr [Joseph] H[opkinson] at large could not be obtained, but that it consisted of a repetition of the principles opened by Mr [Daniel] W[ebster] enforcing and illustrating them by various cases and arguments; and giving full and satisfactory answers to the arguments urged by the counsel on the other side. Something of this, spiced a little if you please with compliment as far as your conscience will allow, will answer all the purpose. I will write to you shortly on our *matter of business.* God bless you   Yours

J Hopkinson

I have heard you Boston folk brag that the *Cod fish* we get are not the the thing; but you have a certain animal called a Dumb fish, much superior. Can you procure me a box & sent [send] it to Philada. Cost & charges will be cheerfully paid by—   J. H

ALS. NhHi. Published in *PC*, 1: 305.

TO JOSEPH HOPKINSON

Boston April 23. 1819

My Dear Sir,

I am quite disappointed about your Speech. Please, pray, to *return* me the notes—possibly I may do something with them. I will do the best for you I can either by writing out a reply from your notes & from my own wits—or stating that you did make a good reply. Let me have the *notes* by return of mail. The cod fish shall be forthwith looked up, & ordered—& perhaps a *cooking prescription* would be a useful accompaniament.

I have talked a little—not much—of going your way this summer. You talk a little about coming this way. Let us have an understanding on this point. My wish is, that you & your daughter would come here—in August.

If this be so settled, the arrangement wd. not be disturbed, if I should happen, at an earlier period, to see you on the Delaware; which, by the way, is exceedingly doubtful. I beg you to look along a little forward, & let me know what you think may be expected. I hope to have a summer of some leisure.

Send me back your notes *instanter*. I have recd [William] Wirt's & [John] Holmes' from [Henry] Wheaton—they are poor & meagre. I can easily so arrange your notes, as not to suffer by comparison—send them —Yrs   D. Webster

ALS. PHi.

FROM WILLIAM WIRT

Washington—April 28. 1819

Dear Sir,

Yours of the 19th. inst.[1] reached me this morning, *via* Richmond Va. I have lately returned from that place, and your letter, I suppose, crossed me on my return. I am extremely obliged to you for your letter, perceiving, as I do, the delicate and friendly motive which suggested it. I had promised to draw out my argument for Mr. [Henry] Wheaton, *if I could find the time*—but I could not and was, therefore, obliged to forward him the very crude draft he had made of it, *together with all my own notes*. Without these it would be out of my power to make even a sketch of what I said, and with them the sketch would scarcely be worth the trouble of making it. I am told that the grounds of argument which I was instructed to draw from [Jeremy] Belknaps history[2] are entirely erroneous and to the prejudice of the cause I was espousing. I am told, moreover, that the first case, as found or agreed, does not present the real merits of the controversy—and that we are to expect these in the succeeding case. To the purpose of truth, then, would it not be well to suspend the publication until the next case shall be heard? This, however is for the consideration of the printer and not for yours. In the posture which the controversy is now represented as having, I would rather decline any hand in the publication, even in preparing, if I could, a statement of my own remarks. There are personal considerations also which lead me to the same conclusion—for my argument was framed under great disadvantage, having to prepare it very hastily and under the pressure of a load of official business which was then wholly new to me.

I do not know whether I acknowledged while in R[ichmon]d a short note recd. from you in the matter of the Bank.[3] I did, as you conjecture, receive a duplicate of the compliment paid you by the P[residen]t of the Bank of the U.S.[4]

Yours, with great respect & esteem   Wm. Wirt

ALS. DLC.
   1. Not found.
   2. *History of New Hampshire,* 3
vols. (Philadelphia, 1784–1792).

3. Not found.
4. See Langdon Cheves to DW,
April 2, 1819, above.

TO TIMOTHY FARRAR, JR.

Boston May 18. [1819]

Dear Sir

I sent you [Benjamin] Trumbull[1] this Morning by Abigail Curtis,[2] who will leave it at your house.

As to Ichabod [Bartlett]'s argument, I am decidedly of opinion, that I would *not* publish any abuse of the Trustees, or of any of the Counsel. If he has not decency enough to leave such slang out, I would not publish his argument,— &, if necessary I would state the reason, in a note. As to mere *nonsense* & *stuff,* I wd. publish it—but nothing in any degree, personal, or injurious to Counsel or parties. You must show the creature to Mr. Mason—& you & he must persuade Bartlett to leave out what is objectionable. He ought to see the propriety of following Mr [George] Sullivan's example in that respect.

It would of course be very desirable to have his argument printed; & I think a little soft persuasion will bring him to have it put right. Ch. Jus. [William] Richardson I should think would not wish that *slang* should appear, as the argument, in his Court. Yrs   D.W.

50 or 60 pages!—Good Heavens!—and all slang!—do get it abridged—

ALS. NhHi.
   1. *A Complete History of the United
States of America, 1492–1792,* 3 vols.

(Boston, 1810).
   2. Not identified.

FROM JOSEPH HOPKINSON

Bordentown May 21. 1819

My dear friend

I return your manuscript with many thanks for the trouble you have taken to give me a respectable position in a book whose importance I estimate as highly as you do. I have made a small addition to the argument you have prepared from my notes; and also furnish some remarks on the topicks you have suggested.

I continue my intention to visit Boston in August; but as I shall see you on the Delaware before that time, I shall have an opportunity to fix my visit with more precision. I will soon write again; but must now put up my packet for you. Yr.   J. H.

ALS. NhD.

TO JEREMIAH MASON

Boston May 27. 1819

Dear Sir

Mr [James T.] Austin read this Morning a mass of papers, about the *new facts*. The Judge [Joseph Story] thought there was nothing in them, but has. taken the papers for a day or two, to examine them before he gives a formal decision. He says, he sees nothing which contradicts any part of the recital of the Charter. We had not much talk about it. Mr. A read & stated all he chose to do, & the Judge intimated, that the *new facts* had no bearing on any part of the Courts Opinion. *The slander causes*[1] *are settled.* How does the Book come on? I believe it will never be finished. Yrs,   D Webster

Copy. NhHi. Published in Van Tyne, p. 82.

1. Not identified.

TO JEREMIAH MASON

[May 29, 1819]
Boston Saturday Evening

My dear Sir

I learn this moment, that you are chosen a Trustee of D College.[1] Under present circumstances, I hope, *earnestly,* you will not decline it. You can relinquish it when you please; but it will do great good, that you should not refuse it.

It will gratify all good people, that you are chosen; & if you hold it but a year, I trust you will accept it Yours as ever   D Webster

Copy. NhHi. Published in Van Tyne, p. 82.
    1. Mason was chosen by the Dartmouth trustees to succeed ex-Gover-

nor J. T. Gilman, who had resigned from the board. Because of other commitments, however, Mason declined to accept the appointment.

TO PHILIP CARRIGAIN

Boston May 30. 1819

My dear Sir,

I am quite obliged to you for your kind & civil letter.[1] As soon as you have completed the collection of the maps,[2] I shall be glad to receive them, & am thankful for being remembered, in this respect. In the mean time I wish you would give me leave to transmit, in any way you may direct, some portion of that "root of evil" to which you refer. Next to food & raiment, I part with what little of that same root I may possess more cheerfully for Books & maps than any thing else.

I thank you for your good wishes, in relation to the College. I hope your influence will be exerted to prevail on the Legislature to forbear any measures of violence or hostility to the Institution. The State can disgrace itself, & can do great injury to the cause of literature, & nothing else, by following the counsels of a few men more distinguished for hot heads than for clear ones.

I am persuaded that almost *all* the intelligent men in the Community think the decision at Washington right. I have never seen *one*, who heard the opinions delivd, or has read them, & who thinks they can be refuted. The opinions of the Chief Justice [John Marshall], [Bushrod] Washington, & [Joseph] Storey, will be published, in the [Wheaton] Reports, & I am sure you will read them with pleasure. I will only add, on this subject, that there has never fallen under my knowledge, on any subject, such a series of direct, palpable, gratuitous falsehoods, as the New Hampshire papers have contained, in the form of "extracts of letters," & otherwise, respecting what transpired in this cause, during the two sessions it was before the Court at Washington.[3]

I hope you will honor us, ere long, with a visit. I expect a very leisure time this summer, & I [sh]ould be glad to see you.

I am, Dear Sir, very truly, Your Ob. sert. D. Webster

N.B. I forgot to say, that the "University," on Thursday presented evidence of certain "new facts" to Judge Storey, for the purpose of ascertaining, whether, if proved, these "facts" would affect the principle of the decision at Washington. The Judge intimated that he thought the facts did not, or would not, affect the decision, one way or another. In his view they were quite unimportant &c.

ALS. NhHi.

1. Not found.

2. Carrigain had a considerable interest in surveying and map-making, publishing in 1816 an excellent map of New Hampshire.

3. The *New Hampshire Patriot* was decidedly anti-Dartmouth College in the dispute (see, for example, issues of March 3, 1818, and February 16, 1819); the *New Hampshire Sentinel* was, in contrast, impartial in its treatment of the subject; and the *Portsmouth Oracle* (see February 13, 1819) was generally sympathetic to DW's position in the case.

TO TIMOTHY FARRAR, JR.

Boston June 10. 1819

Dear Sir

I have written to Judge [Joseph] Storey,[1] enclosing your letter, & desiring him, if he thinks proper, to write a line to the Clerk, directing an order to issue, for plea, answer, or demurrer to be filed Septr. 1.

I have now the Washington arguments, & the opinions have heretofore been forwarded, to you, or to Exeter. I shall send the arguments by the first opportunity.

On reflection, I wish the quotation from [Edward] Stillingfleet,[2] now in my argument, to remain there, as it is, & the additional quotation to be put into a note. Yrs   D Webster

ALS. NhHi. Published in Shirley, *Dartmouth College Causes*, p. 296.
1. Letter not found.

2. Stillingfleet (1635–1699) was Bishop of Worcester.

TO TIMOTHY FARRAR, JR.

Boston June 19. 1819

My dear Sir,

I am placed in a very disagreeable situation with regard to this *Book*— & one from which I must, in some way extricate myself. I have become accountable for the 100 Dlls. to Mr [Henry] Wheaton— & have paid also 15 or 20 Dlls for copies. All this I care nothing about. But where is the Book, & when is it coming out? I have promised Mr Wheaton a printed copy for him to publish by. He wants it; & with all my inquiries, both to you & Mr [George] Lamson, I can get no answer, nor any information? In the mean time, I hear that Mr [Jeremiah] Mason's argument is badly printed, & that the whole thing is about as bad as it can be. What is to be done? In the first place, you must send me back [John] Holmes' & [William] Wirt's argument, as it is, for Wheaton. *He* must have it. He needs it *now*, & has no copy. I plainly see you will not have it in print this *month;*—whereas he wants it this very day. Wherefore please return it, by the mail carrier, on Monday, that I may forward it to him. His Book, at least this case, will be in print probably as soon as you will need it. At any rate, he must have it. I am mortified, beyond measure, at the progress this printing job makes. I do not know that you are at all to blame about it—but I regret the whole undertaking. If you wd. have consented that it should have been printed *here*, it wd. have been done long ago; & if Gentlemen wd. not have furnished their arguments, it would have come out with[ou]t them.

Do write me on Monday, sending me back Holmes & Wirt. Yrs

D. Webster

I think it but fair & right to suggest, to Mr. Lamson, that unless this Book is *well* printed, on good paper, & free from errors, the case at Washington, will probably be printed *here*, in a proper manner.

ALS. NhHi. Published in Shirley, *Dartmouth College Causes*, pp. 296–297.

TO TIMOTHY FARRAR, JR.

Boston June 23. 1819

I send you a copy of the pages you mentioned; beginning a little back of the third, & going on a little beyond the 4th. so as to shew the connexions.

Please examine, & see if it appears to be right, & to make joints. I shall detain the origl—till you can answer this—so that if any thing is wrong, you can let me know. I believe I have followed your directions.

I enclose you also a minute furnished by Judge [Joseph] Storey;[1] to direct the manner of stating the opinions.

I care less about the time when this Book comes out than the *manner*. I am no great judge of these things; but if it should not be thought to be *well printed*, I shall wish it at the bottom of the red sea. I very much wished to see my part of it, as it came out. But in this I cannot probably be gratified. It is not very material. But it is *essential* that the Judges opinions be accurately printed. I made myself answerable for that, both to the Chief Justice [John Marshall], & Judge [Bushrod] W[ashington]. I am fearful of a thousand blunders, in all these opinions. In Judge Storey's particularly, the citations are so numerous, there will be errors, which will not be corrected, unless, he sees the proof. And as the press has waited for every body else, I think, in common decency, he ought to be furnished with the proofs of all the opinions. He will attend to them immediately, & return the proofs in all cases the next mail. I am persuaded that in no other way will the printing of these opinions be accurate. Yrs   D. Webster

ALS. NhHi. Published in Shirley, *Dart-*   1. Not found.
mouth College Causes, pp. 297–298.

TO [JEREMIAH] MASON

Boston, June 28, 1819.
Dear Sir,

I received yours of the 13th,[1] and have felt in too much spleen to answer it. Whoso meddleth with type-setters gets into trouble. You have narrated the progress, present state, and prospects of our book, in a manner to make one's blood run cold.

It appears to me as desperate as it does to you, and I believe the safest way is to make up our minds that we shall have no book; none at least in this generation. I wrote to Mr. [Timothy] Farrar, have got his answer, and written again. He thinks the book will be out at Commencement.[2] If it should not be well printed, and on our good paper, it will not sell, and a new book will be published. I have so stated to Mr. Farrar, and he may be assured it is true.

I suppose you go to Haverhill about this time. My wife and I have made up our minds to a journey, which will occupy us till toward the end of July. We shall go to the North River, and perhaps to the [Saratoga] Springs. We expect to leave here about the 5th July. I am sorry to inform you that Mr. [Christopher] Gore is ill again. His other knee has become affected. It is now some time since this was the case, and I have heard within a day or two of his being a little better, still he is quite unwell. We have no news here, nor is any thing doing.

It is very much my wish that you would not decline the trusteeship. It will give great satisfaction this way, and by staying a single year, you can do a great deal of good. Judge [Joseph] Story is going to Commencement, with his wife. We will make a party, and go your way, and take you and Mrs. Mason. Yours,   D. Webster.

Text from *PC*, 1: 307–308. Original not found.
   1. Not found.

2. Of Dartmouth College on August 25.

TO [JEREMIAH] MASON

Boston, Saturday evening,
8 o'clock, October, 1819.

My Dear Sir,

Enclosed you have a letter from Mr. [Christopher] Gore.[1] Mrs. Webster and I have been there to-day, where we had the pleasure of meeting Mr. [Rufus] King. Mr. King expressed a great wish to see you; said he had thought of going as far as Portsmouth, but could not well go there, without going further, and it would not be convenient at this time to go to Maine. The object of this is to join Mr. and Mrs. Gore, and Mr. King, in the wish that you and Mrs. Mason would come up next week and make us a visit. Mr. King will probably stay at Mr. Gore's until the latter part of next week. I hope you and Mrs. Mason will find it convenient to come up, as it will give us great pleasure to see you, and it will also gratify Mr. Gore and Mr. King. Our household is now well. We have a chamber, as usual, for you, and shall depend on your coming directly here. The circuit court sits here next week; there is nothing to do in it; it is as lean as your Exeter circuit court, and, as far as I now know, will not engage me a single day. On all accounts it would be pleasant to have a visit from you now. I send this by the driver, in order to anticipate a day, as the mail for to-morrow is closed. Please favor me with a line to-morrow afternoon, in answer to this, and be kind enough to say that you will be here on Tuesday.

Mrs. Webster desires me to say to Mrs. Mason that she must come; and that, you know, is the end of a lady's argument.

In the hope of seeing you, I am yours,   D. Webster.

N.B. As I always choose to end my own arguments, I take the liberty to fill this little space in my husband's letter, my dear Mrs. Mason, to beg that you and Mr. Mason will gratify us with a visit next week. We are quite alone, and I am ready to attend you any where, being very much at leisure, and shall be very much disappointed if you do not come. With much love, Truly yours,   G. Webster.

Text from *PC*, 1: 310–311. Original   1. Not found.
not found.

Following the decision in McCulloch v. Maryland, *Webster's interest and participation in the affairs of the Second Bank of the United States increased perceptibly, as the following two letters indicate.*

TO JEREMIAH MASON

Boston Nov. 15. 1819
My dear Sir

Our family is in such a condition as [to] health, that I do not see how it is possible for us to visit you this week. Our little girl[1] has been sick & is now not well; & one of our domestics has a settled & very severe and dangerous typhus fever. Dr. [John Collins] Warren thinks her symptoms better to day; altho she is yet in danger.

I regret this disappointment the more, as there are some topics about which I wish to confer with you. The principal one is the *Bank*. All that was publicly done, you have seen. Mr. [David] Sears[2] tells me, & wishes me to inform you, that there is no intention of discontinuing the N.H. Branch. Perhaps you will not think it worth while to say much about this, however, at present. Our people here are making exertions to collect proxies with a view to the election, the first of January,[3] & we beg you to look out for the N. H. Votes. A list of Directors was pretty much .agreed on at least for the northern states, at Philadelphia. It is <intimated> intended that N. York & Mass shall have three each. N York, [Isaac] Bronson,[4] [Archibald] Gracie[5] & [William] Bayard, probably. Mass [James] Lloyd, [Nathaniel] Silsbee, &, *mirabile dictu* D.W! This last they will be laughed out of the notion of, & therefore pray say not a word about it. Our proxies, here, will be given to Mr. Lloyd, or Mr. Silsbee, both of whom will attend the Election. They should be with power of Substitution, lest accident should happen. It is thought here, that the present is a favorable time to introduce a proper management into the Bank,[6] & I think you will be of that opinion. Will you write me, on the subject, & let me know what number of Votes may be calculated on, in N. H. It is not thought *probable* that any opposition will be made to the Ticket which will be proposed; but it will be well to be prepared agt. surprise.

Wednesday

We see with sincere pain, the annunciation of the death of Dr. [Jesse] Appleton. Few men have made a short life more useful; & his friends must derive great consolation from that reflection.

I have seen [Gilbert] Stewart [Stuart].[7] He says the pictures shall be completed this Week. I think they may be perhaps, next.

Let us hear from you. Yours as usual   D Webster

Copy. NhHi. Published in *W & S*, 16: 54–55.

1. Julia Webster (1818–1848).

2. Sears (1787–1871; Harvard 1807), Boston legislator and banker.

3. In January the Bank's stockholders elected 14 new directors to the 25 member board.

4. Bronson (1760–1838), physician and New York banker.

5. Gracie (1755–1829), prominent New York merchant and banker.

6. The Bank was being reorganized and revitalized at this time under the direction of Langdon Cheves, after a period of considerable difficulty.

7. In addition to fees paid them, the Dartmouth College trustees had requested Mason, Smith, Hopkinson, and Webster to sit for their portraits by Stuart.

TO JAMES LLOYD

Boston Decr. 20. 1819

Sir

I enclose you sundry Proxies of my friends in Portsmouth, & desire of you the favor to vote upon them, at the ensuing Election of Directors. They have not, as far as I know, any particular wishes to express to you, on the occasion, but send their proxies in aid of the general objects, understood by Gentlemen in this part of the Country. We all hope you will find it convenient, yourself, to form one of the Board. I have a few shares in the Bank, but they have not stood in my name long enough to give me a right to vote at this Election. I therefore send no proxie. With great regard, Your obt. Servt   Danl. Webster

ALS. MH.

In December, Massachusetts joined in the growing national debate over the admission of Missouri to the union as a slave state. At that time a public meeting was held at the State House to protest against its admission. Webster assumed a leading role in the meeting as one of a committee of five chosen to draft a memorial to Congress on the subject. According to Fuess (1: 270–271), Webster made a speech, expressing his view that Congress had a moral and humane duty to keep slavery out of Missouri. The memorial, largely drawn up by Webster, expressed the sense of moral outrage against slavery on the part of the meeting's participants and also stated that, under the Constitution, Congress had the right to make the prohibition of slavery a requisite for the admission of any new state to the union. Webster's reference below is to the Memorial to the Congress of the United States, on the Subject of Restraining the Increase of Slavery in the New States to be Admitted into the Union (*Boston, 1819*).

TO RUFUS KING

Boston Decr. 27. 1819

Dear Sir

I send you a Copy of the "Memorial," agreed on here, in relation to the Missouri question; & avail myself of the opportunity to thank you, most sincerely, for the publication of your speeches on that subject.[1]

We have added little or nothing, in this memorial, to the view taken by you; & yet we thought it might be well to state the argument over again, in the hope that some might read it in this shape, who might not see it, better stated, in your admirable speeches.

I beg to assure you of my very great regard, & am yr ob. sert

Daniel Webster

ALS. NHi. Published in *W & S*, 16: 55.

1. See *Papers Relative to Restriction of Slavery: Speeches of Mr. King and Messrs. Taylor and Talmadge* (Philadelphia, 1819); and *Substance of Two Speeches, Delivered in the Senate of the United States on the Subject of the Missouri Bill* . . . (New York, 1819).

TO [DAVID DAGGETT]

Washington Feb. 10. 1820

My dear Sir,

I would not wish that you should put off your journey hither too long. It is, I think, quite uncertain, when the action will come on, but I *must* leave here as early as the middle of the fourth week. I must try to get it on by that time, if it is likely to come on at all. I should not be surprised if the Court should not reach it at all. It is No. 96[1]— & the Court has not, hitherto, usually, and I believe never reached so high a number. But I cannot say of how stubborn materials the docket may be composed. I will keep you duly informed of our progress, thro. the docket, & will take care that no harm happens to you or your clients.

My faith is pretty strong, on the Missouri question. Mr. [Rufus] King has a few words to say tomorrow, & there is some ground to think that the Senate will not *finally* agree to the Amendments recommended by the Com[mitt]ee.[2] I wish you were in it. Yrs   D. Webster

ALS. CtY.

1. *Ricard* v. *Williams*, 7 Wheaton 59.

2. In early January the Senate Judiciary Committee had amended a House bill calling for the admission

of Maine to the Union as a free state   as a slave state.
at the time of Missouri's admission

TO ALEXANDER BLISS

Washington Feb. 11. 1820

My Dear Sir,

Will you have the goodness to inform Mr. [Augustus] Peabody[1] that I have seen Mr. [Anthony] Cazneaue[2] & had a long conversation about the Resolution causes. Mr. Cazneaue is very anxious to know whether it is probable that [Nathaniel] Goodwin[3] will bring suits in Maine. Please ask Mr. Peabody to write me on the subject (as soon as *possible*) & to give me what information he can. Has Goodwin, as yet, become nonsuit, in his causes?

If there is any thing new, respecting any of our causes, I should be glad to know it.

As I do not write to Mrs. Webster today, I will thank you to let her know that I am well. Our Court here goes on, with its causes, and I am in hopes to get thro. with mine, so as to be home about the beginning of the March Term.

The debate still continues here on the Missouri question, & no one sees when it will end. I will thank you to preserve all the papers containing these debates. Yrs   D. Webster

ALS. DLC.

1. Peabody (1779–1851; Dartmouth 1803), Boston lawyer and legislator.
2. Otherwise not identified.
3. Goodwin was from Biddeford, York County, Maine. Otherwise unidentified.

During a private discussion with Henry Baldwin, Pittsburgh congressman and future Supreme Court justice, on the Missouri question, Webster stated an opinion which was later publicly misconstrued. In the exchange of correspondence below, the two tried to clarify the matter.

TO HENRY BALDWIN

Washington Feb. 15. 1820

Sir

May I have permission to see you, at such time & place as may suit your convenience, for the purpose of asking you to correct a misrepresentation, which seems to have gone abroad, respecting expressions said to be used by me, in a late conversation with you. I understand it is reported, that I observed to you, that I considered the question before Congress, as a question of *political power*; & added that if the free states could carry this question *now*, they could hereafter carry any others.[1]

I am sure I said nothing, in any degree like this, for I never, at any time, spoke, or thought of this Question, as being a fit question to be decided on such considerations. After some previous conversation, in which you intimated, I think, (what I had understood before) that your opinion was against the restriction, you lamented the agitation of the question now, & thought it not wise in the Gentlemen from the North to have produced it, since there was the subject of the Bankruptcy Bill, & other subjects deeply interesting to the people of the North towards which it would be desirable to conciliate the dispositions of the South. To this my remark, by way of answer, simply was, that I presumed the people of the North, among other considerations, regarded this question as one which affected their right *to an equal weight in the political power of the Government, & that they would not* think it reasonable to be called on to surrender this, in order to obtain any favorable act of ordinary Legislation. This observation was in reference to the subject of *representation*, which I have always supposed to be one of the objections to making new slave States. I certainly spoke in reference, *solely*, to this mode, in which political power was to be affected; & if I was understood in any other sense, I was greatly misunderstood.

I beg you to be assured that I am quite certain that no intentional misrepresentation could have been made by you. On a subject however, of so much excitement, I am particularly anxious that no remark of mine may be misunderstood, & must rely on you to correct an erroneous impression, as far as may be necessary so to do, whether it arose from any inaccuracy in my own expression, or any other cause. With great respect Yrs   D. Webster

ALS. NhHi. Published in Van Tyne, pp. 83–84; and also in *W & S*, 16: 55–56.

1. Baldwin here inserted his comment: "No such expression used by you or me."

FROM HENRY BALDWIN

[February 15, 1820]

Dear Sir

There was no misapprehension of our conversation. It related to slave representation as the Subject was referred to in the Boston Memorial. I did not think of any other meaning to the word political power. There was no allusion to any election or office. In relation to the relative importance of this question and the Bankrupt law, commerce and manufactures I understood you as expressing your own rather than the opinion of the Northern people. Yours with esteem   Henry Baldwin

ALS. NhHi. Published in Van Tyne, p. 84.

TO [DAVID DAGGETT]

Washington Feb. 19. 1820

My dear Sir,

The Court, at the end of the second week finds itself in the middle of the argument of No. ELEVEN! It has indeed heard the argument in 15—but it has also yet to hear an argument in No. 7. So that No. eleven is now that which marks fairly the extent of the Courts progress thus far. Nos. 14 & 16 will occupy the greater part of the ensuing week, being both causes of great importance and great length. As to *Ricard vs Williams,* No. 96, there is not the least chance of reaching it, I think, this term. I have spoken to Judge [Joseph] Story about it, & told him I wished to write you about it, & wished his opinion. He observed he did not think that there was a possibility of getting to that No. at this term. I shall be sorry if this should prevent your coming here, because all your friends would be glad to see you;—but it does not seem to me to be possible that the case can come on. The most important case I have here is *No. 58*[1]— & I am fearful it will keep me here much later in the term, than I expected it wd. I will write you, however, a week hence, & let you know how we then stand. If it should be morally certain, by the first of March, that Ricard vs Williams cannot come on, I should be glad to have a continuance then entered, & go home.

The Missouri question goes on, as you see. I heard the debate yesterday in the house, on the Senate's amendment. That Honble. Body was treated somewhat freely—not more so than in my opinion it deserves—for this Union of the two States. Yrs   D. Webster

ALS. CtY.

1. Probably *Hughes* v. *Blake,* 6 Wheaton 453 (1821).

TO JOSEPH STORY

Boston April 3. [1820]
Monday Afternoon

My Dear Sir,

We are quite glad to hear that you will be here on Wednesday, & especially that Mrs Story will accompany you, if her health & the weather be good. Please bring her directly to our house, & the earlier she comes & the longer she stays, the more we shall be obliged to her.

I think I perceive proofs of some uncommon occurrences the last day of the Court at W[ashington]. As far as my poor recollection extends I never before knew *one* Judge deliver his opinion, while the rest of the Bench ordered an *ulterius consilium.* These things need explanation.[1]

I have been uncommonly occupied since I came home. Our Court has had a law term of four weeks, & is to assemble, in full bench, again, today week. I believe I shall tax you for an opinion on one case, which I have the charge of. It turns on N. E. Law, which I am heartily sick of.

I have a few new Books. Yrs   D. Webster

I hope to get Mr [Edward] Everett to dine with us. I shall ask Mr. [George] B[lake] to come, & bring his *Shiraz*.²

[John] Brooks 35, [William] Eustis 16: or thereabouts.³

ALS. MHi.

1. On the last day of the term of Court when Chief Justice John Marshall announced the continuance of the *Amiable Isabella* case until the next session of the Court, Justice William Johnson announced that his opinion on the case was already formed, and before a stunned audience he proceeded to give it. It was Johnson's outburst, possibly growing out of his dislike for Joseph Story or a desire to record his opinion because he considered resigning, which Web- ster thought needed "explanation." On the outburst, see Henry Wheaton to Joseph Story, March 17, 1820, in Gerald T. Dunn, *Justice Joseph Story and the Rise of the Supreme Court* (New York, 1970), pp. 200–201.

2. A type of wine.

3. Brooks and Eustis were the leading candidates in the Massachusetts gubernatorial election held that day. DW is here speculating as to the result, which was as he predicted, save that Brooks received only about 28,000 votes to 19,000 for Eustis.

Even though he had been out of New Hampshire for four years and out of office for three, Webster's interest in New Hampshire politics and in public affairs of New England as a whole remained high. To his friends in New Hampshire he offered his opinions on political questions. His election on October 16, 1820, to the Massachusetts Constitutional Convention, marked Webster's debut as a Massachusetts politician. He soon made himself one of the most conspicuous and influential of the convention delegates.

TO JEREMIAH MASON

Boston May 30. 1820.

Dear Sir

I hope you will think a little of districting your State for members of Congress. I deem it an important affair, in the present state of things, & in relation to probable future events. They have done it in Vermont, & I learned there last week that two or three of their most considerable men might perhaps be elected in the fall. I believe I suggested to you also the expediency of separating the Congressional from the State Elections.

The Mass. Legislature assembles Tomorrow. The important business is to decide whether there shall be a Convention, to amend the State Constitution, & to elect a Senator. As there is one Senator from Boston, the other must come from the Country—I suspect it will be [Elijah Hunt]

Mills,[1] George Bliss,[2] of Springfield, or Wm Baylies of Bridgwater. It is possible however it may be a merchant, in which case I think Mr [William] Reed of Marblehead likely enough to be chosen. Very little is said about it, at present.

Our courts are thro. Judge [Joseph] Story adjourned on Saturday, & Chief Jus [Isaac] Parker on the Saturday before. When your legislative labors are over, I hope you will come this way & play a little. If nothing occurs to prevent, I intend being at Concord one day about the 20th of June. I have promised Mr. [Mills] Olcot[t] to be there, if practicable. Your consignment of Books and Potatoes came safe to hand. I have tried the latter article, first, & find it good. My appetite for the first is not at present quite so keen. The first Piscataqua man I see here I shall charge with the conveyance of the two books I promised you.

Mrs Webster desires her regards to Mrs Mason & her daughters. Yrs truly   D. Webster

ALS. MHi. Published in *W & S,* 16: 56–57.

   1. Mills was elected later that session to the United States Senate to fill the vacancy caused by the resignation of Prentiss Mellen.

   2. Bliss (1764–1830; Yale 1784), Springfield lawyer and legislator, and delegate to the Hartford Convention.

TO JEREMIAH MASON

Boston June 15. 1820

My dear Sir

If your Session should prove as short as you anticipate, it will not be in my power to see you at Concord. The Circuit Court sits here, by adjournment, on Monday, which I must attend. If your Session should last thro. next week, I shall probably be up. I have been endeavoring to do something about an answer, in Mr. [Mills] Olcotts case, but have made very little progress in it. I wish he would send me a full copy of the *Bill.*[1]

Our Legislature is wholly engrossed by local subjects, especially by the project of a convention; which it seems we are to have. I have inquired of [Elijah Hunt] Mills, [Warren] Dutton, [Luther] Laurence,[2] & others. They all say the Virginia Resolutions[3] have not been communicated to them!! Whether they were sent last winter—or whether the Gov. has omitted them—or whether Virginia never sent them at all, is more than I know— & more than any body here appears to know.

Mills' election is probably the best thing that could be done. He is always *respectable,* & will be, I think, a safe man. Local causes rendered it convenient to choose a man in his part of the State, & he is generally popular.

I learn, from various sources, that you make quite a *promising Legis-*

lator. I am glad to hear it. So far as I learn particulars, they meet my approbation. I like your idea of discontinuing *joint* Committees—a great *barbarism,* in Legislative proceedings. In the course of time, I expect to hear of some Legislative movements about the Judiciary; if opinion [in] N. H. is as strong on that subject, as it is represented to be by those persons whom I see here from the State.

Our Convention[4] is an important subject. A great many things, of consequence, will be discussed in it—Among others the creation of a Court of Equity. Yrs   D. Webster

ALS. NhD. Published in *W & S,* 16: 57–58.
1. Olcott was involved in a contest with the town of Lebanon which was seeking authority from the legislature to tax the Olcott locks and canals. The legislature responded by drawing up a bill granting the request, only to have it dropped upon the discovery that under existing laws locks and canals were not listed as taxable. W. R. Waterman, "Locks and Canals at the White River Falls," *Historical New Hampshire,* 22 (Autumn 1967): 23–54.
2. Dutton (1774–1857; Yale 1797) was a newspaper editor, lawyer, and

Maine legislator; Lawrence (1778–1839; Harvard 1801), was a lawyer and manufacturer of Groton and Lowell.
3. See *Preamble and Resolutions on the Subject of the Missouri Question, Agreed to by the House of Delegates of Virginia, and the Amendment of the Senate Proposed Thereto* (Richmond, 1820). The resolutions, which strongly supported Missouri's petition to Congress for admission to the Union as a slave state, were passed by the Virginia legislature on February 3, 1820.
4. Constitutional Convention, to meet in late November.

TO JEREMIAH MASON

Boston June 25, 1820
Dear Sir

The first I saw or heard of the N. H. Resolutions[1] was in Mr. [Nathan] Hale's Paper on Saturday. Who sent them to him I know not, & I believe he was altogether self moved in his remarks on that occasion. I met Judge [Joseph] Story at Nahant on Saturday—he had recd. a Copy from you & we had it read after dinner. I saw that you had been obliged to be quite guarded, & yet the whole argument is in it, & some points are put in a new & striking light. We voted it a good thing very unanimously; but then it was after dinner, when if it had not been as good as it was, our patriotism would have prevailed over our criticism. I like very much your allusion to the unparall[el]ed unanimity of the slave holding states in Congress & also your Answer to the Virginia arguments, at the top of page 7. A very excellent argument, agt the notion that the prohibition affects *Sovereignty,* & one which I have not noticed before, is on the third page.

It was a good achievement to bring the N. H. Legislature to these Resolves. I entertain much hope of better times from it; & think you must be satisfied that you did quite right in attending the Session, & taking part in the business of the State.

I regret I could not go to Concord, not however for the reasons you state, but because I wished to see you, on other accounts, & to make some progress in Mr. [Mills] O[lcott]'s business. When you get over your Concord labors, you must come & see us. I expect to be at home all Summer. Mrs W. will not be able at present to leave home, & we shall be in a state of great leisure, if you will come this way & see us.

Mr. [Isaac P.?] Davis tells me he has shipped your wine. Yrs as ever
D Webster

Copy. NhHi. Published in Van Tyne, pp. 84–85.

1. On June 22, in response to Virginia resolutions upholding Missouri's petition for admission to the Union as a slave state, the New Hampshire legislature had adopted resolutions declaring that in admitting states into the Union, Congress had the right to prohibit slavery as a prerequisite for admission, that such a right existed with Missouri, and that "the existence of slavery within the United States is a great moral as well as political evil, the toleration of which can be justified by necessity alone, and that the further extension of it ought to be prevented, by the due exercise of the power vested in the General Government" (8 *Laws of New Hampshire*, 918).

TO JEREMIAH MASON

Boston August 8. [1820]

Dear Sir

I regret that hot weather or any other cause should have deprived us of a visit from you. We are all quite idle here, & should feel much relieved by the coming in of a visitor, to shake off Ennui. I think still you had better come up to see us this Month. In Septr. you will be at your Courts— in October our Courts will commence— & it is not likely we shall all have at any time so much [little] business as at present.

I am in the same predicament as yourself about N York society. At present I know nothing about it. I shall be able however to learn about it, & will tell you what I hear.

I now send you a copy of the Special Verdict, & of the Charter of the Bank, in the case of Foster v Essex Bank.[1] I wish you to make as good an argument for Pl[aintif]f as you can afford for 50 Dollars.

Mrs. Webster & her boy get along very well & she desires her love to Mrs. Mason. Yours as ever   D Webster

Copy. NhHi. Published in *W & S*, 16: 59.

1. See 16 *Massachusetts Reports* 245–274.

TO EZEKIEL WEBSTER

Boston Aug. 17. 1820—

Dear E.

I recd yours,[1] last Saturday. You need not, & I hope do not, give yrself any uneasiness abt. your note. It shall be well taken care of.

Dr. [Nathaniel A.] Haven has drawn on me for 500 Dlls, which draft I have accepted. It is payable some sixty days hence. There will be a small sum remaining due to him, greater or less, according as the proceeds of the Thornton & Unity Lands may turn out. For this sum, whatever it may be—(it cannot be more than 4 or 5 hundred dollars) he has agreed, if I wish it to take my own note. In the meantime, if you will send him a minute of the lots &c conveyed by me to you, he will execute releases such as you may desire. I write to him today to that effect. So much for business.

As to a President,[2] I have weighed the subject very much in my own mind, & conversed on it on every occasion with the friends of the College. My mind is not made up in favor of any candidate. The Gentleman[3] whom you & I thought most of when I saw you is not, I fear, in all respects, the most eligible. I learn that he has not much energy of character, &, as to scholarship, not more than respectable. And if as much fitness for the office could be found in a man 10 yrs younger, it would be much better. The more I think of it, the more I incline to a younger man. At fifty, not enough of life remains to acquire much;—whereas at 30 or 35 a man is young enough to form himself to be President. I cannot yet fix on any body. Mr. [Gardiner] Spring,[4] of N York, (son of the late Dr. Spring) has been mentioned by some. I think Mr. [Nathan] Lord's fitness should be considered. On the whole, my opinion at present is that you should fill up the board, & postpone the appointment of President for the present. I have been industrious to collect the opinions of our best & most intelligent friends in Essex, & it seems to be *against* the appointment which you contemplated as most probable. I am willing you should shew this letter to Mr. [Thomas W.] Thompson, Mr. [Charles] Marsh, & Mr. [Moses] Payson, or other friends. The trustees can inquire, & correspond, thro' the autumn, on this important subject, & when they come to a conclusion, a quorum can meet & make the appointment.

I hope therefore you will on all accounts take further time. It is not only an important question so far as the College itself is concerned, but it is of importance also, generally, to shew that a College, not under Legislative control, can flourish. I believe I may say that *all* our friends this way recommend further consideration.

As to the L.L.D. I thought best to speak directly to the Gentleman concerned. I saw him day before yesterday; & he thinks, so recent are certain things, that a compliment of that sort to him had better be deferred to next year. I told him I would give you this hint. I am, on the whole, of the same opinion.

I hope your board will remember Mr. [Samuel] *Wood*. He at least deserves well of the College—having sent a hundred of us, such as we are, to be educated in it. On Monday the

Charles Baker,
Bloomingburgh
Sullivan County
New York

Above is the address of Mr. Wood's man.   D.W.

ALS [Incomplete]. NhD. Published in part in *PC*, 1: 312–313.

1. Not found.

2. President Francis Brown of Dartmouth College had died on July 27, 1820, and the trustees were now actively engaged in searching for a successor.

3. Probably the Reverend Daniel Dana (1771–1859), a minister in Newburyport, Massachusetts, for the past 26 years. He was selected to succeed President Brown at the August meeting of the trustees but served only a short time, resigning the post less than a year later.

4. Spring was offered the post but declined after Dana resigned.

TO [JOHN GORHAM PALFREY]

[Oct 1820] Saturday.

Dear Sir

The Chief Justice [Isaac Parker] has taken our work off our hands. He has delivd a charge on the subject of revising the Constitution,—which is published in the Northampton paper. It is very long— & excellent. He treats the Religious part of the subject to *my* great satisfaction. It is impossible for me to say any thing so well. I do not think any thing better can be done than to *review* this Charge;—in the Ch[ristian] Dis[ciple][1]— give, as an extract the whole relation to religion, & add the entire & cordial approbation of the Editors. Yrs   D. Webster

ALS. MH.

1. Palfrey was at this time editor of the *Christian Disciple*.

TO JOSEPH STORY

Sunday Eve' [Nov 12, 1820]

Dear Sir

I am glad you are not going to R.I. as you will be much wanted here. We have pressed [William] Prescott into the Service of preparing Resolutions for the introduction & disposition of business. As far as I could form a judgment, he seemed the proper man to bring forward the motion, & he seems willing to do it. His age & character, his known moderation & caution, his respectable standing in the State, at the same time that he is disconnected with the State Government, & so free from all suspicion of bias, for or against change on account of personal convenience, seem to render him the fit man to propose the course of proceeding. We shall expect your effectual support, if his proposition meets with objection. I earnestly trust you will be in town on Tuesday Morning, as there will be many things to be said, & done, & seen to. You will like, among other things, to see the shape in which Mr. P's proposition is to come forward.

I cannot find Smith.[1] It is lost. There is a copy in town which you can get here.

The Book of Constitutions[2] I will endeavor to send you—Tomorrow forenoon.

Pray let me hear that you are in town tuesday morning. Yrs   D.W.

ALS. MHi.

1. Probably William Loughton Smith, *A Comparative View of the Constitutions of the Several States . . .* Philadelphia, 1796.

2. Story had probably requested to borrow either *The Constitutions of the several independent states of America . . .* (Philadelphia, 1781; Boston, 1785), or *The Constitutions of the six-* *teen states which compose the confederated Republic of America . . .* (Boston, 1797). A copy of the former, now in Baker Library, NhD, comes from Ezekiel Webster's library. Annotations therein suggest that Daniel originally gave the volume to his father Ebenezer, who passed it on to Ezekiel.

Named a presidential elector in 1820, Webster cast his vote for James Monroe for president, but he had doubts, as he explained to Mason below, about a vice-presidential candidate. He finally decided to vote for Richard Stockton of New Jersey, an old friend from the Thirteenth Congress.

TO JEREMIAH MASON

Boston Nov 12. 1820

My dear Sir

I have not been able to come to any definite conclusion, on the subject of votes for vice President. There seems to be no way, yet found out, of ascertaining how it would be recd. at Washington, if the votes here should be given for Mr. [John Quincy] Adams. I wish you would see your *friend,* on your way to Concord, & ascertain what he thinks of it. Indeed I know no one more likely to be able to learn from the Gentleman himself, how it would suit. There will be a number of us, of course, in this state, who will not vote for Mr. [Daniel D.] Tomkins, & we must therefore look up somebody to vote for.

If you can, without inconvenience, I hope you [will] see the Ex Governor,[1] as you go to Concord. It is hardly out of your way, I believe. If you learn anything worth communicating, be good enough to write me. Several of our Electors are members of the Convention, & will be here this week. I shall have some conversation with them, and will write you again.

Our Court is adjourned for a month; so that we have nothing to do but attend Convention. I shall follow the course which I intimated to you, & which you approved, in relation to my concern with the Convention.

Mary [Mason] I believe has written to her Mother to day—so that you will learn all the news, if there be any.

With many respects to Mrs. Mason, I am, Dr. Sir, Yours   D Webster

Copy. NhHi. Published in Van Tyne, pp. 85–86.

1. William Plumer, who, as an elec-tor from New Hampshire, cast the only vote against the choice of James Monroe in the election.

TO EDWARD EVERETT

[December 25, 1820]

Dear Sir

I was extremely mortified not to be able to hear you today. The Convention called up some business with which I was particularly charged, & which had been waiting for me. I tried them, repeatedly, to adjourn, but they had not grace enough.

Will you do me the favor to allow me to read yr discourse[1] this Eve'. The Ladies tell me I never heard any thing so excellent. I am very eager to get a sight at it. Yrs affectionately   D. Webster

ALS. MHi.   1. Document not identified.

TO JOHN THORNTON KIRKLAND

In Convention Decr. 30 1820

Ordered,

That Messrs

[Daniel] Webster of Boston
[Henry] Dearborn of Roxbury
[Samuel Sumner] Wilde of N. Port
[Allen] Tillinghast of Wrenth[am]
[Leverett] Saltonstall of Salem[1]

be a Com[mitt]ee to inquire into the Constitutional rights & privileges of Harvd. Col— & to report also an acct. of the donations which have been made to it by the State—[2]

———

Dear sir

I am anxious to see you, on the subject of the above, the very earliest opportunity. Our time is short. If I am not home, when you call, please let me be sent for.

I send this to Cambridge, not knowing whether you are in Town today. This Afternoon—or Eve' or any *lawful* part of Tomorrow—I am at yr service. Yrs   D.W.

If the bearer finds you he will stay [and] bring an answer.

ALS. MH.

1. Wilde (1771–1855; Dartmouth 1789) was a Massachusetts lawyer, delegate to the Hartford and Constitutional Conventions, and Judge of the Supreme Judicial Court of Massachusetts; Tillinghast was a manufacturer from Norfolk County; and Saltonstall (1783–1845; Harvard 1802) was a Salem lawyer, legislator, and congressman.

2. The Committee which DW chaired determined that no fundamental changes need be made in the administration of Harvard "except that the overseers, in electing clergymen to their board, should not confine themselves, as in the past, to only one denomination—the Congregational."

TO JEREMIAH MASON

Boston Jan. 12. 1821

My dear Sir

We learned by Mary's letter of Jane's recovery which gave us great pleasure. We had become a good deal alarmed for her.

You perceive our [Constitutional] Convention is over. We have got out as well as we expected. As soon as our Vol. of debates & proceedings is published, I shall send it to you. It was a great body, in numbers, & tho' I think it generally was well disposed, there was a good deal of inflamable matter, & some *radicalism* in it. We were extremely fortunate, in finding a considerable number of Gentlemen well disposed, who might otherwise have occasioned much trouble. You laugh a little, I know, at our early debates about Rules & Orders &c. But the "rules & orders" brought us out, at last. Without them there is reason to think we might have come badly off. Some of our friends have increased their reputation a good deal. I think Judge [Joseph] S[tory] has done so altho' he had a great deal of that commodity before. [Warren] Dutton, [Samuel] Hoar, & [Leverett] Saltonstall have decidedly risen, not a little. We think three good things done—The Judiciary—The *College*— & *the future Amendment Articles*. As to the rest, there may be different opinions. The House of Reps is not eno[ugh] reduced; but we could go no farther, without departing altogether from [town] Representation. The Senate stands pretty well. Whether the Religious Article is helped or hurt, its friends hardly Know —So I suppose no *great* injury has probably been done it. Some smaller Amendments abt. Militia, &c have passed, which it would have been better to have omitted.

I learn that you have *finished* your Com. Pleas. The consequence, I think, must ere long be, an entire new modification of your Sup. Court.

I hope you will keep in the Legislature long eno[ugh], to pass a law for *Districting* for Members of Congress. I think that quite an object.

I suppose I must leave home for Washington about the 25th. I wish you could make business up here, for a day or two, before that time. I have had no regular *talks*, with any body, since you were here, & I think there were some subjects which we left unfinished.

I want to look into [George] Moore's History of the English Rev.[1] to ascertain a particular fact. I will thank you to give it to the stagecoach driver to be brought to me, Sunday or Monday. It will come safe.

Yours with usual regard   D. Webster

Copy. NhHi. Published in *W & S*, 16: 60.

1. *History of the British Revolution of 1688–89 . . .* (London, 1817).

By 1821 Webster had already laid a foundation for a distinguished political and legal career in Massachusetts. From late January until late March or early April, he was in Washington, appearing before the Supreme Court in several important cases, the most noted being Cohens v. Virginia *(6 Wheaton 430). The remainder of the year, he spent much time in the state courts and in preparation of cases to be argued before the Spanish Claims Commission. In the latter activity, Webster not only enlarged the circle of his acquaintances in Massachusetts but also won their respect, and that of many other prominent merchants and families up and down the entire eastern seaboard.*

Politically, Webster had already distinguished himself in Massachusetts. The popularity of the petition to Congress on the Missouri question, his Discourse at Plymouth commemorating the bicentennial of the landing of the Pilgrims, and his leadership in the constitutional convention had won him the respect of many politicians and voters; and although not an officeholder in 1821, his interest in and comments on the important political issues of the day increased his standing in the eyes of voters and politicians.

Only one indication of his rising status appears in the following letter, in which Webster agreed to the request of his law associate Alexander Bliss to move their offices to more commodious quarters at the corner of Court and Tremont streets.

TO ALEXANDER BLISS

Washington Feb. 9. [1821]

Dr Sir

I recd yrs, thro. the hands of Mr. [Benjamin] Gorham.[1] I am willing to take the new Offices, especially as Mr [William] Prescott is going over head. I confess I have been unwilling to remove, but as you seem to prefer it, I am disposed to submit. I must have a room— & there must be accomodations also for you & the students. I shall leave the matter entirely with you. If we move, I hope you will have the job over, before I return.

Pray let me hear from you often, respecting our business in Court. What causes are tried, & how decided. We are now trying the cause from R. Island—in which Mr Greene was concerned.[2] It looks well, for our side. In a day or two Mr Blake's case will be on.[3]

As to news, here, there is none. My opinion is, it is more probable than otherwise that Missouri will come in, on some terms or other.

I wrote Mrs W. yesterday. It is now mild & fine weather here.

Yrs truly   D. Webster

ALS. DLC.
    1. Gorham (1775–1855; Harvard 1795), Massachusetts lawyer, legislator, and congressman.

2. *The Bello Corrunes,* 6 Wheaton 152 (1821).
    3. *Hughes* v. *Blake,* 6 Wheaton 453 (1821).

TO [DAVID DAGGETT]

Washington feb. 16. '21

My Dr Sir

The Court has yet made very little progress. This is the *fourth* day in which it has been occupied in a western land cause;[1]— & another day may be probably exhausted in it.

Our Ricard & Williams cause is *no:* I think 64. When we shall get near it, I cannot say; certainly not for ten days or a fortnight. I have spoken to Mr. [William] Pinkney about it. He inclines to agree at once to continue it— & I think it probable that may be the course. He says he is not yet prepared, & does not seem to speak of it as a cause expected to come on this term.

You see Congress is hung up again on the Missouri question. It seems nothing can be done until that is *settled;* & it seems no vote, but a vote to *admit,* is to be considered as *settling* the question.

The Bankrupt Bill will probably pass the Senate;[2] but there is no chance I understand of getting it thro. the House. The principal *cause* talked about, this term, is the lottery question, from Virga.[3] Their counsel say, if the Court sustain the jurisdiction, they are instructed to go out of court, & let the *merits* go, as the court see fit.

Yrs truly   D. Webster

ALS. CtY.
    1. Probably *Green* v. *Biddle,* 8 Wheaton 1, involving the constitutionality of a Kentucky "occupying" claimant law, which was decided in a

preliminary fashion in 1821 and finally in 1823.
    2. Congress had under consideration, as it had on several previous occasions, an act to establish a uni-

form system of bankruptcy.
3. *Cohens* v. *Virginia,* 6 Wheaton
264. DW appeared for the state in the
case, but did not participate in the
argument on appellate jurisdiction
which was at the heart of the dispute.

FROM [THOMAS GIBBONS]

E[lizabeth] T[own], N Jersey
2d. April 1821

Sir

The day after you were in N York on your way home from Washington—Capt. [Cornelius] Vanderbilt informed me by letter that you would write me within 10 days after your arrival in Boston of what my situation regarding the Suit of Gibbons vs. Ogden[1] now is—and advising me what measures we should adopt to hasten this cause to a trial before the Supreme Court. I have not yet had the pleasure of receiving such letter of advice, and instruction from you. I shall be very much obliged to you to write me as soon as you can possibly make it convenient. I feel a deep concern in this question, and I want very much to get a decision that will contravene the unconstitutionality of the Laws of New York. The monopolists under these Laws are very vexatious to many citizens in this section of the 2 States. Respectfully &c.

AL copy. NhD.   1. 9 Wheaton 1 (1824).

TO JOSEPH HOPKINSON

Boston April 13. 1821

My dear Sir

It is seldom worth one's while to attempt that, in which he knows he must fail. This consideration restrains me from undertaking to express my surprise at the appointment of these Commissioners. Can you tell me who *Judge* [Hugh Lawson] *White* is or who his associate, *Judge* [John W.] *Green,*[1] is? I confess I was wholly unprepared for such a result, notwithstanding I thought the long delay, & the half apology by way of anticipation which appeared some weeks ago in the [National] Intelligencer,[2] augured ill. As it is, my desire to have much to do before the Board is a good deal *cooled.* I know not how I may finally act, but my present feeling is not to make any effort for business before the Board. I am curious to know what sort of *influence* brought these nominations about. For, even after it was decided that no fit person should be appointed, which, I presume, must have been made a preliminary, still I do not understand how, among the unfit, this trio[3] should have been fallen upon. But away with all these matters, & let me rather ask how Mrs. Hopkinson, & Elizabeth, & the boys—what few there are of them—do?— & tell you, that Mrs. W. and our three children are well. Our little lad who gave me some uneasiness, while at W[ashington] is quite recovered, & has already a sort of fore-the-mast aspect and appearance. Master Danl. Fletcher, who has once honored the middle states with a visit, is now less of a traveller, & cultivates letters, in a neighboring street. Between these two boys, we have a girl, of three years, who, her mother says, must mend her manners much or she will not be numbered among the meek children of Moses   Eliza B[uckminster] is at present with us. I believe you are one of her favorites, for when she read your letter, the other day, tho' not naturally envious, she seemed to think that your horses, cows, and pigs were honored, by your visit [to them], somewhat beyond their deserts.

We do, my dear Sir, most confidently & truly [rely] on your visiting us this year. Just take your wife & daughter—set out— & all will soon be done. Two days from N York will bring you here. We have room enough, in our house, for all of you, and as many more. We expect to be quite at leisure, & shall at least give you a hearty welcome. This visit must not be put off longer.

With very true regard, My Dear Sir, I am Yrs   D. Webster

Mr L. Harris[4] has just arrived. He will, I believe, procure the evidence wished for.

ALS. PHi.

1. Green did not serve on the Spanish Claims Commission and was replaced by Littleton Waller Tazewell of Virginia.

2. March 13, 1821.

3. William King of Maine was appointed the third member of the Commission.

4. Not identified.

TO [NATHANIEL HAVEN]

Boston May 4. 1821

Dear Sir

I postponed writing to you, until I could propose some definite arrangment about this note of a thousand Dollars, & partly because I expect to be in Portsmo. shortly. I regret that you have drawn on me, for I have had so much to pay this Spring, that it puts me to great inconvenience. I was in hopes the note might have rested, a little while, with or without security. As it is, I suppose I must accept your draft, altho' I am quite sorry to see it.

Yours &c   D Webster

ALS. MBNU.

On December 22, 1820, Webster delivered his Discourse at Plymouth *as a part of the bicentennial celebration of the landing of the Pilgrims. The next day, the officers of the Pilgrim Society, the organization which planned the event, asked him to have his address printed for distribution. A few days later he accepted their invitation to publish the speech, but urged that other pressing "engagements" compelled him to postpone its preparation "to a more distant day." On several occasions during 1821, Webster probably reworked the address (as he discusses with Samuel Davis [1765–1829], the corresponding secretary of the Pilgrim Society, below); but not until late autumn in 1821 did the published address appear. Usually Webster rushed to get his orations into print, finding time for the necessary revisions in the midst of other pressing engagements. The delay in publication, Robert C. Winthrop hypothesized* (Scribner's Magazine, 15 [*January 1894*]: 118–128), *arose because Webster had discussed the same questions a week earlier in an address before the Constitutional Convention on December 15, 1820. Since his speech before the convention quickly appeared in print, Webster intentionally delayed the publication of the Plymouth oration to discourage a close comparison of the two addresses. Later in the year, after its belated publication, former President John Adams and New York Chancellor James Kent highly praised the speech.*

TO SAMUEL DAVIS

Boston May 14. 1821

Dear Sir,

I have availed myself of the first leisure which I could command to look over my Discourse, & prepare a copy for the press. A considerable part of it is now ready, & I hope to find time to finish revising the rest within a few weeks.[1]

The printing of it I shall beg to leave wholly to your direction, & I hope you will find it convenient to spend a week here, sometime next month, when we will endeavor to publish it. Your Brother [Isaac P.] & myself contemplate a ride to the Old Colony, about the time of Election when we hope to see you. My engagements however will allow but a short absence from home at that time. Yours very truly   D Webster

ALS. Pilgrim Society, Plymouth.
  1. *A discourse delivered at Plymouth, Dec. 22, 1820. In commemora-*
tion of the first settlement of New England. Boston: Wells and Lilly, 1821.

Ever since the Dartmouth College case the school had been struggling to remain financially solvent. Mills Olcott suggested a resort to the state legislature for public funds, so long as that could be done without yielding actual control in return. In a letter to Webster, June 13, 1821, he described his plan and asked for advice:

> *Some of the friends of old D. College who are here have thought that her real interest might be subserv'd by some Legislative arrangements at this time, whereby not only State patronage but State funds should be obtained. They have thought of a Board of overseers say of 20—to*

include the President of the Senate, the Speaker of the House; the others to be appointed by the Governor & Council—to have a veto upon the appointment, &c of the Trustees & afterwards fill up their own vacancies themselves, & to be somewhat on the footing of Cambridge. A tax is expected to be rais'd for the State Treasury this session from Banks, & from this fund have say $5000 annually for ten years appropriated for D. C. There is no real College man in the Legis., except Bro. Ez[ekiel] & my humble self, & we cannot have the benefit of consulting with Trustees (Copy, NhD, mDWs).

Webster discusses the proposal below in the letters to Olcott and to Ezekiel Webster.

TO MILLS OLCOTT

Boston June 17. 1821

Dear Sir

I wish I had more hope of good than I have, to the College, from the Legislature. Of course you know best the feeling, on such subjects, at present existing, but for myself I do not believe the College could get a dollar from the Genl. Court. They would be very likely to accept the proposition *to appoint overseers*, but as to the money part of the bargain, I do not think they would give a cent. Besides, I do not think the present a favorable moment to create a Board of Overseers, by Executive appointment, with power afterwards of filling their own vacancies. It is easy to see what sort of men would be first appointed, & what sort of men they would perpetuate. All would be *political*, & nothing *literary*. My own impression is, that if the College must *die,* it is better that it should die a natural death. A board of Overseers, such as would probably be appointed, would *negative every important nomination of the Trustees.* Of this, I have no sort of doubt. There are reasons, not applicable to D. College, & to such a board as you would create, which alone presents, *else where,* the utmost embarrassment.

I have given my *opinion,* as you request, & beg you to treat it as entirely confidential. I have no room to state reasons, at large. At any rate, I should not think it expedient to move in the matter without much circumspection, & a previously arranged plan, which should have recd the approbation of the Trustees. Is there any *reliance,* to be placed in the quarter from which the first appointments would proceed? My own judgment & opinion do not answer that question favorably.

I had hoped to be in Concord before you leave it, & still intend so to be, but our Sup. Court is still in session, & may last too long, for my purpose. Mr [George] Blake, with Mrs B & George are gone to Newport, on a little excursion, partly to attend the Circuit Court, & partly for pleasure.

With sincere regard Yrs   D. Webster

ALS. NhD. Published in Shirley, *Dartmouth College Causes*, pp. 12–13.

TO EZEKIEL WEBSTER

Boston June 17. 1821

Dear E.

I have recd yrs of friday.[1] Mr [Mills] Olcott wrote me on this same subject of the Overseers. I am very doubtful whether any good would come of the project. *Who would the Board be?* Every thing depends on that. Har[var]d College would have been prostrate, before now, if a certain party had had the appointment of a board of Overseers. *Look at the Govr. & Council of New Hampshire*— whom will such men appoint? —& whom will their appointees elect, to fill vacancies? In my opinion, *mere political partizans. So it has been found in Maine.* I confess I have a very decided opinion, on this subject; & I do not at all believe you could get a cent, by any concession. They gave their own University *nothing*— they would give the College no more. At least so I think, but you & Mr. Olcott who are on the spot, can judge better. It would be injurious, I think, to propose to take this important alteration in the Charter before the ground was well explored, & some *security* obtained, that the concession should not be abused.

On the whole, it strikes me that the project, so far as it relates to getting money, is impracticable; & the whole of it not without danger.

I hope to be able to leave here about the 25. It depends on the adjournment of the Court, which is still sitting, & I know not exactly when to expect its adjournment.

Your Govr.[2] seems to have made a pretty good speech; certainly better than the average of such things. He talks against a false economy very justly, and as if he had never shared in the benefits derived from the currency of opposite sentiments. I think you will have a pleasant session. Your house has good men eno[ugh] in it to prevent great mischief, even if you shall not effect much positive good; & it is a great thing, now a days, to keep things from growing worse. Yrs   D Webster

ALS. NhD. Published in part in *PC*, 1:   1. Not found.
314–315.   2. Samuel Bell.

FROM JOSEPH GALES, JR.

Washington July 6, 1821.

Dear Sir:

I had the pleasure to receive today your favor of the 2d.[1] I am rejoiced at the stand taken by the *popular* branch of the Legislature of New Hampshire.[2] We have copied the resolutions in question, in such manner as we think will best suit the times.[3] We have, a day or two ago, spoken *plainly* on this subject.[4] *We* must take care not to say too much on it. A few essays in your *Democratic* papers would answer a good purpose in opening the eyes of men to the monstrosity of the Ohio (indeed of the [DeWitt] Clinton & [John] Randolph) doctrines.[5]

We had an Oration here on the Fourth, which will produce a *sensation*.[6] It was Demosthenes redivivus in substance and manner. I have never witnessed any thing superior to the *tout ensemble*.

With great respect, Yr. obed serv   Jo: Gales Jr

ALS. NhHi.

1. Letter not found.

2. On June 27 the New Hampshire House of Representatives passed a resolution supporting a recent Circuit Court decision which denied the right of the state of Ohio to levy a tax on two local branches of the Bank of the United States. The New Hampshire Senate promptly followed suit with a similar resolve. In effect the resolutions placed New Hampshire on record as concurring with the 1819 Supreme Court decision in *McCulloch v. Maryland*, which in part invali-

dated an attempt by Maryland to tax a local branch of the United States Bank.

3. The resolutions appeared in the *National Intelligencer*, July 7.

4. See the *National Intelligencer*, July 4.

5. DeWitt Clinton, like John Randolph of Virginia, was an inveterate opponent of the United States Bank as an unwarranted extension of federal power.

6. John Quincy Adams delivered the oration, which was reported in the *National Intelligencer*, July 7.

TO EDWARD EVERETT

[Boston 9 July 1821]

I think this No. exceedeth all its predecessors in glory.[1] I have read three Art[icle]s—1. Yrs in answer to the New Magazine, of which I do most honestly admire both the right spirit, & the able execution. 2. Florida; by which I am greatly edified & instructed. 3. St Pierre, which is a very entertaining romance.

I verily think we have had nothing so good as this no. *Sic itur ad astra.*
Thine   D. Webster

ALS. MHi. Published in *PC*, 1: 315.

1. *North American Review*, July 1821. Everett was then its editor.

TO JEREMIAH MASON

Boston July 11. 1821

Dear Sir

I received the enclosed yesterday.[1] You will of course have seen that Mr. [Joseph] Gales had even *anticipated* you[r] wishes, & *spoken out* on the subject. What he said you will observe was printed in the Democratic Paper here yesterday. It seems to me that all this works kindly, & will have the best effect. No one can be at a loss now, I think [how] these things are regarded at Washington.

I learned from Judge [Joseph] Story as well as from Yourself that he intends paying you a visit next week. I have promised to go with him. We heard last Evening of the death of Mrs. Websters Mother. This will probably prevent her going, but I intend to persuade her to go, if I can. If she should not, I shall try to pick up some companion—probably I think Mr. [Edward] Everett.

I expect to see the Judge, on his return from Newport, & will fix on the day. I can go any day, as our Courts are now thin. Yrs truly   D.W.

Copy. NhHi. Published in Van Tyne, p. 86.

1. Probably a copy of the *National Intelligencer*, July 4, 1821, which con-tained Gales' editorial regarding Ohio's attempt to tax the local branch of the United States Bank.

TO JEREMIAH MASON

Boston July 15. 1821

Dear Sir,

In the [National] Intelligencer of the 11th you will see some very sound remarks on your Resolutions. They are from the same source, to which my letter was addressed. I have also a letter from the same quarter, which I shall show you. It is quite edifying. Indeed I will, I think, enclose it, tho' I have hardly had time to run over its contents.[1]

I have not heard from Judge [Joseph] S[tory] since I wrote you last. Mrs Webster thinks if I will put off my journey to Monday the 23rd—she will accompany me. I have therefore concluded so to do,— & shall write to the Judge accordingly. If any alteration of this project takes place, it will be by coming on an *earlier* day. I should like much to ride round Winnipesauke Lake—never having yet seen its Eastern shore. I dare say the Judge would like it. The Ladies might have their choice, to remain at Portsmo. or go to the Lake—but I think they would prefer going.

I shall intimate this project to the Judge. Yrs in haste   D. Webster

ALS. MHi. Published in Van Tyne, pp. 86–87.

1. The enclosure, according to Van Tyne, p. 87n, was W. W. Seaton to John C. Calhoun [July 7?, 1821],

Copy, NhHi. See also Calhoun to Wheaton, July 15, 1821, in Hemphill, ed., *Papers of John C. Calhoun*, 6: 259–260, approving the New Hampshire resolutions.

TO JOSEPH HOPKINSON

Boston Aug. 6. 1821

Dear Sir.

Will you do me the favor to inform me whether you suppose any *discussion*, as to what cases are and what are not within the [Adams-Onís] Treaty, is expected at the meeting of the Commissioners in September?

The published order[1] says that the Board will at that time proceed to *decide* whether any memorials which may have been since with the Secretary shall be recd. for examination. Now, as the Memorial is to set forth the facts of the case particularly and minutely, and therefore cannot be varied, are the Commissioners, as you understand the matter, to *decide* at the September meeting, what cases do, & what do not, come within the Treaty? This, as you know, may depend on construction, & interpretation, and no doubt much discussion must be had before the points can all be settled. If these questions or any of them are to be *settled*, at the ensuing meeting, I must attend it, in behalf of certain claimants, as I presume you must. I am anxious therefore, of learning what you think of the probable course of business, at this September meeting.

I regret I had not the pleasure of seeing more of your sailor son. I went into N Hamp. about the time of his arrival, & came home only in season to see him the day before he departed. He appears to be a fine tall fellow, & I look to see him an Admiral.

Mr [William Morris] Meredith informed us that it was expected in Philadelphia that you would ere long resume your residence in that City. I do assure you I learned this with great pleasure altho I fear it may deprive us of the pleasure of seeing you here this Summer. I mentioned it to Judge [Joseph] Story, whose delight was somewhat extravagant on the occasion. If this new arrangement does not prevent, I *confidently* look for you this month. Pray let me hear.

Mrs W. & myself desire to be affectionately remembered to Mrs H. & Eliza.

I am, Dr Sir, as always, Yrs   D. Webster

ALS. PHi.

1. See John Bassett Moore, *History and Digest of International Arbitra-* *tions,* 6 vols. (Washington, 1898), 5: 4501.

TO JEREMIAH MASON

Boston Sep. 3. [1821]

Dr Sir

Some time ago, I was asked about filling up sundry vancancies in the Branch Bk at Portmo. I was asked, inter alia, whether you would be a Director. I s[ai]d, probably, you would, if the Board were to your mind. I believe you are not a stockholder, but the Gentleman who conversed with me, (Mr [David] Sears) hopes you will buy a share or two, & be a Director provided it should happen that others agreeable to you should be appointed.[1] In short, if you chuse to take an interest in the matter, you can probably have a board to your mind. If you hear any thing on this subject, I hope you will not, at present, give a flat refusal.

I send you the policy on the Volant.[2] I have made a little arrangement about it. Judge [Joseph] Story will be here tomorrow to give his judgt in the case here. I hope it will be broad eno[ugh] to cover this. I will let you know.

I send Mr [Alexander] Bliss to Washington, tomorrow, with these *claims*,—not going at present myself, thinking that nothing important can be done this session. So many People are out of Town, that I have as yet been able to do nothing abt. your Bridge. I will see to it, & let you know what can be done, this week. It makes no difference with me whether George [Mason][3] shall come to my office now, or hereafter. I think his intention to be a while at Cambridge a very good one. It will give me pleasure to receive him, when it shall suit his convenience to come.

Very truly Yrs   D. Webster

ALS. NhHi.

1. Although Mason was not appointed a director of the Portsmouth branch of the United States Bank immediately, he became its president in 1828.

2. *Haven et al.* v. *Holland*, 2 Mason 230, a case involving marine insurance.

3. Mason (1800–1865), Jeremiah Mason's son.

TO JEREMIAH MASON

Boston Sep. 12. 1821

Dear Sir

I cannot say much about this Bank matter till I see you. The short of this, is, I recommended the appointments which took place,—partly *because* some of the Gentlemen were *impractible*. I tho't good would come of it, I tho't it time to break up a sort of *knot*.

There is no sort of necessity of presenting any claim, at the present Session of Commissioners nor any *utility*, that I am aware of. In many cases it has been done, & in a great many omitted; as convenience dictated. Several have been drawn very well, in Portsmo. by Mr. [Charles] Cutts. I send you a rough copy of one that happens to lie before me, which was altered in some respects, afterward, in order to set forth the case more exactly, but the *formal part* is such as has been most generally used here.

Mr. [Alexander] Bliss has gone to Washington, & has carried on a pretty large budget of these claims. I cannot say what it may amount to, but most of the claims here go thro. my hands. It has given me three weeks of hard work to prepare them, & will call for as many more. Judge [Joseph] Story has given judgment in the Volant case here. On the facts, as presented, he entertains no doubt, that the Volant did no more than she was authorised to do, with or without letter of Marque. We have one difficulty to meet. *Mr. Gill,*[1] who is a party, really or nominally, in the policy I sent you, was our *best* witness here. I beli[e]ve however we can supply his place pretty well. It will not probably be possible to have a tryal, in Oct. at Exeter; & therefore you can exercise your own judgment, as to sueing at that term. I see no great benefit, in it, but shall leave it to you.

My wife & children are well, but have not yet come into Town. We expect to gather ourselves in Somerset Street next week. Yrs   D. Webster

Copy. NhHi. Published in Van Tyne,   1. Not identified.
pp. 87–88.

TO ALEXANDER BLISS

Boston Sep. 18. [1821]
Dear Bliss

Your several letters to the 13th instant,[1] have been recd. They give great satisfaction to the concerned, & are very honorable proofs of your attention & intelligence. The more detail you give us of all the proceedings of the Board[2] the better. You are very right to stay to see our cases thro. Whatever *formal* difficulties exist may be easily removed by supplemental statements. I am glad, on the whole, that for the present they receive none which are not clearly within the Treaty.

I have not time to say more today but intend writing you again tomorrow. In haste Yrs   D. Webster

ALS. DLC.   2. Spanish Claims Commission.
    1. Letters not found.

TO EZEKIEL WEBSTER

Boston Sep. 26. (Wednesday)
[1821]
Dr E.

I recd. yrs this moment,[1] just as I am setting out for Worcester, for three days. Mr [Nathan] Hale will no doubt publish yr article, if it be wished, but I wish you to consider whether it be not a little *too strong.* Will it not be the means of embroiling you with the other [Dartmouth] Trustees; for it will be known whence the article came. Dr. [Gardiner] S[pring][2] deserves all you say & more too. The question is, how to do him *justice,* without getting into any *inconvenience.* How wd. it do, for some one to publish a short article, lamenting the occurrence, & desiring to know, whether the Trustees did appoint a man, without having any reason to suppose he would accept— & then to publish your piece by way of answer. Any thing will be published that you wish. Give it one more consideration, & let me know next mail.

I have been thinking a good deal abt. President. I shall write you by Wm. Haddock[3] first of next week. My present opinion rather favors the appointment of CHS B HADDOCK.

We are glad you are better. We were much alarmed by William's acct.— D Webster

ALS. NhD.

1. Not found.

2. The Reverend Gardiner Spring of New York City, who was offered the presidency of Dartmouth in 1821 but unexpectedly declined the post.

3. William Haddock (1769–1828) moved to Salisbury from Haverhill, Massachusetts, prior to 1794, where he had been a tanner, currier, and shoemaker. He married DW's sister Abigail and accumulated a small fortune which he later lost through poor investments. Charles Brickett Haddock was his son.

TO EZEKIEL WEBSTER

Boston, October 4, 1821.

Dear Ezekiel,

I like your project of a course of proceeding for the trustees very much. I have no doubt something like that would be very judicious. I think it of great importance that you should come down here before you go to Hanover, if you can possibly. Judge [Joseph] Story and Mr. [Jeremiah] Mason will probably both be here on the 15th, and they both feel a strong wish that the Board should take a right course. If you can possibly come, I hope you will, in the stage-coach on Saturday, the 13th. I have no doubt, by putting all our heads together, we can do something. I would go up and see you if it were not almost impossible, and if it were not much more advantageous that you should be here, where you can confer with many others. Please let me hear, by the earliest mail, whether you can probably come. Yours affectionately, D. Webster.

Text from PC, 1: 316–317. Original not found.

FROM JOSEPH HOPKINSON

Philad: Octob. 14. 1821

My dear Sir

The urgent solicitations of my friends,[1] aided by some other circumstances, have put me down once more in my office in Philadelphia. While I have felt much repugnance to this return to the vexations and fatigues of my profession I am reconciled to the sacrifice by the belief that I owe it to the claims of my friends and the wishes and interests of my family. It is, however, still my intention to retain my country establishment, from which I have removed no furniture; nor will Mrs H. and my family come to the city until some time in December, after her pigs are killed—

her hams cured, and our crops deposited in the barn. We shall still be famous farmers; and boast of our wheat, corn and potatoes as much as ever. You will find me No. 196 Chestnut Street, near 8: Street.

What are you going to do respecting the Spanish claims? I have heard you have made an arrangement with some of the Boston claimants, who have made it worth your attention. If this is the case and you expect to attend the sittings of the Commissioners regularly, I may be able to add something to your business there; which tho' not of itself a sufficient inducement to go, will do well enough as an additional service to a better employment. I have altogether declined it, partly on account of my establishment here; and partly (inter nos) because I perceived in our Claimants a disposition to economize in their allowance of compensation, produced by the *low offers* from men of the South. Walter Jones & Geo Hays are candidates. I do not know the terms of the latter but Jones seems to be willing to take any thing, provided he can get $1000 in hand. I have understood in a way to be relied on that there is a strong disposition in the Commissioners to exclude from the benefit of the Treaty those cases in which the capture was made by french cruisers, the prizes taken into Spanish ports, *but the condemnation in a french port.* Such a decision would cut out a great portion of our claims; and doubtless will seriously affect yours. I am informed an argument will be heard on the point; and if your Clients are deeply interested in it, you should take care to be heard on it.

Let me hear from you I pray you.

Truly & affectionately Your friend & hu[mble] s[ervant]

Jos. Hopkinson

ALS. MHi.

1. See Nathaniel Chapman, *et al.*, to Joseph Hopkinson, October 17, 1820, which is published in part in Burton Alva Konkle, *Joseph Hopkinson, 1770–1842* (Philadelphia, 1931), pp. 231–232. At the zenith of his career Hopkinson had been forced, because of ill health, to reduce his professional activities. Beginning in 1819 he spent much of his time in semi-retirement at his Bordentown, New Jersey, farm.

TO JOSEPH HOPKINSON

Boston Oct. 28. '21

My dear friend

I am truly glad to learn that you have fixed your winter head-quarters in Philadelphia. Since I began to study the law, or to know any thing of its Professors, I have always connected you & the good City of Philadelphia together in my thoughts. I think you should continue united. In the forum of that City you won your laurels, & why should you not there wear them?

The more leisure you find to be spent in Bordentown the better; but still I think it altogether fit & proper that Philadelphia should be regarded by you, as Carthage was by Juno. *Hic illius arma—hic currus fuit.*

It is my expectation to be at Washington the first day of the Session of the Commissioners. I have a good many claims, in number, & not inconsiderable in amount. It is my present purpose to make a business of it, & I shall probably attend the whole sittings of the Board. I shall be glad to do any thing, for any friends of yours, which they may wish. I suppose you will not immerse yourself so much in engagements in the Courts at home as not to attend the Sup. Court at Washington.

We are a good deal disappointed in not having seen you this summer. Mrs W. begins to complain a little, as she thinks she had some right to expect Mrs H. & E. to honor our region with a visit. However, that which is only delayed, is not denied, & our hopes at present repose upon next year.

I beg you to accept Mrs W.'s regards, & to remember us both affectionately to your household. Very truly Yrs   D. Webster

ALS. PHi.

TO EZEKIEL WEBSTER

Boston Sunday Eve' [Oct 1821]

Dear E.

Judge [Joseph] Story has written a letter to Judge [Elijah] Paine.[1] I enclose it by this mail, to the care of Mr [Mills] Olcott. Mr [Jeremiah] Mason has not been here, but is expected on Tuesday. I had a good deal of conversation with him, in the summer, on the subject of the College, & I have no doubt he agrees with the rest of us who think the safe way is to proceed very *slowly*, in relation to the next appointment.[2] My own opinion is most decidedly in favor of postponing any choice till next Spring. I will thank [you] to mention that such is my opinion to Mr. [Charles] Marsh, & Mr. [Seth] Payson.[3] We can lose no great advantage by delay, & a better choice can in all probability be made. I assure you it is the universal sense of all the friends of the College here whom I have spoken with, & I have spoken with many, that the prudent course is to put off the appointment.

I shall be particularly anxious to know the result of your meeting. Affectionately Yrs   Danl. Webster

ALS. NhD. Published in *PC*, 1: 317–318.

1. Paine (1757–1842; Harvard 1781), a trustee of Dartmouth College from Vermont. Letter not found.

2. See DW to Ezekiel Webster, October 4, 1821, above.

3. Both trustees of Dartmouth College.

FROM RICHARD STOCKTON

Princeton 5th. Novr. 1821

My dear Sir,

I was much obliged & relieved by your kind communication respecting *the young Eugen[i]e.*[1] The report here was that she was acquitted, and we had no explanation giving the true state of the affair. You have made the most of the case, and if you can maintain the great point you have taken, you will have done more for the cause of humanity than all the Societies in the U S: put together. If the Flags of nations who have prohibited the Trade shall yet cover it so as that it cant be questioned by an other, for our selves we had better keep our Cruisers at home. It is perfectly known at what rate Americans can be turned into Frenchmen or Spaniards in the West-Indies. I am well informed that a French and Spanish Merchant are now going thro' the U S making proposals to our wealthy merchants to embark their Capital in that trafic. They made their appearance lately at the Coffee house in Phi[ladelphi]a—had a skeme prepared shewing the safety of the project, and that the profits would be immense. They had come on from Baltimore, and the understanding was that they had been very successful. I hope that you will be able to get Robert [Field Stockton][2] out of this scrape, at least without costs and damages—and I trust that he will have too much wit to run any more such risques. He ought to know that as long as the General Govt. is under absolute Southern influence there can be no bona fide wish to put an end to the Slave trade—and consequently that an officer would have no great chance of indemnification in case of damages being awarded against him. I shall rejoice to hear that you maintain the great point even in the Circuit Court. I should think its fate at Washington would be doubtful, especially if it be true as Judge [Joseph] Story in one of the papers is made to say that the Court is called on to Establish a new principle of public Law.

I hope that you will try to stay a day or two with us on your way to W[ashington], I am at last in my new house as I may call it—it will want a little *warming* about the last of January. Mrs. S: has returned safe & sound from N[ew] B[edford] and is highly gratified by her visit. Julia & William are only with us. Miss Annie remains to enjoy *the gaiety* of New Bedford. We all beg to be remembered to [Mrs.] W— and I in particular to my friend Daniel who I hope [torn] has not forgotten the yankee songs I taught him when here.

I am dear Sir very affectionately & truly yours   Rd Stockton

ALS. NhHi.

1. Communication not found.
2. Richard Stockton's son and cap-tain of the frigate which captured the *Jeune Eugénie*, believed to be involved in the slave trade.

TO JOSEPH HOPKINSON

Boston Nov. 24. 1821

My dear Sir

I have recd. yours of the 20th,[1] & am sensible that I owe to *your* kindness the circumstance of being asked for Professional assistance by the Ins: Co: of N. America. I shall be very happy to be employed for them. It is my present purpose and expectation to be in Philadelphia by the first of January. It is possible however that I may not be able to be there till four or five days later. Many of the Memorials of cases in which I am engaged, were presented at the last meeting. In these many supplemental statements have become necessary, & arguments also are required—all to be filed *before* the day of the next meeting. All this I shall of course see performed, & if I should be detained at home a few days too long, I shall seasonably forward them by another hand, & soon follow them. The thing which may *possibly* detain me here a few days longer than I wish, is a family matter that may turn out not to have been luckily timed. In the cases in which your Office is concerned, I suppose no memorials have as yet been filed. In these, therefore, nothing need be done *before* the meeting, except merely to file the memorials, which could be done by the Agent, if I should chance to be a day too late. I trust however I shall be in season, but will give you due notice, so that I may not be expected, if there should remain any doubt of my being in Philadelphia by the 1. or 2. of Jany.

We are all well, & all send love to you, & all that dwell under your roof. Mo. truly Yrs   D. Webster

ALS. PHi.   1. Letter not found.

FROM JOHN ADAMS

Montezillo December 23d. 1821

Dear Sir

I thank you for your Discourse delivered at Plymouth on the termination of the second Century of the landing of our forefathers. Unable to read it, from defect of sight, it was last night read to me, by our friend [William Smith] Shaw. The fullest justice that I could do it, would be to transcribe it at full length. It is the effort of a great mind, richly stored with every species of information. If there be an American who can read it without tears, I am not that American. It enters more perfectly into the genuine spirit of New England, than any production I ever read. The observations on the Greeks, and Romans, on Colonization in general, on the West India Islands, on the past, present, and future, in America, and on the Slave trade, are sagacious, profound, and affecting, in a high degree. Mr [Edmund] Burke is no longer entitled to the praise ["]The most consummate Orator of modern times."

What can I say of what regards myself. To my humble name; "exegisti monumentum aere", marmore et auro, "perennius." This Oration will be read five hundred years hence with as much rapture, as it was heard; it ought to be read at the end of every Century, and indeed at the end of every year, for ever and ever.

I am Sir with the profoundest Esteem your obliged friend And very humble Servant   John Adams

LS. NhHi. Published in *PC*, 1: 318.

TO JOHN BROOKS

Boston Decr. 25. 1821

Sir

I hope you will allow me to say a word on the subject of the appointment of a Judge of the Municipal Court; altho' I do not feel myself authorised often to express any opinion in regard to the official duties of High Magistrates, & appointments to be made by them.

I learn that Mr. [Peter Oxenbridge] Thacher is a candidate for the office, & without any disparagement to the claims of others, I would wish to express an earnest opinion in his favor. Mr. Thacher has heretofore been officially connected with that court, & is well acquainted with its duties; he has been constantly pursuing his Profession, & is fresh in the knowledge of it; a circumstance in my opinion essential to the qualifications of a Judge in a Court of Law at the present time. Mr Thacher's general character is well known, & I think, as far as my knowledge extends, his appointment would be most satisfactory to those whose duties would lead them to transact business in the Court.[1]

I have an acquaintance with Mr Thacher much longer than I have lived in the Commonwealth; I have a high regard for him, & a full conviction that he would fill the situation in the best manner.

I am, Sir, with very true respect, Your Obt. Servt.   D. Webster

ALS. MWelC. Brooks was governor of Massachusetts (1816–1823).

1. Thacher was appointed to the post on May 14, 1823.

FROM JAMES KENT

Albany December 29. 1821

My Dear Sir

Be pleased to accept of my Thanks for the pleasure of the receipt & Perusal of your *Plymouth discourse* which came by yesterday's mail. The

Reflections, the Sentiments, the morals, the Patriotism, the Eloquence, the Imagination of this admirable Production are exactly what I anticipated, elevated, just & true. I think it is also embellished by a Style distinguished for Purity, Taste & Simplicity. Excuse me for this once & I will not trespass in this manner again. I am proud to be able to trace my own Lineage back to the Pilgrims of N. E., & prouder still that I have been thought deserving of the Esteem & Friendship of some of the brightest of their descendants.

Permit Mrs. K. & me to unite in presenting our best respects & the Compliments of the Season to Mrs. W., & be assured of the constant Esteem & Regard of your Friend & most obnt Svt   James Kent

Copy. DLC. Published in *PC*, 1: 319.

TO [JOSEPH] STORY

Philadelphia, January 3, 1821
[1822].

My Dear Sir,

I am not content to wait till I get to Washington, without giving you some account of myself and my travels. I left Boston in the mail stage-coach Saturday noon the 29th, with Mr. [Cyrus] Perkins, T[heophilus] Parsons, and William Gardiner.[1] We kept with the mail to New Haven, where we found ourselves Sunday, 3 o'clock. Here we remained through that day, and finding an accommodation stage-coach going the next day to New York, we took it to ourselves, and reached that city early the evening of the same day. From New York we came hither in a new line of stage-coaches, called the Union line, which we are bound to speak well of. It gave us a whole coach for forty dollars, and allowed us to take our own hours. We left New York at three or four o'clock Tuesday afternoon, lodged at New Brunswick, and arrived here to dine Wednesday, yesterday. Our journey was safe and expeditious. I mention these circumstances for your benefit, knowing that in three weeks you are to be on our track, although I am well aware that Mrs. Story would scold me, if she could scold, for adverting to such a disagreeable topic.

Everybody is in expectation here of receiving your opinion in the case of "The Young Eugenie."[2] It must come out, and that soon. I beg you to tell [Jeremiah] Mason either to publish it at once in a pamphlet, or to let [Nathan] Hale publish it in the paper. I last evening referred some gentlemen to the case of "The Amedie," which they had overlooked. In relation to this case of "The Amedie," I was very negligent, which I confess with shame. I quoted it only from the note in Dodson;[3] whereas the whole case is in Acton,[4] and there is there one pretty strong expression of Sir W.

Grant,[5] not found in the note in Dodson. I mention this lest my unpardonable negligence may have misled you; for not hearing your judgment, I do not know whether you cited the case as from Acton. I think Judge [John] Davis's suggestion, of publishing with the opinion a summary of the English cases, a very good one. Here I find [Joseph] Hopkinson up to his neck in business. He seems to have stepped right off into deep water. He has an interesting charter case, in which he says he made some use of a little bit of an opinion about Dartmouth College.

Adieu, my dear Sir; I shall write you again from Washington, where I hope also to hear from you.

I am, both at home and abroad, yours truly,   D. Webster.

Text from *PC*, 1: 313–314. Original not found.

1. William Howard Gardiner (d. 1822; Harvard 1816), Boston lawyer.

2. The *Jeune Eugénie* case, along with that of the *Amedie* mentioned below and argued in the federal circuit courts, involved the delicate question of maritime search and seizure practices growing out of attempts to suppress the international slave trade.

3. Sir John Dodson, *Reports of cases argued and determined in the High Court of Admiralty, commencing with the judgements of . . . Sir W. Scott, Trinity Term, 1811–[1822]. 2 vols., London, 1815–1828.*

4. Thomas Harmon Acton, *Reports of cases argued and determined before . . . the Lords Commissioners of Appeals in Prize Causes . . . , London, 1811.*

5. Sir William Grant (1752–1832), Master of the Rolls.

FROM ELIZA BUCKMINSTER

Boston Friday 4 Jan. 1822

My dear Sir,

Mrs. Webster desires me to write to you to day, to tell you that she is remarkably well—as well as she can be in your absence, and that the babe grows finely,[1] and seems to be as contented with this world as any one can be who has had as little experience of its changes. Mrs. W. sits up half an hour in the day and has seen nearly all the friends who have called. The children are all well. Hannah keeps them close to herself. I have scarcely had a glymps of them since *I* have been here. Whenever I go into the nursery—Edward cries out *"papa gone"* and wants to come down stairs to find you. Julia is going to pass the day with Mrs. [George] Blake. Daniel has had several New years presents—and I have had a present from Mrs. [Cyrus] Perkins of "Taylors *Holy Living*". Mrs. W. has just received your second letter from New York. She thanks you for writing so often, and hopes soon to hear of your having crossed the Susquehannah in safety. To day, the Misses Inches begin their journey. I hope you will remember your promise to me, to distinguish them a little sometimes. Mrs. [Joseph George] Holman gave a concert last night[2] and sang some of her sweetest songs. I am sure I shall never hear any so sweet, till I hear the angels. I could not find either knife or quill, notwithstanding the abundance you usually have & as I am not very bright this morning I will say adieu.   E.B.

ALS. NhHi.
    1. Grace Webster gave birth to her fifth child, Charles, December 31,

1821.
    2. At Boylston Hall.

TO JEREMIAH MASON

Washington Jan. 10. 1822.

My dear Sir

I arrived here this afternoon, & altho. I have nothing to say about Washington yet, having found yours of the 3rd here,[1] I answer it, respecting the Volant. Mr [Nathan] Appleton will be satisfied, of course, with what you have done. I made an agreement with Mr. A. on this subject, & I think there was a minute made of it, which I have not here—as I recollect, we then expected to recover 2700 Dlls; & you & I were to retain 500; —as the sum recovered is less, perhaps we ought now to retain less—I think you may as well retain *money*, as the note. Mr A. will be satisfied with either. As to the precise amt, leave that till I see him. If you write him, saying that you have adjusted the concern, agreeably to his note to me, & remit him, either the whole money recd, or, say 1200, leaving 478 in your hands, I presume it will be very satisfactory. I have no choice about it, myself, provided you think the 500 Dll. note of Mr. [William] S[ullivan?] will be paid. It is not well for us to run any risks.

I am glad if you think my [Plymouth] discourse leaves me as well as I was before. I have yet seen nobody & nothing here. I saw, while on the road, that Presidential Candidates were springing up in all quarters. As soon as I learn any thing I will write you. Yrs   D. Webster

ALS. MHi.   1. Not found.

TO EZEKIEL WEBSTER

Washington Jan. 13. 1822.

My dear Brother

I have arrived here, safe and sound. While on the way, I caused a suggestion to be made, confidentially, to the Chancellor.[1] He has written me in reply, & I enclose his letter to you.[2] I am sorry he declines. I would not wish you to shew his [lett]er, to any body; nor perhaps say much of the circumstance of any communication being had with him.

I seem to incline to my former opinion; [viz], to appoint some *young* man, already connected with the College.[3] There is much talk here abt.

President. Mr [John C.] Calhoun is, at this moment, much talked of, as the Anti-radical Candidate? What do you think of it? Yrs   D. Webster

ALS. NhD.

1. James Kent of Albany, who was DW's choice for the presidency of Dartmouth College.

2. Letter not found.

3. Bennett Tyler was selected the new president of Dartmouth College on February 13, 1822.

TO [JOSEPH] STORY

Washington, January 14, 1822.

My dear Sir,

I am much obliged to you for yours of the 8th,[1] which I have just received. I came on very safe and sound, and am lodged comfortably, but not on the Capitol Hill; which, for some reasons, I regret. I learn that somebody has made provision for the court at, or near, the old spot. I will, however, speak to Mr. [Elias Boudinot] Caldwell.[2]

There is much stir and buzz about Presidential candidates here. Mr. [Henry] Clay's friends are certainly numerous; whether it be because his is the most recent nomination, or for what other reason, the fact is he is just now much talked about. I think it will be a busy winter, in talking and electioneering. My own opinion is, but I would not intimate it to others, that Mr. Clay considers himself a candidate, and means to run the race. More hereafter on these subjects.

Mr. [Joseph] Hopkinson desired me to beseech you to give him a day, as you come on. I promised him to write you, and mention his request. He wishes much to see you, and to give some of his friends that pleasure. If, on your arrival, you contrive to send him notice, to No. 196, Chestnut street, he will esteem it a great favor.

I am glad your opinion [in the Jeune Eugénie] is coming out. It is much asked for. Mr. [Richard M.] Johnson of Kentucky, has to-day, I learn, made a long speech in favor of his proposed amendment. He has dealt, they say, pretty freely with the supreme court.[3] Dartmouth College, Sturgis and Crowninshield, *et cetera*, have all been demolished. To-morrow he is to pull to pieces the case of the Kentucky betterment law. Then Governor [James] Barber is to annihilate Cohens *v.* Virginia. So things go; but I see less reality in all this smoke than I thought I should, before I came here.

I hope you will call and see my wife, and my boys, what few there are of them; not forgetting Miss Julia.

Give my love to Mrs. Story, and believe me, most truly Yours

D. Webster

Text from *PC*, 1: 319–320. Original not found.

1. Not found.

2. Caldwell (1776–1823), clerk of

the United States Supreme Court and editor of the *Washington Federalist*.

3. Senator Richard M. Johnson had introduced an amendment to the Constitution on December 12, 1821, pro- viding that in all cases involving questions of constitutional law and state authority "the Senate . . . shall have appellate jurisdiction."

Under the Adams-Onís Treaty of 1819 claims of American citizens against Spain were assumed by the United States to the amount of $5,000,000, and a three-man commission was appointed by the President to determine the validity of the claims. The Commissioners were Hugh Lawson White of Tennessee, Littleton Waller Tazewell of Virginia, and William King of Maine. The Commission first met in June 1821 to establish guidelines for claimants, but did not begin to hold hearings until September. By that time Webster already had a considerable backlog of cases, but he waited several months longer before presenting them to see how the guidelines worked in practice and what kind of evidence the Commission would accept. Between the early months of 1822 and the final adjournment of the Spanish Claims Commission he represented claims totaling upward of a million dollars. His commission was generally 5 percent of the award, but in some cases ran as high as 10 percent. A detailed treatment of Webster's work before the Spanish Claims Commission will be found in the legal volumes of this series.

TO ALEXANDER BLISS

Washington Jan. 16. 1822.

Dear Bliss

I am obliged to you for yours, recd yesterday.[1] I think you estimated my services, in Mr [Henry] Cabots case, somewhat too high. Mr [William] Prescot is also to be paid, in the cause. You may send Mr. Cabot a receipt for 150 Dlls, in full for fees in that cause, & pass the money, unless needed for other services, to my credit in the Bank—please ask W. & S.[2] to put the enclosed draft in a way of collection, & hold the money, when recd. to my credit.

The Comm[issione]rs have today stated a pretty strong opinion against the *Contract* cases;[3]—also agt cases, in which, the capture being by Spaniards, and the trial by a Spanish Tribunal, the claimants *compromised*, before final judgment, & claim now for sums thus paid in compromise. Of course this does not touch the case of compromise after judgment by a *French* Court, in Spanish Territory. Such cases will be recd.

I wrote you ab[ou]t *copies*, & need them much. Is there no copy of Mr Cabots Cases, & Mr. [Nathaniel G.?] Snellings?[4]

I find I have one protest, at St. Domingo—viz.—in the Snow Hope.[5] Since I wrote you last it has become less necessary to investigate the history of St. Domingo immediately, since the Comm[issione]rs incline to receive cases, in which it is stated that St. Domingo was Spanish, & leave it to be made out on the proof. Yrs   D.W.

ALS. DLC.

1. Not found.
2. Not identified.
3. These cases before the Spanish claims Commission involved breached contracts between American nationals and the Spanish government.

4. Probably Nathaniel G. Snellings, a Boston businessman who served as a director of the Massachusetts Fire and Marine Insurance Company.
5. Total damages amounting to $31,581.28 were eventually awarded to the snow *Hope* by the Commission.

FROM EZEKIEL WEBSTER

Jany 28. 1822

Dear Daniel,

I never did like John Q Adams. He must have a very objectionable rival whose election I should not prefer. I think it would be difficult for any candidate to divide the votes in New England with him. Although he may not be very popular, yet it seems to be in some degree a matter of necessity to support him—if any man is to be taken from the land of the *Pilgrims*. I should really prefer [John C.] Calhoun, [William] Lowndes—[William H.] Crawford—[DeWitt] Clinton & fifty others that I could mention—but this is high matter & it is very uncertain what political feeling may prevail three years hence.

I am sorry that there was not a better account from Albany. The course you mention is the only one that our condition leaves us— & *that will not be taken.* At least I fear it.[1]

I wrote you in regard to John Flanders' application for a pension— & stated the objection.[2] It seems to be that those troops were on the *Continental* establishment as much as any during the war. In April '75 he enlisted & went to Winter hill—was in Bunker hill battle—went up Kennebec river to Montreal — & helped storm the town. Gen [George] Washington was commissioned June 17. 1775. & probably took the actual command of the forces in July. He was directed to take command of all troops then raised by any of the States & this expedition was under the direction of Congress. I am sorry to trouble you with this & it is the last to which I shall ask your attention. The old man is needy & in my opinion deserving.[3] Affectionately yours as ever   E Webster

ALS. NhD. Extract published in Van Tyne, pp. 89–90.

1. See DW to Ezekiel Webster, January 13, 1822, above.

2. John Flanders (1752–1827), a resident of Boscawen, longtime acquaintance of the Webster family, and a veteran of the American Revo-

lution. See Ezekiel Webster to DW,
January 18, 1822, mDW 3166.
    3. Having consulted with Secretary
of War John C. Calhoun about the
matter, DW wrote to Ezekiel on March

23: "am sorry to say I could do nothing for him. The rule which shuts him
out is imperative; and admits of no
exception" (mDW 3254).

TO JOSEPH HOPKINSON

Washington Feb. 1. 1822

My dear Sir

If, after Church, on the day you receive this, you should call in at Mr.
[John] Inskeeps, you will see, by a letter I have written him,[1] what progress the *claims* of your Office are making. *Thirty six* cases have been
acted on, & only three *rejected;* & one of those *three,* I think, will be restored. Three or four are suspended, but will, most of them, be probably
finally received. Indeed I think we go on *charmingly.* The claims of this
Office have been *exceedingly well prepared,* & in general are good & well
founded claims. The Comm[issione]rs begin to see, I think, now, the *real
commercial* losses, which occasioned the Treaty.

I have not found leisure to write you before, from the pressure of these
concerns. I have been occupied very much, with preparing arguments on
several questions deeply affecting the interest of underwriters. I am not
yet thro', & fear I shall be obliged to keep out of *Court* for the first part of
the session. Affairs are now in their *crisis,* with these claims, & I must
stick to them.

Take your own time to come down for the Vermont cause.[2] You have
stated all the points I can make. The main one is, whether, being a foreign Corporation, holding lands in mortmain, & so not being subject to
any jurisdiction of ours, as to the mode of executing the trust, we must
not consider the case as if the Corporation had been, by the Revolution,
so far as these lands were concerned, *dissolved.*

As to the sum which I let [James Alexander] Hamilton have, if I had
wanted it I had not too much modesty to ask for it. It is quite as safe, at
least, in your pocket as mine; and as I shall probably spend all my money
in Washington, it will be convenient to find in Philadelphia enough to get
home with.

And now, My Dear Sir, what shall I say to your good opinion of my
[Plymouth] Discourse? I will not undertake to tell you—for I could not
tell you—how much I value that good opinion—but I can [say with] truth
that I do not think I wrote a [page of it without] considering *what you
would think of it.* The occasion & the topics were necessarily somewhat
local; but I wished what I said to be so said, as that those not so immediately interested in the occasion might at least not disapprove it. If I

have accomplished that, I am content; but as I know your honesty & sincerity I certainly think much better of my *book* than I ever did before.

I pray you give my love to every dweller under your roof. Yrs ever

D. Webster

ALS. PHi.

1. See DW to John Inskeep, January 30, 1822, mDW 3189.

2. *Society for the Propagation of the*

Gospel in Foreign Parts v. *New Haven*, 8 Wheaton 464. Both Hopkinson and DW acted for the defendants.

TO ALEXANDER BLISS

Washington Feb. 19. 1822

Dear Bliss

Above is a hasty sketch of the decisions in our cases,[1] since I last wrote you. Many are suspended, as *No.* 2, & we expect the general doctrine in that case to be decided tomorrow or next day.[2] I am now much occupied in the Court—having tried three causes in succession.[3] Mr. [William] Pinkney[4] was taken dangerously ill, the day after he finished a *nine hours* speech for your friend Mr Williams. He is better today, but not yet entirely out of danger—cause not yet decided. Bullard & Bell[5] will be continued, I presume, in consequence of his sickness. So will two other causes[6] in which I am concerned, in consequence of the illness of Mr [William] Wirt, who has not been in Court this term. There are two more causes which I must argue, or help to argue—one an important one from Virginia.[7] I hope to bring my concerns in Court to a close about the same time as before the Comm[issione]rs, & to wind up all next week. Let Mrs W. know that I am well at this present writing. Yrs   D.W.

[Webster's Spanish Claims Cases as of February 19, 1822]

968.	Paschal P. Pope & others	
	Ship Topus	Recd. Feb. 14
973	Jos. Coolidge & others	
	Ship Belle Sauvage	Recd. do.
Ship Iris—Brooks & Ward		Recd.
Do	Conway Cl[aiman]t	do.
Brig Nancy—Benj. Smith		do.
Sch. Esther—Israel Thorndike		Rejected as IS
—Alert	Thorndike & Leach	Recd.
Sch. Atlantic Wm. Cottle.		Recd.
S.C.	Josiah Knapp	do.
	Hugh McKullock	Rejected as IS
Ship Galen Caleb Eddy		Recd.

Brig Betsey Abiel Winship	Recd. in part.
W. H. Boardman &c	Recd. as to Fame
	Suspd. as to George
	Rejd. as to Olive
Ship Mercury David Hinkley	Recd.
Ship Galen Jas. Mackay	Do.
Atlantic—Sam. Taylor &c.	Do.
Sch. Sally—Lynde Walter	Rejected as IS.
Louisa Johanna—C. W. Greene	Recd.
Seaflower—Hudson & others	Recd.
Mercury—Dall	Recd.
America—Godfrey & others	Recd.
Endeavour—Woodbury	Do.
S. C. Griffin	Do.
Franklin—Titus Wells &c.	Rejected as IS

Perez Morton—Recd. as to sundries.

P. C. Brooks—Recd.

ALS. DLC.

1. Webster's "sketch" of the Spanish Claims cases appears below.

2. The category of cases subsumed under No. 2 concerned vessels seized by French privateers and brought as prizes to Spanish ports. The *Hawk* was one Webster case in this group, suspended July 7, 1821, but re-examined and disallowed April 9, 1823. Register of the Spanish Claims Commission, Records of the Boundary and Claims Commissions and Arbitrations, DNA, RG 76.

3. *Ricard* v. *Williams*, 7 Wheaton 59; *Brown* v. *Jackson*, 7 Wheaton 218; *the Society for the Propagation of the Gospel in Foreign Parts* v. *New Haven*, 8 Wheaton 464.

4. While arguing the case of *Ricard* v. *Williams*, William Pinkney suffered a heart attack and died on February 25, 1822.

5. See front page of 5 Wheaton.

6. One of which was *Gibbons* v. *Ogden*, 9 Wheaton 1.

7. *Blunt's Lessee* v. *Smith*, 7 Wheaton 248, and *The Santissima Trinidad*, 7 Wheaton 283.

TO ALEXANDER BLISS

Washington Feb 20. 1822.

My dear Sir—

The Commissioners have formally announced their decision, respecting the cases classed as No. 2, *favorable* to those cases. By this decision it is settled, that in cases of American Vessels, captured by French Privateers, carried into Spanish ports, & the property there distributed, *without any condemnation made any where*, the Spanish Govt. is liable; & the Cl[aiman]t has a claim on this fund; at least, if it appear that he has presented his case, previously, to the Govt. so as to bring it within the requisitions in the *fifth* Renunciation;[1] *perhaps*, without this, it might be brought in, under the fourth renunciation.[2]

It will not, however, be enough for claimants to say that they do not know whether there was, or was not, a Condemnation. They must furnish such ground to convince the Commrs that there *was not*, as may be expected in regard to such a negative proposition.

Please communicate this to Mr [Peter Chardon] Brooks, & others concerned. You will see it affects many of my cases. Yrs truly   D. Webster

ALS. DLC.

1. All United States claimants who had sought relief for unlawful seizures which had occurred after the Convention of 1802 and before the treaty of 1819 were covered by this provision of Article Eleven of the treaty.

2. This provision applied to all United States claims arising out of unlawful Spanish seizures.

TO ALEXANDER BLISS

Washington March 2. 1822

Dear Bliss

Mr [William] Pinkney's death [on February 25] having interrupted the Court for Two days, I am so much detained. I shall depart on the 5th inst, & make the best of my way. Pray keep things in Court as quiet as possible. If any thing must be argued, let the other side argue, and reserve for me a right to file a written argument.

Business with the Com[missione]rs goes on well. I have written Mr [Peter Chardon] Brooks a letter today,[1] giving a good account of his concerns—almost all his cases have been *examined* & recd—I think only 5 or 6 exceptions.

I have argued my last cause, & am now preparing to pack up.

The Court has blown your friend Mr Williams' cause[2] into so many atoms, I do [not] think he can ever collect enough of them to fill a nut shell. The cause is decided on grounds that will probably put an end to all controversy about the Dudley Title.

The lawyer at Wilmington, best for you to write to, is—I have forgot who—but will ask again. Yrs   D. Webster

ALS. DLC.

1. Letter not found.

2. *Ricard* v. *Williams*, 7 Wheaton 59.

TO THOMAS GIBBONS

Washington March 2. 1822—

Sir

I have called on Mr [Cadwallader C.] Colden, with a view to ascertain whether it were possible to bring the Steam Boat cause to argument at this Term. He says it is quite impossible; that the Party is now wholly without counsel, owing to the absence of Mr [Thomas Addis] Emmet, & the death of Mr [William] Pinkney; and not being, by the Rule of the Court, *obliged* to enter his appearance at this Term, he cannot consent so to do, under these circumstances.

He assures me, however, that he has no wish whatever to put off the argument, nor to avoid a decision, when it can with propriety be made.

I have examined the Record, & it seems to be right. I shall take home a copy with me. I do not know how to express my regret that we cannot bring this most important cause to a hearing this Term, but it is beyond human effort. The difficulty is, they are not obliged to make any motion, or enter any appearance. All that can be done is to apply to Mr Colden. We have done that, without effect, & can do no more. I do not believe myself, however, that it is possible to dissolve the injunction; nor do I think the Gentlemen concerned will take any course to prevent a decision at the next term.

That we may all live till that time, is the hope of Your Obedient Servt.

Danl Webster

ALS. NhD. Gibbons (1756–1839), was a Revolutionary veteran, lawyer, and politician. His operation of an independent steamboat line from Elizabethtown Point, N.J., to New York City brought on the clash with Ogden, who held a franchise from the Fulton-Livingston monopoly granted by the state of New York.

FROM RUFUS KING

Georgetown Mar 4. 1822

Dr. Sir

As I came from the Senate this morning I stopped at the court Room in hopes that I might find you still there; Having heard that you will leave town tomorrow, I was desirous to say Farewell to you before you leave us —but I had another and more important object: by the mail of this morning I received a letter from my son Mr. Charles King, requesting me to converse with you and to ask your professional assistance in the cause between Judge [William W.] Van Ness[1] of New York, and Messieurs [James Alexander] Hamilton, [Gulian Crommelin] Verplanck and [Charles] King the former Editors of the [New York] American.[2] It was my wish that this application should have been made when the suit was commenced—it was however omitted—and from motives of Regard for the Gentlemen who are the Defendants in the suit, I am still desirous that you should, and shall regard it as an act of Friendship that you would, accept a Retainer in their behalf. I can only add assurances of the Regard & Respect of Dr. Sir your mo. ob. serv. Rufus King

PS Mr. Hamilton to whom I confide this note will as he assures me make you acquainted with the actual state of the Cause.[3]

ALS. NhHi.

1. Van Ness (1776–1823), justice of the New York State Supreme Court.

2. The three defendants were founders of the Democratic weekly *New York American*. On January 26, 1820, an editorial was published in the *American* charging that Judge Van Ness had in 1812 improperly used his office to lobby in the state legislature for chartering the Bank of America. The bank was chartered that year with a capital of some six million dollars, with a bonus of six hundred thousand going to the state. Subsequently a committee was appointed by the Assembly to investigate Van Ness's official conduct in the matter. In the course of the investigation it was alleged that Van Ness had personally received twenty thousand dollars of the state bonus. On April 5, 1820, however, the Judge was officially exonerated from any wrong doing by the committee, and he promptly filed a libel suit against the *American* for recovery of damages. It does not appear that Webster did in fact take any part in the case, which was discontinued by the plaintiff without coming to trial. See James A. Hamilton, *Reminiscences of James A. Hamilton* . . . (New York, 1869), pp. 48–53.

3. King enclosed a note from Hamilton to Webster in which the former requested to confer with Webster on the matter (mDW 3235). For Webster's response to King, see mDW 5794.

FROM THOMAS GIBBONS

E[lizabeth] T[own]
12 March [1822]

Sir,

Your letter of the 2d. Int. is receiv'd. You are pleased to inform me "that you had examined the record and it seems to be right, I shall take home a copy with me." A thorough examination of the record, I would recommend to be done before the present Court adjourns as it is difficult to amend the proceedings, at the 2d. term and if done it generally entitles the adverse party to another term.

You write me that Mr. Colden "assures you, however, that he has no wish what ever to put off the argument nor to avoid a decision when it can with propriety be made." I will here express my opinion of Mr C, and I say in sincerity, that if Mr C, stood alone, if he was the only party in interest, if he had the whole controul of the case on that side, I would take his word as far as he would go—but as he is only an assignee, as he is only a branch of the Bohon Upas[1]—as he is but one member of a large association, a confederate with men who set out upon the plan of enriching themselves, by invading the rights of their own fellow citizens, & the citizens of the adjacents & sister States—acting under laws of a Legislature who profess to reward their meritorious citizens ([as] they call them) with the property of their neighbours—men who combine with them, I cannot but distrust them altho an individual may be found among them of integrity. Yet by their rules a majority must govern, and as a body, I adjudge them an iniquitous confederacy—if a proper agreement could be entered into with Mr C, in writing, I would feel perfectly safe, and would be pleased with such a course, if it can be obtained. Yrs.

AL draft. NhD.

1. A poisonous tree found on the island of Java, the Bohon Upas was celebrated in Erasmus Darwin's poem *The Botanic Garden* (Dublin, 1790, 1793).

TO JEREMIAH MASON

Boston March 23. 1822

My Dear Sir

I came home this day week, after a longer absence than usual, & having had a severe cold on the way, which detained me two or three days at N York. My observation at Washington has not enabled me to say any thing new to you, as Mr. [Rufus] King has probably often written you, & his guesses are worth a great deal more than mine. I have formed, however, one or two opinions which I shall state, without at present giving reasons for them, as to the future events. In the first place, I think it clear there is to be a *warm* contest for the Presidency; & my expectation is, that after sifting out sundry candidates, having less support, the final struggle will be between [William H.] Crawford & [John C.] Calhoun. It would certainly come to this, if the present Congress were to decide the matter, & were now to take sides. Whether the *People* may not interfere, before the time comes, & make a President of somebody else, I know not. The New York dominant party talk mysteriously, & hint that they may bring up Mr. [Rufus] King. Of all this I do not believe one word, I think they are aiming not to serve Mr. King, but to serve themselves *by him;* & I fear he is not quite so fully impressed with this truth as he ought to be. I take the N. York votes to be yet disposed of according to circumstances. Pennsylvania, it is thought, will be unanimous for Mr. Calhoun, & I suppose is the basis of his expected support. I have heard opinions expressed respecting other states, & parts of states, about which speculations have been formed. Maine is expected to go for Mr. *Crawford.* Your Mr. [Isaac] *Hill* is gone to Washington, & in all probability he will pledge N. Hamp. to the same interest. I think the *Intelligencer* lately favours the same interest. The President, as far as he ventures to have any opinion, is I imagine agt. that interest.

We had rather an interesting Court. There were some causes of consequence. Your friend [Littleton Waller] Tazewell (who quotes you on all occasions) made a good speech, in one of those Baltimore Privateering causes.[1] He is a correct, fluent, easy & handsome *speaker*, and a learned, *ingenious & subtile* Lawyer. Our friend Judge [Joseph] Story seems to have drawn up more than his share of Opinions, & I think in general they were very able.

In the Spanish [Claims] Comm[ission], affairs go tolerably well. The general course is favorable to the North, & the real mercantile losses; except only as far as related to the contract cases; which are likely to be forced in against the opinion of the Commrs.

I have a particular reason for wishing to see you between this time & the early part of May; shall you probably be this way? I am, Dr. Sir, yrs as always   D Webster

Did you finally settle the Volant case? Mr. [Harrison Gray] *Otis* will be *Mayor* of the City.[2]

Copy. NhHi. Published in W & S, 16: 67–68.

1. *The Santissima Trinidad*, 7 Wheaton, 283.

2. Otis withdrew from the Boston mayoral race in April, after his candidacy provoked a sizable faction of Federalists, the "Middling Interests" led by Josiah Quincy, to bolt the party.

TO JOSEPH STORY

Boston Saturday noon
[April 6, 1822]

My Dear Sir

Judge [John] Davis has signed or assented to the order, & it is handed to the Clerk. I did not expect or wish it to be exclusive of any other appointment; & if any other appointment should be made, have no objection to give to any other person thus appointed a portion of the business, in which I am concerned.

Mr [William] Prescott is engaged with the College on *Tuesday*. He has promised to dine with me on *Wednesday;*— & I hope you will find *that* day agreeable to you. Pray *come up* on Wednesday;—because I want more of you than I shall get, if you dine with me the day you go home. Mrs S. & Mrs W. will not have half time enough to talk!

We are in a deplorable state here. Nothing seems practicable, but to go forward, & support Mr. [Harrison Gray] O[tis]— & probably be *beaten*. Mr. [Josiah] Q[uincy] has opposed the City from the beginning! He now wraps himself up in mystery, & importance—none of his old friends can get *audience* with him;—tho' I have no doubt a very active communication exists between him, & a certain other quarter.

There will be a *vigorous* effort made for Mr. O.—let the event be what it will. Yrs   DW

ALS. MHi. Published in W & S, 16: 68–69.

TO [JOSEPH STORY]

[Boston] August 6. 1822

My Dear Sir

This gentleman, the Revd Mr [Ralph Randolph] Gurley,[1] comes recommended by our friends at the South, on the subject of the Colonization Society. He has with him some very interesting publications of the African Institution in London as well as the Reports of the society here; & appears to be a very agreeable & intelligent man. I feel inclined to do whatever duty requires, on this subject; You know that my opinion has not been the most favourable; & yet I would wish to pay proper deference to such excellent men as Judge [Bushrod] Washington & Mr [Francis Scott] Key.

Mr. Gurley will probably be in this neighbourhood till commencement; & if you think it proper that some bread should be cast on the waters, in this case, I am willing to follow the example. While I cannot, conscientiously very confidently recommend the cause of this Society as being a great attainable good, I am still willing to confide in those good men who have more confidence, so far as to contribute my own little mite to the object in view. At any rate, my Dear Sir, you have discharged your duty before God & man on the subject of African slavery & you must not be surprised if more should be expected from him who has done so much, so admirably. Yours with perpetual regard yours,   D Webster

Copy. NHi. Published in *PC*, 1: 320–321, where the place of origin is incorrectly given as Washington.

1. Gurley was an agent for the American Colonization Society, founded January 1, 1817, to transport manumitted slaves to Africa. Judge Bushrod Washington was the first President of the Society; William H. Crawford, Henry Clay, and Andrew Jackson were among the vice presidents; and Webster was on the list of initial contributors. Liberia had been established on the West Coast of Africa as an American colony to receive the freedmen only a few months before Gurley's visit.

FROM JOSEPH STORY

Salem, August 6th, 1822.

Dear Sir:

I have had the pleasure of conversing with Mr. [Ralph Randolph] Gurley upon the interesting subject of the African Colonization. My own faith of the practicability of the scheme has never been strong, and I have never affected to disguise it. Still, however, I am ready to accede to any plan to give it a fair chance of success. For, I agree with you in thinking that we ought not to despair, when such men as Judge [Bushrod] Washington and Mr. [Francis Scott] Key are so deeply and earnestly in the belief of its success.

I am ready to subscribe as a donor to the extent of what I think my reasonable share. It has occurred to me, however, that we might do more by a general meeting of friends in Boston to consult on the subject. If it should be thought best to organize an auxiliary society, that may be done with advantage, and will probably secure permanent contributions. If it is thought not best to attempt such an organization, still we could recommend the institution to patronage, and thus, from immediate donations, aid its plan. If neither the one nor the other scheme should be approved, I am still, as one, ready to contribute my mite, and leave the event to Providence. I believe the Colonization Society has now one good effect, and that is to nourish a strong distaste for slavery among the most kind and benevolent of the Southern States; and it gives countenance to them in cherishing a public enthusiasm in favor of the ultimate emancipation of slaves. I think I have perceived a growing feeling of the injustice of slavery among all those who have been ardently attached to its objects. This is no inconsiderable gain.

If in Boston you should think a meeting useful, I incline to think that Mr. [Benjamin] Pickman, [Jr.], Judge [Samuel] Putnam,[1] Judge [Stephen?] White, Col. Timothy Pickering, Mr. [Leverett] Saltonstall, and others might be willing to attend, and aid in the object.

I hope that we may yet live to see the general doctrine, which you have contributed so much to establish, universally admitted, that the slave trade is against the law of nations, as I think it is against the eternal laws of nature.

I am, dear sir, most truly and affectionately, yours,   Joseph Story.

Text from William W. Story (ed.), *Life and Letters of Joseph Story* (Boston: Little & Brown, 1851), 1: 421–422. Original not found.

1. Benjamin Pickman, Jr. (1763–1843; Harvard 1784), Newburyport lawyer, state legislator, and congressman; Samuel Putnam (1768–1853; Harvard 1787), Salem lawyer and Massachusetts legislator.

TO GEORGE BLISS

Boston Septr. 16. 1822

Dr. Sir,

It was well I recd your last letter on Saturday Morning, as I should otherwise have set out *today* for Northampton; your former letter having mentioned the 3rd Tuesday of the Month, as the day of the Court's meeting.[1] Such mistakes are very natural, & not always easily avoided. In this instance, no harm has happened from it.

I have written to N. York, to inquire whether it has yet been decided, *expressly,* in their Court, what shall be considered the legal effect of a creditor's proving his debt, under the Commission. By a letter in answer from Mr. [David B.] Ogden[2] I learn, that the case is not considered as decided, in their Courts, & that one or two suits are now pending, in which the point must arise. Judge [Joseph] Story also informs me that he thinks the same question is before the Court at Washington; a fact of which I was not previously aware. These considerations, perhaps, strengthen the probability, that if we were to argue our cause now, it would not be immediately decided;— & so shew that a written argument is, in all views, likely to be as beneficial to all parties, as an oral argument.[3]

I trust I shall hear, both from you & Mr [Elijah Hunt] Mills, in the course of the week. Yours with regard   Danl. Webster

ALS. NN.
1. Neither letter found.
2. Neither letter found.

3. See *Mason* v. *Haile,* 12 Wheaton 370.

TO JOSEPH STORY

Dorchester, [September 27, 1822]
friday morning

Dear Sir,

I recd your letter, desiring me to be ready to render Professional assistance, if it should be necessary, to Lt. [Horace Cullen?] Story;[1] with which I shall most readily comply. I also wrote a note, expressive of your wish, to Mr. [William] Prescott.[2] For two or three days I have not been much in Town, not having been very well, & being willing to sit down a while, without the sight of a client. I find I am growing rusty, in general knowledge, & unless I can find, or make, some leisure from my office, I shall shortly be neither more nor less than an *attorney.*

I send you two or three English Newspapers, which contain the conversations, in H.C. on the subject of *Piracy.* You will see, among other things, that the Admiralty has gone pretty far, in instructions to search suspicious vessels.

I learn that Spencer Roane is dead. I should not be surprised if P[hilip] P. Barbour should be appointed to the vacant place. I have understood his ultimate object is to be a Judge, & his <peculiar> notions on some leading topics are very likely to recommend him to the Virginia Assembly. In addition to which, it would seem probable that Mr. [Henry] Clay may be a dangerous rival for the chair in the next Congress.[3]

Mr. [Littleton Waller] Tazewell left here on Tuesday. He was very desirous to go to Salem, if time would have allowed, & very much obliged to you for your kindness in inviting him.

Mrs W. desires me to give great love to Mrs Story. She was much disappointed in not seeing her, when your Court sat last. Our hopes now repose on the Oct. Term.

Such a day as we had, at Phillips [Exeter Academy]!⁴ I shall be afraid ever to go again, lest it should be a great falling off.   Yrs truly

D. Webster

ALS. MHi. Published in *W & S*, 16: 70.

1. Probably Joseph's brother, Lt. Horace Cullen Story (1792–1823; Harvard 1811), of the United States Army Corps of Engineers. With Horace's death less than ten months off, DW probably never represented him

in a courtroom. Letter not found.

2. Not found.

3. Henry Clay succeeded Barbour as Speaker of the House in December 1823.

4. Webster was probably referring to commencement exercises held at Phillips Exeter in late August.

FROM STRATFORD CANNING

Exchange Coffee house October 5. 1822.

Dear Sir

Having learnt from the Newspapers that a Society has recently been formed in Boston for the purpose of contributing in various ways to the suppression of the African Slave Trade, I take the opportunity of passing through the City, to send you the inclosed note of fifty dollars, requesting that you will have the goodness to apply it in aid of the funds of that institution, in the success of which, directed as it is to a most humane and useful object, I cannot but take a lively interest.¹

Believe me &c &c &c   Stratford Canning

Copy. Public Record Office, London, F.O./352. Stratford Canning (1786–1880) was British minister to the United States from 1820 to 1824.

1. The Boston *Columbian Centinel,* August 28, 1822, reported that there would be a meeting that evening at the vestry of William Ellery Channing

on Barry Street, "for the purpose of forming a Society auxiliary to the American Colonization Society, or for adopting some other method of affording aid to this institution." It was probably this notice to which Canning referred.

Webster's court and claims commission duties in no way eroded his interest in politics and political questions. He was elected to the Massachusetts House of Representatives (still called the General Court) early in 1822, and attended the first session for a few days in late May and early June, although he participated very little in the general business of the House. He was no doubt an interested observer when Benjamin Gorham, regular Federalist Representative in Congress from Boston, refused to run again. On October 15 the "Middling Interest" Federalists put up Jesse Putnam for Gorham's seat, and three days later the party regulars asked Webster to be their candidate. A Republican caucus endorsed Putnam rather than name a candidate of their own, but the accession of strength was slight. Webster won easily, 2,638 to Putnam's 1,557. Although he would not take his seat in Congress until December 1823, Webster resigned from the Massachusetts House before the second session convened.

FROM THOMAS HANDASYD PERKINS, WILLIAM SULLIVAN,
BENJAMIN RUSSELL, WILLIAM STURGIS, JOHN T. APTHORP

Boston 18 Oct. 1822

Dear Sir

We the undersigned having been chosen (at a meeting of delegates from all the wards, held at Concert Hall, on Thursday Evening last) a Committee to acquaint you that at that meeting you were unanimously selected to be recommended to the support of their fellow citizens, to represent the District of Suffolk in the next Congress of the United States, and having been, by your absence from town, unable to wait upon you personally, have the pleasure to address you, to communicate the above fact; and we beg you to be assured, that in the performance of this duty, we experience a peculiar satisfaction, which will be greatly enhanced by the knowledge of your consent to conform, upon this occasion, to the wishes of your friends, in the number of which we hope to be considered and are with the highest respect and esteem your obedient servants

T H Perkins
Wm. Sullivan.
Benj. Russell.   Committee
Wm Sturgis
Jn. T. Apthorp

LS. NhHi. Published in *PC*, 1: 321, and extracted in Van Tyne, pp. 90–91. Benjamin Russell (1761–1845), Revolutionary veteran, state legislator, and editor of the Boston *Centinel;* William Sturgis (1783–1864), a prominent Boston businessman and banker; and John Trecothic Apthorp (1770–1849), a Boston banker.

TO JOSEPH HOPKINSON

Boston Nov. 13. 1822

Dear Sir,

I enclose a letter for Mr. [John] Innskeep,[1] which I will thank you to read, & send to him. You will see by it that for about three weeks I have been confined to my house by indisposition. I do not think there is any danger of mischief at Washington, especially if we can get a *postponement* of the more interesting questions, which I apprehend will take place. I shall, however, go off immediately as soon as I am well eno[ugh] if it appears at all useful.

I accept with many thanks your congratulation on the election. You judge rightly, that it was a case of *over-persuasion*. In June some of my friends wished me to succeed Mr. [Harrison Gray] Otis, in the Senate, which I had resolution enough to decline. On the late occasion, circum-stances were such that I yielded. My friends thought there was a *claim* in the actual condition of things, & my power of resistance did not hold out. All the good I see from it, is, that perhaps I may help along a law to provide for the payment of our claims, when allowed & settled. I intend to discharge my two-years duty, if I live & enjoy health, punctually & assiduously, & then consider that I have discharged my debts. Yours very truly & sincerely   D. Webster

ALS. PHi.

1. See DW to John Inskeep, November 13, 1822, mDW 3362, dealing with business of the Spanish Claims Commission.

TO JOSEPH STORY

Boston Decr. 18. 1822

Dear Sir,

I meant to have written you earlier, to let you & Mrs. S. know that we got well home, & found all well. What of my dissipation at Salem, & other smaller causes, I have had a return of my cold, but not so as to keep me indoors. Mrs W. thinks she passed a delightful week at Salem, & I do not differ with [her], on that point.

The laughter-moving [Charles] Mathews will no doubt be here this week; & probably the first or the middle of next will be a good time for Mrs S. & yourself to come see him.[1] We shall give you further notice, & hold you to the spirit & letter of the contract; "we four, & no more."

Mr [Lemuel] Shaw having, *at length,* sent you his argument, I suppose you will soon be able to send up an opinion in Barrett v. Goddard.[2] There are reasons, *mihi pertinentes,* which lead me to wish an early judgment in that case. If you will enclose your communication to the Clerk to me, I will present it.

I took the liberty, My Dear Sir, to ask your attention to the concluding part of your opinion in Tappan's case.[3] I think a little more full exposition of the reasons which prevent the application of some of the principles decided to that case, would be useful. The merchants are hard pressed to understand, why there should be so much good law, on one side, & the decision on the other. The opinion has not yet been printed, & altho' it is now better understood, yet when I came home from Salem, I found as great a diversity of opinion as to *which way* the cause was decided, as ever there was about the *place* or *manner* in which Sir Peter Teazle was wounded.[4]

We shall be very glad to hear from you, & to learn that Mrs S. is quite well of her cold.—Yours, most truly,   D. Webster

The good creature, I[saac] P. D[avis] has put a Cask of excellent wine, at 4.25 pr gallon into Mr. [George] Blakes cellar, for J[oseph] S[tory] I P D, G.B., & D.W. in equal quarter parts. He has also, I believe, a couple of dozen [bottles] for you, which is old & excellent.

ALS. MHi. Published in *W & S*, 16: 72.

1. On tour from the Theater Royal in London, Mathews starred in several comedies presented at the Boston Theater in late December and early January. After one of his performances, the *Centinel* of December 28 observed: "Loud and continued peals of laughter followed almost every sentence he uttered."

2. See 2 Federal Cases 911.

3. *Tappan et al.* v. *U.S.*, 23 Federal Cases 690.

4. A character in Richard Sheridan's comedy *School for Scandal*, which played in Boston on September 18, 1822.

TO [SAMUEL JAUDON]

Boston Jan. 1. 1823

My Dear sir,

It is my intention to leave home for Washington this day fortnight. I must stay a few days in N. York, and shall have time to pass as many with you.

I do not see that your friends and mine have, in general, much to complain of, as to the decisions of the Commissioners. In some cases they have disappointed us, it is true, but in those or similar cases they have also disappointed others, who made claims on the fund to a large amount. The general prospect of the S. American cases is not so favorable as it was, even for the best of them. Some of my friends here are affected by this change of appearance, but I suppose Mr [John] Innskeep, Mr. [Daniel] Smith, & Mr [Samuel] Mifflin[1] do not regret it so much.

I am afraid nothing can be done for the New-Jersey.[2] The new ground, assumed by the Commrs, appears formidable. I have considered the other rejected cases, mentioned in your letter,[3] and in one or two of them I think there is ground enough to justify another effort.

I have written to a friend in Providence to obtain the necessary evidence of the citizenship of Capt. Allen, of the Brig Peace, & shall have an answer soon.[4]

Since the latter part of October I have been constantly more or less unwell. At several times I have been confined to my house, for several days together. I hope a journey to the south will do me good, & I intend to set out in such season as to take it leisurely.

Mr [Francis Calley] Gray & Mr [Alexander] Bliss are very well. The latter is hard at work, making up the remainder of our cases. Mr G. is at present occupied in the Legislature, which is now in session.

I beg you to make my regards to our friends. Yrs. very truly

D. Webster

ALS. NHi.

1. Smith was president of the Insurance Company of Pennsylvania. Mifflin was attorney for the Private Underwriters of Philadelphia.

2. DW filed the case of the *New*

Jersey on behalf of the Insurance Company of North America, but the claim was disallowed by the Commission on March 21, 1823.

3. Letter not found.

4. Letters not found.

FROM THOMAS GIBBONS

E[lizabeth] Town N Jersey 14 Jay. 1823

Sir

Your letter of the 2d. of Sepr. last lies before me.[1] I would have acknowledged its receipt before this day, If it had appeared from the state of the business, that it was necessary. I long ago wrote you, that I relied on you as one of my counsel to maintain this case in the Supreme Court,[2] and requested you to hasten this cause; this section of the Union is extremely agitated, from the imposition & exactions of that proud state, New York. In one of my letters written long ago to Mr [William] Wirt, I mentioned to him that he was also to support this cause, and that you would be an adjunct. So much also was written Mr D[avid] B Ogden, and to all of you gentlemen I mentioned that Mr Ogden would be an auxiliary, and I endeavoured to shew how useful I had known, auxiliary or third Counsellors attending at the trial. On the 29th Sepr. last Mr Wirt wrote me, requesting some information on certain points from the Counsel who tried this cause in the Courts of New York[3]—this letter was sent to my son [William Gibbons] then in New York, who made the application, and you have a copy of the answer of Mr Henry (a very able man) to my son inclosed.[4] The original I sent on to Mr Wirt, some time ago, but he has not acknowledged receipt of it. You will please acknowledge receipt of this copy, and at the same time say whether Mr Wirt received that document. I have not had an opportunity of comparing these papers, but I can have no doubt of their being in substance the same. There is something wrong in our Judiciary, that this important tribunal should convene but once in a year. I entreat you to press on the trial, or death will take from me the pleasure of rejoicing with you on the event.

I am very respectfully Your most Ob St.   Th Gibbons

ALS. NjMD.

1. Letter not found.

2. Gibbons is probably referring to his letter of April 2, 1821, above.

3. For the trial record of the case in
New York state, see 4 Johnson Ch.
150 (1819), and 17 Johnson 488

(1820).

4. Not identified; letter not found.

*A crucial question facing politicians in all sections of the Union by 1823
was the presidential succession. The "Era of Good Feelings" was slipping
away fast; a single party, now plagued by factions and interests, filled the
vacuum between the first and second American party systems; and old
political machinery such as the caucus was under general attack. A number of candidates—John Quincy Adams, Henry Clay, John C. Calhoun,
Andrew Jackson, and William H. Crawford—had all entered the field. In
New England, older politicians were in a quandary over whom they should
support: most preferred the selection of a northerner for the office, and
many favored the selection of an old Federalist. The only northern candidate in the race was John Quincy Adams, but his Federalist credentials
were questionable because of his apostasy in 1808. Webster's correspondence in 1823–1824 details the efforts of New Englanders to focus on a
presidential candidate acceptable to them and to the nation. Influencing
their selection were developments in Washington as well as election results in the states. Only reluctantly and late did Webster and his friends
give their support to Adams.*

FROM EZEKIEL WEBSTER

Feby 10. 1823

Dear Daniel,

I want to remind you of Mr [Joseph] Littles application for his pension.[1]
If he should be restored it would be very desirable that it should be done
before the first of March & that he should receive his pay during his suspension. If any more evidence is wanted pray let me know it.

We are likely to have fine sport here till after March Meeting. The
nomination of Judge [Levi] Woodbury[2] puts [Isaac] Hill into hot water.
He has not hesitated in chusing his course— & that is to write against the
Judge. I think you will be very much edified in reading the Patriot. It will
be very refreshing after a severe day's labor. I look on like a spectator at
a bull baiting, pretty indifferent who is the conqueror or the victim. I
have no tears to shed for either. It is for some reasons desirable to have
Woodbury elected. He would not be under the influence of Hill & [Richard
Hazen] Ayer. [Samuel] Dinsmore[3] would be a man of wax merely—Mr
Hill would be the Governor in fact. I am of opinion that the Judge, will
triumph over the General. This is as it should be—the judicial should be
above the military power. Let the event be as it will—we are breaking up
into new parties— & probably with more acrimonious & bitter feelings,
than ever marked the old. I am yours truly   Ezekiel Webster

ALS. NhD. Published with omissions in Van Tyne, p. 91.

1. Little (1761–1843), of Boscawen, New Hampshire, served in the American Revolution and was later pensioned under the Congressional act of April 3, 1818. He was, however, dropped from the rolls on May 1, 1820, and, although DW conferred with Secretary of War John C. Calhoun about the matter, Little's pension was never restored.

2. Levi Woodbury was nominated for governor by the Portsmouth Republicans in January 1823 and subsequently won the election.

3. Ayer (1778–1853) was New Hampshire representative of Dumbarton and Hooksett in the state legislature and a member of the state council for five years; Dinsmoor (1766–1835; Dartmouth 1789) was a Keene lawyer and a former congressman.

TO [JOHN QUINCY ADAMS]

Supreme Court feb. 17. [1823]

Sir

The enclosed is an extract of a letter which I have recd this morning, from Mr. [Isaac] Parker, the Chief Justice of Massachusetts. I know not whether you may deem it to be of any importance, but have thought it might be proper to communicate it.

Yours, with much respect   Danl. Webster

Enclosure

[c. February 13, 1823]

[William H.] Crawfords prospects for the Presidency are certainly on the decline. Mr Adams is gaining fast upon the affections of the people— hardly an opposing Voice in this quarter— & as far as I can learn, there is not an individual in this part of the Country in favor of [Henry] Clay— & in New York the great body of the people are for Mr. Adams. Mathew L. Davis, Wm. P. Van Ness[1]— & the old Burrites are almost the only party who are in favor of Crawford. If the present Legislature were to choose the Electors, Adams would have a unanimous vote. Is not Mr. Clay while he is now at Washington to be pushed, to come out with his threatened exposition of the events at Ghent?[2]

ALS. MHi.

1. Matthew L. Davis (1773–1850) and William P. Van Ness (1778–1826) were early intimates of Aaron Burr. Both had been present at the duel with Hamilton, and Van Ness had been Burr's second. Van Ness was United States Judge for the Southern District of New York from 1812 until his death in 1826. Davis, journalist, politician, and a Grand Sachem of the

Tammany Society, inherited Burr's personal papers, which served as source for his *Memoirs of Aaron Burr*, published in 1836–1837, shortly after Burr's death. Both men were links between the old Burr machine and Van Buren's Albany Regency.

2. Indirectly involved in a feud between his old friend Jonathan Russell and John Quincy Adams over the negotiations leading to the Treaty of

Ghent in 1814, Clay had vowed to "lay before the public a narrative of those transactions as I understood them." He did not make good the promise, probably because he realized in time the political risk involved.

TO EZEKIEL WEBSTER

Washington March 25. 1823

Dear E.

I enclose Mr [Joseph] Little's certificate.[1] You will recollect that he owes me 20 Dolls, borrowed money, which he ought to repay.

I am detained here still, by the affairs of the Commission, & do not expect to leave before 10 or 15 [April]. It is our expectation to go to Dorchester for [the su]mmer, & I intend to move the 2nd day of May. [Soon] after that, I hope you will come down, as I shall want to see you very much on more accounts than one.

You have accomplished a great affair in N. Hamp.[2] I know not whether it is a *triumph,* but it is, at least, a *change,* & for the present it seems for the better. I have seen the returns, & it is clear enough which way the Federal votes went.

As to the great Presidential question, my opinion is, that it was never more uncertain than now, who will succeed. It is time to prepare public opinion, in our quarter, for certain contingencies, which may arise; *Who would N. Hamp. be for, in your opinion, if it were certain that Mr. [John Quincy] Adams could not succeed; or who would she prefer next to him?* I wish you would write me an answer to this question, with or without the reasons, on which your opinion [rests,] so as to reach me here by the 10. or 12 [of April]. This can be done, if you sit right down to it on receipt of this. I would thank you also to express your *own* preference. As [Charles?] Mathews[3] says, "do you catch the idea"? Yours always

D. Webster

You will probably hear from Portsmouth soon, on another subject.

ALS. NhD. Published in *PC,* 1: 322–323.

1. Not found. See letter from Ezekiel Webster, February 10, 1823, above.

2. The election of Levi Woodbury as governor.

3. The actor, mentioned in DW to Joseph Story, December 18, 1822, above.

FROM EZEKIEL WEBSTER

April 3rd 1823

Dear Daniel

I received yours this morning.[1] Of all the Candidates *named* for the Presidency the people of N. Hamp. would undoubtedly prefer Mr Adams. Mr Adams being out of the question—I think Mr [John C.] Calhoun would be their choice. I think [Andrew] Jackson [William H.] Crawford, nor

[Henry] Clay could ever obtain the votes of this state. They would choose to have a northern man for the President, & I think would vote for Mr [DeWitt] Clinton, if there should be any prospect of his being chosen. It seems to me there is among us a pretty strong local feeling, something like a very general wish, that the next President should be from the North. There is a kind of presentiment that after this election—we may give up all expectation. Of all the persons *named,* I reply—Calhoun. Yet if a prominent man from N. England, New York or Pennsylvania, should be put in nomination against him, I think he would succeed in obtaining the electoral votes. Consulting my own feeling & wishes, at this time I should put the Candidates in this order—Adams—Calhoun—Clinton. I am however very incompetent to judge correctly, of their qualifications.

For the time we had to labor, we did something. Every department of the Government, will be, what is called here, anti-[Isaac] Hill. Some good will result from the change, not immediately perhaps—*but in time.* We have not killed Democracy, who could? but we have penetrated its solid columns, we have broken up its line of march. The result of the election was one of the most unexpected, & yet one of the most natural events— that could be imagined. Here is a paradox—I give no more.

I intend to be in Boston the 3rd day of May—as I have some engagements after the 10th, that will require me to be at home. Yours affectionately   Ezekiel Webster

ALS. NhD. Published in part in *PC*, 1: 323–324.

1. See DW to Ezekiel, March 25, 1823, above.

TO ALEXANDER BLISS

Washington April 3. 1823.

Dear Bliss,

I have recd yrs respecting the 589. note, which I had forgotten.[1] If your dr[a]ft comes, I shall accept & pay it; if it does not appear, in a day or two, I will remit the money. In the mean time send the enclosed order to Mr [Samuel Sumner] Wilde, & ask him to give you cash for it.

Three notes of mine will fall due at U. S. Bank. One, 800 Dlls, with Mr [George] Blake's indorsement, April 14—one for $1000, secured by stock, April 14—also— & one for 1000, with Mr. Blake's indorsement, April 21. These days may not be precise, but I believe they are the exact times of renewal. I now send you enclosed, the notes, which you will please to fill up, & take the necessary care of. So much for notes & Banks. This morning the Comm[issione]rs awarded *favorably,* on the case of the Betsey, Halliburton;[2] & the Mary Ann, Anthony—both as to Mr [Abrain] Touro's claim, & Mr [Frederick] Tudors.[3] Tomorrow the Sally[,] Stephenson will be decided.[4]

Nothing said yet about the Mercury[,] Pearson,[5] but my hope has not failed. Not that the case is certain, at all; but I think it *probable* that it will get along. The business before the Board begins to assume the appearance of winding up. Four or five of our cases, set down, are yet to be decided—all not set down are con[tinue]d,—on motion; and two or three that were set down, were, under peculiar circumstances, con[tinue]d also. My opinion is the Comm[issioner]s will get thro by the 15th, & that they will probably adjourn to meet again in October. Many cases have been rejected, this session, but I believe *we* have fared as well as our neighbors. Yrs   D. Webster

ALS. DLC.
 1. Letter not found.
 2. In the case of the *Betsey*, commanded by Captain Halliburton, DW successfully represented several Massachusetts claimants who received an award of $23,000.
 3. Abrain Touro and Frederick

Tudor received a total award of $4,413.57.
 4. The sum of $16,153.78 was awarded for damages to the *Sally*, Stephenson, captain.
 5. Claims filed involving the *Mercury*, Captain Pearson, amounted to $70,671.35.

TO JOSEPH STORY

Washington Ap. 6. [1823]

My Dear Sir,

I was happy to learn, from Mrs W., that you had been heard of, passing thro Boston, & trust you found all safe and well at home. After two long journies, & a long Court, it must be quite agreeable to you to sit down a little time, for rest & repose. I expect to follow your footsteps in a week or ten days, if my affairs get on as fast as I now hope.

You will naturally be anxious to know whether any thing is done here, as yet, in relation to the appointment of your associate upon the Bench. No appointment has been made.[1] Mr [Smith] Thompson will be appointed, if he chuses to take the office, but he has not made up his mind, as I understand, as yet, so to do. If called on *now* to decide, it is said he will *decline*. I cannot account for his hesitation, but on a supposition, which I have heard suggested, but cannot credit, that he thinks it *possible* events may throw another & a higher office in his way.[2]

When a man finds himself in a situation he hardly ever dreamed of, he is apt to take it for granted, that he is a favorite of fortune, & to presume that his blind patroness may have yet greater things in reserve for him.

In the event of his finally declining, those now talked of as prominent candidates are, J[ames] Kent, & *Ambrose Spencer*. If a nomination were now to be made, I think it would be the former of these two names; altho *there are* [those], who wish to give a decisive rebuke to the Buck tails of N. York[3] by appointing Mr. Spencer. What time may produce, no one can say. Mr [Littleton Waller] Tazewell, & some others, have mentioned Mr. [Nathaniel] Macon's name to the Executive. *If he lived in the Circuit, I verily believe he would, at this peculiar moment, be appointed.* There are *two* of the President's advisers who would, I think, give him a decided preference, if locality could be safely disregarded.

On the whole, my expectation is, that the appointment will be delayed, & that, in the end, Mr Thompson will take it.

We have nothing here, I believe, interesting, except the recent news from Europe. Opinion here seems to be that England must, sooner or later, take the part of Spain, if France should not crush her at the first blow; of which I see no great probability, judging by the tardy movement of her Army.[4] It was not so, under Buonapartes reign.

I am in some trouble in relation to the case of *Williams* vs *Reid,* in the Maine Circuit Court.[5] It will not be possible for me to g[et home] in season to be there, especially as the Court is bro[ught] forward a week. I have written to Mr [John Davis] Williams,[6] to that effect, & he & Mr [Simon] Greenleaf[7] must manage as well as they can.

David B. Ogden is here, having been home & returned. Almost every body else is gone. I am thro all laborious duty here, for the present, & am only waiting the decision of my cases. Give my love to Mrs S. & yr children. Yours always— D. Webster

ALS. MHi. Published in *W & S,* 16: 75–77.

1. The death of Supreme Court Justice Henry Brockholst Livingston on March 18, 1823, created a vacancy at a time when several important cases were yet to be heard.

2. Secretary of the Navy in a Cabinet overloaded with presidential aspirants, Thompson hoped that his northern birth would give him an availability not shared by his better known southern colleagues, Crawford and Calhoun. He resigned from the Cabinet at the end of August but did not finally accept the Court appointment until December 1823.

3. The Bucktails were the anti-Clinton, Tammany Hall faction of the New York Republican (soon to be called the Democratic) party, led at this time by Van Buren. The name derived from the fact that the Sachems wore a buck's tail in their hats at Tammany meetings, but the Bucktails formed a larger faction than the Tammany society alone.

4. France had intervened in Spain in early 1823 in order to quash a liberal revolution against King Ferdinand VII.

5. *Williams* v. *Reed,* 29 Federal Cases, 17, 733.

6. Williams (1769–1848), a Boston businessman and banker, one of the directors of the New England Bank and later incorporator of the Provident Institutions for Savings in 1816.

7. Greenleaf (1783–1853), Portland, Me., lawyer and state legislator.

FROM THOMAS JACKSON OAKLEY

Poughkeepsie—April 12, 1823

Dear Webster—

A friend in N. Y. has sent me a Newspaper, called, the "Essex Register" printed at Salem—of the 7th. inst. containing an article, which I inclose.[1]

You will see that this article attributes to me a declaration, at Washington, to some "respectable lawyer from Boston" the import of which is, that I *knew* that the "Hartford Convention" was a "dark transaction" because I had been "consulted" as to its objects and views.

I have not the pleasure of a personal acquaintance, with Mr [Harrison Gray] Otis—but I should be unwilling, if the article alluded to, should fall under his observation, that he should, for a moment, believe, that there is the slightest foundation, for attributing to me such a declaration—and, I request that you will take some opportunity of saying so, to him.

It is possible, that I may have expressed an opinion, at W[ashington] that Mr. O. would lose his election,[2] in consequence of the excitement, that would be raised against him—on the subject of that convention—and, perhaps too, I may have said (for I have always thought so) that that convention, was, (to say the least of it) an act of great indiscretion. But no man—certainly not a "Boston Lawyer", could have so misunderstood my remarks—as to infer, that I spoke of the character of that convention, from any *knowledge* of the objects and views of the Gentlemen, who composed it. I do not now remember, that I was personally known to any one of those Gentlemen—and, most certainly, was never "consulted" on the subject of their meeting at Hartford.

I am very truly Yours &c   Thos. J. Oakley

ALS. MHi.

1. "When the nomination of Mr. OTIS was announced at Washington, Mr. OAKLEY, one of the most distinguished Federalists of New York, said to a respectable lawyer then present from Boston, 'You cannot succeed with this nomination.' The Bostonian replied, 'Why not, Sir? Mr. Otis is a clever fellow.' 'Yes,' says Mr. Oakley, 'but he was a member of the Hartford Convention, and that ought to blast his reputation, and prevent his election to any office whatever.' The Boston lawyer replied, 'The Hartford Convention meant no harm.' Mr. Oakley replied, 'That story will answer to tell those who are ignorant—It will not do to tell me, who was consulted. It was the darkest transaction, Sir, that ever took place in this country.' "

2. Otis ran in April as the Federalist candidate for governor of Massachusetts but was defeated by William Eustis on the issue of his participation in the Hartford Convention.

TO JOSEPH STORY

Boston, May 12, 1823.

My dear Sir,

It will give us great pleasure to go to Portsmouth, especially in company with you and Mrs. Story. I believe there is very little to do in the Circuit Court. For myself I have next to nothing. There will probably be one capital trial, as I learn from Mr. [George] Blake, which he thinks must be postponed for a short time from the commencement of the court; so that on the whole there will probably be no inconvenience in adjourning the court over next week.

I never felt more down sick on all subjects connected with the public, than at the present moment. I have heretofore cherished a faint hope that New England would some time or other get out of this miserable, dirty squabble of local politics, and assert her proper character and consequence. But I at length give up. I feel the hand of fate upon us, and to struggle is in vain. We are doomed to be hewers of wood and drawers of water; and I am prepared, henceforth, to do my part of the drudgery, without hoping for an end. You know I am not disappointed at the result of the election for governor. My "agony" was over before the election took place, for I never doubted the result. Indeed, on the grounds on which the controversy was placed, I could have enjoyed the triumph of neither party. What has sickened me beyond remedy is the tone and temper of these disputes. We are disgraced beyond help or hope by these things. There is a Federal interest, a Democratic interest, a Bankrupt interest, an Orthodox interest, and a Middling interest, but I see no national interest, nor any national feeling in the whole matter.

I am, dear Sir, you true but despairing friend,   D. Webster

Text from *PC*, 1: 325. Original not found.

FROM "FANNY" [?]

Columbia, May 29, 1823.
Sir,

You have probably before this time entirely forgotten that you ever had an acquaintance by the name of Fanny.[1] It is a long time since I have heard any thing of you. I lately, by accident, heard that you were settled in Boston, and in affluence. Very different is my situation. I live in this town with my aged parents, who are unable to do any thing towards supporting themselves. I have one sister; we have nothing but our hands to support our parents and a helpless brother. As a help towards doing this, I took an orphan child under my care. I was to receive six dollars per month for board and tuition; I have kept the child two years, and received but forty dollars, and have no expectation of ever receiving more. His guardian has failed and fled to parts unknown. I agreed with a merchant in this vicinity for some of the necessaries of life, expecting to receive payment quarterly, and pay it to him; he now calls loudly for his pay, and I have nothing to pay with; I expect he will take the steps of the law; in that case you know how dreadful would be the situation of a poor defenceless female. I can do nothing towards paying the debt unless some of my rich friends will help me. The debt due to me is about eighty dollars, and the debt which I owe about fifty dollars. Should you feel able and willing to bestow some pecuniary assistance, you will please to send by mail. I live in Columbia, Brooklyn County, Connecticut. Should you not find it convenient to assist me, I should be glad to hear of your health and happiness and that of your dear ones. If you could make it convenient to answer this the first mail after receiving it, you would much oblige Your unfortunate friend.

P.S. Where is [James] Hervey Bingham,[2] and what is his situation? Do you correspond with him? Perhaps you would be willing to state my condition to him. My great anxiety to do all in my power to render the few remaining days of my parents in some measure comfortable, is all the apology I can offer for thus troubling you.

Text from *PC*, 1 : 326. Original not found.

1. An acquaintance of DW during his Dartmouth days. See DW to James Hervey Bingham, May 18, 1802,

above.

2. On June 9 DW wrote Bingham: "I have sent her a little money, and, according to her request, enclose the letter to you" (*PC*, 1 : 327).

TO SAMUEL JAUDON

Boston June 23. 1823

My dear Sir,

I have recd. your two favors,[1] but wish, instead thereof, you had come yourself & brought another & greater *favor* with you. I have not been doing much about Spanish claims since I came home. Some few little cases are prepared, & for others we must wait still longer for proof.

It is my present expectation to be at the ensuing session; not that I expect to find much to do there, but because some of those interested may imagine my attendance might be useful.

I do not intend however to stay longer than a very few days. As to the cases for rehearing, it strikes me to be as well that they all should lie over to the fall. Towards the close of the Commission would seem to be the proper time for the rehearings.

We begin to talk a little here about the *French* claims.[2] I have been spoken to, to aid in getting them up. I should very much like to have a hand in them, as extensively as I could. If you & I could get the joint agency of the P[hiladelphia] & Boston claims, I think we could do our employers tolerable justice. If your friends have proceeded so far as to frame a Petition, I wish you would send me a copy of it. Yrs very truly

D. Webster

ALS. NHi.

1. Not found.

2. DW was unaware that the United States Minister to France, Albert

Gallatin, had just sailed from the Continent after having failed to reach a suitable accord with the French on the subject of commercial shipping claims. A United States commission to resolve the claims of American citizens was not authorized until the signing of a Franco-American convention on July 4, 1831.

POWER OF ATTORNEY TO AUGUSTUS PEABODY

June 24, 1823

Know all men by these presents that I Daniel Webster of the City of Boston in the State of Massachusetts, Esquire, being one of the associates of Daniel Abbot of Dunstable in the County of Hillsborough and State of New Hampshire, and interested together with him and others in the Nashua Manufacturing Company,[1] divers good causes and considerations me thereunto moving, do hereby nominate and appoint Augustus Peabody of said Boston Esquire, to be my lawful Attorney.

And as to the power and authority which I give to my said Attorney it is as follows. To repair to said Dunstable on the twenty sixth day of June instant, and then and there to meet said Daniel Abbot and his other associates at the house of Moses Tyler, Innholder, where they will meet for the purpose of organizing the Nashua Manufacturing Company under a Charter recently granted by the Legislature of New Hampshire. And at said meeting I authorize my said Attorney to represent and vote for me, and to do and perform, and to assent to, or dissent from any and all acts matters and things that may then and there be done and performed or proposed. And to do and perform all things whatsoever which I legally might do were I personally present touching the premises.

And I do hereby ratify and confirm all and singular the things which my said Attorney shall lawfully do in the premises.

In testimony whereof I have hereunto set my hand and seal, this twenty fourth day of June, in the year of our Lord One Thousand Eight hundred and twenty three. In presence of Saml. B. Walcott

Danl. Webster

DS. NhD.

1. The Nashua Manufacturing Company was incorporated by the New Hampshire legislature on June 18, 1823, to manufacture cotton, woolen, and iron products. The necessary water for power was to be brought by canal from Mine Falls on the Nashua River, about three miles from the site selected for the company's holdings. Capital stock was fixed at $300,000 with a right to increase it to $1,000,000. The capital was divided into 300 shares at $1,000 each. Of these Webster took 60 and Augustus Peabody 75. John Kendrick took 15 shares and the remaining 150 shares were taken in 30-share lots by Daniel Abbot, J., E. and A. Greeley, Benjamin F. French, Foster and Kendrick, and Moses Tyler. The 60 shares subscribed by Webster never actually came into his possession, presumably because he could not raise the money

to pay for them. See Edward E. Parker, *History of the City of Nashua,*

N.H. (Nashua, 1897), pp. 58–59, 435.

FROM BENNET TYLER

Dartmouth College Aug. 23. 1823.

Sir

I have the honour to inform you that the Trustees of this College did at their late Session confer upon you the degree of L.L.D. in testimony of their sense of your literary, scientific and professional eminence, and also in grateful remembrance of the lively interest you have ever taken in the welfare of this literary institution.

With considerations of Respect & esteem I am your Obnt. Servt.

Bennet Tyler

ALS. NhD. The Reverend Bennet
Tyler was President of Dartmouth Col-

lege, 1822–1828.

FROM JOSEPH HOPKINSON

Philad. Sep. 12. 1823

My dear Sir

We have a report here that there is a letter in circulation from Mr [Timothy] Pickering,[1] to whom written I have not heard, in which Mr P— expresses his preference of Mr [William H.] Crawford to Mr [John Quincy] Adams as President because "Mr. C— has always been a *faithful democrat,* and Mr A— is a *dishonest apostate.*" I have not seen the letter, but so it has been recited to me. I feel it impossible, without more direct evidence, to credit this strange tale. To say nothing of the coarseness of the objection made to Mr Adams, hardly becoming a man of P—'s years and standing, I cannot believe he would consider the reason given in favour of Mr Crawford to be of any force. To be a democrat, faithful or unfaithful, has not heretofore been a recommendation with Mr P— for any thing but a gibbet; and altho I doubt not he has abated of such violence, yet I cannot suppose his change so entire as to pass from the gibbet to the Presidential chair. If this was the case, it would seem hardly to be safe for him to urge apostacy upon any man as a crime. I should like to have the truth of this matter that I may do justice to our friend if he is calumniated; and hold my tongue about it if he is not. I have presumed you may be able to give me the information I require, and indeed it might not be amiss to let Mr P— know of the report alluded to.

Mo. truly &c—Yours   Jos. Hopkinson

ALS. DLC.

1. No letter of this character has been found.

TO VIRGIL MAXCY

Boston Sep. 22. 1823

Dear Sir,

I have recd yours of the 15th.,[1] & in a few days will give you my ideas on the subject of it, fully. I am this morning, bound to New Hampshire, so that I have not time to write. On the main subject, I will only say, that in my opinion Mr. [John C.] Calhoun is most likely, next to Mr [John Quincy] Adams, to get the votes of New England, or a great majority of them. Such is the present impression, & I have no doubt of it. The general prospect of his election has certainly brightened exceedingly within three months. At this moment he stands well in N. England; as well as could be expected or wished, considering that New England's first choice is undoubtedly Mr. Adams.

I have written nothing, to any body, on subjects of this sort; but on my return will write you fully what I think. Yours very truly   Danl. Webster

ALS. DLC. Virgil Maxcy (1785–1844) had a varied career as lawyer, state legislator, and diplomat. Born in Massachusetts and educated at Brown, he was for a time a tutor in the South before reading law with Robert Goodloe Harper in Baltimore and settling in Maryland. Though he lived in the midst of faction and personal hostilities, Maxcy managed to retain the lifelong friendship of men as far apart as Webster, Calhoun, and Jackson. He was solicitor of the Treasury under Jackson and was sent as minister to Belgium by Van Buren. He was a guest of President Tyler aboard the Battleship *Princeton* when he was killed by the explosion of one of her guns.

1. Not found.

Returning to Congress after an absence of almost seven years, Webster seized upon the issue of Greek independence for the first major speech of his second period of service in the House. On January 19, 1824, before a packed gallery, he came eloquently to the defense of Greek independence by way of supporting his own proposition that Congress pass a law "defraying the expense incident to the appointment of an agent, or commissioner to Greece, whenever the President shall deem it expedient to make such an appointment." For both the facts and the generalizations in his speech, Webster relied upon Edward Everett, who had recently returned from a trip to Greece and had published several articles on the subject in the North American Review.

TO EDWARD EVERETT

New York Nov. 16. [1823]

I have found leisure here, & not until now, to read your admirable article on the Greeks.[1] Since I left Boston, also, we have had important information from them.[2] I feel a great inclination to say or do something in their behalf, early in the session, if I know what to say or to do. If you can readily direct me to any sources, from which I can obtain more information than is already public, respecting their affairs, I would be obliged to you so to do.

I have not yet seen [Henry] Wheaton,—nor other wise men of Manhattan. Yrs always   D.W.

ALS. MHi. Published in *PC*, 1: 328.

1. "The Ethics of Aristotle to Nicomachus, revised and edited by A. Coray, at the expense of the injured and oppressed Sciotes," *The North American Review*, New Series, 8 (October 1823): 389–424.

2. DW was probably referring to the recent Greek victories at St. Luca and Levadia.

TO JEREMIAH MASON

Princeton Nov. 20 '23

My Dr Sir

We are thus far on our way, well, & without accident. I spent two or three days in N York; & write this principally to give you information of what surprised me, & will equally, I imagine, surprise you. I mean the extraordinary present popularity of Mr. [DeWitt] *Clinton*. I was in no manner prepared to hear the language, held in the City, on that subject. The various Candidates for the Presidency, or their friends, now seem to consider him the most formidable opponent, as far as that State is concerned. What from the natural re-action of popular sympathy, in favor of one who is supposed to have been hardly used, & what from his now acknowledged merits, as connected with the [Erie] *Canal*, he seems rising very strangely. In short his friends speak with great confidence of his success, in that State, & with almost equal confidence of his strength in Ohio. This gives a new aspect to things, & probably renders still more improbable any choice by the Electors. Mr Clinton's friends, & Mr [John C.] Calhoun's friends, at this moment, seem to think the only controversy, in N. York, must be between those two. They admit that Mr. [John Quincy] Adams has a great body of well-wishers, & some active friends; but they think neither class is increasing, at present. And Mr [William H.] Crawford they think—or affect to think—out of the question. In the mean while, it seems to be understood, as far as I could learn, that the friends of Mr Clinton & Mr Calhoun would go along amicably, for the present, at least, & until public opinion should more fully develope itself. In all the middle states there is such a *fashion*—or *passion*, for entertaining projects of internal improvement that considerations of that sort are expected to have influence on the highest elections. Foreign relations being all quiet & pacific, and no high party feelings at present existing, the necessary *excitement* of public sentiment seems only likely to be found in schemes of internal improvement. I believe you & I have the fortune, good or ill, to have committed ourselves in favor of the Constitutional power of Congress to aid such objects.

I hope to find a letter from you at W[ashington]. Mr [Richard] Stockton's good family are all well, & desire their respects to your family. Julia is at New Bedford, for the winter. Yours mo. truly   D Webster

ALS. NhD. Published in W & S, 16: 77–78.

TO EZEKIEL WEBSTER

Princeton Nov. 20. 1823

Dear E,

I left N York yesterday, having remained there two or three days; which was long enough to learn the strange confusion & division of opinion which exists there in relation to prominent public subjects. It seems to be generally believed that Mr. [William H.] Crawford's friends have no longer any reasonable hope of success, in that state. This point being agreed, every thing else is controverted. I was altogether astonished at the confidence which the friends of Mr [DeWitt] *Clinton* expressed, of their ability to secure to him the votes of that State. It is certain, that his popularity has experienced a sudden and most extraordinary revival; so much so as to inspire unlimited expectations. The [Erie] *Canal* has done this. It is said also, with great confidence, that Ohio is better inclined towards Mr. Clinton than any body else. On the other hand, the friends of Mr [John Quincy] Adams, Mr [John C.] Calhoun, & Mr [Henry] Clay say, that altho' Mr. Clinton may be gaining strength, it is improbable he can obtain the votes of New York & impossible, at all events, that he can be Presidt. The friends of Mr Calhoun, especially, regret that Mr Clinton should be brought forward, apprehending it may have the effect of re-uniting the fragments of the old Republican Party[1] in favor of Mr Crawford, thro. the effect of strong feelings of dislike towards Mr. Clinton. As far as I could understand[,] the friends of these two Gentlemen, in that state, are inclined to no mutual hostilities, but willing to leave public sentiment, as between those two, to declare itself. In the meantime it is thought Mr. Adams has a very large, tho' not an increasing number of friends. I should not be at all surprised if the re-action, which has begun evidently to take place in Mr. Clintons favor, together with the *Canal*, & other local considerations, should give him the state. It seems undoubted that the Legislature, which assembles in January, will send the Election to the People, on a general Ticket,— & then, I presume, the friends of the Parties will array themselves.[2] Many of the Federalists in the Western District it is supposed favor Mr Adams; otherwise, in the City, & its neighborhood. This State of N Jersey is thought likely enough to be in favor of Mr Calhoun, unless it should be inundated by an overflow of Mr. Clinton's popularity from N York.

Your friend Mr [Isaac] Hill, of Concord, was this way about a month since. I learn that he said, in New York, that Gov. [Levi] W[oodbury] was hardly likely to have any support at all, at the next election;—that his Excellency had offered *him* terms of reconciliation, which he should not accept; & that he expected to be under the necessity of supporting Mr. [David Lawrence] *Morrill*, altho' he did not much like that Gentleman.

We have got along thus far with[out] accident, & shall resume our jou[rney.]

I hope to find letters from you at [Washington].

Yours affectionately   D Webster

ALS. NhD. Published in *PC*, 1: 328–329.

1. The principal factions of the Republican Party in New York had, since the early years of the nineteenth century, revolved around three major figures: DeWitt Clinton, Robert Livingston, and Aaron Burr.

2. In early November a large number of legislators were elected who were pledged to reforming the caucus procedure of nominating presidential candidates. Primarily of an Anti-Crawford persuasion, they viewed the reform as the only means by which his candidacy could be prevented. Their efforts at reforming the system in a special session of the Assembly in August, however, were unsuccessful.

TO EDWARD EVERETT

Washington Nov. 28. [1823]

My Dear Sir,

I cannot say how much I am obliged to you for your ready attention to my request, & your assurance of future aid. I rely on receiving your *narrative*,[1] as fast as it is composed—if you need a hand to *copy* please call on Mr. [Samuel Baker] Wolcot,[2] at my Office. My wish wd. be to bring forward the subject early in January, if nothing should happen to hasten or retard it. I can say, *to your own ear only*—that the *message* will contain strong expressions of sympathy for the Greeks, & that it probably would not be displeasing to the Executive that, Congress should pass a Resolution, appropriating a fund for some sort of agency to Greece.

You may be assured this subject has been under the consideration of the President; *and also that* YOUR *name has been mentioned* to him as the fittest person for such a service. This mention proceeded from a high source; & yet not from that which would most obviously occur to you.[3] If the measure should be adopted, I verily believe you may have the appointment if you wish it. For the present, I shall mention the subject to very few, nor perhaps will it be worth your while to converse with many. You propose coming here, which will be exactly the right thing to do.

There is nobody, certainly, at all equal to any competition with you, in point of qualification for that place. All that I can do, you may be assured shall be done, to the utmost; & you have other friends—not more zealous or true—but more able & powerful.

I beg of you to write me as often as you can,—on all subjects, but especially on the *Greeks*. It is very probable some other Gentlemen may anticipate me, in this business—the Chairman of the Com[mitt]ee of foreign relations for example. But that will not be material, as I co[uld] say any thing I may be prepared to say, as well on another's motion as my own. My real difficulty is *ignorance*—& with this candid acknowledgment I bid you, adieu! Yrs mo. truly   D W.

Mrs W. desires her faithful regards to you & yours. If you see Eliza [Buckminster], & Mrs [Henry Holton] F[uller] give them our love—et quoque Mr F[uller] and the President [John Thornton Kirkland].

ALS. MHi.

1. "Life of Ali Pacha," *The North American Review*, New Series, 9 (January 1824): 106–140.

2. Wolcott (1795–1854; Harvard 1819), law student in DW's office.

3. On October 30 Everett had written Secretary of State John Quincy Adams: "If such a course should be adopted, I wish you would persuade the President to make me Secretary of the Commission." Adams, however, refused to make solicitations on Everett's behalf for the post, although Secretary of War John C. Calhoun did urge the President to appoint Everett.

TO [JEREMIAH] MASON

Washington, November 30, [1823]

Dear Sir,

We arrived here on Wednesday evening safe and well, after a journey which, on the whole, was pleasant and agreeable. Our lodgings were ready and are very comfortable.

The attendance of members is uncommonly large, and we shall have a quorum, no doubt, to-morrow. Mr. [Henry] Clay arrived last evening. He will doubtless be Speaker, although I understood Mr. [Philip P.] Barbour's friends intend to run him. It will not go. Mr. Clay's popularity as Speaker is great, and he is in many respects a liberal and honorable man. His health is not good, but I fancy not so bad as to induce him to decline the chair.

Although I think him tolerably liberal, and not unfriendly in his general feeling, yet I do not suppose that, in the organization and arrangement of the affairs of the House, he will venture to disregard old lines of distinction.

Mr. [Rufus] King has arrived, but I have not seen him. Both your senators [Samuel Bell and John F. Parrott] are here.

I have not seen much here yet to add to my stock of knowledge on the subject of the Presidential election. It looks to me, however, at present, as if it might happen that Mr. [William H.] Crawford would ere long be given up, and his friends go off in a direction to Mr. Clay.

It appears to me to be our true policy to oppose all caucuses; so far our course seems to me to be clear. Beyond that I do not think we are bound to proceed at present. To defeat caucus nominations, or prevent them, and to give the election, wherever it can be done, to the people, are the best means of restoring the body politic to its natural and wholesome state.

Mrs. W. sends a great deal of love to you all.

Yours, most truly,   D. Webster

P.S. I hope you have not abandoned an idea which you intimated to me at Dorchester. I think you will do exceedingly right to take that step, and am sure you will not regret it.

It will excite no jealousy or suspicion here, at all; and you have reasons which will allay any that might arise at home.

Text from *PC*, 1: 329–330. Extract published in Van Tyne, p. 93. Original not found.

TO EZEKIEL WEBSTER

Washington Dec. 4— [1823]

Dear E.

I have recd yours, covering three letters, today.[1] My information as to what Mr [Isaac] H[ill] said in New York was from the Editor of the "Statesman," but I suppose he would not wish to have it known.[2] He is now here; I shall see him, & will endeavor to put him in the right way. Mr. [John F.] Parrott lodges in the same House with us. He said today, speaking of N.H. affairs, that if there were *any* objection to Gov. [Levi] W[oodbury] he could not be chosen; that Mr. [David Lawrence] Morrill was talked of, but he thought *that* wd. hardly do, & that if Judge [Arthur] L[ivermore] were a candidate, *he* probably might & would succeed.

One thing I hold to be *material*—get *on without a Caucus*. It will only require a little more pains. It is time to put an end to *Caucuses*. They make great men little, & little men great. *The true source of power is the People.* The Democrats are not Democratic enough. They are real aristocrats. Their leaders wish to govern by a combination among themselves, & they think they have a fee simple in the people's suffrages. Go to the *People*, & convince them that their pretended friends, are a knot of self-interested jobbers, who make a trade of patriotism, & live on popular credulity.

We have as yet done little or nothing here. The choice of Speaker should be considered as indicating nothing but a sense, in the House, of Mr. [Henry] Clay's fitness for that place. He had nearly all the Northern votes. How he will discharge the important duties of the chair, in arranging the business of the House, we shall know tomorrow. I have no doubt of the liberality of his feelings, & can hardly persuade myself that he will be *afraid* to shake off trammels. Yet, in the present condition of things, he *may,* perhap[s keep] on the safe side—as he may think it. We shall see.

[N]othing very new, & important, has transpired, relative to the Presidential election. I remain of opinion *the choice must come to the House.*

I shall write you often, & should be glad to hear from you twice a week. These are interesting times— & we ought to keep awake. What think you of doing or *saying* something in favor of the *Greeks?* Mr. [Stephen] Longfellow has not yet arrived. I note yr request— & will see him. Yrs faithfully   D.W.

ALS. NhD. Published in *PC*, 1: 330–331.
 1. Not found.
 2. Nathaniel H. Carter and George W. Prentiss both edited the *New York Statesman* in 1823. DW, however, was probably referring to Carter, a fellow New Hampshireman and Dartmouth College alumnus (1811).

TO EDWARD EVERETT

Washington Decr. 5. [1823]

My dear Sir

I have gone thro your two manuscripts, with the map before me, & think I have mastered the campaign of 1821–1822—historically & topographically. My wonder is, where & how your most extraordinary industry has been able to find all the materials for so interesting and detailed a narrative. I hope you will send me a digested narrative of the events of this year, so far as they are to be learned from the last accounts.

I have spoken to several Gentlemen on the subject of a motion respecting Greece, & all of them approve it. My only doubt, at present, is as to the manner. The object which I wish to bring about, and which I believe may be brought about, is the appointment of a Commissioner to go to Greece. Two modes present themselves. A motion to that effect, & a speech in support of it, giving some account of the rise & progress of the Greek Revolution, & shewing the propriety & utility of the proposed mission.

The other is, to raise a Com[mitt]ee on the subject, & let there be a report, containing the same matter. The first would be the easier to be done; the last would be the more grave & imposing. Whichever may be adopted, your communications are invaluable; & I wish you would tell me frankly how far I can use them without injury to your January Article in N. A.[1]

We can wait until that article is *out*, if you think best—but my impression is we should do well to bring forward the subject within ten or twelve days from this time, while the House is not yet much occupied, & while the Country feels the warmth communicated by the Presidents Message. I intend to see, in the course of this day and tomorrow, Mr. R[ufus] King, Mr [Henry] Clay, & perhaps the President, & learn their views of this matter.

I shall send you every thing, in the shape of a document, that is printed this session. These are interesting times—let us improve them. Yours most devotedly   D. W.

ALS. MHi. Published in *PC*, 1: 331–332.

   1. "Life of Ali Pacha," *The North*

American Review, New Series, 9 (January, 1824): 106–140.

TO EDWARD EVERETT

Decr. 6. 1823

My D Sir

There was, as I believe a meeting of the members of Administration yesterday; at which, inter alia, they talked of Greece. The *pinch* is, that in the Message the President has taken, as is supposed, pretty high ground as to *this Continent;* and is afraid of the appearance of interfering in the concerns of the *other continent* also.[1] This does not weigh greatly with me—I think we have as much Community with the Greeks, as with the inhabitants of the Andes, & the dwellers on the borders of the Vermilion Sea. It was, or I am not well informed, stated, yesterday, that there ought to be a Commiss[ione]r, & that you ought to be persuaded to go. Go you will— & go you shall—if you chuse so to do.

If nothing should occur to alter my present purpose, I shall bring forward a motion on the subject *on Monday*— & shall propose to let it lie on the table for a fortnight.

If you can find any tolerable map of Modern Greece, I wish you would send it to me, for *Mr.* [John C.] *Calhoun.* I write this at his request, who desires me to say to you that he is as friendly to the Greeks as yourself.

I am glad to see that you publish in the [Boston] Daily [Advertiser] yr narrative. It will be well recd—& do much good.

There seems to be here a good natured & liberal spirit, on all subjects. Yrs mo. sincerely   D. Webster

ALS. MHi. Published in *PC*, 1: 332–333.

   1. On December 2 the Monroe Doctrine had been quietly announced in the President's opening message to Congress. The first draft contained an endorsement of the Greek Revolution and the appointment of a special United States agent. Secretary of State John Quincy Adams, the pri-

mary author of the doctrine, had res-
ervations and the appointment was
dropped, although Monroe's message

did ultimately express support for the
Greeks.

TO GEORGE BLAKE

Washington Dec 20 [1823]

My dear Sir

I believe Mrs W. is meditating a letter to Mrs B. today—but as she told me this morning it was uncertain whether *engagements of business* would allow her time to write, she directed me to indict a line to Mrs B to be enclosed in this, which I told her I was about writing to you.

The object of this is to call your attention to Mr [Timothy] Fuller's[1] Resolution, respecting the Law of 1814—that partial, & odious act.[2] The Resolution is now before our Com[mitt]ee. We shall act upon it soon— & probably report a Bill to *repeal* the act of 1814—probably in *12 days* we shall be acting on the matter in our House.[3] I wish you, therefore to do two things—*First,* to write to me, giving me your ideas, and any information which you may think useful; &, secondly, to write to *Mr [Elijah Hunt] Mills*, to look after the matter, if it should get to the Senate.

I have a belief—perhaps it is unfounded—that it will pass our house. I shall be very glad, if the first thing I do here, in addition to its being just & proper, shall also be something not unfavorable to you.

As to the business of the Court, I have not yet paid much attention to it. My Spanish claims have called for all the time at my command. They are now pretty much finished—at least so far as not to be extremely burdensome, on my time.

As to great political affairs, we, who are not in secrets, know here very little more than is known in Massachusetts. Some say there is to be a Caucus, & some say there is not. I think it yet uncertain, whether there will be one or not. I suppose the Members of the House have all their preferences, but, so far, there is great *abstinence*, in the House, from all topics connected with the election. I hope this will last.

I write this in the *House,* (not now in session) & your friend Mr [James] Buchannan is here, & desires me to make his remembrances to yo[u] and Mrs Blake. He means to write to you soo[n] and he just now says, "Mr Blake is [one] of the most agreeable men I have ever known." What a poor judge of such matters, he is! If he always judges as wrong, he will not do to be followed!!!—

Pray let me hear from you soon; & believe me, most truly,

Yrs always   Danl. Webster

ALS. DLC. Published in *PC,* 1: 333–334.

1. Fuller (1778–1835; Harvard 1801), Boston lawyer and congress-

man.

2. The act of April 18, 1814, had decreased "the compensation to clerks, marshals and attorneys in the Courts

of the U. S."

3. Fuller's repeal resolution was passed by the House on February 27, 1824.

TO MRS. GEORGE BLAKE

Washington Dec 20 1823

My Dear Madam

It is Mrs Webster's intention to write you immediately, in her proper person, in answer to yours of the eleventh. Not to suffer, however, so great a favor to remain altogether unnoticed, even for a short time, she *commands* me to write to you, to acknowledge its receipt, & to assure you of the pleasure it gives us to hear from you. It is true that we find objects here which may well enough fill up the attention, for a time; and, truth to tell, I really think Mrs W. likes Washington tolerably well. Nevertheless, we need your & Mr B's Society *very much.* There is nobody here, to come in, of an evening, & pull off his over shoes, coats, & handkerchiefs, & sit down to a regular social talk, like your Husband. For my part, I would give something just to *see* that *blue* handkerchief. Our Evenings are sometimes not a little lonesome. However, I, sometimes, (tho seldom) take a *nap;* and as you speak of dreaming away the long nights, you hit me on a tender point—since I am always accused, (very *unjustly,* of course) of no little love of the good thing, sleep. However, I will not altogether deny it, & in respect to good dreams, I am, I am sure, surpassed by nobody. I believe I have a talent, that way. Our Evening parties are not yet numerous. We have been but to *two:* one at Genl. [Jacob Jennings] Browns, night before last— & one at Mrs [John Quincy] Adams—ten days ago. Report runs that the drawing Room, at the white House, will be opened on New Year's day, and afterwards as usual. There are several handsome female faces here, that I have not seen before; especially two or three ladies from the South. We may be in some danger, My Dear Lady, of losing the reputation of the North, if you do not come on to sustain us against this Southern competition. You must remember that our Northern forces are much weakened since your beautiful friend Miss Dickinson[1] stays out of combat. For this, as well as other reasons, I hope you will allow me to *entreat* you to accompany your Husband.

You have a great friend here, in the person of Master Edward [Webster]. He desires all sorts of affectionate remembrance. I think both he & his sister [Julia] may speak well of the bread & butter of the Potomac. I will thank you to remember me to Miss Helen;[2] I regret that you are so soon to lose her present society. Give our love to George. Mrs W. will probably write you in a day or two.

Yrs, with most sincere regard,   Danl. Webster

ALS. DLC. Published in *PC*, 1: 334–
335.

1. Not identified.
2. Not identified.

TO EDWARD EVERETT

Sunday Eve' 21st Dec. [1823]

My Dear Sir

Two days ago I recd your Greek statistics; & today your letter of the 15.[1] I pray you not to think that my engagements are such as to make your correspondence inconvenient. In the first place, I write you only when I can *with convenience;* and, as to my duties in the Judiciary Com[mitt]ee, most of the topics coming up there are pretty familiar to me, & are consequently disposed of without great labor.[2]

As to the Greek subject, the Resolution will be taken up *tomorrow* fortnight (not yesterday fortnight) as mentioned in yesterday's Daily Int[elligencer]— I believe there will be a good deal of discussion, altho I fancy pretty much on one side. While some of our Boston friends (as I know) think this Resolution even *Quixotic*—leading to *Crusade,* &c—it will be objected to strongly by many, on acc[ount] of its tame, milk-&-water character. The Merchants are naturally enough a little afraid about their cargos at Smyrna—besides Greece is a great way off, &c.

I find your communications of the utmost utility. In regard to the history of the Campaign, I could have done nothing without your aid.

My intention is to justify the Resolution agt two classes of objections— those that suppose it not to go far enough— & those that suppose it to go too far—Then to give some little history of the Greek Revolution—express a pretty strong conviction of its ultimate success, & persuade the House, if I can, to take the merit of being the first Govt. among all the civilized Nations, who have publicly rejoiced in the emancipation of Greece— &c. There will be Speeches eno[ugh]— & some of them no doubt tolerably good. Whatever occurs to you—if it be but a *scrap*—in season to be sent here, pray forward it. Mr [John C.] C[alhoun] is greatly obliged to you for your *map.* I hope to hear from you a short word, at least, every day or two. Yours always truly   D.W.

I feel now as if I could make a pretty good speech for my friends the Greeks—but I shall get *cool,* in *14 days,* unless you keep up my temperature.

ALS. MHi. Published in part in *PC*, 1:
335–336.
1. Not found.
2. Speaker of the House Henry Clay had appointed DW chairman of the
Judiciary Committee soon after his return to Congress in November.

TO JEREMIAH MASON

Washington Decr. 22. 1823

My Dr Sir,

Will you be kind enough to read, in a late No. of the Nat[ional] Int[elli-gencer], a Report of the Judiciary Com[mitt]ee of H. R. of last year, on the subject of the *Courts;*[1] & write me your opinion freely, thereon. Soon after New Year's day we must report some measure on that subject; & I should be particularly glad to know what you think of the matter.

I incline to think there will be no Caucus at present. Possibly, the cause of one of the candidates has been so much identified with a Caucus, that some *sort* of a Caucus will be convened, during the Session,—but at this moment I imagine, it would illy succeed, if attempted. I cannot help having a half-suspicion that some doubts of Mr [William H.] Crawford's *health* is entertained;[2] & that *this* has some effect in the postponement of a *Caucus.* It is said your Mr [Ichabod] *Bartlett* is in favor of a Caucus; your other members agt it. I suspect this is true, but I cannot vouch for it.

Yrs always   D. Webster

ALS. MHi. Published in Van Tyne, pp. 93–94.

1. The report contained three plans to reorganize the federal court system so that "the natural increase of business . . . both in the old and new states . . . could be expedited." The three proposals were: 1. "to increase the number of circuits to nine and add two more Judges to the Supreme Court. 2. to establish Circuit Courts throughout the US . . . and to provide for the eventual reduction of the number of Judges of the Supreme Court to five. 3. to establish two Circuit Courts in the western States, with the same general powers and jurisdiction as are now possessed by the Circuit Courts of the US . . ." *National Intelligencer,* December 20, 1823.

2. In September Crawford had suffered a severe stroke. The fact that he was seriously incapacitated was kept secret for several months in order to protect his bid for the Presidency. Ill health did not prevent his nomination by a rump caucus in February 1824.

FROM THOMAS HANDASYD PERKINS, *et al.*

Boston Decr. 23. 1823

Sir

The Subscribers amongst others of your Constituents in Nov. 1821 forwarded a Petition to Congress praying for the establishment of an uniform system of Bankruptcy.[1] The same reasons still urge them to wish the passage of such a Bill; they are of Opinion that longer experience of the evils of the existing laws, has increased the friends to that Petition.

Believing therefore that the wishes of a great proportion of your Constituents will be gratified, and the Community at large benefited, by the enacting of uniform national laws upon the subject of Bankruptcy, they request that the Petition here refered to may again be called up and presented for the consideration of Congress, in such manner, and at such time as you may deem expedient.

Very respectfully your friends & Constituents.

T H Perkins
Theodore Lyman jr.
Lynde Walter
Giles Lodge[2]

LS. NhHi.

1. Document not found.

2. Walter (1767–1844) and Lodge were Boston merchants.

FROM JOEL ROBERTS POINSETT

[1823?]

Dear Sir

I saw the President and shewed him the modification you proposed.[1] He still objects on the ground, that such measures ought to originate with the Executive, and that your resolution proposes to go further than he wishes. He intended only to express his wishes for the success of the Greeks. I think it important to the cause you advocate that some expression favorable to the Greeks should pass the house, and propose to offer a substitute for your resolution. If the Friends of a positive measure in their favor are most numerous your resolution will pass, if on the contrary the majority are of opinion that we ought to confine ourselves to an expression of sympathy and interest in their cause, mine will be adopted. I propose to offer at the same time a resolution in relation to the free governments south of us, which I have no doubt your remarks will induce the house to adopt, for the cause is the same.[2]

Altho on this subject I differ from you more in the form than in the substance I do so with much regret and with some compunctions of conscience, for at first I did not perceive the inconveniences of adopting this measure, which have on reflection occurred to me.

With great regard and respect Yours sincerely,   J. R. Poinsett

ALS. DLC.

1. Concerning DW's proposal of December 8th that a special commissioner be sent to Greece.

2. Poinsett introduced both resolutions into the House on January 20,

1824. The second, which would have given congressional approval to the Monroe Doctrine, was withdrawn after Poinsett discovered that a similar proposal had already been made.

TO EDWARD EVERETT

Jan. 2. 1824

Dear Sir,

I send you the answer, to the call for information respecting the Greeks.[1] If I mistake not, it will, with the Country, very much *raise* the

Greek stock. As to the danger from my motion, of offending the Turk, I think we may disregard that, when we see the Sec. of State corresponding with [a] G[reek] Agent in London, wishing him & his nation all success, & *publishing the correspondence.*[2]

It is possible my motion may be put off till we get an answer to Mr [Rollin C.] Mallary's motion,[3] so as to debate our whole foreign relations at once. *We shall have the nation;* & if Mr Monroe does not do, speedily, as much as I have suggested, he will soon be obliged to do more.

I mean to say as much to him, this day or tomorrow.   D.W.

ALS. MHi. Published in *PC*, 1: 338.

1. On December 18, 1823, Lewis Williams of North Carolina had introduced a resolution requesting the president to submit to the House of Representatives information "relating to the present condition and future prospects of the Greeks"; and on December 31, such a report had been submitted to the House. It was to the latter report that DW directed Everett.

2. About the same time that he was trying to negotiate a commercial treaty with Turkey, Secretary of State Adams had cautiously written Andreas Luriottis, Greek agent in London, that the U.S. hoped for Greece's success against the Turks.

3. Mallary's motion had called for information respecting Spain and the South American colonies.

In the early 1820's, Webster became identified as one of the chief American exponents of the "cause of humanity," as Bates described him below. His stand on two issues had resulted in this widespread identification: in 1819–20 he opposed the admission of Missouri as a slave state, and in 1823–24 he was one of the foremost proponents of American support of the Greeks in their fight for independence. Champions of many causes were soon turning to Webster for support.

In the letter below, Bates solicited Webster's assistance in his bid for reappointment as collector of customs in Bristol, Rhode Island. Named to the post by President Monroe, Bates had been unwavering in his prosecution of Bristol merchants engaged in the illicit slave trade. Those efforts, he explained, had caused James De Wolf, United States senator and one of the leading figures in the slave traffic, to oppose his reappointment. A Massachusetts congressman, Webster apparently did not intervene in the Senate debate over Bates' renomination. De Wolf succeeded in getting his Senate colleagues to block Bates's confirmation, and shortly afterward Bates left Bristol for New York City.

FROM BARNABAS BATES

Bristol, R.I. Jany 5, 1824.

Sir,

The interest which you have always manifested in the cause of humanity, & more especially in the abolition of the odious traffick in human flesh, induces me to address you on the present occasion. You are not insensible, I presume Sir, of the difficulties which I have been obliged to encounter in the suppression of a trade which has so long disgraced the District in which I reside, & in enforcing the revenue laws which for a series of years had been shamefully violated. Certain powerful individuals who have been made rich by this trade have from my first appointment arrayed themselves in opposition to me, & have made several unsuccessful attempts to effect my removal. I should feel no anxiety on the subject at the present time, were it not that the term for which I was appointed expires in April next and my principal opponent holds a distinguished station in the Congress of the U.S. which enables him to oppose with efficiency my reappointment, & that he with his friends are making great exertions to accomplish the object which they have so long desired. The great object which that gentleman has in view is to obtain the office for one of his own family, & more especially for a person whom he can direct & control. His list of candidates contains, I have heard, the names of Jonathan P. Hall, his son in law, John D[e] Wolf & Levi D[e] Wolf his brothers, John d[e] Wolf, Jr. & John Howe his nephews, & Luke Dowry & Robert Rogers Jr who married his nieces, Hersey Bradford his wife's brother, & Byron Diman his Clerk; as the subject is managed with great secrecy there may be others of his family of whom I have not heard. I am aware that, through the agency of the gentleman above alluded to, several charges have been preferred against me to the President, but what they are I cannot learn: but if they are of a nature to impair the confidence which the government has placed in me, I earnestly solicit an investigation of my official conduct, or at least that I may know what they are that I may have an opportunity to show that they are unfounded, & also have been fabricated by those who have been detected in violating the revenue laws, or who wish the appointment for themselves or their friends. Uncommon exertions have also been made to obtain signatures to remonstrances, & considering the situation of the District it is not surprising that a great number of persons should be willing to lend their assistance. By the suppression of a lucrative traffick, a great number of persons, mariners, & mechanicks of various kinds, were deprived of their usual employments, & viewing the present Collector to be the cause of this stagnation of business, they would be easily influenced to do any thing to cause his removal. If we add to these, a number of wealthy & powerful individuals who had enriched themselves by this illicit traffick, and about ten different candidates with their friends & expectants, it may easily be accounted for why such a formidable number should be arrayed against me. However, in justice to the citizens of the District generally, I would state that at present they are quiet & satisfied, and having engaged in lawful branches of commerce are willing to have the revenue laws faithfully executed: they are likewise desirous that I should be appointed. As evidence of this about one hundred persons residing in the District have petitioned the President to reappoint me, & have stated that it would be an acceptable appointment to the citizens of the State. This petition contains the names of several respectable merchants, the High Sheriff of the County, the Clerk of the Sup. Jud. Court, a majority of the Justices of the Peace in the Town of Bristol, and a large number of the principal landholders, who of course can have no other motive in requesting it, than that the laws may be enforced.

Another petition has been forwarded from Providence in my behalf which contains the names of twenty six gentlemen of the first respectability. Among these are Nicholas Brown, Thomas P. Ives, Edward Carrington, Moses Brown[,] Wm. Church, William Jenkins, Tristam Burgess, Thomas Burgess, Philip Crapo, Benjamin F. Hoppin, Thomas C. Hoppin, Thomas Arnold, & others of equal respectability. With the character & standing of these gentlemen you are no doubt well acquainted. President [Asa] Messer & Judge [Wheeler] Martin have also written to the President of the US. Were more names necessary, I could obtain in this District more than any other person.

I am apprized, however, that I must principally rely on the assistance of my friends in Washington, or the unwearied exertions of Mr. D[e] Wolf will be successful. For this reason, Sir, I take the liberty to solicit your aid & influence which I know is great, & will have much more effect than any thing which he can possibly do. May I take the liberty to beg of you to ascertain whether the charges have made an unfavourable impression upon the President & Heads of Department, & if so to obtain a copy of them & forward it to me; likewise to advise me of any measures necessary to be adopted to secure my reappointment, & whether it would be useful for me to visit Washington this winter.

For any further particulars respecting my situation, I would respectfully refer you to the Hon. S[amuel] Eddy from this State, & the Hon. John Reed from Massachusetts.

I remain, Sir, very respectfully your obliged friend & Obt. Servt.

Barn[abas] Bates

ALS. NhD.

TO NATHAN APPLETON

Washington Jany 12 1824

Dr. Sir

I transmit you a copy of the bill proposing an augmentation of duties, recently reported by the committee on manufactures. I shall be much obliged to you for the communication of such observations as may occur to you, on the examination of this bill.

It is probable that the subject may be acted upon in about three weeks, or a month, and the importance of the subject I hope may excuse me for asking for the benefit of your opinions respecting it.

I am Sir with great regard yours   Danl. Webster

Copy. NhD. Published in Van Tyne, pp. 101–102; *W & S*, 16: 79.

FROM THOMAS HANDASYD PERKINS

Boston January 26. 1824

My dear Sir

To give you my individual opinion on the subject of the Tariff, would be to repeat what has been published over and over again in the papers of this town—there is a meeting in this town this Eve on this subject, and if they take my advice they will send a deputation to Washington, of some of their practical men. If the law as reported shall pass two years will not pass away before you are called upon, and successfully in my opinion to revise your proceedings. The uncertainty which results from such a state of things both to the Merchant and the Manufacturer is one of the worst consequences of the measure. The last two or three papers of Hale[1] have contained some interesting remarks on the subject.

In the Legislature are pending several subjects which create a considerable degree of interest. A Vote has been taken in the Senate, and in favor of which all the Suffolk Senators who were present, voted in the affirmative, for fixing the number of the Judges to four. We were governed in a considerable degree in our vote by the belief that if the expense of the Superior Court was diminished in this way, the advocates of reduction of the Salaries, might be satisfied to let the salaries remain untouched. There is one other reason which operated on my mind however, which was as to who would be nominated to fill the fifth place if such was to be filled. It seems to be understood that [Levi] Lincoln is to be nominated, but we [are] as yet not satisfied that another opening would be as well filled. King[2] of Concord, whom you have known in the house, advocated very strongly the retaining the Old number—it is *possible* he may suppose that this may make an opening for him as M.C. The Granting a Charter to Amherst College has passed the Senate, that is so far as to authorise a bill to be brought in, and will pass the house. If this had been an original proposition, it is doubtless the case that the Suff[olk] Senators would have opposed it, but under all the circumstances, and from motives of policy they voted for it. The Applicants have always considered that Harvard Coll. was sub rosa always using its influence against them. They are now concerned to the Contrary, and I hope will create a favourable interest in the question of renewing the Grant to the Colleges of Harvard & Williams, which expires in February. The reduction of Sallarys of the Govr. Judges &c is assigned for tomorrow, and in the spirit of economy which prevails, I fear may be carried. The question of a New Bridge from Charlestown to this City has been three afternoons & evenings before a joint Committee—the intention of abolishing the tolls for foot passengers, or rather exacting no toll for them will make it popular, with those who care more for half pence than principle. I doubt its success; as I do that of another application for a Bridge to So. Boston. You will see by the papers that the Resolution of the amiable [Seth] Sprague to expunge certain Resolutions of 1813 from the Records prevailed.[3]

All we could do, and indeed all we wished then to do, was to keep "*hands off*" from the Record Book and it was understood in the debate that their interpretation of *expunge* was to *preserve it*, as they declared their intention to be, to let the Record book remain inviolate. Tho' last not the least in interest, is the subject which will be shortly before us, which is the progress of the Commissioners who represent the State in the claim for remuneration for services during the war. It is generally understood here that had Mr [George] Sullivan cooperated with General [William] King, or rather had he no[t] prevented the latter from acting jointly with him—much would have been done before this; but that at present things were rather worse than better than they were, when Mr S. first presented himself at Washington. I had thought of writing to Genl. King, and requesting to state to me the facts which kept them aloof, that I might have authority to state, (what I now believe) from an authentic source. My friend [Albion Keith] Par[r]is, was joined to the Commission from his knowledge of the details of the accounts, and from the interest he feels that the negotiation should be brought to a favourable issue. I cannot but suppose he would have been in favour of considering Genl. King a joint agent for the common good. There may be time to receive a letter from Washington, before this subject is finally acted upon, and if upon your suggestion General King should think proper to write to me or any other Gentleman here, such a letter as might be shewn, and which would evince the desire he has had to act in concert with Mr S. it might be useful. I hope Par[r]is has not joined in the opposition to Genl. King as I think him very essential in auditing the accounts, and in all the details with which he is so familiar. Let me know how this is, or if Genl. King should write to me on the subject, if he can and will exhonorate Major Par[r]is from any share of the obstinacy of his Colleague I shall be glad.

If you think proper to shew Genl. King this letter you will do so. Report says that Sullivan has acted under the instructions of the Governor in endeavouring to go alone—if so he may get off under the wing of his patron.

Dr. [John Thornton] Kirkland & myself *dined** with the "young fry" on Saturday, and found the "Old fish" nothing to them. Compliments to the Ladies. Yrs. always   T H Perkins

* at P. Jacksons
ALS. DLC.
  1. The *Boston Advertiser*, edited by Nathan Hale.
  2. Not identified.

3. Seth Sprague had proposed the expunging of the resolutions disapproving the War of 1812 from the records of the Massachusetts legislature.

TO EZEKIEL WEBSTER

Washington Jan. 27. [1824]

I have omitted, for a long time, to write to you, principally because I have had nothing important to say, & partly because I have had little leisure. I shall send you my Greek Speech, in a pamphlet, in a few days. You notice the occurrence between Mr Speaker [Henry Clay] & Mr [Ichabod] Bartlett.[1] I am inclined to think Mr. B. will find it necessary to do something, in consequence of what happened, by way of obtaining a pacific explanation. He will, as you see, get *no explanation,* in the House: & yet, it wd. seem he is bound to obtain explanation. I presume some friends will undertake to set matters right. I can hear nothing of *Lewis.*[2] One of the Alabama members, Col [John] McKee, lives at the very spot you mention—the falls in the Black Warrior— & says there is no such man there —possibly Lewis has changed his name.

I have conversed abt. the mail contracts. There is the best disposition at the Department, to do what is right, but the question is, *how?* The contracts are not out till *next year*— & if a law were to pass, excluding Printers, still, Printers' friends would bid. *Some one else must offer lower* —there is no other remedy.

I have asked Mr [Stephen] Longfellow, as you wished. He did not recommend Mr Kelly.[3]

The Presidential question is still in the clouds. We know no more here than you do, & such as you & I have nothing to do but keep quiet.

I think your course is right, about your next Govr. Take care to open the door— & let the People say who shall go in. For certain reasons, I should [wish] Mr [Arthur] Livermore might be chosen. For certain others, I should not regret Mr. [William] Morrill's election. Let us know how things are going on.

Of all yr Reps I have seen most of Mr [William] Plumer—& am, thus far, quite well pleased with him. Yrs always   D.W.

Feb. 10. I wrote this a fortnight ago & mislaid it. There is nothing new since. I *will* write you in a day or two.

ALS. NhD. Published in part in *PC*, 1: 344–345.
　1. For the misunderstanding between Ichabod Bartlett and Henry Clay involving Webster's Greek resolution, see *The Papers of Henry Clay,* ed. James F. Hopkins and Mary W. M. Hargreaves (Lexington, Ky., 1963), 3: 612–614, 616–618.
　2. Not identified.
　3. Not identified.

FROM JEREMIAH MASON

Portsmouth Feby 1st. 1824

My dear Sir

I cordially congratulate you on your defense of your resolution in favour of the Greeks. The universal praise is no louder than is deserved. In my opinion, your first speech is the best sample of Parliamentary eloquence & statesmanlike reasoning, that our Country can show. You were eminently judicious in avoiding all declamation on the antient glories of Greece, to which the subject so obviously led. Except Genl. [Alexander] Smyths speech,[1] which has not yet come to hand, I read this whole debate, which I have not, for a long time, done with any other Congress debate of equal length. The attempt to give a meaning to your resolution, which does not belong to it, was certainly unfair, & the final disposition of it evasive & mean. I suppose this may be attributed, in some degree, to the cause suggested by Mr. [Henry] Clay. I have no doubt that reason operated with our Mr. [Ichabod] Bartlet[t], & I am glad to see him so well castigated for it. I hope it will do him good.

On the whole you personally have nothing to regret on this subject. You have acquired all the credit the subject & occasion were capable of giving, without any responsibility for the final success of the proposed measure. And indeed the impression on the public mind will be quite as strong, as would have been made by passing the resolution by a lean majority.

I see the N York Legislature is for a caucus, & consequently, I suppose, for [William H.] Crawford. What is to be the result? Will there be a Congressional caucus? And if so will it be composed exclusively of self-styled republicans?

The proposed tariff begins to invite attention in this quarter. Our Salmon Falls woolen manufacturers would like the increased duty on imported woolen cloths, & some think this necessary. But they are alarmed by the extravagant measure proposed on wool & indigo. This seems to me a strange way of encouraging manufactures. The cost of the wool is more than one third the price of the cloth. The duty on this article in 1827 is to be 50 pr. Cent. It is idle to expect that enough will be produced in the

Country for its consumption by that time. No rate of duty would effect it. The quantity of wool now produced in the Country bears a small proportion to what is wanted. The change in agricultural production must be slow & gradual. To our common farmers a sudden change is impracticable, without ruin. I expected no good from the tariff mongers. I suppose this bill is the result of some bargain between different interests, & that the owners of a few merino flocks are let in for a share.

I lately returned from the first Court in the new County of Merrimac. There was the greatest congregation of lawyers I ever saw in this State. Your brother was in high spirits, though somewhat perplexed in making a selection among the numerous cattle proposed for the office of Governour.

With my & Mrs. Masons kindest regards to Mrs. Webster I am as ever Truly yours,   J Mason

ALS. DLC.
1. Delivered on January 26. A congressman from Virginia, Smyth

(1765–1830) was a lawyer, state legislator, and 1812 war veteran.

TO [EDWARD EVERETT]

Washington Feb. 13. [1824]
Mr. [Alexander] Bliss can furnish you the Report of the Comm[issione]rs under the Louisiana Treaty. There is a copy, in my Drawers, in the Office. I am glad you are about to try your hand at a Memorial on the subject of French Spoliations. It is a good subject.

I have sent you sundry Speeches; if you think it worth while, you may send one to any friend on the other side the Atlantic. There is no export duty; it is *casus omissus* in the new Tariff. On this same Tariff we are now occupied. It is a tedious disagreeable subject. The House, or a majority of it—are apparently *insane*—at least I think so. Whether any thing can be done to moderate the disease, I know not. I have very little hope. I am aware that something is expected <for> [from] me, much more than I shall perform. It would be easy to make a *Speech*,—but I am anxious to do something better,—if I can;—but I see not what I can do.

The Caucus is tomorrow. I intend to learn what transpires in it, & write a line to Mr [Nathan] Hale, after it is over in the Evening. Thine—
D.W.

ALS. MHi. Published in PC, 1: 345.

The case of Gibbons v. Ogden (9 *Wheaton* 1), *or the Steam Boat case, as it is commonly known, greatly extended the power of the federal government over internal commerce. The issue revolved around the right of a*

New York steamship line to exclusive control over navigation in New York waters. Webster, appearing with William Wirt for the plaintiff, Thomas Gibbons, played a decisive role in the case. The Supreme Court eventually decided the case in 1824 in favor of Gibbons, who thereafter was permitted to operate a rival line.

TO JOSEPH HOPKINSON
                                            Washington Feb. 14. [1824]
My Dear Sir,

The Steam Boat cause is not yet decided. I suppose we shall hear from the Court in four or five days. There is *no doubt* but the decision will be *against* the New York monopoly;—at least so far as respects Vessels going from other States to New York—which is the present case. Be assured the result is certain.

I shall "do the needful," as the Merchants say, in regard to the cases to be mentioned to the Commrs, in Mr [Daniel] Smith's claim. Yrs
                                            D. Webster

ALS. PHi.

TO JEREMIAH MASON
                                            Washington Feb. 15. 1824
My Dear Sir

The Caucus was holden last night, & you will see its result. The number attending was smaller than was expected; & it seems to me the measure is more likely to *hurt* than to *help* Mr. [William H.] Crawford. You will observe that a majority of *three States* only attended. This is an awful intimation of what will be the consequence, if the Election should come into the H of R., and I fully believe it must come there. It does, on the whole, now seem to me extremely probable that Mr Crawford's prospects are at an end. Even, with New York, he can have little hope. The Penna. Convention will meet the 4th March, & I presume will nominate either [Andrew] Jackson or [John C.] Calhoun, & probably the *former*. If so Mr. Calhoun will be no longer a candidate. Then the question is, who will be the *three* Candidates presented to the House. Mr. [John Quincy] Adams certainly will be one. If Mr. Crawford gets N. York, he will be one; but if he should not, & I doubt whether he will, he will not come into nomination; in which case the other two will be [Henry] Clay & Jackson. Mr. Crawford being out of the case, Virginia, it is thought by Mr. [Littleton Waller] Tazewell would be not unlikely to go for Mr. *Adams*, & she might influence Maryland & N. Carolina—so that the present aspect of affairs looks to me favorable to that Gentleman. But the Moon does not change so often as the prospects of these Candidates. One thing is observable;

they are all, just now, very civil towards *Federalists*. We see & hear no abuse of us, except in some places in N. England. I hope all our friends will see the propriety of keeping very quiet at present. Our time for action has not come, but is approaching. I hope your Election of Governor will not be made to mingle Presidential matter with it. I presume the old Democratic regular party—or its accustomed leader, in N. H. will now feel authorised & obliged to support Crawford. Others of the party will not —there will of course be a schism— & it will be time enough six months hence to decide what course of conduct the case requires from Federalists.

The Election in Mass is important, in the same view. I think it not unlikely it may result in a Federal Legislature—which, if done without bringing up the question of President, may be of some importance.

The Court is going on very well; the business this term is likely not to be as heavy as usual. We have no opinion, yet, in the Steam Boat cause; but I presume there can be no doubt how it will go. The case of *collision*, is, I think, unquestionably made out; & I have no doubt the Court will decide, that so far as respects commerce between different states, (which is this case) the law of N. York is inoperative. Possibly the navigation of the N York waters between port & port, in her own territory, may be subject to a different consideration.

I have as yet reported no bill on the Judiciary, but incline to think we shall recommend a *partial* system of Circuit Judges. If we had more confidence, as to the course the appointing power would take, we might act differently. I find your Mr. [William] Plumer, [Jr.,] also who is on the Com[mitt]ee with me, a very pleasant & respectable man. I see more of him than of all the rest of your delegation.

Of the compliments my Greek Speech has recd. I value your letter more than all;[1] for altho. you say of course, as much as you think, I presume your real opinion is so favorable as that you believe the Speech respectable. I am quite satisfied with that. The Motion ought to have been adopted, & would have been, by a general vote, but for certain' reasons, which the Public will never know, & which I will not trouble you with now. I could divide the House, very evenly on the subject, now— &, perhaps carry a vote. Whether I shall stir it again, must be considered. Mr. *Adams'* opposition to it was the most formidable obstacle. You saw how Messrs Clay & [Ichabod] Bartlett settled their matter; or rather how some body else settled it for them. I presume you are right, as to the motive which led B. to speak a conned speech agt. my motion. That was all fair enough; at least I could not complain. But when he brought into debate his broad Dover-Court wit, I thought it better to settle the account on the spot.

A similar motive, I fancy, influenced a few other *creatures* from N. England;—but I am bound to say, that out of N England I do not think it influenced more than two or three members.

Mrs. Webster and our children here are quite well. We all send our love to Mrs. Mason & the family; among whom we hear you have the pleasure to recon Julia Stockton.[2] Her brother left here for home three days ago. He is to come back, in a fortnight or three weeks.

Yrs Always   D Webster

Copy. NhHi. Published in *W & S*, 16: 80–81.

1. See Jeremiah Mason to DW, De-cember 29, 1823, above.

2. Julia Stockton was probably then a house guest of the Masons.

TO JOSEPH HOPKINSON

March 17. '2[4]

Dr Sir

I recd in due time your kind letters,[1] transmitting the Clerks Certificate, as to the Donaldson Ex[e]c[uti]on. They answered the purpose; & the good Judge's claim has been allowed.[2]

I send you my Greek Speech, as I promised. Greece being laid out of the case, I hope the general doctrines are right. I took some pains with it —more than I am likely to do with another.

The Senate adjourned today, & I wait only a day or two for the Court, when I shall set forth, for the North.

I confess, My Dr Sir, I do not see any promise of good from my remaining in my present situation; & I go home in great doubts, whether I shall return;—tho' I say nothing of this to the many. I believe we are to have a day of small things, & of bitter things; more small, & more bitter, by much, than the state of things which was introduced in 1801. I rejoice that *you* are out of it; & in an honorable & useful situation for life. And I rejoice, that by good fortune & good advice, *I* have been led to follow such a course, that no change can make me a loser. I have never yet answered, nor sought to answer, one selfish end by the means of my public situation;— & tho' I have done little good, that little has been, at least, *disinterested*. I shall see you, as I go along, and we must have some hours talk, the world shut out; but I cannot stay long with you. My boy Edward,[3] (yr friend) wants the company of his play-fellow, & urges me to come home. Always, most sincerely, Yrs   D. Webster

ALS. PHi.

1. Not found.

2. Probably the claim of John J. Donaldson, Philadelphia merchant, before the Spanish Claims Commission.

3. Edward (1820–1848; Dartmouth 1841), worked with the Maine Survey team, and later served with the Massachusetts Volunteers in the Mexican War. On January 23, 1848, he died at San Angel, Mexico.

TO [JOSEPH] STORY

Washington, April 10, 1824.

My dear Sir,

I am happy to hear, through Mr. [James William] Paige, that you were at home so seasonably and so safe; and I hope to learn soon from yourself, that you had the pleasure of finding Mrs. Story and the children well. I have not had an earlier opportunity of writing to you, although I wished to call your attention to two or three things, in regard to which you promised me the benefit of your opinions. We have had a busy time of it since you left us. For myself, I am exhausted. When I look in the glass, I think of our old New England saying, "As thin as a shad." I have not vigor enough left, either mental or physical, to try an action for assault and battery. However, the fine weather has come on, I have resumed the saddle, and hope to "pick up my crumbs" again soon. You see the condition of the tariff. The great struggle has been on the iron; and our majority yesterday was unexpectedly great. The speeches on the side of the bill have been very impressive and captivating on the general question; on the ability of protecting domestic industry, raising prices of agricultural products by manufactures, working up our own materials, &c. Accompanying sentiments of this sort, we have had much from the Philadelphia school, of the adverse balance of trade, exportation of specie, loss of foreign markets, &c. But I think some impression has been made against arguments of this class. For myself, I have really wished some proper and reasonable bill to pass, that the business might be settled. I would not oppose the bill, I think, if hemp should be struck out, and some other minor amendments made. The molasses, I presume, will come out. The minimum ought to be struck out of the woollens. And if possible, there should be a change in a variety of provisions about hardware. It is a great object to settle the concerns of the community; so that one may know what to depend on. I am apprehensive, however, that our vote yesterday has made the bill so unacceptable to its friends, that it is very probable they may abandon it.

I shall call up some bills reported by our committee, as soon as possible. The gentlemen of the West will propose a clause, requiring the assent of a majority of all the judges to a judgment, which pronounces a state law void, as being in violation of the constitution or laws of the United States. Do you see any great evil in such a provision? Judge [Thomas] Todd told me he thought it would give great satisfaction in the West. In what phraseology would you make such a provision?

As to the bankrupt law, pray give me your ideas of an outline, as I must bring forward some resolutions on that subject before the end of the session. I know how much you are employed, but still I must have one half hour.

Mrs. Webster desires her best regards to Mrs. Story and yourself. I will also beg to be remembered to Mrs. Story. I hope you will allow me to hear from you soon. With constant regard, yours,   D. Webster.

P.S. *Sunday Morning.*—I hardly know what our votes of yesterday indicate, as to the final decision on the tariff. My impression rather is, that the bill will hardly get through our House. It certainly would not, if there were not so many members who vote on the judgment of their constituents, not on their own.

Text from *PC,* 1: 348–349. Original not found.

TO JEREMIAH MASON

April 19. 1824

Dear Sir

I hear nothing further about the resignation.[1] The members here now think it has not taken place. I hope it has not. Possibly the events of the Summer may enable you to get up a respectable interest for Mr. [Nathaniel A.] Haven.

The Senate will probably take up the Tariff Bill tomorrow, & an attempt will be made to commit it to a Select Comm[itt]ee. It is generally thought the Senate will a good deal modify, or altogether reject, the measure. But this is not very certain, as the Majority is not large, either way. We have heard a great deal of *nonsense,* on this subject, & some of it from high quarters. I think, you will be surprised at Mr. [Henry] Clays Speech. It is printed, & I shall send you a Copy. My speech will be printed, & you will get it.[2] Whatever I have done, in other cases, I must say, that in this, I have published it *against* my own judgment. I was not expecting to speak, at that time, nor ready so to do. And from Mr. Clays ending, I had but one night to prepare.

The ideas are right enough, I hope, but as a *speech* it is clumsy, wanting in method, & tedious.

We have rather a calm about the Presidential Election. There is nothing, in my opinion, at present, to change the expectation that Messrs Adams, Crawford, & Jackson, will come to the House.

In two or three days I believe we shall try to fix a day for adjournment. I hope very much to get home before you go to Concord, & to see you. I will keep you informed of the events, bearing on this point, & if I get home you must come up to Boston.

Among other things I hope you mean to district the state for the choice of members to Congress.

My great business of the Session remains yet undone; that is, to get thro the law for paying the Spanish claims. We apprehend some trouble about it, from quarters where we did not expect it. Mr. [Rufus] *King* thinks we ought to take stock, payable, both as to *principal & interest,* out of the Florida land sales; I hope he will withdraw his opposition to the proposed Bill (which provides for payt. in cash) or that we shall be able to overcome it.

Mrs. W. and the children are very well. We all begin to be very desirous of going home.

Please remember us most affectionately to your family.

Yours very truly   D. Webster

Copy. NhHi. Published in *W & S,* 16: 84.

1. The rumor that John Sherburne, had resigned as New Hampshire attorney general had been circulating for some time. (On the rumor, see

Jeremiah Mason to DW, April 12, 1824, mDW 4100).

2. For DW's speech on the tariff question, see *Annals of Congress,* 18th Cong., 1st sess., 1823–1824, pp. 2026–2068.

TO JEREMIAH MASON

Washington May 9. 1824

My Dear Sir

It seems now to be extremely uncertain whether I shall see you before you go to Concord. The Houses will probably not agree to adjourn until the 20th or 25th; & I may be detained beyond that time, as the Commi[ssi]on of Spanish Claims closes the 8th of June.

There are several things, on which to say a few words; which I must *write,* since there is so little hope of a Communication *ore tenus.*

First as to *President*

I have not observed any great recent change, in appearance, as to this Election. Mr Adams appears, however, to be *increasing* in strength.

The novelty of Genl Jackson is wearing off & the contest seems to be coming back to the old question between Mr. Adams & Mr. Crawford. They, with Jackson, will I think, come into the House,— & my belief, at present, is that Mr. Adams will be chosen. But Mr Crawford's friends are, nevertheless, as confident as ever.

As to the feelings of these two Gentlemen, & their friends, towards *Federalists,* you know my opinion. It has not essentially changed except that circumstances have compelled them all to treat us with increasing respect. The events of the winter, with the common operation of time, have very much mixed up Federalists with some or other of the parties; and tho' it is true that some men make great efforts to keep up old distinctions, they find it difficult. Of Mr. Crawford's friends, the *South* are liberal, & the *North* are not. I have reason to think the Caucus address very disagreeable to Mr. C himself, & many of his friends. It was the work of the North.

Mr. Adams, I think, sees also that *exclusion* will be a very doubtful policy. And in truth I think a *little* better of the kindness of his feeling towards us, than I have done.

I have always taken it for granted that Mr Adams wd. get N. Hampshire, certainly, as agt. Mr Crawford, if for no other reason, on account of Mr. Crawford's supporters, there. At least I have not seen how *Federalists* could possibly join with those who support Mr C. The company he keeps, at the North, is my strongest objection to him.

I hope you will get thro. the Session without committing yourselves. The Electors, I presume will be chosen by the People; & you will see perhaps clearer in August or September than in June. Still I fancy you will find a very great majority of the Legislature favorable to Mr. Adams.

As to Senator, I feel much more interest on the subject than the other. I have constantly cherished a sort of hope that you would consent to come here once more, & that events might possibly bring you in. How that is, I cannot now see, at this distance; but if the good people are willing you should come, I hope most earnestly you will. I like Mr. [John F.] Parrotts <concern> course, & conduct very well, & should much prefer him to any others, likely to be chosen, unless it be yourself. He could, undoubtedly, be provided for, under the next administration, in some agreeable mode, as he is generally respected. If, however, it comes at last to a question, between him, on one side, & Gov. [Levi] Woodbury, or Gover. [David Lawrence] Morrill, &c. &c. on the other, I think there ought not to be a moment's hesitation.

I trust you will not forget the Districting of the state. That is a great operation, as far as it is desirable to complete the destruction of the Caucus system.

We do not hear yet from Mr. [Ninian] Edwards. Some think he will not come back, in season for this Session. I imagine we shall wait till about the 24th. & if he is not here by that time, that Congress will adjourn, leaving the Com[mitt]ee to take his evidence, when he comes. There will be a great call for a Report, as far as practicable, before the House adjourns, which perhaps must be made.

Our Bill for paying the Spanish awards which I told you was, with me, the great business of the Session, has passed the House. It was violently opposed, however, by Mr Clay, Mr. [John] Randolph & others. Strange as you may think it, Mr. [Rufus] King has a great inclination to oppose it in the Senate. I trust however he will finally not do so. It will pass, I hope, without great difficulty.[1] If it should, the awards I presume will be paid immediately after the 8th. of June.

Mrs. Webster sends her love to your Household, we are all quite homesick. Yours always   D Webster

Copy. NhHi. Published in *W & S*, 16: 85–86.

1. For the act of Congress authorizing the Secretary of the Treasury to create a stock not exceeding $5,000,000 "to provide for the awards of the commissioners under the treaty with Spain," see 4 *U.S. Stat. at Large*, 33–34.

FROM THOMAS HANDASYD PERKINS

Boston May 12th. 1824

My dear Sir

I am quite in a stew about the Tariff Bill—if the time of its taking effect is not put off so far as to put all vessells engaged in similar voyages from distant Countries on the same footing, when they could not have heard of any change being contemplated in the duties, it will be most oppressively injurious. The Philadelphia & N. York ships are all or mostly in—and these folks pay 18 per Ct. duty—those arriving after 30th. June 30 per Ct. Silk goods at this time are not worth the cost, and the *present duty,* with the charges of importation—if 12 per Ct. are added it will give us a *loss on a ship we expect in August of $40,000 extra duty on her silks. She sailed with the vessells or about the time with the vessells already arrived.* Three or 4 ships have arrived at Philadelphia within a few days, which gives them an advantage over those which will arrive two months hence of what may be considered a decent profit on a voyage. The reason why the vessells in question are not already here is, that they *carried produce and stopped at Batavia, Manilla &c.* and *those* which have arrived carried *Spices* & made direct passages.

If the Bill get within your reach, I flatter myself your exertions will be made to get the alteration made.

I see the bill for raising the means of paying the awards has gone a step forward in the House & I presume will be go[t] thro' the Senate. I am told you intend to come here and return again, to be in at the death of the Commission.

We choose our Representatives to day, who I suppose will be Democratic, as that seems to be the favorite rule now adays.

Yr. friend & Serv.   T H Perkins

ALS. DLC.

FROM GRACE FLETCHER WEBSTER

Sunday evening [June 6, 1824]

My dear Husband,

We have been to Point Breeze to pay our respects to the Count [Joseph Bonaparte][1]—we found them standing in the door all ready for a little excursion on the water. They very politely urged us to accompany them & stay to supper—but we had taken the children with Mrs [Joseph] H[opkinson]'s woman and Jenette[2] and they were walking in the grounds and I feared Julia might be unhappy to see me launched off again in a boat. I therefore told Mrs Hopkinson if it would be equally agreeable to her we would accompany the party to the barge and then return which we did— after walking a long way we came to the same covered way which you doubtless remember. There are many relicts of broken statuary of the finest marble hudled to gether in the remaining part of one of the wings of the former Palace. It looks more like things we read of, than anything I ever saw before. You will see I soon forgot that I promised never to write excepting just to say we are well—because you do not take the trouble to read your letters—but this I expect you to read every word, that is if you can—as it is to be conveyed to Philadelphia by hands that once swayed a Sceptre.

Mrs. H. desires to be especially remembered to you. Goodnight and pleasant dreams to you my dear Love. Yr   G.W

PS The Count goes to P[hiladelphi]a at four in the morning and offered to take any communication for Mrs H. so these letters are to be put in an Envelope to Mr H.

ALS. NhHi. Published in part in Van Tyne, p. 549.

1. Joseph Bonaparte, Comte de Survilliers. For brief remarks on the Websters' friendship with Bonaparte, see Georges Bertin, *Joseph Bonaparte en Amerique* (Paris, 1893), pp. 171– 172; and Charlemagne Tower, "Joseph Bonaparte in Philadelphia and Bordentown," *Pennsylvania Magazine of History and Biography*, 42 (1918): 308.

2. Not identified.

TO SAMUEL JAUDON

Boston July 4. 1824

My Dear Jaudon,

I should have written you yesterday, according to my promise, thro Mr [Alexander] Bliss, but was not able. From the time I entered my office at 8 oclock till the mail closed at one, I was occupied by friends or *claimants*. This latter class I find in very good humor, & well satisfied. The parties in interest have taken up the *Mercury*, & will, I trust, be able to say how I shall pay the money, by the time I receive it.

I send you proof that Mary L. Pickard is Adm[inistratri]x of Mark Pickard;—her power of Atty to Charles Barnard, & his to you. These will enable you to get that award.

I took a minute to shew whether Ritchie, as Adm[inistrato]r of Scobie, was interested in this award, made in the Jane, Knight, to Mark Pickard, surviving partner—but my minute is imperfect— & does not enable me to say. I will thank you to look to the papers, and inform me, particularly, how it is.[1]

I do not think I shall send you any further powers—unless one should fall in tomorrow or next day. I suppose you may be proposing to leave Washington, & I would not detain you. You will have recd. several. I will thank you when you leave, to forward me an exact list of the unpaid awards.

You make me smile here, while alone, at the civil things you report from the conversations of Washington, respecting myself. There is no danger of their turning my head. When I go to England, you shall go too.

Mrs Webster desires her especial regards to you & Mrs. J. Julia & Ned still insist on having that baby bought. I write this at Dorchester, where I found all the household assembled on Thursday Evening. We are all well; & our place here looks pleasant & agreeable. I met here also my Brother from N. Hamp. Yrs always   D. Webster

ALS. NHi.
   1. All of the above were claimants

whom DW had represented before the Spanish Claims Commission.

FROM JOEL ROBERTS POINSETT

Charleston 14th July 1824
My dear sir

I am waiting with some impatience for the list of books you led me to expect *Judge [Joseph] Story* would furnish me with. I relied entirely upon him for the law books and if I do not receive his list shortly the judges and law members will be disappointed. If you receive it be so good as to forward it to me here. I shall not proceed to England this summer as I had promised myself and as my health required. There exists here a state of things I could not have anticipated, an union of Mr. [John Quincy] Adams's and Mr. [William H.] Crawford's friends, which will render the opposition to me very formidable, for I can not unite with the latter. I am unwilling to add to the difficulties my friends will have to encounter by absenting myself from the Country. But for this unseasonable and somewhat unnatural alliance by which Mr. Adams's friends must be sacrificed I might have succeeded, as I have all along been anxious to do, to unite the South and the East—the only natural alliance for both divisions of the Country.

With great regard and esteem Yours very truly   J. R. Poinsett

Do you really intend to introduce the Bankrupt bill at the next session?

ALS. ScU.

TO WILLIAM GASTON

Boston Sept. 8. 1824.

My Dear Sir

More difficult problems were never presented, than those contained in your letter, (which I suppose you have forgotten) of April last.[1] They were difficult then, & after waiting four or five months, I do not see that time has done much towards their solution. It seems to me vain to conjecture, even now, what will be the result of the election. I have an impression that Mr Adams' chance is best;—but others, close about me, think differently. All New England may be put to his credit—so, I suppose, may New Jersey, & the greater part of Maryland—as to the rest, I have no means of knowing in what States his friends may confidently expect votes for him. From the beginning I have supposed the election would come to the H. of R. & still continue of that opinion. If Pennsylvania adheres to General Jackson, & S. Carolina also, Mr Crawford, Mr Adams, & Genl. Jackson will come into the House, I should conjecture, in the order in which I have named them.

If S. Carolina should go for Mr Adams, it might put him possibly at the head of the list, & bring in Mr Clay instead of Genl. Jackson. How the election would terminate, in either of these cases, I cannot, with any certainty, foresee. My opinion, however, such as it is, I have already intimated. We are putting to the proof the most delicate part of our system, the election of the Executive. In the absence of such persons as are very prominent, & highly distinguished, for character & service, the choice falls necessarily among a greater number, & among those also whose merits may not be supposed to be very unequal. In such case, local considerations, personal considerations, & a hundred other *small* considerations will have their influence. The result, I fear, will be a general failure in the election, by the Electors, in time to come. And the consequence of this will be, as is obvious, a diminution of the weight & authority of the Executive Magistrate, & a continued devolution of more & more of the authority properly belonging to that department on Congress. When we have strong parties again, we shall have a chance for Presidents, who shall be elected thro' their own favor & popularity;—so we may also, if war or troublous times should bring forth great talents, united with great services. Otherwise I am fearful the President's Office may get to be thought too much in the gift of Congress.

In this part of the Country, there is no great warmth about the approaching election. Mr Adams' friends seem to be most numerous; but the other Candidates are neither feared nor greatly disliked, except by the public writers.

Our portion of the Country is at this time exceedingly prosperous, upon the whole; & having had a little excitement from the visit of the good Lafayette, we are going on again in our every day pursuits. Our Congressional elections take place in Nov. No nominations have yet been made. Most of our present members will probably be reelected. It is *possible* that our friend Mr [Jeremiah] Mason may be chosen Senator again, from N. Hampshire—but this is only possible. The times, tho' tolerably good, are not quite good enough I fear for that.

I see Roger Vose now & then. He is as formerly, except that silver locks render his venerable appearance more venerable. He can laugh yet— & cause others to partake in the same exercise.

Poor [John] Lovat [Lovett], you know, has been deceased some years. I had a short visit last year from Mr. Morris S. Millar [Miller]. He is what they call in N. York a *Bucktail*. He & Mr [Zebulon R.] Shepherd [Shipherd] think that opposition to the war was carried too far!

We have, My Dear Sir, a great many good people in New England, who would be glad to see your face. Some of us think you bear a resemblance to the better class of Yankees. If you regard this as a reproach, come and disprove it. Yours always affectionately   Danl. Webster

LS. NcU. Published in Van Tyne, pp. 107–109; *W & S*, 16: 89–90.

1. See William Gaston to DW, April 11, 1824, mDW 4094.

FROM WILLIAM GASTON

Newbern October 10th. 1824

My dear Sir

I had the pleasure to receive your late letter, which revived many agreeable recollections of common pursuits and common enjoyments.[1] The period seems to be fast advancing on me in which we take more delight in remembering the past than in attending to the present. You are not quite as far advanced as I am in the journey of life, yet sufficiently forward to be disposed now and then to look behind and think with regret on pleasures past never to return. I fancy that I shall never laugh again as I have done with [John] Lovett and [Roger] Vose—and never unbend with such social ease as I was wont to do with [Jeremiah] Mason and [Robert H.] Goldsborough and [John Whitefield] Hulbert[2] and yourself over a glass of hot toddy in a cold winter's night at Crawford's [Hotel]. If we had not much wit we had, what Dr. Primrose declares to be much better, much and hearty mirth.

On the subject of the Presidential Question I have but a word to say, which perhaps may be acceptable as a matter of intelligence. There are two tickets voted for in this State—the Caucus or [William H.] Crawford ticket, and the Anti-Caucus or People's Ticket. I hold it to be morally certain that the last will succeed. It is not a pledged ticket, but will probably vote for Jackson. The electoral vote of North Carolina may be pretty confidently set down to him. The Anti-Caucus Ticket is generally (not universally) upheld by the Federalists in this State. They deem this a fit occasion on which to break down the practise of a Congressional Caucus —and they feel themselves insulted by the language used towards them in the Manifesto of Messrs. [Benjamin] Ruggles [Martin] Van Buren & Co.[3]

In some of the States, and I believe in Massachusetts, there is a General Rule of Court requiring that applicants for admission to the Bar should be natural-born or naturalized citizens of the U. States. An interesting case has lately occurred in which the Judges of our Supreme Court have applied the same rule.[4] The case has been brought under my notice, and at the next term of our Court will probably be again brought before the Judges. I believe that under the Statutes of No. Ca. the Courts are bound to admit all applicants who have competent law knowledge and fair characters. In examining the subject however I am led to enquire into the origin of these General Rules existing in other States. Will you have the goodness to let me know what Statutory provisions exist in Massachusetts under which your Judges admit attor[neys] and consellors to practice?

I have more than once since I saw you planned a visit to New England, and had nearly this summer carried the plan into operation. I went as far as Philadelphia and proposed such a trip to my eldest daughter then quitting school at that place. But she was so anxious to rejoin her sisters whom she had not seen for a long time that I was induced to return Southwardly. Next summer I hope to see Boston.

Present me most kindly and respectfully to all enquiring friends, and believe me Very affectionately your's   Wm. Gaston

ALS. NhHi. Published in *W & S*, 16: 90–91.

1. See letter of September 8, above.

2. Hulbert (1770–1831), lawyer and Massachusetts congressman.

3. A reference to the decision of the congressional caucus, chaired by Ruggles of Ohio and engineered by Van Buren.

4. *Ex Parte Thompson,* 3 Hawke 355–357.

FROM NOAH WEBSTER

Cambridge. Eng. Oct. 16. 1824

Dear Sir,

I take the liberty to inclose to your care, & commend to your friendly attention & aid, a petition[1] which to me is interesting, & I should hope, not wholly uninteresting to my fellow citizens. You will readily perceive the necessity of my coming to England to excute the work in hand, in the first instance, as no printer in America would probably hazard the expense of types, for such an expensive work, until the value & probable sales could be better known than by conjecture. I should hope that no objection at all can be raised against my request. The term of five years will be short enough to enable me or my heirs, to ascertain public opinion, & if favorable, to procure the necessary apparatus to print the work in the United States. The work will probably consist of two Quartoes, or of one Quarto, (the Synopsis) & two large Octavos.[2]

I will thank you to take charge of the petition, & attend to it through its several stages, & if possible procure an act for the exemption requested. I will thank you also to make my request to Gentlemen of my acquaintance in both houses, that they would lend their aid in obtaining a favorable result.

I shall probably remain here till next summer, as I have some months labor yet to bestow on the Work.

Accept the respects of Sir Your Obedt Servt   Noah Webster

ALS. DLC.

1. The petition, dated October 16, 1824, is endorsed in Daniel Webster's hand "Petition of Noah Webster; praying that copies of his 'Dictionary of the English Language,' & of his 'Synopsis of Languages' may be imported into the United States, free of duty, for 5 years." It was introduced by DW on December 27, 1824, and referred to the Committee of Ways and Means. A bill was reported January 10, 1825, and became law on March 3, 1825.

2. Noah Webster was engaged in lexicographical study in England, and the work to which he referred, *An American Dictionary of the English Language,* was finished in 1825 but not published until 1828.

TO EZEKIEL WEBSTER

Saturday Morning Oct. [23?] 1824

Dear E.

The matters of business I wrote you about in my last,[1] have all been attended to, on my part. From what I learn, there is some ground of hope that something may be made out of that concern, if we look well after it. I trust you will omit *nothing*, on your part.

As to politics, we are all in a ferment; as you will see. By the way— Govr. [David L.] Morrill has been in Town— & I have heard of his saying that he should favor the election of Genl. [James] Miller[2] & *yourself.* That he should give his support to the gallant General is easy enough to be believed—but how he should happen to think so well of you as to say, voluntarily, that he should support your election, can be accounted for only on the principle of the near approach, or actual arrival—of the "era of good feelings."

But to advert to matters that come nearer home—Mrs W. wants half a dozen blls of your *best potatoes*, sent down by the Boat. The flour has arrived—&c. Yrs in haste   D. Webster

ALS. NhD. Published in *PC*, 1: 346–347.

1. Not found.

2. Miller (1776–1851), Greenfield lawyer, veteran of the War of 1812, former governor of Arkansas Terri-tory. Both Miller and Ezekiel Webster were talked of as candidates for Congress. The former was elected, but decided to accept instead the post of customs collector at Salem, Massachusetts.

FROM GRACE FLETCHER WEBSTER

Dec 4th. [1824]
Sat. morning

My dear Husband,

I have not written to you for several days—indeed, I am surprised to find how many, I believe not a line since monday. I have been a good deal occupied, but still not sufficiently so as to have prevented me from writing a line. [James] William [Paige] told me he would write you yesterday. I supposed he told you dear little Charles [Webster][1] is sick of a lung fever—he is better this morning the Dr thinks and I hope he will soon get over it. He has had a very heavy cold for rather more than a week—but I thot he would get along as he has done frequently before. Wednesday I gave him an Emetic, which appeared to relieve him. He was playful Thursday, which was our Thanksgiving, and never talked more than he did till he went to sleep—in the Evening—and he had not been in bed I believe more than ten minutes before he was taken in very great distress—every breath was with a groan. I sent immediately for Dr. [John C.] W[arren]—he gave him Emetics and other medicine which relieved him in some measure. Yesterday he was bled by leaches which I tho't a great relief. I hope you will not be too anxious. I think he is doing very well to day—and trust he will soon be quite well again. Julia and Edward are all but sick—poor Eddy has been fasting since Wednesday. The poor fellow calculated as much on a plum-pudding Thanksgivin[g]day as if he had never heard of one but instead of puddings and pies, he and Charley had to stay in the nursery and eat water gruel. Julia's greatest trouble is that she can not go to school. She is looking on to see me write and says ask Papa what he makes such a X for on his letters and wishes me likewise to remember that she sends love and kisses, how many hundreds of times have I written to you love and kisses. I think you must be tired of both.

Charley asked me this morning—["]Where is Papa I [miss] him, why dont he come home[,"] said [he]. To confess the truth this has been a very long fortnight since you left. It seems as [if] you had been gone long enough to return.

I received a letter from you yesterday from Philadelphia[2]—which amused Mrs [George] B[lake] very much. She said a part of that was me[a]nt for herself. My head feels so much confused I hardly know what I write. I hope you will excuse all that is as it should not be. [Ever?] and from Your afft[ectiona]te.   G.W.

ALS. NhHi. Published in part in Van Tyne, pp. 549–550.

    1. Born on December 31, 1821,

Charles died in Boston on December 19, 1824.

    2. Not found.

Webster returned to Washington alone in December 1824, having left his family in Boston. Soon after taking his lodgings, he and Mr. and Mrs. George Ticknor headed into Virginia to visit former presidents Jefferson and Madison. For five days they were guests at Monticello, and on the evening following their departure, Webster dictated to Mrs. Ticknor the following account of their conversation. While at Jefferson's home, Webster learned of the illness of his son Charles, then almost three years old, but not until after his return to Washington did he get the news of the boy's death on December 19.

TO JOSEPH GALES & WILLIAM WINSTON SEATON

Capitol Hill Decr. 9. [1824]
Thursday Morning

Private
Messrs G. & S.

I am going into Virginia, for a few days. Leave of absence will be asked for me this morning. These are times when the most common & natural occurrences are often *conjectured* to be connected with some unavowed object. If any *wise acre* should intimate that my absence is connected with any thing political, I will thank you to say—that you understand— (& so the truth is)—that I am merely gone, with some private friends from Boston, on a visit to Mr [Thomas] Jefferson.

Yrs with regard,   D. Webster

ALS. NhD.

TO [WILLIAM PLUMER, JR.]

Monticello, Decr. 18. [1824]
Saturday Morning

My Dear Sir

If I am inquired for, have the goodness to say I may be expected either on Tuesday or Wednesday Morning. We should have left here yesterday morning, for W., but for the rain, which fell in torrents all day. This morning the streams are very full, & we doubt the expediency of setting out.

I have found my visit here very pleasant. It has not only gratified a natural desire to see a distinguished & extraordinary man, but allowed an opportunity for much interesting & instructive conversation.

Yours, with true regard Danl. Webster

The rain fell here yesterday & last night 5 inches.

ALS. Nh. Published in Van Tyne, p. 110; W & S, 16: 92.

FROM JAMES WILLIAM PAIGE

Sunday Dec 19. 1824—

Dear Sir,

In my letter yesterday I mentioned that Charles [Webster's] Fever had abated & that the pressure on his Lungs increased—which Doct [John C.] Warren tho't no unfavorable symptom. In the evening he was more troubled with *phlegm* & Mrs Webster gave him the usual *syrup* to relieve him—which did not operate so favorably as it had done before— & I wrote a note to Doct Warren, between 11 & 12 o'clock saying to him what we had done—& asked what to do further. He sent us a prescription & direction, but Charles grew worse & we sent for Dr [Jacob] Bigelow (being very near) & at the same time for Doct Warren—both of which were soon here & did every thing they could to remove the Phlegm from his throat—but he was so weak that the medicine had no effect upon him. His stomach seemed entirely insensible to any medicine—altho any thing that could be tho't of—was resorted to. By giving wine & water he revived a little— & lingered along untill Seven this morning—when sad as it may be I am under the necessity of informing you that a few minutes past *Seven this morning he breathed his last*— & we trust is in a happier world where all pain will cease. You may rest assured that nothing was left undone—that could have been of service to him.

Little did any of us think that our next letter to you, would be of this character. Mrs Webster is as well & resigned to her lot as could be expected. Cousin Eliza [Buckminster] is with her & a no small comfort. Danl, Julia & Edward were much affected at the loss of poor Charlie & E. in particular seemed very much grieved— & also Danl. Julia shew[ed] less feeling, but may have felt as bad.

Poor Charles suffered very much all the latter part of the night but at last went off without a single struggle. Doct Warren after being with us some time said he could do no more but got Doct [John B.?] Brown[1] to spend the residue of the night with us.

The children send much love to you— & with much Respect I am most truly yours   J. W. Paige

ALS. NhHi. Published in part in Van   1. Physician on Sumner Street.
Tyne, pp. 552–553.

NOTES OF MR. JEFFERSON'S CONVERSATION 1824 AT *Monticello*
1825

Mr Jefferson is now between eighty one & eighty two, above six feet high, of an ample long frame, rather thin & spare. His head, which is not peculiar in its shape, is set rather forward on his shoulders, & his neck being long, there is, when he is walking or conversing, an habitual protrusion of it. It is still well covered with hair, which having been once red, & now turning grey, is of an indistinct sandy colour. His eyes are small, very light, & now neither brilliant, nor striking. His chin is rather long, but not pointed[,] his nose small, regular in its outline, & the nostrils a little elevated. His mouth is well formed, & still filled with teeth; it is generally strongly compressed, bearing an expression of contentment & benevolence. His complexion formerly light, & freckled, now bears the marks of age & cutaneous affection. His limbs are uncommonly long, his hands & feet very large, & his wrists of a most extraordinary size. His walk is not precise & military, but easy & swinging; he stoops a little, not so much from age, as from natural formation. When sitting he appears short, partly from a rather lounging habit of sitting, & partly from the disproportionate length of his limbs. His dress when in the house, is a grey surtout coat, kerseymere buff waistcoat, with an under one faced with some material of a dingy red. His pantaloons are very long, loose, & of the same colour as his coat. His stockings are woollen, either white or grey, & his shoes of the kind that bear his name. His whole dress is neglected but not slovenly. He wears a common round hat. He wears when on horseback a grey strait bodiced coat, & a spencer of the same material, both fastened with large pearl buttons. When we first saw him he was riding, & in addition to the above, wore round his throat a knit white woollen tippet, in the place of a cravat, & black velvet gaiters under his pantaloons.

His general appearance indicates an extraordinary degree of health, vivacity, & spirit. His sight is still good, for he needs glasses only in the evening[,] his hearing is generally good, but a number of voices in animated conversation, confuses it.

———

Mr J. rises in the morning, as soon as he can *see* the hands of his clock, (which is directly opposite his bed,) & examines his thermometer immediately, as he keeps a regular meteorological diary. He employs himself chiefly in writing till breakfast, which is at nine. From that time till dinner, he is in his library, excepting that in fair weather he rides on horseback from seven to fourteen miles. Dines at four, returns to the drawing room at six, when coffee is brought in, & passes the evening, *till nine* in conversation. His habit of retiring at that hour is so strong, that it has become *essential* to his health & comfort. His diet is simple, but he seems restrained only by his tastes. His breakfast is tea & coffee, bread, of which he does not seem afraid, though it is always fresh from the oven, with sometimes a slight accompaniment of cold meat.

He enjoys his dinner well, taking with meat a large proportion of vegetables. He has a strong preference for the wines of the Continent, of which he has many sorts of excellent quality, having been more than commonly successful in his mode of importing, & preserving them. Among others we found the following, which are very rare in this country, & apparently not at all injured by transportation. L'Ednau, Muscat, Samian, & Blanchette de Limoux. Dinner is served in half Virginian, half French style, in good taste & abundance. No wine is put on the table till the cloth is removed.

———

In conversation, Mr J. is easy & natural, & apparently not ambitious; it is not loud as challenging general attention, but usually addressed to the person next him. The topics when not selected to suit the character & feelings of his auditor, are those subjects with which his mind seems particularly occupied, & these at present, may be said to be Science & Letters, & especially the University of Virginia, which is coming into existence almost entirely from his exertions, & will rise it is to be hoped, to usefulness & credit under his continued care. When we were with him, his favorite subjects were Greek & Anglo-Saxon, & historical recollections of the times & events of the Revolution & of his residence in France, from 1783–4 to 89.

———

In the course of the evening when the preceding was written, from Mr Webster['s] dictation, the gentlemen by uniting their recollections, preserved the following anecdotes of several great men, from Mr Jeffersons conversation.

———

Patrick Henry

was originally a bar-keeper. He was married very young, & going into some business on his own account, was a bankrupt before the year was out. When I was about the age of fifteen, I left the school here, to go to the College at Williamsburgh. I stopped a few days at friends in the county of Louisa. There I first saw & became acquainted with Patrick Henry. Having spent the Christmas holidays there, I proceeded to Williamsburgh. Some question arose about my admission, as my preparatory studies had not been pursued at the school, connected with that Institution. This delayed my admission about a fortnight, at which time Henry appeared in Williamsburgh, & applied for a license to *practise* law, having commenced the Study of it, at, or subsequently to the time of my meeting him in Louisa. There were four examiners, [George] Wythe, [Edmund] Pendleton, Peyton Randolph, & John Randolph. Wythe, & Pendleton at once rejected his application; the two Randolphs were by his importunity prevailed upon to sign the license, & having obtained their signatures, he applied again to Pendleton, & after much entreaty, & many promises of future study, succeeded in obtaining his. He then *turned out* for a practising Lawyer. The first case which brought him into notice, was a contested election, in which he appeared as Counsel, before a Committee of the House of Burgesses. His second was the *Parsons cause,* already well known. These & similar efforts, soon obtained for him so much reputation, that he was elected a member of the Legislature.

He was as well suited to the times as any man ever was, & it is not now easy to say, what we should have done without Patrick Henry. He was far before all, in maintaining the spirit of the Revolution. His influence was most extensive, with the Members from the Upper Counties, & *his* boldness & their votes overawed & controlled the more cool, or the more timid Aristocratic gentlemen of the lower part of the State. His eloquence was peculiar; if indeed it should be called eloquence, for it was impressive & sublime beyond what can be imagined. Although it was difficult when he had spoken, to tell what he had said, yet while he was speaking, it always seemed directly to the point. When he had spoken in opposition to *my* opinion, had produced a great effect, & I myself been highly delighted & moved, I have asked myself when he ceased, "What the Devil has he said," & could never answer the enquiry.

His person was of full size, & his manner & voice free & manly. His utterance neither very fast nor very slow. His speeches generally short from a quarter to an half hour. His pronunciation, was vulgar & vicious, but it was forgotten while he was speaking.

He was a man of very little knowledge of any sort, he read nothing & had no books. Returning one November from Albemarle Court, he borrowed of me Hume's Essays, in two vols. saying he should have leisure in the winter for reading. In the Spring he returned them, & declared he had not been able to go farther than twenty or thirty pages, in the first volume. He wrote almost nothing, he *could not* write. The resolutions of '75 which have been ascribed to him, have by many, been supposed to have been written by Mr [Thomas] Johnson, who acted as his second, on that occasion. But if they were written by Henry himself, they are not such as to prove any power of composition. Neither in politics nor in his profession was he a man of business, he was a man for debate only. His biographer [William Wirt] says, that he read Plutarch every year,—I doubt whether he ever read a volume of it in his life. His temper was excellent, & he generally observed decorum in debate.

On one or two occasions I have seen him *angry*— & his anger was terrible. Those who witnessed it, were not disposed to rouse it again. In his opinions he was yielding & practicable, & not disposed to differ from his friends. In private conversation he was agreeable, & facetious & while in genteel society appeared to understand all the decencies & proprieties of it; but in his *heart*, he preferred low society, & sought it as often as possible. He would hunt in the pine woods of Fluvannah, with overseers, & people of that description, living in a camp for a fortnight at a time without a change of raiment. I have often been astonished at his command of proper language; how he obtained the knowledge of it, I never could find out, as he read so little & conversed little with educated men.

After all, it must be allowed that he was our leader, in the measures of the Revolution, in Virginia. In that respect more is due to HIM than to any other person. If we had not had *him*, we should probably have got on *pretty* well, as you did, by a number of men of nearly equal talents, but he left us all far behind. His biographer, sent the sheets of his work to me, as they were printed, & at the end asked for my opinion. I told him it would be a question hereafter, whether his work should be placed on the shelf of *history*, or of *panegyric*. It is a poor book, written in bad taste, & gives so imperfect an idea of Patrick Henry, that it seems intended to show off the *writer*, more than the subject of the work.

———

Throughout the whole revolution Virginia, & the four New England States, acted together; indeed *they made* the Revolution. Their five votes were always to be counted on; but they had to pick up the remaining two for a majority, when & where they could.

———

The Virginia Fast.

About the time of the Boston Post Bill, the patriotick feeling in Virginia, had become languid, & worn out, from some cause or other. It was thought by some of us, to be absolutely necessary to excite the people, but we hardly knew the right means. At length it occurred to us to make grave faces, & propose a Fast. Some of us, who were the younger members of the Assembly, resolved upon the measure. We thought Oliver Cromwell would be a good guide in such a case. So we looked into [John] Rushworth, & drew up our Resolutions after the most pious & praiseworthy examples. It would hardly have been in character for *us* to present them ourselves; we applied therefore to Mr [Robert Carter] Nicholas a grave and religious man.

He proposed them in a set & solemn speech; some of us gravely seconded him, & the Resolutions were passed unanimously. If any debate had occurred, or if they had been postponed for consideration, there was no chance that they would have passed[.] The next morning Lord Bottetourt [Norborne Berkeley], the Governor, summoned the Assembly to his presence, & said to them, "I have heard of your proceedings of yesterday, & augur ill of their effects. His Majesty's interest, requires, that you be dissolved, & you *are* dissolved." Another Election taking place soon afterwards, such was the spirit of the times that every member of the Assembly without an *individual* exception, was re-elected.

———

Our Fast produced very considerable effects. We all agreed to go home & see that preachers were provided in our Counties, & notice given to the people. I came home to my own County, provided a Preacher, & notified the people, who came together in great multitude wondering what it meant.

———

Lord Bottetourt was an honourable man. His Government had authorized him, to make certain assurances to the people here, which he made accordingly. He wrote to the Minister, that he had made those assurances, & that unless he should be enabled to fulfil them, he must retire from his situation. This letter he sent unsealed to Peyton Randolph for his inspection. Lord B's. great respectability, his character for integrity, & his general popularity, would have enabled him to embarrass the measures of the Patriots exceedingly. His death was therefore, a fortunate event for the cause of the Revolution.

He was the first Governor in Chief, that had ever come over to Virginia. Before his time we had received only Deputies, the Governor residing in England, with a salary of £5,000, & paying his Deputy £1,000.

———

When Congress met, Patrick Henry, & Richard Henry Lee, opened the general subject with great ability & eloquence;—so much so, that [William] Paca & [Jeremiah Townley] Chase,[1] delegates from Maryland, said to each other, as they returned from the House, "We shall not be wanted here,—these Gentlemen from Virginia will be able to do every thing without us." But neither Henry nor Lee, were men of business,— & having made strong & eloquent general speeches, they had done all they could. It was thought advisable that two papers should be drawn up,— one an address to the People of England; & the other an address I think to the King. Committees were raised for these purposes, & Henry was at the head of the first, & Lee of the second. When the address to the People of England was reported, Congress heard it with utter amazement. It was miserably written, & good for nothing. At length Governor [William] Livingston of N. Jersey ventured to break silence. After complimenting the author, he said, he thought some other ideas might be usefully added to his draft of the address. Some such paper had been for a considerable time contemplated, & he believed a friend of his, had tried his hand in the composition of one. He thought if the subject were again committed, some improvement in the present draft might be made. It was accordingly recommitted, & the address which had been alluded to by Governor Livingston, & which was written by John Jay, was reported by the Committee, & adopted as it now appears. It is in my opinion one of the very best state papers, wh. the Revolution produced.

———

Richard Henry Lee, moved the Declaration of Independence, in pursuance of the Resolutions of the Assembly of Virginia, & only because he was the oldest member of the Virginia delegation.

———

The Declaration of Independence was written in a house on the North side of Chesnut St. Philadelphia, between Third & Fourth, not a corner house. Heiskells Tavern which has been pointed out as the house, is not the correct one.

———

For depth of purpose, zeal, & sagacity, no man in Congress *exceeded*, if any equalled Sam Adams; & none did more than he, to originate & sustain revolutionary measures in Congress. But he could not speak, he had a hesitating grunting manner.

John Adams was our Colossus on the floor. He was not graceful, nor elegant, nor remarkably fluent; but he came out occasionally with a power of thought & expression, that moved us from our seats.

———

I feel much alarmed at the prospect of seeing General [Andrew] Jackson, President. He is one of the most unfit men, I know of for such a place. He has had very little respect for Laws or Constitutions,— & is in fact merely an able military chief. His passions are terrible. When I was President of the Senate, he was a Senator; & he could never speak from the *rashness* of his feelings. I have seen him attempt it repeatedly, & as often choak with rage. His passions are no doubt cooler now;—he has been much tried since I knew him—but he is a *dangerous man.*

—————

When I was in France, the Marquis de Chastellux carried me to Buffon's residence in the country, & introduced me to him. It was Buffon's practice to remain in his study till dinner time, & receive no visitors under any pretence, but his house was open, & his grounds; & a servant showed them very civilly, & invited all strangers & friends to remain & dine. We saw Buffon in the garden, but carefully avoided him, but we dined with him & he proved himself then as he always did, a man of extraordinary power in conversation. He did not declaim—he was singularly agreable.

I was introduced to him as Mr Jefferson, who in some notes on Virginia, had combatted some of his opinions. Instead of entering into an argument, he took down his last work, presented it to me, & said, "When Mr J. shall have read this, he will be perfectly satisfied that I am right."—Being about to embark from Philadelphia, for France, I observed an uncommonly large Panther skin, at the door of a hatters shop. I bought it for half a Jo, ($16) on the spot, determining to carry it to France to convince Mons. Buffon, of his mistake in relation to this animal; which he had confounded with the Cougar. He acknowledged his mistake, & said he would correct it in his next volume. I attempted also to convince him of his error in relation to the common Deer, & the Moose of America; he having confounded our Deer, with the Red Deer of Europe, & our Moose with the Rein Deer. I told him that our Deer had horns two feet long—he replied with warmth, that if I could produce a *single* specimen with horns *one* foot long, he would give up the question. Upon this I wrote to Virginia for the horns of one of our deer, & obtained a very good specimen, *four* feet long.—I told him also, that the Rein-deer could walk under the Belly of our Moose; but he entirely scouted the idea. Whereupon I wrote to General [John] Sullivan of N. Hamp. & desired him to send me the bones, skin, & antlers of our Moose, supposing they could easily be procured by him. Six months afterwards, my agent in England, advised me, that Gen. Sullivan had drawn on him for 40 Guineas. I had forgotten my request, & wondered why such a draft had been made, but I paid it at once. A little later, came a letter from Gen. Sullivan, setting forth the manner in which he had complied with my request. He had been obliged to raise a company of nearly twenty men; had made an excursion towards the White Hills, camping out many nights, & had at last, after many difficulties, caught my Moose, boiled his bones in the desert, stuffed his skin, & remitted him to me. This accounted for my debt, & convinced M. Buffon. He promised in his next volume, to set these things right also: but he died directly afterwards.

———

Madame Houdetot's society was one of the most agreeable in Paris, when I was there. She inherited the materials of which it was composed, from Mad. de Tencin, & Mad. de Geoffrin. St. Lambert was always there, & it was generally believed that every evening on his return home, he wrote down the substance of the conversations he had held there, with D'Alembert, Diderot, & the other distinguished persons, who frequented her house. From these conversations, he made his books.

———

I knew the Baron de Grimm very well,—he was quite ugly, & one of his legs was shorter than the other. But he was the most agreable person in French society, & his opinion was always considered decisive, in matters relating to the Theatre & to Painting. His persiflage was the keenest, & most provoking I ever knew.

———

Mad. Necker, was a very sincere & excellent woman, but she was not very pleasant in conversation, for she was subject to what in Virginia, we call the *Budge,* that is, she was very nervous & fidgetty. She could rarely remain long in the same place, or converse long on the same subject. I have known her get up from table five or six times in the course of a dinner, & walk up & down her Saloon, to compose herself.

———

Marmontel was a very amusing man. He dined with me, every Thursday, for a long time, & I think told some of the most agreable stories, I ever heard in my life[.] After his death I found almost all of them in his Memoirs, & I dare say, he told them so well, because he had written them before in this book.

———

I wish Mr [John] Pickering would make a practical Lexicon. It would do more than any thing else in the present state of the matter, to promote the study of Greek among us. Jones' Greek Lexicon is very poor. I have been much disappointed in it. The best I have ever used is the Greek & French one by Planche.

———

Copy in Mrs. George Ticknor's hand. NhHi. Published in *PC,* 1: 364–373.   See mDW 4495–4497 for three pages of DW's notes (AD), from which he probably dictated his memorandum to Mrs. Ticknor.

delegate to the Continental Congress, 1783–1784.

1. Chase (1748–1828), Maryland

FROM EZEKIEL WEBSTER

December 28. 1824

Dear Daniel,

The Concord Register, under its editorial head—gives a pretty correct account of the closing scene in our Senate.[1] The Journal of the same day —last Saturday—has a statement under the hand of Mr [Nathaniel A.] Haven.[2] I think our Senate are in a very promising way to be as immortal, as the New York *seventeen*. If a majority of our Senate, are to be believed, Mr [Jeremiah] Mason was chosen. When you have the facts—I should like very well to have an article appear in the Nat. Intel. on the extraordinary conduct of a majority—who denied the inquiry into the mistake, &c &c. It should appear as editorial. If it could not appear in the Int. it might perhaps be inserted in the Nat. Journal. A well written article would count here. Our object now is to secure such a Senate & House— as will elect Mr Mason next June. We feel the importance of having a man of such talents and integrity in our National Councils. We shall make an effort—from a sense of duty. If you notice any thing that will have a favorable bearing—please to forward it. We had a campaign of seven weeks. We kept our armour buckeled on—& slept upon our arms— & the N Hampshire troops never did themselves more credit, since they fought at Bunker hill & Bennington. Yours &c   E Webster

ALS. MHi. Published in *PC*, 1: 358–359.

1. On December 25, the Concord *Register* had carried an editorial on the failure of the legislature to elect a senator. The specific question to which Ezekiel referred was that of the

votes in the Senate for Jeremiah Mason.

2. Haven's letter on the indecision of the Senate appeared in the Portsmouth *Journal of Literature and Politics*, December 25, 1824.

TO JEREMIAH MASON

Washington Decr. 29. [18]24

My dear Sir,

We have heard of the adjournment of the Legislature of N. Hamp. without having effected a choice of Senator. Seeing, towards the close, that the Senate were equally divided, I had some hope that a choice might be made. But, on a general view, the result is more favorable than there was reason to expect. So decisive a feeling in the House, & on equality in *such a Senate*, were circumstances shewing very solid strength. I am sure, My Dear Sir, you have no reason to regret the occurrences of the

session. They have shewn to the public your personal weight & consideration with the State; & they have, also, given an opportunity for the people
of the State to learn your standing with the Community, generally. Public
opinion, wherever expressed, has been uniformly in your favour. Here,
I may assure you, all considerable men, of all parties & all associations,
have felt & expressed the same wishes. Mr Parrot is generally respected,
& while *he* was of the number of candidates, being the present incumbent, a desire to have you here was, naturally, a little mitigated by a feeling of unwillingness to dispossess *him*. But, he being out of the case, if
there were any who did not *wish* you success, there was none who ventured to *express* such feelings. Looking at the matter, at a distance, &
judging only from the operation of general causes, I should think your
election was *only postponed*. Nothing else can happen, certainly, if the
House, now soon to be elected, be like its predecessor. I should not think
it of first importance to turn out these Senators. If the *House* remain of
the same opinion, the Senate must come to it.

I have been home from Va a week. My intention was to go to Richmond
& Norfolk, from Monticello, but intelligence from home induced me to
return, without accomplishing that part of my intention. We were two
days at Mr Madisons. He was very agreeable, & treated us with much
hospitality. He keeps alive a stronger interest in passing events than his
more advanced friend. Mrs. Madison is in perfect health, & remembers
all her Washington acquaintances. At Mr Jefferson's, we remained five
days. This was something longer than our intention, but there came rains,
which prevented our departure. Mr. Jefferson is a man of whom one may
form a very just account, as to person & manners, from description, &
pictures. We met him in the road, & I knew him at once, although he was
on horseback, & something straiter, & freer from the debility of age, than
I had expected. We found him uniformly pleasant, social, & interesting.
He talked less of present things than might be expected, altho' in the
intercourse with gentlemen under his own roof, he did *not keep back* his
opinions, on men or things. But if I were to say what appeared to be the
leading topics, with him, & those to which his mind habitually turned itself, I should mention *three*—early anecdotes of Revolutionary times—
French society—politics— & literature, such as they were when he was
in France—and Genl. Literature, & the Va. University.

On these three general topics he has much to say, & he says it all well.

Since I returned here, I have not been in[1] the way of hearing much
said on the election of President. It wd. be difficult, in my opinion, to say
which of the two leading candidates has the best chance—but if I were
to express an opinion, such as it is—it wd. be, at this moment, that Mr
[John Quincy] *Adams'* chance is best. New England, 6— New York—

Delaware— Va— Geoga— N. Carolina— Ohio— Louisiana— Illinois— out of these *14,* I think it not unlikely Mr Adams may get *13.* He *may,* also, get N. Jersey. It seems to me that there is, at this moment, rather a re-action agt. Genl. [Andrew] Jackson—a *feeling,* somewhat adverse to giving the Presidency to *mere* military character.

I propose to do nothing this Session, myself, but a few *useful & neces-sary* things—such as to provide for some crimes, now unprovided for, &c. My health is very good. You see what Mr. [John] Randolph said, about his letter. He had *talked* with some of the Comm[itt]ee & told a *story* (material or immaterial) which he thought they would confirm. I had not been spoken to. It occurred to me, at the moment, to be the right course to put the main question to him, cooly & quietly, & let him answer or evade it, as he chose. His course was open enough to remark—but I did not wish to have a quarrel—or to go farther than the strict necessity of self-defence. Whether I judged right or not, I cannot tell.[2]

I should be glad to hear from you, now that you have returned from your Concord expedition. Give my remembrances affectionately to your family, & believe me truly Yrs   Danl. Webster

ALS (incomplete), Typed copy. NhHi. Published in *PC,* 1: 360–362.

1. The text to this point is taken from a typed copy, NhHi.

2. Toward the end of the previous session of Congress, DW and several other members of the House had been appointed to a special committee to investigate misconduct charges made by the recently appointed Minister to Mexico, Ninian Edwards, against William H. Crawford, Secretary of the Treasury. John Randolph, another member of the committee, sailed for Europe before the committee adjourned; before his departure, how-ever, he left an open letter claiming responsibility for having persuaded the committee members to give Crawford an opportunity to respond to Edward's charges. The committee members, Webster included, denied Randolph's claim, and in the succeeding second session of the Eighteenth Congress, the quesion had again come up. Again, DW denied Randolph's claim, and Randolph responded to DW's denial with a challenge (*Register of Debates in Congress,* 18th Cong., 2nd sess., 1824–1825, pp. 56–58; Fuess, 1: 318–319).

TO [EDWARD EVERETT]

Washington Decr. 31. [1824]

Dear Sir

I have waited on Mr [John C.] Calhoun, with your letter,[1] & said, also, what I thought would be useful.

The world rings with your Plymouth Speech;[2] even before the echoes of the P.B.K. Oration[3] have entirely subsided. Yrs always   Danl. Webster

P.S.—& *P.M.* I am much obliged to you for your kind letter,[4] which has just come to hand. I know that my presence at home could not have altered the course of things, in respect to our little boy.[5] The loss I feel, heavily, but I hope not to be too much depressed by it. The oftener you call & see Mrs W. the more she & I shall be obliged to you.

I shall certainly take care to secure snug quarters for your family & mine next year.[6]

ALS. MHi. Published in W & S, 16: 93.

1. Not found.

2. On December 22, 1824, Everett had delivered an oration, "The First Settlement of New England," at Plymouth.

3. "The Circumstances Favorable to the Progress of Literature in Amer-

ica," delivered at Cambridge on August 26, 1824.

4. Not found.

5. Charles, who died on December 19, 1824.

6. Everett had just been elected, and Webster reelected, to the 19th Congress.

TO JOSEPH HOPKINSON

Decr. 31. [1824]

My D Sir

I delivered the Medals, immediately on my return from Va. & must beg your pardon for omitting to do so before I left Washington.

I am very glad you think well of my course, in regard to Mr Randolph's remarks. No one could conjecture in what direction he would move; & therefore it was impossible to decide, before hand, what conduct to pursue, in answering what he might say.

Many observations, besides those which I made, were obvious enough; but I did not wish to do more than the necessity of self defence strictly enjoined. My visit to Va. was not unpleasant. Mr Jefferson is full of conversation, & as it relates, pretty much, to by-gone times, it is replete with information & useful anecdote. All the great men of our Revolutionary epoch necessarily had a circle of which they were, severally, the centre. Each, therefore, has something to tell not common to all. Mr [John] Adams & Mr Jefferson, for example, tho' acting together, on a common theatre, at Philadelphia, were nevertheless far apart, when in Massachusetts & Virginia, & each was at home, in the midst of men, & of events, more or less different from those which surrounded the other. I heard Mr Jefferson talk over the events of his early life, as your friend [David] Hunter[1] represents the young Indians to listen to the tales of the age-stricken warriors; not without occasionally feeling, like them, an impulse to raise the war song, & grasp the tomahawk. Mr Jefferson's conversation is little on present things; partly perhaps from the prudence of forbearing to engage in questions which now d[ivide] the community, but most[ly] fro[m] a greater love for other top[ics]. Early Revolutionary events, politic[al] occurences, in both Hemispheres, about the time he was in France,

& general literature & the *University of Va.* would seem to be his favorite subjects.

I believe we have nothing new here on the subject of the elections.

You will see that we have lost one of our little boys. His birth was announced to me, I remember when at your House, three years ago. Ys. mo. truly   Danl. Webster

ALS. PHi.

1. Hunter (1802–1886), a grandson of Richard Stockton, at this time a young lieutenant, two years out of West Point.

TO JEREMIAH MASON

Washington Dec. 31st. [1824]

D Sir

Since I wrote you two or three days ago,[1] I have seen the nomination of your judges—& of Mr [Ichabod] Bartlett, among others. I know not, whether he will accept the appointment, but he has as yet, I understand from him, not made up his mind to reject it. I should not be surprised if he should take the place. In that event, I suppose it probable Mr. [William] Plumer [Jr.] might be again a Candidate for Congress. You know the opinions which I have generally entertained of him. Certainly, he acts *here* with fairness & liberality; & I should have faith to believe that, in regard to passing events at home he might be inclined to give his assistance to the liberal side. If this vacancy should occur, it wd. be filled, I presume, by an election thro the State. Hereafter, when you vote by Districts, another Gentleman's turn may probably come. I have been inclined to throw out these ideas, in the hope of hearing from you, or Mr [Nathaniel A.] Haven, if the vacancy should occur, & if you should wish to say any thing on the matter. Yrs always   D.W.

I have seen Mr Haven's statement of the extraordinary incidents occuring in yr Senate the last day of the Session. I incline to think, you had, in truth, 7 *votes*.[2]

ALS. MHi.

1. See DW to Jeremiah Mason [December 29, 1824], above.

2. See Note 2, Ezekiel Webster to DW, December 28, 1824, above.

Calendar, 1797–1824

(Items in italic are included in this volume. Page numbers are in boldface.)

1797

Sept 21	Account with Richard Lang. AD. NhD. mDWs. (Runs to 1801, July 4). Details DW's purchases and payments with a Hanover storekeeper.

1798

[Dec 20]	Poem addressed to George Herbert. ADS. NhD. mDW 1. Published in *PC*, 1: 71–72.	
[Dec 22]	*To Joseph Warren Brackett.*	**25**
[1798–1799?]	"Hail Poesy, thou nymph of every grace!" AD. NhD. mDW 39358. Poem. *PC*, 1: 155–156.	

1799

[Feb 25]	Poem addressed to George Herbert. ADS. NhD. mDW 3. *PC*, 1: 72. Signed "Mela."	
[July]	*Constitution of the Federal Club.*	**25**
[Aug 27]	"Hope." Copy. NhHi. mDWs. *Dartmouth Gazette.* Aug 27, 1799. Essay and poem signed "Icarus."	
[Aug 27]	*To Moses Davis.*	**26**
[Oct 21]	"Charity." Copy. NhHi. mDWs. *Dartmouth Gazette,* Oct 21, 1799. Essay and poem signed "Icarus."	
[Oct 28]	"Fear." Copy. NhHi. mDWs. *Dartmouth Gazette,* Oct 28, 1799. Essay and poem signed "Icarus."	
[Nov 25]	Essay on Man and War. Copy. NhHi. *Dartmouth Gazette,* Nov 25, 1799. Signed "Icarus."	
[Dec 2]	Essay on Pennsylvania election. Printed. *Dartmouth Gazette,* Dec 2, 1799. Signed "Icarus."	
[Dec 9]	"Winter." Copy. NhHi. mDWs. *Dartmouth Gazette,* Dec 9, 1799. Poem signed "Icarus."	
[1799?]	"A Hint to the Ambitious and other poems." AD in DW's and others' hands. NhD. mDW 194.	
[1799?]	"Human Redemption." Printed. Bela Chapin, *Poets of New Hampshire.* (Claremont, 1883), pp. 27–28. Poem.	

1800

Jan 1	To John F. Carey. Printed. *Putnam's Magazine,* 7 (April 1910): 862–863. *Zion's Herald* (January 4, 1933); cover and p. 10. "Happy New Year . . ."

Feb 5	*To [James Hervey] Bingham.*	**27**
Feb 11	To [James Hervey] Bingham. Printed. *PC*, 1: 80–82. Relates news of college friends and reading from Salisbury, N.H.	
[Feb 17]	Political Essay. Copy. NhHi. mDWs. *Dartmouth Gazette*, Feb 17, 1800. Discusses political developments on European continent.	
[Feb 24]	To [Moses Davis]. Copy. MWalB. mDWs. *Dartmouth Gazette*, Feb 24, 1800. "Icarus" comments on Napoleon Bonaparte.	
[April 21]	"Spring." Copy. NhHi. mDWs. *Dartmouth Gazette*, April 21, 1800. Poem signed "Icarus."	
April 25	To Ezekiel Webster. ALS. NhD. mDW 14. *PC*, 1: 83–84. Banters with Ezekiel on philosophical questions; discusses Massachusetts and New Hampshire politics.	
[April 28]	Poem. Copy. NhHi. mDWs. *Dartmouth Gazette*, April 28, 1800.	
May	From Habijah Weld Fuller. ALS. NhD. mDWs. Poem.	
July 30	Minutes of the Alpha Chapter, Phi Beta Kappa, recorded by DW, Secretary. ADS. NhD. mDWs. Through August 18.	
Aug 4	"Incidents at Home." Printed. *Dartmouth Gazette*, Aug 4, 1800. Reply to Joseph Dennie's criticism of DW's Fourth of July oration.	
Nov 27	To Moses Davis. Copy. NhHi. mDWs. *Dartmouth Gazette*, Dec 6, 1800. "Icarus" comments on presidential election.	
[Dec 6]	"Jacobinic Deglutition." Printed. *Dartmouth Gazette*. Dec 6, 1800. Comments on politics.	
[Dec 13]	"Question—By a Jacobin." Printed. *Dartmouth Gazette*, Dec 13, 1800. Discusses Jefferson's views of government.	
[Dec 13]	"Winter." Copy. NhHi. mDWs. *Dartmouth Gazette*, Dec 13, 1800. Poem signed "Icarus."	
Dec 25	*Argument for the Acquisition of the Floridas.*	**29**
Dec 26	From Benjamin Gilbert. ALS. NhHi. mDW 24. Sends DW on errand to gain information on land ownership.	
Dec 28	To [James Hervey] Bingham. Printed. *PC*, 1: 84–86. Comments on Jefferson's election and the Hanover scene.	
[1800?]	"Robin, no more thy morning song." AD. NhD. mDW 39471. Poem.	
[1800–1805?]	"The force of nervous sensibility." ADS. MH. mDW 39484. Poem.	

1801

Jan 5, 7	From Moses Davis. ALS. NhHi. mDW 9. Relates

	circumstances of trip to Concord; points out inaccuracies in the *Dartmouth Gazette,* temporarily edited by Webster.	
Jan 7	*To [George] Herbert.*	**30**
Jan 9	To Samuel Ayer Bradley. ALS. NhD. mDW 26. Discusses life in Hanover in winter.	
Jan 17	To [James Hervey] Bingham. Printed. *PC,* 1: 86–87. Plans to leave for Concord next day.	
Jan 26	To Habijah Weld Fuller. ALS. NhD. mDW 30. *PC,* 1: 87–89. Says he has been sick; encloses poem.	
[Feb 11]	Poetical Epistle. Copy. NhHi. *Dartmouth Gazette,* Feb 21, 1801. Poem on Federalists and Antifederalists.	
Feb 13	"To General Eleazar Wheelock Ripley." Printed. Lucy Crawford, *History of the White Mountains* (1886), pp. 225–228. Poem.	
Feb 16	To Samuel Ayer Bradley. ALS. NhD. mDW 37. About to set out again for Hanover; inquires after Bradley's health.	
May 4	*Is Deception Ever Justifiable?*	**32**
June 14	To [James Hervey] Bingham. Printed. *PC,* 1: 90. Writing from Thompson's law office in Salisbury of friends he has seen.	
Aug 28	Promissory note to [H. W. Fuller]. ADS. NhD. mDWs.	
Sept 10	To [James Hervey] Bingham. ALS. NhD. mDWs. *PC,* 1: 90–92. Discusses his situation in Salisbury; reading law.	
Sept 22	To [James Hervey] Bingham. Printed. *PC,* 1: 92–94. Discusses his situation in Thompson's law office.	
Oct 3	To Nathaniel Coffin. ALS. MH. mDW 84. *PC,* 1: 94–95. Reading law in Thompson's office; Dartmouth commencement.	
Oct 26	*To [James Hervey] Bingham.*	**33**
Dec 8	To [James Hervey] Bingham. Printed. *PC,* 1: 98–101. Discusses his and Ebenezer's efforts to keep Ezekiel in college; old friends; reading of law; and Jefferson's appointment of postmaster in Salisbury.	
Dec 26	*To Judah Dana.*	**36**

1802

Jan 9	Store Account with John and Robert Bradley. AD. NhD. mDWs. Elizabeth Porter Gould, *John Adams and Daniel Webster as Schoolmasters* (Boston, 1903), pp. 51–52. Runs to 1804, April 29.
Feb 20	To Samuel Ayer Bradley. ALS. NhD. mDW 90. Teaching school in Fryeburg.
Feb 20	To Habijah Weld Fuller. ALS. MeHi. mDW 93. *PC,* 1: 104–106. Teaching in Fryeburg, writing poetry.
Feb 21 – July 24	Sports of Pequawket. Copy. NhHi. mDW 98. Poems

	and essays composed in Fryeburg. Signed variously "Gratian," "Ic[arus]," "L," and "DW."	
Feb 25	*To [James Hervey] Bingham.*	**36**
Feb 25	From C.D. ALS. NhHi. mDW 114. Letter from a female admirer in Hanover.	
March 3	To Samuel Ayer Bradley. ALS. Fryeburg Academy. mDW 116. *W & S*, 16: 4–5. Fryeburg scene.	
March 19	To Samuel Ayer Bradley. ALS. NhD. mDW 120. Friendly reminiscences.	
May 18	*To [James Hervey] Bingham.*	**38**
[c. June 6]	To John Porter, enclosing poem of June 4 addressed to John Porter and Nehemiah. ALS. NhD. mDW 128. *PC*, 1: 113–115. Poem with brief comments on politics.	
June 7, 9	To Thomas Abbot Merrill. ALS. NhD. mDW 132. *PC*, 1: 116–117. Comments on Fryeburg friends, his reading habits.	
June 11	To Habijah Weld Fuller. Copy. NhD. mDWs. *PC*, 1: 118. Mentions that he is to leave Fryeburg; discusses ambition.	
[July 10]	Essay on Government. Copy. NhHi. mDWs. *Dartmouth Gazette*, July 10, 1802. Signed "Icarus."	
July 22	To James Hervey Bingham. Printed. *PC*, 1: 119–121. Reports news of college friends.	
[Aug 7]	Essay on Newspapers. Copy. NhHi. mDWs. *Dartmouth Gazette*, Aug 7, 1802. Signed "Icarus."	
Aug 29	To Habijah Weld Fuller. ALS. NhD. mDWs. *PC*, 1: 121–122. Discusses his illness, friends, and money problems.	
Sept 7	From Daniel [Abbott]. ALS. NhHi. mDW 148. Mentions that he is seeking admission to bar.	
Oct 23	From Ezekiel Webster. ALS. NhD. mDW 150. Discusses college life.	
Nov 4	*To Ezekiel Webster.*	**43**
Nov 6	From Ezekiel Webster. Printed. *PC*, 1: 123–124. "Money, Daniel, money."	
Nov 26	From Moses Davis. ALS. NhHi. mDW 157. *PC*, 1: 125. Requests DW to write New Year's Address for *Dartmouth Gazette*.	
Dec 18	*To Jacob McGaw.*	**43**
Dec 21	To James H. Bingham. Printed. *PC*, 1: 127–128. Discusses the study of law; brief reference to politics.	
Dec 21	To Habijah Weld Fuller. ALS. NhD. mDWs. *PC*, 1: 126–127. Discusses friends; now in Salisbury, with visits to Concord and Hanover.	
[1802]	Poem addressed to Habijah Weld Fuller. Copy. MeHi. mDW 165. *PC*, 1: 101–102.	
[1802]	Poem addressed to DW. ADs. NhD. mDWs. From Habijah Weld Fuller.	

[1802?]	To Thomas Abbot Merrill. AL (incomplete). NhD. mDW 88. Discusses a date.
[1802–1803]	To John Porter. ALS. NhD. mDW 171. Reminisces of college life and friends.
[1802–1808]	To Nathaniel [Sawyer]. Typed copy. NhD. mDW 38832. Chats about the writing of letters and of "attending to *things literary*."

1803

Jan 1	The News Boy's Message to the Patrons of the *Dartmouth Gazette,* and Carrier's address [Jan 1, 1803]. AD in DW's and others' hands. NhD. NhHi. mDW 174. *Dartmouth Gazette,* Jan 1, 1803. Poem.
Jan 4	To Thomas Abbot Merrill. ALS. NhD. mDW 200. PC, 1: 128–130. Contemplates letterwriting and the reading of law.
Jan 14	To [Amos Jones] Cook. ALS. NhD. mDWs. PC, 1: 130–131. Reminisces about Dartmouth College, friends, and study of law.
Feb 22	To James Hervey Bingham. Printed. PC, 1: 132–133. Discusses politics, college friends.
Feb 26	To Jacob McGaw. ALS. Mrs. Lester W. Parker, Brimfield, Mass. mDW 204. Reminisces on his friendship with McGaw; study of law.
March 26	To John Porter. ALS. NhD. mDW 208. May possibly be going to Fryeburg for visit.
April 8	From James Hervey Bingham. ALS. NhHi. mDW 210. PC, 1: 134–135. Philosophizes about law and life.
May 3	To Habijah Weld Fuller. ALS. MeHi. mDW 124. PC, 1: 106–107. Comments on stay in Maine, friends, law study, and *Literary Tablet.*
May 13	From Ezekiel Webster. ALS. NhD. mDW 214. PC, 1: 135–136. Cannot accept Davis' request to edit anonymously the *Dartmouth Gazette.*
May 18	To James H. Bingham. Printed. PC, 1: 136–137. Discusses friends and the pursuit of eminence.
May 21	From Ezekiel Webster. ALS. NhD. mDW 217. PC, 1: 138. Needs money; discusses Davis and *Literary Tablet.*
May 28	From Ezekiel Webster. ALS. NhD. mDW 220. PC, 1: 138–139. Discusses antifraternity sentiment at Dartmouth.
June 15	Account Book. ADS. MH. mDW 39488. Runs to 1810, June 12.
June 30	*To Samuel Ayer Bradley.* **45**
July 2	To Habijah Weld Fuller. Printed. PC, 1: 140–141. Discusses travels around New Hampshire and friends he saw.

July 30	To Thomas Abbot Merrill. ALS. NhD. mDW 228. *PC*, 1: 141–142. Solicits letter.	
Aug 3	To Thomas Abbot Merrill. ALS. NhD. mDW 232. Comments on Dartmouth College developments.	
Sept 3	To James Hervey Bingham. Printed. *PC*, 1: 142–144. Writes on Dartmouth commencement, politics, college friends.	
Sept 24	*To Samuel Ayer Bradley.*	46
Sept 28	To James Hervey Bingham. Copy. NhHi. mDW 240. Van Tyne, pp. 14–15. Writes from Hanover of friends there.	
Oct 6	*To [James Hervey] Bingham.*	47
Oct 6	To Habijah Weld Fuller. Printed. *PC*, 1: 146–147. Discusses trip to Hanover.	
Oct 18	From Ezekiel Webster. Printed. *PC*, 1: 147–149. Discusses his study at Dartmouth.	
Oct 23	To Ezekiel Webster. ALS. NhD. mDW 241. Urges Ezekiel to take teaching post; mentions forthcoming trip to Dartmouth.	
Nov 11	To Thomas Abbot Merrill. ALS. NhD. mDW 244. *PC*, 1: 149–151. Mentions that he's giving up poetry for law.	
Dec 11	To John Porter, ALS. NhD. mDW 248. Declines writing anniversary poem for Phi Beta Kappa.	
Dec 23	To James Hervey Bingham. Printed. *PC*, 1: 153–155. Discusses letters from friends and his and Ezekiel's ramblings on "poverty."	
Dec	To Thomas Abbot Merrill. ALS. NhD. mDW 252. *PC*, 1: 151–153. Mentions Porter's request for anniversary poem and Webster's declining to write it.	

1804

Jan 18	To Moses Davis. Copy. NhD. mDW 256. *PC*, 1: 156–157. Sends condolences on death of Mrs. Fuller, a mutual friend.	
Feb 5	To Moses Davis. ALS. NhD. mDW 261. *PC*, 1: 158–159. Talks of old friends and electioneering in New Hampshire.	
March 10	From Ezekiel Webster. ALS. DLC. mDW 264. Comments on the advantages of a college degree.	
March 16	To Thomas Abbot Merrill. ALS. NhD. mDW 268. *PC*, 1: 160–162. Reflects on ambition and friendship.	
March 16	*To [James Hervey] Bingham.*	49
April 3	*To [James Hervey] Bingham.*	50
April 4	*From Ezekiel Webster.*	52
May 1	To Thomas Abbot Merrill. ALS. NhD. mDW 276. *PC*, 1: 166–167. Banters with Merrill on philosophy of life.	
May 5	*To Ezekiel Webster.*	53

May 10	From Ezekiel Webster. ALS. NhD. mDW 284. *PC*, 1: 169–170. Comments on his short supply of money and DW's coming to Boston.
May 28	To Thomas Abbot Merrill. ALS. NhD. mDW 288. *PC*, 1: 170–172. Discusses matrimony philosophically and his intentions to go to Boston.
June 10	*To Ezekiel Webster.* 54
June 17	From Ezekiel Webster. ALS. NhD. mDW 296. *PC*, 1: 174–175. Discusses DW's coming to Boston and New Hampshire political campaign.
June 18	*To Ezekiel Webster.* 56
June 18	To James Hervey Bingham. Printed. *PC*, 1: 175–176. Comments on politics, classmates, and travel to East Andover with Miss Poor.
July 12	*To Timothy Farrar.* 57
July 12	From Jacob McGaw. ALS. NhD. mDW 308. Van Tyne, pp. 15–16. Remarks on recent trip to Fryeburg.
July 12	To Ellen [Thompson]. Printed. Boston *Evening Transcript*, Aug 14, 1906. Declares himself a "free, single, untied man again."
July 17	Student Law Diary of DW. AD. NhD. mDW 311. *PC*, 1: 178–184. Runs to 1805, March 5.
July 24	Communication signed "W." Printed. Boston *Repertory*, July 24, 1804.
July 27	Communication signed "W." Printed. Boston *Repertory*, July 27, 1804.
Aug 4	From Augustus Alden. ALS. NhD. mDW 335. Discusses his law studies and Dartmouth friends.
Aug 4	To James Hervey Bingham. Printed. *PC*, 1: 185–186. Discusses his arrival in Boston and reading of law in Christopher Gore's office.
Aug 8	From Daniel [Abbot]. ALS. NhD. mDW 337. Requests DW to have summons served.
Aug 10	Communication signed "W." Printed. Boston *Repertory*, Aug 10, 1804.
Aug 15	From James Hervey Bingham. ALS. NhD. mDW 339. Inquires of DW's whereabouts; discusses his own life in Charlestown.
Aug 20	From Daniel [Abbot]. ALS. NhD. mDW 343. Has received the money DW sent.
Aug 25	From Jabez Bradford Whitaker. ALS. NhD. mDW 346. Comments on DW's presence in Boston.
Sept 3	To Jacob McGaw. ALS. Mrs. Lester W. Parker, Brimfield, Mass. mDW 350. Remarks on trip to East Andover and Fryeburg the previous spring and on the recent election in New Hampshire.
Sept 11	From Daniel Abbot. ALS. NhD. mDW 354. Instructs DW on the collection of a debt.
Sept 13	From Joseph Warren Brackett. ALS. NhD. mDW 357. Discusses his trip to New York and Pennsylvania.

Sept 14	*To [James Hervey] Bingham.*	**58**
Sept 21	From Parker Noyes. ALS. MHi. mDW 361. Requests DW to get him a pamphlet on the Massachusetts legislature.	
Sept 23	From F[reeborn] Adams. ALS. NhD. mDW 363. Former classmate now physician in S.C. discusses his practice and Webster's study of law.	
Sept 29	Poem by "Massachusetts." Printed. *Columbian Centinel,* Sept 29, 1804.	
Oct 2	*"W."*	**59**
Oct 6	From Ebenezer Webster to DW and Ezekiel Webster. LS. NhHi. mDW 367. *PC,* 1: 187–188. Discusses his and the family's health.	
[Oct 6]	From Mitty [Mehitable] Webster (enclosed with Ebenezer W. to DW and EW). ALS. NhHi. mDW 367. Van Tyne, p. 14. Relates news of family and friends in Salisbury.	
Oct 10	From Moses Davis. ALS. NhD. mDW 371. Requests DW to purchase some type and to write for *Dartmouth Gazette.*	
Oct 17	*From Thomas W. Thompson.*	**61**
Oct 17	To Habijah Weld Fuller. Copy. NhD. mDWs. *PC,* 1: 191–192. Relates news of old college friends.	
Oct 19	Communication signed "W." Printed. Boston *Repertory,* Oct 19, 1804.	
Oct 20	To Moses Davis. Copy. NhHi. mDW 383. Van Tyne, pp. 16–17. Will purchase plates for *Dartmouth Gazette;* remarks on Federalist victories in New Hampshire.	
Oct 31	From Moses Davis. ALS. NhD. mDW 387. Expects plates soon; comments on politics.	
Nov 3	From Moses Davis. ALS. NhD. mDW 391. Still hopes to receive plates soon; urges Webster to write for paper.	
Nov 3	From John Nelson. ALS. NhD. mDW 394. Asks DW's assistance in getting into a good law office in Boston, perhaps Gore's.	
Nov 4	From Jabez Bradford Whitaker. ALS. NhD. mDW 398. Introduces S. M. Richmond of Providence.	
[Nov 6]	To Ezekiel Webster. ALS. NhD. mDW 400. *PC,* 1: 192. Implores Ezekiel to maintain secrecy of his trip to Albany.	
Nov 9	To Ezekiel Webster. ALS. NhD. mDW 403. *PC,* 1: 192–193. Writing from Springfield, details his trip west to Albany.	
Nov 10	From James Hervey Bingham. ALS. NhD. mDW 406. Details for DW the legal opportunities in the Cheshire area.	
Nov 15[?]	*To Ezekiel Webster.*	**63**
Nov 30	*To Thomas Abbot Merrill.*	**65**

Nov 30   To Thomas W. Thompson. ALS. MH. mDW 418.
Boston *Evening Transcript*, Aug 14, 1906. Details
his study of law thus far and requests statement
from Thompson for use in gaining admission to
bar.

Dec 2   From Habijah Weld Fuller. ALS. NhD. mDWs. Writes
of old girl friend and of politics.

Dec 10   From Thomas W. Thompson. ALS. NhD. mDW 422.
Has complied with DW's request of Nov 30; discusses New Hampshire politics.

Dec 14   "W." to the Editor of the *Repertory*. Printed. Boston
Repertory, Dec 14, 1804.

Dec 21   From Sally (Sarah Ann) Webster (with postscript:
Ebenezer Webster to DW and Ezekiel Webster),
ALS. NhD. mDW 427. *PC*, 1: 196–197. Mentions
DW's New York trip.

Dec 21   *From Ebenezer Webster, to DW and EW.*   67

Dec 29   To Judah Dana. ALS. Steptoe & Johnson, Attorneys.
Washington, D.C. mDWs. *W & S*, 16: 670. Requests
of Dana a statement that he read law in his office
while teaching at Fryeburg Academy.

1805

Jan 2   To James Hervey Bingham. Printed. *PC*, 1: 198–199.
Discusses trip to Albany.

Jan 18   *From Judah Dana.*   67

Jan 26   From Samuel Osgood. ALS. NhD. mDW 434. Seeks
DW's assistance in getting into law office in Boston.

Jan 28   From James Hervey Bingham. ALS. NhD. mDW 437.
Relates a narrative of smallpox inoculation in
Alstead.

Feb 19   Petition concerning a justice of the peace for Bos-
cawen. ADS by Benjamin Jackman, Joseph Little,
DW et al. Nh-Ar. mDWs. Recommends Joseph
Gerrish.

March 10   To Habijah Weld Fuller. ALS. NhD. mDWs. *PC*, 1:
199–201. Discusses trip to Albany and mentions that
he may be leaving Boston soon.

March 10   To Thomas Abbot Merrill. ALS. NhD. mDW 441. *PC*,
1: 201–202. Mentions that he's leaving Boston;
discusses reading, politics.

March 23   From Gore, Miller, and Parker. ALS. MHi. mDW 445.
Employ DW to collect debts.

March   To Grace Fletcher. Printed. *Century Magazine*, New
Series, 7 (March 1885): 723. Invites her to ride to
Dunstable.

April 1   From Gore, Miller, and Parker. ALS. NhD. mDW 447.
Sends information on a Mr. Putney, from whom
DW is to collect debt.

April 2   From Samuel Osgood. ALS. NhD. mDW 451. Asks
                 for advice on studying law in Boston.
April 15   From Andrew Lovejoy. ALS. NhD. mDW 455. In-
                 quires if DW is interested in debt collection case.
April 23   From Daniel [Abbot]. ALS. NhD. mDW 457. Inquires
                 about money DW had sent him.
April 23   From Gore, Miller, and Parker. ALS. NhD. mDW 460.
                 Send additional recommendations on collection of
                 certain debts.
April 24   From Gore, Miller, and Parker. (Enclosure: Gore,
                 Miller, and Parker to DW, April 23, 1805; Caleb
                 Putney to John Gore & Co., March 30, 1805). ALS.
                 NhD. mDW 463. Enclose copy of Putney letter.
April 25   To Ezekiel Webster. ALS. NhD. mDW 468. PC, 1:
                 202–204. Discusses his loss of $85 and the conse-
                 quences of it.
[April] 27   From Daniel Abbot. ALS. NhD. mDW 473. Sends in-
                 formation regarding a deed question.
April 27   From S. Green. ALS. MHi. mDW 475. Encloses letter
                 from John Callender, to be kept private.
April 29   To Samuel Ayer Bradley. ALS. MH. mDW 477. Dis-
                 cusses the Putney case he was handling for Gore,
                 Miller, and Parker; did not lose the $85.
April 30   *To Ezekiel Webster.*   **68**
May 4   *To James Hervey Bingham.*   **69**
May 6   From John Callender. ALS. NhD. mDW 489. Thanks
                 him for letter on the Carrigain and Dix matters.
May 7   From Isaac Brooks. ALS. NhD. mDW 491. Reports the
                 results of his search through deeds on the Putnam
                 matter.
May 12   *To Ezekiel Webster.*   **70**
May 12   From Ezekiel Webster. ALS. NhD. mDW 496. PC, 1:
                 207–208. Responds to DW's letter of April 30; in-
                 quires of his law practice.
May 13   From Samuel Osgood. ALS. NhD. mDW 500. Plans to
                 enter Olcott's office; thanks DW for his advice.
May 14   To Thomas Abbot Merrill. ALS. NhD. mDW 504. PC,
                 1: 208–209. Recounts his leaving Boston; recent
                 reading.
May 16   To Ezekiel Webster. Printed. PC, 1: 209. Reports on
                 family's health and requests Ezekiel to send him
                 blank books.
May 17   *From Peter Thacher.*   **71**
May 18   From Peter Thacher. ALS. NhD. mDW 511. Sends
                 note for collection and forwards latest work of
                 Dr. Caustic.
May 19   From Ezekiel Webster. ALS. NhD. mDW 513. PC, 1:
                 211. Sends trunk, blank books, and volume from
                 Thacher.
May 23   From Ezekiel Webster, ALS. NhD. mDW 516. Van

	Tyne, p. 22. Inquires about clerk's office; tired of teaching.	
May 25	*To Ezekiel Webster.*	71
May 30	From Ezekiel Webster. ALS. NhD. mDW 525. *PC*, 1: 211–212. Describes results of Massachusetts election.	
June 4	From Boott & Pratt. ALS. MHi. mDW 529. Instruct DW on Timothy Dix debt.	
June 13	[Power of attorney from Benjamin Ingham transferred by William Bolton to DW]. DS by Bolton. NhD. mDW 531.	
June 14	From R. G. Amory. AL. NhD. mDW 533. Sends DW debt for collection.	
June 14	From James Hervey Bingham. ALS. NhD. mDW 535. Talks of his small law practice and desire to live near Webster.	
June 26	"The Hermit." Printed. *Literary Tablet*, 2 (June 26, 1805): 84. Poem signed "Monos."	
June 28	From John Nelson. ALS. NhD. mDW 539. Discusses his study of law and law practice.	
June 29	From Joseph Warren Brackett. ALS. NhD. mDW 543. Details his recent career and reports of old college friends.	
June ?	To Ezekiel Webster. ALS. NhD. mDW 547. *PC*, 1: 212. Reached home from Boston "alive" last evening; send some "gaiters."	
July 9	From William Henry Woodward. ALS. NhD. mDW 549. Asks DW to correct and serve writs on several people in Boscawen area.	
July 10	From Ezekiel Webster. ALS. NhD. mDW 552. *PC*, 1: 212–213. Thinks of leaving Boston and resettling in New Hampshire once school is out.	
July 15	From Skinner & Hurd. ALS. NhD. mDW 556. Instruct DW on action against Timothy Dix.	
July 17	From Moses Davis. ALS. NhD. mDW 558. Asks DW to begin writing for *Dartmouth Gazette* again.	
July 17	From Reuben D. Mussey. ALS. NhD. mDW 561. Inquires of the prospects for a physician in Boscawen.	
July 25	From John Nelson. ALS. NhD. mDW 563. Recommends R. D. Mussey to DW.	
July 28	To Ezekiel Webster. ALS. NhD. mDW 565. *PC*, 1: 213–214. Reports on his activities since he left Boston in late June; need to borrow money.	
July 31	From Nathan Smith. ALS. NhD. mDW 568. Recommends R. D. Mussey to DW.	
Aug 1	From Ezekiel Webster. ALS. NhD. mDW 570. *PC*, 1: 214–215. Sends gaiters and briefly comments on yellow fever epidemic and politics.	
Aug 9	*To Ezekiel Webster.*	72

Aug 12   From Jonathan Howard. ALS. NhD. mDW 573. Requests him to take charge of note for collection.

Aug 12   From William Henry Woodward. ALS. NhD. mDW 575. Thanks DW for his prompt attention to the Lovejoy and Taylor matters.

Aug 14   From Ezekiel Webster. ALS. NhD. mDW 577. *PC*, 1: 215–216. Perplexed about accepting clerkship.

Aug 19   From Peter Thacher. ALS. NhD. mDW 580. Will send DW additional writs soon; comments on DW's poor health.

Aug 27   From Solon Stevens. ALS. NhD. mDW 583. Reports on cases he had handled for DW.

Aug 31   From Samuel Salisbury, Jr. ALS. NhD. mDW 586. Instructs DW on action to be taken against Old Store.

Sept 12   From Gore, Miller, and Parker. ALS. NhD. mDW 590. Instructs DW on action in several matters.

Sept 12   From Sewall, Salisbury & Company. ALS. NhD. mDW 592. Instruct DW on disposal of collateral goods.

Sept 15   From Ezekiel Webster. ALS. NhD. mDW 595. *PC*, 1: 216–217. Comments on yellow fever epidemic, Dartmouth College, and the New Hampshire legislature.

Sept 24   To Ezekiel Webster. ALS. DLC. mDW 599. Been away from Boscawen on court tour; urges Ezekiel to come to Boscawen.

Sept 27   *From Benjamin Porter.*   73

Sept 29   From Samuel Salisbury. ALS. NhD. mDW 603. Further instructs DW on sale of certain goods.

Sept 30   From Solon Stevens. ALS. NhD. mDW 606. Encloses material on a legal case.

Oct 5   From Charles H. Atherton. ALS. NhD. mDW 608. Informs DW of the conditions expected for the repayment of his notes.

Oct 13   *To Ezekiel Webster.*   73

Oct 17   From John Callender. ALS. NhD. mDW 613. Inquires of the progress of DW's action against the Carrigains.

Oct 17   From Ezekiel Webster. ALS. NhD. mDW 616. *PC*, 1: 217–218. Details reasons for his not coming to Salisbury; pressed for money.

Oct 18   To B. J. Gilbert. ALS. DGU. mDW 620. Instructs Gilbert to hold note of person in debt to him.

Oct 21   From Isaac Brooks. ALS. NhD. mDW 622. Encloses Dix deed.

Oct 25   From William Henry Woodward. ALS. NhD. mDW 624. Encloses writ.

Oct 31   From Caleb Bingham. ALS. NhD. mDW 626. Sends note for collection.

Nov 7	From Benjamin Orr. ALS. NhD. mDW 628. Instructs DW on the collection of certain debts.	
Nov 11	*From Benjamin Porter.*	**74**
Nov 12	From George Woodward. ALS. NhD. mDW 630. Encloses money from a Mr. Porter.	
Nov 13	From Jabez Bradford Whitaker. ALS. NhD. mDW 632. Congratulates DW on his successful law practice.	
Nov 15	To Ezekiel Webster. ALS. NhD. mDW 634. *PC*, 1: 218. Urges him to come to Boscawen.	
Nov 25	From Hazen Kimball. ALS. NhD. mDW 636. Responds to DW's instructions on collecting debt in Savannah.	
Dec 3	From Gore, Miller, & Parker. ALS. NhD. mDW 640. Instructs DW on collection of debt.	
Dec 7	To James Hervey Bingham. Printed. *PC*, 1: 219. Expects to be in Portsmouth on visit soon; hopes to see him there.	
Dec 14	To Noah Emery. ALS. MB. mDW 643. Requests him to send blank writs.	
Dec 15	To Ezekiel Webster. ALS. NhD. mDW 645. Reports death of their sister, Abigail Haddock.	
Dec 19	From James Hervey Bingham. ALS. NhD. mDW 648. After six months' silence, would like to hear from DW.	
Dec 26	Promissory Note. ADS by DW & others. NhD. mDW 39492.	
Dec 30	From Sewall, Salisbury & Company. ALS. NhD. mDW 651. Instruct DW on action in a case.	
[1805–1807]	From George Woodward. ALS. NhD. mDW 653. Instructs DW to convey message on debt to John Chandler.	

1806

Jan 10	*From Thomas W. Thompson.*	**74**
Jan 12	From Benjamin Porter. ALS. NhD. mDW 659. Questions chances of further purchases of Coös bank stock in Boscawen and Salisbury area.	
Jan 19	To James Hervey Bingham. Printed. *PC*, 1: 219–223. Discusses his activities—legal, social, and political —over the past few months.	
Jan 21	From Jonathan Gore. ALS. NhD. mDW 661. Instructs DW on a legal case.	
Jan 28	From Jonathan Gore. ALS. NhD. mDW 663. Reports that action of B. Porter against him is completed.	
Jan 29	*From Thomas W. Thompson.*	**76**
Feb 3	From George Woodward. ALS. NhD. mDW 667. Instructs DW on case against Caleb Putney.	
Feb 8	From James Hervey Bingham. ALS. NhD. mDW 669.	

April 24	From Gore, Miller & Parker. ALS. NhD. mDW 735. Instruct DW on securing certain notes.
April 25	From M. Blood. ALS. NhD. mDW 738. Instructs DW on certain actions against Timothy Dix.
May 7	From Gore, Miller & Parker. ALS. NhD. mDW 740. Report to DW on the Lewis debt.
May 8	From Samuel Ayer Bradley. ALS. NhD. mDW 742. Asks for further instructions from DW on Wardwell case.
May 19	*From Benjamin Porter.* 83
May 24	From Boott & Pratt. ALS. NhD. mDW 748. Report their disappointment with T. Dix's payments.
May 28	From John Penhallow. LS. NhD. mDW 751. Asks DW to handle a trespassing case.
June 4	From Gore, Miller & Parker. ALS. NhD. mDW 753. Asks for immediate reply to their letter of April 24.
June 15	From Samuel Osgood. ALS. NhD. mDW 755. Discusses his decision to enter ministry.
June 16	From Sewall, Salisbury & Co. ALS. NhD. mDW 759. Ask if DW has made any collections on their behalf.
July 7	From Ephraim Paddock. ALS. NhD. mDW 761. Provides information on a Mr. King, involved in a lawsuit.
July 10	To Noah Emery. ALS. William Upton, Concord, N.H. mDWs. Orders blank writs.
July 12	From Barrack Chase. ALS. NhD. mDW 763. Provides information on an assault and battery case.
July 16	From Daniel Abbot. ALS. NhD. mDW 686. Asks DW, "a great 'cricket' in the Law," for an opinion.
July 31	From Joseph Flanders. ALS. NhD. mDW 765. Sends an account of debts and debt collection in which DW had interest.
Aug 6	From William Henry Wilkins. ALS. NhD. mDW 767. Discusses problems of his involvement with Dix.
Aug 7	From Daniel Campbell. ALS. NhD. mDW 771. Sends DW a note for collection.
Aug 19	To [Samuel Ayer Bradley]. ALS. NhD. mDW 773. W & S, 16: 670–671. Makes arrangements with Bradley to go to Dartmouth commencement.
Aug 23	*To Thomas W. Thompson.* 84
Aug	Subscription Paper (for purchase of lottery tickets—proceeds to benefit Fryeburg Academy). Printed. *Fryeburg Webster Centennial* (1902), pp. 50–53.
Sept 1	From Peter Thacher. ALS. NhD. mDW 789. Discusses various cases he's working on; mentions that critics have noticed DW's Phi Beta Kappa address.
Sept 3	*From Cyrus Perkins.* 84
Oct 7	From Benjamin Orr. ALS. NhD. mDW 794. Discusses cases he's asked DW to work on.

April 28	From D. Holmes. Printed form with ms insertions. NhD. mDW 867. Note of $400 due at Hillsborough Bank.
May 14	From Peter Thacher. ALS. NhD. mDW 869. Encloses note for $500 loan.
May 16[?]	From Cyrus Perkins. ALS. NhD. mDW 871. Will arrive in Concord May 30 to proceed to Hopkinton court.
May 29	From Daniel Abbot. ALS. NhD. mDW 873. Hopes to see him shortly after the Hopkinton Court recesses.
May 29	From John Johnson. ALS. NhD. mDW 876. Sends note for collection.
June 9	*From Nathaniel Adams.* 94
June	Petition for incorporation of Religious Society of Boscawen. ADS by DW. Nh-Ar. mDWs. Written by DW as agent for the Society.
July 15	From Abraham Hinds. ALS. NhD. mDW 880. Will forward money he has collected for DW as soon as convenient mode found.
July 17	From Gore, Miller & Parker. ALS. NhD. mDW 882. Send notes for collection.
July 22	From Ebenezer Frothingham. ALS. NhD. mDW 884. Asks DW to secure property for certain notes he holds.
July 25	From B. Hallyn & Co. ALS. NhD. mDW 886. Ask DW to attach property of certain individuals to secure notes.
July 25	From Jonathan Porter. ALS. NhD. mDW 888. Sends notes to be secured.
July 28	From Peter Thacher. ALS. NhD. mDW 890. States that he does not now need the $500 until September.
July 30	From Gore, Miller & Parker. ALS. NhD. mDW 893. Ask for information on Ezra Flanders.
July 31	From Jonathan Porter. ALS. NhD. mDW 895. Sends information on a draft DW is trying to collect or secure.
Aug 3	From Gore, Miller & Parker. ALS. NhD. mDW 897. Addressed to DW at Portsmouth; ask DW to check into several writs.
Aug 8	*To Thomas Worcester.* 95
[Aug 8?]	[Confession of faith]. AD draft. NhD. mDW 906.
Aug 13	From Gore, Miller & Parker. ALS. NhD. mDW 910. Send other instructions regarding writs.
Aug 17	To Parker Noyes. ALS. MBBS. mDW 912. Sends him a "little business" for Strafford.
Aug 18	To Samuel Ayer Bradley. ALS. NhD. mDW 914. Sends instructions regarding a suit against a Mr. Simson.
Aug 20	Certificates of Concord Bank Stock. DS with ms insertions. NhHi. mDW 39495, mDW 39497.
Aug 21	From Jonathan Porter. ALS. NhD. mDW 916. Asks

	DW for information on matters he has entrusted to him.	
Sept 1	*From Ebenezer Frothingham.*	97
[Sept 4]	To "Cousin[?]." Printed. *Century Magazine*, New	
[1807]	Series, 7 (March 1885): 722. Will leave for home at three o'clock.	
[*Sept*] 4	*To Grace Fletcher [Webster].*	97
Sept 5	To Jonathan Porter. ALS. NhD. mDW 921a. Reports on cases and writs he has handled for him.	
Sept 8	To Mills Olcott. ALS. NhD. mDW 922. Asks for assistance in the collection of a note.	
Sept 30	From Jonathan Porter. ALS. NhD. mDW 924. Responds to DW's report of September 5.	
Oct 22	From Skinner & Hurd. ALS. NhD. mDW 926. Send instructions on note collection.	
Oct 26	To Samuel Ayer Bradley. ALS. NhD. mDW 928. Reports on *"Mrs. Lyman."*	
Oct 30	To Ezekiel Webster. ALS. NhD. mDW 932. Details arrangements to be made before court convenes.	
Nov 5	To Ezekiel Webster. ALS. NhD. mDW 934. Sends recommendations on how to conduct debt collecting.	
Nov 25	From William Webster. ALS. NhD. mDW 937. Asks for further instructions regarding writs sent to him.	
Nov 30	To William W. Woodward. ALS. NhD. mDW 939. Orders books for himself and a clergyman friend.	
Dec 1	To Noah Emery. ALS. MB. mDW 942. *W & S*, 16: 10. Asks for documents in case involving Ezekiel Webster.	
Dec 2	To Samuel Ayer Bradley. ALS. NhD. mDW 944. Discusses *"Mrs. Lyman"* and legal matters.	
Dec 2	To Habijah Weld Fuller. Printed. *PC*, 1: 226–227. Thinks of getting married.	
Dec 5	From Samuel Dorr & Company. ALS. NhD. mDW 948. Send instructions regarding note collection.	
Dec 8	To Moody Kent. ALS. NhHi. mDW 950. Sends writ to be served.	
Dec 12	To Ezekiel Webster. ALS. NhD. mDW 952. Needs money; discusses executions; might sell his horse if Ezekiel can get it to Portsmouth.	
Dec 12	From Gore, Miller & Parker. ALS. NhD. mDW 956. Instruct DW to secure a debt of a Mr. Lewis.	
Dec 16	*To Ezekiel Webster.*	98
Dec 26	To Ezekiel Webster. ALS. NhD. mDW 961. Reports that he desperately needs money; instructs Ezekiel to institute several suits.	
[1807–1816]	Epitaph for R[ichard] C[utts] S[hannon]. AD. NhD. Bell, *Bench and Bar of New Hampshire* (1894), p. 633.	

1808

Jan 9	*To Thomas W. Thompson.*	**98**
Jan 15	To Samuel Smith. ALS. NhD. mDW 965. Seeks information on the responsibility of John Levan of Peterborough.	
Jan 18	To S[imon] N. Dexter. ALS. NNPM. mDW 967. Describes action taken in several cases.	
Jan 27	To Samuel Ayer Bradley. ALS. NhD. mDW 968. Is sending horses on since he is detained in Salisbury on business.	
Feb 4	To Ezekiel Webster. ALS. NhD. mDW 970. Sending important papers to Kelly and Col. Webster.	
Feb 27	*To James Hervey Bingham.*	**99**
March 2	To S[imon] N. Dexter. ALS. MHi. mDW 976. Reports that Wilkins & Co. was closed yesterday.	
March 3	*To Ezekiel Webster.*	**100**
March 3	To Mills Olcott. ALS. NhD. mDW 977. Encloses note for his action against a Thetford man.	
March 6	*To [Samuel] Smith.*	**101**
March 9	To Ezekiel Webster. ALS. NhD. mDW 982. PC, 1: 229–230. Has received blank writs; "sue everybody."	
March 11	To Ezekiel Webster. ALS. NhD. mDW 985. Explains his views on a debtor case.	
March 16	To Ezekiel Webster. ALS. NhD. mDW 989. Enclose writs against Bean & Keith, traders in Wentworth.	
April 2	Stock Certificate, Concord Bank. DS by DW and others. NhD. mDW 39499.	
April 8	To Simon N. Dexter. ALS. NhD. mDW 993. Reports on case he was handling for Dexter.	
April 16	To Ezekiel Webster. ALS. NhD. mDW 995. Sends notes involving several cases.	
May 5	To James Hervey Bingham. ALS. NhD. mDWs. PC, 1: 230–231. Reports on his law practice—earning a small living, but shall never be rich; to get married in June.	
May 19	*To John H. Crane.*	**102**
May 25	Petition for incorporation of Grafton Bar Library Association. ADS by Moses Dow, A. Sprague, DW et al. Nh-Ar. mDWs.	
June 7	Writ of attachment. DS by Abiel Foster. NhHi. mDWs.	
June 24	Receipt for legal fees. AD. MWalB. mDW 39501.	
June 28	*To Samuel Ayer Bradley.*	**102**
July 11	*To Mills Olcott.*	**103**
July 18	To Judah Dana. ALS. NhD. mDW 1004. Inquires if Fessenden still plans to read law in his office; must turn away another student if he does.	
July 25	*To Thomas W. Thompson.*	**105**

1809

July 29	Receipt. ADS. MH. mDW 39503. From George Woodward, $1000 for Jeremiah Smith.
Aug 3	*From Charles March and Alfred G. Benson.* **110**
Aug 7	To Ezekiel Webster. ALS. NhD. mDW 1075. Reports that he has made a settlement with Lewis.
Aug 8	From David Webster. ALS. NhHi. mDW 1077. Discusses several note settlement cases.
Aug 15	Certificates of transfer of Concord Bank Stock. DS. NhHi. mDW 39504, 39505.
Aug 28	To Ezekiel Webster. ALS. NhD. mDW 1080. Sends instructions and documents involving several cases.
Sept 1	To Ezekiel Webster. ALS. NhD. mDW 1082. Discusses several cases and points of law.
Sept 27	To Samuel Ayer Bradley. AL incomplete. NhD. mDW 1090. Informs him of the disposition of several cases.
Oct 24	*To Jeremiah Smith.* **111**
Oct 30	*To Mills Olcott.* **111**
Nov 4	*From Noah Webster.* **112**
Nov 4	From James Hervey Bingham. ALS. NhHi. mDW 1097. Asks DW to enter certain cases on the Hillsborough court docket.
Nov 11	Promissory note. ADS. OCHP. mDW 39508. For $146.16 to March & Benson of New York for the Madeira wine.
Dec 4	*From William Webster.* **113**
Dec 5	Promissory note. ADS. MB. mDW 39510.
Dec 12	From S. P. Webster. ALS. NhHi. mDW 1104. Sends note for collection.
Dec 14	To Thomas W. Thompson. ALS. CSmH. mDWs. Has no doubt of Thompson's fidelity and friendship.
Dec [15]	From Ezekiel Webster. ALS. NhD. mDW 1106. Sends accounts of several cases.
Dec 23	*From S. R. Miller & Co.* **113**

1810

Jan 8	From S. R. Miller & Co. ALS. NhHi. mDW 1112. Send statements of accounts with Garland.
Jan 14	From Munroe & Francis. ALS. DLC. mDW 1114. Send draft on DW for $100 on his bill.
Jan 15	From Samuel Dorr. ALS. NhD. mDW 1116. Inquires of the standing of John Weare of Andover.
Jan 20	To Jonathan Hartwell. ALS. Shattuck Hartwell, North Muskegon, Mich. mDWs. Discusses land mortgages, overdue payments, and other legal matters.
Jan 23	To Joseph Langdon. ALS. NhD. mDW 1118. Informs

May 22	From Timothy Bigelow. ALS. NhD. mDW 1172. Sends note for collection or for getting security.
June 2	*From Samuel Fessenden.* **118**
June 5	To Timothy Bigelow. ALS. MHi. mDW 1178. Believes he can get security for notes.
July 14	From Samuel Ayer Bradley. ALS. DLC. mDW 1180. Asks DW to commence action in Strafford County.
[p/m July]	To Ezekiel Webster (with enclosed promissory note of Samuel Albree). ALS. NhD. mDW 1184. Asks that Ezekiel make writs against Albree.
Aug 1	*To [Federalist Committees in New Hampshire].* **119**
Aug 27–28	*To Ezekiel Webster.* **120**
Sept 1	From S. R. Miller & Co. ALS. NhHi. mDW 1191. Inform DW of their agreement with Kelly.
Sept 10	To Ezekiel Webster. ALS. NhD. mDW 1194. Sends list of civil actions he wants entered in Grafton.
Sept 15	To Samuel Ayer Bradley. ALS. NhD. mDW 1197. Responds to Bradley's letter of July 14 and explains a New Hampshire statute.
Nov 9	From Edward St. Loe Livermore. ALS. NhD. mDW 1200. Sends authorities for argument used in court case.
Nov 26	To Samuel Ayer Bradley. ALS. NhD. mDW 1202. Requests Bradley's services on enclosed writs.
Nov 26	To Noah Emery. ALS. NhD. mDW 1205. Asks for dedimus in *Brown* v. *Evans.*
Nov 27	*To Ezekiel Webster.* **120**
Nov 29	[Deed from John Ham to Thomas Brown]. Printed form with ms insertions in DW's hand. WaU. mDW 1210.
Dec 31	To Mills Olcott. ALS. NhD. mDW 1213. Recommends course of action in Lewis case.

1811

Jan 4	From Alexander Townsend. ALS. NhHi. mDW 1215. Authorizes DW to discharge a note.
Jan 8	From Peter Thacher. ALS. NhHi. mDW 1217. Inquires of DW his knowledge of a deposition.
Jan 28	To [Moody?] Kent. ALS. NhD. mDW 1219. Forwards him executions for collection.
Jan 29	From William Thurston. ALS. NhHi. mDW 1211. Requests DW to check into the authenticity of a signature on a note.
Jan 30	To Samuel Ayer Bradley. ALS. NhD. mDW 1223. Reports on certain legal matters and invites him for a visit to restore his health.
[Feb]	To Ezekiel Webster. ALS. NhD. mDW 1226. *PC*, 1: 232. Sends him some imported items.

Aug 15	From William Little. ALS. NhHi. mDW 1284. Discusses payment of an account.
Aug 29	To ? ALS. NhHi. mDW 1286. Sends instructions for payment of a note.
[Aug 30]	To Samuel Ayer Bradley. Typed copy. NhD. mDW 1287. States fee for legal services.
Sept 2	From Alexander Townsend. ALS. NhHi. mDW 1288. Asks for DW's opinion on a case.
Sept 9	To Ebenezer Thompson. LS by proxy. NhD. mDW 1291. Forwards note for collection.
Sept 10	From Robert Ilsley. ALS. NhHi. mDW 1293. Urges DW to press for payment on a note.
Sept 14	*To Ezekiel Webster.* **125**
Sept 18	From Alexander Townsend. ALS. NhHi. mDW 1299. Forwards notes for collection.
Oct 24	*To William A. Kent.* **126**
Nov 26	To Samuel Ayer Bradley. ALS. NhD. mDW 1304. Discusses his plan of action in Ruggles matter.
[Nov 28]	To [Samuel Ayer Bradley] (enclosure: deposition of Richard Pickering). ALS. MeBP. mDW 1306. Makes suggestions on the Ruggles matter.
Nov 29	To Moses Paul Payson. ALS. MHi. mDW 1311. Discusses executions to be served and remittance of money.
Dec 18	To Nicholas Emery. ALS. CtY. mDW 1313. Discusses a theft case.
[Dec 23]	To Noah Emery. ANS. NhD. mDW 1316. Orders blank writs.
Dec 29	*From Paul Revere and Sons.* **127**

1812

Jan 11	To Ezekiel Webster. ALS. NhD. mDW 1319. Instructs Ezekiel to take deed to Lewis land for what Lewis owes him.
Jan 17	*From James A. Geddes.* **127**
Jan	Account of Clement March. AD. MWalB. mDW 39516. (Runs to 1814, Jan). Statement of DW's fees.
Feb [?]	To Ezekiel Webster. ALS. NhD. mDW 1324. Asks Ezekiel to have the Kelly land surveyed, since he is selling it to Pickering.
March 21	To William A. Kent. ALS. NhHi. mDW 1327. Comments on the security of Upham's note.
April 3	To Charles H. Atherton. ALS. Amherst Historical Society, Amherst, N.H. mDWs. Expresses pleasure at learning "the favorable course of action in Boston."
April 13	To Paul Revere & Sons. ALS. MHi. mDW 1329. Sends report on debt collection matter.

May 14   From ? Gile. AL. NhHi. mDW 1331. Discusses question of who invented fliers for spinning cotton yarn.

June 19   From S. R. Miller & Company. ALS. NhHi. mDW 1335. Urge DW to communicate with them on certain cases.

July 28   *To Timothy Farrar.*   **128**

Aug 1   To Moody Kent. ALS. NhHi. mDW 1342. Mentions the scheduled anti-war gathering at Brentwood.

Aug 6   Property Deed, Isaac Waldon to Joseph Sheafe. ADS. MHi. mDWs. Signed by DW.

Sept [p/m 19]   From Thomas Oliver Selfridge. ALS. DLC. mDW 1383. Discusses matter of captured sailors and wages to be paid.

Sept 26   *From Horace Binney, Joseph Hopkinson, and William Meredith.*   **130**

Oct 1   [Court order conferring degree of barrister-of-law on DW et al.]. ADS. NhHi. mDW 1389.

Oct 3   "DeWitt Clinton." Printed. Portsmouth *Oracle.* Oct 3, 1812. DW expresses a preference for the election of Clinton over Madison.

Oct 6   *To Joseph Smith.*   **130**

Oct 8   To Benjamin J. Gilbert. ALS. DGU. mDW 1393. Introduces John P. Lord.

Oct 8   To Mills Olcott. ALS. Richard S. Rolfe, Concord, NH. mDW 1395. Introduces John P. Lord.

Oct 9   *To Timothy Farrar, Jr.*   **131**

Oct 15   *To John Pickering.*   **133**

Oct 16   To Noah Emery. ALS. NhD. mDW 38362. Requests copies of *Austin* v. *Penhallow.*

Oct 29   From Timothy Pickering. ALS draft. MHi. mDW 1405. Instructs DW to commence suit against Portsmouth *Gazette* editor.

Nov 4   Receipt to Jonathan Merrill. ADS. NhD. mDW 39518. For $292.18.

Nov   To Ithamar Chase (from Daniel French and DW). ALS by Daniel French and DW. Nh-Ar. mDWs. Recommend Joseph Bartlett for a justice of the peace for Rockingham County.

[Nov]   Petition of Jeremiah Gerrish, Stephen Gerrish, and DW. ADS. Nh-Ar. mDWs. Ask to be relieved of their obligations as co-signers of a Timothy Dix note.

Dec 2   Credentials of DW as Representative of New Hampshire. ADS. DNA, RG 233. mDW 40774.

Dec 9   *To Samuel Ayer Bradley.*   **133**

Dec 11   *To Timothy Pickering.*   **133**

Dec 11   To John Pickering. ALS. MHi. mDW 1409. W & S, 16: 12. Asks about bringing the libel suit against *Gazette* editor in Circuit Court.

Dec 23   From Timothy Pickering. ALS draft. MHi. mDW
1414. Agrees to institution of suit in a circuit court
of the United States.

1813

Jan 10   To Jedidiah Morse. ALS. NhHi. mDW 1415. Asks for
letter of introduction to the Rev. Dr. Austin of
Worcester.

[Feb 15?]   To Noah Emery. ALS. MB. mDW 1416. W & S, 16:
13. Requests copy of the case *Austin* v. *Penhallow*.

Feb 18   From John Givan. ALS. NhHi. mDW 1418. Urges DW
to take action on note to be collected.

March 4   To Timothy Farrar, Jr. ALS. NhHi. mDW 1421.
W & S, 16: 671–672. Desires to form law partner-
ship with Farrar in Portsmouth before Congress
convenes.

March 8   Deed: Transfer of land from Daniel Webster to
Joshua Pickering. Printed DS. Morristown National
Historical Park. mDWs.

March 29   [Partnership agreement with Timothy Farrar, Jr.].
ADS by DW and Timothy Farrar. NhHi. mDW
1425.

April 24   To John Pickering. ALS. MHi. mDW 1431. W & S,
16: 13. Discusses action in suit against *Gazette*
editor; asks for letter from Timothy Pickering.

April 27   From Timothy Pickering. ALS draft. MHi (enclosure: John Pickering to [Timothy Pickering]. April
27, 1813. ALS draft. MHi). mDW 1434. Sends
statement of reasons for action against *Gazette*
editor.

May 1   To Paul Revere & Sons. ALS. MHi. mDW 1439. Will
be in Boston on May 10 and will call on them.

May 1   From John Givan. ALS. NhHi. mDW 1441. Sends instructions on forwarding money collected for him.

May 17   From Thomas W. Thompson. ALS. DLC. mDW 1443.
Discusses politics in New Hampshire—resignations,
removal from office, etc.

May 23   From Edward St. Loe Livermore. ALS. NhD. mDW
1445. Reports death of Captain Ham.

May 25   From Joseph Bartlett. ALS. NhHi. mDW 1452. Inquires about developments in Washington; asks
DW for recommendations for "justiceship."

May 27   To Charles March. ALS. NhHi. mDW 1463. W & S,

16: 16. Reports committee appointments in House of Representatives.

May 27   To Ezekiel Webster. ALS. NhD. mDW 1465. Reports committee appointments in the House of Representatives.

May 28   *To Samuel Ayer Bradley.*   **140**

May 28   To Charles March. ALS. NhHi. mDW 1473. W & S, 16: 16. Describes action in House on seating of delegates.

May 29   *To Ezekiel Webster.*   **141**

May 31   To Ezekiel Webster. ALS. NhD. mDW 1482. Reports discussion on the seating of a stenographer.

May 31   *To Charles March.*   **142**

May 31   *From Charles March.*   **143**

June 1   To Timothy Farrar, Jr. ALS. NhHi. mDW 1488. Encloses $100; discusses stenographer's petition.

June 2   To Ezekiel Webster. ALS. NhD. mDW 1492. Discusses election of printer in House and election of senator in New Hampshire.

June 3   *To Charles March.*   **144**

June 3   To Charles March. ALS. NhHi. mDW 1497. Van Tyne, p. 36. Mentions the nomination of Swedish and Russian minister, French decrees.

June 4   *To Ezekiel Webster.*   **144**

June 4   To [James Hervey] Bingham. Printed. *PC*, 1: 232–234. Discusses slow progress in House; Washington society.

June 4   From Ezekiel Webster. ALS. NhD. mDW 1501. *PC*, 1: 232–233. Describes political organization of New Hampshire legislature and election of senator.

June 5–7   *From Ezekiel Webster.*   **144**

June 6   *To Charles March.*   **146**

[June 7]   *To Charles March.*   **147**

[June 8]   To Charles March. ALS. NhHi. mDW 1515. Van Tyne, pp. 38–39. Reports that his resolutions on Berlin and Milan decrees not brought forward yet.

June 8   From Ezekiel Webster. ALS. NhD. mDW 1517. Conveys the news of Mason's election as senator.

June 9   To Charles March. ALS. NhHi. mDW 1522. W & S, 16: 19. Reports slow progress in House.

[June 10]   *To Charles March.*   **147**

June 10   "Resolutions requesting the President to inform House of Representatives when U.S. first learned of French decree." *Annals of Congress*, 13th Cong., 1st sess., 1813–1814, pp. 150–151.

[June 11]   To Charles March. ALS. NhHi. mDW 1528. W & S, 16: 20. Reports that his resolutions on the French decrees are to come up tomorrow.

June 12   *To Moody Kent.*   **148**

Sept 8	From Thomas J. Oakley. ALS. DLC. mDW 1604. Asks about the effect of a foreign judgment in New Hampshire.
Sept 16	To Moses Paul Payson. Copy. NhHi. mDW 1608. Details judgments recovered and remarks on a "strange" speech in Portsmouth.
Sept [?]	To Noah Emery. ALS. NhD. mDW 1609. Requests copies of *Eastman* v. *Tay* for Ezekiel.
Oct 14	Petition for Justice of the Peace for Newmarket. ADS by Daniel R. Rogers, DW et al. Nh-Ar. mDWs. Recommends Seth R. Shackford.
Oct [?]	*To Thomas W. Thompson.* 157
Nov 3	From John Coyle. ALS. DLC. mDW 1611. Inquires about DW's arrangements for a "mess" in Washington.
Nov 20	From Charles March. ALS. NhHi. mDW 1613. Has paid DW's draft for $970.
Nov 20	From Samuel C. Webster. ALS. NhHi. mDW 1615. Reports that he has completed levies on Fulton's farm.
Nov 25 – Dec 8	DW's account with Samuel C. Webster. AD. NhHi. mDWs. For various errands.
[c. Dec 26]	From D. W[aldron]. ALS (incomplete). NhHi. mDW 1619. Van Tyne, pp. 48–49. Describes fire at DW's home and in Portsmouth.
Dec 29	*To Ezekiel Webster.* 159
Dec 30	To Timothy Farrar, Jr. ALS. NhHi. mDW 1623. Responds to news of fire; sends money.
[Dec ?]	To William A. Hayes. ALS. NhHi. mDW 1626. Will try to pay off debt soon.

1814

Jan 6	*To Isaac P. Davis.* 159
Jan 6	"Conscription." Printed. *Columbian Centinel,* Jan 15, 1814. Essay.
Jan 27	To Edward Cutts, Jr. ALS. MB. mDW 1632a. Suggests that Cutts squelch rumor that Boston men are taking up a collection for him, if such a rumor is prevalent in Portsmouth.
Jan 27	Petition from Portsmouth asking that direct taxes and internal duties go for relief from fire destruction, referred to Committee on Ways and Means. ADS. DNA. RG 233. mDW 40765.
Jan 30	*To Ezekiel Webster (with postscript to Grace Fletcher Webster).* 160
Feb 3	To [Timothy Farrar, Jr.] ALS. NhHi. mDW 1637. Discusses prospects of peace, certain pseudonymous newspaper articles and inquires about money.

Feb 5	*To Ezekiel Webster.*	**162**
Feb 7	To Charles B. Haddock. Printed. *PC*, 1: 241–242. Reminisces about study and reading in college.	
Feb 7	From Timothy Pickering. ALS draft. MHi. mDW 1645. Questions wisdom of dropping libel suit against Weeks, *Gazette* editor.	
Feb 8	*To [Benjamin J. Gilbert?].*	**163**
Feb 11	*To [?].*	**163**
Feb 14	To [Timothy Farrar, Jr.]. ALS. NhD. mDWs. Inquires about certain court cases, receipt of money from New York; reports on developments in Congress.	
Feb 14	Receipt of payment of Jeremiah Gerrish. AD in DW's hand. NhD. mDW 39519.	
Feb 19	Petition of Asa McFarland and others asking for legislation prohibiting the distillation of grain into spirits. Referred to Committee on Ways and Means. ADS. DNA, RG 233. mDW 40760.	
Feb 24	Petition of J. Salter, Jr. complaining of delay in relation to the trial of the ship *Rose* in the District of New York and praying relief. Referred to the Committee on the Judiciary. ADS. DNA, RG 233. mDW 40689.	
[Feb 28]	*To [Nathaniel Appleton Haven] enclosing to [Isaac P. Davis].*	**165**
March 25	To Robert Brent. AD. DNA, RG 99. mDW 57117. Presents back-pay claims of Stanton Smiley, deceased soldier.	
March 26	Petition of sundry inhabitants of Portsmouth for legislation allowing transportation by water of lime from Thomastown and Campden in Maine to Portsmouth during the continuation of the Embargo. Referred to Select Committee. ADS. DNA, RG 233. mDW 40770.	
March 28	*To Ezekiel Webster.*	**167**
May 9	From Joshua Pickering. ALS. NhHi. mDW 1668. Instructs DW on the collection of rent on certain property.	
May 15	To Israel W. Kelly. ALS. NhHi. mDW 38658. Expects to be in Hopkinton with the Titcomb execution on Friday.	
June 11	To Shubael Hurd, Jacob Smith, and Charles Willey. ALS. NhD. mDW 1671. Thanks them for the expression of their sympathy in his recent misfortune.	
June 20	To [David Daggett]. ALS. CtY. mDW 1672. On behalf of Parish Committee, inquires about a Connecticut ministerial candidate.	
[June 20]	*To Moses Paul Payson.*	**168**
June 25	Political essay on Portsmouth election of councillor. Printed. Portsmouth *Oracle*, June 25, 1814.	

June 29   To James Thom. ALS. PHi. mDW 1676. Van Tyne, p. 49. Invites him and others to the Washington Benevolent Society gathering on July 4.

July 21   From William Jenks (to DW et al.). ALS copy. MHi. mDW 1679. Cannot accept the invitation to become minister of the North Parish, Portsmouth.

Aug 1   From John Chandler. ALS. DLC. mDW 1682. Sends note for collection.

Aug 1   From Joshua Pickering. ALS. NhHi. mDW 1684. Inquires about rent due him; remarks that fleet of 10 sailing vessels has just left Sackets Harbor for Niagara.

Aug 5   From Miles R. Burke. ALS. NhHi. mDW 1687. Requests DW to collect notes and debts.

Aug 9   From James Monroe. Printed LS. ICHi. mDW 1691. Informs him that Congress is to convene on September 19.

[c. Aug 12]   *To John Kelly.*   **169**

Aug 16   Essay on Jay Treaty. Printed. Concord *Gazette,* Aug 16, 1814.

Aug 17   To William Jenks. ALS. MHi. mDW 1693. Renews the call of the North Parish.

[Aug]   To Ezekiel Webster. ALS. NhD. mDW 1695. Intends to come to Boscawen after Gilmanton court; wants to see Flanders, if he wants to buy the lot.

Sept 3   Committee for Defense of Portsmouth to [John Taylor Gilman]. ALS by John Goddard, J. Mason, DW, et al. Nh-Ar. mDWs. Requests the governor to detach regiments for defense of Portsmouth.

[c. Sept 5–6]   To Samuel Ayer Bradley. ALS. NhD. mDW 1697. Introduces a Captain Humphries.

Sept 10   *Notice of Portsmouth Committee of Defense.*   **169**

Sept 21   From Jonathan Cass. ALS. NhHi. mDW 1701. Asks if New Hampshire will ever be returned to sound principles.

Sept 29   To Samuel C. Webster. ALS. NhD. mDWs. Sends instructions on certain cases.

Sept 30   Credentials of DW (elected as Representative from New Hampshire from March 4, 1815 to March 4, 1817). Printed D with ms insertions. DNA, RG 233. mDW 40791.

Oct 17 (1)   *To William Sullivan.*   **170**

Oct 17 (2)   *To William Sullivan.*   **171**

Oct 19   Petition for post road from Exeter to Concord. Referred to Committee on Post Offices and Post Roads. ADS. DNA, RG 233. mDW 40695.

Oct 20   To Ezekiel Webster. ALS. NhD. mDW 1711. W & S, 16: 30. Discusses trip to Washington, Pennsylvania election, war news, and his decision on the tax question.

Oct 24	[Certificate of Membership in American Antiquarian Society]. Printed DS with ms insertions. MWA. mDW 1715.	
[Oct 25]	*To Nathan Hale.*	**172**
Oct 27	To Nathan Hale. ALS. MHi. mDW 1717. Sends abstract of conscription bill.	
Oct 27	Editorial on Direct Taxes. Printed. *National Intelligencer*, Oct 27, 1814.	
Oct 29	*From Ezekiel Webster.*	**172**
Oct 30	To David Lewis. ALS. PPL. mDWs. Asks for his opinion, as a merchant, on Dallas' plan for a national bank.	
Oct 30	*To [Timothy Farrar, Jr.?].*	**174**
Oct 30	*To Ezekiel Webster.*	**175**
Nov 8	To [Ezekiel Webster]. ALS. NhD. mDW 1731. *PC*, 1: 246. Describes discussion in Congress on conscription.	
Nov 12	Petition for establishment of postal route from Concord to Fryeburg. Referred to Committee on Post Offices and Post Roads. ADS. DNA, RG 233. mDW 40701.	
Nov 21	*To Ezekiel Webster.*	**176**
Nov 28	To [Nathaniel Appleton Haven?]. ALS. NhHi. mDW 7139. Makes recommendations regarding the New Hampshire elections.	
Nov 29	*To Ezekiel Webster.*	**177**
Dec 14	Petition of J. B. Eastman for settlement of claims against British. Referred to Committee of Claims. ADS. DNA, RG 233. mDW 40686.	
Dec 14	Petitions of Francestown and Ipswich protesting Sunday mails. Referred to Postmaster General. ADS. DNA, RG 233. mDW 40703, 40705.	
Dec 17	Petitions of Bedford, Hampton, Hamstead, protesting Sunday mails, referred to Postmaster General. ADS. DNA, RG 233. mDW 40707.	
Dec 22	To Moody Kent. ALS. NhHi. mDW 1770. *W & S*, 16: 32. Discusses New Hampshire and national politics.	
Dec 22	*To Ezekiel Webster.*	**178**
Dec 28	To Daniel Gookin. ALS. MB. mDW 1777. Discusses seamen question—shortage, bounties, etc.	
Dec 28	Petitions of Londonderry, Mt. Vernon, Northampton, Boscawen, Atkinson, Washington, Epping, Raymond protesting Sunday mails. Referred to Postmaster General. ADS. DNA, RG 233. mDW 40717.	
Dec 31	To [Jacob McGaw]. ALS. Mrs. Lester W. Parker. Brimfield, Mass. mDW 1781. Reminisces about Fryeburg; describes Washington.	
[1814?]	To William Sullivan. AN. NhExP. mDW 39360. Denies that a "doggerel" sent by Grace Fletcher is his.	

Feb [15?] To John Bell. ALS. CtY. mDW 1878. Reports that he has requested that *Lord* v. *Bell* not be called before court until he reaches home.

[Feb 15] To William Hale. ALS. NhHi. mDW 1879. Discusses his congressional pay.

March 15 Receipt for payment by William [Rice]. ADS. NhHi. mDW 39521.

March 22 To Paul Revere and Sons. ALS. MHi. mDW 1881. Authorizes company to draw on him for amount of note and interest.

[April 1] From Nathaniel Appleton Haven and John Haven. DS. MBNU. mDWs. Statement of DW's account with the Havens.

May 8 From [John Lovett]. AL. NhHi. mDW 1883. Discusses friends in Congress.

June 16–27 From James Hervey Bingham. ALS. NhHi. mDW 1885. Encloses minutes in case of *Chamberlain* v. *Crane.*

June [Argument for the plaintiff in *Webster* v. *Inhabitants of Orono*]. Copy. DLC. mDW 1884–a.

July 1 To James Hervey Bingham. Copy. NhHi. mDW 1889. *W & S,* 16: 33–34. Discusses several court cases.

July 5 From John Pickering. ALS. NhHi. mDW 1890. Discusses use of word "liability" in legal and lay circles.

July 24 From Nathaniel Appleton Haven and John Haven. DS. MBNU. mDWs. Statement of DW's account with company.

Aug 4 To William Hale. ALS. NhHi. mDW 1893. Informs him of a hearing before which Hale is to appear.

Aug 5 *From John Wheelock.* 188

Aug 16 *From Josiah Dunham (enclosure: Thomas W. Thompson to Ebenezer Adams, July 13).* 188

Aug 25 *To [Josiah Dunham].* 191

Aug 26 *To Nathan Hale.* 194

Sept Receipt for $7.60, in the case of *Harris* v. *Austin,* September term, 1815. DS. DLC. mDWs.

Dec 13 To Amos Avery Brewster. ALS. NhD. mDW 1914. Encloses deed from DW to Cyrus Perkins for delivery.

[1815?] Petition on Justice of the Peace for Portsmouth. ADS by John Langdon, Isaac Waldron, DW, et al. Nh-Ar. mDWs. Recommend Edmund H. Quinn.

1816

Feb 9 Petition of Daniel C. Akerman and John Underwood on behalf of ropemakers of Portsmouth. Referred to Committee of Commerce and Manufactures. ADS. DNA, RG 233. mDW 40783.

Feb 9 Petition of Lucy Dix for back pay of husband. Re-

July 1	To [Richard?] Bradley. ALS. NhHi. mDW 1947. Reports the payment of a note.
July 13	From R[obert] B[rent]. Letterbook Copy. DNA, RG 99. mDW 57116. Reports on the claim of David G. Allen for back pay.
July 17	To William Hale. ALS. NhHi. mDW 1949. Makes arrangements for settlement of a note in Dover.
July 29	To Alexander Bliss. ALS. DLC. mDW 1952. Has shipped to Boston five boxes of his books.
July 30	*To [Joseph] Story.* **201**
Aug 12	From Nathaniel Pierce Hoar. ALS. DLC. mDW 38651. Sends his best wishes on the eve of DW's move to Boston.
Aug 12	Catalogue of books in the Law Library of Daniel Webster. AD, not in DW's hand. NhD. mDW 1955.
Aug 14	Memoranda of Professional Fees. ADS. MHi. mDW 1961. Runs through 1818, August 14.
Sept 23	From Samuel L. Knapp. ALS. Morristown National Historical Park. mDWs. Introduces Edmund Kimball.
[Sept ?]	To Ezekiel Webster. ALS. NhD. mDW 1982. Discusses several court cases.
[Sept ?]	To Octavius Pickering. ALS. Boston Bar Association, Boston, Mass. mDWs. States that Ninian C. Betton entered his law office on September 1.
Oct 3	To Jeremiah Mason. ALS. NhHi. mDW 1984. Discusses several court cases.
Oct 9	To James Hervey Bingham. ALS. OClWHi. mDW 1986. W & S, 16: 34. Describes how he would proceed in a certain court case.
Oct 10	To Moses Paul Payson. ALS. MHi. mDW 1988. Van Tyne, pp. 70–71. Inquires for Mrs. Webber, widow of the president of Harvard, about lands and taxes.
Oct 14	To [Timothy Farrar, Jr.?]. ALS. NHi. mDW 1991. Forwards several notes to collect or secure.
Oct 14	To Moses Paul Payson. ALS. MHi. mDW 1993. Sends note for collection.
Oct 29	*To Jeremiah Mason.* **202**
Nov 9	*To Nathan Appleton Haven.* **203**
Nov 18	*To James William Paige.* **205**
Dec 2	To Alexander Bliss. ALS. DLC. mDW 2004. Reports his arrival in Washington; comments on a legal question raised by Bliss.
Dec 6	Petition on Justice of the Peace for Concord. ADS by John Carter, DW, et al. Nh-Ar. mDWs.
Dec 9	To [Joseph Story]. ALS. MHi. mDW 2007. W & S, 16: 36–37. Discusses judiciary bill, bankruptcy bill, and president's recommendation for reorganizing the courts.

Dec 13	To James Madison and Mrs. Madison (from DW and Mrs. Webster). AL in Mrs. W's hand. CSmH. mDW 2011. Accept invitation to dine.	
Dec 14	To Alexander Bliss. ALS. DLC. mDW 2013. Encloses statement in Staver case.	
Dec 30	To Henry Wheaton. ALS. NNPM. mDW 2016. Discusses *Ariadne* case.	
Dec 31	Summons for Jeremiah Gerrish to appear in court. AD in DW's hand. NhD. mDW 39523.	
[1816–1827]	To ? ALS. NN. mDW 39277. Discusses a note due in March.	
[1816–1827]	To Alexander Bliss. ALS. DLC. mDW 38267. Instructs Bliss to send letters to Mr. Sedgwick and to keep a record of the letters sent.	
[1816–1827]	To Alexander Bliss. ALS. DLC. mDW 38262. Reports that he is ill and cannot get out of the house; requests Bliss to get his cases continued.	

1817

Jan 2	*To [William Sullivan].*	**205**
Jan 3	To Alexander Bliss. ALS. DLC. mDW 2027. Sends instructions on notes to be collected; very concerned over illness of daughter.	
Jan 3	To Ezekiel Webster. ALS. NhD. mDW 2030. Instructs Ezekiel on securing note; Mrs. W. will probably return home to see Grace.	
Jan 8	From James Sheafe and John Haven (to DW and William Hale). LS. NhHi. mDW 2032. Ask attention to certain papers.	
Jan 9	*From William Sullivan.*	**208**
[Jan 11]	To James William Paige. ALS. MH. mDW 2038. Has arrived in New York and should arrive in Boston January 14.	
Jan 11	From William Sullivan. ALS. NhHi. mDW 2041. Reports on Grace's health and urges DW to send Mrs. Webster on home.	
Jan 13	From George Sullivan. ALS. NhHi. mDW 2044. Reports on Grace's health.	
Jan 19	*To Ezekiel Webster.*	**209**
Jan 22	From Thomas W. Thompson. ALS. NhD. mDW 2050. Discusses the Dartmouth College question.	
[Jan 26]	*To Ezekiel Webster.*	**209**
Jan 31	From Nathan Appleton Haven (to DW and William Hale). ALS. NhHi. mDW 2056. Reports he is enclosing resolutions adopted at a meeting of the merchants and shipowners of Portsmouth.	
Feb 10	From Isaac Fiske. ALS. Boston Bar Association, Boston, Mass. mDWs. Introduces a Mr. Whiting.	
Feb 17	Petition protesting Sunday mails, referred to Select	

	Committee. Printed D with ms insertions. DNA, RG 233. mDW 40786.	
Feb 24	To Alexander Bliss. ALS. DLC. mDW 2061. Will check at War Department on the matter of paying back wages to administrators.	
April 9	To Ezekiel Webster (enclosure: George Sullivan to [Ezekiel Webster], April 9). ALS. NhD. mDW 2064. Discusses George Sullivan's purchase of Sanbornton Turnpike stock.	
[May 25]	*To Ezekiel Webster.*	210
June 2	To William H. Crawford. Copy. DNA, RG 59. mDWs. Recommends Samuel D. Harris for vacancy in Boston Custom House.	
June 13	[Appointment as Justice of the Peace, Suffolk County]. Printed form with ms insertions. NhExP. mDW 2071.	
June 21	To Charles Brickett Haddock. ALS. NhD. mDW 2072. PC, 1: 264–265. Discusses questions of choosing a profession and studying Latin.	
June 28	*To Jeremiah Mason.*	211
June 30	To the Secretary of the Suffolk Bar Association. ALS. Boston Bar Association, Boston, Mass. mDWs. Certifies that Ninian C. Betton has read law in his office since July 1, 1816.	
Aug 9	To Alexander Bliss. ALS. DLC. mDW 2079. Have arrived at Boston; should be home on Monday, August 10.	
Aug 18	To [Moody?] Kent. ALS. NN. mDW 2081. Sends instructions regarding a note.	
Aug 21	Statement of Account between DW and Jeremiah Gerrish. ADS. NhD. MWalB. mDW 39525.	
Sept 4	*To [Jeremiah] Mason.*	212
Sept 5	To Abel Harris. ALS. CSmH. mDW 2083. States that Harris suit will be continued if continuance can be obtained.	
Oct 4	[Certificate for Edmund Kimball]. ADS. DLC. mDW 2087. States that Kimball has read law in DW's office since October 1, 1816.	
Oct 4	To the Secretary of the Suffolk Bar Association. ALS. Boston Bar Association, Boston, Mass. mDWs. States that Martin Whitney has read law in his office since January 30, 1817.	
Oct 12	Statement of Account between John Peirce and DW. ADS. NhD. mDW 39529.	
Nov 11	To Nathaniel Appleton Haven. ALS. MBNU. mDWs. Is willing to answer Haven's draft for $500.	
Nov 11	To James William Paige. ALS. MHi. mDW 2089. Denies that any of his friends spoke disrespectfully of Mrs. Greenleaf.	
Nov 15	To Francis Brown. ALS. NhD. mDW 2093. Mentions	

the decision on the Dartmouth case at Plymouth and intention to appeal to Washington; will decide within a few days whether he will go to Washington next winter.

Nov 20   *From Joseph Hopkinson.*   213

Nov 27   To Francis Brown. ALS. NhD. mDW 2101. States that he will go to Washington to argue college cause.

Nov 27   *To [Jeremiah] Mason.*   214

Dec 8   To Francis Brown and Charles Marsh. ALS. NhD. mDW 2104. Shirley, *Dartmouth College Causes,* p. 5. Discusses possibility of bringing suit in circuit court.

Dec 8   *To Jeremiah Mason.*   215

Dec 8   To Jeremiah Smith. Printed. *PC,* 1: 267–268. Discusses the Dartmouth College cause.

Dec 16   *From Isaac Hill.*   215

Dec 23   To Theodore Eames. ALS. NhD. mDW 2112a. Tries to collect fees owed him.

Dec 23   To Nathaniel A. Haven. ALS. MBNU. mDWs. Directs Haven to see him in Boston and to bring his letters to a shipowner.

Dec 24   To Nathaniel Appleton Haven. ALS. NhD. mDW 2113. Reports that Ezekiel is in town and would like Haven to come down with legal papers.

Dec 27   To Isaac Hill. ALS. NhHi. mDW 2116. States that he cannot comply with Hill's request to publish the argument of counsel in the Dartmouth College case, which is still pending.

Dec 31   From William Sullivan and William C. Jarvis. ALS by Sullivan and Jarvis. MHi. mDW 2118. Decline to admit certain papers in evidence.

[1817?]   To Alexander Bliss. ALS. DLC. mDW 38265. States that he will not be back in Boston until Tuesday morning.

[1817–1822] To Alexander Bliss. AL incomplete. DLC. mDW 38269. Sends recommendations on legal matters.

[1817–1825] To John Quincy Adams. AL. MHi. mDW 2120. Declines dinner invitation.

[1817–1825] To John Quincy Adams. AL. MHi. mDW 2122. Declines dinner invitation.

[1817–1825] To John Quincy Adams. AL. MHi. mDW 2124. Declines dinner invitation.

[1817–1825] To John Quincy Adams. AL. MHi. mDW 2126. Accepts dinner invitation.

1818

Jan 3   To [David Daggett]. ALS. CtY. mDW 2128. Encloses papers of a Mr. Searle, Boston merchant, and comments on tax question in Congress.

Jan 4	To Ezekiel Webster. ALS. NhD. mDW 2130. Shall get Ezekiel's trunk on the stage tomorrow morning.
Jan 8	To [Ezekiel Webster]. ALS. NhD. mDW 2132. Has drawn on Ezekiel for $100.
Jan 9	To [David Daggett]. ALS. CtY. mDW 2134. Introduces a Mr. Goddard and urges Daggett to press for action on Goddard's petition.
Jan 9	To Nathaniel Appleton Haven. ALS. NhD. mDW 2137. States that he cannot serve as counsel to Mr. Mesland; comments on *Volant* case.
Jan 9	To Jeremiah Mason. ALS (signature removed). MHi. mDW 2139. *PC*, 1: 269–270. Is detained in Boston by Mrs. Webster's ill health; wants to discuss Dartmouth case with him.
Jan 9	*To [Jeremiah] Smith.* 216
Jan 12	From Samuel Bell. ALS. NhD. mDW 2144. Sends him fees, part payment of legal fees in *Bullard* v. *Bell*.
Jan 12	Account with Elijah Chamberlain. ADS. MWalB. mDW 39531.
Jan 12	From John C. Chamberlain. ALS. NhD. mDW 2147. Sends description of Webster's land and account of debts he has collected.
Jan 12	To Nathaniel Appleton Haven. ALS. Robert E. McLaughlin, Portsmouth, N.H. mDW 2143. States that draft for $500 has been paid; requests that New Hampshire bank not draw on him until he returns to Washington.
Jan 15	To Samuel Ayer Bradley. ALS. NhD. mDW 2150. Sends Bradley some unidentified papers relating to Dartmouth College.
Jan 16	From Jonathan Mason. ALS. DLC. mDW 2152. Acknowledges receipt of petition forwarded by DW for national bankruptcy legislation; discusses the burying of "old party distinctions," New England politics.
Jan 20	From Thomas L. Winthrop, et al. LS. Morristown National Historical Park. mDW 2156. Sends DW an account of the New England Mississippi Land Company, for which DW is to appear before Supreme Court as counsel.
Jan 21	To Joseph Hopkinson. Typed extract. DLC. mDW 2179. Reports that the record in the Dartmouth College case is prepared.
Jan [c. 23]	*To [Jeremiah] Mason.* 216
Jan 24	To Nathaniel Appleton Haven. ALS. MBNU. mDWs. Wants to know what Haven will allow on certain land as payment for some of DW's debts.
Feb 14	To Francis Brown. ALS. NhD. mDW 2180. Reports that Dartmouth College case will probably be argued in the current term of the Supreme Court.

Feb 22	*To Jeremiah Mason.*	**217**
Feb 27	*To [William Sullivan].*	**219**
[March 10]	Notes for draft of argument in Dartmouth College case. AD. NhD. mDW 2188.	
[March 10]	Argument in Dartmouth College case, in part. AD. NhD. mDW 2383.	
March 11	To Francis Brown. Copy, incomplete. NhHi. mDW 2415. Van Tyne, pp. 75–76. Dartmouth College case "came on yesterday."	
March 13	*To [Francis] Brown.*	**221**
March 13	To Jeremiah Mason. Printed. PC, 1: 275–276. Discusses the arguments in the Dartmouth College case before the Supreme Court.	
March 13	*To William Sullivan, endorsed to Mrs. Grace Fletcher Webster.*	**222**
March 14	To R. G. Harper. ALS. MdHi. mDW 2454. Expresses "regret of Mrs. Harper's illness."	
March 14	To Jeremiah Smith. Printed. PC, 1: 276–277. Reports that the college cause has been argued and discusses the argument.	
March 22	*To [Jeremiah] Mason.*	**222**
March 30	To Francis Brown. Printed. PC, 1: 279. Expresses approval that a new case is to be brought forward in circuit court.	
[March]	To [William Wirt]. ALS. MdHi. mDW 2455. Asks to borrow several law books.	
April 1	To [Henry Wheaton]. ALS. NNPM. mDW 2456. Sends his argument in Bevan's case.	
April 6	To [Octavius Pickering]. ALS. Boston Bar Association, Boston, Mass. mDWs. States that Martin Whiting has read law in his office since March 1, 1817.	
April 12	To Francis Brown. Printed. PC, 1: 280. Discusses the Dartmouth College case in the circuit court.	
April 22	To Benjamin J. Gilbert. ALS. DGU. mDW 2457. Asks that George Woodward be informed of his inability to attend Haverhill Court.	
April 22	To [John Thornton Kirkland]. AD. MH. mDWs. Encloses argument in Dartmouth College case for his examination.	
April 23	*To [Jeremiah] Mason.*	**223**
April 28	To Jeremiah Mason. Printed. PC, 1: 282–283. Discusses developments in Dartmouth College case.	
April 28	From Isaac Parker. Printed. John M. Shirley, *Dartmouth College Causes* (St. Louis, 1879), pp. 250–252. Thanks DW for the argument he sent him; discusses the Dartmouth College case and urges the printing of the arguments.	
May 9	To Joseph Hopkinson. ALS. PHi. mDW 2726. Discusses Dartmouth College case before the circuit court in New Hampshire.	

May 9   From Joseph Hopkinson. ALS. MHi. mDW 2459. Gratified that he learned to know DW in Washington.

May 12   *To [Jeremiah] Smith.*   **225**

May 14   To Joseph Story. Printed. *PC*, 1: 282. Asks Story to assist Isaac P. Davis in his efforts to secure appointment as appraiser.

May 26   To Jacob McGaw. ALS. Mrs. Lester W. Parker, Brimfield, Mass. mDW 2465. Acknowledges receipt of a writ; the long friendship which has existed between him and McGaw.

June 6   To [Alexander Bliss]. ALS. DLC. mDW 2467. Sends money for the payment of notes due at the bank.

June 18   To Ezekiel Webster. ALS. NhD. mDW 2470. Will be happy to settle accounts with a Mr. Briton.

June 26   From Ezekiel Webster. ALS. NhD. mDW 2472. Discusses settlement of debts and certain court cases.

June 28   To Ezekiel Webster. ALS. NhD. mDW 2475. Suggests that Ezekiel may use money Col. Webster has for him until Ezekiel comes to Boston.

June 29   To Nathaniel Appleton Haven. ALS. MBNU. mDWs. Discusses arrangements he's making to pay Lang's note.

June 29   To Jeremiah Mason. Copy. NhHi. mDW 2478. Van Tyne, pp. 76–77. Enquires when Mason expects to be in Boston to visit him; also mentions New Hampshire elections, and relates a discussion on a point of law with Judge Story.

July 1   To Nathaniel Freeman. ALS. NN. mDW 2480. Expresses the belief that "our cause will be continued to March term."

July 2   To Jeremiah Smith. Printed. *PC*, 1: 283–284. Asks to borrow Chalmers' "opinion on eminent men" for John Quincy Adams.

July 3   To Joseph Hopkinson. ALS. PHi. mDW 2483. Reports on the reception in New England of the argument of the Dartmouth case; has had arguments printed for a few friends.

July 7   From Jeremiah Smith. Printed. *PC*, 1: 284. Has received Smith's letter and books; will forward both to Adams.

July 8   To Ezekiel Webster. ALS. NhD. mDW 2487. Has purchased Sullivan lands in Salisbury for $1500.

July 16   *To [Francis] Brown.*   **225**

[c. July 16]   To [Daniel] Dana. AN. NhD. mDWs. Sends him outline of the plaintiff's argument in the Dartmouth College case.

July 16   To Ezekiel Webster. ALS. NhD. mDW 2494. Has had to cancel plans to come to Boscawen; inquires if he can come to Boston.

July 17   *From Daniel Putnam.*   **226**

July 19   To Ezekiel Webster. ALS. NhD. mDW 2499. Reports on the travel and health of Mrs. Ezekiel Webster, who is visiting them in Boston.

July 24   From Abel Parker ("To the anonymous Reviewer of General Dearborn's defense of his attack on General Putnam"). Printed. *New Hampshire Patriot,* Aug 4, 1818. Discusses the Putnam question.

July 27   *To Jacob McGaw.*

July 27   To Enoch G. Parrott. ALS. NhHi. mDW 2504. Will try to sell property to pay off Parrott's note.

July 27–28   Account with Elijah Chamberlain. ADS. MWalB. mDW 3951.

July 28   To Thomas Eames. ALS. DLC. mDW 2506. Discusses possibility of appealing case.

Aug 6   From Josiah Webster. ALS. NhHi. mDW 2510. Reports on note collection.

Aug 8   To Judge Abel Parker (anonymous). Printed. *Columbian Centinel,* Aug 8, 1818. Responds to Parker's letter of July 24.

Aug 12   To James Hervey Bingham. Copy. NhHi. mDW 2513. Sends note for collection.

Aug 15   Memoranda of Professional Fees. Printed. *PC,* 1: 291–296. Runs through 1819, August 12.

Aug 16   To Joseph Story. Printed. *PC,* 1: 286. Discusses with Story the proceedings of Parliament relating to "redressing abuses in charities."

Aug 27   *To Ezekiel Webster.*

Aug 31   George Sullivan and Daniel Webster to the Public. Printed. *Columbian Centinel,* Sept 2, 1818. Discusses the state lottery.

Sept 8   From Francis Brown. ALS. NhHi. mDWs. Shirley, *Dartmouth College Causes,* pp. 264–266. Discusses his meeting in Albany with Chancellor James Kent.

Sept 9   *To [Joseph] Story.*

Sept 13   To Ezekiel Webster. ALS. NhD. mDW 2517. Discusses payment of a note to J. Gerrish and mentions that he is going to Exeter.

Sept 15   From Francis Brown. ALS. NhD. mDW 2519. Shirley, *Dartmouth College Causes,* pp. 268–270. Is on way home from Albany where he has talked with Chancellor James Kent.

Sept 26   From Francis Brown. ALS. NhD. mDW 2533. Shirley, *Dartmouth College Causes,* pp. 272–274. Fears that the defense argument is being circulated.

[Sept] 28   To Francis Brown. ALS. NhD. mDW 2537. Discusses the impact of the argument being circulated.

[Oct] 5   To William Wirt. Printed. Everett Pepperell Wheeler,

	Daniel Webster: The Expounder of the Constitution (New York, 1905), pp. 32–33 (misdated by Wheeler). Denies saying deficiencies in his Dartmouth College cause argument were supplied by Wirt's argument.	
Oct 10	*From George Farrar.*	**232**
Oct 11	*To Ezekiel Webster.*	**233**
Oct 13	From William Wirt. LC. DLC. mDW 2547. Mentions cases coming up before the Supreme Court and responds to the rumor of DW's drawing a part of his argument from Wirt.	
Oct 23	To Nathaniel Appleton Haven. ALS. MBNU. mDWs. Asks that deed be sent to Ezekiel.	
Oct 23	To Jeremiah Mason. ALS. MHi. mDW 2458. Discusses the "New Ipswich occurrence," to come before court.	
Oct 23	Promissory note to Exeter Bank. ADS by DW and Ezekiel Webster. MB. mDW 39536.	
Oct 25	To Ezekiel Webster. ALS. NhD. mDW 2551. Sends instructions regarding Haven deed and payment of debts.	
Oct 26	From Thomas Jackson Oakley. ALS. NhHi. mDW 2555. Discusses the New Ipswich occurrence, involving the custody of a child.	
Nov 4	*From Francis Brown.*	**233**
Nov 9	*To [Francis] Brown.*	**234**
Nov 14	To [David Daggett]. ALS. CtY. mDW 2563. Mentions article on maritime law by Story; urges judiciary and bankruptcy legislation by Congress.	
Nov 15	To Ezekiel Webster. ALS. NhD. mDW 2565. Directs EW to pay certain amounts to Miss Wiggin and Mrs. Rice.	
Nov 17	From Joseph Hopkinson. Printed. *PC*, 1: 288–289. Relates a conversation with Pinkney on the Dartmouth College case.	
Nov 27	From Hugo Beyerman. ALS. DLC. mDW 2568. Thanks DW for books and confirms his friendship for DW.	
Nov 28	To Cyrus Perkins. Copy. NhHi. mDW 2572. Van Tyne, pp. 77–78. Thanks him for eulogy on W. W. Woodward and comments on Dartmouth College case.	
Dec 1	To Jeremiah Mason. ALS. NhHi. mDW 2574. Discusses a slander case coming before Essex court.	
Dec 2	Receipt for account between William Tolford and DW. ADS (by proxy). NhHi. mDW 39537.	
Dec 4	From Josiah Webster. ALS. NhHi. mDW 2577. Enquires of the state of certain notes sent him for collection.	
Dec 6	*To [Francis] Brown.*	**236**
Dec 12	To Jeremiah Mason. ALS. MHi. mDW 2579. Discusses	

several cases in which they are mutually involved or interested.

Dec 12 *To [Henry Wheaton].*   **237**

Dec 16 To Ezekiel Webster. ALS. NhD. mDW 2584. Has paid Samuel Smith $150 for Ezekiel.

Dec 18 From Timothy Farrar, Sr. ALS. NhHi. mDW 2586. Discusses the Ipswich child custody matter.

Dec 19 *From Thomas Addis Emmet.*   **237**

Dec 27 To Francis Brown. ALS. NhD. mDW 2591. Discusses the Lang case and compensation for representing Dartmouth College.

Dec 28 *From William Pinkney.*   **238**

[1818] To Samuel Ayer Bradley (enclosure: William C. Bradley to Samuel Ayer Bradley [1818]). ALS. NhD. mDW 2598. Invites Bradley to dine with him and Mr. [Hugo] Beyerman.

[1818] To Samuel Ayer Bradley. ALS. NN. mDW 2601. Wants to see him today.

[1818] To Messrs. H. & T. ALS (signed page in another hand). NhD. mDW 2603. Discusses maritime law and wages to seamen.

[1818?] Writ of Error to N.H. Superior Court of Judicature in *Trustees of Dartmouth College* v. *William H. Woodward*. Printed D. PHi. mDWs.

1819

Jan 2 To Jeremiah Smith. Copy. NhHi. mDW 2606. *W & S*, 16: 43. Discusses Goodridge and Dartmouth College cases.

Jan 2 *From Timothy Farrar, Jr.*   **238**

Jan 8 *From Timothy Farrar, Jr.*   **239**

Jan 10 *To [Francis] Brown.*   **240**

Jan 17 To Timothy Farrar, Jr. ALS. NhHi. mDW 2613. Reports he has "nothing new respecting our case."

Jan 17 To John Pitman. ALS. RPB. mDW 38800. Has no objection to Pitman's going to Washington, but fears that Pitman would sustain more losses than gains in doing so.

Jan 28 From Julia Stockton. ALS. NhHi. mDW 2615. Reports that Robert Field Stockton will be in Washington on February 1.

Feb 1 *To Timothy Farrar, Jr.*   **241**

Feb 2 To Francis Brown. ALS. NhD. mDW 2620. *PC*, 1: 300. Reports that "all is safe" with Dartmouth case.

Feb 2 To Timothy Farrar. ALS. NhHi. mDW 2622. Shirley, *Dartmouth College Causes*, pp. 302–303. Reports that "a judgment has been pronounced in our favor this morning."

Feb 2 To [Jeremiah Smith]. ALS photocopy. MH. mDW

scribes his effort to adjust his concerns with the
John Gore estate.

June 13   To Ezekiel Webster. ALS. NhD. mDW 2757. Prepares
to leave for Rhode Island (to appear in Circuit
Court).

June 19   *To Timothy Farrar, Jr.*   263

June 23   *To Timothy Farrar, Jr.*   263

June 26   From [David Daggett]. AL. CtY. mDW 2767. Responds to DW's legal queries.

June 28   *To [Jeremiah] Mason.*   264

July 1   To Joseph Hopkinson. ALS. PHi. mDW 2769. Sends
box of fish with instructions on preserving them.

July 2   To Russell Freeman. ALS. NhD. mDW 2773. Reports
that Davis will argue cause in Essex in November.

Aug 3   From James Kent (to Joseph Story and DW). ALS.
MHi. mDWs. *MHi Proc.*, Second Series, 14 (1900,
1901): 413–414. Mentions that DW will be able to
give Story the reasons for his not preparing a
review of the "Dartmouth question."

Aug 10   To Jeremiah Mason. Printed. *PC*, 1: 308. Mentions
trip to Philadelphia and Albany, and proposed
journey into New Hampshire.

Aug 15   Memoranda of Professional Fees. Printed. *W & S*,
17: 545. Runs through 1832, September 10.

Aug 27   From Ezekiel Webster (with DW to Nathaniel A.
Haven, Sept 7, 1819). ALS. Robert E. McLaughlin,
Portsmouth, N.H. mDW 2775. Reports the sale of
the Fowler place in Bridgewater.

Aug 30   From Isaac Fiske. ALS. Boston Bar Association,
Boston, Mass. mDWs. Introduces Frederick Hobbs,
who wishes to read law in DW's office.

Sept 7   To Nathaniel A. Haven (with Ezekiel Webster to DW,
Aug 27, 1819). ALS. Robert E. McLaughlin, Portsmouth, N.H. mDW 2775. Requests Haven to forward EW a release of the Fowler place; DW will
then see Haven paid in ninety days.

Sept 17   To Joseph Story. ALS. MiU-C. mDW 2777. Asks to
use Story's minutes of a case.

Sept 21   To Henry Wheaton. ALS. NNPM. mDW 2781. Comments on Wheaton's Volume 4 and makes a correction.

Sept 26   To Francis Brown. Printed. *PC*, 1: 309. Will write
himself, or get others to write, letters of introduction for Brown.

Sept 27   To Ezekiel Webster. ALS. NhD. mDW 2783. Instructs
EW on the payment of certain debts.

Oct 5   To Francis Brown. Printed. *PC*, 1: 309–310. Sends
money and letters of introduction.

Oct 6   To Henry L. DeKoven. ALS. Ct. mDW 2785. Discusses
a suit he is handling for him.

Oct [?]   *To [Jeremiah] Mason.*   265

Nov 2   To Francis Hopkinson. ALS. Bordentown Historical
Society. Bordentown, N.J. mDW 2787. Introduces
Martin Whiting.

Nov 15   *To Jeremiah Mason.*   **266**

Nov 19   To John Marshall. ALS. NhD. mDW 2791. Introduces
[Benjamin Joseph?] Gilbert.

Nov 28   To William Bainbridge. ALS. NhD. mDWs. Expresses
his strong friendship and high regard for Bainbridge.

[Nov]   To Dudley Atkyns Tyng. ALS. NhD. mDWs. Cannot
take time to write up arguments in Dedham cause.

Dec 15   Memorial to Congress on restraining increase of
slavery in new States to be admitted into Union.
Printed pamphlet.

Dec 20   *To James Lloyd.*   **267**

Dec 25   To Langdon Cheves. ALS. ScHi. mDW 2796. Introduces Francis C. Gray.

Dec 27   *To Rufus King.*   **268**

[1819]   *Welsh* v. *Barrett* [re] motion for a new trial. AD.
NhD. mDW 2800.

[1819]   To Jeremiah Mason. Printed. *PC*, 1: 311–312. Sends
him "the creature," probably *Report of The Case of
the Trustees of Dartmouth College against William
H. Woodward* (1819).

1820

Jan 4   To William Sullivan. ALS. NhD. mDW 2808. Affirms
that Richard Fletcher read law with him in Portsmouth, 1808–1811.

Jan 17   To [David Daggett]. ALS. CtY. mDW 2810. Requests
Daggett to introduce John Pitman to one of Daggett's neighbors.

Jan 25   To Charles Marsh. ALS. NhD. mDW 2811. Sets out
for Washington day after tomorrow; glad to hear
favorable accounts from Brown.

Jan 25   To James William Paige. ALS. MHi. mDW 2813.
Prepares to leave for Washington; instructs Paige
on the payment of certain accounts.

Feb 10   *To [David Daggett].*   **268**

Feb 11   *To Alexander Bliss.*   **269**

Feb 13   To John Quincy Adams. AL. MHi. mDW 2823. Accepts
invitation to dinner.

Feb 14   To Alexander Bliss. ALS. DLC. mDW 2825. Discusses
several cases before courts.

Feb 15   *To Henry Baldwin.*   **269**

[*Feb 15*]   *From Henry Baldwin.*   **270**

[Feb 15]   To ? ALS. NhHi. mDW 2832. Requests that his
correspondent forward the record in the Connecticut case, *Ricard* v. *Williams.*

Feb 15	To Alexander Bliss. ALS. DLC. mDW 2834. Has received the record in the Connecticut case he requested.
Feb 19	*To [David Daggett].* **271**
Feb 24	To ? ALS. NhD. mDW 2839. Tries to collect a debt for a client.
Feb 26	To [David Daggett]. ALS. CtY. mDW 2841. Informs Daggett that the Connecticut case will not be argued this term.
Feb 27	To Alexander Bliss. ALS. DLC. mDW 2842. Discusses progress of Supreme Court and tries to line up cases on the Massachusetts and New Hampshire dockets.
March 30	To ? ALS. NHi. mDW 2846. States that he and Prescott "are not a little surprised that Mr. Marston declines agreeing to demur this cause."
April 3	*To Joseph Story.* **271**
April 12	From John C. Chamberlain (with DW to Nathaniel Appleton Haven, April 17, 1820). ALS. NhD. mDW 2854. Discusses sale of DW's Unity lot.
April 17	To Nathaniel A. Haven (with John C. Chamberlain to DW, April 17, 1820). ALS. NhD. mDW 2852. Requests Haven to forward deed and discusses a case regarding Greenleaf.
[c. April]	To Ezekiel Webster. ALS. NhD. mDW 2857. Discusses payment of notes and sale of land.
May 1	Receipt to Leeds & Co. ANS. MWelC. mDW 39540.
May 30	*To Jeremiah Mason.* **272**
June 15	*To Jeremiah Mason.* **273**
June 16	To Jeremiah Mason. ALS. MHi. mDW 2867. Requests Mason to serve a note against Daniels.
June 21	From Mills Olcott. ALS. NhD. mDWs. Remarks on Gordon Whitmore's bill in equity against him.
June 23	To Leverett Saltonstall. ALS. NhD. mDWs. Report in Thurston case ready to be delivered on payment of fees.
June 24	To Ezekiel Webster. ALS. NhD. mDW 2869. Has paid bill for EW; Daniel coming to Boscawen for a visit.
June 25	*To Jeremiah Mason.* **274**
June 28	To Leverett Saltonstall. ALS. NhHi. mDW 2876. Remarks that he has paid for and received the report in the Thurston case.
July 5	To Ezekiel Webster. ALS. NhD. mDW 2879. Encloses deed and informs him that Haven is selling the Thornton land.
July 6	To Nathaniel Appleton Haven. ALS. NhD. mDW 2881. Informs him that auditors have made their report in the Greenleaf case and Haven's claim is allowed.
July 6	From Mills Olcott. ALS. NhD. mDWs. Sends documents relating to the Whitmore matter.

July 17   To John Quincy Adams. LS. DNA, RG 59. mDW
2884a. Asks for a certified copy of a deed to certain
Georgia lands.

July 20   From Josiah Quincy. Printed LS. DLC. mDW 2885.
Informs DW of his election as a fellow of the
American Academy of Arts and Sciences.

July 25   From John Quincy Adams. LC. DNA, RG 59. mDW
55663. Encloses copy of William Hull deed.

Aug 2   To Ezekiel Webster. ALS. NhD. mDW 2887. Discusses
certain lots in New Hampshire and sends him a
copy of the Haven pamphlet.

Aug 5   To Ezekiel Webster. ALS. NhD. mDW 2889. Asks EW
to check on certain cases before the New Hampshire courts for him.

Aug 8   *To Jeremiah Mason.*   275

Aug 12   To Jonathan Davis. ALS. MHi. mDW 2893. Reports
that causes with Goodwin are settled.

Aug 17   *To Ezekiel Webster.*   276

Aug 20   To Alexander Bliss. ALS. DLC. mDW 2901. Asks that
carriage be sent to Sandwich for family.

Aug 21   To William Davis and Barnabas Hedge (from DW
et al.). LS. MBBS. mDW 2903. Asks for meeting of
persons in Massachusetts interested in the tariff
question.

Aug 22   Share of Stock in the Boston Library. Printed DS.
MBAt. mDW 39541.

Aug 23   To Nathaniel Appleton Haven. ALS. NhD. mDWs.
Discusses money he owes to the Havens.

Aug 23   To Nathaniel Macarty. ALS. MWA. mDW 2907.
Sends $6.00 to the American Antiquarian Society
in accordance with its rules.

[Aug 29]   To Alexander Bliss. ALS. DLC. mDW 2909. Discusses
his vacation at Sandwich and instructs him to pay
certain notes.

[Aug 30]   To Grace Fletcher Webster and Mrs. George Blake
(from DW and George Blake). ALS. NhD. mDW
2912. Report on their vacation.

Aug [?]   To Nathaniel Terry. ALS. CtHt-W. mDWs. Introduces
Davis, Solicitor-General of Massachusetts.

[Sept 3]   To Alexander Bliss. ALS. DLC. mDW 2913a. Discusses the election of Mason's successor to
Congress.

Sept 18   To the Secretary of the Suffolk Bar Association. DS.
Boston Bar Association. Boston, Mass. mDWs. Re-
ports that William J. Haddock entered his office to
read law on September 11, 1820.

Sept 22   Affidavit in *Thomas Gibbons* v. *Robert Montgomery
Livingston.* ADS by Lewis Willett. NhD. mDW
39542.

Oct 23   To William M. Davis. ALS. MHi. mDW 2914. Reports

that he believes Davis' election is "entirely and
unquestionably *legal*."

[Oct ?]	To [John Gorham Palfrey].	277
Nov 3	Receipt to Jonathan Davis. ANS. MHi. mDW 39544.	
Nov 9	To Ezekiel Webster. ALS. NhD. mDW 2918. Expects him to come down to convention so that matter with Haven can be adjusted.	
[Nov 12]	To Joseph Story.	277
Nov 12	To Jeremiah Mason.	278
Nov 15	Motion for the attendance of Chaplains to the Convention. Printed. *Journal of the Massachusetts Constitutional Convention*, p. 15.	
[Nov 18?]	To Lemuel Shaw. ALS. MH. mDWs. States that he has examined the amendments and believes them "essentially right."	
Nov 22	Certificate of DW as presidential elector. Printed form with ms insertions. NhHi. mDW 2924.	
Nov 28	[Conveyance of pew, St. Paul's Church, Boston, to DW, and subsequent transfers of same]. Printed form with ms insertions; additions by DW et al. NhD. mDW 2925.	
Nov 28	From R. Heriot. ALS. NhD. mDW 2931. Discusses a shipping case involving the *Alexander*.	
[Nov 29]	Committee Report, Massachusetts Constitutional Convention, on revision of Chapter 6, Section II, of Massachusetts Constitution. ADS. M-Ar, Constitutional Convention Papers. mDWs.	
[Nov 29]	Committee Report, Massachusetts Constitutional Convention, on Oaths and Affirmations. ADS. M-Ar, Constitutional Convention Papers. mDWs.	
[Nov 29]	Committee Report, Massachusetts Constitutional Convention, on amending the Constitution. ADS. M-Ar, Constitutional Convention Papers. mDWs.	
[Dec 6]	Minutes of the Massachusetts Electoral College. AD. DLC. mDWs.	
Dec 7	Dearborn Resolutions, Massachusetts Constitutional Convention, on Lt. Governor and Council (with ANS by DW). AD. M-Ar. Constitutional Convention Papers. mDWs.	
Dec 13	Resolutions, Massachusetts Constitutional Convention, respecting amendments. AD. M-Ar, Massachusetts Constitutional Convention Papers. mDWs.	
Dec 13	Resolution on unfinished business. Printed. *Journal of the Massachusetts Constitutional Convention*, pp. 259–260.	
Dec 23	From Samuel Davis. Printed. *A Discourse delivered at Plymouth, December 22, 1820* [p. 3]. Expresses appreciation to DW for delivering address.	
[Dec 25]	To Edward Everett.	279
Dec 25	Amendment and comments on judges and office	

Dec 25

holding. Printed. *Journal of the Massachusetts Constitutional Convention*, p. 403.

Resolution, Massachusetts Constitutional Convention respecting Sheriffs (with ANS by DW). AD. M-Ar, Massachusetts Constitutional Convention Papers. mDWs.

Dec 26

To Samuel Davis. Printed. *A Discourse delivered at Plymouth, December 22, 1820* [p. 4]. Will send copy of address for printing as soon as time permits its preparation.

Dec 30

To John Thornton Kirkland. 279

Dec 30

Resolution on removal of judges. Printed. *Journal of the Massachusetts Constitutional Convention*, p. 489.

[c. 1820?]

[Opinion regarding Estate of John Simpson]. DS, with citation in DW's hand. NC-Ar. mDW 2942.

[1820–27?]

To Nathan Hale. ALS. MHi. mDW 38428. Discusses a hearing involving a Mr. Fletcher.

[182–]

To Jeremiah Mason. ALS. MHi. mDW 2939. Discusses a case involving a Mr. Wyman.

1821

Jan 3

From John Pierce, Secretary of the President and Fellows of Harvard College. ADS. M-Ar, Massachusetts Constitutional Convention Papers. mDWs. Reports that Harvard College assents to the resolutions proposed by the convention committee.

Jan 4

Committee Report, Massachusetts Constitutional Convention, on Harvard College. AD & ADS. M-Ar, Massachusetts Constitutional Convention Papers. mDWs.

Jan 5

Amendment to proposal on qualification for voting. Printed. *Journal of the Massachusetts Constitutional Convention*, p. 553.

Jan [6]

Resolution, Massachusetts Constitutional Convention on Article III of Declaration of Rights (with ANS by DW). AD. M-Ar, Massachusetts Constitutional Convention Papers. mDWs.

Jan 8

Amendment to resolution on jury trials. Printed. *Journal of the Massachusetts Constitutional Convention*, p. 572.

[Jan 8?]

Draft of resolution on taxing non-resident landowners addressed to DW. AD. M-Ar, Massachusetts Constitutional Convention Papers. mDWs.

Jan [8?]

Resolution, Massachusetts Constitutional Convention, on taxing non-resident landowners for support of public worship. AD. M-Ar, Massachusetts Constitutional Convention Papers. mDWs.

Jan 9

Resolution and comment on the question of final

Aug 19	To James William Paige. ALS. MHi. mDW 3023. Asks Paige to send gunpowder to Sandwich, where he is vacationing.
[Aug 23]	To Alexander Bliss. ALS. DLC. mDW 3026. Expects to get home on Saturday and to be in office on Monday.
[Aug ?]	[Agreement with Peter Chardon Brooks, et al. Spanish Treaty Claimants]. DS by Brooks, et al. NhHi. mDW 3028.
[Aug ?]	[Agreement with Nathaniel West, et al. Spanish Treaty Claimants]. ALS. NhHi. mDW 3032.
Sept 1	To [William Davis]. ALS. MBBS. mDW 3034. Discusses the case of the *Washington* before the Claims Commission.
Sept 3	To William King. ALS. DLC. mDW 3036. Introduces Alexander Bliss.
Sept 3	*To Jeremiah Mason.* 290
Sept 3	From Nathaniel Gilman. ALS. NhHi. mDW 3042. Discusses claims under Spanish treaty.
Sept 4	To William Wirt. ALS. DLC. mDW 3044. Introduces Alexander Bliss.
Sept 7	To Alexander Bliss. ALS. DLC. mDW 3046. Instructs him not to allow doubtful claims to be decided by the claims commissioners.
[Sept 7]	To Leverett Saltonstall. ALS. DLC. mDWs. Discusses the Thurston case.
Sept 10	From Dudley L. Pickman and Stephen White. ALS. NhHi. mDW 3049. Request DW to take charge of their claims under the Spanish Treaty.
Sept 11	To Alexander Bliss. ALS. DLC. mDW 3052. Discusses several claims before the commissioners.
Sept 12	*To Jeremiah Mason.* 291
Sept 13	To Alexander Bliss. ALS. DLC. mDW 3057. Sends a memorial for filing before the claims commission.
Sept 18	*To Alexander Bliss.* 292
Sept 19	To Alexander Bliss. ALS. DLC. mDW 3061. Discusses memorials and the claims commission.
Sept 19	To Nathaniel Appleton and John Haven. ALS. NhD. mDW 3064. Discusses the case of the *Volant*.
Sept 20	To Alexander Bliss. ALS. DLC. mDW 3066. Discusses claims cases.
Sept 21	To William Woart. ALS. NN. mDW 3069. Discusses his case, also before the claims commissioners.
Sept 24	To Joseph Story. Printed. *PC*, 1: 316. Discusses several recent cases; invites Story to join him and friends on September 25.
Sept 25	To Thomas G. Fessenden (signed William Prescott, DW). Printed. *New England Farmer*, 1 (Sept 7, 1822): 47. Recommends Fessenden's publication on the law of patents.
Sept 26	*To Ezekiel Webster.* 292

pp. 88–89. Recommends Chancellor James Kent
for presidency of Dartmouth College.

Jan 3   *To [Joseph] Story.*   299

Jan 3   [Agreement with Insurance Company of North America]. DS. NhHi. mDW 3131. Spanish claims.

Jan 4   To Alexander Bliss. ALS. DLC. mDW 3134. Encloses draft to pay note if it is not renewed.

Jan 4   *From Eliza Buckminster.*   300

Jan 4   [Agreement with Insurance Company of Pennsylvania]. ADS. NhHi. mDW 3139. Spanish claims.

Jan 5   [Agreement with Private Underwriters of Philadelphia, per Samuel Mifflin]. AD in DW's hand; signed by Mifflin. NhHi. mDW 3142. Spanish claims.

Jan 10   *To Jeremiah Mason.*   301

Jan 11   To John Quincy Adams (enclosure G[eorge] B[lake] to DW, Jan 2, 1822). AL. DNA, RG 59. mDWs. DW forwards letter to Blake.

Jan 11   To Alexander Bliss. ALS. DLC. mDW 3148. Discusses case in Essex court and tells Bliss to forward other memorials.

Jan 13   To Alexander Bliss. ALS. DLC. mDW 3150. Needs copies of memorials relating to claims; general instructions for preparing them.

Jan 13   *To Ezekiel Webster.*   301

Jan 14   *To Joseph Story.*   302

Jan 16   *To Alexander Bliss.*   303

Jan 17   To Willard Peale. ALS draft. NhHi. mDW 3163. W & S, 16: 64–65. Discusses policy procedures adopted by the Spanish claims commissioners.

Jan 18   To [Thomas Wren Ward]. AL draft. CtY. mDW 3154. Discusses Spanish claims case.

Jan 18   From Ezekiel Webster. ALS. NhD. mDW 3166. Inquires about the status of John Flanders' claim for a Revolutionary War pension.

Jan 19   To Alexander Bliss. ALS. DLC. mDW 3169. Discusses policies adopted by claims commissioners.

Jan 22   To Stephen Codman. ALS. NhHi. mDW 3173. W & S, 16: 65. Reports that the case of the *Levant* was called up and received yesterday by the claims commission.

Jan 23   To Edward Cutts, Jr. ALS. NhHi. mDW 3175. Asks for more information relating to Sheafe's case of the *Betsy.*

Jan 24   From Thomas Astley (enclosed with Samuel Mifflin to DW, Jan 26, 1822). ALS. DLC. mDW 3179. Forwards Mifflin's letter.

Jan 24   From J[ohn] I[nskeep]. ALS draft. Insurance Company of North America, Philadelphia, Pa. mDWs. Responds to DW's letter regarding claims awarded by the commissioners.

Jan 26	From Samuel Mifflin (to DW?) (with Thomas Astley to DW, Jan 24, 1822). ALS. DLC. mDW 3178. Sends information regarding claims.
Jan 28	*From Ezekiel Webster.* 304
Jan 30	To James Trecothick Austin. ALS. NhD. mDW 3187. Expresses pleasure to be associated with him in the Atkins' case.
Jan 30	To John Inskeep. ALS. Insurance Company of North America, Philadelphia, Pa. mDW 3189. Discusses Spanish claims cases.
Feb 1	*To Joseph Hopkinson.* 305
Feb 2	To John Inskeep. ALS. Insurance Company of North America, Philadelphia, Pa. mDW 3196. Reports on cases decided by the claims commissioners.
Feb 2	From Samuel Hubbard. ALS. DLC. mDW 3198. Desires to retain DW in the Hull court martial.
Feb 4	To Alexander Bliss. ALS. DLC. mDW 3200. Discusses claims commission cases.
Feb 4	From J[ohn] I[nskeep]. ALS draft. Insurance Company of North America, Philadelphia, Pa. mDWs. Expresses pleasure with DW's success before the claims commission.
Feb 6	To Samuel Hubbard. ALS. NhD. mDWs. Expresses his willingness to be retained for Commodore Hull; knows little of public affairs.
Feb 6	To James William Paige (with postscript to Grace Fletcher Webster). ALS. NhHi. mDW 3204. Van Tyne, p. 90. Comments on his activities in Washington before the commission and the court.
Feb 9	Note in the case of the *Louisa Joanna.* ANS. DNA, RG 76. mDWs.
Feb 16	From Benjamin Pickman. ALS. NhHi. mDW 3208. Inquires about his claim before the commissioners.
Feb 19	*To Alexander Bliss.* 306
Feb 20	*To Alexander Bliss.* 307
Feb 20	To [Samuel Davis]. ALS. CCC. mDW 3216. Discusses policy decisions by the commissioners.
Feb 21	From [Thomas Gibbons]. AL copy. NhD. mDW 3221. Discusses his case before the Supreme Court.
Feb 22	To Alexander Bliss. ALS. DLC. mDW 3223. Reports on claims and Supreme Court cases.
Feb 23	To John Quincy Adams. AL. MHi. mDW 3225. Declines invitation to dinner.
Feb 23	From J[ohn] I[nskeep]. ALS draft. Insurance Company of North America, Philadelphia, Pa. mDWs. Discusses cases before the claims commissioners.
Feb 28	From S. Pleasanton. LC. DNA, RG 206. mDWs. Reports on the claim of the United States to certain funds of Moses Myers & Son of Boston, then under attachment.

Feb 28	Petition in the case of the brig *Betsy*. DS. DNA, RG 76. mDWs.	
March 2	*To Alexander Bliss.*	308
March 2	*To Thomas Gibbons.*	308
March 4	*From Rufus King.*	309
March 4	From [James A.] Hamilton (enclosed with Rufus King to DW, March 4, 1822). AN. NhHi. mDW 3235. Requests few minutes conversation with Webster.	
[March 5]	To Rufus King. ALS. NHi. mDW 5794. States that he has received King's letter of March 4, and that he will gladly render any "professional services" needed to Charles King and James A. Hamilton (incorrectly dated [1826?] on microfilm).	
March 5	To Lemuel Shaw. ALS. MH. mDW 3239. Reports a discussion with President Monroe involving Mr. Thomas Melville.	
March 12	*From Thomas Gibbons.*	310
March 12	To Alexander Bliss. ALS. DLC. mDW 3242. Sends news that he is sick in New York with a cold; wants to get on home.	
March 20	To James Monroe. Copy. MH. mDW 3248. Discusses the Thomas Melville matter.	
March 23	*To Jeremiah Mason.*	311
March 23	To Ezekiel Webster. ALS. NhD. mDW 3254. Reports his arrival in Boston, his inquiry into the Flanders' claim for a pension.	
March 27	[Appointment as justice of the peace]. Printed form with ms insertions. NhHi. mDW 3257.	
April 2	To Samuel Jaudon. ALS. NHi. mDW 3259. Discusses cases before claims commission.	
April 5	To Joseph Story. ALS. MHi. mDW 3263. W & S, 16: 68. Discusses appointment of claims commissioners and the Boston mayoral election.	
[*April 6*]	*To Joseph Story.*	312
April 10	To [William D.] Sohier. ALS. PPL. mDWs. Introduces William B. Parker.	
April 19	To Samuel Jaudon. ALS. NHi. mDW 3269. Discusses claims commission cases.	
April 20	From John Halkett (with enclosures: J. H. to John Quincy Adams, March 5, 1822, draft revised by DW; Halkett to William Crawford, March 10, 1822). ALS. NhHi. mDW 3275. Discusses his land claims.	
May 13	From David Daggett. ALS. DLC. mDW 3296. Reports on the DeForest case.	
May 15	To Samuel Jaudon. ALS. NHi. mDW 3298. Details procedure to be followed in preparing memorials to be presented to the claims commission.	
May 16	To John Pierce. ALS. MH. mDW 3303. Accepts	

	appointment as member of the board of overseers of Harvard College.
May 23	To Samuel Jaudon. ALS. NHi. mDW 3306. Discusses Spanish claims.
May 23	From Samuel Bell. ALS. DLC. mDW 36888. Introduces Russell Jarvis.
May 26	To Samuel Jaudon. ALS. NHi. mDW 3309. Proposes certain procedures in drafting memorials for claimants.
June 4	Petition for the regulation of the Boston House of Industry. ADS. M-Ar. mDWs.
June 5	To Samuel Jaudon. ALS. NHi. mDW 3312. Sends Bliss on to handle claims commission cases.
June 5	To James Strong. ALS. DLC. mDWs. Discusses the preparation of the case of the *Frederick* for presentation to the claims commissioners.
June 8	To Alexander Bliss. ALS. DLC. mDW 3318. Sends memorials from Portsmouth.
June [8?]	Bill for the regulation of the Boston House of Industry. AD draft. M-Ar. mDWs.
June 8	To Joseph Hopkinson (enclosed with DW to Alexander Bliss, June 9, 1822). ALS. DLC. mDW 2989. Introduces Alexander Bliss.
June 9	To Alexander Bliss. ALS. DLC. mDW 3320. Sends note to John Inskeep and memorials.
June 10	To Alexander Bliss. ALS. DLC. mDW 3322. Sends additional memorials from Portsmouth.
[June 19?]	Index of papers in the case of the *Nautilis*. ADS. DNA, RG 76. mDWs.
June 22	To Alexander Bliss. ALS. DLC. mDW 3324. States that he can come to Washington now if he is needed.
[June 22]	Memorial on William Boyd to Spanish Claims Commissioners. DS by DW. DNA, RG 76. mDWs.
June 25	Affidavit of Samuel Upton. Copy. NhHi. mDW 39547.
June 25	From Samuel Upton. Copy. NhHi. mDW 39549. Gives conditions of business agreements with DW.
July 10	To William Sullivan. ALS. Morristown National Historical Park. mDW 3328. Expresses his regret at having to decline an honor intended for him by the bar.
July 17	Promissory Note of Samuel Upton. ANS. NhHi. mDW 39551.
July 17	Promissory Note of Samuel Upton. ANS. NhHi. mDW 39552.
July 27	To Samuel Jaudon. ALS. NHi. mDW 3331. Discusses Spanish claims cases.
July 29	To Jeremiah Smith. Copy. NhHi. mDW 3335. *W & S*, 16: 69. Discusses case involving Edsons.
July 30	To Samuel Jaudon. ALS. NHi. mDW 3337. Remarks on the Mifflin claims case.

	North America, Philadelphia, Pa. mDWs. Discusses claims in Washington, in response to DW's letter of November 13.
Nov 23	To Jeremiah Mason. Typed copy. NhHi. mDW 3374. Reports a chance meeting with George W. Mason, about to embark on a western tour.
Dec 9	To [Charles Brickett?] Haddock. ANS. NhD. mDW 38421. Asks Haddock to deliver papers to Theodore Lyman and to receive money.
[Dec 10]	To Alexander Bliss. ALS. DLC. mDW 3385. Urges Bliss to send copy of Bliss' argument in *Barrett* v. *Goddard* to Shaw.
[Dec 11]	To Alexander Bliss. ALS. DLC. mDW 3387. Reports his being detained in Salem by many causes; instructs Bliss to pay several notes.
Dec 11	From Samuel Upton. ALS. NhHi. mDW 3376. Reports that the negotiations with Lyman have been completed and money turned over to Haddock.
Dec 18	*To Joseph Story.* 318
Dec 20	To [William H.] Gardiner. ALS. DLC. mDW 3382. States that John Everett has entered his office as a law student.
Dec 20	Credentials of DW (elected Representative from Massachusetts commencing March 4, 1823). DS. DNA, RG 233. mDW 41292.
Dec 30	To David Daggett. LS. CtY. mDW 3384. Asks to borrow volume on old land titles.
[1822]	To [John Halkett]. AL incomplete. NhHi. mDW 3390. Regrets that he missed DW in [Philadelphia?].
[1822]	Note in the case of the brig *Betsey*. ANS. DNA, RG 76. mDWs.
[1822]	Memorandum on the case of the brig *Neptune*. Copy. MBevHi. mDWs.
[1822–1824]	Petition in the case of the schooner *Lucy*. ADS. DNA, RG 76. mDWs.
[1822–1824]	To Nathan Hale. ALS. Edward W. Stack, Glen Head, N.Y. mDW 38439. Asks Hale to get an article published for him in either the *Patriot* or the *Centinel*.

1823

Jan 1	*To [Samuel Jaudon].* 319
Jan 7	To [David Daggett]. ALS. CtY. mDW 3394. Discusses a document he had written Daggett about and asks his assistance for Mr. Blake.
Jan 14	*From Thomas Gibbons.* 320
Jan 14	[From Portsmouth Customs Collector's Office]. ALS fragment. DLC. mDW 3401. Reports that he is forwarding a copy of the register of the brig *Hannah*.
Jan 22	To Alexander Bliss. ALS. DLC. mDW 3398. Sends

	back material, incorrectly forwarded to DW in New York.	
Jan 25	To Samuel Jaudon. ALS. NhD. mDW 3402. Arranges to meet Jaudon in Philadelphia on his way to Washington.	
Feb 5	Deed to Tomb lot, St. Paul's Church, Boston, Mass. Printed with ms insertions. MWalB. mDW 3404.	
Feb 7	Agreement with James Thomson, Spanish Treaty Claimant. DS by Thomson. NhHi. mDWs.	
Feb 10	From Isaac Parker. ALS. DLC. mDW 3408. Discusses a claim against the United States government, New York and Massachusetts politics.	
Feb 10	*From Ezekiel Webster.*	321
Feb 13	From George Manners. ALS. NhHi. mDW 3415. Retains DW in a Matthews libel suit.	
Feb 15	From Willard Phillips. ALS. NhHi. mDW 3421. Discusses problems of the Tappan case.	
Feb 17	*To [John Quincy Adams] (enclosure: from Isaac Parker, c. Feb 13, 1823, extract 2 pp.).*	322
Feb 17	To William A. Coleman. ALS. NN. mDW 3425. Sends $100 to cover his book purchases.	
Feb 23	To Alexander Bliss. ALS. DLC. mDW 3428. Reports the receipt of his package containing material on claims cases.	
Feb 26	To Alexander Bliss. ALS. DLC. mDW 3432. Discusses numerous claims cases.	
March 3	From Dudley L. Pickman. ALS. NhHi. mDW 3439. Discusses a claims commission case.	
March 8	To Alexander Bliss. ALS. DLC. mDW 3443. Reports on activity of the Spanish Claims Commission.	
March 13	To Alexander Bliss. ALS. DLC. mDW 3447. Asks Bliss to make arrangements to have a bill for $500 he accepted from Wheaton paid.	
March 14	To William M. Davis. ALS. MHi. mDW 3449. Discusses the Davis claim before the commissioners.	
March 16	From Julia Stockton. ALS. NhHi. mDW 3451. Reports on the health of the Stockton family and inquires of mutual friends in Boston.	
March 18	To Ezekiel Webster. ALS. NhD. mDW 3454. Reports that he has attended to Mr. Little's claim.	
March 18	Application for the Union Insurance Co. ADS. DNA, RG 76. mDWs. Spanish claims.	
March 20	To Alexander Bliss. ALS. DLC. mDW 3456. Reports that he's tired of the business in Washington and urges Bliss to plan on coming there to represent claimants.	
March 21	To Alexander Bliss. ALS. DLC. mDW 3460. Forwards money to take care of the Wheaton bill.	
March 25	To Alexander Bliss. ALS. DLC. mDW 3461. Reports on cases before the claims commission.	

March 25   To Jeremiah Mason. ALS. NhD. mDW 3465. *W & S*, 16: 74–75. Discusses a pension fraud, the presidential election, and New Hampshire politics.

March 25   *To Ezekiel Webster.*   **323**

March 30   To Alexander Bliss. ALS. DLC. mDW 3472. Instructs Bliss on payment of a note and discusses his possible arrival in Boston.

[March?]   To [Edward Everett]. AL. MHi. mDW 3476. Suggests that Everett come into town by way of Medford.

[March]   Report on the petition of Walley & Foster, Boston merchants. AD. DNA, RG 233. mDW 41118.

April 3   *From Ezekiel Webster.*   **323**

April 3   *To Alexander Bliss.*   **324**

April 5   From Joseph Anderson. ALS. NhD. mDW 3484. Reports that the Treasury Department has authorized Mr. Blake to retain DW as counsel.

April 5   From James Strong & Robert C. Cornell. ALS. DLC. mDWs. Discusses the case of the *Frederick* before the claims commissioners.

April 6   To [Isaac Parker]. ALS. NN. mDW 3487. Discusses a claim of the United States against Parker.

April 6   *To Joseph Story.*   **325**

April 6   From Joseph Nourse. ALS. DNA, RG 76. mDWs. Discusses Spanish spoliation claims under the Florida treaty.

April 7   To Joseph Nourse. ALS. NN. mDW 3494. Will undertake the Sheafe claim before the commission on a ten percent basis.

April 8   To Alexander Bliss. ALS. DLC. mDW 3497. Discusses his finances and claims commission cases.

April 10   To Alexander Bliss. ALS. DLC. mDW 3501. Reports on decisions by the claims commissioners and on a decision by the Treasury Department.

April 10   To Jeremiah Mason. Printed. *PC*, 1: 324–325. Urges Mason to take care of a court case in Portland since he cannot get home in season to appear.

April 12   To Alexander Bliss. ALS. DLC. mDW 3504. Reports on claims commission cases.

April 12   *From Thomas Jackson Oakley.*   **326**

April 12   From James Sheafe. ALS. NhHi. mDW 3511. Discusses his claims under the Florida treaty.

April 14   From James Sheafe. ALS. NhHi. mDW 3515. Further discusses his claims.

April 15   From Benjamin Guild. ALS. DLC. mDW 3518. Informs DW of his election as a trustee of the Massachusetts Society for Promoting Agriculture.

April 22   To Ezekiel Webster. ALS. NhD. mDW 3520. Announces his arrival in Boston.

April 24   [Waiver in agreement with Massachusetts Fire and Marine Insurance Company]. DS, by Jonathan Mason, et al. NhHi. mDW 3522.

[June 26]	To John Quincy Adams. ALS. MHi. mDW 3545. Introduces General Iredell and a Mr. Hitchcock.
July 2	To Jeremiah Nelson. ALS. Carl H. Pforzheimer Library. mDW 3547. States his anticipated departure for Washington.
July 2	Promissory Note of Alfred Curtis. ANS. NhD. mDW 39569. For payment of bonds.
July 14	To Alexander Bliss. ALS. DLC. mDW 3549. Discusses cases before the claims commission.
July 15	From James Sheafe. ALS. NhHi. mDW 3553. Discusses his claims under the Florida treaty.
July 15	Brief on the claims of the *Minerva*. ADS. DNA, RG 76. mDWs.
July 16	To James Lloyd. ALS. MH. mDW 3557. Reports on cases taken up by the claims commissioners.
July 17	To James Lloyd. ALS. MH. mDW 3560. Relates that the claim of the *Washington* has been allowed.
July 18	To Alexander Bliss. ALS. DLC. mDW 3562. Reports the results of several claims.
July 18	To Jeremiah Nelson. ALS. The John Rylands Library, Manchester, England. mDW 3566. Discusses Nelson's claims under the Florida treaty.
July 19	Promissory note to Alfred Curtis. ANS. MHi. mDW 39570. For $1000.
July 19	Promissory note to Alfred Curtis. ANS. MHi. mDW 39572. For $1000.
July 21	Application for postponement of cases before the Spanish Claims Commission. ADS. DNA, RG 76. mDWs.
July 22	To Alexander Bliss. ALS. DLC. mDW 3570. Reports his anticipated departure for Philadelphia and discusses several claims cases.
July 24	From John Cowper. ALS. NhHi. mDW 3574. Reports on the claim of the ship *James*.
July 29	To Samuel Lewis Southard [with reply, Aug 11, 1823]. ALS. NjP. mDW 3576. Discusses the possibility that he may recommend Dr. Judson to Dartmouth College for an honorary degree.
Aug 10	To Charles Brickett Haddock. ALS. Sanborn C. Brown, Lexington, Mass. mDW 3578. Recommends Dr. Judson for consideration for an honorary degree.
Aug 11	From Samuel Lewis Southard. AD draft. NjP. mDW 3576. Thinks Dr. Judson is certainly worthy of a Dartmouth College honorary degree.
Aug 23	*From Bennet Tyler.* 331
Aug 26	From Morrell Watson. ALS. NhHi. mDW 3581. Requests information on a court case in which DW represented him.
Sept 6	From W. A. Hill (enclosed with DW to John Quincy

	Adams, Sept 15, 1823). ALS. MHi. mDW 3588. Questions the advisability of Adams' visiting New York at the time.	
Sept 12	To Ezekiel Webster. ALS. NhD. mDW 3583. Inquires if he might visit EW the last of the month.	
Sept 12	*From Joseph Hopkinson.*	331
Sept 15	To John Quincy Adams (enclosure: W. A. Hill to DW, Sept 6, 1823). ALS. MHi. mDW 3589. Forwards Adams the letter from Hill.	
Sept 21	To Joseph Story. ALS. MHi. mDW 3591. Expects visit from Story presently.	
Sept 21	To Ezekiel Webster. ALS. NhD. mDW 3593. Expects to arrive in Boscawen next Wednesday with Mrs. Webster.	
Sept 22	*To Virgil Maxcy.*	332
Sept [?]	From S. B. Forbes. ALS. NhD. mDW 3594. Appeals to DW for financial assistance.	
Oct 1	To the Secretary of the Suffolk Bar Association. ALS. Boston Bar Association, Boston, Mass. mDWs. Reports that George W. Adams is a law student in his office.	
Oct 1	To the Secretary of the Suffolk Bar Association. DS. Boston Bar Association, Boston, Mass. mDWs. Reports that John Langdon Elwyn has read law in his office for a year.	
Oct 6	To the Secretary of the Suffolk Bar Association. ALS. Boston Bar Association, Boston, Mass. mDWs. Reports that Elwyn "sustains a good moral character."	
Oct 9	To James Lloyd. ALS. MH. mDW 3606. Asks if he might borrow Lloyd's copy of Treaty of Ghent.	
Oct 10	From Peter Chardon Brooks. ALS. NhHi. mDW 3609. Waives limit of 5 percent fee to DW for his services before the claims commission.	
Oct 13, 15	Deed transfers between Israel W. Kelley and Daniel Webster. ADS. MWalB. mDW 39575, 39577.	
Oct 17	To John Quincy Adams. ALS. DNA, RG 76. mDW 55612. Discusses the claims of Sheafe against the British government under the Treaty of Ghent.	
Oct 17	From Christopher Gore. ALS. MiU-C. mDW 3611. Invites DW and Joseph Story for a visit.	
Oct 21	To Joseph Hopkinson. ALS. PHi. mDW 3614. Replies to Hopkinson's letter of Sept 12 regarding an alleged statement by Pickering; discusses Adams' candidacy for presidency.	
Oct	Account with Alfred Curtis. AD. NhHi. mDW 39581. Payment of notes.	
Nov 3	To William Channing Woodbridge. ALS. NhD. mDW 3618. Discusses sources for gaining a knowledge of European criminal and civil codes.	

Nov 4   [Power of Attorney to Augustus Peabody]. DS. NhD. mDW 3622. To represent DW at meetings of the Nashua Manufacturing Company.

Nov 4   Promissory Note of Samuel Upton. ANS. NhHi. mDW 39583. For $116.84.

Nov 5   From Nathaniel Amory. ALS. DNA, RG 76. mDWs. Spanish claims.

Nov 7   To Ezekiel Webster. ALS: NhD. mDW 3624. Instructs him to take care of several notes.

Nov 10   To Samuel Jaudon. ALS. NHi. mDW 3626. Asks Jaudon to request the claims commissioners to postpone his cases until he returns to Washington.

[Nov 11]   To James William Paige. ALS. MHi. mDW 3634. Reports the progress of his trip toward Washington.

Nov 13   From James Sheafe. ALS. NhHi. mDW 3628. Discusses his cases before the claims commissioners.

Nov 14   From Nathaniel Amory. ALS. DNA, RG 76. mDWs. Spanish claims.

Nov 16   *To Edward Everett.*   **332**

Nov 20   *To Jeremiah Mason.*   **333**

Nov 20   *To Ezekiel Webster.*   **334**

[Nov 20]   [Memorandum on case of the *Apollo*]. AD. NhHi. mDW 3677.

Nov 22   From James Sheafe. ALS. NhHi. mDW 3648. Forwards memorials in several of his claims cases.

[Nov 24]   To James William Paige. ALS. MHi. mDW 3652. Requests that several local newspapers be sent to him in Washington.

Nov 24   From Henry Preble. ALS. DNA, RG 76. mDWs. Spanish claims.

Nov 24   Lewis Tappan to DW. Manufactures Committee. Enclosure: petition of Massachusetts Wool Manufacturers for additional duty on foreign wool. ALS. DNA, RG 233. mDW 41104. Forwards petition of Massachusetts wool manufacturers.

Nov 25   From Samuel Ayer Bradley. ALS. DLC. mDW 3655. Introduces Stephen Longfellow, Jr., congressman from Maine, to DW.

Nov 26   From Samuel Ayer Bradley. ALS. DLC. mDW 3658. Again remarks on the character and health of Longfellow.

Nov 27   From John Paine. ALS. DNA, RG 233. mDW 41058. Encloses draft of a bill relating to public acts, judicial proceedings.

Nov 28   To Alexander Bliss. ALS. DLC. mDW 3662. Discusses several legal matters, the claims commissioners, arrival of congressmen, and Clay's illness.

Nov 28   To Robert H. Douglas. ALS. NhD. mDWs. Inquires about the money he holds for Mr. Welles, acquired through the sale of a schooner.

Nov 28	*To Edward Everett.*	**335**
Nov 28	To Samuel B. Walcott. ALS. MHi. mDWs. Reports the receipt of several packages in Washingon forwarded by Walcott.	
Nov 29	To Alexander Bliss. AL. DLC. mDW 3669. Asks Bliss to look for and forward several legal documents.	
Nov 29	To Josiah Whitney (enclosed in Josiah Whitney to William King, March 15, 1824). Copy. MeHi. mDWs. Reports the receipt of his papers regarding claims.	
Nov 30	*To Jeremiah Mason.*	**336**
Nov 30	From Henry Wheaton. ALS. DLC. mDW 3671. Discusses cases before the Supreme Court and briefly comments on politics.	
[Nov]	To Edward Everett. ALS. MHi. mDW 3675. *PC, 1*: 327. Looks forward to Everett's coming to Washington; briefly discusses the Greek question.	
Dec 1	To [Nathan Hale?]. ALS. MHi. mDW 3680. Discusses the election of Clay as Speaker of the House and the appointment of a minister to France.	
Dec 1	From Eliza Buckminster. ALS. NhHi. mDW 3681. Reports her findings, per DW's request, on the character and ability of a Mr. Towle.	
Dec 1	From [Henry Wheaton?]. ALS. NhHi. mDW 3683. Relates his fears that he may be removed as court reporter.	
Dec 2	To Alexander Bliss. ALS. DLC. mDW 3686. Reports the loss of a claims case, despite all the pains they had taken.	
Dec 2	To Alexander Bliss. ALS. DLC. mDW 3689. Discusses the case of the *Mary*.	
Dec 2	To Josiah Whitney (enclosed in Josiah Whitney to William King, March 15, 1824). Copy. MeHi. mDWs. Reports reluctance by the commissioners to accept his request for delay.	
Dec 3	To Alexander Bliss. ALS. DLC. mDW 3690. Discusses case before claims commission.	
Dec 4	To Alexander Bliss. ALS. DLC. mDW 3693. Discusses the case of the *Mary*.	
Dec 4	*To Ezekiel Webster.*	**337**
Dec 4–11	Bill to alter the times of holding the district court in Mobile. AD. DNA, RG 233. mDW 40796.	
Dec 5	*To Edward Everett.*	**338**
Dec 6	*To Edward Everett.*	**339**
Dec 8	Resolution to provide for appointment of Commissioner to Greece. AD. DNA, RG 233. mDW 40926.	
Dec 9	To Peter Chardon Brooks. Copy. NhD. mDW 3078. Discusses the case of the *Betsey* and other claims.	
Dec 9	To Edward Everett. ALS. MHi. mDW 3712. Reports on the reception of his resolution to appoint a com-	

	missioner to Greece and thanks Everett for several documents on the Greek question.	
Dec 9	From Charles Jared Ingersoll. ALS. NhHi. mDW 3713. Sends DW a pamphlet and requests copy of his Plymouth oration.	
Dec 10	To Mr. and Mrs. John Quincy Adams. AL. MHi. mDW 3716. Accepts dinner invitation.	
Dec 10	From Samuel Fessenden. ALS. NhHi. mDW 3717. Asks DW to represent him in a court matter.	
Dec 11	From E. Brooks. ALS. DNA, RG 76. mDWs. Spanish claims.	
Dec 11	From Edward D. Parry. ALS. DNA, RG 76. Spanish claims.	
Dec 12	To John C. Calhoun. ALS. DNA, RG 94. mDWs. Recommends George E. Chase as cadet to West Point.	
Dec 13	From Samuel Fessenden. ALS. NhHi. mDW 3721. Asks DW for a legal opinion.	
Dec 15	From Charles W. Greene. ALS. NhHi. mDW 3725. Reports on the health of DW's two children, Daniel and Charles.	
Dec 16	To Alexander Bliss. ALS. DLC. mDW 3729. Discusses cases before the claims commissioners.	
Dec 16	Report on the petition of Alexander MacTier of Boston. AD. DNA, RG 233. mDW 41041.	
Dec 16	Report giving concurrent jurisdiction to the Superior Courts. AD. DNA, RG 233. mDW 41039.	
Dec 17	To Alexander Bliss. ALS. DLC. mDW 3732. Reports on the status of certain cases before the claims commission.	
Dec 17	From Charles Pelham Curtis. ALS. DLC. mDW 3734. Asks DW to present a petition before Congress of a woman who lost her husband in battle.	
Dec 18	To Alexander Bliss. ALS. DLC. mDW 3737. Reports that the case of the *Betsey* has been allowed by the commissioners.	
Dec 19	To Alexander Bliss. ALS. DLC. mDW 3739. Asks him to forward a document to a client.	
Dec 19	From E. Brooks. ALS. DNA, RG 76. mDWs. Spanish claims.	
Dec 20	*To George Blake.*	**340**
Dec 20	*To Mrs. George Blake.*	**341**
Dec 21	To Alexander Bliss. ALS. DLC. mDW 3749. Asks Bliss to check about his notes at the bank.	
Dec 21	*To Edward Everett.*	**342**
Dec 22	From Zeb Cook, Jr. ALS. DNA, RG 59. mDW 55509. Recommends George B. Adams for a Spanish consular post.	
Dec 22	*To Jeremiah Mason.*	**343**
Dec 23	From David B. Ogden. ALS. DNA, RG 76. mDWs. Spanish claims.	
Dec 23	*From Thomas Handasyd Perkins, et al.*	**343**

Dec 23 From R. B. Magruder. ALS. NhHi. mDW 3759. Discusses the question of debtors to the U.S. and asks Webster's opinion.

Dec 23 Bill concerning costs of certain cases. AD. DNA, RG 233. mDW 40801.

Dec 23 Bill to repeal an act to lessen compensation for marshalls, clerks, and attorneys. AD. DNA, RG 233. mDW 40799.

Dec 24 To [Joseph Gales & W. W. Seaton?]. ALS. NN. mDW 3767. Calls their attention to resolutions presented to the Kentucky House of Representatives.

Dec 24 To Leverett Saltonstall. ALS. NhD. mDW 3769. Expresses willingness to be associated with Saltonstall in a case.

Dec 25 From "Vigilans" [with "Vigilans" to John W. Taylor, Dec 25, 1823]. ALS. NHi. mDW 3772. Asks DW to postpone indefinitely his resolution on Greek independence and to substitute resolution favoring freedom of slaves.

Dec 26 To Joseph Story. Printed. *PC*, 1: 412–413. Comments on his work with Spanish claims; discusses judiciary reform, and asks for Story's views (undated, but under 1826 in *PC*).

Dec 27 To T. G. Thornton. ALS. NhExP. mDW 3777. Responds to Thornton's request for attention to the construction of a pier at the mouth of the Saco River.

Dec 27 From Josiah Whitney. ALS. DNA, RG 76. mDWs. Spanish claims.

Dec 29 From Jeremiah Mason. ALS. NhHi. mDW 3778. Mason, *Memoir*, pp. 278–281. Discusses Supreme Court reforms proposed by Congress.

Dec 30 To Alexander Bliss. ALS. DLC. mDW 3786. Reports on claims commission cases; relates "a general blowup" on the West Indian cases.

Dec 30 From Thomas Lindall Winthrop, et al. LS. NhHi. mDW 3789. Encloses a memorial on the affairs of Greece.

Dec 30 Report on the subject of a uniform system of bankruptcy throughout the U.S. AD. DNA, RG 233. mDW 41045.

Dec 31 To Alexander Bliss. ALS. DLC. mDW 3791. Instructs Bliss to give his attention to one of DW's court cases.

Dec 31 From C. W. Owen. ALS. DNA, RG 233. mDW 41169. Discusses the application of Alabama for custody of Africans imported in the vessels condemned in the District of Alabama.

Dec To Mrs. George Blake. ALS. DLC. mDW 3794. Forwards letter from Mrs. Webster.

[Dec ?] *From Joel Roberts Poinsett.* **344**

Dec Report of Whole House Committee concerning costs
of certain cases. AD. DNA, RG 233. mDW 40801.
Dec Resolutions of the Judiciary Committee (18th Congress). AD. DNA, RG 233. mDW 40925.
[1823] Protection of the Officers of the U.S. in performance
of their duties. AD. DNA, RG 233. mDW 41089.
[1823] To John Quincy Adams. ALS. MHi. mDW 3802. Will
call at the Department of State later to see the
papers sent to Chile.
[1823] To Jeremiah Mason. Copy. NhHi. mDW 3814. Introduces Richard Haughton, editor of the *Washington Republican.*
[1823?] To Jeremiah Mason. Copy. NhHi. mDW 3815. *W & S,*
16: 75. Makes plans to see Mason; discusses a
John Quincy Adams oration.
[1823–1824] To Alexander Bliss. ALS. DLC. mDW 3806. Sends
bank note.
[1823–1825?] To John Quincy Adams. ALS. MHi. mDW 3804.
Hopes to be well enough to call at State Department later in the week.
[1823–1827] To Alexander Bliss. ALS. DLC. mDW 3808. Instructs
Bliss on payment of notes.
[1823–1827] To Alexander Bliss. ALS. DLC. mDW 3810. Sends
draft to repay Paige loan.
[1823–1827?] To Alexander Bliss. ALS. DLC. mDW 3812. Sends
check for $800.
[1823–1827] To Alexander Bliss. ALS. DLC. mDW 2874. Asks Bliss
to mail something for him.

1824

Jan 1 To [Francis] Baylies. ALS. NhD. mDW 38220. Re-
quests Baylies to come by his study.
Jan 1 From James Tallmadge and Cornelius C. Cuyler.
DS. DLC. mDW 3817. Send copy of resolutions of
citizens of Poughkeepsie on the question of Greek
independence.
Jan 2 *To Edward Everett.* 344
Jan 2 To Thomas Gibbons. ALS. NjMD. mDW 3821. Reports
that the Steamboat cause is No. 29 on the court
docket.
Jan 2 To Elizabeth Langdon Elwyn. ALS. PHi. mDW 3822.
PC, 1: 337–338. Invites her to Washington and
reports on Washington society.
Jan 2 From Timothy Pitkin. ALS. NhHi. mDW 3825. Dis-
cusses national politics and a Spanish claims case.
Jan 3 From James Dill. ALS. DNA, RG 233. mDW 41077.
Urges DW to support a bill authorizing the pur-
chase of a courtroom and offices for the district of
New York.

Jan 3   From Isaac Parker. ALS. DLC. mDW 3829. Asks
         Webster's attention to the Isaac McLellan case,
         pending either in the Treasury Department or
         Congress.

Jan 4   To Alexander Bliss. ALS. DLC. mDW 3833. Discusses
         two cases before the claims commissioners.

Jan 4   To Joseph Story. Printed. *PC*, 1: 338–340. Discusses
         proposed legislative reform of Supreme Court.

Jan 4   From Joseph Story. Printed. *Life and Letters of
         Joseph Story*, 1: 435–437. Discusses judiciary re-
         organization.

Jan 5   From Charles H. Atherton. ALS. DNA, RG 233. mDW
         41082. Offers suggestions for amending naturaliza-
         tion laws.

Jan 5   *From Barnabas Bates.*   345

Jan 5   Petition of Thomas Winthrop and others of Boston
         on the subject of the Greeks. ADS. DNA, RG 233.
         mDW 41283.

Jan 6   To Alexander Bliss. ALS. DLC. mDW 3841. Sends
         money.

Jan 6   From Isaac P. Davis. ALS. NhHi. mDW 3843. Thanks
         DW for canvasback ducks; refers to Lowell's essays
         on the Greek question.

Jan 6   To William Gibbons. ALS. Robert Carver, Summit,
         N.J. mDWs. Reports to Thomas Gibbons' son that
         the steamboat cause is No. 29 on the Supreme
         Court docket.

Jan 6   From Stephen Pleasanton. ALS. DNA, RG 233. mDW
         41055. Submits bill, drafted in part by the Secre-
         tary of the Treasury, regarding sale and conveyance
         of lands assigned to the United States by insolvent
         debtors.

Jan 6   Report on the case of Peter Jackson. AD. DNA,
         RG 233. mDW 41047.

Jan 7   Receipt to Asa Handy. ANS. NIC. mDW 39585. For
         $175.

Jan 8   To Alexander Bliss. ALS. DLC. mDW 3847. Inquires
         about the location of the Sheafe memorial on the
         Calliope.

Jan 9   To William Plumer, Jr. ALS. Nh. mDW 3849. Van
         Tyne, p. 101. Urges Plumer to speak in behalf of
         DW's Greek resolution, if it meets Plumer's appro-
         bation.

Jan 9   From Leverett Saltonstall. ALS. DLC. mDW 3851.
         Asks when the *Argonaut* case is to be argued.

Jan 9   From James Sheafe. ALS. NhHi. mDW 3855. Sends
         papers relating to his case.

Jan 10   To Alexander Bliss. ALS. DLC. mDW 3859. Discusses
         several cases before the claims commission.

Jan 10   From Joseph Story. Printed. *Life and Letters of*

	Joseph Story, 1: 438–439. Discusses the reorganization of the judiciary.
Jan 10	From Samuel Upton. ALS. DNA, RG 59. mDW 55434. Sends memorial of Peters Pond & Co.
Jan 10	Petition of Massachusetts dealers in straw bonnets. ADS. DNA, RG 233. mDW 41216.
Jan 12	*To Nathan Appleton.* 347
Jan 12	To [Enoch Silsby?]. LS. NhD. mDW 3863. Sends copy of tariff bills and asks for his opinion on it.
Jan 12	To Thomas Wren Ward. ALS. MHi. mDW 4639. Asks Ward's opinion on the proposed tariff bill.
Jan 12	Memorial of Edmund Winchester and others asking a repeal of duties on imported tallow. ADS. DNA, RG 233. mDW 41208.
Jan 13	From Robert C. Cornell and James Strong. ALS. DLC. mDW 3865. Discuss the probability of a rehearing of their case before the claims commissioners.
Jan 14	From Henry Alexander Scammell Dearborn. ALS. NhHi. mDW 3867. Asks DW to support increased pay for customs house officials.
Jan 14	From A. R. Govan. ALS. DNA, RG 233. mDW 41074. Requests citizenship for G. C. Memminger
Jan 17	Petition in the case of the *Nancy.* DS. DNA, RG 76. mDWs. Spanish claims.
Jan 19	Memorial of Thomas Sewall and others in relation to the Greeks. ADS. DNA, RG 233. mDW 41275.
Jan 21	From Jedidiah Morse. ALS. DLC. mDW 3914. Asks DW to attend annual meeting of the Society for the Benefit of Indian Tribes and to speak in their behalf as he has done in the case of the Greeks.
Jan 22	From John Codman. ALS. NjR. mDW 3917. Hopes DW can take on legal defense of his estate against encroachments by the city of Boston.
Jan 23	From Abiel Holmes. ALS. DLC. mDW 3921. Thanks DW for package he sent; comments on the Greek question and South American independence.
Jan 23	From Joseph Hopkinson. ALS. NhHi. mDW 3925. *PC,* 1: 341–343. Praises DW's Greek speech; comments on his own recent publications.
Jan 24	From J. Gales, Jr. ALS. DNA, RG 233. mDW 41067. Makes suggestions for amending the bill to punish more effectively offenses against the United States.
Jan 24	From A. Picquet. ALS. NhHi. mDW 3928. Discusses a financial matter to which he directs DW's attention.
Jan 26	From Elizabeth Langdon Elwyn. ALS. NhHi. mDW 3931. Discusses proposed visit to Washington.
Jan 26	*From Thomas Handasyd Perkins.* 348
Jan 26	Petition of John Burnstead and other merchants of Boston asking for a duty on sales at auctions. ADS. DNA, RG 233. mDW 41188.

Jan 26	Petition of Inhabitants of D.C. asking for government equity. DS. DNA, RG 233. mDW 41134.
Jan 27	*To Ezekiel Webster.* 350
Jan 27	From Asahel Stearns. ALS. DLC. mDW 3945. Commends a holder of Georgia Land Office certificates to DW's attention.
Jan 27	Bill for the punishment of crimes against the United States, and for other purposes. AD. DNA, RG 233. mDW 40814.
Jan 29	Resolution to allow publishers of newspapers to accompany their papers with bills or memoranda of account. AD. DNA, RG 233. mDW 40970.
Jan 30	From J. McLean. Letterbook copy. DNA, RG 28. mDW 57043. Reports that Boston postmaster is furnished with wrapping paper and twine by the Post Office Department.
Jan 30	Committee on the Judiciary. Report on repealing the 25th section of the act to establish judicial courts in the U.S. AD. DNA, RG 233. mDW 41053.
Jan 30	Bill to alter the times of holding the circuit court in the District of South Carolina. AD. DNA, RG 233. mDW 40883.
Jan 31	To John Quincy Adams. ALS. DNA, RG 59. mDW 55433. Encloses memorial forwarded by Samuel Upton.
Jan 31	From Morris S. Miller. ALS. NhD. mDW 3947. Sends melon seeds and invites the Websters to visit him in Utica during the summer.
[Jan]	To Edward Everett. ALS. MHi. mDW 3949. *PC*, 1: 341. Reports that he will send large number of copies of his Greek speech to New England.
Feb 1	From Joseph Hopkinson. ALS. NhHi. mDW 3950. *PC*, 1: 343–344. Praises DW's Greek speech and urges him to publish it.
Feb 1	*From Jeremiah Mason.* 351
Feb 2	Petition of Massachusetts book sellers. ADS. DNA, RG 233. mDW 41212.
Feb 3	From Zabdiel Sampson, et al. LS. NhHi. mDW 3958. Ask DW to support their memorial to Congress for the preservation of Plymouth harbor.
Feb 5	To Joseph Hopkinson. ALS. PHi. mDW 3962. Discusses his Greek speech, cases before the Supreme Court, and the claims commission.
Feb 6	From A Friend to Justice. ALS. NhHi. mDW 3967. Alludes to possible impropriety in the Boston post office.
Feb 7	From Nicholas Biddle. ALS draft. DLC. mDW 3972a. Praises DW's Greek speech and thanks him for copy.
Feb 9	From William Meredith. ALS. NhD. mDW 3973. Thanks DW for copy of his Greek speech.

Feb 9   Petition of City Council of Boston on surrounding islands. ADS. DNA, RG 233. mDW 41201.

Feb 9   From Alfred Curtis. ALS. NhHi. mDW 39586. Reports that he has drawn on DW for money.

Feb 10   From John J. Bryant. ALS. NhD. mDW 3975. Suggests that DW send the *National Intelligencer* and perhaps a small bank note to one of DW's strong supporters in New Hampshire.

Feb 10   From D. Sheffey. ALS. DNA, RG 233. mDW 41097. Asks DW's support for the establishment of an additional U.S. court at Staunton.

Feb 15   To Ezekiel Webster. ALS. NhD. mDW 3986. Van Tyne, p. 102. Discusses the meeting of the congressional caucus on the presidential question.

Feb 16   From James Kent. ALS. MeHi. mDW 3989. Thanks DW for copy of his Greek speech.

Feb 17   To Jonathan Goodhue. ALS. NNS. mDW 3991. Sends draft for collection.

Feb 18   To [John C. Calhoun]. ANS. DNA, RG 99. mDW 57134. Endorses the recommendation of John S. Tyler by a group of Boston men for office of sutler in the army.

Feb 18   To William Gibbons. ALS by William Wirt and DW. Robert Carver, Summit, N.J. mDWs. Discuss their fees for arguing the case of *Gibbons* v. *Ogden.*

Feb 18   From Timothy Upham. ALS. NhD. mDW 3993. Thanks DW for his Greek speech and briefly discusses New Hampshire politics.

Feb 18   Katherine Dexter, Power of Attorney to DW. DS. DNA, RG 76. mDWs. Spanish claims.

Feb 18   Agnes Prince, Power of Attorney to DW. DS. DNA, RG 76. mDWs. Spanish claims.

Feb 19   From Thomas March. ALS. NhHi. mDW 3996. Discusses a dispute between himself and Charles March.

Feb 19   William H. Boardman, Power of Attorney to DW. DS. DNA, RG 76. mDWs. Spanish claims.

Feb 20   Samuel Brown, Power of Attorney to DW. DS. DNA, RG 76. mDWs. Spanish claims.

Feb 20   Isaac P. Davis, Power of Attorney to DW. DS. DNA, RG 76. mDWs. Spanish claims.

Feb 20   David Eckley, Power of Attorney to DW. DS. DNA, RG 76. mDWs. Spanish claims.

Feb 20   Thacher Goddard, Power of Attorney to DW. DS. DNA, RG 76. mDWs. Spanish claims.

Feb 20   Henry Ladd, Power of Attorney to DW. DS. DNA, RG 76. mDWs. Spanish claims.

Feb 20	Jacob Sheafe, Power of Attorney to DW. DS. DNA, RG 76. mDWs. Spanish claims.
Feb 21	Jonathan Amory and Francis Amory, Power of Attorney to DW. DS. DNA, RG 76. mDWs. Spanish claims.
Feb 21	Thomas Cushing, Power of Attorney to DW. DS. DNA, RG 76. mDWs. Spanish claims.
Feb 21	Richard Derby, Power of Attorney to DW. DS. DNA, RG 76. mDWs. Spanish claims.
Feb 21	Ebenezer Francis, Power of Attorney to DW. DS. DNA, RG 76. mDWs. Spanish claims.
Feb 21	Ebenezer Gay, Power of Attorney to DW. DS. DNA, RG 76. mDWs. Spanish claims.
Feb 21	Nathaniel Gilman, Power of Attorney to DW. DS. DNA, RG 76. mDWs. Spanish claims.
Feb 21	Benjamin P. Homer, Power of Attorney to DW. DS. DNA, RG 76. mDWs. Spanish claims.
Feb 21	William Mackay, Power of Attorney to DW. DS. DNA, RG 76. mDWs. Spanish claims.
Feb 21	Samuel W. Pomeroy, Power of Attorney to DW. DS. DNA, RG 76. mDWs. Spanish claims.
Feb 21	Andrew Ritchie, Power of Attorney to DW. DS. DNA, RG 76. mDWs. Spanish claims.
Feb 21	Hannah Smith, Power of Attorney to DW. DS. DNA, RG 76. mDWs. Spanish claims.
Feb 21	Israel Thorndike, Power of Attorney to DW. DS. DNA, RG 76. mDWs. Spanish claims.
Feb 21	Benjamin M. Watson, Power of Attorney to DW. DS. DNA, RG 76. mDWs. Spanish claims.
Feb 21	Francis Welch, Power of Attorney to DW. DS. DNA, RG 76. mDWs. Spanish claims.
Feb 21	Arnold Welles and John Welles, Power of Attorney to DW. DS. DNA, RG 76. mDWs. Spanish claims.
Feb 21	Moses Wheeler, Power of Attorney to DW. DS. DNA, RG 76. mDWs. Spanish claims.
Feb 22	To Alexander Bliss. ALS. DLC. mDW 4001. Discusses payment of a bank note and power of attorney forms which he will expect to be forwarded.
Feb 22	To Ezekiel Webster. ALS. NhD. mDW 4004. *PC*, 1: 346. Sends Ezekiel a book and discusses national politics.
Feb 22	From Thomas Handasyd Perkins. ALS. DLC. mDW 4007. Reports on the discussion of the Massachusetts claims in the legislature.
Feb 22	From William Prescott. ALS. NhHi. mDW 4011. Discusses the activity of the Massachusetts legislature.
Feb 23	From J. B.[?] Davis. ALS. DNA, RG 233. mDW 41157. Encloses petition of Ezra Davis.
Feb 23	Elizabeth Amory, Power of Attorney to DW. DS. DNA, RG 76. mDWs. Spanish claims.

Feb 23 — Nathan Bridge, Power of Attorney to DW. DS. DNA, RG 76. mDWs. Spanish claims.

Feb 23 — Benjamin Bussey, Power of Attorney to DW. DS. DNA, RG 76. mDWs. Spanish claims.

Feb 23 — Samuel Cobb, Power of Attorney to DW. DS. DNA, RG 76. mDWs. Spanish claims.

Feb 23 — Charles W. Greene, Power of Attorney to DW. DS. DNA, RG 76. mDWs. Spanish claims.

Feb 23 — Theodore Lyman, Power of Attorney to DW. DS. DNA, RG 76. mDWs. Spanish claims.

Feb 23 — Daniel Sargent, Power of Attorney to DW. DS. DNA, RG 76. mDWs. Spanish claims.

Feb 23 — Remonstrance of Massachusetts merchants against duty on sales at auction. DS. DNA, RG 233. mDW 41260.

Feb 24 — To Alexander Bliss. ALS. DLC. mDW 4015. Asks Bliss to secure power of attorney documents from certain claimants.

Feb 24 — Charles Brown, Power of Attorney to DW. DS. DNA, RG 76. mDWs. Spanish claims.

Feb 24 — Joseph Foster, Power of Attorney to DW. DS. DNA, RG 76. mDWs. Spanish claims.

Feb 24 — Stephen Gorham, Power of Attorney to DW. DS. DNA, RG 76. mDWs. Spanish claims.

Feb 24 — Jonathan Merry, Power of Attorney to DW. DS. DNA, RG 76. mDWs. Spanish claims.

Feb 24 — Lucy Rand, Power of Attorney to DW. DS. DNA, RG 76. mDWs. Spanish claims.

[Feb 24] — Bill to amend further the judicial system of the United States. AD. DNA, RG 233. mDW 40886.

Feb 25 — John J. Apthorp, Power of Attorney to DW. DS. DNA, RG 76. mDWs. Spanish claims.

Feb 26 — To Alexander Bliss. AL. DLC. mDW 4018. Encloses check for $700 to take care of a debt.

Feb 26 — From Richard Bland Lee. ALS. DNA, RG 233. mDW 41072. Discusses political and judicial disfranchisements of inhabitants of the District of Columbia.

Feb 26 — William Moody, Power of Attorney to DW. DS. DNA, RG 76. mDWs. Spanish claims.

Feb 27 — Rufus G. Amory, Power of Attorney to DW. DS. DNA, RG 76. mDWs. Spanish claims.

Feb 27 — Henry Sigourney, Power of Attorney to DW. DS. DNA, RG 76. mDWs. Spanish claims.

[Feb 28] — To John C. Calhoun. ALS. MHi. mDW 4020. W & S, 16: 91–92. Discusses the location of a road from Boston to Watertown.

Feb 28 — John Brazer, Power of Attorney to DW. DS. DNA, RG 76. mDWs. Spanish claims.

Feb 28 — Nathaniel Dorr, Power of Attorney to DW. DS. DNA, RG 76. mDWs. Spanish claims.

Feb 28	Henry Hatch, Power of Attorney to DW. DS. DNA, RG 76. mDWs. Spanish claims.
Feb 28	John Hancock, Power of Attorney to DW. DS. DNA, RG 76. mDWs. Spanish claims.
Feb 28	Jonathan Mason, Power of Attorney to DW. DS. DNA, RG 76. mDWs. Spanish claims.
Feb 28	Jonathan Mason and Thomas Perkins, Power of Attorney to DW. DS. DNA, RG 76. mDWs. Spanish claims.
Feb 28	Perez Morton, Power of Attorney to DW. DS. DNA, RG 76. mDWs. Spanish claims.
Feb 28	Thomas Perkins, Power of Attorney to DW. DS. DNA, RG 76. mDWs. Spanish claims.
Feb 28	Charles Taylor, Power of Attorney to DW. DS. DNA, RG 76. mDWs. Spanish claims.
Feb 28	Nathan Whiting, Power of Attorney to DW. DS. DNA, RG 76. mDWs. Spanish claims.
March 1	Charles P. Curtis, Power of Attorney to DW. DS. DNA, RG 76. mDWs. Spanish claims.
March 3	Petition of Ezra Davis. ADS. DNA, RG 233. mDW 41158.
March 3	Petition of Massachusetts merchants against abolishing the office of measurer in the Customs. ADS. DNA, RG 233. mDW 41278.
[March 5]	To Alexander Bliss. ALS. DLC. mDW 4024. Discusses his finances.
March 5	From William Sullivan. ALS. DLC. mDW 4027. Discusses a legal matter and Massachusetts politics.
March 5	From Samuel Upton. ALS. DNA, RG 206. mDWs. Annexes schedule of his bonds.
[c. March 5]	To Stephen Pleasanton. ALS. DNA, RG 206. mDWs. Sends Samuel Upton's letter on the Customs House bonds.
March 7	To Joseph Hopkinson. ALS. PHi. mDW 4031. Questions the possibility of presenting claims before the commissioners.
March 8	From [Anon]. AL. NhHi. mDW 4035. Discusses militia bill under consideration in Congress.
March 8	From William Gibbons. ALS. NhHi. mDW 4038. States that his father agrees to fees stated in letter of February 18.
March 8	Oliver Keating, Power of Attorney to DW. DS. DNA, RG 76. mDWs. Spanish claims.
March 11	From Stephen Pleasanton. LC. DNA, RG 206. mDWs. Encloses letter and draft of a bill from Mr. Bibb, Attorney of the United States for the district of Kentucky.
March 13	To James William Paige. ANS. MHi. mDW 4040. Reports that passage of a tariff bill in its present shape is unlikely.

March 14   To Ezekiel Webster. ALS. NhD. mDW 4044. *PC*, 1:
                  347–348. Discusses the New Hampshire gubernato-
                  rial election, the tariff, and presidential prospects.

March 14   From Isaac Parker. ALS. DLC. mDW 4048. Inquires
                  about cases before the Supreme Court, praises
                  DW's Greek speech, and comments on presidential
                  candidates.

March 17   *To Joseph Hopkinson.*   355

March 19   From Benjamin Joseph Gilbert. ALS copy. NhD.
                  mDW 4056. Asks DW to assist his son in securing
                  an appointment as a midshipman.

March 19   Bill to alter the time of holding the district court of
                  the United States in the District of Illinois. AD.
                  DNA, RG 233. mDW 40909.

March 20   From Jeremiah Mason. ALS. NhHi. mDW 4059.
                  Discusses New Hampshire and Massachusetts pol-
                  itics, presidential election, and claims cases.

March 23   From Richard Bland Lee. ALS. DNA, RG 233. mDW
                  41149. Discusses governmental reform for the Dis-
                  trict of Columbia.

March 23   From Richard Bland Lee. ALS. DNA, RG 233. mDW
                  41146. Discusses political and civil rights for the
                  inhabitants of the District of Columbia.

March 23   From Thomas Swann. ALS. DNA, RG 233. mDW
                  41101. Discusses bill providing for the security of
                  money.

[March 24]   To Alexander Bliss. ALS. DLC. mDW 4067. Sends
                  check for payment of a note.

March 24   To S[tephen] Pleasanton. AD. DNA, RG 206. mDW
                  57178. On behalf of the Committee on the Judici-
                  ary, inquires about instructions issued to district
                  attorneys by the Treasury Department.

March 24   From S[tephen] Pleasanton. AD. DNA, RG 233. mDW
                  41095. Transmits the instructions Webster re-
                  quested.

March 25   To John C. Calhoun. ALS. DNA, RG 156. mDWs.
                  Recommends Major John Peter for appointment as
                  paymaster at the Harpers Ferry armory.

March 27   To Alexander Bliss. ALS. DLC. mDW 4069. Discusses
                  note payments.

[March 27]   To Nathan Hale. ALS. MHi. mDW 4073. *W & S*, 16:
                  82. Discusses the Civil Appropriations Bill, the
                  tariff, and a claims question.

[March 29]   To Nathan Appleton. ALS. MHi. mDW 4077. Wel-
                  comes Appleton to Washington and invites him to
                  dinner.

March 29   From Jeremiah Mason. ALS. NhHi. mDW 4078. Asks
                  DW when he thinks the current session of Congress
                  will adjourn; wants to see him before the New
                  Hampshire legislature convenes.

March 30   To the Board of Commissioners under the Spanish

	Treaty. ADS. DNA, RG 76. mDWs. Motions and affidavits for continuance.
March 31	To Nathan Appleton. Copy. NhHi. mDW 4080. Arranges to meet Appleton in the evening.
[March]	To Alexander Bliss. ALS. DLC. mDW 4081. Discusses a New England Mississippi Land Company claim and Florida treaty claims.
[March]	Report of the Committee on the Judiciary on protection of federal officers. AD. DNA, RG 233. mDW 41089.
April 2–5	Account with Alfred Curtis. ANS. NhHi. mDW 39588.
April 3	From William Gibbons. ALS. NhHi. mDW 4084. Sends drafts covering DW's fees.
April 5	To Jeremiah Mason. Copy. NhHi. mDW 4086. Van Tyne, p. 103. Discusses the race for a judgeship in New Hampshire.
April 6	To [Thomas Gibbons?]. ALS. Robert Carver, Summit, N.J. mDWs. Received payment.
April 6	To Jeremiah Mason. Copy. NhHi. mDW 4087. Van Tyne, pp. 103–104. Discusses the New Hampshire senatorial race.
April 7	From Stephen Pleasanton. LC. DNA, RG 206. mDWs. Discusses the Upton bonds.
April 10	To Ebenezer Clough. ALS. NhD. mDW 4088. Accepts Clough's retainer fee.
April 10	From S. B. Parkman. ALS. DNA, RG 76. mDWs. Spanish claims.
April 10	From [Samuel L. Southard]. AN. DNA, RG 233. mDW 41064. Asks DW to read letter from William Bainbridge.
April 10	*To Joseph Story.*
April 11	To Isaac P. Davis. ALS. NhHi. mDW 4091. *PC,* 1: 383–384. Discusses family, weather, and the tariff.
April 11	From William Gaston. ALS. NhHi. mDW 4094. Van Tyne, p. 107. Queries DW on the presidential election.
April 12	From Theodore Lyman, Jr. ALS. DLC. mDW 4096. Discusses the tariff and Massachusetts politics.
April 12	From Jeremiah Mason. ALS. NhHi. mDW 4100. Mason, *Memoir,* p. 286. Discusses the rumor of Judge Sherburne's resignation and proposes a replacement for him.
April 14	To [Edward Everett]. ALS. MHi. mDW 4103. Forwards a letter and an article.
April 16	From Ebenezer Clough. ALS. NhD. mDW 4090. Thanks DW for his letter of April 10.
[April 17?]	To J. Gales and W. W. Seaton. ALS. NhD. mDW 4051. Asks how promptly they could get his tariff speech printed.

356

April 17	To Enoch Silsby. ALS. NhD. mDW 4104. Asks Silsby and other shipowners and manufacturers to send a memorial to Congress on the tariff question.
April 17, June 3	From Stratford Canning. ALS. NhHi. mDW 4107. *W & S*, 16: 111n. Introduces four Englishmen who will be visiting America to DW.
April 18	To Ezekiel Webster. ALS. NhD. mDW 4111. *PC*, 1: 349–350. Discusses tariff question.
April 19	*To Jeremiah Mason.*
April 19	To Dudley L. Pickman. ALS. NhD. mDWs. Informs him that the claims commission has disallowed his case.
April 22	To Alexander Bliss. AL. DLC. mDW 4116. Asks him to give legal assistance to Samuel Lord in Boston.
April 22	From Samuel Humphreys. ALS. DNA, RG 76. mDWs. Spanish claims.
April 22	From William Sturgis. ALS. NhHi. mDW 4118. Discusses his objections to the tariff bill.
[c. April 22]	Petition in the case of the brig *Nora*. DS. DNA, RG 76. mDWs. Spanish claims.
April 24	To Alexander Bliss. ALS. DLC. mDW 4122. Discusses his departure from Washington and the proposed plan of payment of Spanish claims.
April 24	From Daniel Brent. Letterbook copy. DNA, RG 59. mDW 55664. Returns papers borrowed from DW.
April 24	To Gorham Parsons. ALS. NhD. mDW 4126. Reports that claims are likely to be paid in cash; if so will probably remain in Washington until June.
April 25	To Alexander Bliss. ALS. DLC. mDW 4129. Discusses note payments and Clough retainer fee.
April 26	From Dudley L. Pickman. ALS. DNA, RG 76. mDWs. Spanish claims.
April 27	To Alexander Bliss. ALS. DLC. mDW 4132. Discusses health and certain claims and court cases.
April 27 [1824–1826]	To Samuel L. Southard. ALS. MHi. mDW 4134. Recommends the appointment of a Mr. Howe as surgeon's mate in the navy.
April 28	From Dudley L. Pickman. ALS. NhHi. mDW 4137. Urges Webster to press his claim before the claims commission.
[April]	To Alexander Bliss. ALS. DLC. mDW 4141. Discusses his personal finances.
May 1	To Alexander Bliss. ALS. DLC. mDW 4143. Instructs Bliss to pay certain accounts.
May 4	To Alexander Bliss. ALS. DLC. mDW 4146. Discusses a Whitney case and cases before the claims commission.
May 4	To James Monroe (from DW et al). Copy. DNA, RG 77. mDWs. Discusses the survey of land in Massachusetts.

357

May 4	From Henry Alexander Scammell Dearborn. ALS. NhHi. mDW 4149. Van Tyne, pp. 104–105. Remarks on DW's speech on the Greek Revolution and the tariff.
May 4	From Benjamin Pickman. ALS. NhHi. mDW 4153. Discusses his claim under the Florida treaty and DW's and Clay's tariff speeches.
May 4	To Joseph Story. PC, 1: 350–351. Describes the debate on the Supreme Court in Congress.
May 4	Resolution by DW relating to suits on validity of treaties. AD. DNA, RG 233. mDW 41000.
May 5	From Peter Oxenbridge Thacher. ALS. DLC. mDW 4156. Praises DW's speech on the tariff; discusses the West and the tariff question.
May 8	From Dudley L. Pickman and Stephen White. ALS. NhHi. mDW 4159. Discuss Spanish claim cases.
May 9	To Alexander Bliss. ALS. DLC. mDW 4162. Instructs Bliss on the handling of court cases during DW's absence from Boston.
May 9	*To Jeremiah Mason.* 358
May 10	To Alexander Bliss. ALS. DLC. mDW 4170. Asks Bliss to inform clients on the method of payment of their claims.
May 10	From John Randolph. ALS. DSI. mDW 4173. Inquires about documents received from the Treasury Department.
May 11	To John Quincy Adams. AL. MHi. mDW 4176. Accepts dinner invitation.
May 11	From Christopher Gore. ALS. NhHi. mDW 4177. PC, 1: 351. Praises DW's tariff speech.
May 12	To [?] Adams, from DW and Bliss. ALS in Bliss' hand. NhHi. mDW 4180. Discuss his claim under the Florida treaty.
May 12	To Robert Rantoul. ALS. MBevHi. mDW 4187. Reports that claims under the Florida treaty are to be paid by the Treasury Department and not the commissioners.
May 12	*From Thomas Handasyd Perkins.* 360
May 19	To Alexander Bliss. ALS. DLC. mDW 4189. Reports the receipt of several powers of attorney.
May 20	To Alexander Bliss. ALS. DLC. mDW 4191. Reports passage of claims bill through Senate; expects Congress to adjourn in a week.
May 22	To [Edward Livingston]. ALS. DNA, RG 76. mDWs. Discusses a Spanish claims case.
May 22	From Edward Livingston. ALS. DNA, RG 76. mDWs. Discusses a Spanish claims case.
[May 23]	To Alexander Bliss. ALS. DLC. mDW 4195. Instructs Bliss to take care of several notes.
May 24	To [Daniel Parker?]. Copy. DNA, RG 107. mDWs.

	Offers legal opinion to Parker, who wished to be considered as an assignee of John H. Piatt.
May 26 [1824–1826]	To Alexander Bliss. ALS. DLC. mDW 4589. Asks him to inquire into a case for George McDuffie.
May 26	From Isaac Morris. ALS. DLC. mDW 4202. Inquires if DW knows of a Daniel D. Rogers in Massachusetts.
May 26	Resolution by DW to establish uniform system of bankruptcy. AN. DNA, RG 233. mDW 41002.
May 28	To ?. Copy. NhD. mDW 4204. Discusses illness of William H. Crawford and its effect on the presidential contest.
[c. May 29]	Petition in the case of the brig *Alert*. DS. DNA, RG 76. mDWs. Spanish claims.
[May]	To [Alexander Bliss]. ALS. DLC. mDW 4205. Recommends either a continuance or an appeal in the case involving Whitney.
[May]	To Alexander Bliss. ALS. DLC. mDW 4207. Discusses form of powers of attorney and the bill for paying claims, under consideration in Congress.
[May]	To Alexander Bliss. ALS. DLC. mDW 4209. Instructs Bliss on the proper form required in the powers of attorney.
[May]	To Alexander Bliss. ALS. DLC. mDW 4211. Reports on claims matters.
[May]	To Alexander Bliss. ALS. DLC. mDW 4213. Reports on procedure in claims payments.
June 2	From William Savage. ALS. DNA, RG 59. mDWs. Recommends J. Hill Clark for appointment as consul in the Hamburg area.
June 3	To Alexander Bliss. ALS. DLC. mDW 4216. Reports his arrival in Philadelphia; instructs Bliss on payment of notes.
June 3	To James William Paige. ALS. MHi. mDW 4219. States his itinerary for the next few weeks.
June 5	To James William Paige. ALS. MHi. mDW 4222. Reports Mrs. Webster's departure for New York and Boston and his, for Washington.
June 5	To Ezekiel Webster. ALS. NhD. mDW 4224. *W & S*, 16: 87–88. Discusses New Hampshire and national politics.
June 6	To Alexander Bliss. ALS. DLC. mDW 4228. Instructs Bliss on payment of notes and reports on decisions by the claims commissioners.
June 6	From Grace Fletcher Webster. ALS. NhHi. mDW 4230. Reports on visit with the Hopkinsons at Bordentown.
[*June* 6]	*From Grace Fletcher Webster.* 360
June 7	To Alexander Bliss. ALS. DLC. mDW 4237. Concerned that he has not yet received the powers of attorney.

June 9 To Mrs. George Blake. ALS. DLC. mDW 4239. *PC*, 1: 352. Reports a change in Washington society when the Blakes left; plans to "play" when he gets to Boston.

June 9 To James Monroe. ALS. DNA, RG 59. mDWs. Recommends Tobias Watkins for an office.

June 9 From Grace Fletcher Webster. ALS. NhHi. mDW 4272. Reports her arrival in Princeton.

June 9 To Thomas Wilson. ALS. NIC. mDW 4243. Encloses check for $1812.57, for deposit in his account.

June 9 Memoranda of Commissions on Spanish Claims. AD. MWalB. mDW 4245. Runs through July 7.

June 10 To Ezekiel Webster. ALS. NhD. mDW 4276. Gives brief report of occurrences in Washington.

June 12 From Grace Fletcher Webster. ALS. NhHi. mDW 4278. Reports her arrival in New York.

June 12 Bank draft for $40,018.81. ANS. NhD. mDW 39546.

June 12 Bank draft for $4,929.20. ANS. NhD. mDW 39590.

June 12 Bank draft for $25,373.05. ANS. NhD. mDW 39591.

June 12 Bank draft for $57,652.51. ANS. NhD. mDW 39592.

June 12 Bank draft for $59,296.11. ANS. NhD. mDW 39593.

June 13 To Alexander Bliss. ALS. DLC. mDW 4281. Instructs Bliss to take care of several of his debts.

June 13 Power of Attorney to transfer 58 shares of Concord Bank Stock to DW from Cyrus Perkins. ADS. NhHi. mDW 39596.

June 14 To Alexander Bliss. ALS. DLC. mDW 4283. Discusses the final reports of the claims commissioners.

June 14 From Grace Fletcher Webster. ALS. NhHi. mDW 4291. Thanks Webster for two letters.

June 15 To Alexander Bliss. ALS. DLC. mDW 4293. Urges him to send powers of attorney.

June 15 Bank draft for $8,875.54. ANS. Robert C. Laserte, Leominster, Mass. mDW 39594.

June 16 To George Blake. ALS. DLC. mDW 4296. *PC*, 1: 352–353. Reports on his activities in Washington.

June 16 To Robert Rantoul. ALS. NhD. mDW 4300. Reports that awards payments have been arranged through the Bank of the United States in Philadelphia.

June 17 To Gabriel Richard from DW et al. LS by DW et al. Detroit Archdiocesan Chancery Archives. mDW 4303. Give a legal opinion in an ecclesiastical matter.

June 17 From Hutchins G. Burton. ALS. NhD. mDW 4305. Praises Webster's speech on the tariff.

[June 18] To Alexander Bliss. ALS. DLC. mDW 4309. Needs powers of attorney to expedite claims awards.

[June 19] To Alexander Bliss. ALS. DLC. mDW 4313. Instructs Bliss on the matter of powers of attorney.

June 19 Bank draft for $653.13. ANS. NhD. mDW 39595.

June 19   Bank draft for $939.87. ANS. R. A. Martin, Henniker, N.H. mDW 39595a.

June 20   To Alexander Bliss. ALS. DLC. mDW 4317. Discusses claims commission matters.

June 20   To Alexander Bliss. ALS. DLC. mDW 4320. Reports the receipt of several letters and powers of attorney.

June 20   To Alexander Bliss. ALS. DLC. mDW 4322. Reports that he is now making payments to several claimants.

June 21   To Thomas Wilson. ALS. OClWHi. mDW 4325. Encloses Treasury draft for $2,911.05, to be credited to his account.

June 24   To Alexander Bliss. ALS. DLC. mDW 4326. Reports on payments of claims.

June 25   To Alexander Bliss. ALS. DLC. mDW 4329. Discusses the payment of claims awarded under the Florida treaty.

June 25   To John Inskeep. ALS. Insurance Company of North America, Philadelphia, Pa. mDW 4332. Expresses his high regard for Samuel Jaudon.

June 25   To Samuel Jaudon. ALS. NHi. mDW 4335. Reports from Philadelphia on the payment of claims.

June 28   To Alexander Bliss. ALS. DLC. mDW 4339. From New York, instructs Bliss on the payment of notes.

June 28   From William Pickman. ALS. NHi. mDW 4342. Reports on error in DW's payment of claims and suggests method of settlement.

[June]   To Alexander Bliss. ALS. DLC. mDW 4346. Sends enclosed note to pay debt to William Appleton.

[June?]   To James Monroe, from DW et al. LS. DNA, RG 59. mDWs. Express their high regard for Tobias Watkins, Secretary of the Spanish Claims Commission, and recommend him for some office.

[July 2]   To Samuel Jaudon. ALS. NHi. mDW 4348. Asks Jaudon for an opinion on a claims case.

July 2   From James Gore King. ALS. NHi. mDW 4350. Acknowledges receipt of check in the amount of his claim.

July 2   From Benjamin Pickman. ALS. NHi. mDW 4352. Acknowledges receipt of check in the amount of his claim.

July 3   To John P. Kennedy. ALS. Henry N. Ess, III, New York, N.Y. mDWs. Discusses the payment of a claim.

July 4   *To Samuel Jaudon.*   **361**

July 4   To [?]. ALS. PU. mDW 4354. Wishes to purchase a book.

July 6   Bank draft of $6948.63 to Samuel G. Perkins. ADS. MHi. mDWs.

July 7	Bank draft for $2697.23. ANS. NhD. mDW 39599.
July 8	Bank draft for $1485.18. ANS. NP. mDW 39600.
July 8	Bank draft for $2620.58. ANS. NhHi. mDW 39604.
July 10	Bank draft for $2983.05. ANS. NhHi. mDW 39602.
July 10	Bank draft for $435.43. ANS. NhHi. mDW 39602.
July 10	Bank draft for $717.24. ANS. NhHi. mDW 39602.
July 10	Bank draft for $435.33. ANS. NhHi. mDW 39604.
July 12	Transfer of Stock in Concord Bank. Printed DS. NhHi. mDW 39607.
July 12	Bank draft for $873.59. ANS. Mr. John W. King, Concord, N.H. mDW 39609.
July 12	To Samuel Jaudon. AL. NHi. mDW 4359. Discusses claims commission cases.
[July 12]	From John C. King. ALS. MHi. mDW 4367. Discusses the settlement of his claim.
July 13	To Samuel Jaudon. ALS. NHi. mDW 4369. Sends information on claims cases.
July 13	Account with Alfred Curtis. ANS. NhHi. mDW 39610.
July 14	To Samuel Jaudon. ALS. NHi. mDW 4373. Sends several powers of attorney from claimants under the Spanish treaty.
July 14	*From Joel Roberts Poinsett.* 362
July 24	From Cornelius Peter Van Ness. Copy. Vermont State House. mDW 4380. Asks DW for his opinion on Vermont law involving lands originally granted to the Society for the Propagation of the Gospel.
July 31	To Samuel Jaudon. ALS. NHi. mDW 4382. Remarks on Jaudon's return to Philadelphia and reports on a claims case.
July 31	To Cornelius Peter Van Ness. Copy. Vermont State House. mDW 4385. Responds to Van Ness' letter of July 24; states that Van Ness' question was "so general" that he does not understand what he wants.
[July]	Bank draft for $456.45. DS. MWalB. mDW 40677.
Aug 10	To James William Paige. ALS. MHi. mDW 4387. Sends check and reports the good health of family.
Aug 15	To [Edward Everett]. ALS. MHi. mDW 4389. Discusses Massachusetts politics.
Aug 15	To [John Collins] Warren. Printed. George Washington Warren, *History of the Bunker Hill Monument Association*, pp. 98–99. Discusses purchasing land for the Association.
Aug 19	From John C. Calhoun. Copy. DLC. mDW 4391. Introduces a Dr. Everett.
Sept 8	*To William Gaston.* 363
Sept 8	From W[illiam] S[ullivan]. Copy. MHi. mDWs. Discusses loan for Bunker Hill Monument Association.
Sept 13	To Samuel Jaudon. ALS. NHi. mDW 4396. Asks for

	information on his bank account; comments on the presidential race.	
Sept 14	To William B. Swett & Co. ALS draft. NhHi. mDW 4400. Instructs him to pay a note on a law suit.	
Sept 18	From Cornelius Peter Van Ness. Copy. Vermont State House. mDW 4404. Clarifies his earlier query involving a Vermont law.	
Sept 20	Circular to raise funds for monument at Bunker Hill, written by E. Everett and signed by DW et al. Printed in Warren, *History of the Bunker Hill Monument Association*, pp. 109–116.	
Sept 24	From W. M. Gibson. ALS. NhHi. mDW 4407. Discusses the possibility of his purchasing the claims of some southerners, thereby to "free them from embarrassment."	
Sept ?	To Mrs. George Blake. ALS. NhD. mDW 4409. Requests to borrow a house servant for a day.	
Oct 10	*From William Gaston.*	364
Oct 14 [1824–1826]	To Joseph Story. ALS. MiU-C. mDW 4415. Responds to Story's declining dinner invitation.	
Oct 16	*From Noah Webster.*	365
[Oct 16]	To Edward Everett. AL. MHi. mDW 4417. Requests a conference with Everett on some unstated matter.	
Oct 18	Purchase of pew by DW in Brattle Square Church, Boston. Printed. DS. MWalB. mDW 36913.	
Oct 20	From S[amuel] L. S[outhard]. Copy. DNA, RG 45. mDWs. Asks DW to request that a payment made by the U.S. in 1823 shall be refunded.	
Oct 20	From Cornelius Peter Van Ness. Copy. Vermont State House. mDW 4422. Requests DW to answer Van Ness' letter of September 18, since the Vermont legislature has convened.	
Oct 21	From Samuel F. Halsey. ALS. NhHi. mDW 4424. Discusses his lawsuit against Sweet.	
Oct 23?	*To Ezekiel Webster.*	366
Oct 26	To Cornelius Peter Van Ness. Copy. Vermont State House. mDW 4429. States that he is unable to make any suggestions for Van Ness.	
Oct 26	Bank draft for $93. ANS. NhD. mDW 39615.	
[Oct?]	To [Edward Everett]. ALS. MHi. mDW 4432. Wants to see Everett about the Evans' business.	
[Oct?]	To [Edward Everett]. AN. MHi. mDW 4433. Mentions that there is a "wrong impression" about the "Salem document."	
Nov 1	Credentials of DW as member of Congress. DS. DNA, RG 233. mDW 42202.	
Nov 2	To R. W. Greene. ALS. MWA. mDW 4434. Reports his willingness to be retained by a client if acceptable fees be forwarded.	
Nov 3	From Parker Noyes. ALS. M. H. Cannon, Webster,	

	N.H. mDW 4437. Asks DW for letters of introduction for Henry Greenleaf.	
Nov 6	To Jeremiah Mason. *PC*, 1: 353–354. Urges Mason to visit him; discusses New Hampshire politics.	
Nov 6	Bank draft for $1,000. ANS. NhD. mDW 39616.	
Nov 8	From James A. Holden (enclosed with DW to John Quincy Adams, Jan 20 [1825]). ALS. DNA, RG 59. mDWs. Solicits commercial agency at Aux Cayes.	
Nov 10	From Estwicke Evans. ALS. DLC. mDW 4440. Discusses donations for Greeks and his planned trip to Greece.	
Nov 14	To Jeremiah Mason. Copy. NhHi. mDW 4444. Van Tyne, p. 109. Discusses national and New Hampshire politics.	
[Nov 18]	To Ezekiel Webster. ALS. NhD. mDW 4445. Discusses the presidential election.	
Nov 25	To Alexander Bliss. ALS. DLC. mDW 5146. Instructs Bliss on the payment of a note and reports the presidential returns of Ohio and North Carolina.	
Dec 1	Bank draft for $290.46. ANS. NhD. mDW 39612.	
Dec 4	To Grace Fletcher Webster. Printed. *PC*, 1: 355. Reports on his Washington quarters.	
Dec 4	*From Grace Fletcher Webster.*	367
Dec 6	To Grace Fletcher Webster. Printed. *PC*, 1: 355–356. Reports again on his lodgings and social life in Washington.	
Dec 6	From Grace Fletcher Webster. ALS. NhHi. mDW 4451. Reports on Charles' illness and on friends in Boston.	
Dec 7	From Grace Fletcher Webster. ALS. NhHi. mDW 4454. Gives DW a report on Charles' health and the news from Mrs. Elwyn.	
Dec 8	To Grace Fletcher Webster. *PC*, 1: 356–357. Sends gifts for the children; reports on Washington friends.	
Dec 8	From Grace Fletcher Webster. ALS. NhHi. mDW 4457. Discusses family and Charles' illness.	
Dec 9	*To [Joseph] Gales & [W. W.] Seaton.*	368
Dec 9	From Samuel May (enclosure: DW to John Quincy Adams, n.d. AN). ALS. DNA, RG 59. mDWs. Recommends his nephew, Henry Archibald, for a consulate.	
Dec 9	From Josiah Quincy. ALS. DLC. mDW 4462. Discusses his negotiations for the purchase of George's Island.	
Dec 9	From Grace Fletcher Webster. ALS. NhHi. mDW 4465. Discusses Charles' illness.	
[Dec 10]	From Grace Fletcher Webster. ALS. NhHi. mDW 4469. Reports on Charles' health.	
Dec 11	From William Russell. ALS. DNA, RG 233. mDW	

Dec 29	To Ezekiel Webster. ALS. NhD. mDW 4565. *PC*, 1: 362–363. Discusses his grief over Charles' death, his trip to Virginia, and congressional politics.	
Dec 29	From Grace Fletcher Webster. ALS. NhHi. mDW 4569. Harvey, *Reminiscences*, p. 322. Reports on the kindness expressed by friends during Charles' illness.	
Dec 31	*To [Edward Everett].*	380
Dec 31	*To Joseph Hopkinson.*	381
Dec 31	*To Jeremiah Mason.*	382
Dec 31	To Ezekiel Webster. ALS. NhD. mDW 5186. Discusses the appointment of Ichabod Bartlett as Chief Justice of the Court of Common Pleas of New Hampshire.	
Dec 31	From Grace Fletcher Webster. ALS. NhHi. mDW 4581. Harvey, *Reminiscences*, p. 323. Reveals her thoughts of Charles to DW on Charles' birthday.	
[1824]	To John Quincy Adams (enclosed with Samuel May to DW, Dec 9, 1824). AN. DNA, RG 59. mDWs. Introduces Samuel May and supports his recommendation.	
[1824]	To George Ticknor. ALS. NhD. mDW 4585. Will be unable to visit him this evening.	
[1824]	To Nathan Appleton. ALS. MHi. mDW 4587. Requests Appleton to visit him in the evening.	
[1824]	Promissory note payable to DW. ANS. NhD. mDWs.	
[1824]	From Caleb Kirk. ALS. DNA, RG 267. mDWs. Discusses a court case.	
[c. 1824]	From Eli Kirk Price. ALS. PPAmP. mDW 4597. Asks DW's attention to reform of patent laws.	
[1824?]	[Memorandum of interview between DW and J. H. Causten]. AD in Causten's hand. DLC. mDW 4601.	
[1824–1827]	To Alexander Bliss. ALS. DLC. mDW 4591. Instructs Bliss on payment of notes.	
[1824–1828]	To Samuel Lewis Southard. ALS. NjP. mDW 4595. Introduces Samuel Jaudon.	

Index

Daniel Webster is abbreviated DW within entires. The entry for Webster is confined to personal details and his writings and speeches. For material on his career, see especially under the following entries: Banking; Boscawen; Boston; Dartmouth College case; Education; Land; Law; Massachusetts; New England; New Hampshire; Politics and political campaigns; Portsmouth; Presidential elections and politics; Spanish claims; United States; United States Congress; United States Supreme Court. Page-entry numbers between 383 and 475 refer to material in the Calendar. Numbers set in italic indicate pages where individuals are identified. Individuals in the *Dictionary of American Biography* and the *Biographical Directory of the American Congress* are not identified in the notes.